BOURDIEU AND
HISTORICAL ANALYSIS

D1572351

POLITICS, HISTORY, AND CULTURE
A series from the International Institute at the University of Michigan

SERIES EDITORS
George Steinmetz and Julia Adams

SERIES EDITORIAL ADVISORY BOARD

Fernando Coronil	Nancy Rose Hunt	Julie Skurski
Mamadou Diouf	Andreas Kalyvas	Margaret Somers
Michael Dutton	Webb Keane	Ann Laura Stoler
Geoff Eley	David Laitin	Katherine Verdery
Fatma Müge Göcek	Lydia Liu	Elizabeth Wingrove

Sponsored by the International Institute at the University of Michigan and published by Duke University Press, this series is centered around cultural and historical studies of power, politics, and the state—a field that cuts across the disciplines of history, sociology, anthropology, political science, and cultural studies. The focus on the relationship between state and culture refers both to a methodological approach—the study of politics and the state using culturalist methods—and to a substantive one that treats signifying practices as an essential dimension of politics. The dialectic of politics, culture, and history figures prominently in all the books selected for the series.

BOURDIEU AND HISTORICAL ANALYSIS

EDITED BY PHILIP S. GORSKI

DUKE UNIVERSITY PRESS

DURHAM AND LONDON 2013

© 2013 Duke University Press

All rights reserved

Printed in the United States of America on acid-free paper ∞

Typeset in Minion Pro by Keystone Typesetting

Library of Congress Cataloging-in-Publication Data appear on the last printed page of this book.

Chapter 9, "T. H. Marshall Meets Pierre Bourdieu: Citizens and Paupers in the Development of the U.S. Welfare State" by Chad Alan Goldberg, was originally published in *Political Power and Social Theory* 19 (2008), 83–116. © Emerald Group Publishing Limited, all rights reserved.

CONTENTS

ACKNOWLEDGMENTS

Most of the essays below were first presented at a conference sponsored by the Center for Comparative Research at Yale University. Special thanks are due to Taly Noam for her invaluable assistance in organizing the conference and preparing the manuscript. Thanks are also due to Courtney Berger and Christine Choi of Duke University Press for bringing the manuscript to fruition.

PHILIP S. GORSKI

BOURDIEU AS A THEORIST OF CHANGE

It is not difficult to imagine some readers repeating the title of this book in the form of an incredulous question: Bourdieusian theory and historical analysis?! Wasn't Bourdieu first and foremost a theorist of social reproduction rather than a theorist of historical transformation? While the question is a legitimate one, the incredulity is misplaced. As we will see, it is based on certain misconceptions about Bourdieu's work, misconceptions that are unfortunately quite widespread, particularly in the Anglophone world. These misconceptions are the result of how Bourdieu's works were received, especially by English-speaking audiences and, more specifically, of the *order* in which they were read and the impact which this had on *how* they were read. Once these misunderstandings have been dispelled, it will become clear that the project suggested by this title is firmly rooted in Bourdieu's own work. The main purpose of this brief introduction is therefore quite modest: to convince the reader that the title needn't be followed by a question mark and that Bourdieu himself was something of a historical analyst.

It is one thing to show that a Bourdieusian approach to historical analysis is possible and quite another to assess whether it is fruitful. That requires that one put Bourdieu's concepts to work, see where they come up wanting, reflect on how they can be elaborated and refined, and compare the approach as a whole to its rivals. And that is what the essays in this volume seek to do. While all of the contributors to the book are deeply knowledgeable about and appreciative of Bourdieu's work, they do not all come to the same assessment about his approach to sociohistorical change. Some find it compelling and complete, while others feel it should be revised or even supplemented with other theories. The aim of the volume, then, is not to compile a catechism but to initiate a discussion.

Before turning to the question of what historical research can do with Bourdieu's approach, however, I want to first see what Bourdieu himself did with it, and how it is that he nonetheless came to be styled a reproduction theorist. My answer to this latter question is twofold: Bourdieu's reputation is due both to the historical reception of his work and to the interpretive scheme that resulted from this initial reception. Once we have grasped this, we are able to see Bourdieu's work in a new and different light. We can see that it provides conceptual tools for analyzing macrosocial change and historical crisis. What is more, we will see that Bourdieu's initial question was about transformation rather than reproduction, that this question never disappeared from his view, and that it reemerged with great force at the end of his career. In sum, we will find that our understanding of his *oeuvre* has been too much influenced by a one-sided understanding of his midcareer work.

Reception, or How Bourdieu Became a Reproduction Theorist

I begin, as Bourdieu himself might have, with a holistic and objectivizing style of analysis, looking at Bourdieu's *oeuvre* as a whole and how it has been cited by others. This will help readers to map the received Bourdieu into the space of possible Bourdieus. For the purposes of this analysis, I wish to stipulate that some of Bourdieu's work emphasizes reproduction while other parts of it highlight transformation. The theme of reproduction, for example, is especially prominent in the work on class, culture, and education in France that defines the middle period of Bourdieu's work. Here, I am thinking especially of two empirical monographs, *Reproduction* (1977) and *Distinction* (1984b), and of two programmatic works, *Outline of a Theory of Practice* (1977) and *The Logic of Practice* (1990a [1980]), all four of which were originally published between 1970 and 1980. The theme of transformation, by contrast, is much more salient in the early work on the crisis of peasant societies contained in *The Algerians* (1962), *The Bachelors' Ball* (2008c), and other books, and in the later work on literature, most notably *The Rules of Art* (1996a), but it is also evident in the major research monographs of the 1980s, *Homo Academicus* (1984b) and *The State Nobility* (1996b [1989]) and even in *The Political Ontology of Martin Heidegger* (1991a), which was originally published in article form in 1975, then republished in book form in 1988.

Given the bulk of the midcareer work, one could argue that Bourdieu was foremost a theorist of social reproduction. But a closer examination of his early and late work suggests that one could just as easily argue that Bourdieu was first and last a theorist of social transformation and, indeed, that the concern with historical change is a red thread, sometimes thicker, sometimes thinner, that traverses his entire life's work. All in all, I would argue, the work of the 1970s has loomed much too large in our understanding of Bourdieu's project and occluded a more balanced appreciation of his writings.

Why did this work loom so large though? A first clue can be gleaned from a comparison of the dates when his books were first published in French with the dates when they were first translated into English (see appendixes 1 and 2). The first thing to notice here is that one of Bourdieu's books on Algeria (*Travail et travailleurs en Algérie* [1964]) has never been translated, while a second (*Le déracinement* [1964]) was translated only in 2010. Meanwhile, *The Bachelors' Ball*, which contains a series of essays on the crisis of peasant society written over the course of three decades, was translated only in 2007. What is more, the one book from this period which *was* translated early, *The Algerians* (1962), is arguably the one that has the least to say about change. The second thing to notice is the titles of the works that were translated during the late 1970s: *Reproduction* (1977), *Algeria 1960* (1979a), *The Inheritors* (1979) and, most important, *Outline of a Theory of Practice* (1977). The appearance of these books laid the foundations of Bourdieu's reputation, and drew attention to *Distinction*, the book from 1979 (translated 1984) that cemented it. Given this translation history, it is perhaps not surprising that Bourdieu was so quickly labeled a reproduction theorist by English-speaking social scientists.

Once affixed, the label stuck—tenaciously. The two books that established Bourdieu's reputation in the Anglophone world—*Outline of a Theory of Practice* and *Distinction*—are massively cited. As of this writing, Web of Science lists 6,289 total citations for *Distinction* in the social sciences and humanities, and 4,906 for *Outline of a Theory of Practice*, with *The Logic of Practice* running a distant third at 2,807.[1] To put this into perspective: Max Weber's *Protestant Ethic* (Weber, Baehr, and Wells 2002) collects only a bronze medal in this competition, with 4,439 total citations! By contrast, *The Algerians*, Bourdieu's first book and the first to be translated into English, has accumulated only 114 citations, while *The Bachelors' Ball* has received 35 and *Le déracinement* a mere 15.

The dominance of *Distinction* and *Outline of a Theory of Practice* in Anglophone social science is overwhelming. Taken together, they account for over half of all citations of Bourdieu's published books in English-language social science articles (see table 1). In French-language social science articles, by contrast, they account for just over one-quarter of all citations. Table 2 tells a similar story. Here, we see that the United States and England account for a larger percentage of all social science citations of *Distinction* and *Outline of a Theory of Practice* than France, the reverse being true for *The Rules of Art* and *State Nobility*.

Could the dominance of *Outline of a Theory of Practice* and *Distinction* in Anglophone social science simply be owing to the fact that they have been

TABLE 1 Results of Searches for Bourdieu's Works in the *Social Science Citation Index*, 1958–2010

Title	Pub. Date Fr./Eng.	Total Citations	U.S.	Eng.	Fr.
Algerians	1958/1962	95	27	12	9
Uprooting	1964/2010	61	20%	20%	16%
Inheritors	1964/1979	367	27	11	25
Craft of Sociology	1968/1991	132	7%	10%	40%
Reproduction	1970/1977	1035	37	12	12
Outline of a Theory	1972/1977	4117	47	17	3
Algeria 1960	1977/1979	104	42%	21%	6%
Distinction	1979/1984	4608	34	21	5
Sociology in Question	1980/1993	459	13	26	13
Logic of Practice	1980/1990	2152	34	20	6
Lang and Sym. Power	1982/1991	1416	40	18	3
Homo Academicus	1984/1988	668	27	21	6
In Other Words	1987/1990	878	31	20	7
Pol. Ontol. of Martin H.	1988/1991	54	33	30	2
State Nobility	1989/1996	395	24	20	13
Rules of Art	1992/1996	263	28	20	12
On Television	1996/1998	111	42	11	7
Pascalian Meditns.	1997/2000	398	24	24	6
Firing Back	1998	83	20	30	7
Masculine Dom'n.	1998/2001	315	25	18	13
Soc. Struct's. of Econ.	2000/2005	141	21	20	14
Bachelors' Ball	2002/2007	24	21	25	17
Sketch for Self-Anal.	2004/2008	30	27	30	13

Source: Based on "cited reference" searches in the *Social Science Citation Index* for French original and English translation of each work.

available in translation for a longer period of time? It is a fair question, but that is not what the evidence suggests. Since its translation in 1979, *Outline of a Theory of Practice* has been cited an average of 85 times per year in English language social science articles. The equivalent figure for *Distinction* is 114.[2] This is many multiples more than the average citation rates for *Homo Academicus* (17), *The State Nobility* (6.9), *The Rules of Art* (8.0), and *The Political Ontology of Martin Heidegger* (1.4). The books on Algeria, meanwhile, average less than 1 citation per year.

These averages could be misleading; influential books tend to receive increasing numbers of citations per year and may reach their peak citation rates

TABLE 2 Anglophone Citation Dominance of Selected Bourdieu Works in the *Social Science Citation Index* during Their Initial Reception, 1964–1984

Title	Pub. Date Fr./Eng.	Total Citations	U.S.	Eng.	Fr.
Inheritors	1964/1979	367	27	11	25
Reproduction	1970/1977	1035	37	12	12
Outline of a Theory	1972/1977	4117	47	17	3
Algeria 1960	1977/1979	104	42%	21%	6%
Distinction	1979/1984	4608	34	21	5

Source: Based on "cited reference" searches in the *Social Science Citation Index* for French original and English translation of each work.

only after several decades. It could be that the more historical works of the middle and later periods are simply further back on the trend lines. But that is not what the evidence suggests. Figure 1 charts the number of English-language citations for *Distinction, Outline of a Theory of Practice, The Rules of Art* and *Homo Academicus* in the first fifteen years following translation. *The Rules of Art* and *Homo Academicus* have indeed gradually trended upward, but the trend lines are much, much flatter than those for *Outline of a Theory of Practice* and *Distinction*.

It could also be that the stature of *Outline of a Theory of Practice* and *Distinction* is owing to their universally recognized quality and originality. If so, we would not expect to find any significant differences in the English and French citation patterns. On the other hand, if the pattern of English translation and reception did play a role, we would expect these citation patterns to be very different. Tables 3 and 4 provide some support for both hypotheses.

While the rankings are slightly different, the top four works are the same. This suggests that quality and originality do go some distance toward explaining which works are cited most. But they do not go the whole distance. For there are at least two notable differences between the French and English citation patterns. The first is that the French citations are much more evenly distributed across Bourdieu's works. The standard deviation for the English-language distribution is 13.4, while that for the French-language distribution is 5.4. A second and related difference is that the books on Algeria and the three other historically oriented works noted above account for over 13 percent of all French citations, but only about 6 percent of the English citations. So while Bourdieu's works on reproduction are the most influential in both the Anglophone and Francophone worlds, his works on transformation appear to have been less influential in the former than the latter.

In sum, if we imagine a two-dimensional space of possible Bourdieus, with

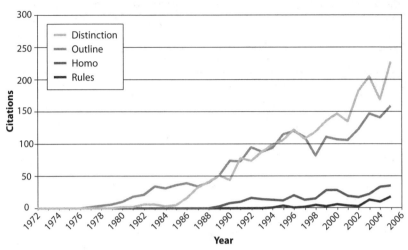

Figure 1. Citations in English language articles for four books.

transformation theorist forming the left pole and reproduction theorist the right pole, then the "actual" Bourdieu, the Anglophone Bourdieu of the moment, is much closer to the right pole than the left. This cannot be explained solely, or even primarily, by Bourdieu's work. Rather, it is at least partly the result of a particular historically conditioned pattern of reception, translation, and appropriation. This book seeks to revise this reception and push Bourdieu closer to the transformation pole.

Interpretation, or Re/Reading Bourdieu as a Theorist of Change

Bourdieu's reputation as a reproduction theorist has influenced not only how his work has been received, but also how it has been interpreted; that is, it has influenced not just *which* works are read, but also *how* those works are read. Indeed, it has even determined how two of his best-known concepts are understood, the signature concepts of cultural capital and habitus. Both are typically understood as being the central mechanisms in a general theory of social reproduction (Lareau and Weininger 2003) especially by sociologists of education (Conway 1997; Richter 2002; Sullivan 2001), but also by students of stratification (Hartmann 2000) and even historians of the family (MacHardy 1999).

There is nothing wrong with using these concepts in this way, for they are indeed powerful tools for explaining the persistence of inequality in contemporary societies. The problem is that many scholars seem to believe that this is what these two concepts were designed to do and that they are incapable of doing other analytical work (Archer 1993; Kingston 2001). Such an interpretation might appear plausible if one's reading of Bourdieu started and ended

TABLE 3 Percentage of Total English Language Citations in Bourdieu Works

Title	Percentage of Total English Language Citations
Distinction	27.6
Outline of a Theory of Practice	26.1
The Logic of Practice	10.8
Reproduction	8.6
Language and Symbolic Power	7.7
Homo Academicus	3.8
Sociology in Question	2.5
Practical Reason	2.0
State Nobility	1.5
Pascalian Meditations	1.4
Rules of Art	1.3
The Inheritors	1.1
Masculine Domination	0.9
On Television	0.8
Craft of Sociology	0.7
Love of Art	0.6
Photography	0.5
Free Exchange	0.5
The Algerians	0.4
In Other Words	0.4
Political Ontology of Martin Heidegger	0.3
Le déracinement	0.2
Firing Back	0.2
Travail et travailleurs en Algérie	0.2
Leçon sur la leçon	0.2
Algeria, 1960	0.1
Science of Science and of Reflexivity	0
Social Structures of the Economy	0
Standard Deviation	10.0

with the much-cited works of the 1970s, in which Bourdieu invoked the concepts of habitus and cultural capital in order to explain the persistence and reproduction of social inequality in postwar France, a society in which many material and symbolic goods are distributed through the educational system on a meritocratic basis that is supposed to reflect natural abilities. But it is much harder to sustain if one starts with the less-cited work of the 1960s on

TABLE 4 Percentage of Total English Language Citations in Bourdieu Works

Title	Percentage of total English language citations
Distinction	21.8
Reproduction	14.9
The Logic of Practice	13.2
Outline of a Theory of Practice	12.8
The Inheritors	8.7
Craft of Sociology	6.9
Sociology in Question	6.8
Language and Symbolic Power	6.0
	5.3
Homo Academicus	5.3
State Nobility	5.0
In Other Words	4.1
Rules of Art	3.6
Masculine Domination	3.5
Practical Reason	3.1
Pascalian Meditations	2.6
Travail et travailleurs en Algérie	2.6
Le déracinement	1.6
The Algerians	1.5
Love of Art	1.4
Social Structures of the Economy	1.3
Firing Back	0.7
Leçon sur la leçon	0.6
Algeria, 1960	0.5
Photography	0.5
Political Ontology of Martin Heidegger	0.3
On Television	0.2
Free Exchange	0.1
Science of Science and of Reflexivity	0

the crisis of peasant societies. Consider the notion of habitus. As Wacquant (2004: 391) points out, Bourdieu introduced this concept in 1962 in an article on the peasants of the Béarn "not to provide a lynchpin for the process of social reproduction . . . but to describe the traumatic disjuncture between the embodied abilities and expectations of rural men and those of their women-folk" and the forced celibacy and failed reproduction of peasant households that was its tragic result. Bourdieu then redeployed the habitus concept in his subsequent writings on Algeria to explain the slow speed and crisis-filled character of economic change in colonial societies. As he later explained, "The relationship between structures and habitus was constituted as a theoretical problem in relation to a historical situation in which that problem was in a sense . . . in the form of a permanent *discrepancy* between the agents' economic dispositions and the economic world in which they had to act" (Bourdieu 1979a: vii).

It might be objected that the habitus concept is really being used here in essentially the same way: in the early work it is used to account for the breakdown of social reproduction; in the middle work it is used to account for the success of social reproduction. While there is admittedly some truth to this interpretation, it is still much too simplistic and one-sided—and for at least two reasons: first, because Bourdieu's early writings on peasant societies are concerned, not just with the way in which an unchanging habitus frustrates economic change, but also with the ways in which economic change reshapes the habitus (Bourdieu 1979a: 54, 64); and second, because he is concerned throughout with the connection between social dispositions and political positions, with understanding which classes and class-fractions are most likely to pursue social change by revolutionary means (Bourdieu 1979a: 92–93). So reproduction is not the only dependent variable nor is the habitus just an independent variable for explaining reproduction.

And whatever validity a reproductionist reading might have for Bourdieu's early work, it cannot possibly be sustained for his later works or even for one (little-read) midcareer work, *The Political Ontology of Martin Heidegger*. The subject of this short study is the "revolutionary philosophical coup" carried out by Heidegger in "*creating*, at the heart of the philosophical field, a new position, in relation to which all the other positions would have to be redefined" (Bourdieu 1991a: 46), by reasserting the foundational significance of ontology and relegating epistemology—the cardinal question of Western philosophy at least since John Locke—to a subordinate status. The philosophical coup, Bourdieu contends, also had a political dimension: for Heidegger's radically ontological language contained politically conservative undertones that were clearly perceived by his listeners, if not necessarily consciously. Moreover, Bourdieu argues, Heidegger's success was probably partly a function of his peculiar habitus: "It seems likely that Heidegger's social trajectory helps to explain his absolutely exceptional polyphonic talent, his gift for making connections between problems which previously existed only in fragmentary form, scattered around the political and philosophical fields, while yet giving the impression that he was posing them in a more 'radical' and more 'profound' manner than anyone before him. His rising trajectory, leading across different social universes, predisposed him better than a plane trajectory to speak and think in several spaces at once, to address audiences other than his peers" (Bourdieu 1991a: 47). In the book on Heidegger, a charismatic habitus serves as the sociopolitical catalyst of historical and cultural change.

The same could be said for *The Rules of Art*, in which Bourdieu analyzes the role of an anticharismatic intellectual, Gustave Flaubert, in creating ex nihilo another new position within the cultural field: avant-garde literature. Indeed, the only real difference between the two works is that *The Rules of Art* is more deeply researched and more fully conceptualized—and focused on a figure whom Bourdieu finds more sympathetic. The method, however, is exactly the same. And given that the Heidegger book was originally published in 1975, we are forced to abandon not only a one-sidedly reproductionist reading of Bourdieu's work but even a reproductionist reduction of his middle period.

If *The Rules of Art* is an empirically fleshed-out version of the historical method developed in *The Political Ontology of Martin Heidegger*, then *Homo Academicus* can be seen, to some degree, as a more conceptually elaborated version of the political sociology of *Algeria 1960*. In *Algeria 1960* and indeed throughout his early writings Bourdieu struggles to answer that perennial question of Marxist theory, a focal point for many "soixante-huitards," namely, the identity of the "revolutionary subject," even as he reframes the question itself. The question, as he poses it in *Algeria 1960*, is, What kind of economic position creates a revolutionary disposition and, more specifically, are workers or peasants more likely to revolt? (Bourdieu 1979a: 92–94). Unfortunately, Bourdieu does not manage to free himself from the simplistic assumptions of a naïve Marxism in *Algeria 1960*; he remains ensnared in an overly holistic, materialistic, and deterministic approach that seeks to mechanically read political disposition off of economic position. The same cannot be said of *Homo Academicus*. One of the central aims of this monograph, if by no means the only one, is to understand both the why and the who of May 1968, the near-revolution that briefly joined students, intellectuals, and workers in a frontal challenge to the Gaullist regime. By treating the university system as an autonomous field with its own stakes and rules rather than as an ancillary of the capitalist economy or the bourgeois state, and by analyzing the internal vertical and horizontal divisions within this field—its hierarchies and orthodoxies—Bourdieu is able to show how morphological changes within the university system, such as the rapid expansion of the student population, created an increased oppositional potential within the teaching corps and to identify with great precision just where this potential lay. Further, by juxtaposing the crisis within the university field and that in the economic field proper, he is also able to show how students, teachers, and workers came to see their plights as homologous and to explain not only why they allied but why that alliance unraveled. The events of May, he concludes, resulted from a "conjunction of independent causal series" within the university and the economy and a "synchronization" of the crises within both fields.

I have focused mainly on how the habitus concept figures in Bourdieu's analyses of social struggle and historical transformation, as both a cause and an effect. But what of his other signature concept, cultural capital? Is it solely a means of explaining reproduction? or can it, too, be used to analyze struggle and transformation? An initial answer to that question may be found in *The State Nobility: Elite Schools in the Field of Power*. As the subtitle suggests, the central topic of this book is the French system of *grandes écoles*, the highly selective institutions of higher education where the political, intellectual, and economic elites of France are trained. As one might expect, one of the principal arguments of the book, developed in parts 1 and 2, is that the grandes écoles are a key institution in the larger machinery of social reproduction in modern France and cultural capital one of the chief mechanisms through which that machinery accomplishes its work. In parts 3 and 4, however, Bourdieu shifts to a dynamic historical perspective that emphasizes conflict and transformation. In part 3, for example, he analyzes long-term shifts in the distribution of power and prestige among the various grandes écoles in terms of social struggles and morphological shifts both within the university field and within the wider "field of power" (Bourdieu 1996b [1989]: 266, 272). And in part 4 he situates these changes in a much longer historical time frame and identifies various types of long-term changes in the field of power, including a secular shift in the relative weight of economic and cultural capital in favor of the latter; the growing importance of educational institutions in the distribution and sanctification of cultural capital, at the expense of the church; and the consequent intensification of struggles within the cultural field between the bearers of the different types of secular cultural capital (Bourdieu 1996b [1989]: 132, 198). Here, too, *The Rules of Art* can be seen as the endpoint insofar as it picks up where *The State Nobility* leaves off and completes the circle. For it is concerned not only with struggles within the cultural field but also with the emergence of a new subtype of cultural capital (literary capital), a new type of artistic habitus (the avant-garde), and an autonomous field of literary production.

Integration: Reproduction and Transformation in Bourdieusian Theory, or *Plus ça change, plus c'est la même chose*

To accuse Bourdieu of being a reproduction theorist, then, is to confess that one has not read that much of his work or that one has not read it very closely.

Careful readers of Bourdieu's work have long recognized that his conceptual framework can be used to study sociohistorical transformation (Harker 1984), and increasing numbers of scholars are now trying to develop and apply his ideas in this way (Boyer 2003; Crossley 2003; Garcia 1999; Gartman 2002). That said, it would be silly to argue that Bourdieu was not also a reproduction theorist or to deny that reproduction was a major theme in his work. He was both—a theorist of reproduction and a theorist of transformation—as any student of society and history should be. What are the historical and social sciences, after all, if not sciences of continuity and change? Indeed, I would argue that one of the advantages of the Bourdieusian framework is that it allows one to analyze social reproduction and transformation and historical continuity and rupture, even simultaneously, and that that in fact is what most of Bourdieu's work does to one degree or another.

Distinction, for example, is widely understood to be a book about social reproduction. And not without reason: the main point of that book, at least its main political point, is to show that the spread of meritocratic principles and the expansion of higher education in France since the Second World War have not had the equalizing and leveling effect that had been hoped for or claimed. Instead, the effect has been to change the relative values of economic and cultural capital, that is, their exchange rate, and to increase the importance of educational credentials in social reproduction. But it is not only about reproduction and continuity—whence the words *change* and *increase* in the previous sentence. Even *Distinction* is not just about reproduction. A quick glance at that book's table of contents makes that clear enough: chapter 2, "The Social Space and Its *Transformations*"; chapter 4: "The *Dynamics* of Fields" (emphasis added), and so on. And a closer reading of the contents makes it clearer still. After all, isn't the central theoretical point of the book that the reproduction of distinctions requires the transformation of distinctions? That the maintenance and transmission of class privilege within social space and across historical time involve continual adjustments and occasional reversals of aesthetic judgment within symbolic space and across cultural time? In short, doesn't the cultural domination of the socially dominant involve an endless run on a cultural treadmill? If *Distinction* seems to be about reproduction, this is not because Bourdieu is blind to transformation but because he wishes, for both political and intellectual reasons, to highlight the one rather than the other. Implicit within its pages is another book about the endless transformations in symbolic space—changes in taste and judgment—produced by the thirst for social distinction. But that is not the book Bourdieu wanted to write.

What of the more historical works that emphasize transformation? Not surprisingly, they often include secondary storylines about continuity. In the second half of *The State Nobility*, for example, where Bourdieu situates recent transformations of the French field of power within a longer time horizon, he argues that "the field of power has undoubtedly included constants through the most varied historical configurations, such as, for instance, the fundamental opposition in the division of the labor of domination between temporal and spiritual or cultural power holders—warriors and priests, *bellatores* and *oratores*, businessmen . . . and intellectuals" (Bourdieu 1996b [1989]: 266). The players have changed, but the game has not. In *Masculine Domination* (Bourdieu 2001b) Bourdieu sets himself the task of "neutralizing the mechanisms of the neutralization of history" (2001: viii) by *"reconstruct[ing] the history of the historical labor of dehistoricization"* (2001b: 82). In truth, Bourdieu does not complete this task; indeed, he barely even begins it. But one thing that his analysis does do is to highlight the extraordinary continuity in the basic categorical oppositions (wet/dry, inside/outside, and so on) that underlie gender inequality across space and time, a continuity that is all the more striking, if he is correct, when contrasted with the churning of categories closer to the surface of consciousness. In this case, Bourdieu suggests, historical change and cross-societal variation on the surface of symbolic space conceal extraordinary stability and solidity at a deeper and less visible level, thereby giving the illusion that "the more things change, the more they remain the same."

Overview

Having argued that the application of Bourdieu's approach to sociohistorical analysis is in keeping with the general spirit of Bourdieu's work, I want to see now what fruits this project might bear, and how the quality of the harvest might be improved. It is time, in other words, to see what kinds of historical work we can and cannot do with the conceptual tools and methodological strategies Bourdieu has developed, and whether we might want to alter or add to them in any way. The contributors to this book are not all of one mind on this. Some find the tools quite adequate to the job at hand; others suggest various ways of sharpening them; and still others would like to supplement them with tools borrowed from entirely different theories. In short, the chapters herein run the gamut from orthodox to heterodox.

The volume is in three parts. The first, "Situating Bourdieu," consists of three chapters. The first, by David L. Swartz, offers a brief, essential primer on Bourdieu's three master concepts, field, capital, and habitus, and identifies six analytical strategies that underlie his work. The next, by Craig Calhoun, suggests that we can learn a great deal by viewing Bourdieu as a historical sociologist and shows that much of his work can be seen as an attempt to conceptualize and explain four major processes of social transformation. The third and final chapter in part 1, by the French social historian Christophe Charle recounts Bourdieu's influence on French historiography and the academic stakes it involved.

The second part, "Theoretical Engagements," is composed of five chapters that juxtapose Bourdieu's approach with that of a major competitor and adjudicate their relative strengths and weaknesses by means of historical analysis. Chapter 4, by Ivan Ermakoff, seeks to clarify the relationship between rational choice theory and practice theory, taking as its starting point Bourdieu's puzzling pronouncement that "in times of crisis, rational choice may take over." The fifth chapter, by George Steinmetz, using the examples of colonial statehood Bourdieu's self-analysis argues for the fundamental complementarity of Bourdieusian socioanalysis and Lacanian psychoanalysis. Chapter 6, by Mustafa Emirbayer and Erik Schneiderhan, reflects on the limitations of Bourdieu as a theorist of democracy and democratization and argues that on these subjects John Dewey's pragmatism provides an approach that is at once compatible and superior. In chapter 7 Gil Eyal compares Bourdieu's field-theoretic approach to Bruno Latour's actor-network theory, showing how the latter helps us to better comprehend the "spaces between fields" created and occupied by code-switching social entrepreneurs such as "Israeli defense intellectuals." The eighth and concluding chapter of part 2, by Charles Camic, draws on recent work in the sociologies of knowledge and science to highlight ambiguities and shortcomings in Bourdieu's work on these subjects.

While the chapters in part 2 mainly use empirical examples as an occasion for theoretical reflection, those in part 3, "Historical Extensions," do the reverse: they put Bourdieu to work, showing how his concepts and methods can be used to illuminate subjects old and new. In chapter 9, for example, Chad Alan Goldberg uses Bourdieu's concept of "classification struggles" to analyze the policy battles of the New Deal. Then, in chapter 10, I propose a theory of "nation-ization struggles," showing how it might resolve certain perennial debates in the literature of nationalism. In her chapter, Gisèle Sapiro uses Bourdieu's concept of "synchronization"—a concept little used by American analysts—to explain the changing stakes and struggles within the field of French literature during and after the Second World War. In chapter 12 Robert Nye applies Bourdieu's approach to the analysis of gender to the case of early modern France. Finally, Jacques Defrance presents a comparative and historical analysis of the genesis of the modern sports field in France, delving deeply into a subject Bourdieu touched on only superficially.

The conclusion, "Bourdieusian Theory and Historical Analysis: Maps, Mechanisms, and Methods," shows how each of Bourdieu's master concepts can be used to track and explain social transformation, in both objectivizing and subjectivizing modes.

I have chosen to arrange the contributions in this way in the hope that it will enable the reader to evaluate more easily the fruitfulness of the Bourdieusian program for themselves. But this is certainly not the only way in which the contributions could have been arranged—or might be read; they could also have been arranged thematically, and readers interested in how Bourdieu's approach can be applied to a particular topic might prefer to read the volume in this way. Some of these thematic groupings are not immediately obvious from the chapter titles, so it may be useful to indicate them here. For example, those curious about what a Bourdieusian style of political sociology might look like will be interested not only in the essays by Goldberg and me, which deal, respectively, with the symbolic moment of political struggles over social policy and the politics of nationalism and nationalist movements; they may also wish to read Ermakoff's discussion of parliamentary abdications in France and Germany between the wars, Steinmetz's analysis of German colonialism in China and Africa (Steinmetz 2007b, 2008), or Sapiro's discussion of the synchronization of the French literary and political fields during the Nazi occupation. Those interested in the relationship between social class and bodily habitus, by contrast, will find much material in Defrance's analysis of the role of competitive sports in the formation of bodily habitus in modern France and in Steinmetz's insights about how colonial administrators' evaluation and appropriation of native culture were shaped by their class location and social trajectory. Those working on the sociology of intellectuals or the production of culture will naturally want to read Sapiro's piece on French literature alongside the chapters by Camic and by Emirbayer and Schneiderhan. No doubt still other constellations are possible.

Notes

1. All of the figures given in this paragraph are based on a "cited references" search for the French original and English translation of each book in Web of Science in late August, 2010, including the Social Sciences Citation Index, the Humanities Index, and Social Science and Humanities Conference Proceedings.
2. Based on a "cited reference" search in the Social Sciences Citation Index from the year of translation through the end of 2009.

PART I **Situating Bourdieu**

1 DAVID L. SWARTZ

METAPRINCIPLES FOR SOCIOLOGICAL RESEARCH IN A BOURDIEUSIAN PERSPECTIVE

In recent years the sociology of Pierre Bourdieu has been widely referenced across a broad range of subfields in American sociology (Sallaz and Zavisca 2007). Not only referenced but also engaged substantively and critically, Bourdieu's work has become a leading reference for framing much substantive research and theoretical discussion. A review of the leading journals and several recent books shows numerous creative efforts to apply key ideas of Bourdieu to new settings and issues not examined by the French sociologist himself. His pivotal concepts of capital, habitus, and field plus his central arguments about symbolic domination and social distinction are being applied, expanded, modified, and elaborated in a great variety of recent pieces of research. Frequently missing, however, from the many efforts to work with his concepts is an understanding of the broader framework of metaprinciples that guided Bourdieu in his work. Yet metatheoretical considerations decisively shaped Bourdieu's understanding of sociological research. I will argue here that one can identify at least six orienting principles in Bourdieu's sociology that would be useful to keep in mind as one attempts to extend his thinking to new areas of investigation: (1) focus on multiple forms of power and domination, particularly cultural and symbolic ones, (2) challenge received views of the social world, (3) employ relational analysis, (4) connect micro and macro levels of analysis, (5) adopt a self-critical, reflexive posture in sociological work, and (6) include an intellectual activist orientation for a public sociology.

Neither Grand Theory nor Empiricism

One might begin, as Bourdieu himself always did, by identifying who or what he argued against—his intellectual enemies. Bourdieu conducted empirical research, yet his conceptual language is fundamentally antipositivist. He developed his concepts out of critical reflection in particular empirical domains, but his concepts do not designate particular empirical phenomena as the positivist tradition would require. Bourdieu does not see himself employing concepts as definitions for which one can pin down precise empirical content. His concepts are not intended to be reflections of empirical reality. Rather, his concepts try to convey a certain way of approaching the study of the social world; they are orienting tools for research. He thinks of his concepts as agendas of questions for research rather than as ready-made answers (Bourdieu and Wacquant 1992: 110).

We would do ourselves a disservice as well to veer from the path Bourdieu designated if we were to focus, say, on just what habitus means or what exactly the empirical content of a field is. We need to approach his concepts, as Brubaker (1993: 220) insightfully suggests, as "designators of particular intellectual habitus or sets of habits." Bourdieu wants them read and applied in a "dispositional manner."[1]

On the other hand, his concepts are not purely theoretical constructs either. One does not find in capital, field, and habitus a tightly structured theory of the social world as exemplified in the work of Talcott Parsons and Niklas Luhmann. Bourdieu's concepts are not expressions of "grand theory," as C. Wright Mills put it.[2] His concepts are tools for conducting empirical research rather than formal constructs, definitions, or abstract, fixed propositions.[3] They attempt to assemble in diverse ways a variety of relevant empirical materials for sociological investigation. They developed out of a research orientation and stem from efforts to understand certain empirical phenomena.

Some Key Metaprinciples in Bourdieu's Sociology

How might one draw upon core concepts of Bourdieu's sociology for carrying out new sociological research? One way is to focus on the overarching metaprinciples and intellectual dispositions that animated Bourdieu's work. His master concepts—field, capital, and habitus[4]—are situated within a broader framework of metatheoretical principles and intellectual dispositions that oriented Bourdieu's conceptual development and his employment of concepts in his research (Brubaker 1985; Swartz 1997). I want to outline six guiding principles that traverse Bourdieu's conceptual orientation and suggest that they might serve as important guides in how one applies his concepts in various areas of investigation.[5]

The perspective I outline recommends that we approach Bourdieu's concepts as "tools for research" that embody certain sociological dispositions. It is a dispositional perspective, a kind of sociological habitus that I am after rather than a strictly theoretical reading or empirical application of Bourdieu. While it is very tempting to talk about field, capital, and habitus as theoretical constructs and thereby evaluate them in terms of logical consistency, contradiction, affiliation with theoretical traditions, indebtedness to classical theorists, and so on, I recommend that we think of them more as forms of sociological practices that have a practical, dispositional orientation for understanding the social world. As Brubaker (1993: 212) advises, "Resist the temptation to 'talk about concepts' instead of 'making them work.'" To illustrate with his concept of field: the strategy I am proposing is not to give a correct definition of the concept of field but to identify key metaprinciples that Bourdieu used to guide his own field analyses. To this end, I posit six guiding principles that I think characterize Bourdieu's work and can be usefully employed for approaching new areas of sociological investigation.

A SOCIOLOGY OF POWER AND DOMINATION

First is Bourdieu's objective to do a sociology of power with particular attention to forms of domination. Indeed, the analysis of power stands at the heart of Bourdieu's sociology. He is a conflict theorist who stresses the competitive, stratified character of social worlds and who sees them firmly ordered by mechanisms and processes of domination and reproduction. He proposes a theory of symbolic power, violence, and capital that stresses the active role symbolic forms play as resources that both constitute and maintain social hierarchies. Bourdieu's perspective challenges the commonly held view that symbolic power is simply symbolic. His sociology sensitizes us to the more subtle and influential forms of power that operate through the cultural resources and symbolic categories and classifications that interweave everyday life with prevailing institutional arrangements. Rejecting both Marxist and non-Marxist forms of economic reductionism, he identifies a wide variety of valued resources beyond sheer material interests that function as resources of power and that he calls forms of capital, such as social capital and cultural capital.[6] Furthermore, individuals and groups struggle over the very definition and distribution of these capitals in distinct power arenas Bourdieu calls fields. He sees concentrations of various forms of capital in specific areas of struggle, such as the field of power, the political field, and the state. Bourdieu's sociology offers conceptual tools for analyzing three types of power: power vested in particular resources (capitals), power concentrated in specific spheres of struggle over forms of capital (fields of power), and power as practical, taken-for-granted acceptance of existing social hierarchies (symbolic power and violence).[7]

BREAKING WITH RECEIVED VIEWS

For Bourdieu social science begins with an "epistemological break" with the received views of the social world. This second principle represents in fact "the most crucial research operation," regardless of the substantive domain under investigation (Bourdieu and Wacquant 1992: 224). Inspired in part by Emile Durkheim (1966), Bourdieu's method calls for breaking with received categories by constructing a conceptual model of the social world that explains the social world by situating the actors and their categories within a broader social and historical framework of which they are the product (a view not usually available to insiders). Constructing the object means refusing to take insider behaviors and claims at face value or refusing to focus on those units most immediately and directly visible, such as individuals, social groups, and organizations. To do so would be to miss the underlying dynamics and processes of conflict that have generated their immediate visibility.[8]

In order to facilitate the critical questioning of the taken-for-granted, Bourdieu advises that we "mobilize all the techniques that are relevant and practically usable, given the definition of the object and the practical conditions of data collection" (Bourdieu and Wacquant 1992: 237).[9] Constructing the field of practices is his key methodological device for breaking with received views of the social world. Fields show that views are generated out of competing positions that bring into play different power resources (capitals) and relations of hierarchy and domination among the relevant players. A related privileged intellectual tool for doing so is social history (Bourdieu and Wacquant 1992: 238). History appears as a privileged instrument for breaking with received views that strike the uncritical observer as self-evident, commonsensical, and only natural.

THINKING RELATIONALLY

Breaking with the most immediately visible forms of social life, such as individuals, social groups, and organizations, calls for relational thinking. Social realities obtain sociological significance only by comparison to others. Focus not on the immediately visible units but on the structure of relations that unite and differentiate them (Bourdieu and Wacquant 1992: 107). Focus on fields of relations rather than on individual entities that are artificially extracted from their context.[10] Bourdieu was among the first contemporary sociologists to criticize sharply "substantialist" thinking.[11] Thinking relationally means not looking for intrinsic properties of individuals or groups but constructing their relational attributes. Relationality for Bourdieu means conceptualizing capitals, individuals, groups, organizations, and even nations, as interdependent units in terms of broad networks of relations that shape their action beyond individual consciousness or direct contact or control. This sets Bourdieu apart from methodological individualism and interactionist perspectives that focus attention on individuals and units of exchange between individuals.

INTEGRATING SUBJECTIVE AND OBJECTIVE FORMS OF KNOWLEDGE

It is also Bourdieu's ambition to offer and call for a sociology that integrates subjective and objective forms of knowledge into what he calls a "general science of practices" (Swartz 1997: 56). He contends that the social sciences have for too long been plagued by a series of classic antinomies that have limited the development of a comprehensive view of human action. Bourdieu's conceptual strategy is to overcome these classic dualisms by forging concepts that will permit integrating subjective and objective forms. He offers a conceptual program that would weave together the following four dualisms: (1) theory versus empirical research, (2) agency versus structure, (3) symbolic forms versus material objects of social life, and (4) micro versus macro levels of analysis.[12]

Bourdieu emphasizes that theorizing and empirical investigation must go hand in hand. Theory without an empirical object is vacuous and sociological significance does not emerge automatically from empirical realities. This call to combine theory and empirical investigation is such a commonplace in sociology today that few would dispute its charge. Still one finds journals and books specialized in one or the other. Bourdieu calls for a social scientific practice that resolutely practices both simultaneously.

The sociological habitus Bourdieu would have us cultivate is one that motivates us to seek out and demonstrate the intrinsically *dual* character of social life—its objective and subjective features. Bourdieu heightens our awareness of the duality of social life and shows how, via theory, method, and available data, we frequently are tempted to give fractured portrayals of that totality. We need to develop dispositions to seek out the rich, often subtle ways in which the social world is simultaneously subjective and objective, internal and external, symbolic and material, individual and collective, free and constrained and to integrate these dual moments into our sociological accounts. His concepts are oriented toward that kind of integrating view of the social world. This would mean that characteristics of individual actors, their views, the forms of power they represent as well as the organizational structures—locally, nationally, and internationally—they inhabit should be taken into account.

REFLEXIVITY

Fifth, all of Bourdieu's concepts are to be employed reflexively.[13] They call for critical examination of all assumptions and presuppositions not only of the sociological object investigated but also of the stance and location of the researcher. Reflexivity arises from the need to control the relationship of the researcher to the object of inquiry so that the position of the researcher is not unwittingly projected into the object of study.

Three principal sources of such projection are considered: the habitus of the researcher, the intellectual field position of the researcher, and what Bourdieu considers the most difficult bias to overcome, that of the "theoreticist" bias inherent in the scholarly gaze itself (Bourdieu 1990c; Swartz 1997: 271–77). Habitus and particularly field are key tools for implementing this reflexivity for dealing with these effects that distort an adequate portrayal of human action. Using the language of habitus acts as a reminder that practical, not theoretical, knowledge guides much human action. It reminds us as researchers to take care to avoid the "scholastic fallacy" of mistakenly thinking that human action follows directly our rational theoretical models of human action.

The concept of field offers a more sociological view of reflexivity as opposed to one that depicts the researcher as a kind of ethical hero who would simply display his or her value commitments for all to see. Bourdieu's field analytic perspective shows that even good-faith observations of the social world are situated ones. But more important than situating observations as representing points of view that bear traces of field positions is showing the overall relational character of various viewpoints, which is exactly what field analysis does.

The researcher always faces the danger of being captured by a particular viewpoint, a partial viewpoint in the field of analysis. Field construction, as Dezalay and Garth (2002: 11) insightfully recommend, is best approached from multiple points of entry. The researcher needs to collate multiple data sources and methods so as not to limit her or his view by embracing any one.

CONCEPTUAL ARMS FOR COMBAT

Sixth, and most challenging, if not controversial, Bourdieu's master concepts of field, capital, and habitus are more than just research tools. They are also arms for intellectual combat. They are oriented toward trying to achieve specific corrective effects in the practice of sociology. Their intended meanings and empirical content vary in emphasis from study to study. Bourdieu and Wacquant (1992: 80) often "twists the stick in the other direction," as he sometimes put it, to obtain desired effects. Choice of terminology, theoretical content he loads into concepts, and empirical referents he selects all reflect his effort to break with received views, both intellectual and lay. To understand Bourdieu, we need to understand whom he is arguing against. It is always important to read Bourdieu's use of his concepts in light of the specific intellectual fields he is trying to influence, which is true of any intellectual work, including our own. Perhaps one of the positive contributions of Bourdieu is to increase our self-awareness of just how much our own work is shaped by opposing views in the professional fields in which we work that we try to correct, react to, ignore, or sidestep. Using concepts is a way of acting on an intellectual field, and we would do well to understand and be explicit about that in our own work.

But Bourdieu's concepts are more than tools for jockeying for better position in intellectual fields. They are also instruments of struggle against symbolic power. This gives an activist dimension, a political dimension, to Bourdieu's work and concepts. There is no armchair theorizing in Bourdieu. His work is not purely academic. His concepts are "instruments of combat."[14] He wishes to change the world by changing the way we see it. Since Bourdieu believes that the social world is governed by symbolic violence, which takes the form of taken-for-granted classifications and categorizations, he sees his sociology as one of exposing that important dimension of social life for what it is—an expression of power and domination. His texts and conceptual language are "instruments of struggle" that represent a "practical strategy" of trying to change our way of thinking about the social world.

We can see this activist orientation at two levels. First and foremost is to change the way sociologists view the social world. He wants to make sociology critical but not theoreticist, empirical but not positivist, and more relational and reflexive. He wishes to build up the intellectual and scientific legitimacy of sociology by protecting and increasing its autonomy from external political, economic, cultural, and social forces. This is the key objective of most of Bourdieu's work. But making sociology more scientific and critical was never an end in itself. His was also a political strategy to debunk existing power arrangements in larger society in hopes of creating the possibility of more rational, open, and egalitarian social relations. Acts of research are fundamentally to be political acts in that they debunk taken-for-granted assumptions about how the social world is ordered. Sociology is a struggle against symbolic violence. There is, therefore, a type of intellectual role to be played as well as a cognitive orientation to understanding social life.[15] This aspect of his work became more apparent in his later years.

A practical implication for us is that we should think of his concepts as tools that embody sets of dispositions and strategies for both understanding *and acting upon* the social world. The master concepts are more than theoretical markers or organizers and empirical indicators; they invite us not only to view the world differently but also to act upon it. It is those dispositions (and their underlying principles) and strategies that we need to understand if we are to appropriate from Bourdieu's work a set of thinking tools for analyzing social relations.

This intellectual activism may be the most challenging of Bourdieu's metaprinciples for our consideration. For Bourdieu the objective of sociology should be to expose symbolic violence, to attack dominant representations that justify dominant social relations and hide underlying power relations. This activist orientation poses a challenge to mainstream sociology, which is strongly influenced by a positivist sense of objectivity. Are we ready to follow in this direction or is there something problematic about this political activist orientation?

Taking the Concepts into Research

I want to consider how Bourdieu's theoretical triad—field, capital, and habitus —embody these orienting principles and might be employed in new sociological research.

All three concepts are constructed against the most visible, obvious, taken-for-granted units that immediately invite our attention and catch the naked eye: individuals, social groups, and organizations and the transactions that occur among those units. Empirical objects must be sociologically constructed. They need to challenge received views. Bourdieu also sees all of his master concepts linked relationally. Definitionally they do not stand alone in Bourdieu's thinking (Bourdieu and Wacquant 1992: 96). Strictly speaking, Bourdieu does not offer a theory of fields, a theory of capital, or a theory of habitus as stand-alone conceptual perspectives. A tendency in Americans' appropriation of Bourdieu is to extract one concept from the overall orienting framework and to try to test it empirically. In the sociology of education, for example, one finds the theory of cultural capital, as if that could be operationalized nonrelationally (Lareau and Weininger 2004; Swartz 2005). But if one wants to follow Bourdieu's mode of thinking one cannot carry out field analysis without employing the concepts of capital and habitus.

FIELDS AND CAPITALS

Field is a prime conceptual instrument by which Bourdieu constructs his sociological objects of research. He (Bourdieu and Wacquant 1992: 97) offers the following definition of *field*: "In analytic terms, a field may be defined as a network, or configuration, of objective relations between positions. These positions are objectively defined, in their existence and in the determinations they impose upon their occupants, agents or institutions, by their present and potential situation (*situs*) in the structure of the distribution of species of power (or capital) whose possession commands access to the specific profits that are at stake in the field, as well as by their objective relation to other positions (domination, subordination, homology, etc.)."

Fields are arenas of struggle over what Bourdieu calls *capitals* (valued resources—see definition below). They are structured spaces configured around specific types of capital or combinations of capital. The configured relationships of capitals should be the focus of research. Fields are analytic constructs, not simple reflections of social reality.

The concept of field draws on Bourdieu's fundamental presupposition (metatheoretical disposition) that social units develop their identity in opposition to others and that an adequate grasp of their sociological character requires that they be situated within this broader arena of opposing relations. The concept encourages the researcher to seek out arenas of conflict and struggle that develop with the emergence of particular kinds of valued resources, or capitals.

In conventional methodological language, the field is the unit of analysis and is constructed from different observational units, whether those units are individuals, groups, organizations, social interactions, or artifacts. We do not actually observe fields directly; we construct them from the relevant empirical realities that operate interrelationally. A field perspective, therefore, includes not just one type of social unit, say, churches in the field of religion, but all types of units that are implicated in any significant way in religious activity, such as seminaries, schools of religion, publications, publishing houses, tv and radio broadcasting, music and mass media, and so forth.

How might one construct a field? First, identify some arena of struggle. Ask what the struggle is over? (Where is the fire?) Do not think of it simply in topological terms, such as the space of all higher education institutions or the arena of religion that would include all places of worship. That would be too empiricist and too abstract. Population ecology is not a Bourdieusian field. All nonprofits do not constitute a field. Start with a struggle. What are some people struggling over? That will help identify valued resources that function as power resources (capitals).

How are the structures of fields to be mapped out? Here Bourdieu introduces his concept of capital that is relationally interdependent with that of field. The concept of capital permits Bourdieu to map out the structure of the field. Resources become capital when they function as a "social relation of power" by becoming objects of struggle as valued goods (Bourdieu 1986b, 2000a: 11–13; Swartz 1997). Bourdieu shifts from a substantialist view of capital that roots value entirely in economic possession to a broader conception that includes a variety of cultural and social resources as well. Thus the various types of capital derive their value not from their intrinsic properties but from particular fields where they operate and form specific differences vis-à-vis other types of capital. As Bourdieu (Bourdieu and Wacquant 1992: 101) puts it, "A capital does not exist and function except in relation to a field." The various types of capital are relational and oppositional in the sense that one type of capital is always pitted against another, particularly cultural capital versus economic capital.

The term *capital* also reflects Bourdieu's constructionist orientation to break with received views of valued resources. Calling culture a form of capital, for example, especially in the French context with its strong literary and philosophical tradition, demarcates an analytical posture and form of analytical consciousness that distances the researcher from widely idealized views of culture. Calling religion or spirituality a form of capital might achieve a similar break with received views in the United States.

The struggle for capital occurs in two ways. First, efforts to turn some resource into a capital—a source of power that socially differentiates. Bourdieu speaks of this type of capital struggle when he talks about the struggle over definitions and classifications. Second, struggle over distributions of capital. Bourdieu speaks of this as forms of strategies whereby actors accumulate, transmit, exchange, and convert one type of capital for another in order to maintain or improve their position in some social hierarchy. Capitals function, in Bourdieu's thinking, both as weapons and as stakes in the struggle to gain power in fields.

Capitals vary not only in type (economic, social, cultural, and so forth) but also in degree of valuation within a field. The holders of a master in business administration may have more authority than holders of a doctorate in engineering in an organizational field increasingly oriented toward marketing and sales. Capitals can vary in their symbolic worth, or symbolic capital, to the extent they are accorded positive recognition and authority within a field.

Once the relevant capitals have been identified, try to identify all the important players and their respective and relative positions. Actors bring to fields of struggle distinct profiles of capital holdings. And they occupy positions that require distinct configurations of capitals. Identifying the relevant players and the forms of capital they bring to the struggle are simultaneous tasks, not separate stages in the research process. Researchers should try to identify the dominant, dominated, and intermediate positions in terms of the volume and mix of relevant capitals. Look for significant differences or oppositions. This will give the structure of the field.

Field positions are relational and oppositional. Fields are polarized between those players who occupy dominant positions in terms of their volume and mix of capitals and try to maintain their dominance by defending the status quo, and the challengers, who attempt to restructure the capital configuration of the field by trying to accumulate more capital or to introduce new forms of capital. The challenge of heterodoxy to orthodoxy can be thought of in terms of conflict over capitals. Some positions are rising in importance whereas others are declining. New positions emerge around new configurations of capital. Old ones disappear.

The tasks of constructing the field of positions by identifying the relevant players and their positions will call for developing a basic, yet fairly extensive knowledge of the field. Bourdieu strongly advises using ethnographic observation of behavior, statements, and the compiling of statistical regularities of practices, both material and symbolic, of the significant players. Bourdieu (Bourdieu and Wacquant 1992: 230) recommends using the technique of a cross-tabular analysis at an early stage of the research process as a way of identifying the relational character of those traits that group and discriminate different individuals, groups, organizations, and institutions. Cross-tabulate potential players with all the properties that seem pertinent. Select the columns of properties that differentiate the greatest number of agents to identify the system of variation among agents. This will eventually yield the relevant capitals and the principal positions structuring the struggle and a map of positions showing proximity and opposition as captured in the graphic display of correspondence analysis, Bourdieu's preferred statistical technique for showing relationality and field properties.[16]

The researcher will also need to familiarize himself or herself with the history of the struggle and the players involved. Constructing the field will require the researcher to digest vast amounts of relevant historical material.[17] This enormous task will be guided by a sense of the craft rather than by textbook methodological guidelines. Bourdieu likens learning the art of constructing the object to that of an apprentice following the example of the mentor, that of the workshop or laboratory rather than the lecture hall or textbook in methodology.[18] The researcher begins with early intuitions about organizing principles of the struggle and puts them to the empirical test, refining them as more data are gathered and begin to form a coherent picture. Bourdieu (Bourdieu and Wacquant 1992: 227–28) stresses that the research task of constructing the object or field is not accomplished by a sudden gush of theoretical inspiration or by following a "methodological blueprint drawn up in advance" but by a "protracted and exacting task that is accomplished little by little." Constructing fields of struggle is not for the fainthearted or for the nine-to-five schedule; it requires a tremendous amount of work.

POSITIONS AND STANCES

Integrating subjective and objective dimensions of social life means mapping out as well the field of stances (*prises de position*), that is, actual practices (physical and symbolic—acts and expressions) of agents, in addition to the field of positions. Here also one will find a structure of oppositions, a field differentiated by the dominant expressions of orthodoxy and the challenging expressions of heterodoxy. Bourdieu (Bourdieu and Wacquant 1992: 105) sees these tasks as "methodologically inseparable." Generally he suggests that in "situations of equilibrium" these two fields, positions and stances, tend to fit such that the positions tend to generate the stances. This, for example, is his overall finding in *Homo Academicus* (1988a [1984b]).

The fit Bourdieu frequently posits between the field of positions and the field of stances can lead to a form of field position reductionism as I charged in an earlier work (Swartz 1997: 241), and many others have noted as well. Elsewhere Bourdieu seems to accord more autonomy to the field of stances, suggesting a relative autonomy of culture within fields as well as the relative autonomy of cultural fields themselves from other fields.[19] But there is ambiguity in Bourdieu's position here. I would say that his conceptual frame is open to significant mismatch between stances and positions, and this can be the source of change. But Bourdieu himself tended not to stress this option for two reasons: (1) because he was sharply critical of all forms of Sartrian voluntarism, and (2) because he saw academics, writers, and artists, excessively prone to stress, by professional ideology, their belief in their capacity to transcend traditional constraints of subjective bias. Bourdieu saw his work as an empirically informed reminder that choice, insight, and creativity do not simply drop out of the sky.

RELATIONS BETWEEN FIELDS

Constructing the field leads the researcher as far as the effects of the field can be discerned. Bourdieu (Bourdieu and Wacquant 1992: 109) says there are "*no transhistoric laws of the relations between fields*." Relations between fields are historical, not fixed. Neither are they teleological; they can be reversed. Fields can lose autonomy, as he thinks is occurring in the contemporary artistic field in the face of the economic interests of publishers, galleries, museums, and mass marketing.

A relational understanding of fields also means there can be no a priori answer to the question of field boundaries; they are a matter of empirical investigation (Bourdieu and Wacquant 1992: 100, 104). They cannot be decided by some operationalist imposition on the part of the researcher. Indeed, Bourdieu stresses that boundaries themselves are frequently contested. That it may be very difficult for the researcher to say exactly where one field ends and another begins is not a problem of method but conveys a realistic account of the practical and contested character of social reality itself.

Many have observed circularity here in Bourdieu's program and one he freely admits: fields are defined by their effects and their effects define fields. Yet it is important here as elsewhere to stress that Bourdieu's concepts are not straightjackets but are designed to foster research. The constructionist and relational principles undergirding concepts like field motivate the search for a much broader range and mix of types of data than appears in much conventional sociology.

Constructing the research object within a field of relations facilitates the reflexive practice of social science since the researcher is less likely to input essentialist characteristics into the object of investigation or to project the researcher's own field position into the research object.

HABITUS

The space of positions and the space of stances, Bourdieu argues, are homologous and mutually constitutive. Occupants of opposing positions by virtue of their capital holdings (volume and mix) tend to assume stances that are similarly opposed. And the stances they uphold tend to reinforce oppositions in their positions. This homology of structures occurs because of the third key concept, habitus.

Habitus gives the fit between positions and stances. Stances are mediated by actor strategies shaped by the habitus. More generally, habitus aligns actors to field positions. So field placement of actors in fields is provided by habitus. Field and habitus go together; they are relational.

Habitus also provides a basis for homologies across different fields where actors occupy homologous positions in different fields. It is habitus that helps create homologies between fields.

One of the most widely cited definitions of habitus goes as follows: "A system of lasting, transposable dispositions which, integrating past experiences, functions at every moment as a matrix of perceptions, appreciations, and actions and makes possible the achievement of infinitely diversified tasks, thanks to analogical transfers of schemes permitting the solution of similarly shaped problems" (Bourdieu 1977: 82–83).[20] The concept embodies a theory of action that is practical rather than discursive, prereflective rather than conscious, embodied as well as cognitive, durable though adaptive, reproductive though generative and inventive, and the product of particular social conditions though transposable to others. The concept of habitus invites us to think of social practices in dispositional terms, and by this Bourdieu means that practices are created and regulated by internalized, generalized, and transposable dispositions rather than by rules, norms, or external structures or by conscious intentions or calculations. A dispositional reading of the concept encourages the researcher to identify those dispositions from past socialization that actors are likely to bring, unconsciously for the most part, to situations of action.

The concept of habitus offers a programmatic research agenda for addressing the agency/structure issue. The research agenda derives from Bourdieu's theory that action is generated by the encounter between opportunities and constraints presented by situations and the durable dispositions that reflect the socialization of past experiences, traditions, and habits that individuals bring to situations. His programmatic agenda mounts a challenge to academic sociology by claiming that micro and macro and objective and subjective levels of analysis are not to be separated by forms of theoretical or methodological specialization. He argues that theory and empirical research must proceed simultaneously on both levels rather than, as is frequently the practice today, confining attention to just one type of data or level of analysis.

Ethnographic observations of self-presentation, both bodily and symbolically, in the manner shown by Erving Goffman, are useful data resources for constructing the habitus.[21] I think looking for behavioral and symbolic expressions that indicate aspirations and expectations for the future is one promising source of data for describing habitus. What seems reasonable or unreasonable, likely or unlikely, natural or unthinkable for group members? Who are the entitled? Who self-exclude?

This alignment between the dispositions of habitus and the expectations of field positions is seldom perfect. Expectations from the past seldom fit exactly with existing opportunities. There is a dynamic of adaptation and adjustment. Some degree of change is almost always occurring. In extreme situations, where sharp disjuncture occurs between the expectations of habitus and the opportunities and constraints offered by field positions, crisis can occur, motivating or creating the conditions for significant transformation.

Thus research must include not only the identifying of fields of struggle and their relevant capitals but also the kinds of habitus brought by agents to their respective positions and the social trajectories they pursue with the fields of struggle. The research program consists of three steps: (1) identify the field being analyzed vis-à-vis the field of power, (2) map out the structure of the relations between the positions (on the basis of the types and amounts of capital) within the field, and (3) analyze the habitus of the agents (Bourdieu and Wacquant 1992: 104–5) and, in doing so, employ the various metaprinciples.

In sum, Bourdieu's concepts are not straightjackets but are designed to foster research. The various metaprinciples undergirding concepts like capital, field, and habitus motivate the search for a much broader range and mix of types of data and levels of analysis than appears in much conventional sociology. I have identified six metaprinciples that I believe will be helpful for orienting new research in a Bourdieusian perspective. Sociology, for Bourdieu, was, after all, a program for doing actual research.

Notes

While a few supporting references have been added and several editorial adjustments made, this chapter preserves the character of the oral presentation originally delivered at the conference on "Bourdieuian Theory and Historical Analysis" at Yale University from April 28 to May 1, 2005.

1. I recommend looking at the last section of *An Invitation to Reflexive Sociology* (Bourdieu and Wacquant 1992), "The Practice of Reflexive Sociology (The Paris Workshop)," for a useful reminder of how Bourdieu wanted students to adopt his manner of sociological research. Here Bourdieu seems more interested in developing among his students a set of dispositions for research than in elaborating a battery of well-defined concepts for careful empirical operationalization.

2. Bourdieu seldom discusses the ensemble of his conceptual tools. "The Forms of Capital" (Bourdieu 1986b) is one place where he lays out his thinking about the term *capital*. *An Invitation to Reflexive Sociology* (Bourdieu and Wacquant 1992) is one notable effort to clarify his sociological approach and to respond to several of its critics.

3. Bourdieu (Bourdieu and Wacquant 1992: 228) warns against using concepts like field, capital, and habitus as "'theoretical' instruments . . . in themselves and for themselves, rather than to put them in motion and make them *work*."

4. While capital, habitus, and field are widely recognized today as Bourdieu's master concepts, there is a broader array of concepts, including symbolic power and violence, doxa, classification struggles, and reflexivity, that will interest researchers as well. The general orienting principles I outline here apply in general to all of Bourdieu's concepts, not just to field, habitus, and capital.

5. The perspective I outline here benefits enormously from the seminal paper "Social Theory as Habitus" by Rogers Brubaker (1993). It also benefits from Bourdieu's "The Practice of Reflexive Sociology (The Paris Workshop)," which, as noted, appears as part 3 in *An Invitation to Reflexive Sociology* (Bourdieu and Wacquant 1992). I highly recommend both for insights into how Bourdieu thought about his concepts, particularly in his later years.

6. Bourdieu (1986b).

7. David Swartz (2013).

8. Further, drawing inspiration from the French philosopher of science Gaston Bachelard (1949, 1980, 1984), Bourdieu holds that the logic of scientific investigation is one of ongoing and renewed critical examination of existing scientific understandings of the social world. Scientific work progresses polemically by negation; it refuses to grant existing, established scientific procedures and theories some universal status or nonhistorical truth. Earlier conceptualizations and constructs are to be displaced and replaced by new, more encompassing understandings. Why is this necessary? Because social scientific conceptualizations can become invested in existing power relations that must always be subjected to challenge. Science needs to break with the taken-for-granted in order to reveal those power relations.

9. See Champagne et al. (1989) for illustrated techniques and cases by Bourdieu's colleagues on how to construct objects of sociological research in a Bourdieusian perspective.

10. Bourdieu (Bourdieu and Wacquant 1992: 228) admonishes researchers to "*think relationally*," to see the object of research not in terms of intrinsic features but as constituted extrinsically by a "space of relations." For example, relational thinking in terms of studying social stratification would mean not taking groups defined as populations, a realist view of actual groups, but to construct a space of relations that maps individuals and groups in terms of the distributions of power resources (their capital holdings) over which there is conflict.

11. Mustafa Emirbayer (1997) argues that relational thinking is important for social theorizing and sees Bourdieu as a key source of inspiration for advancing this kind of logical method.

12. See Brubaker (1985) and Swartz (1997: 52–60, 84–88, 96–98) for analyses of the dualisms that Bourdieu challenges.

13. Reflexivity is an enduring theme throughout Bourdieu's work. One finds it in *The Craft of Sociology* (Bourdieu et al. 1991), *Pascalian Meditations* (Bourdieu 2000b), and *Science of Science and Reflexivity* (Bourdieu 2004d [2001c]).

14. This is an important theme in the Bourdieu documentary, "Sociology is a Martial Art" (Carles 2001).

15. See Bourdieu (2008 [2002]) and Swartz (2003) for illustrations of his political activism as an intellectual.

16. Correspondence analysis is a structural statistical procedure that is a graphical variant of discriminate analysis and multidimensional scaling. It is a technique for displaying the association between rows and columns of a data matrix as points in multidimensional space such that similarities and dispersions of clusters of points are emphasized and readily visible. For Bourdieu (Bourdieu and Wacquant 1992: 96) it "is a relational technique of data analysis whose philosophy corresponds exactly to what, in my view, the reality of the social world is. It is a technique which 'thinks' in terms of relation, as I try to do precisely with the notion of field."

17. It is difficult to construct a field by looking simply at cross-sectional survey data. One needs some history to understand the changing dynamics of struggle over different types of capital.

18. In a critical jab at the French university tradition of instruction in sociology Bourdieu (Bourdieu and Wacquant 1992: 224) writes, "Thus the sociologist who seeks to transmit a scientific habitus has more in common with a high-level sports coach than with a Professeur at the Sorbonne."

19. Bourdieu (1996a [1992]: 256–57) writes, "However great the effect of the field, it is never exercised in a mechanical fashion, and the relationship between positions and position-takings (notably works of art) is always mediated by the dispositions of agents and by the space of possibles which they constitute as such through the perception of the space of position-takings they structure."

20. A later and more frequently employed formulation defines habitus as "systems of durable, transposable dispositions, structured structures predisposed to function

as structuring structures, that is, as principles which generate and organize practices and representations that can be objectively adapted to their outcomes without presupposing a conscious aiming at ends or an express mastery of the operations necessary in order to attain them" (Bourdieu 1990a: 53).

21. Brubaker (1985: 768) likens the task to one of "Proustian sensitivity" in Bourdieu's deft hands.

FOR THE SOCIAL HISTORY OF THE PRESENT
Bourdieu as Historical Sociologist

It is typical to approach the work of Pierre Bourdieu through the analytic concepts he made influential: habitus, symbolic violence, field, capital, practice, and so forth. This is not inappropriate, but it does risk making these appear as components in an abstract theoretical system rather than as working concepts shaped by the contexts in which they were deployed. Bourdieu's work can also be described in terms of the wide range of topics he addressed: exchange relations, migrant labor, education, cultural hierarchies, social domination, art, and many more. Focusing on disparate topics has contributed, however, to a fragmentary reading of Bourdieu, connecting him to different subfields of sociology or anthropology rather than drawing on his work for help in integrating social analysis.

To bring out the core of Bourdieu's analytic perspective it is helpful to see him as a historical sociologist. I obviously don't mean he inhabited a subdisciplinary specialty. Nor is the point just that Bourdieu's concepts are useful to those doing historical analysis, though this is certainly true. I do not mean simply that several of his studies were based on historical research, though many were. I mean much more basically that social transformations—and their limits and unintended consequences—were core foci of his sociological project.

Bourdieu was not always explicit about the historical specificity of his work, especially in his early studies. This resulted in ambiguity about when his analytic concepts were meant to be universal, general to modernity or states or capitalism, or specific to a particular context. Bourdieu was also shaped deeply by an ethnographic approach, writing in an elastic ethnographic present, and by a variety of philosophical and theoretical resources. Nonetheless, I suggest, grasping the way in which historical transformations shaped his approach does much to clarify it. As he said, "One of my constant struggles, particularly through *Actes de la recherché en sciences sociales*, has been to promote the development of a unified social science in which history would become a historical sociology of the past and sociology would become a social history of the present" (Bourdieu and Raphael 1995: 113).

Bourdieu's engagement with four specific social transformations shaped both his theory and his empirical approach:

1. *The way state power and market expansion and intensification produced a deracination or uprooting of "traditional" ways of life, specifically peasant life.* Bourdieu explored how long-established practices and cultural systems worked in slow-changing societies in which neither state nor economy exerted a constant or differentiated influence and then what happened to them in colonial Algeria, especially Kabylia, and in his native region of the Béarn in the Pyrenees mountains of southwest France.

2. *The creation of what other social theorists have called modern society by the differentiation of state and market power and more generally the making of fields.* Bourdieu saw each field as a domain of relative autonomy marked off from others by its distinctive hierarchy, values, struggles, styles of improvising action, and forms of capital. He analyzed the genesis and structure of a wide range of fields from law and religion to art and literature. Implicitly, he studied the production of a "fielded" society, centrally in the nineteenth century and the first part of the twentieth.

3. *The great economic expansion and welfare state project of the post–Second World War era.* Called in France *les Trente Glorieuses* (the thirty glorious years), this period promised greater equality, opportunity, and social participation but also reproduced old inequalities in new contexts and structures, and it often legitimated them by apparent meritocracy and the logic of individual responsibility for social fate. Bourdieu emphasized the false promises of equality but also the real investments people made even in institutions that didn't live up to their promises.

4. *The massive attack on the state or, more precisely, on the idea that the state should act centrally to achieve social welfare, that is often called neoliberalism.* Though this had older roots, it came to the center of attention in the 1990s, sometimes appearing as an American model imposed on Europe. Neoliberalism portended a destruction of social fields, especially those dependent on public support, and a violent reduction of the pursuit of different values to brutal market logic. This turned Bourdieu's attention more directly to what investment in different fields and the state itself had achieved, and what hopes they still offered—though also to the limits their frequent conservatism imposed on struggles for a better society.

In what follows I present these four transformations not in chronological order, as above, but in the order of Bourdieu's most sustained engagement with each—that is, 1, 3, 2, 4—though they overlap in his work. Algeria is the crucial starting point.

Algeria: Tradition, Uprooting, Old Practices, and New Logics

In 1955, late in the era of French colonial rule, Bourdieu was sent to do military service in Algeria.[1] He stayed on to teach at the University of Algiers and became a self-taught ethnographer. Bourdieu did not simply study Algeria but sought out its internal variants, regional and so-called minority communities that were stigmatized and marginalized not only by French colonialism but also by the construction of Algerian national identity as modern and Arab in opposition to rural, tribal, and traditional. *Sociologie d'Algerie*, Bourdieu's first book, describes in some detail not only "Arabic-speaking peoples," especially those along the coast and in the central plain, but also Kabyles, Shawia, and Mozabites, each of which groups had a distinct culture and traditional social order. Colonialism and market transformations were disrupting each group and, along with opposition to French rule, pulling members of each into a new, more unified Algerian system of social relations (Bourdieu 1962).

Behind Bourdieu's studies of social change, therefore, was an account of the traditional other vis-à-vis modernization, the less rapidly changing peasant culture and economy (Bourdieu 1962). The Kabyle had been Emile Durkheim's primary exemplars of traditional, segmentary social organization in *The Elementary Forms of Religious Life* (Durkheim 2001) and already had a role in France as representative of a certain type of the premodern. But at the same time, the very term *Kabyle*, the name of the group Bourdieu studied most, is derived from the Arabic word for "tribe" and marks a similar view from the vantage point of Arab modernity. It was an ascribed identity, a reminder of marginalization, even if it is now claimed. The Kabyle were dominated by France and by the dominant Algerians alike, yet they were being drawn into a new order, uprooted from traditional agricultural occupations and ways of life, working at a disadvantage in cities and struggling to keep communities together in the countryside. This double domination informed both Bourdieu's analyses of Algeria and his development of a theory of symbolic violence.[2]

Conducting research in Kabyle villages and with Berber-speaking labor migrants to the fast-growing cities of Algeria's coastal regions, Bourdieu addressed themes that ranged from the introduction of money into marriage negotiations to cosmology and the agricultural calendar to the economic crisis facing those who are forced into market relations for which they are not prepared (Bourdieu and Sayad 1964; Bourdieu 1977, 1979a). Bourdieu proved himself an extraordinarily keen observer of the interpenetration of large-scale social change and the struggles and solidarities of daily life. Among other reasons, his native familiarity with the peasant society of Béarn gave him an affinity with the traditional agrarian societies of rural Algeria that were being destroyed by French colonialism.

With Abdelmalek Sayad, Bourdieu studied peasant life and participation in the new cash economy that threatened and changed it (Bourdieu and Sayad 1964).[3] He studied the difficult situation of those who chose to work in the modern economy and found themselves transformed into its underclass, not able to gain the full status even of proletarians because of the ethnonational biases of the French colonialists (Bourdieu 1962; Bourdieu, Darbel, Rivet, and Seibel 1963) Yet at the same time, he found people unwittingly collaborating in their own disadvantages, reinforcing by misrecognition what was forced on them by circumstance.

Bourdieu initially represented the lives of the ostensibly original inhabitants of Algeria in fairly conventional terms, echoing many aspects of the more critical end of the modernization theories of the day. Increasingly, though, he began to develop not only a challenge to the idea of benign modernization, but also a much richer, more sophisticated analysis of how a traditional order could be created such that it reproduced itself with impressive efficacy without any conscious intention of doing so, or any template for that reproduction, or exercise of power in its pursuit. This was made possible, Bourdieu argued, by the very organization of social practices, combining the symbolic and the material seamlessly in a "polythetic" consciousness and inculcating practical orientations to actions in the young through experiences repeated in everyday life. The spatial organization of the household and the calendar of agricultural production were not only cultural choices or responses to material conditions, but also media of instruction organizing the ways in which the world appeared to members of the society and the ways in which each could imagine himself and improvise action (Bourdieu 1977).[4] This social order did not admit of divisions into different fields of activity with diverse specific forms of value or claims on the loyalties of members. Kinship, poetry, religion, and agriculture were not distinct, as family, art, religion, and the economy were in more allegedly modern societies. Kabyle could live in a *doxic* attitude, reproducing understanding of the world as simply the taken-for-granted way it must be, while the development of discrete fields was linked to the production of orthodoxies and heterodoxies, competing claims to right knowledge and true value.

Recognizing that the traditional order was sustained not by simple inertia or the force of cultural rules, Bourdieu turned attention to the ways in which continuous human effort, vigilance toward proper action that was simultaneously an aspect of effective play of the game, achieved reproduction. Analyzing the traditional Kabyle idea of honor (*nif*), for example, Bourdieu realized that this was both the focus of long-term investments (hence a form of cultural capital) and at risk in every interaction. Nif was constitutive of the very sense of self as a man of honor (and indeed profoundly gendered). Sustaining nif demanded a sense of appropriate timing, judgment not just following rules. This was a game peasants could play effectively in their villages. They were prepared for it by explicit teaching and by learning from all their practical experiences, usually not explicitly but tacitly, deployed in proverbs and cultural analogies or embodied as second nature or habitus. People who could play the games of honor with consummate subtlety in peasant villages, however, often found themselves incapacitated by the games of rationalized exchange in the cities. Labor migration and integration into the larger state and market stripped peasant habituses of their efficacy and indeed made the very efforts that previously had sustained village life and traditional culture potentially counterproductive. Both the accumulated cultural capital and the sense of self were violently devalued.

More generally, most Berbers had at best weak preparation for participation in the modern society of Algeria—notably, the fields of economy and politics. Apparent opportunities were in fact undercut by such inequalities of preparation to take advantage of them. At first, Bourdieu looked to education as a vehicle for equipping the marginal and dominated with the capacity to compete effectively in the new order.[5] Eventually, he saw education as more contradictory, providing necessary tools but only in a system that reinforced and legitimated subordination. Kabyles and other Berbers not only wound up being dominated but colluded in their own subjugation because of the ways in which they felt themselves to be different and disabled. Experience constantly taught the lesson that there was no way for "people like us" to succeed. Occasional exceptions were more easily explained away than the ubiquitous reinforcement that inculcated pessimism as habitus. Feeling fundamentally ill-equipped for the undertakings of Algeria's new modern sector, they transformed a fact of discrimination into a principle of self-exclusion and reduced ambition.

This was a theme to which Bourdieu returned in his studies of the village culture of Béarn in the 1960s. If his rural youth attuned him to certain aspects of Algerian experience, his analyses of Algeria opened his eyes to key dimensions of the world of his youth. There was a match even to linguistic reinforcement of a sense of difference; Bourdieu's family spoke Gascon when he was a child. Yet Béarn was being incorporated into centralizing France, and, for all the universalism of republican ideology, on unequal terms. Bourdieu took up a variety of themes, from matrimonial strategies to gender relations. Writing of bachelors at a rural village ball, he observed peasant men standing back from the dance, seemingly shy, unable, or unwilling to approach attractive girls who had found work and new aspirations in the expanding economy of nearby cities. The bachelors literally embodied the contradictions of social change as they came to judge their own bodies as rough and clumsy by urban standards, not least the standards of women they might have wished to marry but who embraced new opportunities as well as new cultural styles (Bourdieu 2008c).

Bourdieu fused ethnography and statistics, theory and observation, to begin crafting a distinctive approach to social inquiry aimed at informing progressive politics through scientific production. In some ways, it may have helped to be self-taught because this encouraged Bourdieu to ignore some of the artificial oppositions structuring the social sciences, for example, between quantitative and qualitative inquiry. Research also gave Bourdieu an approach to practical action at a time when he felt caught uncertainly between political camps. At one point he drew heavily on Frantz Fanon, for example, and then vehemently rejected the revolutionary politics that had initially attracted him, seeing it as naively and sometimes dangerously romantic (Bourdieu 1962; Lane 2000). Convinced that total revolution was impossible, but also that the French state was insupportable, Bourdieu sought, without complete success, an approach that would give adequate weight to the power of social reproduction without simply affirming it.

At the heart of Bourdieu's approach to practice lay the notion of habitus. The concept is old, rooted in Aristotle's notion of bodily "hexis" and transmuted and transmitted by Thomas Aquinas in his approach to learning and memory. It is used by a range of modern thinkers, including G. W. F. Hegel, Edmund Husserl, and Marcel Mauss. Norbert Elias had recovered the term to help grasp the transformations of manners in modern European history.[6] Bourdieu's concept was specifically more social and more bodily than, say, Husserl's usage, which focused on the background understandings latent in any act. Though Husserl understood action, including perception, in individual and cognitive terms, he did stress the importance of dispositions and horizons of potential acts. Maurice Merleau-Ponty, a more proximate source for Bourdieu, stressed the generative role of the habitus, the ways in which embodied knowledge transmutes past experience into dispositions for particular sorts of action, not only in familiar but also, though less effectively, in new situations. As Bourdieu writes, "The conditionings associated with a particular class of conditions of existence produce *habitus*, systems of durable, transposable dispositions, structured structures predisposed to function as structuring structures, that is, as principles which generate and organize practices and representations that can be objectively adapted to their outcomes without presupposing a conscious aiming at ends or an express mastery of the operations necessary in order to attain them. Objectively 'regulated' and 'regular' without being in any way the product of obedience to rules, they can be collectively orchestrated without being the product of the organizing action of a conductor" (Bourdieu 1990a [1980]).

Habitus is important to the project of understanding how a traditional society works—how honor is achieved and respect demonstrated, for example, in ways that can never be reduced to or reproduced by following rules. But it is not a concept limited to or definitive of traditional social order. In all settings people improvise new actions based on past learnings embodied as habits and seldom made explicit. And in times of transition some suffer difficulties in generating appropriate actions for new circumstances. If habitus is central to mastery, whether of a craft or of social games, it is also central to subordination. People learn from past experience, for example, to limit their aspirations. Habitus is an internalization of social structure and a capacity to generate creative responses. Even the responses that succeed in breaking with some dimensions of old structures or in adapting to new circumstances remain marked by learning that situates individuals in structures and shapes their trajectories through them. Habitus is a condition of doing anything and at the same time a powerful factor in the reproduction of established patterns of action. Among other things, the habitus can lead to a naturalization and internalization of the inequalities also reproduced by symbolic violence.

With concepts like habitus and also symbolic violence and power, Bourdieu sought a way to move beyond the dualisms of structure and action, objective and subjective, social physics and social semiotics and especially to inject a stronger account of temporality and temporal contingency into social analysis.[7] His effort was not merely to forge a theoretical synthesis but to develop the capacity to overcome some of the opposition between theoretical knowledge based on objectification of social life and phenomenological efforts to grasp its embodied experience and (re)production in action. Human social action is at once "structured" and "structuring," Bourdieu argued, indeed structuring *because* it is structured, with the socialized body as "analogical operator of practice." Habitus is internalized experience, embodied culture and history.

There is no simple, context-free or transhistorical solution to the riddle of structure and agency. Rather, their mutual constitution and subsequent interaction must be worked out in analysis of concrete empirical cases. In his analyses of Algeria, Bourdieu is attentive to contemporary history—French colonialism, expanding markets, urbanization—but does not delve into the history of Kabylia. He allows it to appear largely as the traditional, unchanging other to the historical transition he studies.[8] This is not equally true in his studies of France, where he works by reconstituting, first, the social genesis and makeup of objective social worlds, or fields, within which agents develop and operate, and, second, the socially constituted dispositions, or habitus, which fashion the manner of thinking, feeling, and acting of these agents. This double historicization calls for field and habitus to be related in analysis of specific temporal processes and trajectories. Moreover, it must be complemented by the historicization of the analytic categories and problematics of the inquiring scholar. Only in this way can social scientists do the necessary, if hard, labor of "conquering and constructing social facts," that is, of distinguishing the hidden forms and mechanisms of social reality from the received understandings of previous academic knowledge, folk knowledge, and the everyday preconceptions of culture more generally. On this basis, empirically based reflexive analysis can also establish the social and epistemological conditions for both the objective and subjective perspectives themselves and for avoiding the pitfalls of what Bourdieu later termed "the scholastic bias," that is, the tendency of social analysts to project their own (hermeneutic) relation to the social world into the minds of the people they observe (Bourdieu 1998d).

These studies helped forge Bourdieu's theory of practice and informed his entire intellectual trajectory, including both academic endeavors and his later political critique of neoliberalism. Near the end of his life, he wrote, "As I was able to observe in Algeria, the unification of the economic field tends, especially through monetary unification and the generalization of monetary exchanges that follow, to hurl all social agents into an economic game for which they are not equally prepared and equipped, culturally and economically. It tends by the same token to submit them to standards objectively imposed by competition from more efficient productive forces and modes of production, as can readily be seen with small rural producers who are more and more completely torn away from self-sufficiency. In short, *unification benefits the dominant*" (Bourdieu 2003b: 93). Unification could be a project not only of the colonial state but also of national states, the European community, and the World Trade Organization.

Les Trente Glorieuses: Education, Inequality, and Reproduction

When Bourdieu returned to France the postwar economic boom was in full swing. Urbanization was extremely rapid. Homeownership was on the rise.

Personal consumption was expanding rapidly. Widespread ownership of cars, for example, offered both convenience and a sense of movement into the middle class and simultaneously expanded the distances within which village and small town residents could work. New hobbies like photography spread.[9] At the same time, the distinctive European welfare state model was being created; France was a leading exemplar. Social mobility and greater equality were promised. Expansion of educational opportunities was a central part of the promise.

In 1964, in collaboration with Jean-Claude Passeron, Bourdieu published *The Inheritors*, the first of several groundbreaking studies of schools, cultural distinction, and class division (Bourdieu and Passeron 1977, 1979). The theme was straightforward but powerful. Education appeared to be neutral and available on an open, meritocratic basis, but in fact it reproduced class bias. It did this partly by embracing hierarchy and distributing success in ways that rewarded prior family accumulation and transmission of cultural capital. Schooling thus achieved its apparent meritocracy by an act of symbolic violence; it legitimized the prevailing social order by manipulating the categories through which it was produced and reproduced. Pedagogical work imposed a "cultural arbitrary" but made it appear neutral or universal. Familiarity with bourgeois language, for example, translated into differences in performance on academic tests. Read in English narrowly as texts in the sociology or anthropology of education, *The Inheritors* and *Reproduction* were also more general challenges to the French state. Bourdieu saw the sociology of education not simply as a specialized pursuit but as being at the very core of sociology because of the insight it offered into the reproduction of inequality in modern societies as they came to rely more and more on both credentials reflecting specialized training and the certification of high levels of attainment of canonical general knowledge, or culture.

In France the national education system stood as perhaps the supreme exemplar of the pretended seamless unity and neutrality of the state in its simultaneous roles as representative of the nation and embodiment of reason and progress. Bourdieu showed not merely that it was biased, a fact potentially corrigible, but that it was biased in principle. This was read by some as a blanket condemnation; Bourdieu was seen nearly as antischooling. Bourdieu's disappointment was in fact more complicated. He worried later that this loose reading of his work encouraged teachers simply to adopt lax standards in order not to be seen or to see themselves as agents of symbolic violence. Poor teaching and weak standards did not eliminate class inequality, after all. In fact, they reduced the extent to which schools could give students a chance to overcome inherited, familial differences in cultural capital.

Bourdieu's early work on Algeria suggests that he started out with a conviction that reformed educational institutions and access could provide the dominated and marginalized with effective resources for political and economic participation. They might remedy the poor preparation of ex-peasants for the new commercial society and postcolonial politics. If only they could be organized to provide fair, open, and effective access to high-value cultural goods, he implied in concert with many educational reformers, then educational institutions could be the crucial means for improving society. By the mid-1960s, however, he saw education failing to play this role (Robbins 2004; Grenfell 2005). This was not narrowly a failing of schools, however, but a contribution of the educational field to the field of power more generally, a contribution organized in part by the ways in which schools and teachers related to the overall organization of cultural hierarchy, markets, and especially the state. Schools were organized not merely to teach, after all, but to perform selection and exclusion. They simultaneously maintained and disguised the class structure. This was an issue that Bourdieu addressed in a range of further works, including books on higher education and in *Distinction*, his great study of the hierarchical organization of cultural taste. Education did not have to be merely a process of reproduction, but it would take self-conscious reform, reform aided by the reflexive view sociological research provided, to change this outcome. This would also require political will.

Bourdieu's view of the educational system reflected the disappointed idealism of one who had invested himself deeply in it and owed much of his rise from provincial obscurity to Parisian prominence to success in school. As he wrote in *Homo Academicus*, he was like someone who believed in a religious vocation then found the church to be corrupt. "The special place held in my work by a somewhat singular sociology of the university institution is no doubt explained by the peculiar force with which I felt the need to gain rational control over the disappointment felt by an 'oblate' faced with the annihilation of the truths and values to which he was destined and dedicated, rather than take refuge in feelings of self-destructive resentment" (Bourdieu 1988: xxvi).[10] The disappointment could not be undone, but it could be turned to understanding and potentially, through that understanding, to positive change.

Educational institutions were central to Bourdieu's concern, but his sense of disappointment and his critical analyses both reached widely. All the institutions of modernity, including the capitalist market and the state itself, share in a tendency to promise far more than they deliver. They present themselves as working for the common good but in fact reproduce social inequalities. They present themselves as agents of freedom but in fact are organizations of power. They inspire devotion from those who want richer, freer lives, and they disappoint them with the limits they impose and the violence they deploy.

In educational institutions, particular systems of categories, contents, and outcomes are presented as necessary and neutral. Forming the taxonomic order of both the way academics think and the way the system is organized, these impressively protect against internal critique and therefore against successful reform and improvement. One senses Bourdieu's outrage at professors who can't see the system reflexively and critically even while he explains their complacency and incapacity sociologically: "The homology between the structures of the educational system (hierarchy of disciplines, of sections, etc.) and the mental structures of the agents (professorial taxonomies) is the source of the functioning of the consecration of the social order which the education system performs behind its mask of neutrality" (Bourdieu 1988: 204). In short, the educational system is a field. It has a substantial autonomy, which it must protect, and a distinctive form of capital which depends on that autonomy for its efficacy. It is internally organized as a set of transposable dispositions and practical taxonomies that enable participants to understand their world and to take effective actions, but that also produce and reproduce specific inequalities among them and make these appear natural. These can be challenged, as indeed Bourdieu did by analyzing them, but it should not be thought that they can simply be dispensed with, at least not without losing the basic goods they are organized to deliver. The benefits are bound up with the distortions, providing the larger field of power with powerful legitimation through the process of the conversion of educational capital into more directly economic, political, or other forms.

This happens, like much else, through a dialectic of incorporation and objectification (Bourdieu 1977, 1990a). The education system depends on the inculcation of its categories as the mental structures of agents and on the simultaneous manifestation of these as material structures of organization. This enables the production of objective effects that do not cease to be objective and materially powerful simply by pointing to the subjective moments in their creation. It is true that there is "symbolic aggression observable in all examination situations" (and Bourdieu goes to great lengths to document and analyze such things as the terms teachers use in commenting on examination papers) but it is not true that this is explicable simply as the psychological attitude of individual agents. Rather, it is a disposition inculcated by agents' own trajectories through the educational field (as students as well as teachers) and both reproduced and rendered apparently neutral by its match to the categories of organization and value in the field as a whole.

More generally, the social order is effectively consecrated through the educational system because it is able to appear as neutral and necessary. In one of Bourdieu's favorite metaphors for describing his work, Mao Zedong's notion of "twisting the stick in the other direction," he turned the structuralist analysis of taxonomies in another way by mobilizing it for a critical account of the logic of practice.[11] In the context of les trentes glorieuses, this was central to showing how certain organizations of inequality could produce compliance rather than protest and to exposing the false promises of visions that a rising tide lifts all boats—which helped his work contribute in due course to protest. For Bourdieu it was especially important to analyze the idealization of culture because it figured centrally in French nationalism and the legitimation of both state power and market expansion. Charles de Gaulle established a Ministry of Culture in France in 1959, appointing André Malraux to head it and charging it with both the celebration of high culture and the production of a cohesive account of Frenchness through an inventory of the heritage each locality brought to the whole. When Bourdieu undertook to demonstrate that culture was a realm not of simple, disinterested ideals but one that operated on the base of its own economy, albeit one that reversed certain evaluative premises of the business economy, this was not simply an exercise in value-neutral sociology of culture but a politically salient engagement with continuing transformations in French society (Bourdieu 1993c).

Bourdieu's studies of education were part of a broader approach to culture, power, and inequality. Informed by a series of empirical studies of art and artistic institutions starting in the 1960s (Bourdieu, Darbel, and Schnapper 1990; Bourdieu, Boltanski, Castel, Chamboredon, and Schnapper 1990), this line of work is most widely known through *Distinction*, Bourdieu's monumental study of the social organization of taste. The politics and historical context of this body of work are not always clear. It is work that comes to terms with historically transformed structures of class inequality and explores the potential for new kinds of struggles over inequality. These could include direct action like strikes but also necessarily would need to include struggles over classification.

Distinction is an analysis of how culture figures in social inequality and how the pursuit of distinction or differential recognition shapes all realms of social practice. It is also an effort to "move beyond the opposition between objectivist theories which identify the social classes (but also the age or sex classes) with discrete groups, simple countable populations separated by boundaries objectively drawn in reality, and subjectivist (or marginalist) theories which reduce the 'social order' to a sort of collective classification obtained by aggregating the individual classifications or, more precisely, the individual strategies, classified and classifying, through which agents class themselves and others" (Bourdieu 1984a: 489). Bourdieu develops the argument that struggles over classification are themselves important and largely ignored aspects of class struggle, though also struggles that must include questioning conventional, inherited definitions of class. Here Bourdieu is not only bringing Weberian attention to prestige, but also addressing the changes in structures of inequality wrought by credentialism, professionalization of work, the delivery of state welfare services—and the list would eventually include questions of citizenship and the status of immigrants.

Bourdieu drew from structuralism many specifics of his argument that classification is materially efficacious. But classification is, for Bourdieu, an exercise of political power and potentially challengeable by a political and also cultural struggle. In a sense he offered a more precise and empirical account of the production of hegemony than Antonio Gramsci or than Louis Althusser's notion of ideological state apparatuses. This is not the impersonal power of Michel Foucault but a more directly transitive power, wielded by agents in defense of their interests and in support of their projects. As Bourdieu was fond of pointing out, the root of *categorize* also means to accuse, and deployment of categories was often an act of symbolic violence.

Distinction, however, is also a response to Immanuel Kant's Third Critique (Kant 1987) and to subsequent philosophical disquisitions on judgment. Much as Durkheim (Durkheim 1951) had sought to challenge individualistic explanation of social facts, so Bourdieu sought to uncover the social roots and organization of all forms of judgment. Kant's argument had sought an approximation in practical reason to the universality available more readily to pure reason. He had seen this as crucial equally to artistic taste and political opinion. But he had imagined a standpoint of disinterested judgment from which practical reason and critique might proceed. Bourdieu accepted the analogy between art and politics, but not this idea of disinterest or of a place outside social struggles from which neutral knowledge might issue. He was not precisely against universality so much as a critic of the illusion of the universal deployed to justify the arbitrary. He shared this critique of ostensible neutrality with Foucault and other poststructuralists but he differed importantly in arguing that knowledge not only buttresses the hierarchies of the social world but also can be an effective part of the struggle to change that world. The key is to recognize that knowledge is never produced from a standpoint outside world or struggle, and adopt a reflexive approach. The world-as-it-is-perceived issues out of and bolsters the world-as-it-is, but a struggle over classification may actually change the world. And—crucial to Bourdieu—that struggle need not be simply a matter of power but can be conducted as a matter of knowledge that transcends mere power even if it does not escape struggles over power and recognition altogether. It is the job of the scientific field to organize collective interests in the pursuit of truth. In short, we needn't go down a simplistically conceived Nietzschean path toward a choice between simple embrace of the will to power or a futile resistance to it. On the contrary, "there is, as Nietzsche pointed out, no immaculate conception; but nor is there any original sin—and the discovery that someone who discovered the truth had an interest in doing so in no way diminishes his discovery" (Bourdieu 2000b: 3).

Philosophy, art, and even science may operate with a denial of interest (Bourdieu 1975, 1997). Economics and less academic discourses about economic matters commonly embrace interest. But they operate with a presumption of neutrality and objectivity that renders them vulnerable to a closely related critique. For if the cultural world is the economic world reversed, as Bourdieu famously put it (Bourdieu 1993c), it is also true that much liberal economics turns precisely on the denial of cultural significance, the positing of "interests" as objective, and the perception of economic systems as matters of necessity rather than products of choice and power and therefore potentially to be improved by struggle. There is no disinterested account of interests, no neutral and objective standpoint from which to evaluate policy, not even academic economics (Sayer 1999). But this doesn't remove economic matters from science, it simply extends the demand for a truly reflexive social science and for an overcoming of the oppositions between structure and action, objective and subjective to economics and economic analysis. The economy has no more existence separate from or prior to the rest of society than art or philosophy. It is not merely necessity, to which we may only adapt, any more than artistic creativity is simply freedom with no social base.

Fields, Specific Capital, Monopolies, and "Non-Domination"

As Bourdieu's analysis of the limits of les trente glorieuses matured, he became increasingly engaged in the analysis of social fields. This was his approach to problems of social differentiation. It led him to questions about the historical genesis and structure of such fields and to further development of his account of the forms of capital and their convertibility. In addition to the book-length works on education and art, Bourdieu published substantial articles on the religious, scientific, philosophical, and juridical fields. In these and other investigations he laid the basis for a general theory of fields as differentiated social microcosms operating as spaces of objective forces and arenas of struggle over value that refract and transmute external determinations and interests. This became increasingly a theory of the distinctive nature of modern society as "fielded" society, organized by the ways in which fields worked internally, related to each other, and mediated the influences of state and market.

This took Bourdieu into the study of longer-term historical transformations—for example, as the modern French religious field was shaped by a long Catholic history, the Protestant Reformation, the creation of a state church and secular opposition to it. In this connection he introduced the notion of "structuration" (later taken up by Anthony Giddens) to call attention to the fact that cultural and social structures were always incompletely solidified and hence potentially changing (Bourdieu 1991c). Fields represent Bourdieu's specification of what Max Weber called the different value-spheres of modern society. But he sees these relationally, and always as objects and sites of struggle.

Bourdieu's initial engagement with fields focused largely on their conservatism and especially the way in which their actual operation could undercut the universalism of much modern ideology. Modern states and markets both unified society and presented individuals as equal in their rights to property and political subjectivity. But this was a formal universality imposed on people who actually differed in their resources and preparation. Treating people equally, without actually empowering them equally, reinscribed inequality in less straightforward form. And imposing centralization and integration onto larger-scale units such as nation-states and international markets could actually deprive ordinary people of collective resources.

However, if fields demonstrated the illusory character of universal promises, they also presented a better grounding for republican arguments about a good society. Bourdieu argued first for replacing the exclusive emphasis on individuals as rights bearers—a dominant operationalization of autonomy in the sense Kant theorized it—with more attention to "non-domination," which was achieved collectively (Pettit 1997). Second, he emphasized the importance of the "specific capital" of each field, the good that it distinctively valued and produced. The convertibility of capital demanded attention precisely to the extent that it could not be accomplished by simple reduction to cash transactions without destroying the logic of fields. This was republican in the strong sense that it focused on the decentralized social production of public goods.[12]

Each field is created through struggles among its members as they compete with each other to produce and be recognized for producing its distinctive value. Indeed, the very definition or constitution of that distinctive value is a product of their struggles, but it becomes also the basis for their collective autonomy. Historically, fields represent successful claims to distinctive kinds of value and to distinctive capacity to provide that value to society more generally. This capacity implies field-specific knowledge and other resources, like capital, and it implies a division of labor among fields. Lawyers should govern matters of justice, scientists matters of truth, priests access to salvation, and real estate agents the sale of homes. The implicit premise of every field is that it needs autonomy since outsiders lacking its specific knowledge will not be able to judge the quality of internal production. Outsiders buying medical services pay more for the labor of those held in high regard by other doctors; absent this field-specific hierarchy they might pay less but risk getting substandard care. Succeeding in such a claim to autonomy, Bourdieu argued, is the "critical phase" in the emergence of a field (Bourdieu 1996a).

The organization of fields is not necessarily fair, and the pursuit of field-specific standing may distort the distribution of socially valued goods, as Bourdieu argued was the case in education. Indeed, the definition of each field embodies a cultural arbitrary, a historically achieved demarcation that did not have to exist in that form. These can be challenged; their seeming necessity can be unmasked. But at the same time, fields are productive; they organize the actual delivery of distinctive goods. To abolish them without providing a new structure for the provision of important goods would be devastating. In this way, Bourdieu roots republican virtue not in abstract idealism but in partially self-interested competition for distinction.

This is a central reason Bourdieu was at pains to challenge conventional views of culture as disinterested pursuit of beauty or truth or justice. The issue is not disinterest but distinctive interests. The literary field recognizes writers, the artistic field painters, and the legal field judges only for their contributions to and achievements in their field. These may come in agonistic relations to other participants in that field. But it is a debased version of field-specific pursuit of distinction to rely on capital from outside the field, that is, to get your book reviewed favorably because your father owns the paper, to get your painting into the museum because your brother-in-law is a financial donor, to get a seat as a judge purely on the basis of politics without legal achievements. Within every field some participants are more attentive to external arbiters of value or providers of resource—the state or market actors—and others more focused on the pure form of the field's specific value. Valuing art for art's sake is crucial to the existence of a field of art, even if it may sometimes be hard to convert the symbolic capital of fellow artists' esteem into cash. Legitimate achievement and recognition depend on the autonomy of the field's specific capital from capital in general or from equally short-circuiting relations to political power.

Bourdieu was hardly anticulture. The point of exposing the misrecognition of its character in idealist accounts was not to debunk it but to make possible radically different social relations to it. Just as Karl Marx argued that capitalism produced wealth that it could not effectively distribute to all its partici-pants, so Bourdieu argued that artists produce work of great value. Likewise, science and education do in fact produce and reproduce knowledge. But in the social structures of modern society, they do so inseparably from inequalities in capacity and opportunity to appropriate that knowledge: "Economic power lies not in wealth but in the relationship between wealth and a field of eco-nomic relations, the constitution of which is inseparable from the develop-ment of a *body of specialized agents*, with specific interests; it is in this relation-ship that wealth is constituted, in the form of capital, that is, as the instrument for appropriating the institutional equipment and the mechanisms indispens-able to the functioning of the field, and thereby also appropriating the profits from it" (Bourdieu 1977: 184–85, 2000b). It would make no sense to start socialism or any more egalitarian society by willfully abolishing all the mate-rial wealth accumulated under capitalism and previous economic systems. But it would be necessary to transform the system of relations that rendered such wealth as capital and distributed it unequally. Knowledge, like cultural achievements generally, constitutes a specific form of capital, a kind of re-source deployed by those with power in relation to specific fields, for example, legal, medical, academic. But knowledge need not be organized this way.

Bourdieu's deepest work on fields as well as his most sustained historical research focused on literature and was capped by *The Rules of Art*, an inves-tigation of the symbolic revolution wrought in literature by Gustave Flaubert, Charles Baudelaire, and others (Bourdieu 1977, 1996a). Bourdieu's greatest unfinished work is probably its companion study, a sociogenetic dissection of Édouard Manet and the transformation of the field of painting in which he played a pivotal role. Both center on the organization of cultural production in the late nineteenth century, when the French state took on its modern form, secularizing definitively, establishing its monopoly and standardization of education, and so forth.

In *The Rules of Art* Bourdieu addresses the point at which the writing of realistic novels separated itself simultaneously from the broader cultural field and the immediate rival of journalism. He takes up the specific empirical case of Flaubert and his career in relation to the constitution of the field as such and the broader patterns implicit in it. The emphasis on Flaubert was, among other things, a riposte to and critical engagement, often implicit, with Jean-Paul Sartre's famous, largely psychological analysis. *The Rules of Art* contested the view of artistic achievement as disinterested and a matter simply of indi-vidual genius and creative impulses. It showed genius to lie in the ability to play the game that defines a field as well as in aesthetic vision or originality.

Flaubert was the mid-nineteenth-century writer who, more than anyone else, with the possible exception of Baudelaire, created the exemplary image of the author as an artistic creator working in an autonomous literary field. The author was not merely a writer acting on behalf of other interests: politics, say, or money. A journalist was such a paid writer, responsible to those who hired him. An author, by contrast, was an artist. This was the key point for Flaubert and for the literary field that developed around and after him. What the artistic field demanded was not just talent or vision but a commitment to art for art's sake. This meant producing works specifically for the field of art.

Writers like Flaubert and Baudelaire made strong claims for the value of their distinctive points of view. This has encouraged the analysis of their products as simply embodiments of their psychological individuality. On the other hand, they wrote "realistic" novels, engaging the social issues of their day from poverty to the Revolution of 1848 and the Paris Commune. This has encouraged others to focus on the ways in which they reflected one or another side in those issues, interpreting them, for example, as social critics or as voices of the rising middle class. Bourdieu showed how this misses the decisive importance of the creation of a field of literature as art. This meant, first, that when Flaubert and Baudelaire wrote about the issues of their day, they claimed the distinctive authority of artists. Indeed, they helped to pioneer the idea that artists might offer a special contribution to social awareness that reflected precisely their disinterestedness, the fact they were not simply political actors. Second, though, Bourdieu showed that the appearance of disinterestedness is misleading. It is produced to the extent that artists are motivated by interests specific to the artistic field and their place within it and not merely serving as spokespeople for other social positions. In other words, artists are disinterested in the terms of some other fields precisely because of the extent to which they are interested in the field of art. The autonomy of this field is thus basic to the production of artists in this sense.

The modern artistic field is defined by the difference between producing art for its own sake and producing art for the sake of religion, as (to take painting as a case) in medieval decorations of churches, or for the sake of memory and money, as in some portraiture. The new, more autonomous approach does not mean that the painter stops wanting food or fame or salvation, though he may not consciously recognize how much he is driven by these desires. Rather, what it does is orient his creative work specifically to the field of art and to the standards of judgment of others in that field. The artist in this sense doesn't just produce more of what the market wants but endeavors to create works that embody his distinctive vision and place in the field. He seeks recognition from other artists, and in his work marks off his debts to but also distinctions from them. It is because it becomes a field in this way, oriented to an internal communication and accumulation of specifically artistic capital, that the production of art becomes partially autonomous from popular and even elite tastes. Art may guide tastes, not just be guided by them, or it may operate outside the world of everyday tastes, but it may not be reduced to them. This liberates art from determination by its immediate social context, but it does not liberate artists from all interests in achieving distinction or accumulating capital. On the contrary, they are driven to innovate rather than just reproducing the masterworks of a previous generation and to innovate in ways that derive much of their form from the existing state of communication in the art field. The artistic habitus thereby enables a regulated improvisation, working with the symbolic materials at hand to express at once the artist's original vision and the artist's individual claims on the field of art. Because the art field is autonomous, its works can be understood only by those who master its internal forms of communication. This is why ordinary people find much modern art hard to understand, at least until they take classes or read the guiding statements offered by museum curators. From the mid-nineteenth century, art could become increasingly abstract partly because it was the production not simply of beauty or of a mirror on the world but of a communication among artists. This communication was driven simultaneously by the pursuit of distinction and of art for art's sake.

When we set out to understand the "creative project" or distinctive point of view of an artist like Flaubert, therefore, the first thing we need to grasp is his place in and trajectory through the field of art or, more specifically, the field of literature as art. This, Bourdieu recognizes, must seem like heresy to those who believe in the individualistic ideal of artistic genius. It is one thing to say that sociology can help us understand art markets, but Bourdieu claims that sociology is not just helpful for but crucial to understanding the individual work of art and the point of view of the artist who created it. Bourdieu takes on this task in an analysis simultaneously of Flaubert's career, or his own implicit analysis of it in the novel *Sentimental Education*, and of the genesis and structure of the French literary field. In doing so he accepts a challenge similar to that Durkheim took in seeking to explain suicide sociologically: to demonstrate the power of sociology in a domain normally understood in precisely antisociological terms.

At its center, Bourdieu's analysis is the demonstration that Flaubert's point of view as an artist is shaped by his objective position in the artistic field and his more subjective position-takings in relation to the development of that field. For example, it is important that Flaubert came from a family that was able to provide him with financial support. This enabled him to participate fully in the ethic (or interest) of art for art's sake while some of his colleagues, perhaps equally talented, were forced to support themselves by writing journalism for money. This is different from saying simply that Flaubert expressed a middle-class point of view. In fact, it suggests something of why middle- and upper-class people who enter careers like art that are defined by cultural rather than economic capital often become social critics. Their family backgrounds help to buy them some autonomy from the immediate interests of the economy, while their pursuit of distinction in a cultural field gives them an interest in producing innovative and incisive views of the world. The objective features of an artist's background influence his work not so much directly as indirectly through the mediation of the artistic field. And without the field, there are not artists in the same sense.

Within that field, Flaubert or any other artist occupies a specific position at any one point in time and also a trajectory of positions through time. The position of an individual artist is shaped by the network of relationships that connect him to and differentiate him from other artists and by his position in the hierarchies of artistic producers defined both by the external market and the internal prestige system of the field. The actual position the artist occupies, however, is only one among a universe of possible positions. He could have made different friends and enemies, could have used his talent better or worse at earlier times, could have traveled abroad rather than staying in Paris. In this sense, the artist's biography, including both the objective resources he starts with and the uses he makes of them, describes a trajectory through the space of objective positions in the field, which itself may be developing and changing. This trajectory is produced partly by choices, by the way the artist played the game, and by material factors. The way the artist plays the game is itself shaped by the objective circumstances he has experienced and internalized as habitus. As he sets out to produce any new work, the artist starts from an objective position in the field and also engages in new position-takings. That is, he chooses consciously or unconsciously from among the range of possible moves open to him.

In line with Bourdieu's overall approach, what we see here is the deep way in which subjective and objective dimensions of fields and practices are bound up with each other. "Paradoxically," he writes, "we can only be sure of some chance of participating in the author's subjective intention (or, if you like, in what I have called elsewhere his 'creative project') provided we complete the long work of objectification necessary to reconstruct the universe of positions within which he was situated and where what he wanted to do was defined" (Bourdieu 1996a). One important way in which the field as a whole shapes the work of a Flaubert, say, is by granting him the freedom to innovate and to construct a vision of the world that is not immediately constrained by economic logic or political power. Put differently, the artist gains his freedom in relation to his broader social context precisely by accepting the determinations that come with investment in the artistic field. "The posts of 'pure' writer and artist, like that of 'intellectual', are institutions of freedom, which are constructed against the 'bourgeoisie' (in the artist's terms) and, more concretely, against the market and state bureaucracies (academies, salons, etc.) through a series of ruptures, partially cumulative, which are often made possible only by a diversion of the resources of the market—hence of the 'bourgeoisie'—and even of state bureaucracies." That is, the pure writer needs resources from somewhere. "These posts are the end point of all the collective work which has led to the constitution of the field of cultural production as a space independent of the economy and politics; but, in return, this work of emancipation cannot be carried out or extended unless the post finds an agent endowed with the required dispositions, such as an indifference to profit and a propensity to make risky investments, as well as the properties which, like income, constitute the (external) conditions of these dispositions" (Bourdieu 1996a: 257).

In this sense, the artist is not so much disinterested as differently interested. The illusion of disinterest is produced by the way economic and cultural dimensions of modern societies are ideologically opposed to each other. The field of cultural production is defined as the economic world reversed. It is one of the central contributions of Bourdieu's theory, however, to show that this is a misrecognition, and the opposition is really between different forms of capital. Directly economic capital operates in a money-based market that can be indefinitely extended. Cultural capital, by contrast, operates as a matter of status, which is often recognized only within specific fields (here again, Bourdieu follows Weber). To convert all specific capitals into monetary capital is to undo the field structure of modern society and the main bulwark for the pursuit of specific capitals, distinctive values, and thus republican virtues.

Contesting Neoliberalism: Sociology in Action

Bourdieu did not develop any detailed account of the economy as such, partly because his concerns lay elsewhere and partly because he questioned whether any such object existed with the degree of autonomy from the rest of social life that conventional economics implied.[13] His account of the different forms of capital involved no account of capitalism as a distinctive, historically specific system of production and distribution. This was perhaps implied by his treatment of the corrosive force of markets in Algeria and by his critique of neoliberal economic policies. In each case the more inclusive, larger-scale organization of economic life also entailed a greater reduction of other values to economic ones and a specification of economic values as those of private property. "Economism is a form of ethnocentrism," Bourdieu wrote. It removes the elements of time and uncertainty from symbolically organized exchange; it desocializes transactions, leaving, as Bourdieu follows Marx (and Thomas Carlyle) in saying, no other nexus between human and human than "callous cash payment." It treats precapitalist economies through the categories and concepts proper to capitalism (Bourdieu 1990a). Among other things, this means introducing what Bourdieu calls monothetic reason, in which analysts imagine reality decomposed into elements that mean only one thing at a time, as though all goods were defined only by their prices. Precapitalist thought in general and much ordinary thought even in capitalist societies is, Bourdieu suggests, polythetic, constantly deploying multiple meanings of the same object. "Practice has a logic which is not that of the logician"[14] (Bourdieu 1990: 86). It puts symbols and knowledge together practically, that is, in a philosophically unrigorous but convenient way for practical use.

Bourdieu devoted a good deal of effort to challenging such economism. But he did this not to suggest an alternative view of human nature in which competition did not matter so much as an alternative view of the social world in which other kinds of goods and relationships were the objects of investment and accumulation. This led him to the influential idea of different, partially convertible forms of capital, notably, cultural, social, and symbolic capital:

> The social world can be conceived as a multi-dimensional space that can be constructed empirically by discovering the main factors of differentiation which account for the differences observed in a given social universe, or, in other words, by discovering the powers or forms *of capital* which are or can become efficient, like aces in a game of cards, in this particular universe, that is, in the struggle (or competition) for the appropriation of scarce goods of which this universe is the site. It follows that the structure of this space is given by the distribution of the various forms of capital, that is, by the distribution of the properties which are active within the universe under study—those properties capable of conferring strength, power and consequently profit on their holder. . . . these fundamental social powers are, according to my empirical investigations, firstly *economic* capital, in its various kinds; secondly *cultural* capital or better, informational capital, again in its different kinds; and thirdly two forms of capital that are very strongly correlated, *social* capital, which consists of resources based on connections and group membership, and *symbolic* capital, which is the form the different types of capital take once they are perceived and recognized as legitimate (Bourdieu 1987b: 3–4).

Economic capital is that which is "immediately and directly convertible into money" (Bourdieu 1986b: 243). Educational credentials (cultural capital) or social connections (social capital) can be converted only indirectly, through engagement in activities that involve longer-term relationships like employment, family, or marriage. Different social fields create and value specific kinds of capital. Their role in producing such specific capitals is precisely their importance to republican values of nondomination and Bourdieu's reason for defending them against reduction to immediately monetary values.

Bourdieu focuses on showing that what economism takes as the universal characteristic of human nature, that is, material, individual self-interest, is in fact historically arbitrary, a particular historical construction. "A general science of the economy of practices" would "not artificially limit itself to those practices that are socially recognized as economic." It would "endeavor to grasp capital, that 'energy of social physics' in all of its different forms, and to uncover the laws that regulate their conversion from one into another" (Bourdieu and Wacquant 1992: 118). Capital is thereby analogous to energy, and both to power. But "the existence of symbolic capital, that is, of 'material' capital misrecognized and thus recognized, though it does not invalidate the analogy between capital and energy, does remind us that social science is not a social physics; that the acts of cognition that are implied in misrecognition and recognition are part of social reality and that the socially constituted subjectivity that produces them belongs to objective reality" (Bourdieu 1990a).

Bourdieu's work at its most basic is a challenge to false oppositions: the interested and disinterested, the individual and the collective, and the sociocultural and the economic. "A presupposition which is the basis of all the presuppositions of economics" is that "a radical separation is made between the economic and the social, which is left to one side, abandoned to sociologists, as a kind of reject"(Bourdieu 1998a: 31).[15] This in turn undergirds "a political vision that leads to the establishment of an unbreachable frontier between the economic, regulated by the fluid and efficient mechanisms of the market, and the social, home to the unpredictable arbitrariness of tradition, power, and passions" (Bourdieu 2001a: 29–30). Economics is able to claim a falsely asocial and acultural individual subject, and the social, including culture, is posited as the noneconomic realm, the realm at once the economically unimportant and of the pure aesthetic—never a true commodity but claimable only after the fact as an economic good. When the production of knowledge is structured by such presupposed categories, failure to take seriously the social costs of neoliberalism, the social conditions on which such an economy depends, and the possibilities of developing less damaging alternatives is almost inevitable.

Bourdieu's analyses lay the basis for an empirical science that would address the practices of knowledge at the same time as it produced knowledge of social practice. The issue remained central in his challenge to neoliberalism: "The implicit philosophy of the economy, and of the rapport between economy and politics, is a political vision that leads to the establishment of an unbreachable frontier between the economic, regulated by the fluid and efficient mechanisms of the market, and the social, home to the unpredictable arbitrariness of tradition, power, and passions" (Bourdieu 2001a: 29–30). This "frontier" is reinforced by both academic preconceptions and folk understandings and structures the apparently objective categories and findings of economic analysis.[16] As the habitus internalizes history and makes it seem natural, so too do the categories of academic thought. The production of knowledge structured by such presupposed categories undergirds the failure to take seriously the social costs of neoliberalism, the social conditions on which such an economy depends, and the possibilities of developing less damaging alternatives.

Bourdieu was politically engaged with historical struggles and transformations throughout his career. We might follow Vincent in thinking of him as embodying, like Durkheim, the type of Scholar-Republican (Vincent 2004). Nonetheless, he usually chose to avoid the nonautonomous media field in favor of emphasizing his more specific contributions as a scientist (Bourdieu 1998a; Benson and Neveu 2005). He decried the example of Sartre as a "general intellectual," analogous to the depredations of capital in general versus field-specific capital. Yet in resistance to neoliberalism and related public issues like the rights of immigrants, Bourdieu shifted his personal style of engagement. He marched, he signed petitions, he wrote polemical essays.[17] Bourdieu saw the rise of neoliberalism as a basic challenge to the era of the welfare state and economic expansion he had spent most of his career analyzing. The new context and new issues, like the plight of undocumented workers, made protest politics compelling. The failure of the socialist party to rise to the new challenges made them necessary.

But despite the stylistic shifts, Bourdieu's political actions were fully consistent with and understandable in terms of his scientific sociology (Wacquant and Bourdieu 2005). Bourdieu's challenge to threatened collapse between political and economic and, indeed, scientific and economic fields in the 1990s and early 2000s is of a piece with his rejection of a collapse between academic and political fields in 1968, and both are informed by his theory of quasi-autonomous social fields and by his analysis of the disruption of traditional life and marginalization of former peasants in Algeria.

Bourdieu drew on his earlier analyses of how the culturally arbitrary and often the materially unequal come to appear as natural and fair to inform his critique of the imposition of neoliberal economic regimes. Rhetoric and specific patterns of social relations and state action were deployed to make it seem necessary to abandon the gains of long social struggles in order to compete with Asia, to integrate with Europe, or to benefit from new technologies. Imposition of the American model of dismantling or reducing state institutions was given the appearance of false necessity. And so Bourdieu took care to emphasize another side from his earlier arguments during les trentes glorieuses. He insisted that institutions like education do provide opportunities for ordinary people even while in their existing form they reproduce distinctions like that of ordinary from extraordinary (Bourdieu 1998e).

Calling this the "American model" annoyed Americans who wished to distance themselves from government and corporate policies. The label nonetheless captured a worldwide trend toward commodification, state deregulation, and competitive individualism exemplified and aggressively promoted by the dominant class of the United States at the end of the twentieth century. Bourdieu identified the American model with five features of American culture and society which were widely proposed as necessary to successful globalization in other contexts: (1) a weak state, (2) an extreme development of the spirit of capitalism and (3) of the cult of individualism, (4) exaltation of dynamism for its own sake, and (5) neo-Darwinism with its notion of self-help (Bourdieu 2001a: 25–31).

Whatever the label, Bourdieu meant the view that institutions developed out of a long century of social struggles should be scrapped if they could not meet the test of market viability. Many of these, including schools and universities, are state institutions. As he demonstrated in much of his work, they are far from perfect. Nonetheless, collective struggles have grudgingly and gradually opened them to a degree to the dominated, workers, women, ethnic minorities, and others. These institutions and this openness are fragile social achievements that open up the possibility of more equality and justice, and to sacrifice them is to step backward, whether this step is masked by a deterministic analysis of the market or a naked assertion of self-interest by the wealthy and powerful. This does not mean that defense must be blind, but it does mean that resistance to neoliberal globalization, even when couched in the apparently backward-looking rhetoric of nationalism, can be a protection of genuine gains and, indeed, a protection of the public space for further progressive struggles.

Bourdieu was concerned above all that the social institutions that supported reason—by providing scholars, scientists, artists, and writers with a measure of autonomy—were under unprecedented attack. Reduction to the market threatened to undermine science; reduction to the audience-ratings logic of television entertainment threatened to undermine public discourse:

> If one wants to go beyond preaching, then it is necessary to implement practically . . . the *Realpolitik* of reason aimed at setting up or reinforcing, within the political field, the mechanisms capable of imposing the sanctions, as far as possible automatic ones, that would tend to discourage deviations from the democratic norm (such as the corruption of elected representatives) and to encourage or impose the appropriate behaviors; aimed also at favouring the setting up of non-distorted social structures of communication between the holders of power and the citizens, in particular through a constant struggle for the independence of the media. (Bourdieu 2000b: 126)

The problem was not internationalization as such. Bourdieu himself called forcefully for a new internationalism, saw science as an international endeavor, and founded *Liber*, a European review of books published in six languages. The problem was the presentation of a particular modality of globalization as a force of necessity to which there was no alternative but adaptation and acceptance.

In his own life, Bourdieu recognized, it was not merely talent and effort that propelled his extraordinary ascent from rural Béarn to the Collège de France, but also state scholarships, social rights, and educational access to the closed world of "culture." This recognition did not stop him from engaging in critical analysis. He showed how the classificatory systems operating in these institutions of state, culture, and education all served to exercise symbolic violence as well as and perhaps more than to open opportunities. But he also recognized the deep social investment in such institutions that was inescapably inculcated in people whose life trajectories depended on them: "What individuals and groups invest in the particular meaning they give to common classificatory systems by the use they make of them is infinitely more than their 'interest' in the usual sense of the term; it is their whole social being, everything which defines their own idea of themselves" (Bourdieu 1984a: 478).

Neoliberal reforms thus threaten not only some people with material economic harms, but also social institutions that enable people to make sense of their lives. That these institutions are flawed is a reason to transform them and the classificatory schemes central to their operation and reproduction. Those flaws do not form a basis for imagining that people can live without them, especially in the absence of some suitable replacements. Moreover, the dismantling of such institutions is specifically disempowering, not only economically depriving. That is, it takes away material goods in which people have an interest as well as undercutting their ability to make sense of their social situation and create solidarities with others.

A central strength of global capitalism is its ability to control the terms of discourse and, most especially, to present the specific emerging forms of globalization as being both inevitable and progressive. Consider the force of this message in the rhetoric of the European Union and the advocates of a common currency. Globalization appears as a determinant force, an inevitable necessity to which Europeans must adapt; capitalism appears as its essential character; the American model is commonly presented as the normal, if not the only, model. Yet European unification is held to be liberal, cosmopolitan, and progressive (Bourdieu 1998a; Calhoun 2002, forthcoming). To assert, as Bourdieu did, that the specific pattern of international relations—like relations within nations—is the result of the exercise of power is to open up the game, to remove the illusion of necessity. To reveal the power being wielded and reproduced when apparently open political choices are structured by a symbolic order organized to the benefit of those in dominant positions, whether or not they are fully aware of what they do, is to challenge the efficacy of doxic understandings. These are basic acts of critical theory and both consistent with and informed by Bourdieu's work since his early Algerian studies.

Conclusion

Bourdieu was famous long before the struggle against neoliberal globalization of the 1990s. In June 1968 some students had actually carried copies of his book *The Inheritors* onto the barricades. But Bourdieu had stayed more or less apart from that struggle, turning his attention to scientific, albeit critical, research. Some of this research produced *Homo Academicus*, a book partly about the relationship between the university microcosm and the larger field of power in 1968, but the book appeared over fifteen years later. One reason Bourdieu was not a vocal public activist in 1968 was that he did not think the crucial issues of power and inequality were well joined in the struggles of that year. Neither their romanticism nor the predominant versions of Marxism appealed to him, and he resisted especially leftist tendencies to collapse the scientific and political fields. Moreover, he worried that naïve over-optimism encouraged actions that would set back rather than advance the causes of liberation and knowledge. Not least of all, there was a superabundance of symbolically prominent intellectuals in 1968. By the early 1990s this was no longer so. Sartre and Foucault were both dead, and a number of others had abandoned the public forum or simply appeared small within it.

It was as a social scientist that Bourdieu in the last years of his life turned to analyze the impacts of neoliberal globalization on culture, politics, and society. "The social sciences," he wrote, "which alone can unmask and counter the completely new strategies of domination which they sometimes help to inspire and to arm, will more than ever have to choose which side they are on: either they place their rational instruments of knowledge at the service of ever more rationalized domination, or they rationally analyse domination and more especially the contribution which rational knowledge can make to *de facto* monopolization of the profits of universal reason" (Bourdieu 2000b: 83–84). Though he was accused of simply adopting the mediatic throne Sartre and Foucault had occupied before—and certainly he never fully escaped from that mediatic version of politics—he offered a different definition of what a public intellectual might be. Citing the American term, he wrote of "one who relies in political struggle on his competence and specific authority, and the values associated with the exercise of his profession, like the values of truth or disinterest, or, in other terms, someone who goes onto the terrain of politics without abandoning the requirements and competences of the researcher" (Bourdieu 2001a: 33). He contrasted such a "specific intellectual" to the "general intellectual" (Sartre was the obvious model) who spoke on all matters, claiming a right conferred more by personal eminence or authenticity than by professional expertise or perspective. If the tradition of Émile Zola legitimates intellectual as political forces in France, it was nonetheless important to recognize the difference between simply claiming a new sort of aristocratic-clerical right to speak in public and bringing analyses with specific scholarly bases into public debate.

Basic to Bourdieu's interventions as a public intellectual, in this sense, was the importance of creating the possibility of collective choice where the dominant discourse described only the impositions of necessity. This was one reason he embraced the deep connections of history and sociology. History demonstrates that existing relations are made, not necessary. And in a sense sociology demonstrates the same thing in reverse, that history is not the mere positivistic narrative of facts but the result of socially organized conflicts and struggles.

Especially from the early 1990s Bourdieu worked to protect the achievements of the social struggles of the twentieth century, including pensions, job security, open access to higher education, and other provisions of the social state, against budget cuts and other attacks in the name of free markets and international competition. In the process he became one of the world's most famous critics of neoliberal globalization.[18] He challenged the neoliberal idea that a specific model of reduction in state action, enhancement of private property, and freedom for capital was a necessary response to globalization, itself conceived as a quasi-natural force.

Bourdieu's approach was to rethink major philosophical themes and issues by means of empirical observation and analyses rooted in "a practical sense of theoretical things" rather than through purely theoretical disquisition (Brubaker 1993). Only relatively late, in *Pascalian Meditations*, did he offer a systematic explication of his conception of social knowledge, being, and truth. In this book, he started once again with the premise that the knowledge produced by social analysts must be related to the conditions of intellectual work and to the peculiar dispositions fostered by the scholastic universe. He laid out his philosophical anthropology, in which human action is guided not by interests but by the struggle for practical efficacy and pursuit of recognition, whose form will be determined by particular locations in collective and individual histories. He clarified his agonistic view of the social world, anchored not by the notion of reproduction but by that of struggle, itself internally linked to recognition. And he showed why epistemic, as distinguished from narcissistic, reflexivity mandates a commitment to "historical rationalism," not to relativism.

Historical rationalism was a theme derived from Bourdieu's teachers Gaston Bachelard, Jules Vuillemin, and Georges Canguilhem, who also shaped many others of his poststructuralist generation, including Foucault and Jacques Derrida. Bourdieu's debt to it helps us see why, even while he was an important master of structuralist analysis, he also rejected the structuralist refusal of history. Bourdieu was not, like Foucault in 1966, a theorist of deep epistemic ruptures. Rather, he wrestled with the complexities of partial transformation and partial reproduction; with the multiple, ubiquitous temporalities of social life; and with the embeddedness of knowledge itself in historical practice.

In this we see the specificity of Bourdieu as historical sociologist. It is of a piece with Bourdieu the scholar-republican and Bourdieu the village scholarship student excelling in the very intellectual institutions that disappoint him. It is a view of the complexity of social life, the inevitability of misrecognition as a dimension of recognition, the embeddedness of real achievements in regrettable inequalities. Yet it is also a view that humanly created histories are available to humans to change—but only with recognition of their social character and only if we also work reflexively to discern the partiality of our own socially created perspectives.

Notes

1. Assignment to Algeria was in fact the military's punishment for Bourdieu's rebellious attitude after his initial posting in Versailles. See Wacquant (2002: 17).
2. At the same time, Bourdieu's account exaggerated and sometimes idealized the stability and autonomy of traditional Kabyle society in order to make a sharper

contrast to the social upheavals of colonial Algeria. Indeed, his account was based on reconstructions articulated by Kabyles who were situated in a kind of "structural nostalgia" as they contemplated the relationship between their traditional ways of life and both forced resettlement by the French and the difficulties of life as urban labor migrants; on structural nostalgia see Herzfeld (1997); on this dimension of Bourdieu's account, see Silverstein (2004).

3. An exceptional scholar in his own right, Sayad remained a close friend and interlocutor of Bourdieu's until his death in 1998. See Saada (2000); Bourdieu and Wacquant (2000); and also Bourdieu's introduction to Sayad (1999).

4. The analysis of the Kabyle house is one of the classics of structuralism. Originally written in 1963–64, it was first published in 1969 in an homage to Lévi-Strauss.

5. For decades Bourdieu quietly supported students from Kabylia in the pursuit of higher education, a fact that speaks not only to his private generosity and sense of obligation, but also to his faith that, for all their complicity in social reproduction, education and science remained the best hope for loosening the yoke of domination. He also helped Berber emigrants in Paris found a research center, the Centre de Recherches et d'Etudes Amazighes (CERAM), and was a founder of a prominent support group for imprisoned and threatened Algerian intellectuals, the Comité de soutien aux intellectuels algériens (CISIA).

6. Bourdieu seems not to have been aware of Elias until much later. See Chartier (1993). Elias and Bourdieu share a variety of themes, tastes, and some other concepts, though there are also striking differences, not the least of which is the extent to which Elias focused on long-term historical change whereas Bourdieu, while dealing intensively with shorter-term processes of change, often left questions of large-scale, epochal historical change implicit. See "Habitus, Field of Power and Capital: The Question of Historical Specificity" in Calhoun (1995).

7. Bridget Fowler (1987) rather strangely sees the concept of practice as "associated with [Bourdieu's] conversion to structuralism," thus missing some of the other sources on which it drew—notably Marx and Marxism, but also a tradition from Aristotle through phenomenology—and the extent to which it marked an effort to transcend limits of structuralism.

8. This is not to say that Bourdieu is unaware of earlier patterns of change, but that he emphasizes the attitude he would come to describe (following Aristotle) as *doxa*. This is the un-self-aware inhabitation of culture as taken-for-granted reality that is disrupted by heterodoxy. Orthodoxy may present itself as an attempt to return to earlier tradition but generally cannot reestablish the doxic attitude; it can only restate some contents in a contention with heterodoxy and an effort to enforce cultural conformity. See also Weber (1951: 296) on the difference between tradition and traditionalism.

9. Bourdieu's study of photography is precisely of the "middle-brow" art of these hobbyists. He also studied museum attendance and other kinds of growing cultural engagement, though generally finding that despite expanding numbers stratification remained powerful. See Bourdieu, Boltanski, Castel, Chamboredon, and Schnapper (1990); and Bourdieu, Darbel, and Schnapper (1990).

10. Bourdieu's disillusionment with the educational system was not simply an immediate response to his experience at the École Normale, though that was certainly among its roots. See accounts in Lane (2000); Calhoun (2011).

11. Bourdieu complained about the misunderstanding of those who seized on the analytic devices he took up from one or another established approach, missing the fact that he was already exaggerating in order to twist the stick in the other direction, and then labeled his approach by the strategically deployed concept—perhaps most famously the idea of strategy itself that he used as a way of injecting dynamism into structuralist analysis (Bourdieu 2000b, 1993b; Calhoun 1993a: 263–75).

12. As Julian Vincent suggests, this connected Bourdieu to a strong French intellectual tradition with a great deal of affinity to sociology; Durkheim was a prominent exemplar. More recently it has been the basis for engagements with Bourdieu's work on the part of republican historians. See Vincent (2004).

13. See Bourdieu (2000a), which takes up but moves well beyond arguments about "embeddedness" following Polanyi.

14. Compare Pascal's most famous line, "The heart has its reasons, of which reason is ignorant."

15. Bourdieu's emphasis was especially on the separation of the economic from both the social and the cultural, but the opposition of the latter two can also be equally pernicious, as in specious ideas of division of labor between sociology and anthropology in the United States, or the construction of "sociology of culture" within American sociology—rather than, say, the "cultural sociology" of central Europe.

16. Bourdieu's understanding of the historical process by which this tacit understanding of market society was established was close to—and indebted to—that of Karl Polanyi (Polanyi 2001).

17. For evidence that this wasn't altogether new despite the suggestion of many of Bourdieu's critics that his campaigns of the late 1990s marked a complete reversal, see Bourdieu (2002c).

18. Bourdieu published a host of essays collected in *Acts of Resistance, Firing Back*, and *Interventions*. Bourdieu's essays were only a part of his struggle "against the tyranny of the market." He gave speeches and interviews, appeared on the radio and at public demonstrations, launched a nonparty network of progressive social scientists called *Raisons d'agir* (Reasons to act) and a book series by the same name, and helped forge links among intellectuals, cultural producers, and trade union activists.

3 CHRISTOPHE CHARLE
translated by Grey Anderson

COMPARATIVE AND TRANSNATIONAL HISTORY AND THE SOCIOLOGY OF PIERRE BOURDIEU
Historical Theory and Practice

I can say that one of my most steadfast ambitions, particularly in *Actes de la recherche en sciences sociales*, has been to promote the growth of a unified social science, in which history would be a historical sociology of the past and sociology would be a social history of the present.
—PIERRE BOURDIEU (1999 [1995])

Little practiced in France, comparative history and historical sociology have, since the 1960s, expanded greatly in Germany, the United States, England, and even Italy. This resistance of French historians derives from long-standing a priori objections to comparison that are rooted in the complicated history of the relationship between history and sociology in France. After a reflection on the relevance, scope, and limits of comparative history, particularly in the social and cultural sphere, I will examine how I personally have tried to apply the sociological propositions of Pierre Bourdieu to new themes and national areas in order to combine comparative and transnational approaches.

History, Sociology, and Comparison: Historiographical Reminders
In the controversy at the beginning of the twentieth century between François Simiand and Charles Seignobos, Simiand criticized the "historicizing" history personified by Seignobos for having rejected comparison, the only means for arriving at a genuine explanation. Simiand writes, in his famous article of 1903, "Only comparison makes determination and classification feasible and understanding possible" (1987 [1903]). During the interwar period some historians saw in comparative history a means of struggle against the nationalism, cultivated by traditional historiography, that was responsible for the

catastrophe of 1914. This was the inspiration for the Congress of Historical Sciences in Oslo and for Marc Bloch in the paper he gave there in 1928: "Toward a Comparative History of European Societies" (1953).

In this address Bloch rejects overly large-scale comparisons such as those preferred by the Durkheimians and Max Weber, for example, the comparative study of religions, kinship systems, and so forth, and later by Fernand Braudel and his "world-economies." The author of *Feudal Society* instead looks to comparison as a way of controlling against false similarities, which sometimes result in overgeneralizations, or, conversely, as a procedure for unearthing similarities hidden because of the lack of a shared vocabulary: he thus observes that while there are certainly enclosures in France as well as in England, they are hidden from the view of French historians for want of a specific name. These early analyses pose one of the crucial questions of comparison: the scale of analysis, and the usage and definition of similarities and differences as categories, pertinent or not, of comparison.

Nonetheless, it would be difficult to cite even a few names of comparativists among later French historians, particularly in social and cultural history. In 1995 Heinz-Gerhard Haupt offered three reasons for the insignificance of the comparative approach within French historical production:[1] the mainly local and regional subjects of doctoral theses, the frequent politicization of historical debates involving a national perspective, and the importance of the founding myth of the French Revolution as the irreducible origin of contemporary history.

This founding event, which in France serves as a caesura between modern and contemporary history, is certainly responsible for a large part of the resistance of recent history to the comparative project. From the moment one thinks of the history of France as an exception born of the French Revolution, its comparability with the destiny of other Western nations becomes problematic. Political history is not the only branch of French historiography to think of itself as radically different in comparison to the evolution of other European nations. Economic history emphasizes the originality of the French process of industrial development in comparison to that of England; historical demography has scrutinized, since the 1950s, the origins of the early Malthusian rupture that characterizes the French population from the end of the eighteenth century; social history highlights the originality of a nation in which the peasantry, the middle classes, and foreign workers play a larger role than elsewhere; and intellectual history seeks the roots near and remote for a distinctive cultural model centered on contentious dialogue with the state and the Catholic Church. If need be, French historians attempt to measure French influence on neighboring nations or France's reaction to foreign influences, but the correlation is always founded on an imbalance according to the country of the observer, and a prejudice in favor of that country as tutor of mankind [*instituteur du genre humain*]. A chosen nation for progressive historians, a cursed nation since the Revolution for conservative historians, France cannot, in any case, be placed on the same map as its neighbors because it is implicitly incomparable, in both senses of the word.

These prejudices, transmitted from generation to generation of contemporary historians, have been a decisive obstacle to comparison. While not denying French specificities, France is not, in this respect, radically different from other Western nations. All of these nations, to the extent that their national ideology—indeed, nationalist ideology—has asserted itself, have in turn considered themselves to be unique, whether one thinks of the various theories of the German *Sonderweg*, the twofold celebration of English industrial leadership and the inimitable constitution of Great Britain (the Whig interpretation of history), or the notion of American exceptionalism.

In fact, there are other reasons, proper to the discipline of history, that account for the difficult emergence of comparative history. The abundance of research and publications demands an increasing specialization at the expense of any synthesis or comparison. Such specialization is reflected in the distribution of university chairs, dominated by national specializations (French history, German history, and so on), and in constraints imposed on the size of dissertations. The prolonged domination of political history within contemporary history too often turns historians away from looking for more global explanations, independent of singular contexts.

At the same time, these academic hindrances are not at all unavoidable, as shown by the following foreign examples: in the United States, Arno J. Mayer and Charles Tilly; in Germany, Jürgen Kocka, Hartmut Kaelble, Heinz-Gerhard Haupt, Hannes Siegrist, and Ute Frevert; in England, Eric Hobsbawm, Linda Colley, Geoffrey Crossick, Chris Bayly, Jay Winter, among others; all have no French equivalents in comparative history, at least in the older generation.

It is also true that the theoretical and methodological debates that run through comparative history may account for the timidity of French historians. No fewer than seven preliminary questions must be posed.

The Seven Questions to be Resolved by Comparative History
CONSTRUCTING THE OBJECT

As Nancy L. Green (1990) has shown, the same historical object can be compared in very different ways. Her demonstration begins with the case of the Jews: comparison can be religious with respect to Protestants and Catholics, social with respect to other ethnic minorities, or national (Jews from different countries); the same word, in appearance, in fact refers to different points of view on the object. One can even deconstruct the object itself: eastern Jews and southern Jews, the Jewish proletariat and the Jewish bourgeoisie, assimilated Jews and Orthodox or particularist Jews, in various contexts.[2] As comparison involves research operations demanding in terms of time and theoretical elaboration, it requires a more refined reflexivity than the classical history of a single context, and it demands that the chosen object be deconstructed, then reconstructed. This was one of the precepts of the sociology taken from Durkheim by Bourdieu, and this analysis is accomplished by placing the object in relation to several contexts.

THE SCALE OF DIVISION

Contemporary history coincides more or less with the emergence of nations; but the national point of view (induced by the structuring even of historical sources by the state in the contemporary epoch) risks changing the emphasis of observation by condemning as secondary or as relics phenomena that have taken place on a scale different from that of the nation, or by inappropriately generalizing in order to reintegrate them into the national context. In fact, what is called national in contemporary history is often a local monograph that has been taken as unduly representative for want of the ability to make repeated case studies. Hannes Siegrist (1995), in his comparative social history of lawyers in three countries, has shown the specificity of the villages and regions inside Germany, Switzerland, and Italy. The oppositions are less between national traditions than between typologies of the towns of practice: a lawyer from Geneva may be closer to a lawyer from a large French or Italian city than a lawyer from a small Swiss canton or a small German village.

THE ANALYTIC FRAMEWORK (*TERTIUM COMPARATIONIS*)

The analysis of any historical object involves a framework of questioning and interpretation. To compare two historical objects, even those that are related or thought to have points in common, one must create a shared framework for the two contexts. This obligation has justified the rejection of comparison by hostile historians on the grounds that it reduces the dimensions of the object and forfeits part of its meaning. One of the supporters of the cultural transfer approach, Michel Espagne (1999 [1994]), has insisted on the negative effects of comparison in cultural history. According to him, the shared analytic framework, especially in cultural history, depends on a *tertium comparationis*, yet this framework tends to make use of a euphemized vocabulary that poorly accounts for the specificities of each context, given that every language, as the expression of a national culture, carves up reality differently. Depending on the vocabulary one accepts, one thus risks conveying implicit value judgments born of the reciprocal perspective of the compared cultures. Comparison will thus inevitably affirm national specificity by the very fact of its parallel approach, which accentuates discordances; at the same time, comparison will not take account of all of the transgressions, exchanges, and transfers that occur through migrations, retranslations, readings, and productive misunderstandings of breaches against the national. Comparison, far from struggling against nationalism and ethnocentrism, will thereby follow its cultural interests in hardening frontiers. Yet one can take lessons from this warning without thinking that the study of transfers advocated by Espagne suffices to exhaust the program of a sociocultural comparative history.

To guard against the dangers cited by Espagne, I suggest turning to a comparison of several frameworks applied to different analyzed contexts in order to expose their relativity and to rectify the effects of reading that they engender. Thus in *Les intellectuels en Europe au XIXe siècle* (1996), I tried to read the situation of German intellectuals within a French framework and that of French intellectuals within an English framework.[3] In each case unusual perspectives became apparent. In this way, rather than opposing unattached French avant-garde intellectuals who have undertaken noble humanist causes to German mandarins imbued with nationalism and respect for order, an image one might derive from a hasty comparison of the works on these two countries that unduly privilege these two types because they are the dominant representations that each nation makes of its intellectuals, one witnesses the appearance of an avant-garde every bit as vigorous, indeed, even more radical, in Germany. One accordingly restores French mandarins, often forgotten by the cultural pantheon established by the avant-garde and later academics, to their true place as keepers of academic legitimacy, defenders of the nation, and every bit as conservative as their German counterparts.

THE USE OF TRANSNATIONAL CONCEPTS

In history and in the social sciences more generally, we continually and unreflectingly use transnational concepts that orient our comparative perspective without our conscious awareness, whether because we privilege a lexicon that is not in circulation in the other country or because we translate the lexicon of one country into that of another, since there must be a common conceptualization in order to translate comparison into a propositional language. And yet the social sciences, nationally framed, do not generally have access to a single shared vocabulary, as chemistry or physics, for example, do, but to several vocabularies, as Jean-Claude Passeron has demonstrated in *Le raisonnement sociologique* (1992).

When confronting situations in multiple countries, one must a fortiori seek to bring together [*mettre en rapport*] conceptualizations linked to national and theoretical traditions appropriate to each context. Thus in the collective work directed by Jürgen Kocka on the European bourgeoisies, the articles by different authors employed concurrently a period vocabulary ("*Bürgertum*," "bourgeoisie," "middle class"), borrowings from sociology (dominant class, ruling class, elites, upper classes), problematics particular to the central country of inquiry (feudalization of the bourgeoisie, persistence of the aristocratic model, *Bildungsbürgertum*, proletarian intellectuals), and alternative problematics from other contexts: professionalization, or the merging of elites, in accordance with Anglo-Saxon sociological models; notables and competition between social fractions, according to the French tradition; the educated bourgeoisie (Italy); intelligentsia (Central and Eastern Europe), and so on (Kocka and Frevert 1988). Comparativists must remain conscious of the inevitable effects of this theoretical melting pot, not in order to practice a lazy eclecticism but to measure the effects of construction that the usage of any given terminology entails. As Bourdieu (1999 [1995]: 172) reminds us, "Sociological concepts must be picked up with a pair of historical 'tweezers,'" for they are themselves the product of transfers and comparisons between university traditions that circulate within the social sciences through favored authors and concepts, and they can become obstacles to a true comparison by imposing underlying problematics that are uncontrolled in their effects.

THE NEAR AND THE FAR

The first theorists of comparison in the social sciences privileged the long-distance comparison of global phenomena: suicide in the case of Durkheim, for example, and the great world religions in the case of Weber. By this means they sought to understand the essential specificities of modern society in comparison to ancient societies, or those of Western capitalist society in comparison to the rest of a world not yet conquered at that time by the development of modern capitalism. American sociologists of the 1960s gladly took up this cavalier perspective with modernization theory, opposing either the West to the rest of the world, Europe to America, or the North to the South. Insofar as noncomparative history has increasingly turned its back on macrohistory, comparative history has also freed itself from this type of rapprochement between large groups situated at the level of global structures inherited from older sociological approaches.

Comparative history is henceforth meant to be a microhistory, like the other branches of current historiography. It is here that one can fruitfully put to use the notion of the field developed by Bourdieu, that is to say, of relatively autonomous social worlds moved by a specific principle of struggle and of competition. However, this implicitly supposes that the various segments of reality—social, cultural, biographical, and so forth—that we bring together be divided in such a way that they occupy, *grosso modo*, a comparable position within the wider reality, a difficult postulate to establish given that most often general comparative inquiry has not itself been undertaken, and we therefore are unable to situate the specific fields we compare in their own diverse contexts. The risk lies not, as in the macro approach, in comparing categories devoid of reality [*vides du réel*], but in comparing shifting categories and in seeking to explain differences which are insignificant and do not refer to anything but our ignorance of their true context. This danger is not very great for the relatively classic types of history: demographic history, economic history, and even the history of political structures, which involve relatively similar models from one country to another.

It is a much riskier undertaking where social and cultural processes are concerned. Thus in *Fields of Knowledge* (1992), Fritz K. Ringer, a historian who explicitly draws on Bourdieu, compares the social composition of French and German biographical dictionaries and purports to deduce from them the specific characteristics of intellectual and social elites in the two countries. His comparison of seemingly proximate realities suffers, however, from many uncertainties for want of a prior reinsertion of his object into a larger context: uncertainties concerning the nature of the dictionaries selected and their function, the criteria implicit in the editorial choices, the classifications used by the editors in their entries according to the rules of the biographical genre in each cultural context, and finally the starting date and speed of the publication process for each dictionary, which can result in an implicit or explicit variation of the criteria of composition for the individual entries. In France, for example, the *Dictionnaire de biographie française*, begun in the 1930s by teams strongly influenced by an outmoded vision of history, is still unfinished today. In Germany, the first series of the German biographical reference dictionary is finished, but finished according to the criteria of nineteenth-century biographies. A second version, begun in 1953, is much more modern than the corresponding French version, but it is likewise uncompleted. These considerations, for two objects that appear very similar, in fact strongly bias the results of the comparison and what it really reveals about elites in the two countries.

RESEMBLANCES AND DIFFERENCES, STATISTICAL OR DYNAMIC EXPERIMENTATION?

The sixth problem to be resolved is that of the purpose of comparison. The inventory of resemblances and differences, the most simple operation of comparison, does not exhaust its function. On the contrary, this juxtaposition [*mise en parallèle*] raises new questions, such as the interplay of hypotheses and evidence via the labeling and balancing of distinguishing factors. Some comparativists suggest an analogy with experimentation in the natural sciences: the historian deals with events or processes that have only occurred once. If he nevertheless wants to suggest an interpretation and an explanation, he can compare [*mettre en parallèle*] two analogous processes in two different contexts in order to weigh and rank the factors' significance. What will interest a comparative historian here is less the frame of each process than the process itself in the abstract, in both cases constructed from shared or divergent elements that can allow for the isolation of key factors from secondary ones specific to each case.

This mode of sociological comparison generally displeases historians, who miss what is for them the spice of historical work, namely, infinite contextual particularity. Nevertheless, even the most historicist of historians unknowingly practice a spontaneous comparison when, for example, they propose a periodization. Every periodization entails attributing to one factor a dominant role over the others. As Robert Tombs (1994) has shown, for example, one can interpret the social and political history of France in entirely different ways depending on how one delimits the French Revolution: 1799, as in textbooks, 1880, as per François Furet (1992 [1988]), 1950, as per Henri Mendras (1988), and so on. The choice of dates boils down to a comparison of what is considered typical of the Revolution and decisive of the future, with an implicit comparison between the different possible types of revolution: revolution as rupture and disorder (the first date, with France unique and off to the side) or revolution as the completion of the liberal and democratic process (the second date, with France drawn nearer to the Anglo-Saxon countries when it equips itself with a durable parliamentary regime). In the third revolutionary periodization, revolution as delayed modernity, the political rupture of 1789 stabilizes the peasantry on a long-term basis, and the true economic and social rupture ("the second French revolution," in the words of Mendras) is not completed until the point at which the peasantry disappeared, belatedly aligning France with the most developed nations.

To such implicit or truncated comparisons, one might oppose straightforward comparisons between processes which seek to draw out their laws, such as that carried out by Theda Skocpol (1979) in her analysis of the three great revolutions in France, Russia, and China. Likewise, Arno Mayer's book *The Persistence of the Old Regime* (1981) rests on an analogy and an explicit comparison between the revolutionary turmoil of the years 1789–1848 and what he calls the thirty years' war of the twentieth century (1914–45), conceived as an attempt at counterrevolution on the part of the elites of the Old Regime which resulted in a double catastrophe, military (the massacre of the two wars) and social: the definitive end of these ancien régime elites in Central and Eastern Europe, ruined by the Russian Revolution, German and Austrian inflation, wartime deaths, and the Sovietization of the USSR satellite states. However, in coming to grips with these processes, Mayer is obliged to neglect whatever diverges from his schema, that is to say, the internal contradictions of or between nations and empires; paradoxically, this approach, which is meant to be Marxist, becomes excessively Paretian: history is then nothing more than a cemetery of aristocracies from which politics and the masses have been expelled.[4]

No doubt these global and experimental forms of interpretation that break with the usual reference points of social, political, or cultural history can have a stimulating effect on historical thought, but they also risk caricaturing the real through typification. Their chief virtue is to inspire complementary analyses of phenomena neglected by the usual procedures of exposition. Mayer's book is undoubtedly at the origin of this remarkable vogue for research in most countries on the nobility and, more so, on elites. Scholars need to revisit this subject, much as Kocka did for the bourgeoisie, in new systematic comparisons because the bibliography Mayer drew upon is now outdated. Moreover, Maria Malatesta's (1999) synthetic work on landed aristocracies strongly nuances the decadent vision Mayer offers of the old elites, responsible, according to him, for choosing war in 1914.

THE STANDARD OF SOURCES USED

The choice of a model of comparison and generalization determines the standard for evidentiary sources. The major criticism historians level at sociologists is that, owing to the enormity of the subjects they take on, they reprocess sources secondhand on the basis of existing works. The historian, especially if he has chosen the micro approach and social or cultural themes, must instead concern himself with inspecting these works, their sources and their divisions, because at this level the smallest uncontrolled bias (consider the critical commentary on Ringer) leads to blunders that can run counter to the facts.

To respond to this problem, I have been obliged in my comparative works to apply the following five principles:

1. Avoid binary comparisons, which congeal oppositions between simplistic models; from which arose the analysis of three, four, five, or six areas in *Histoire des universités* (Charle and Verger 2007 [1994]), *La crise des sociétés impériales* (2001), *Les intellectuels en Europe au XIXe siècle* (1996), and *Théâtres en capitales* (2008).
2. Favor the micro scale to the macro social vision so as to control against

the inevitable bias of sources on a more global scale, which refers back to national structures and thus to a perspective fixed by the state.

3. Practice a fine-grained semantic history and exercises in cross-fertilizing translation [*traductions croisées*] in order to master the multiple harmonics of terms and concepts that are often only euphemistic versions of much richer specific terms, revelatory of past struggles between groups and ideas.

4. Carry out cross-fertilizing transfers [*transferts croisés*] of perspectives to free oneself from national historiographic traditions (approach French history from an English or German point of view and vice versa).

5. Conduct wide-ranging research with the support of international working groups to take advantage of reciprocal assessment and expert knowledge of sources by many historiographic and theoretical cultures.[5]

Following these general considerations, let us see how they have put into practice and put to the test conceptualizations born of Bourdieu's propositions.

For a Transnational Usage of Bourdieusian Concepts
THE UNIVERSITY FIELD

My initial choice to begin comparisons by privileging German-speaking countries and the sociocultural history of intellectuals and higher education stemmed from the pragmatic desire both to recycle the expertise I had accumulated on these subjects with regard to France and to enrich the collective biographies I had already assembled by putting them into a comparative perspective.[6] One might equally note that comparison was here not just my own approach qua historian, but also that of the very groups and institutions of the period I was studying. This convergence offered a double advantage: on one hand, it had already given rise to very rich source materials oriented in part by a problematic connected to my own, and, on the other hand, it permitted a comparison not only of objective evidence but also of interpretations and representations of historical "realities," themselves produced by actors in the history that was to be reconstructed. These shared views and this reflexive perspective [*perspective en abyme*] permitted the deployment of richer hypotheses without thereby trapping me in a purely external sort of history or, conversely, making me prey to the sort of complaisant genealogy or celebration so common in the historiography of the academy and academics, especially in the case of Germany. Comparison is one means of gaining a critical perspective on history, but that perspective is sharpened further when it is confronted with the double critical examination of the witnesses and actors being studied.

To give an example of this productive echo, I will summarize the first chapter of *La République des universitaires* (1994a), in which I analyze the critical examination of the German academy and academics offered by young French academics sent out on a mission to analyze the specificities of German universities at the beginning of the Third Republic. Had I limited myself to the study of discourse, I would have certainly shed some light on the representations these reformers made of the German academy, and what they retained from their comparison once they were in a position to influence the reform of higher education, a useful history but one already accomplished in part on a scholarly or technical level. To avoid the simple genealogy of ideas, I had first put together systematic social biographies of these academics (1985, 1986, 1988, 1989), which I then compared to larger samples of elites.[7] I also tried to draw up a similar portrait of the Berlin academics evoked in the laudatory or critical texts of these missionaries to Germany.

Through this two-tier comparative analysis, I was therefore able to establish at which points the assessments of French educators were distorted by prejudice or self-interest (which is particularly the case for anything having to do with the financial aspects of academic careers in Germany) and at what moment their critical examination corresponded with what a comparison could establish today (thus with respect to the social position or eminent stature, by French standards, of German academics). I was also able to do this for the shadowy areas and blind spots that academic propriety obliged them to repress but that often constitute missing links for understanding the inner workings of a particularly well-supervised milieu (everything that has to do with political, familial, and religious affiliations, in particular).

More generally, *La République des universitaires*, in which German universities are always in the background of the analysis of academic milieus of the Third Republic, permitted me to understand the specificities of the evolution of the French university much better than if I had limited myself to an internal social history of university professors of the period. The comparison, having emerged from a will to understand the difference in political attitude between French and German academic intellectuals, ended up equally putting into question the received wisdom of my own academic formation concerning the French *homo academicus*. In *Naissance des "intellectuels"* (1990a) I had related the birth of "intellectuals" to a particular moment in the evolution of the elites of the Republic and the entrance of a portion of the academic avant-garde into this struggle as a prolongation of their reformist struggle in the university. The comparative deepening of the social history of this group across the Third Republic as a whole, in comparison with the German evolution, allowed me to understand why the resurgence of this universalizing intellectual function was one of the compensations for the recurrent French academic unease, born of the "conflict of the faculties" that can certainly be found elsewhere, but in a more acute and more fundamental form in France because reproduced and amplified by each successive reform of the contemporary university. It is therefore not an accident if Bourdieu's analysis of the roots of May 1968 in the university also has recourse to this scheme of the conflict of the faculties. Each French academic crisis replays it: at the end of the nineteenth century, in the interwar period, in the 1960s, and yet again today. The conflict exists in a more or less latent state in every university system, but it is more acute in France than elsewhere. The French Revolution, in destroying guilds and notably the university guild, left French academics bereft of a coherent social identity and incited them to define themselves against other faculties, administrative power, political power, and foreign models.

THE INTELLECTUALS

My second comparative work (*Les intellectuals en Europe au XIXe siècle* [1996]) revisited some of these themes but ventured into much more difficult territory in enlarging the Franco-German frame to all of the major European countries, and in extending the period of observation to an entire century. *Les intellectuals en Europe* defined itself as a synthetic work, that is to say, as a research program as much as a definitive assessment. It did not seek to establish itself as a vulgate so much as a first draft of possible lines of interpretation and points to be further developed.

The Franco-German comparison had allowed me to relativize notions of the academy and academics by juxtaposing different developmental models, while multinational comparison on a European scale allowed me to locate intellectual cycles that varied from one country to another. Processes with an indirect influence also appeared, often by the intermediary of other, smaller countries that escaped nationalistic hardening or shared multiple cultures (Belgium, Switzerland, and Italy, in particular). Thanks to the *longue durée* and to variations in national unity, I was also able to develop a more complex typology of intellectual figures and to introduce five additional explanatory factors showing, in a different fashion, French specificities:

1. The spatial and political organization of the state according to centralist or polycentric models results in considerable differences concerning the functioning of intellectual fields and their relationship to the power of intellectuals (here one finds the link, which Bourdieu [1971a] had insisted upon early on, between the intellectual field and the field of power).

2. The specific relationships between the state and religion weigh much more heavily on intellectual life than one would like to admit in France owing to the culture of secularism [*laïcité*]. Historically, the figure of the "intellectuel" has not defined itself in the same way when faced with Catholic, Protestant, Jewish, or Orthodox clergy. Here I reworked the analyses of "prophet" functions and of ordinary clergy that Bourdieu (1987a [1971]) also deploys in his interpretation of Weber's sociology of religion in order to define two types of intellectuals in the romantic period.

3. The unequal involvement of traditional elites (the nobility, high-ranking public officials) in intellectual life and the hierarchies between different types of capital strongly differentiate the various European intellectual fields. The primary battle of intellectuals in the nineteenth century is to gain recognition of the value of their cultural, symbolic, or scholarly capital as equivalent to forms of economic or social capital. The success of this secular struggle, however, varies unequally according to the development of relationships of force between elites and the degree to which intellectuals are integrated in the field of power.[8]

4. The variable relationships between men and women in social and intellectual life also oppose a Latin and Catholic cultural area, in which high-society women protect artists and men of letters, to a more Protestant area, in which such women themselves have precocious access to intellectual production (cf. the importance of female novelists from the eighteenth century on in England),[9] and in which, on the contrary, salons and patronage scarcely play a role in the intellectual or literary field.

5. The effects of linguistic unity or plurality, of the unity or multiplicity of religious denominations in a given national area, the unequal degree of international openness of national intellectual fields, and the age of the nation all also modify the degree of autonomization possible for intellectual fields and the diverse competing groups. These themes were developed a bit later in a more widely Bourdieusian perspective by Pascale Casanova (2004 [1999]) and Blaise Wilfert (2009).

To understand these multiple dimensions, I tried to combine a number of methods and approaches previously tested in the German and French cases:

Morphological analyses of intellectual fields allowing for the definition of periods of expansion and crisis, periods of liberation and reaction (here one finds certain schemas regarding the processes of professional solidarity [*défense du corps*] described in the buildup to the crisis of 1968 in *Homo Academicus* (Bourdieu 1988 [1984]) or in my own *La crise littéraire à l'époque du naturalisme* [1979]), the degree of unification or

decentralization of the intellectual field, and its degree of nationalization or extroversion. In certain dominated nations, the "true intellectuals" are often exiles who find refuge in already constituted nations;
Paris has thus served in some periods as a substitute capital for the
intellectual fields of oppressed nations: Italians, Poles, Germans, people
of the Balkans, Latin Americans, German Jews, or persecuted Russians,
and so on. This is a reminder that the intellectual field is not identical to
a given objective geographical space. Indeed, this was the focus of the
last research projects directed by Bourdieu, which concerned the international circulation of ideas and the transformations of publishing on a
global scale.[10]

Well-constructed collective biographies of sample groups of intellectuals
can reveal the large variables that structure fields and the differentiation
of trajectories around the poles of different fields and the specificities of
the societies compared. These methods, employed by Bourdieu and his
team in the 1970s on French elites, the *grandes écoles*, academics, and
bishops, thus show their fruitfulness on a larger scale.

The study of the representations of intellectual groups (endogenous or
exogenous representations, themselves to be resituated in the field of
political struggles) that appear across critical moments as well as debates concerning the place of intellectuals, changes in terminology, and
the borrowing or refusal of foreign terminologies. These analyses of the
political conjunctures that create major confrontations bring to light
the fault lines of intellectual milieus (on the model of the Dreyfus
affair), as, for example, around 1848.[11]

This last opening leads to research concerning the networks and transfers
that supplement these one-to-one comparisons.

COMPARISONS, NETWORKS, AND TRANSFERS

Some critics of Bourdieu have occasionally accused him of being a prisoner of
a Franco-French vision of sociology owing to the centrality he accords the
state, the strong relationship he establishes between culture and politics, and
the value he accords to national standardization inherited from the process of
state formation in France. The notions of habitus and field would accordingly
be useful only to analysts of countries close to the centralized French model
(for example, Russia, Spain, Greece, Portugal, Mexico, Argentina) and much
less adapted to analyses of decentralized countries or those weakly unified on a
national level, where the state is uninterested in culture.

Having undertaken the social history of both types of countries, I willingly recognize that the transfer of principles of analysis to countries homologous to France is much easier for the reconstruction of Bourdieusian schemas (see my comparative study of the role of intellectuals in France, Russia, and Spain in *Les intellectuals en Europe au XIXe siècle* [1996]). At the same time, as shown above by the Franco-German comparison regarding universities, it is unclear that the application of Bourdieu's schema to countries highly similar to France is really the most productive method of moving forward with the initial theory. Rather, I believe that it is by turning to the cases most different from France that Bourdieu's theorization may best be shown to be most enriching, not only for a French analyst but also for analysts from the culture in question.[12]

In accord with the method of cross-fertilizing transfers [*transferts croisés*] evoked earlier, it is the very discrepancy between Bourdieusian concepts and societies distant from France that grants the analysis additional heuristic value. Not only because it requires that both the case considered and the tools used be better thought out, but especially because in this manner it raises questions which sociologists and historians of these societies, being under the sway of their national habitus and received academic blindness, do not think of themselves. The American historian Thomas Bender (2006), the product of an entirely different methodological orientation, has shown all the potentialities of this decentering with respect to American history in replacing it in a global European or, indeed, Western perspective during the nineteenth century. Stefan Collini (2006), the English historian, likewise little concerned with sociology while being very familiar with French scholarship, has similarly enriched his discussion of English intellectuals by crossing his deep knowledge of British historiography and English intellectual debates with perspectives borrowed from French historians, notably my own works, and thus indirectly with Bourdieu's approaches.[13]

For this cross-fertilizing transfer [*transfert croisé*] to be possible and fruitful, it is necessary to combine the comparative approach with the transnational approach and to do so by means of transfers. Nations divergent from the French model are constantly, by virtue of the very history of their relations with France, confronted by it and constantly defined and redefined in comparison to it[14] (the converse, moreover, being every bit as true, as we have seen with respect to France in the academic domain). The initial hypothesis of comparison, according to which cases can be isolated and a more general theory drawn from their variations, is in fact only an approximation of historical, social, and cultural reality. All European national areas and Western national areas more generally, insofar as they have participated in a common heritage, an intertwined history, and continuous rivalry and emulation for at least three centuries, may be considered as interconnected fields requiring, on a larger scale, an approach in terms of a transnational or international field, depending on the case. I tried to show this with respect to the European intellectual field at the fin-de-siècle moment of crisis, for French, German, and British societies during the period I defined as the crisis of imperial societies (1900–1940), for the relations between French and English intellectuals in the second half of the nineteenth century, and with respect to European cultural capitals and the theatrical market in Paris, Berlin, London, and Vienna after 1860.

In this manner the European intellectual field considered as a transnational ensemble and not as a comparison of closed national fields, arises in the 1900s out of an earlier and double reorganization. On one hand, academic reforms, notably in France, Italy, Central Europe, and, later, Spain, gradually bring universities into conformity with the German research standard, defined in the "human sciences" by the philological paradigm, and in the "natural sciences" by the experimental laboratory protocol.[15] On the other hand, the growing disassociation of national literary fields, itself the product of the nationalization of European societies, increasingly obeys the French model, which is structured around oppositions between literary autonomy/economic heteronomy, and avant-garde/commercial literature/academic literature. This is evidenced in the remarkable diffusion of French practices of distinction and advancement to writers elsewhere in Europe: the literary manifesto, investigations and polemics between schools, sociability within closed urban circles, positioning with respect to classics or national and political issues, and the launching of reviews free of concerns about profitability thanks to patronage or cultural activism.

This double, parallel process, overlapping but finally contradictory, results in intellectual competition on a European scale between three national poles which define the internal and external strategies of diverse intellectual groups in each linguistic area, without, however, now being able to ignore the tensions in the neighboring area owing to translations and multiple cultural transfers. In the first place, a German norm places the university-affiliated state intellectual in the position of dominant legitimacy, close to power and defender of a pure scientific or scholarly ideal; this figure is opposed to the free intellectual, "without ties" (according to Karl Mannheim's well-known expression), who is relegated to a dominated position but with a social situation that improves through the decades I investigated thanks to the growing prospects afforded by journals with large circulations, the press, and the commercial literary sector. In the second place, a traditional French norm, inherited from the Enlightenment and romanticism, always claims hegemony in the intellectual field for the man of letters independent of power but protected from it through institutions of sociability as such: salons, journals, professional associations for the defense of artistic or literary property, and so on. He is in touch with the general public but increasingly hostile toward a writerly craft more and more subjected to the laws of the market, as in Anglophone countries, more and more critical of emergent internationalist, scientist, and materialist pretensions, and also concerned about competition from the new figure of the savant, whom he identifies with an intellectual "Germanization." Finally, a new norm is affirmed, first in France but soon in all of Europe, in a dominated position, that of the intellectual in the sense that word took on during the Dreyfus affair. It combines traits borrowed from the academic model as it was re-formed by the Republic (autonomy, as in Germany, but political independence and concern for social responsibility, unlike in Germany) and from the literary and artistic avant-garde stemming from the principle of art for art's sake, opposed at once to scholarly orthodoxy and lettered orthodoxy of the old academic type (*la vieille Sorbonne* of Napoleon) and to the social and political conformism of the established literary field.[16]

In a very simplified manner, the space of struggles and antagonisms resulting from these three concurrent positions may be sketched out, as much on a national as on an international scale, according to a series of principles of solidarity, opposition, and equivalence of one level of observation to another on a generic model: the avant-garde is to the literary establishment what the new generation of scientists is to the established scholar (in France); the intellectuals in France are to anti-Dreyfusard intellectuals or German mandarins (*Gebildete*) or English scholars what Italian or Spanish intellectuals or German modernist avant-gardes are to the dominant men of letters of their respective countries or to the dominant academics of other countries; or even, globally, the Italian, Spanish, or German literary field is to the French literary field what the French academic field (or Italian, or Spanish, or even English before its reforms) is to the German academic field; finally the Latin nations are to the nations of the North what Catholic nations are to Protestant nations, what intellectual fractions are globally to traditional elites, what the popular classes are to the dominant class, and what women are, culturally and socially, to men, colonized people to imperial nations, and so forth.

This interplay of slippages and analogies between multiple cultural and social oppositions also underlies many of the polemics which marked the period (the theme of Anglo-Saxon superiority and the social-Darwinian debate between rising and decadent nations), in some new, emergent conflicts (the affirmation of intellectuals in the political field, the emergence of the feminist movement, the workers' movement, forerunners of the anticolonial struggle, debates concerning the "failure of science" or, on the contrary, its superiority) and in a transnational manner, permitting or preventing alliances between the dominated and dominant in homologous positions in their specific subfields within the transnational, global field. This underlying unification, far from erasing national antagonisms, exacerbates and retranscribes them according to logics proper to each space of reference and to unequally consistent or advanced interplay and framing [*emboîtement*] in the larger space. As the majority of works of intellectual history either limit themselves to a few dominant figures, with no effort made to reconstitute their position in the double international and national space, or resign themselves to partial monographs on certain groups, they grasp only in a roundabout way the intercalation of short, medium, and long-term relations that condition the fashions, the possibilities, and the intensity of expression of the writers, academics, or ideological groups under consideration. I tried to restore this internal and external double logic with respect to anglophile French intellectuals, for example; through a social microhistory of the elites in different imperial societies charged with foreign relations, with respect to the process of triggering the war of 1914; and on the subject of the relationship between intellectuals and modernity and new relations of domination between French and German intellectuals in the 1950s.[17] Rather than engaging in a long theoretical debate, I have preferred to demonstrate the interest and fruitfulness of this method with documentary evidence and applied theoretical constructions.

Conclusion

If the diverse concepts and principles of Bourdieu's sociological method may be mobilized by a historical and comparative-retrospective sociology equally well for elites, culture, intellectuals, and universities, it is because he himself constructed his theoretical project on the basis of a critical reading of the founding fathers of sociology, who advocated the comparative method, but also because he realized the extent of the contribution of ethnological currents, a discipline he himself practiced, to microhistory. Bourdieu always insisted on the double reflexivity in our relation to the object imposed by the sociohistorical comparative approach, a posture he borrowed from the philosophy of science notably inspired by Bachelard. Because of the international impact of his later work, Bourdieu was himself obliged to constantly attend to the translation and retranslation of his perspectives and principles in multiple national contexts, where his theses could be misinterpreted owing to intellectual presuppositions or national cultural traditions divergent from those of France. His last research projects were increasingly comparative. In an unpublished text that he communicated to me along these lines, he defined the program I have set out here as the question of "how to become an ethnologist of one's own society, of one's own historical experience, the socioanalyst of one's own social unconscious?"[18]

Notes

1. See also Kaelble 1999.
2. For an attempt at a comparative sociology of Jews in Europe, see Karady 1999.
3. For a partial English translation, see Charle 2004c.
4. Mayer's (2000) comparative analysis of the French and Russian revolutions corrects this bias.
5. Collective books have resulted from this: Charle, Keiner, and Schriewer 1993; Charle, Schriewer, and Wagner 2004; Charle, Vincent, and Winter 2007; Charle and Roche 2004; Charle 2009.
6. Cf. Charle 1994a; Charle and Verger 2007 [1994].
7. Cf. Charle 2006b [1987]; the results are summarized in English in Charle 1994b.
8. I took up this point in greater detail with respect to theater writers in chapter 4 of Charle 2008.
9. Cf. Cohen 1999.
10. See issues 144 and 145 of *Actes de la recherche en sciences sociales*, particularly Bourdieu 2002a.
11. See Charle 2002.
12. Bourdieu himself demonstrated so implicitly (Bourdieu 1991 [1988]), 2008.
13. Cf. my review (Charle 2007b).
14. Colley 1992; Tombs and Tombs 2006; and Stedman Jones 2004 have demonstrated this for different periods in the case of England.
15. See Weisz 1983; Charle 2004b.
16. See Charle 1998 and chapters 2 and 3 of Charle 1990b.
17. See Charle 2005, 2007a and chapter 5 of Charle 2001.
18. Pierre Bourdieu, "Les spécificités des histoires nationales: Histoire comparée des différences pertinentes entre les nations," personal communication with the author (2001).

PART II   **Theoretical Engagements**

RATIONAL CHOICE MAY TAKE OVER

Times of crisis, in which the routine adjustment of subjective and objective structures is brutally disrupted, constitute a class of circumstances when indeed "rational choice" may take over, at least among those agents who are in a position to be rational.

—PIERRE BOURDIEU AND LOÏC WACQUANT, *AN INVITATION TO REFLEXIVE SOCIOLOGY*

In this chapter I weave variations on a single theme: Pierre Bourdieu, rational choice, and historical analysis. For this purpose, the statement quoted as epigraph will be my running thread and my lead. Why this thread in particular? The motivation is threefold. First, the quotation brings us straight to the subject matter. Bourdieu sets the stage for a possible modus vivendi with rational choice against the backdrop of historical time. History adjudicates the relevance of alternative theoretical frameworks. These frameworks can coexist provided they acknowledge where they stand. Crisis is the domain of rational choice. The theory of practice reserves for itself the time of patterns, structures, and routines.

Second, the quotation is paradoxical. There is no want of disparaging rebuttals of the fundamentals of rational choice in Bourdieu's oeuvre. In contrast, this short statement asserts the possibility of a peaceful coexistence. Rational choice has its raison d'être, however qualified it might be. A modus vivendi is conceivable once domains of competence have been identified. Indirectly this statement reveals how Bourdieu typifies rational choice and its (restricted) domain of expertise. One interesting issue is whether rational choice analysts might recognize themselves in this characterization. A further issue is whether and how they could make sense of the claim given the explicit tenets of their theoretical framework.

Third, the quotation is intriguing. Interpreted literally, it suggests that in situations of a fit between subjective and objective structures, actors are not properly rational, at least not rational in the sense rational choice conceives rationality. What does it mean to say that when the fit is disrupted, "'rational choice' may take over"? Why would rational choice take over? Which conception of rationality is implied here?

To address these points, I develop the argument here in four steps. Drawing on Bourdieu's theoretical elaborations, I first consider the analytical rationale for apportioning classes of historical situations between theoretical frameworks. Second, I ask whether the conception of rational choice implied by Bourdieu's proposal accords with the rational choice analysts' own understanding of their core claims. The third section adopts a more empirical outlook and discusses Bourdieu's account of the crisis of May 1968 in France. My purpose in the third section is to gauge the fit between, on the one hand, the empirical account of a case which, in Bourdieu's analytical framework, has emblematic status and, on the other hand, the short pronouncement presented in the epigraph. Finally, I develop the implications of these observations for the analysis of historical change.

As this outline suggests, the structure of this chapter varies the standpoints between theoretical frameworks and genres of inquiry. In the first two sections the discussion is pitched at the level of generality presumed by Bourdieu for the purpose of assessing the validity of a general claim. The upshot of this discussion corroborates a broader point: whether we adopt the bearings of the theory of practice or those of rational choice, the claim does not stand firm. It leaves out too many qualifying clauses. The third section shifts to a more empirically grounded type of inquiry. I develop the argument about a modus vivendi between these two frameworks by engaging empirical observations mostly derived from the case which Bourdieu analyzes at length: May 1968 in France.

A word on the core concepts and assumptions that identify the two frameworks I consider: the key concepts of rational choice revolve around the notion of utility maximization (Green and Shapiro 1994: 14). Actors seek to optimize their interests (Coleman 1990: 14–15), assuming that their beliefs and intentions are consistent (Elster 1986: 12–13; Tsebelis 1990: 18, 24–27). The key concepts of the theory of practice are the habitus and the field. The habitus is a system of enduring dispositions, cognitively informed by a system of classification, that constitutes a generative principle of practices (Bourdieu 1984a: 110, 1990a [1980]: 56–57). A field is the system of objective relations—between positions differentiated in terms of various forms of capital—that at once gives shape and validates this system of dispositions (Bourdieu 1996a: 83, 182–84).

Rationale

What justifies the claim that in crisis situations rational choice can take over? Answering this question requires, first, that we clarify how Bourdieu construes the core assumptions and internal logic of rational choice and, second, that we identify the defining features of crisis conjunctures. These two sets of considerations combined together justify the claim. I start with the characterization of rational choice and follow up with an analytical definition of crises. The fit between the object crisis and the framework rational choice becomes much clearer and less intriguing once we place consciousness at the center of the stage, as Bourdieu invites us to do. Crisis situations are amenable to the tools of rational choice because they elicit a heightened level of consciousness. Routine patterns and conjunctures are propitious to the theory of practice since they make reflexivity superfluous.

CONSCIOUSNESS AND ITS AFFIDAVITS

In the shadow theater which Bourdieu imputes to rational choice, the main character is, as we might have expected, the individual actor, and this main character has several typical features. First, her knowledge is unencumbered. She has complete and perfect information (Bourdieu 1988: 61, 63). Second, this agent is freed from the debilitating impact of constraints. That is, she is freed from representations about herself that limit her capacity. Third, reflexivity and consciousness are her hallmarks. The rational choice actor is the epitome of a consciousness that calls herself to order. This last premise is the arch stone of the edifice. I therefore start with this assumption.

Three features. The rationality of rational choice designates a conscious mode of action in which actors intentionally select a course of action geared to material interests after having assessed the probable consequences of alternative options.[1] As Bourdieu writes, "The 'rational actor' theory, which seeks the 'origin' of acts, strictly economic or not, in an *'intention' of 'consciousness,'* is often associated with a narrow conception of the 'rationality' of practices, an economism which regards as rational . . . those practices that are *consciously oriented* by the pursuit of maximum (economic) profit at minimum (economic) cost" (1990a [1980]: 50, emphasis added).[2] The rational choice actor is a consciousness *en acte*, fully aware of the ins and outs of her action and its material consequences.

This representation has two correlates. One is the assumption of full knowledge. The information available to this actor is complete and perfect (Bourdieu 1990a [1980]: 50, 61, 63). "The champions of rational action theory believe" that "social agents are conscious and knowing subjects acting with full knowledge of the facts" (Bourdieu 1998d: 24). The world is, so to speak, transparent to the designs and intentions of the actor.[3] This knowledge applies to material interests and to the options available to fulfill these interests. A second correlate is that consciousness is not warped by a sense of constraints. These have no grip upon mental structures (Bourdieu 1990a [1980]: 50). The rational choice actor is mentally unburdened by the limits of her practice. The world is transparent also in the sense that it does not play tricks with consciousness. It is what it is.

Autonomy under influence. Under Bourdieu's lens, the rational choice actor is the epitome of a conscious subject loaded with the plenitude of full knowledge, eluding the mental grip of constraining conditions and enacting the principle of her autonomy. As such, this actor turns out to be almost the exact negative of the agent conceptualized by the theory of practice. Whereas, according to Bourdieu, reflexivity and awareness are the centerpieces of the rational choice edifice, the theory of practice investigates the rationality of action embodied in a practical sense informed by habitual experience. In this realm of experience, consciousness is subsidiary. The habitus is "a spontaneity without consciousness or will" (Bourdieu 1990a [1980]: 56). Similarly, practice logic is "a logic in itself without conscious reflexion" (Bourdieu 1977: 92). Individuals are inhabited by dispositions that shape their sense of the possible and their capacity for improvisation. The "ontological complicity between the habitus and the field is 'infra-conscious'" (Bourdieu 1998d: 79).

This contrast explains why the prototype which Bourdieu imputes to rational choice borrows her features as much from Jean-Paul Sartre as from Jon Elster. Consciousness, full knowledge, autonomy: this conceptual language is not incidental. Bourdieu combines the critique of the Sartrean conception with the critique of rational choice in the same chapter and under the same heading: "The imaginary anthropology of subjectivism" (Bourdieu 1977: 42–51). Both proceed from the same erroneous anthropological postulates evoking "the ultra-finalist subjectivism of a consciousness 'without inertia'" (Bourdieu 1990a [1980]: 46).[4] Consciousness is indeed the dividing line with the realm of action investigated by the theory of practice.

The paradox is that this ultrafinalist conception ends up offering a strict determinist conception of action (Bourdieu 1990a [1980]: 46, 1998d: 24–25). The rational choice actor asserts her autonomy of choice by engaging in intricate strategic considerations aimed at her self-interest. However, since the choice criteria and the mental processes at play are assumed to have universal validity, actors confronted with the same decision problem behave in the same way given their overriding interest in maximization. Hence, rational choice oscillates between, on the one hand, the fantasy of a psyche that demonstrates autonomous mastery and, on the other hand, an "intellectual determinism" that could be couched in very mechanical terms if it were not for a "few differences in phrasing" (Bourdieu 1990a [1980]: 46).[5]

PRACTICE DISRUPTED

Let us now consider the second term of the equation: crisis conjunctures. Here the focus is on the disruption of habitual patterns. Times of crisis are times of disjuncture. Practices do not produce their anticipated effects. Dispositions inherited from the past are dysfunctional, out of phase and disconnected from situational challenges or imperatives. They have lost their relevance. As a result, actors are at odds with the world that is emerging before their eyes. Bourdieu (1988: 183–84) evokes the shock (*stupeur*) experienced by French academics in May 1968 as they experienced their world turned upside down—a shock not so different from the old Kabyle peasants' incredulity when confronted with "the heretical methods of cultivation practiced by the young" (183).

If times of crisis are situations in which, since dispositions are being de-coupled from their structural conditions, the habitus is "out of sync," then the theory of practice a priori has little to say. The domain of predilection of the habitus is a realm of experience marked by the concordance between structures and practices when actors can develop their practical sense thanks to the fit between structures and expectations. Experience confirms expectations, which in turn reinforce structures. Once the fit becomes problematic, the relevance of the theory becomes questionable. It makes sense a priori to look for another ship to carry the day.

Still, this does not tell us why rational choice would carry the day. The justification for the proposal lies in the impact of disjuncture on actors' dispositions. In times of concordance, actors can afford to be irreflexive. In times of rupture, this luxury becomes problematic. The point is no longer to make virtue out of necessity but to figure out where the necessity lies and, accessorily, why virtue has been lost. Actors realize that their dispositions no longer provide them with a sense of the game. They have lost their practical understanding. The loss compels them to gauge and reflect on their own presumptions. Their understanding of practice becomes less practical, less implicit, and less obvious as it becomes loaded with a sense of disjuncture.

Moments of crisis are thus times of greater awareness. They bring to light background assumptions. In the process of departing from a practical sense that has become obsolete and irrelevant, actors accede to a state of consciousness which for the most part eludes them in highly predictable and recognizable situations, when their habitus provides them with the appropriate cognitive and bodily clues.[6] The hiatus between what used to be their practical sense and the social world as they now experience it—far removed from the "sanctity of what had always been" (Weber)—goads their awareness.[7]

Now we can connect the dots. Crises are the domain of predilection of rational choice because, according to Bourdieu, they induce a higher level of consciousness and reflexivity. The "double consciousness" characteristic of actors mobilizing the categories of two distinct symbolic universes (e.g., religious and economic) "is at the basis of a very great (partial) lucidity which is manifested above all in situations of crisis and among people in precarious positions" (Bourdieu 1998d: 113). As consciousness asserts itself and actors shift from an irreflexive mode to a more reflexive one, so does their propensity for instrumental rationality, self-awareness, and a conscious assessment of the future. Actors objectify the ins and outs of their behavior.[8] Their action, being *deliberately* oriented toward a goal, fits the theoretical postulates of rational choice.

The Pundits' View

Does this characterization accord with rational choice analysts' own conceptions? Can there be a rational choice justification for the suggestion that its conceptual tools and assumptions apply to crisis situations in the first place? As mentioned at the outset of this chapter, I use the rational choice label to designate studies that either assume or demonstrate the prevalence of strategic rationality geared to a criterion of optimization. This definition is more specific than conceptions broadly equating rational choice with strategic rationality.[9] It is also consistent with the way in which systematic commentators characterize the framework (Green and Shapiro 1994: 14–15).

CORE ASSUMPTIONS

Optimization. For the proponents of rational choice, optimization, not consciousness, is the central assumption. At best, consciousness and reflexivity can be construed as derivations of the search for maximization. The issue, however, is not decisive. Of greater significance is the analysis of the logic of optimization and the criteria relevant to capture analytically this logic. In this analytical universe the reference to consciousness does not have the centrality Bourdieu assigns to it.[10] True, Elster (1983b: 117–18) elaborates the contrast between "sour grapes" and "character planning" as revolving in part on this criterion. "Sour grapes" designates a causal and unconscious adaptation to constraints. It operates "behind the back" of the actor, who downgrades the options which she cannot reach as a way to cope with the frustration. "Character planning" on the other hand, designates a process of deliberate preference adjustment.

Yet the distinction between sour grapes and character planning takes place within a broader discussion of the rationality of beliefs ("thick rationality") that is peripheral to the technical specifications of instrumental rationality ("thin rationality").[11] Among rational choice circles, most of the debate about the distinction between rational and nonrational action has focused, first, on the distinctiveness of purposive action in contrast to expressive or impulsive action (Coleman 1990: 16–17) and, second, on criteria of choice and belief consistency (Elster 1983b: 6–7; Tsebelis 1990: 24–27). From the standpoint of rational choice, the theory of rational action is a theory of consistency.

Similarly, for a critic of rational choice as systematic as Herbert Simon, the main issue is less consciousness than cognitive capacity: rational choice stumbles against the limited cognitive power of the human mind. Choices are constrained not only because of the objective characteristics of the situation, but also because of the way in which human beings process information. These are internal constraints. Rational choice lacks realism inasmuch as it is oblivious to these limitations and to the correlate power of framing effects. Selective attention is one facet of this limited cognitive capacity (Simon 1985: 302; Tversky and Kahneman 1986: 260). Hence, we cannot a priori assume that "all alternatives are known to the agent without cost"—a claim which Coleman (1990: 506) depicts as standard in rational choice.

Complete information. This brings up a second issue: full knowledge. The imputation of complete information is problematic. A great deal of the analytical refinements yielded by rational choice concerns the engineering of decisions with incomplete information (Harsanyi 1967, 1995: 292).[12] Individuals face a decision that can be costly to themselves and others. Yet they do not have all the information required to assess the costs involved. The decision is risky and entails a significant amount of uncertainty. Rational choice has identified several decision criteria, such as the minimax criterion and the principle of expected utility maximization, to assess the rationality of decisions made with incomplete information.[13] Most of the critical debate has focused on the empirical plausibility of these criteria. Thus the cardinal assumption made by rational choice is *not*, as Bourdieu presumes, that actors are fully informed about the ins and outs of their choice. It is that actors make the best possible use of the information available to them.[14]

Constraints. What about constraints? The cognitive and dispositional impacts of these constraints is not at the center of the rational choice analysts' agenda. The latter confine their domain of investigation by treating values (normative beliefs) and normative preferences as given. This methodological decision implies no definite stance on the relationships between social positions and normative beliefs. For instance, North, who interprets economic developments in light of a "neoclassical model of the state," has no difficulty acknowledging that "people differently positioned in terms of experience have differing rationalizations or views of the world around them and have no way to confirm or reject definitely these different views" (1981: 50).[15]

The impact of constraints on preferences and dispositions, however, is not outside the purview of a rational choice theory focused on cost considerations. The constant call to order imposed by constraints has a psychological cost. It is costly to experience dissonance. In internalizing or rationalizing these constraints and in molding their dispositions so that these anticipate the structure of objective relations, actors minimize the costs inherent to dissonance. This rationality fits the standards of rational choice.[16] It is less costly to make virtue out of necessity than to engage in a fruitless denial of reality that would amount to a denial of structures. Better make peace with constraints that appear indomitable than exhaust oneself in vain, with glory perhaps, but in vain. Sour grapes illustrates an adaptive process of this kind (Elster 1983b: 118).

MODUS VIVENDI?

I now address the second question raised at the outset of this section: from the standpoint of rational choice can we justify Bourdieu's proposal for a division of intellectual labor, as stated in the epigraph? There is no definite answer to that question. Or, rather, one should say, two rational choice answers are possible, and they are at odds with one another. One draws attention to the incentives for strategic rationality generated by the prospect of having to bear significant, tangible costs. The other states that times of rupture are also conjunctures in which the standard scope conditions of rational choice are open to question. It is therefore far from clear whether in these conjunctures individuals are in a position to be strategically rational in the sense postulated by rational choice. I discuss each answer in turn.

Cost assessment. The first answer emphasizes the shift to instrumental rationality geared to an optimal assessment of consequences. When individuals are confronted with new options that are risky as a result of the uncertainty begotten by the future and the incomplete character of the information available, they can no longer rely on the cognitive short circuits which routine situations give way to and make possible. Given these risks, their prime consideration is to minimize potential future costs (Lindenberg 1989: 55). Threats to basic (material) interests are very powerful incentives to "face reality" (Elster 2000: 692).[17] Cost considerations are now at center stage. Actors develop an instrumental understanding of their behavior geared to a principle of cost avoidance. They pay greater attention to assessing consequences.

Scope conditions. The second answer, by contrast, questions the relevance of rational choice in crisis situations given the model's scope conditions. For individuals to deploy their strategic capacity, certain minimal cognitive conditions are required. Actors must be able to exercise their judgment and apply some criteria of consistency to uphold this judgment (Schumpeter 1942: 253). They need to be able to map out risks and alternatives and to assess how the consequences of their choices will affect their welfare (Taylor 1988: 91). If uncertainty blurs the future to the point of incapacitating their ability to discern alternative courses of action and to make reasonable assessments, then a very different mode of action might be at play—one regulated by the explicit script of ideological pronouncements. Hence rational choice applies if in a minimal sense actors can identify which alternatives they face. Situations of disequilibrium or unstable equilibria do not fit this prerequisite (North 1990: 22).

A reversal in stance. This line of argument reverses the assertion quoted in the epigraph. It is in routine times, when institutional conditions are well established, that actors can fully exercise their capacity for instrumental rationality, for when institutional conditions are well established the scope conditions of rational choice can be reasonably assumed to be in place (Simon 1978: 14). Individuals can develop the cognitive resources to learn the rules of the game. They can also stabilize their judgments. Bourdieu's views of historical processes are congruent with this interpretation. Whether we adopt the grid of reading of rational choice or of the theory of practice, we are witnessing actors who primarily seek to preserve, consolidate, or expand their interests. "Agents . . . have no other choice than to struggle to maintain or improve their position in the field, thus helping to bring to bear on all the others the weight of the constraints" (Bourdieu 1990e: 196; quoted by Calhoun 1993a: 143).

Not surprisingly, commentators have noted the parallel between this view of history and rational choice. Postone, LiPuma, and Calhoun (1993) emphasize the drive for maximization: "Unaware of some true possibilities, unable to take full advantage or conceive of other possibilities due to their class habitus, agents nonetheless seek to *maximize* benefits, given their relational position within a field" (5, emphasis added). Biernacki (1995) points out that "like rational choice theorists, [Bourdieu] underscores the agents' *unceasing* manipulation of their symbolic and material environment" (22, emphasis added). Steinmetz (1999) makes consonant observations: "Bourdieu . . . evokes a quasi-Hobbesian world of struggle for competitive advantage, one that in many ways recalls microeconomic descriptions of rational actors pursuing their material interests" (28).

In documenting the constant struggle for competitive advantage as it takes place in history and different institutional contexts, ethnographically oriented accounts actually flesh out historical actors who, in their rational choice guise, often look shallow and devoid of substance, as if their main reason for showing up on the stage was to corroborate the plausibility of theoretical claims. Given rational choice analysts' insistence on agency (for example, Coleman 1986: 1312), this lack of substance is surprising. It becomes less so when we take cognizance of the status granted to theoretical arguments in historical explanations that have the rational choice label. Theory basically has it all. As sites of agency, actors cannot be expected to deviate from the model. De facto they do not. As a result, narratives ensconced in the rational choice mold make them highly predictable.

To recapitulate: When we try to uncover the analytical underpinnings of the claim that rational choice takes over in times of crisis, the inquiry proves inconclusive and the claim elusive, irrespective of the theoretical standpoint we adopt. It is not so clear why rational action should become the dominant mode when the correspondence between dispositions and objective relations gets disrupted. There is no sound theoretical reason for arguing that in such conjunctures actors are more likely to behave as rational choice would lead us to expect. The difficulty is compounded when we pause on a case that has acquired paradigmatic status, given the amount of attention Bourdieu devoted to it: the crisis of May 1968 in France. For in this case, the concept that comes forward is deprivation and its correlates, not a greater sense of rationality.

Maladjusted Expectations

Two concepts stand out in Bourdieu's (1988) analysis of the crisis of May 1968: "dispossession" and "maladjusted expectations." "Dispossession" refers to a situation in which people do not get what they believe they are entitled to. The frustration thus generated is the proximate cause of the crisis. "Maladjusted expectations" describe the generating mechanism. People cannot fulfill their aspirations. In May 1968 students could not expect positions that would fulfill their social expectations (Bourdieu 1988: 168). Hence they felt deprived and they revolted.

Why were their expectations maladjusted? According to Bourdieu (1988), the discrepancy between aspirations and abilities had its origin in the "increase in the number of students" (163; see also 166; Bourdieu 1998d: 21). This increase in number contributed to the devaluation of educational credentials, and, by way of consequence, it caused a generalized "downclassing." Bourdieu (1988: 163) analyzes the hiatus between "the statutory expectations . . . and the opportunities actually provided" as a structural phenomenon. The more widely shared this experience, the greater its social significance and the greater its objective character—objective in the sense that it can be assessed by independent external observers.

Whether we consider the basic mechanism at play (the expectation-capabilities gap), its diffuse character resulting from macrosocietal factor (devaluation), and the type of explanation being set forth (psychological versus political), the parallel is striking between this explanatory account of May 1968 and the relative deprivation explanation of collective unrest (e.g., Davies 1962; Feierabend and Feierabend 1966, 1972; Gurr 1970). In both cases, the starting point of the analysis is the presumption of a discrepancy experienced by individual psyches, and in both cases the discrepancy results from a societal process, the significance of which can be assessed from an external (objective) standpoint independent of the groups of actors thus affected. Relative deprivation arguments track unrest back to economic slowdown or downturns. Bourdieu's explanation tracks collective dissatisfaction back to academic devaluation.

As Tilly noted in 1975, this representation of collective upheavals "has been around a long time. Individuals anger when they sense a large gap between what they get and what they deserve" (1975: 495). The apparent power of this explanation is that, from a retrospective viewpoint, it is "true by definition" (Tilly 1975: 486, 493), that is, by definition, people who revolt are angry. It seems therefore obvious and commonsensical to argue that deprivation is the main causal factor of rebellion and unrest. If people rebel because they are frustrated, in times of wealth they can be frustrated only because things do not go well enough: opportunities do not match up with their aspirations.

Whether we give credence to this explanatory account or not, it is at odds with a rational choice argument. From a rational choice standpoint, we expect actors appraising costs and benefits, assessing consequences, and devising plans and strategies. These actors would not necessarily act alone contra Tullock's (1971) mistaken assumption. In times of disruption and uncertainty, we may safely assume that they will strive to act as members of a group or within a collective setting (Ermakoff 2008: 181–82). Yet they act by paying close attention to the possible consequences of their action for their own status and welfare as well as for those whom they define as peers.

The dispossession/maladjusted expectations argument does not portray actors reflecting about options for the purpose of protecting themselves against the worst, preserving their interests, or taking up opportunities. Rather, it portrays actors venting their frustration and being swept away by the perception that "everything is possible" (Bourdieu 1988: 162). The claim stated in the epigraph does not apply. Rational choice does not analytically take over. It has stepped back away from the scene. Bourdieu describing the crisis of May 1968 contradicts Bourdieu stating the broad relevance of rational choice when the focus is on crisis situations.

Faced with these contradictory assessments, one is tempted at first to conclude that they are mutually exclusive and cannot both be relevant. A closer focus shows that this conclusion is mistaken. Some actors are quite strategic as they opt for a course of option. They ponder the pros and cons, assess likelihoods as much as they can, and decide for the line of conduct that seems to them the best one given the circumstances. Others let themselves be carried out by the spirit of the time. Their action is mainly expressive and devoid of a master plan. The conjuncture displays both modes of action. This variance does not simply concern types of individuals. It is also diachronic within the same individual psyches.

Moments and Modes

These few remarks underscore a broader point. Times of crisis elicit a multiplicity of modal responses (Ermakoff 2010: 542–44). Some actors become self-centered and instrumental. Others adopt a line of conduct that is mainly expressive. Still others elaborate an ideological definition of the situation (Gilcher-Holtey 1995: 47–50). Bourdieu refers to the strategic mode when he sets forth his claim about rational choice taking over. He points to the expressive mode when he provides an analytical account of the May 1968 demonstrators' subjective dispositions. Both modal responses take place within the same conjuncture, and each is amenable to a different theoretical framework. Instrumental action a priori fits rational choice axiomatic claims. Action geared to a set of symbolic categories that are normatively laden belong to the domain proper of the theory of practice. The meaning and resonance of these symbolic categories rest on the living legacy of past practices.

To illustrate the plurality of responses elicited by times of disjuncture, suffice to note the contrast between Bourdieu's general remark about rational choice coming to the fore in such conjunctures and his remarks about actors stubbornly, "contrary to all reason," sticking to a set of dispositions leading them to "social death" (Bourdieu 2000b: 161). For instance, the "inheritors of great families in Béarn condemning themselves to celibacy" (Bourdieu 2000b: 161), the "elects of the French elite schools endorsing a model of career" that "condemned them to give way to newcomers" (Bourdieu 2000b: 161), and the "pathological traditionalism" of the Algerian fellah organizing agrarian production for the satisfaction of immediate needs in a context marked by dramatic impoverishment and the breakdown of the collective structures conducive to provident behaviors (Bourdieu and Sayad 1964: 18–19).

Here the actors are far removed from a strategic response to the crisis. The prevailing mode is adherence to a behavioral script at odds with the strategic imperatives of adaptation or innovation imposed by shifting constraints. Only in an awkward sense can this script be assumed to exemplify value rationality. The extent to which actors invest tradition with value varies. The scions of the French elite schools are very likely to proclaim aloud their sense of value. This type of consideration is obviously foreign to Algerian peasants struggling with the necessities of daily survival in the coercive environment of a colonized society. In addition, these cases involve actors with vastly different resources. We would expect students of the French elite schools to display the greatest capacity for adaptive rationality à la rational choice. Bourdieu suggests that even they may be trapped in self-defeating reproductive strategies.

UNCONDITIONAL CLAIMS, LOST CAUSE

Two implications follow. First, apportioning classes of historical conjunctures among theoretical frameworks does not do if there is no one-to-one correspondence between these classes of situations and the types of action to which the frameworks supposedly apply. Second—and related—theories of action cast in broad, unconditional terms are bound to miss the mark. By design, these theories cannot cull the multiplicity of modal responses elicited by a situation of disruption (Ermakoff 2010: 530, 549). Furthermore, because these theories are cast in such general and unconditional terms, it is always possible to find instances that invalidate their unconditional scope. Indirectly, this observation points to the key issue. No modal response has exclusive privilege. The challenge is to identify and theorize the factors conditioning their possibility.

This last point is consistent with Bourdieu's (1977: 63, 1998d: 93) critique of the universalist pretensions of rational choice. Individuals situated in time and space rely on categories and taken-for-granted assumptions that inform their practices and understandings. From this perspective, reason can indeed be said to be "historical through and through" (Bourdieu 1998d: 138). The "rational habitus which is the precondition for appropriate economic behavior is the product of particular economic condition" (Bourdieu 1990a [1980]: 64). Yet rational choice analysts proceed as if this historical and institutional variation was of no consequence to actors' preferences. Postulating a model of action that is atemporal and universal, they abstract actors away from the situational context of their practice.[18] "Actors are always assumed to be equally rational" (Kiser and Schneider 1995: 789).

In short, rational choice errs in substantializing a model of action that is valid only in specific circumstances (Bourdieu 1998d: 93). It is typical of the scholastic illusion whereby the analyst imputes to actors his own intellectualist disposition (Bourdieu 2000a: 19). That is why this model rests on "anthropological fictions" (Bourdieu 1990a [1980]: 47). "The pure model of rational action cannot be regarded as an anthropological description of practice. . . . real agents only very exceptionally possess the complete information and the skill to appreciate it, that rational action would presuppose" (Bourdieu 1990a [1980]: 63). By way of consequence, analyses of historical change should start by acknowledging the variation inscribed in the genealogy of practices and the conditions that shape this formative process. The anthropology posited by rational choice needs to be made situation- and institution-specific (Katznelson and Weingast 2005: 7–12).

COMPLEMENTARY

We cannot explore this variation without examining how collective and individual actors construe their interests and act accordingly. For this purpose, both frameworks are necessary. This point holds for conjunctures of disruption as well as for times of routine expectations—times in which expectations are bounded by a sense of rules and which as a result could be called institutional, insofar as such rules define our understanding of institutions. Whichever class of conjuncture we are considering, the analytical grids provided by rational choice and the theory of practice complement one another in highlighting different facets of preferences and actions. In so doing, they help hone specific empirical claims.[19]

I first consider institutional times. These are times pervaded by a sense of the familiar. Actors know what to expect. They elaborate their strategies of action in light of what they assume to be regulated patterns of behaviors. These reveal shared normative definitions and more or less implicit rules of behavior. Documenting these shared understandings is the domain proper of the theory of practice. Bourdieu's analytical framework highlights repertoires of action which actors regularly enact as they seek to preserve, consolidate, or expand their interests. This framework also highlights the "feel for the game" and the institutional factors shaping this practical sense. The focus here is on actors' understanding of the rules at play and the consequences of breaching them.

Given the values at stake and actors' understanding of what they deem acceptable and worthwhile, rational choice provides tools for analyzing the type of inferences which actors draw and the strategies which they deploy given the configuration of resources they have, the constraints they face, their beliefs about other agents' assets, including those of their competitors, and the likely strategies of these agents. This set of tools has relevance when the stakes are high and relations geared to these stakes are competitive. In these settings, individuals are most likely to think about consequences, their potential costs and best strategies.

What about processes of historical change in times of disruption? Is there room for collaboration between the two frameworks? We are then considering conjunctures in which the sense of the familiar has collapsed. The prospect of mutual regulation is dubious. Bearings have been blurred. Times of disruption call into question the prospect of patterned relationships not only with competitors and opponents but also with peers and allies, all the more so in that the disruption is dramatic and actors experience it as a challenge to their vested interests. The point is critical. Such conjunctures make the need for coordination with peers more pressing and obvious (Ermakoff 2008; Laitin 1998: 24). Ultimately, the goal is to ensure coordination of action. Group members need to achieve a shared understanding of where they stand.

In this type of collective conjunctures, the theory of practice helps understand how individuals draw on their stock of culturally shaped expectations and on their experience of past practices to draw inferences about their peers' and their competitors' beliefs (Schelling 1960: 90–118; O'Neill 2001: 45–62). In particular, this approach to past practices highlights the relative salience of symbols and past events in the collective memory of the group under consideration. Rational choice, for its part, investigates how actors make their strategic bids in light of this knowledge. More broadly, it highlights dynamics of strategic inferences.

The pas de deux I have just sketched is based not on a distinction of classes of situations but on the distinction between different moments in collective and individual decision-making processes (Ermakoff 2008: chapter 6). The theory of practice and rational choice complement one another insofar as they offer tools and hypotheses for analyzing the beliefs and behavioral choices of actors departing from past patterns and in so doing enacting historical change.[20] This observation is not confined to times of crisis. It applies as well to all the micro adjustments which over time produce gradual changes and contribute to large-scale shifts (Ermakoff 2010: 530–38). What is specific about situations of rupture is that they expand the scope of uncertainty. As a result, these situations contribute to making the reconfiguration of patterns and processes more highly visible and more synchronic in time.

Conclusion

In line with Bourdieu's suggestion and in contradistinction to canonical representations of academic turfs of war, my discussion has emphasized the need for and the possibility of analytical collaboration between two frameworks which critics and proponents alike invite us to view as antithetical. There are multiple venues for setting up the antithesis. One can focus on key concepts, on underlying anthropological conceptions, on predictions, on core hypotheses, or on research agendas. All this is fine for scholastic purposes (as Bourdieu would say). If, however, the point is to theorize processes of change through the lens of their etiology and as they take place in time and space, the confrontation breaks down. Rational choice and the theory of practice shed light on how individuals and groups position themselves, engage in conflict relations, deal with uncertainties, and devise lines of conduct. In so doing, both frameworks complement one another.

Bourdieu therefore is right. An analytical modus vivendi indeed is possible. Yet, this conclusion has paradoxical implications for his own proposal—that is, rational choice takes over in times of crisis while the theory of practice reserves for itself "institutional times" as I have defined the term, that is, as conjunctures in which a shared sense of rule regulates patterns of relations and expectations. If both frameworks are valid, they cannot be valid at once. Their ontology sets them far apart. Furthermore, they cannot be valid at the level of generality posited by Bourdieu in the epigraph. Their validity is necessarily conditional. Their truth resides in their qualifying clauses.

Indirectly, I have underscored this point when I considered the possibility for rational choice analysts to justify Bourdieu's claim from the standpoint of their own theoretical framework. This exercise—a scholastic one for sure—led to a reversal of claims. A priori, it is perfectly plausible to argue that the tools and assumptions of rational choice apply in the first place to institutional times. The problem here is the lack of specification. In the end, we do not know what makes one framework more likely to be relevant and valid than the other. Both are true when pitched at this level of generality because both can be equally deemed to be true. The flipside of this point is that it is always possible to turn up instances that flatly refute each. The cast shed on May 1968 by a relative deprivation argument is an instance of that kind. It illustrates the paucity of broad pronouncements that forget to specify their conditions of possibility.

The additional implication is that our focus should be on qualifying clauses. There is one clause of this kind in the epigraph: "'rational choice' *may* take over, *at least* among those agents who are in a position to be rational" (Bourdieu and Wacquant 1992: 131, emphasis added). Not everybody is in a position to be rational in the sense postulated by rational choice (as the theory of practice depicts it). Actors are more or less equipped to be deliberately instrumental and self-reflexive. The capacity is a potentiality inscribed in their habitus. Yet even for those "in a position to be rational," the claim remains hypothetical (rational choice "*may* take over"). We are left with a question mark. When, that is, under which conditions, does rational choice take over? The shift to rational choice is conditional on preexisting dispositions. It is also conditional on something else that remains to be specified.

Notes

1. The proponents of a "utilitarianist vision" make two anthropological assumptions. First, they "pretend [that] agents are moved by conscious reasons, as if they consciously posed the objectives of their action and acted in such a way as to obtain the maximum efficacy with the least cost." Second, "they reduce everything that can motivate agents to economic interest, to monetary profit" (Bourdieu 1998d: 79). The rational choice framework "reduces the universe of exchanges to mercantile exchange" (Bourdieu 1986b: 242).

2. Bourdieu emphasizes the same point in his exchange with Wacquant: rational choice conceives action as determined by the conscious aiming at goals explicitly defined (Bourdieu and Wacquant 1992: 125).

3. "The rational calculator that the advocates of rational action theory portray as the principle of human practices is no less absurd . . . than the angelus rector, the far-seeing pilot to which some pre-Newtonian thinkers attributed the regulated movement of the planets" (Bourdieu 1998d: 133).

4. Wacquant and Calhoun (1989) propose a similar characterization, with Coleman as exemplar: "It is striking to observe how much Coleman endorses as obvious the subjectivist philosophy of rational action, understood as a *self-reflexive* sequence [*enchaînement réfléchi*] of *conscious* decisions by an actor free of all economic conditioning" (47; my translation, emphasis added).

5. "If choices are made to depend, on the one hand, on the structural constraints (technical, economic, or legal) that delimit the range of possible actions and, on the other hand, on preferences presumed to be universal and conscious, then the agents . . . constrained by the logical necessity of 'rational calculus', are left no other freedom than adherence . . . to the objective chances" (Bourdieu 1990a [1980]: 46).

6. "In contrast to what happens in situations of concordance when the self-evidence linked to adjustment renders invisible the habitus which makes it possible, [in moments of crisis] the relatively autonomous principle of legality and regularity that habitus constitutes *appears very clearly*" (Bourdieu 2000b: 160; emphasis added).

7. On a more micro scale, these faltering moments take the form of flickering bouts of reflection quickly engulfed by the force of habit: "Habitus has its 'blips', critical moments when it misfires or is out of phase: the relationship of immediate adaptation is suspended, in an instant of hesitation into which there may slip a form of reflection which has nothing in common with that of the scholastic thinker and which, through the sketched movements of the body . . . remains turned towards practice and not towards the agent who performs it" (Bourdieu 2000b: 162).

8. By contrast, individuals who remain stuck in the confines of their condition are not in a position to realize the structural logic that keeps them stuck. "Absolute alienation deprives the individual of the consciousness of alienation" (Bourdieu 2008a: 210). The Algerian urban underclass in the early 1960s is a case in point: "They are poverty and destitution, suffering and misery. They are not removed enough from their condition to constitute it as an object" (Bourdieu 2008a: 209).

9. See, for instance, Levi: "rational choice—that is, the theory of individual strategic

decision making" (1988: 7–8). Contrast with O'Neill's definition: "Rational choice theory refers to the general approach that parties pursue their material self-interest, pay attention to objective likelihoods and maximize their expectations in a conscious, calculated way" (2001: 259). In light of this definition, O'Neill observes that one can work within a strategic paradigm—"players judge likelihoods and pursue goals" (259)—without endorsing the core assumptions of rational choice such as the assumptions of objective probabilities and maximization. This point is important and helps avoid confusions and misunderstandings.

10. Collins, who extends rational choice to the determinants of emotional action—"individuals apportion their time to . . . various activities to maximize their overall flow of emotional energy" (1993: 205)—explicitly states the subsidiary character of consciousness for the viability of rational choice: "If an unconscious mechanism exists that leads toward medium-run optimizing outcomes, then individuals who rise to the level of conscious calculation would tend to come to the same conclusions as the nonconscious behavior" (205).

11. "We should evaluate the broad rationality of beliefs and desires by looking at the way in which they are shaped" (Elster 1983b: 15).

12. A point of precision: to say that actors know about alternative options is not to say that they have complete information about these alternatives.

13. Tsebelis (1990: 26) observes that "the overwhelming majority of rational-choice studies assumes that rational actors maximize their expected utility."

14. "The choice-theoretic approach to economics assumes that in making choices values exist but are fixed, and people are acting rationally in the sense of making efficient use of information" (North 1981: 49).

15. This observation underlines North's critique of Stigler and Becker (1977). They ignore "the ethical and moral judgments that are an integral part of an individual's ideological makeup" (North 1981: 49).

16. Personal commitments, for instance, can be analyzed as "acquired by rational choice, by comparing the advantages and the disadvantages associated with any commitment (including advantages and disadvantages of a purely subjective psychological nature)" (Harsanyi 1969: 523). This assumption is one of the four "motivational postulates" which, according to Harsanyi, are required by rational choice models of noneconomic social behavior.

17. In making this claim, Elster retrieves Schumpeter's (1942: 253) basic argument about the conditions fostering individual rationality.

18. The "illusion of ahistorical universalism" that is characteristic of the concepts and categories of economics is based on the forgetting of their genesis" (Bourdieu 2000a: 16).

19. The exchange between Gorski (1995) and Kiser and Schneider (1995) is instructive in this regard. Beyond the paradigmatic oppositions that frame the exchange (Gorski 1995: 783; Kiser and Schneider 1995: 789–90), the debate ultimately boils down to a critical assessment of the evidence available and its significance. Analytically, this discussion points to a qualified argument about the role of religious affiliations in strategies of institution building.

20. Along consonant lines, Sewell's call for a more direct engagement with the "dialectical complexity" of social action enacting historical change does not foreclose a priori the analytical relevance of rational choice. This engagement will have to "borrow heavily from anthropology and history" (1987: 170). Still, "Coleman's problematic . . . can help to illuminate real instances of social change" (169).

TOWARD SOCIOANALYSIS
The "Traumatic Kernel" of Psychoanalysis and
Neo-Bourdieusian Theory

Far from being hostile to psychoanalysis, [Pierre Bourdieu] reckoned
that there was no fundamental difference between his conception of the
unconscious and Freud's: "It's the same thing: confronted with the
unconscious action of dispositions we notice resistances, displace-
ments, repression, negations."
—VINCENT DE GAULEJAC, *"DE L'INCONSCIENT CHEZ FREUD À
L'INCONSCIENT SELON BOURDIEU"*

In this chapter I explore the possibility of reconstructing Bourdieusian theory
by bringing it into closer dialogue with psychoanalysis.[1] Bourdieu gestured
repeatedly toward such a merger through his reliance on psychoanalytic terminology, ideas, and arguments, through his embrace of the idea of socioanalysis (*la socioanalyse*), and in discussions specifically on the topic (Bourdieu
1994a: xxvii).[2] Bourdieu's writing includes such concepts as the unconscious,
misrecognition, projection, reality principle, libido, ego splitting, negation
(*dénégation*), repression (*refoulement*), phallonarcissism, compromise formation, and anamnesis.[3] I suggest that Bourdieu's recurrent use of psychoanalytic concepts is more than just an "analogical usage of psychoanalytic notions
within sociological research" (Fabiani 1984: 92). Bourdieu's core concepts can
best be modeled as deep causal mechanisms (Bhaskar) by rethinking them
along psychoanalytic lines. In doing so we are simultaneously moving from
sociology to socioanalysis, moving toward a merging of disciplines.

One barrier to this project concerned Bourdieu's ambivalent relationship
to psychoanalysis and his hostile comments about Jacques Lacan, the thinker
whose ideas can, I submit, contribute the most to a rethinking of the core
Bourdieusian concepts. Bourdieu's apparent rapprochement with Sigmund

Freud and certain ego-analytic traditions contrasts sharply with his studious avoidance of any open engagement with Lacan. Bourdieu's rare mentions of Lacan are derisive and distorted. In *The Rules of Art*, for example, he dismisses Lacan as a sort of intellectual punster engaging in "the intellectual play on words" (Bourdieu 1996a: 247). And while Bourdieu insists on Lacan's noble status and his "great importance in the [academic] field," he did not include him in his dataset for the correspondence analysis in *Homo Academicus*, because Lacan "did not hold an official position in the university." Whether the academic field, Bourdieu's ostensible object of analysis, is coterminous with the university field is a question Bourdieu does not address here. Bourdieu's exclusion of Lacan from the academic field is not only arbitrary but also a symbolic repetition of the "refusal to permit him to lecture at the Ecole Normale Supérieure" (Bourdieu 1988a: xxi).

Lacan also appears as the source of a joke originating with Lacan and repeated by Bourdieu on several occasions from 1975 through the 1990s, namely, the "distressed complaint of the Jew to his pal": "Why do you tell me you are going to Cracow so I'll believe you are going to Lvov, when you really are going to Cracow?" According to Bourdieu, this linguistic subterfuge was used by Martin Heidegger "to encourage the belief, by proclaiming what he is really doing, that he is not really doing what he has always done" (Lacan 2002: 164).[4] What Bourdieu does not seem to realize is that he himself may be discussing Lacan repeatedly, obsessively, in order to encourage the belief that he is not really talking about Lacan, not really presenting a theory that makes better sense when it is reconstructed on a psychoanalytic basis. For I contend that Lacan is the key to reconstructing two of Bourdieu's most important concepts, concepts that will remain mysterious and unfinished until their psychic foundations are filled in: symbolic capital and habitus.[5]

Many of Bourdieu's formulations during the 1980s and 1990s could be drawn directly from Freud or Lacan, although they are often hedged about with a *cordon sanitaire* of Bourdieu's own coinages. Bourdieu writes in *Language and Symbolic Power*, for example, that "in all cases of camouflage through form . . . the tabooed meanings . . . remain misrecognized in practice; though present as substance they are absent as form, like a face hidden in the bush. The role of this kind of expression is to mask the primitive experiences of the social world and the social phantasms which are its source, as much as to reveal them" (Bourdieu 1991e: 142–43). *Phantasie* (or fantasy) is a core concept of Freud and is even more central for Lacan, as is the concept of camouflage (Heath 1986; Riviere 1986).[6] Several years later, in *The Rules of Art*, Bourdieu writes, "What indeed is this discourse which speaks of the social or psychological world *as if it did not speak of it*; which *cannot speak* of this world except on condition that it only speak of as if it did not speak of it, that is, in a *form* which performs, for the author and the reader, a *denegation* (in the Freudian sense of *Verneinung*) of what it expresses?" (Bourdieu 1996a: 3). Bourdieu also introduces at this moment the idea of the "social libido which varies with the social universes where it is engendered and which it sustains (*libido dominandi* in the field of power, *libido sciendi* in the scientific field, etc.)" (Bourdieu 1996a: 172). This opening to psychoanalysis becomes even more explicit in *The Weight of the World*, which declares sociology and psychoanalysis to be identical enterprises: "This is not the place to question the relation between the mode of exploring subjectivity proposed here and that practiced by psychoanalysis. But, at the very least, it is necessary to guard against thinking of these relationships as alternatives to each other. *Sociology does not claim to substitute its mode of explanation for that of psychoanalysis*; it is concerned only to construct differently certain givens that psychoanalysis also takes as its object" (Bourdieu 1999: 512, emphasis added). This book also contains the following passage, which is incomprehensible without its psychoanalytic foundations: "Such limitation of aspirations shows up in cases where the father has been very successful. . . . But it assumes all its force when the father occupies a dominated position . . . and is therefore inclined to be ambivalent about his son's success as well as about himself. . . . At one and the same time he says: be like me, act like me, but be different, go away. . . . He cannot want his son to identify with his own position and its dispositions, and yet all his behavior works continuously to produce that identification" (Bourdieu and Accardo 1999: 510). In psychoanalysis, the young boy's first symbolic identification is with the imago of the father, but the Oedipal structure makes this identification fundamentally impossible or at least contradictory: "There issues forth an impossible double command: to be like the father, but not to be like the father with respect to his sexual power" (Bryson 1994: 233). According to Freud, the relationship of superego to ego is not exhausted by the precept, " 'You *ought to be* like this (like your father),' " but "also comprises the prohibition: 'You *may not be* like this (like your father)' " (Freud 1962: 34). Freud's analysis does in fact suggest the centrality of social class in generating psychic variations, for example, in his discussion of the "family romance" in which an older child's "imagination becomes engaged in the task of getting free from the parents of whom he now has a low opinion and of replacing them by others, who, as a rule, are of higher social standing" (Freud 1953: ix, 238–39). But Freud was less explicit than Bourdieu about the different conditions in which parents occupied "a dominated position" or were "very successful," and this is one of the reasons sociology needs to be integrated into psychoanalysis and vice versa.

Bourdieu's wide-ranging writings could be mined for any number of theoretical influences. Bourdieu relies heavily on the language of Marxism, for example, and he once described his field theory as a "generalized Marxism" (Bourdieu 1993c: 273, n. 7). But here, too, in the relation to Marxism, Bourdieu's work is marked by deep ambiguities as to whether he is fully embracing the Marxist definition of words like *capital* or the Marxist account of the labor theory of value (Calhoun 1993a; Desan 2010; Steinmetz 2009a). Cultural capital is not extracted via an exploitative process like the labor process in Marx. Cultural domination in Bourdieu is often a zero-sum game governed by monopolization of cultural capital, while capital accumulation is, for Marx, inherently expansive. Nonetheless, Bourdieu's core theoretical project of analyzing semiautonomous fields of practice and their irreducible stakes of competition and axes of recognition can stand alone, without these Marxian concepts, indeed as a generalized sociology of cultural, political, and scientific practice—one that finally takes seriously the neo-Marxist slogan of the relative autonomy of the so-called superstructures. But Bourdieu's theory cannot do without psychoanalysis, whose concepts go to the very heart of the sociologist's main concerns. Psychoanalytic theory is not so much an influence on Bourdieu as an essential component of his theory or, rather, of a reconstructed version of his theory.[7]

The entire sweep of Bourdieu's theory of subject formation is framed in terms of the internalization, incorporation, and embodiment of societal conditions and the reconstitution of those external conditions through the "regulated improvisations" of individual and collective practice.[8] This model closely tracks the psychoanalytic interest in the individual's interiorization of social history (Freud) and incorporation into the symbolic order (Lacan). One of Bourdieu's more remarkable openings to the logic of psychoanalysis occurs in the section of *Pascalian Meditations* (2000b) in which he addresses the genesis of subjects who are suited to operate competitively in social fields. In a passage that tracks the shift in an individual's transition from self-love toward a "quite other object of investment" that "inculcate[s] the durable disposition to invest in the social game," Bourdieu works through a development described by Freud as the Oedipal story and by Lacan as the entry into the symbolic order:

Sociology and psychology [*sic*] should combine their efforts (but this would require them to overcome their mutual suspicion) to analyse the genesis of investment in a field of social relations, thus constituted as an object of investment and preoccupation, in which the child is increasingly implicated and which constitutes the paradigm and also the principle of investment in the social game. How does the transition, described by Freud, occur, leading

from a narcissistic organization of the libido, in which the child takes himself (or his own body) as an object of desire, to another state in which he
orients himself towards another person, thus entering the world of "object
relations," in the forms of the original social microcosm and protagonists of
the drama that is played out there? (Bourdieu 2000b: 166)

As we will see below, Bourdieu locates the motor of this shift in the "search for
recognition," a phrase that brings his interpretation even closer to the Lacan-
ian/Žižekian reading of Freud through G. W. F. Hegel's *Phenomenology*.

Bourdieu's most explicit discussion of psychoanalysis occurs in *Masculine
Domination* (Bourdieu 2001b). This is hardly surprising since the subject
matter here is psychoanalytic home turf. Bourdieu acknowledges as much
toward the end of the book, where he writes that "researchers, *almost always
schooled in psychoanalysis*, discover, in the psychic experience of the men and
women of today, processes, for the most part deeply buried, which, like the
work needed to separate the boy from his mother or the symbolic effects of
the sexual division of tasks and times in production and reproduction, are
seen in the full light of day in ritual practices" (Bourdieu 2001b: 81–82). But
Bourdieu begins this book with one of his characteristic defensive moves,
categorizing psychoanalysis *tout court* as essentialist and dehistoricized—the
same misleading criticisms that have often been launched at Bourdieu's own
approach (Bourdieu 1977: 92–93, 2001b: viii).[9] With respect to the centrality of
"sexual attributes and acts" in Kabyle society, Bourdieu notes that there is "a
danger of misinterpreting their deep significance if one approaches them in
terms of the category of the sexual itself," a remark that appears to be targeting
a naturalistic version of psychoanalysis (Bourdieu 2001b: 7). In fact, Lacan
argues along lines that are quite compatible with Bourdieu's antinaturalism
that the "very delimitation of the 'erogenous zone' that the drive isolates from
the function's metabolism" is "the result of a cut"—a symbolic cut, that is—
"that takes advantage of the anatomical characteristic of a margin or border."
The symbolic order, the order of language, is a system of differences; similarly,
"the characteristic of being partial . . . is applicable not because these objects
are part of a total object, which the body is assumed to be, but because they
only partially represent the function that produces them" (Lacan 2002: 303).
The terminology differs, but both writers reverse the doxic direction of causality between the biosexual and social orders.

Psychoanalytic theory has long been concerned with the problem Bourdieu sets out to explain here: the ways in which masculine domination is
historically reproduced as an apparently dehistoricized form of practice. The
meaning of the psychoanalytic expression "the unconscious does not have a

history," like Louis Althusser's formula "ideology has no history" (1971: 159), does not mean that the unconscious (or ideology) takes the same form everywhere or that it is eternal because it is determined by some permanent natural foundation. Instead, this formula underscores the ways in which the past is constantly being "actualized" within the unconscious through the mechanism Freud calls "the return of the repressed." Likewise, for Bourdieu, the (masculine) habitus is, on the one hand, historical—a "product of all biographical experience"—while at the same time it presents itself in an *eternalized* form (Bourdieu 2001b, viii; Gaulejac 2004: 75). But once again, in his discussion of habitus, Bourdieu rejects the language of fantasy and the imaginary, warding off any serious mixing and mingling with psychoanalysis and insisting that "we are very far from the language of the 'imaginary' which is sometimes used nowadays" (Bourdieu 2000b: 171). In one particularly dogged example of never pronouncing those two accursed names, Bourdieu refers in his footnote to Cornelius Castoriadis rather than to the more obvious intertexts, Lacan's writings on the imaginary, in which the term was first introduced and developed as a scientific concept, and Althusser's use of the idea of the imaginary in his theory of ideology.[10]

Bourdieu also reveals his deep connections to psychoanalysis when he mentions in this text that he is relying on the Mediterranean cultural matrix for his model of masculine domination. Whereas Freud drew on ancient Greek myth, Bourdieu deploys Kabyle society as a "paradigmatic realization" of what he calls the "phallocentric" tradition. From there, Bourdieu's account takes on an increasingly psychoanalytic tone, interpreting masculine domination as being rooted in unconscious structures centered on "phallonarcissism." Bourdieu notes that "the link (*asserted by psychoanalysis*) between phallus and *logos* is established" in Kabyle society (Bourdieu 2001b: 17, emphasis added). But Bourdieu does not make the obvious additional reference here to Lacan, who first developed the theory of the phallus-*logos* connection (Lacan 2002: 280). In Bourdieu's discussion of the "somatization of the social relations of domination" in the creation of sexed bodies, the difference between Bourdieu and Freud almost disappears:

> The work of symbolic construction is far more than a strictly *performative* operation of naming . . . it is brought about and culminates in a profound and durable transformation of bodies (and minds), that is to say, in and through a process of practical construction imposing a *differentiated definition* of the legitimate uses of the body, in particular sexual ones, which tends to exclude from the universe of the feasible and thinkable everything that marks membership of the other gender—and in particular all the

potentialities biologically implied in the "polymorphous perversity," as Freud puts it, of every infant. (Bourdieu 2001b: 23)

Here Bourdieu takes for granted the ego-psychoanalytic notion of the denial of "the female part of the male" and "severing attachments to the mother" (Bourdieu 2001b: 26). Moreover, Bourdieu explicitly argues that male domination, rather than class domination, "constitutes the paradigm (and often the model and stake) of all domination" (Bourdieu 1990b: 30–31; Moi 1999: 289).

The word *socioanalysis* (*socioanalyse*), which points toward psychoanalysis (*psychoanalyse*) as its template, also appears in *Masculine Domination* (Bourdieu 2001b: 3). Bourdieu had already used this word in the 1960s but in a context of the sociology of knowledge rather than psychoanalysis (Bourdieu, Passeron, and Chamboredon 1968: 102). The word *socioanalyse* was used in 1983 by Bourdieu's psychoanalytically oriented colleague Francine Muel-Dreyfus, who presented sociology as a "psychoanalysis of the social world" (Fabiani 1984a: 92; Muel-Dreyfus 1983). By the beginning of the 1990s Bourdieu was equating the word *socioanalysis* with efforts to reconcile psychoanalysis and sociology and praising "the great vigilance of certain recent attempts to advance in this direction," especially in the work of Jacques Maître (Bourdieu and Accardo 1999: 512, n. 7).[11]

The word *socioanalysis* moves us away from disciplinary and scientific names based on *Logos* (sociology, and so forth), which suggest a unitary "word of God" (Johnson 1981: ix) approach to knowledge, and toward the word *analysis*, which suggests breaking up a complex topic, substance, or event into smaller parts. In this respect the idea of analysis is more compatible with the conjunctural, contingent, overdetermined approach to explanation recommended by Althusser and Roy Bhaskar and adopted explicitly by Bourdieu in *Homo Academicus* (Althusser 1979: 87–128; Bourdieu 1988: 173; Steinmetz 2011).

Despite Bourdieu's rapprochement with psychoanalysis at the level of his language and occasionally at a more systematic theoretical level (a rapprochement he shares with his erstwhile critic Judith Butler [1997]) he never fully acknowledged its implications for his theoretical approach. Bourdieu protested somewhat feebly that he "would have needed a second life" ("il lui aurait fallu une deuxième vie") to master psychoanalysis and that he told himself he wasn't "up to the task" ("tu n'es pas à la hauteur").[12] But this is unconvincing, since Bourdieu mastered one new field after the other throughout his life, working in areas typically associated with philosophy, anthropology, history, art history, and political science, as well as sociology.

Among the problems that psychoanalysis addresses in more satisfactory ways than orthodox Bourdieusian theory are the following: the misrecognition of the social-real; the internalization of contradictory interpellations and their fragmentation (or potential integration into a unified habitus); the transformation of originally symbiotic subjects into agents equipped with the desire to compete in social fields, agents who can sublimate, in Freud's terms, or submit to the demands of the big Other in the field of the Symbolic, in Lacan's. Psychoanalysis offers a richer array of concepts for analyzing the idiosyncratic sense that individuals make of shared social conditions and the paradox of an unconscious agency.[13] The relative autonomy of fields ultimately depends on the interest and ability of participants to orient themselves toward a field's autonomous logics and to resist being subjected to external forces and powers like the economy or the state. In this respect, sociological autonomy needs to be connected to psychic ego autonomy (Steinmetz 2009b).

Above all, Lacanian theory helps specify the core Bourdieusian concepts of symbolic capital and habitus. After discussing these two concepts I will turn briefly to Bourdieu's self-analysis, a text in which his proximity to psychoanalysis appears in sharp relief. This text also gestures toward the possibility of a transdisciplinary form of socioanalysis through an equal-sided synthesis of psychoanalysis and Bourdieusian sociology that would render both theories more adequate.

Symbolic Capital, Field Theory, and the Lacanian Symbolic

Lacanian theory allows us to reground Bourdieu's concept of symbolic capital in the symbolic order and in the related dynamics of recognition and misrecognition that are so central to symbolic identification. The symbolic, for Lacan, is the realm of language, difference, metonymy, and the law—the realm of socially sanctioned, official ego ideals. The relationship of the subject to the symbolic is thus a relation of "dependence on the Other, locus of signifiers" (Julien 1994: 167). Symbolic identifications are linked to the ego-ideal (*Ich-ideal*), which "constitutes a model to which the subject attempts to conform" (Laplanche and Pontalis 1974: 144). In Lacan's later writings, symbolic identification is understood more specifically as identification with the place from which we are observed, the location from which we "look at ourselves so that we appear to ourselves likeable, worthy of love" (Žižek 1989: 105). The "demand of the *Ichideal*," according to Lacan, thus "takes up its place within the totality of the demands of the law" (Lacan 1988: 134).

The ego-ideal for Lacan is the "position of the subject within the symbolic, the norm that installs the subject within language" (Butler 1997). Subjects seek to recognize the normative injunctions of the symbolic order, and they seek to be recognized by those who issue these injunctions. This is recognition in

Hegel's sense, as *Anerkennen* or *Wiedererkennen*, rather than simply *Erkennen* (or knowledge). In his Jena *Realphilosophie*, analyzed trenchantly by Axel Honneth (1995), Hegel observes that "in recognition, the self ceases to be this individual" and that "Man is necessarily recognized and necessarily gives recognition . . . he *is* recognition" (Hegel and Rauch 1983: 111).

In *Pascalian Meditations* Bourdieu began to think systematically about the psycho-sociogenesis of the individual's capacity and desire to reorient itself from narcissistic to other-oriented practice as a precondition for the operation of the competitive field. But he never, to my knowledge, discussed the ironic relevance of the Lacanian Symbolic for his own analysis of "symbolic domination." Why did Bourdieu feel the need to complement his category of cultural capital with symbolic capital? Why this theoretical stuttering? None of his other categories take this doubled form. Other influences are named: Bourdieu refers to Émile Durkheim as a sociologist of symbolic forms and attributes to Ernst Cassirer the idea that symbolic form is the equivalent of forms of classification (Bourdieu 1991e: 164). In 1983 he defines *symbolic capital* as capital "insofar as it is represented, i.e., apprehended symbolically, in a relationship of knowledge" (Bourdieu 1986b [1983]: 255). This suggests that, at this early stage in Bourdieu's development of the concept, *symbolic* is simply another word for the semiotic. Several years later, however, Bourdieu noted that symbolic capital is "cultural capital which is acknowledged and *recognized* . . . in accordance with the categories of perception that it imposes," and "symbolic capital . . . is the power granted to those who have obtained sufficient recognition to be in a position to impose recognition" (Bourdieu 1990e: 135, 138). By the time he wrote *Pascalian Meditations*, Bourdieu had connected the topic of symbolic capital directly to the "search for recognition." As Bourdieu writes,

> Absorbed in the love of others, the child can only discover others as such on condition that he discovers himself as a "subject" for whom there are "objects" whose particularity is that they can take him as their "object." In fact, he is continuously led to take the point of view of others on himself, to adopt their point of view so as to discover and evaluate in advance how he will be seen and defined by them. His being is being-perceived, condemned to be defined as it "really" is by the perceptions of others. . . . Symbolic capital enables forms of domination which imply dependence on those who can be dominated by it, since it only exists through the esteem, recognition, belief, credit, confidence of others. (Bourdieu 2000b: 166)

Bourdieu also seemed to make the crucial (Hegelian) observation that it is not only the dominated but also the dominant who depend on the "esteem, recognition, belief, credit, confidence of others" (Bourdieu 2000b: 166). In Hegel's words, lord and bondsman "recognize themselves as mutually recognizing one another" (Hegel 1967: 235). Symbolic capital, Bourdieu now argued, can be perpetuated only so long as it succeeds in generating a system of mutual interdependence in which all of the actors in a given field depend on recognition from all of the others, and grant recognition to all of the others, even if this is recognition of an inferior status. Along similar lines, we are told in *Masculine Domination* that manliness "is an eminently *relational* notion, constructed in front of and for other men," in a kind of field of men (Bourdieu 2001b: 53). This formulation again suggests that both dominated and dominant depend on recognition.

For the most part, however, Bourdieu falls back on a populist political vision that prevents him from noticing that his own concept of symbolic capital requires a universalization of the desire for recognition to all actors in a given field. The dominated may develop a "taste for necessity," preferring their own (dominated) tastes to those of the elite. At the same time, they recognize that the cultural capital of the dominant groups is more valuable or distinguished. Where this is not the case—where the dominated and dominant fail to mutually recognize shared definitions of distinction—there is an ongoing struggle over the "dominant principle of domination" (Bourdieu 1996b: 376). Fields can become unsettled; practices may fail altogether to cohere in fieldlike ways, existing "*hors-champ*" (outside of all fields).[14]

Lacan offers a solution to this problem. He borrows the notion of desire (*Begierde*) from Hegel, "who argued that desire was the 'desire for another desire'" (Braungardt 1999). Bourdieu's notion of symbolic capital is based on the premise of reciprocal demands for recognition by all actors in a field, recognition of the variable cultural positions, habituses and tastes, and recognition of their hierarchy. But why should the dominant partner in a hierarchical relation seek recognition from the subordinated other? The answer is that both dominant and dominated are subjects of an encompassing system that is itself structured around a hierarchical system; both are subject to the Symbolic order.

What we have, then, are two different axes of recognition and misrecognition. On the one hand there is the axis along which the Law confronts the "infinity of individuals." Althusser, who reframed Lacan's symbolic order as the system of ideology, described ideology as "speculary, i.e., a mirror structure . . . the Absolute Subject occupies the unique place of the Centre, and interpellates around it the infinity of individuals into subjects in a double mirror-connexion such that it subjects the subjects to the Subject, while giving them . . . the Subject in which each subject can contemplate its own image"

(Althusser 1971: 180). Among the "infinity of individuals," however, are diverse social classes and groups, each of which can "contemplate its own image" in the social mirror of the other classes and groups. The Symbolic order demands recognition from the subject and grants him a sliver of recognition in the guise of the policeman's call: "Hey, you there!" (Althusser 1979: 174). The dominant and the dominated both demand recognition of their respective tastes and practices. These tastes and practices differ from and reciprocally implicate one another.

Recognition is also doubled by misrecognition, both with respect to the subject's overarching relationship to the Symbolic Order and with respect to its relationship to other classes and groups in the social fields. This is a relation of misrecognition, insofar as the image offered up for the purposes of ego-formation and identification is always generated elsewhere, outside the subject, and it is always an inverted, reversed, or otherwise distorted representation of the real. This is a relation of misrecognition insofar as the dominated tend to embrace their own condition of domination, and insofar as the dominant believe that their tastes and practices are genuinely superior in an objective or absolute sense.

The desire among dominated groups for the approval of, or recognition by, those who dominate them is somewhat paradoxical, and neither Bourdieu nor Hegel really makes sense of this puzzle. Bourdieu called attention to the central role of *amor fati*, or the "taste for necessity," in social reproduction. By failing to account for the genesis of amor fati, however, Bourdieu runs the risk of a kind of social scientific functionalism. By contrast, psychoanalytic theory offers an account of the way in which the desire for submission emerges from the very genesis of the subject. It emphasizes the contradictory demand to be both like and unlike the father. Psychoanalysis offers a definition of the masochist as one who "locates enjoyment in the very agency of the Law which prohibits the access to enjoyment," suggesting another account of this desire for recognition, one that is always controversial because it is so damaging to a different sort of *amour propre* (Žižek 1997).

Lacan's theory of the symbolic order thus sketches out some of the micro-foundations or, better, the psychofoundations that underpin Bourdieusian fields and permit their operation by giving rise to subjects suited for working in a competitive but mutually recognizing manner. The subject's ineluctable entry into the symbolic explains the desire to have his or her cultural capital recognized; it also explains why others have the capacity and motivation to classify that cultural capital. The "social libido" that Bourdieu invokes needs to be thematized within this wider theoretical framework.

Habitus and the Imaginary

The other key concept in the Bourdieusian theoretical lexicon is habitus. Bourdieu's notion of habitus has been praised for overcoming the mind-body and objectivity versus subjectivity distinctions that have been so deeply engrained in Western philosophy. The *integrative* power of habitus also makes it certainly important to Bourdieu's approach. Given the array of different social fields and spaces in which people operate and the historical layering of experiences and socializations, the ability of the habitus to integrate disparate experiences is a genuine achievement. By contrast, the idea of fragmented subjectivities in postmodern social theory does not do justice to the fact that many people do not suffer from a subjective sense of their own fragmentation or exhibit signs of disorientation or discontinuity, even though they are subjected to the same complex postmodern conditions as people who do feel fragmented. But while Bourdieu's concept of habitus is often mobilized to make sense of the seemingly mysterious integration of the disparate historical experiences that make up a biography, he also became increasingly interested in cases in which the habitus is internally contradictory, split, or unresolved.

Bourdieu introduced the word *habitus* when he was analyzing the subjectivity of the Algerian Kabyle, French colonial subjects, in order to explain a disjuncture between ingrained habit and the requirements of colonial economic modernity. There is little acknowledgment in his later writing on habitus that colonial ethnologists and sociologists had long dealt with this exact problem. Bourdieu was analyzing the subjectivity of colonial subjects who had been described for more than a century by Europeans as suffering from a kind of cultural schizophrenia or unstable code switching, a disunity of habitus (Steinmetz 2007b). French socioethnographers, including many of those to whom Bourdieu referred in his early writing on Algeria, had been theorizing cultural hybridity and transculturation among the colonized since the beginning of the twentieth century. The difference between describing the culture of the colonized as an unstable mix versus a stabilized integration of indigenous and European culture was at the core of practical discussions of alternative forms of colonial native policy and also within academic social science (Bastide 1958, 1970–71). Bourdieu's first comments on habitus thus stand in a long and evolving tradition of French and international ethnological research on colonized cultures subjected to foreign conquest.

Bourdieu's concept of habitus as durable and transposable dispositions came to encompass two opposing conceptions: a "permanent *discrepancy* between the agents' economic dispositions and the economic world in which they had to act" versus the idea that habitus does in fact successfully update itself to meet changing requirements of the situation (Bourdieu 1979a: vii).[15] Later Bourdieu added a third possibility, the idea of a cleft or divided habitus. Here he accounted for his own divided habitus by referring to the radical disjuncture between his social origins and his exalted position at the Collège de France (see below).

We could call these three main orientations of habitus the integrated, disjunctural, and split forms. As for the first, integrated form, we need to ask: how does the subject accomplish the task of integration? And why does it sometimes fail? Lacan and Freud provide crucial missing elements for the argument. Just as the Lacanian concept of the symbolic order makes sense of the subjective structures that underlie Bourdieu's fields, so the Lacanian concept of the Imaginary illuminates the curious capacity of the habitus to integrate disparate experiences and identifications so that practice usually does not appear to be disjointed. A cluster of linked concepts—mirror stage, bodily ego, plenitude, ideal ego, and imaginary identification—points toward a possible solution to this arduous problem of integration.

As noted above, the starting point for human subjects, according to Lacan, is not competitive aggressiveness (in contrast to the anthropological Hobbesianism of a thinker like Carl Schmitt), but symbiotic helplessness. Lacan postulates that the subject continues to experience a fragmented body image because of this early experience. Recurrent adult fantasies of the "body in pieces" harken back to this early experience, along the general lines of the "return of the repressed." Lacan discusses the production of a "succession of phantasies that extends from a fragmented body image to a form of its totality that [he calls] orthopaedic." As Kaja Silverman points out, Freud maintains that the ego is "first and foremost, a bodily ego; it is not merely a surface entity" (Silverman 1996: 1). As Lacan writes,

> Whatever in man is loosened up, fragmented, anarchic, establishes its relation to his perceptions on a plane with a completely original tension. The image of the body is the principle of every unity he perceives in objects. . . . Because of this . . . all the objects of his world are always structured around the wandering shadow of his own ego. They will all have a fundamentally anthropomorphic character, even egomorphic we could say. Man's ideal unity, which is never attained as such and escapes him at every moment, is evoked at every moment in this perception. . . . The very image of man brings in here a mediation which is always imaginary, always problematic, and which is therefore never completely fulfilled. (Lacan 1991: 161)

Habitus in Bourdieu, like the psychoanalytic concept of a roughcast "bodily ego," thus overcomes the body–mind split.

The key word in the last quotation from Lacan is *imaginary*. For Lacan the initial identifications that constitute the subject begin in the mirror phase, when the watery subject—the *hommelette*, or man-omelette—identifies with the totalizing and alienating external image of itself.[16] The core structure of specular identity in the realm of the imaginary is this sense of plenitude and wholeness. Imaginary identification is identification with an image that Lacan (following Freud) calls the ideal-ego (*Idealich*), that is, an image "in which we appear likeable to ourselves . . . representing 'what we would like to be'" (Žižek 1989: 105).[17] The earliest imaginary identifications provide a template for later ones that are similarly characterized by a striving for wholeness.[18] The notion of imaginary identification can be connected to the overarching psychoanalytic concept of fantasy, which has been used to great avail by theorists of nationalism, communism, totalitarianism, and postfascism. Fantasy scenarios express a conscious or unconscious wish. Imaginary identification is one site for such wishful scenarios (Inderbitzin and Levy 2001).[19]

Although Lacan initially restricted imaginary identifications to the mirror phase, in his later writing the imaginary was no longer a separate stage or realm but a dimension of subject-formation that persists throughout a life while coming under the sway of the symbolic order. As Althusser writes, the "imaginary. . . . is stamped by the seal of . . . the symbolic" (Althusser 1971: 214). The imaginary is therefore as much a realm of signifiers as the symbolic. The symbolic order guides subjects toward specific images for imaginary identification, yet the subject continually slips from symbolic identifications back into imaginary ones. Although neither realm can be said to be fundamentally more estranged than the other, the imaginary offers forms of identifications that deny difference, estrangement, and the loss of symbiotic plenitude; they disavow their debt to the Other. The imaginary is a sort of estrangement from the subject's "inevitable estrangement" (Weber 1991). There is a perpetual "oscillation of the subject" between ideal egos and ego ideals (Lagache 1961: 41).

We could therefore posit that the sense of embodied "ideal unity" expressed in bodily habitus is generated in the realm of the imaginary and imaginary identifications. Although, as noted, Bourdieu often erects a protective fence around psychoanalytic concepts, in this context he writes that, "Habitus of necessity operates as a *defence mechanism* against necessity" (Bourdieu 2000b: 232–33). This suggestion of a defense mechanism comes very close to the psychoanalytic ideas of fantasy and the ideal-ego: Imaginary identifications can be defenses against the grueling necessity of symbolic identifications, even as they fall inexorably under the latter's dominion. And while these imaginary identifications of the subject-body as a unified whole are just as much fantasies as the idea of the body in pieces, they provide the psychic conditions of possibility for a temporarily, apparently unified habitus.

As noted, Bourdieu introduced the idea of habitus in his work on French colonial subjects, the Algerian Kabyle. But he could not explain why some colonized subjects moved from a traditional to a modern habitus, while others retained or returned to more traditional identifications. Bourdieu suggested in the 1950s that the "economic world imported by colonization" was a completely modern, capitalist one (Bourdieu 1979a: 3). In the second edition of *Sociologie de l'Algérie* he included a new discussion of French land policy, which had produced a "*tabula rasa* of a civilization that could no longer be discussed except in the past tense" (Bourdieu 1961: 125). This perspective on colonialism overlooked the fact that in Algeria, as in other overseas colonial empires, modern colonizers often sought to strengthen indigenous modes of life rather than erase them. This policy of fortifying tradition was ubiquitous in modern European colonial empires and was known as "indirect rule" in the British Imperium and "associationism" in French colonial theory, and took the form of a kind of "salvage colonialism" in the German colonies in the Pacific and some African colonies (Steinmetz 2004; 2007b). It also underwrote forms of anthropology that prioritized the study of static indigenous cultures apparently untouched by external European conquest and rule. In practice European colonial rule manufactured a hierarchical plurality of symbolic orders within the colonies, for metropolitan civil servants, white settlers, and for each of the various tribes (Coquery-Vidrovitch 1969; Mamdani 1996).

The disjuncture between habitus and the demands of modern capitalism was thus much more than a cultural lag, as Bourdieu described it. The formulae Bourdieu uses to describe this disjuncture—the "hysteresis of habitus" and the "Don Quixote effect"—turn habitus into a memory of an earlier socio-historical formation that no longer exists. This mode of analysis tends to obscure the coexistence of diverse symbolic and social orders in colonies and in other social orders. A habitus that is out of sync with the demands of a dominant symbolic order may be perfectly adjusted to another, dominated order and may even constitute a form of resistance, a refusal to adopt new identifications that correspond to the demands of the dominant order. Since Bourdieu never fully analyzed the history of French colonial native policy in Algeria prior to the wartime interventions in the 1950s, he overlooked the ways in which the disjuncture between Kabyle and the new economic world may have reflected vital symbolic and imaginary identifications rather than passively reflecting vanished conditions. The "world in which [the colonized] had to act" (Bourdieu 1979a: vii) was more than just a modern Europeanized economic world. Bourdieu did of course analyze the traditional world extensively, but he kept this part of his work separate from his texts on colonial destruction and displacement, producing, as it were, two separate Algerias (Martin-Criado 2008; Hammoudi 2009; Silverstein and Goodman 2009). If Bourdieu had brought the two projects together, he would have been able to argue that some forms of habitus that were obsolete from the standpoint of European and postcolonial policies of resettlement and proletarianization continued to be reinforced and ratified by subaltern symbolic systems and by systems originating in the "associationist" native policies of the colonial state itself.

The model I am proposing of a hierarchical plurality of symbolic orders is not unique to colonial or imperial contexts. There may also be a plurality of social spaces, to use Bourdieu's terms, or Symbolic Orders (in the Lacanian sense) within a given territory and not just a plurality of fields.[20] The result of moving between symbolic orders and social spaces will usually be disjunctural or split forms of habitus, or forms of practice that appear clumsy or illegible. By contrast subjects are often able to move successfully among fields within a given social space, since social space corresponds to a given symbolic order.

What can we conclude from the forgoing discussion? We can define a *split* habitus as the product of sustained subject formation in two or more discrepant positions in a given social space or symbolic order. Bourdieu presents himself as an example of this in his auto-analysis. A disjunctural habitus, by contrast, suggests a more radically divided social condition, such as colonialism, in which there is more than one social space or symbolic order. The condition of "double consciousness" analyzed by W. E. B. Du Bois and many other colonial theorists points to this doubling of symbolic or social orders. Both the split and the disjunctural habitus can be distinguished from the run of the mill situation in which a modern person is active in more than one field within a single social space or symbolic order. In this unexceptional condition, habitus will be adjusted consciously and unconsciously to fit the demands of the new field, but the field-specific performances of a given subject will appear continuous and integrated.

The idea of a multiplicity of symbolic orders systems goes beyond Lacanian theory, of course, but it brings us back to sociology and history. Or perhaps this is the moment at which history, sociology, and psychoanalysis join forces to become historical socioanalysis. Bourdieu's *Sketch for a Self-Analysis* resonates in many respects with psychoanalysis and is suggestive of a neo-Bourdieusian historical socioanalysis (Steinmetz 2009b). Just as Lacan fills in some of the missing elements of Bourdieu's theory, Bourdieu shows in this text how sociology can complement psychoanalysis.

Bourdieu's *Sketch for a Self-Analysis*

This is a short book with a long, complicated history. It first took shape as Bourdieu's final public lecture at the Collège de France in March 2001. That lecture was published later that year as a forty-page concluding chapter entitled "Esquisse pour une auto-analyse" (Sketch for a Self-Analysis) in the book *Science de la science et réflexivité* (Bourdieu 2001c; Schultheis 2002: 114). In the final months of 2001 Bourdieu turned this chapter into a short book, which he decided to publish first in German translation. It appeared shortly after Bourdieu's death as *Ein soziologischer Selbstversuch* (Bourdieu 2002b). The French manuscript was then published in 2004 under the title of the final chapter of *Science de la science* (Bourdieu 2004c).

The first thing one notices about this book is that its title in both German and French resonates strongly with psychoanalysis.[21] The most famous case of self-analysis (or *auto-analyse*) is Freud's; other renowned psychoanalysts, including Karen Horney, have written on the topic of self-analysis (Horney 1942). In a letter to Wilhelm Fliess, Freud wrote, "I can only analyze myself with the help of knowledge obtained objectively (like an outsider)."[22] Bourdieu treated the idea of a "self-socio-analysis" in much the same terms. Similarly, Bourdieu elaborated the idea of "the *objectification of the subject of objectivation*, of the analyzing subject" (Bourdieu 2003a: 282). Freud concluded that self-analysis was a necessary complement to the training of psychoanalysis, though it could not replace it, since there were "definite limits to progress by this method" (Laplanche and Pontalis 1974: 413). Subsequent psychoanalytic theorists have agreed (Abraham and Jones 1927; Anzieu 1986: 303–11). Bourdieu did not comment on the specific obstacles to self-objectification and its methodological difference from the objectification of others.

After initially presenting his book as a self-analysis, Bourdieu quickly relabels it a "self-socioanalysis" (une auto-socioanalyse) (Bourdieu 2004c: 11), the same phrase he and his coauthors Jean-Claude Chamboredon and Jean-Claude Passeron had used in the 1968 book *The Craft of Sociology* (Bourdieu, Chamboredon, and Passeron 1991: 74). Bourdieu announces his goal as one of retaining "all the features that are pertinent from the point of view of sociology, in other words, that are necessary for sociological explanation and understanding, and only those" (Bourdieu 2008b: 1). Attempting to present the text as something other than a self-psychoanalysis and as something other than an autobiography, Bourdieu does not begin with his childhood, his parents, or his ancestors. Instead, the narrative opens directly in the sociological, social-symbolic thick of things: Bourdieu's years at the Ecole Normale Supérieure (ENS). For Bourdieu the educational field takes precedence even over the family. "To understand is first to understand the field with which and against which one has been formed [*avec lequel et contre lequel on s'est fait*]. That is why, at the risk of surprising a reader who perhaps expects me to begin at the beginning, that is to say, by evoking my earliest years and the social universe of my childhood, I must, as a point of method, first examine the state of the field at the moment when I entered it, in the 1950s."[23] But it is not really obligatory for a psychoanalytic account (or an autobiography, for that matter) to begin at the beginning. Indeed, most psychoanalytic case studies begin with the symptoms that have brought the client to the analyst. Furthermore, psycho-analysis is one of the most narratively sophisticated of the human sciences, meaning that psychoanalytic writers often manipulate and hold in tension what the Russian formalists called story and plot.[24] The psychoanalytic pro-cess and the psychoanalytic case report do not take the form of stories told from beginning to end, with plot and story merging into a single identical linear path. Instead, these narratives are often marked by repeated, looping returns to different moments in the past as diverse memories are awakened in the present and new connections made across the timeline of the story. By the time Freud was analyzing Dora he had adopted the technique of letting the patient "choose the subject of the day's work," which meant that "the patient's story emerged piecemeal, in fragmented and disconnected form, with past and present interwoven, calling for new narrative strategies" (Lunbeck and Simon 2003: 13). The dislocation of plot and story in Bourdieu's autoanalysis is in this respect perfectly compatible with psychoanalysis and is indeed closer to the novelistic forms used by psychoanalysis than to the ostensibly nonnarra-tive forms of positivist sociology.

Following the strategies of denegation discussed above, Bourdieu oscillates between explicitly psychoanalytic and more narrowly sociological language. In the first section of the text he summarizes what he calls the "collective *fantasy*" (*fantasme collectif*) and "community of the *unconsciousnesses*" (*com-munauté des inconscients*) among the "scholarly aristocracy" at the ENS (Bour-dieu 2004c: 19; 2008b: 7–8). The remainder of this first section seems to answer the question that concerns us but that Bourdieu's text has not explicitly asked concerning his relationship to psychoanalysis. In summarizing the state of the academic field at the ENS after the war, Bourdieu depicts the dominant pole as organized around Jean-Paul Sartre and existentialism and the domi-nated grouping as based initially among "marginal . . . authors, hidden from celebrity," but who nonetheless founded the history of philosophy and sci-ence: Gaston Bachelard, Georges Canguilhem, and Alexandre Koyré. These were philosophers with "lower-class or provincial origins, or brought up outside France and its academic traditions" (Bourdieu 2008b: 10). Bourdieu describes himself as being closest to this group, especially to Canguilhem, during his time at the ENS and after he passed the *agregation* (the highly competitive examination for positions in the public education system) (Bourdieu 2008b: 26–28). The dominated philosophical tradition represented by Bachelard, Canguilhem, and Koyré was completely dominant in Bourdieu's main epistemological text from the 1960s, *The Craft of Sociology* (Bourdieu, Chamboredon, and Passeron 1991). This philosophical tendency, according to Bourdieu, gave rise to the "leaders of the anti-existentialist revolution in philosophy," who were "more distant from the core of the academic tradition, such as Althusser, Foucault, and some others." Bourdieu characterizes this group as developing a "philosophy without a subject," and he reminds his readers that social scientists, Durkheim in particular, had made similar arguments a century earlier (Bourdieu 2004: 23). The problem with this account, for Bourdieu, is that it locates him in precisely the same social location in the French intellectual field as Bachelard and Althusser, who were deeply engaged with psychoanalysis, and by extension also with Lacan.

In response to this threat of contamination, Bourdieu's text moves abruptly forward in time from the 1950s to the French intellectual field of the 1970s. Bourdieu now discerns a completely different axis of polarization, pitting sociology and the social sciences against a camp that includes Althusser, Foucault, and the other "nephews of Zarathustra" (Pinto 1995) along with psychoanalysis. Psychoanalysis, Bourdieu now asserts, was allied in France with "spiritualism" and, "more precisely, with Catholicism," and was situated "on the side of the most noble and pure intellectual activities." Bourdieu harshly criticizes Lacan for combining "the obscurities and audacities of a [Stéphane] Mallarmé and of a Heidegger." But this unconvincing denunciation cannot sharply separate Bourdieu from Freud, who was neither Catholic nor noble and whose writing style was crystalline and scientific, not obscure or audacious. Bachelard, one of Bourdieu's earlier heroes, cannot be assimilated to obscurantism. Althusser can hardly be tarred with the brush of social class "nobility." Moreover, in his dialogue with Jacques Maître, Bourdieu embraced "a kind of social psychoanalysis" and argued "transgressively" that the interview itself is a "spiritual exercise."[25]

The next section of his auto-analysis moved back in time to the second half of the 1950s and the early 1960s, the time of his research in Algeria and his natal village in rural Béarn. According to Bourdieu, this "return to the origins" in Béarn was also a "*return of the repressed*, but a controlled one." The need to control the experience is owing to "the emotional atmosphere" and the "very painful" interviews he conducted there. As we know from Bourdieu's publications on this period, his father often accompanied him in his work in Béarn, and "through his presence and his discreet intercession, helped [Bourdieu] to elicit trust and confidence" (Bourdieu 2004c: 82–83).

Bourdieu's familial story—specifically, the relation to his father—is finally broached near the end of the *Sketch for a Self-Analysis*, when Bourdieu narrates his inaugural lecture at the Collège de France. Two psychoanalytic concepts structure this segment. The first is ambivalence. Bourdieu interprets his entire stance toward intellectual life under the heading of a "sense of ambivalence" rooted in the "lasting effect of a very strong discrepancy [*décalage*] between high academic consecration and humble social origins" (Bourdieu 2004c: 135, 127). In psychoanalysis, ambivalence points to "conflicts in which the positive and negative components of the emotional attitude are simultaneously in evidence and inseparable, and where they constitute a non-dialectical opposition which the subject, saying 'yes' and 'no' at the same time, is incapable of transcending" (Laplanche and Pontalis 1974: 28). As noted above, this is also where Bourdieu returns to the idea of a split or "cleft" habitus (*habitus clivé*). The second concept in this discussion is guilt. Bourdieu says that his lecture was accompanied by a "sense of guilt towards [his] father, who had just died in a particularly tragic way." Bourdieu makes a "magical connection between his [father's] death and a success [he] constructed as a transgression and a treachery" (Bourdieu 2004c: 138). Lacan might read the sense of guilt as intrinsic to the entrance into the symbolic order per se. A sense of guilt would be especially strong in the context of a challenge to that order (Butler 1997: 106–31). And, indeed, Bourdieu goes on to describe his lecture as a "challenge to the *symbolic order* [*un défi à l'ordre symbolique*]" (Bourdieu 2004c: 138; italics mine). It is worth noting the linguistic slippage from *space* to *order* in this context: Bourdieu's more usual phrase was symbolic space (*espace symbolique*). Bourdieu's entry into the Collège de France recalls for him the original traumatic entry into the symbolic order itself, the realm of official ego-ideals.

Toward Socioanalysis

My conclusion is that Lacanian psychoanalysis and Bourdieusian socioanalysis need one another. Bourdieu had already suggested the necessity of combining a sociological sense of lifelong transformations with a psychoanalytic account of the original constitution of the subject. In his interview with Maître he observed that psychoanalysis often stops "at the moment when the social begins to transform desire (*au moment où le social commence à travailler le désir.*")

What is needed, Bourdieu argued, is a "theory of the socialization of the libido" (Bourdieu 1994a: xvii). As I have suggested here, what is also needed is a more thorough specification of the psychic underpinnings of the social.

Bourdieu argued that "sociology does not claim to substitute its mode of explanation for that of psychoanalysis; it is concerned only to construct differently certain givens that psychoanalysis also takes as its object" (Bourdieu 1999: 512). But social analysis requires an integration of the ontological levels of the psychic and the social (Bhaskar 1979). If Bourdieu had explored this relationship in more depth, he might have seen that they were not alternatives, but that psychoanalysis filled some of the lacunae in his own theoretical approach. Bourdieu's signal contributions, including the concepts of habitus and symbolic capital, need to be reconstructed in dialogue with psychoanalytic theories of the imaginary integration of bodily imagery and symbolic recognition and misrecognition. Bourdieusian theory needs to specify its own psychofoundations, and it needs to select a version of psychic theory that best fits with its aspirations to remain on the side of antipositivism or nonpositivism. Bourdieu's situationally determined reluctance to fully engage with the most powerful theorists of the psychic, such as Lacan, should not continue to afflict his followers.

Notes

1. The source of the epigraph is Gaulejac (2004). In a recent paper (Steinmetz 2009b) I examined the possibility of intergrating Bourdieu's theory of scientific autonomy with the psychoanalytic theory of ego autonomy in order to better understand scientists' susceptibility to heteronomization, that is, to aligning their research with extrascientific powers.

2. I am grateful to Françine Muel-Dreyfus for bringing this article to my attention and for her critical comments on an earlier draft of my article.

3. Freud did not invent the term *unconscious*, but he gave it its distinctive contemporary definition (Rand 2004).

4. Bourdieu first refers to this story in his article of 1975 on Heidegger, expanded into Bourdieu 1991a. It appears again in Bourdieu 1991e: 146.

5. It follows that the third key Bourdieusian concept, *field*, also makes most sense when reconstructed along these lines. As I have argued elsewhere, fields cannot be understood solely as agonistic Kampfplätze but are also arenas of mutual identification, recognition, and even love (Steinmetz 2008). For a parallel effort to integrate Bourdieu's theory with Lacanian psychoanalysis, see the important book by Hage (2000). I am grateful to Ghassan Hage for discussing some of the issues in this paper with me in Melbourne in August 2010. For an execellent but more orthodox reading of the idea of the unconscious in Bourdieu, see Chevallier and Chauviré (2010).

6. Contrary to Jean-François Fourny, there is no systematic Lacanian or Freudian

usage according to which *phantasy* or *phantasm* designates a collective and unconscious form while *fantasy* refers to a conscious one (Fourny 2000). Fourny's excellent article overlaps with my efforts to integrate Bourdieu and psychoanalysis; the main difference is that I argue that a more systematic integration of Lacan can strengthen Bourdieu's theory, and vice-versa, yielding a transdisciplinary, neo-Bourdieusian and neo-Lacanian "socioanalysis."

7. Bourdieu's relationship to psychoanalysis is both deeper and much more problematic than his relationship to nonpsychoanalytic psychologists; but see Lizardo's excellent article (2004) on the importance of Jean Piaget to Bourdieu's idea of habitus.

8. It is crucial to recognize that Bourdieu is not an ahistorical "reproduction theorist." Both social reproduction *and* social change, constraint *and* freedom, are at the core of Bourdieu's project. See Steinmetz (2011). The same is true of Freud, for whom two individuals confronted by the same Oedipal drama may make very different sense of it.

9. Here, psychoanalysis is reduced to a form of biological reductionism, ignoring Freud's shift from the theory of childhood abuse in the early *Studies in Hysteria* to the theory of sexual fantasy he developed in the course of his self-analysis. In *Five Lectures on Psycho-Analysis* (1905) Freud insisted that the child's taking one or both of its parents as "the object of its erotic wishes" "usually follows some indication from the parents" rather than emerging quasi-naturally from a biological foundation. Freud also insisted on the "plasticity of the components of sexuality" (Freud 1977: 51, 61). For a more detailed discussion of the tension between biological and sociological modes of interpretation in Freud, see Elliott (2005). On the accusations against Bourdieu of antihistoricism, see Steinmetz (2011) and Gorski's introduction to this volume.

10. Castoriadis's original theory of the imaginary was developed in an act of theoretical suppression directed at Lacan, his former master theorist. See Stavrakakis (2002).

11. Bourdieu praised Maître's efforts to specify the "relations between sociology and psychoanalysis." See Bourdieu 1994a.

12. Unattributed comment from the public, quoting a comment by Loïc Wacquant, in Corcuff (2004: 95). Second quote from Bourdieu (2003c: 29).

13. This will seem like a startling claim only to those who have restricted themselves to Freud's more schematic overviews of his theory or approached psychoanalysis through the work of hostile critics. But even the various case studies in Freud's earliest work on hysteria reveal an enormously wide array of symptoms among his women patients (Breuer, Freud, and Brill 1950). The distinction between the positive and negative Oedipus complex in Freud's mature theory points to different alternative paths that people can take in response to identical social predicaments. Indeed psychoanalysis emphasizes the infinitely creative nature of the unconscious and the huge variety of forms of psychosexual development. Freud's concept of *working through* "characterizes the role of the patient in analysis" and is concerned with "the labor of the patient" in recognizing and overcoming resistances—in other words, the conscious and unconscious agency of the subject. See Sedler (1983).

14. Comments by Lilian Mathieu in Corcuff (2004: 239). I discuss settled and unsettled fields in Steinmetz (2007a).

15. Wearing his "therapeutic" hat, Bourdieu also suggested that habitus could be deliberately remade through "repeated exercises . . . like an athlete's training" (Bourdieu 2000b: 172).

16. This need not be a literal reflection in a mirror but can also be the image or even the voice of another human, perhaps a mother or caretaker (Silverman 1988).

17. See also Lacan (1988); Lagache (1961).

18. Freud already recognized that identifications need not involve explicitly erotic cathexes (Freud 1955).

19. See, in addition, the special issue of *La Psychanalyse* 8 (1964) entitled "Fantasme, Rêve, Réalité."

20. Even within a given social space it is possible that habituses generated and reinforced within one field may be "discrepant" or ill-fitting when they are imported into other fields. There needs to be as much attention to discrepancies as to homologies among the fields in a given social space.

21. The German title has less explicitly psychoanalytic associations. A more accurate German translation of Bourdieu's original title would have been something like *Umriss einer Selbstanalyse.*

22. Freud 1897: 271.

23. Bourdieu 2004c: 15.

24. The story, as Bordwell and Thompson (1979: 50) point out, is the "series of causal events as they occur in chronological order and presumed duration and frequency." In most narratives, however, the "events are not presented in exact chronological order; the order in which they occur in the actual text is their *plot* order" (50). Bourdieu (1986a) was familiar with these narratological categories.

25. Bourdieu continues that he "always felt this," that is, that the sociological interview is a spiritual exercise, but that he had been suffering from a "sort of positivist repression, . . . this form of masochism identified with professional virtue" (Bourdieu 1994a: v–xxii).

DEWEY AND BOURDIEU ON DEMOCRACY

"Democracy is belief in the ability of human experience to generate the aims and methods by which further experience will grow in ordered richness." So asserted John Dewey in "Creative Democracy—The Task Before Us," a speech given on the occasion of his eightieth birthday; his words nicely encapsulate the classical pragmatist vision of a democratic way of life. Democracy was, in Dewey's view,

> faith that the process of experience is more important than any special result attained, so that special results achieved are of ultimate value only as they are used to enrich and order the ongoing process. . . . All ends and values that are cut off from the ongoing process become arrests, fixations. They strive to fixate what has been gained instead of using it to open the road and point the way to new and better experiences. . . . The task of democracy is forever that of creation of a freer and more humane experience in which all share and to which all contribute. (Dewey and Bentley 1991 [1949]: 229)

From Dewey's perspective, it was important for political philosophy and social science to study the ideal conditions necessary for the sustenance of a democratic way of life, to determine the difficulties and obstacles standing in the way of their realization, and to indicate some strategies for bringing about a more genuinely creative and progressive society. It was crucial that democratic scholarship provide "intelligent insight" (Dewey 1985 [1916]: 225) into the possibilities for social and political reconstruction. Dewey himself noted that, with the advent of industrial capitalism, a more class-structured society had arisen whose structures of inequality and ethos of possessive individualism were highly corrosive of democratic habits and mores. A "Great Society" (Dewey 1988d [1927]) was coming about in which possibilities for self-development through associated life and participatory democratic action were increasingly stunted; the task for democratic thinkers and activists was to turn that Great Society into a "Great Community."

Dewey's vision, while deeply rooted in what he characterized as "the socio-logical standpoint" (Dewey 1972 [1897]: 70), was ultimately limited in its possibilities for development because he was not a sociologist but a philoso-pher. Despite his concern for the concrete, for a return to actual lived experi-ence, he lacked the conceptual and methodological tools necessary to turn his philosophical vision into a sociological and historical research agenda.[1] In particular, he was unable to say much of substance concerning the pervasive threats to democracy posed by class divisions and other forms of societal antagonism. His theory of creative democracy could not bridge the divide separating it from any systematic analysis of domination—and hence could not speak as compellingly as Dewey would have liked to the problems and challenges of his day.

Half a century after Dewey, however, there did appear on the scene a sociological enterprise making good on much of the unrealized promise of classical American pragmatism. Pierre Bourdieu was not directly influenced, to be sure, by the pragmatist tradition of social and political thought, a tradi-tion lacking in visibility in the French intellectual life of his formative years. But he was certainly familiar with it, cited the major thinkers from it favorably and often, and indicated in *An Invitation to Reflexive Sociology* (Bourdieu and Wacquant 1992), not to mention also *Pascalian Meditations* (2000b [1997]), an awareness of the continuities between his own thinking and that of Dewey in particular. These thematic continuities were striking and many-sided, and we shall discuss a number of them in the section that follows. However, Bour-dieu's approach also went beyond Dewey's stated philosophic program; it provided a critical and reflexive sociology of domination and symbolic vio-lence in modern society, a perspective that greatly enhances the analytic pow-ers of democratic scholarship. In so doing, it supplied what was missing in Deweyan pragmatism.[2]

Even as we acknowledge that Bourdieu went a considerable distance be-yond Dewey, however—but in a direction Dewey himself might have affirmed —it is also important that we reread him with Dewey squarely in mind. This is because, rightly or wrongly, historical sociologists of democracy have over the years had little actual use for Bourdieu's work. Regardless of their orientation to democratic studies—whether that be the historical study of citizenship and social rights; research on civil society and the public sphere; inquiries into the mechanisms of democratization; or studies of the relations among associa-tionalism, trust, and social capital—many scholars of democracy have consid-ered Bourdieu's *oeuvre* to be oddly lacking in promising leads or insights.

Indeed, they have more often characterized it as a one-sidedly pessimistic account of domination than as a forward-looking, generative inquiry into the conditions of possibility for human freedom, creativity, and liberation. Far from seeing Bourdieu's sociology as an exciting fount of ideas regarding democratic prospects, "a major untapped store of concepts, theories, and insights for rethinking the links between freedom, justice, and politics" (Wacquant 2005: 10), they have perceived it as a gloomy compendium of all the forces and dynamics that make democracy *im*possible.

This is in some ways puzzling, for Bourdieu worked throughout his life, especially in his later years, in the service of progressive social and political causes; indeed, few if any major sociologists of the latter half of the twentieth century were more deeply immersed in democratic struggles. Moreover, Bourdieu's writings not only explored in comprehensive fashion the institutions and practices of modern democratic politics, they also constituted in themselves a democratic political intervention, aiming time and again to raise the level of debate in the political public sphere.[3] In light of this, the lack of resonance between Bourdieu and the critical sociology of democracy seems thoroughly unnecessary and, indeed, something of a lost opportunity.

In our view, pausing to let the Bourdieusian wine breathe—that is, reflecting on it from a Deweyan perspective or, to pursue the metaphor further, in a Deweyan air—will allow certain of its features that have been understated or underappreciated to stand out more distinctly. It will conduce to a better understanding of Bourdieu's insights into the importance of practical intelligence, the transformative potentialities of social action, and the concrete strategies to be pursued if a fuller realization of the universal is to be effected in different spheres of modern social life. In addition, reflecting on Bourdieu from a Deweyan perspective will allow for some of the genuine shortcomings in Bourdieu's way of thinking to be identified and reconstructed. Indeed, Bourdieu did have much to learn from Dewey's theory of creative democracy. In his overriding concern to uncover the workings of power and domination, he failed to appreciate fully the possibilities of creative and democratic action. If an approach stressing in equal measure both domination and democracy is to be our goal, then it will be useful to reconsider Bourdieusian sociology while keeping Dewey's theory of democracy very much in mind.

Such is our agenda in this chapter. In the first major section, we identify the key similarities and continuities between Deweyan pragmatism and Bourdieusian sociology. Some of these parallels were noted by Bourdieu himself, but others were not. In a comprehensive overview we point out some of the striking affinities between the two bodies of work. In the next two sections, we indicate some of the important ways in which Bourdieu can be said to have gone beyond Dewey, at least in terms of grasping the main contours of modern social life and its inner dynamics of domination, reproduction, and transformation. Then, in the final major section of the essay, we turn to specifying what Dewey nonetheless continues to offer, which in a phrase can be summed up as a more vital and compelling vision of creative democracy. Putting the two together, we develop some tentative ideas regarding the social conditions of possibility for creativity and freedom.

I

Many of the ideas we develop here could also be elaborated with reference to classical pragmatists besides Dewey, not to mention other social thinkers of the day, such as Jane Addams, the important theorist of racial democracy Alain Locke, and later social critics in the pragmatist camp like the young Sidney Hook and perhaps C. Wright Mills, both of whom were also oriented toward critical social science, and perhaps still other, more recent figures. However, it is the sheer breadth of Dewey's work, which encompasses the history of philosophy, the theory of action, and democracy, among other topics, which makes him the most appropriate and useful of all the authors in that tradition to consider in tandem with Bourdieu. So in the present context, we shall confine ourselves to highlighting a few important issues in Dewey's work, issues that will prove especially instructive when we turn later to considering Bourdieusian sociology.[4]

The first of these issues is Dewey's antifoundationalism, developed through an elucidation of philosophy's age-old denial of experience and of practice. In Dewey's view, the ancient Greeks distanced themselves from the analogical reasoning of myth and practice and moved toward reasoning through logic. They created an intellectual space in which to contemplate the troubles of the world and to add to a canon of received truth. The result of this "quest for certainty," to invoke the title of one of his major works, was a disastrous division between the ideal and the material, thinking and acting, theory and practice.[5] Modern philosophy, too, was lent a dualistic cast by René Descartes's search for "clear, distinct, and certain" foundations of knowledge and his sharp divide between Body and Mind, the material and the mental. As Stephen Toulmin (1990: 75) noted in a work deeply influenced by Dewey's *The Quest for Certainty* (1988e [1929]), "The Cartesian program for philosophy swept aside the 'reasonable' uncertainties and hesitations of [past philosophy], in favor of new, mathematical kinds of 'rational' certainty and proof. . . . That change of attitude—the devaluation of the oral, the particular, the local, the timely, and the concrete—appeared a small price to pay for a formally 'rational' theory grounded on abstract, universal, timeless concepts."

Dewey sought to recover, by contrast, the world of experience and practice. This world, he pointed out in *Experience and Nature* (1988c [1925]), was characterized, among other things, by uncertainty as well as stability; knowledge should aspire to practical judgment, not theoretical certitude. In addition, the world of experience was marked by ceaseless change. Even seemingly substantial objects were only relatively so: experience was a flow of events, "an affair of affairs" (Dewey 1988c [1925]: 83). Moreover, this world of affairs was eminently relational: for Dewey, there could be no separation of the qualities of the affairs of experience one from another, as in the Cartesian dualism of things experienced and those who experience them. Dewey was highly critical of philosophers and social thinkers who remained caught up in these binaries. What was required, he believed, for an adequate grasp of the nature of experience was a "trans-actional approach," one involving "the seeing together, when research requires it, of what before had been seen in separations and held severally apart" (Dewey and Bentley 1991 [1949]: 112).

One of the pillars of Dewey's faith was the notion that humans could intervene in the stream of events or affairs of experience and redirect their course. The better they understood how experience was ordered, the more effective those practical interventions would be. Dewey conceived of inquiry as a process that both began and ended in "directly experienced subject-matter" (Dewey 1988c [1925]: 11). It began with experience in the sense that experience posed to inquiry its questions and problems. Experience presented to people a roadblock, a fork in the road, new situations for which their regular channels of thought and action would not suffice, conflicts or ruptures in practice that caused them perplexity. It also provided them the data and the raw materials for their investigations. Inquiry ended with experience in the sense that its findings then had to be put to the pragmatic test, to see how much they helped to illuminate experience and to allow for its practical reconstruction. The process of thinking, Dewey observed, was "not aimless, random, miscellaneous, but purposeful, specific, and limited by the character of the trouble undergone" (Dewey 1988a [1920]: 161). Humans systematically examined the facts of the situation, critically observed what was before them, and sought in creative ways—and in an experimentalist spirit—to clarify what was causing their perplexity and to attend to it.

This was surely true of ordinary everyday inquiry, but it was also and especially true of the sort of empirical inquiry that characterized modern experimental science, a particularly effective method, in Dewey's view, for comprehending and acting upon the world of events. This method now promised to bring theory back into a more meaningful connection with practice: no longer did practice have to proceed blindly or by trial and error or in accordance with custom and authority; it could now call for guidance on a knowledge that had for its own part forsaken the quest for certainty: "The new scientific development," Dewey wrote, "effects an exchange of reason for intelligence.... A man is intelligent . . . in virtue of his capacity to estimate the possibilities of a situation and to act in accordance with his estimate. In the large sense of the term, intelligence is as practical as reason is theoretical" (Dewey 1988e [1929]: 169–70).

Dewey noted that intelligence could be brought to bear upon even the most mundane of our everyday practices. Typically, humans engaged in a relatively unreflective form of action. "Men do not, in their natural estate, think," he observed, "when they have no troubles to cope with, no difficulties to overcome" (Dewey 1988a [1920]: 160). This did not mean, however, that they were mere automatons. In his understanding, which has been described by a recent commentator (Joas 1996) as a "non-teleological interpretation of the intentionality of action," habits were "acquired predisposition[s] to *ways* or modes of response, not to particular acts"; they were a form of embodied history, "human activity which is influenced by prior activity and in that sense acquired; which contains within itself a certain ordering or systematization of minor elements of action; [and] which is projective, dynamic in quality, [and] ready for overt manifestation" (Dewey 1988b [1922]: 32, 31).

Dewey by no means saw such habitual activity in a denigratory light, although he did note that in many instances it could be unimaginative and deadening (and this applied as well to the habits of thought of philosophers and social thinkers). What he envisioned was that habits could themselves be made more intelligent, indeed, that not only intelligent habits but also habits of intelligence could take root and thrive. Such an eventuality—and here we return to Dewey's distinctive vision of democracy—would require a reconstruction not only of habits but also of the social conditions of their production and reproduction. To achieve it would require an extended process of reform, one aided and abetted by a critical and pragmatic science of society.

Turning to Bourdieu, we see remarkable similarities to Dewey. Like Dewey, Bourdieu eschewed the search for foundations, or what he called the "illusion of foundations," saying, in *Pascalian Meditations* (Bourdieu 2000b [1997]: 115), that philosophy and the social sciences are properly "sciences without a foundation, forced to accept themselves as historical through and through, destroying every founding ambition." Throughout his work, he rejected the division between theory and practice, focusing attention instead on the level of concrete, lived experience and avoiding the abstractions and idealizations that prevail in so much of sociology and democratic theory. *Skholé*, or conditions of leisure and separation from the practical necessities of life, were what especially conduced to the development of scholastic dispositions and tendencies of thought. Such ways of thinking were much in evidence in the philosophy and social thought of his times.

Bourdieu argued that overcoming the limitations of scholasticism had, as one of its prime consequences, the uncovering of the distinctive logic of practice. Much like Dewey, he developed a theory of practical action that stressed its nonteleological nature—how action is "directed towards certain ends without being consciously directed to these ends, or determined by them" (Bourdieu 1990e: 10)—avoiding simultaneously the shortcomings of both intentionalist finalism and mechanistic causalism. In his theory, social agents were neither rational calculators nor automatons; his alternative way of thinking consisted in allowing actors agency without conceding that their actions are the product of a utility function. Central to all of this was the idea of the habitus, understood by Bourdieu as a system of dispositions or a "feel for the game . . . *acquired through experience*" (Bourdieu 1990e: 9).

Like Dewey, Bourdieu was suspicious of the intellectual dispositions and habitus of *homo academicus*. In his view, philosophers and social thinkers tended to approach issues in a relatively unreflexive and taken-for-granted fashion, relying on the *doxic* prenotions and habits of thought of both their scholastic environments and their broader social lifeworld. In particular, he inveighed against tendencies, all too common in academia, to think in substantialist rather than relational terms (he derived this idea not from Dewey but from a contemporary of Dewey's, Ernst Cassirer), to rely on standard epistemological couplets and dualisms, many with deep roots in Cartesian philosophy, and to dehistoricize and naturalize social reality. Bourdieu also criticized—again, in a fashion very reminiscent of Dewey—the false division between theory and substantive research, arguing that the two were inseparable, both of them mere aspects of scientific research practice. In his view, the task before us was to cultivate a new "scientific habitus," a new "*modus operandi* [to] practically guide and structure scientific practice" (Bourdieu and Wacquant 1992: 161).

Like the democratic community of science envisioned by Dewey, Bourdieu offered a vision of "a genuine scientific field" both conducive to the development of such a habitus and fueled by the research activities generated by it. This field would revolve around "rational communication" and function as "a space where researchers agreed on the grounds of disagreement and on the instruments with which to resolve these disagreements and on nothing else" (Bourdieu and Wacquant 1992: 176). In such a field, individual scientists or scholars would advance their own particular interests by also advancing the universal, or knowledge of the truth about the social world. This new "*Real-*

politik of reason" would presuppose the continued autonomy of scientific inquiry vis-à-vis outside societal forces, particularly those emanating from the economy, politics, or state bureaucracy, an autonomy that Bourdieu, especially in his later years, was less and less inclined to take for granted.

Scientific work, however, would by no means confine itself to the ivory tower. The field of science would ideally be restricted and autonomous—but also open to the larger world. In something akin to a pragmatist Deweyan spirit, Bourdieu's work emphasized not only the need for a steep "entrance fee" into the world of scientific research but also, on the other end, the need or "duty to exit"—and hence the broader moral-practical mission of a scholarship with commitment (Bourdieu 2003b). Good intentions may not make for good science, he often pointed out, but ultimately science and scholarship have a duty to intervene in the larger world of social relations: "I believe that when sociology remains at a highly abstract and formal level, it contributes nothing. When it gets down to the nitty gritty of real life, however, it is an instrument that people can apply to themselves for quasi-clinical purposes" (Bourdieu and Wacquant 1992: 198).

Accordingly, Bourdieu devoted himself to sociological inquiries intended to shed light on the causes and effects of human suffering. He uncovered the social mechanisms whereby actors deprive themselves and others of possibilities of liberation, growth, and creativity—in a word, of a democratic way of life. From his earliest studies of colonial Algeria and provincial Béarn, to his midcareer work on education, politics, and social class in France, to his researches, later in life, on global neoliberalism and the retrenchment of the welfare state, he pursued scholarly work as a way of engaging indirectly in democratic politics. (Few scholars of the twentieth century since Dewey had taken on such a sweeping range of topics in the interest of social critique.) Moreover, Bourdieu undertook this work without succumbing either to the party line of sectarian leftist politics or to the empty sloganeering of a mainstream pseudo-Left. Like Dewey in this respect as well, he elevated the democratic ideal above all the seducements of conventional or even radical politics.

II

In all these ways Bourdieu's thought was strikingly reminiscent of Dewey's, despite being the product of an altogether different intellectual culture and despite Bourdieu's living—and writing—some half a century or more after Dewey himself. As we noted, however, Bourdieu superseded Dewey in important respects. Despite Dewey's remarkable breadth, his capacity to address powerfully core issues in social and historical inquiry and to anticipate and chart many of the directions in which these investigations would unfold, his democratic agenda was necessarily constrained by the fact that he approached social science questions from a lay humanistic perspective and, beyond that, by the state of development—theoretical as well as methodological—of the social sciences themselves in his day. By contrast, Bourdieu—himself trained as a philosopher at the Ecole Normale Supérieure, where he began his studies just a few months before Dewey's death, but more and more oriented toward ethnology and sociology over his subsequent years—was in a much better position to elaborate and implement the program Dewey had been calling for but was unable adequately to pursue.

In particular, Bourdieu was able to develop transactional, relational thinking in the direction of a theory of social fields, or of spaces of forces and of struggles. Often, when Dewey spoke of the democratic ideal and of social obstacles thereto, he committed what Bourdieu called the "short-circuit fallacy"—that of focusing on the social space as a whole without taking account of the mediating effects of the structures and dynamics of specific fields. Indeed, when speaking of the social space, Dewey placed primary analytic weight upon divisions based on class, very broadly defined, and did so in a loose, unsystematic fashion. By contrast, Bourdieu was able to work out a sophisticated theory of historical differentiation, one that owed much to Max Weber's idea of the growing autonomy of life-spheres, which took seriously the internal organization and logic of multiple social microcosms and which raised the question, both logical and empirical, of their interrelation. Modern society, he claimed, is marked not by the ascendancy of any one singular logic like that of class relations but by the existence of a number of more or less independent social universes which, although mutually determinative, nonetheless obey, to some extent, their own inner laws and principles. "What happens in [any one of these fields]," he wrote, "cannot be understood by looking only at external factors" (Bourdieu 1998c: 39).

This field-theoretic approach, which also involves a dramatic reworking of the ideas of capital and interest or *illusio*, constituted one of Bourdieu's most important advances vis-à-vis the theory of modernity elaborated by Dewey. It enabled him to explore systematically all the disparate domains of social life in which something approaching freedom and creativity could take hold: the state and politics and also the family, gender relations, art, the economy, and education. Democratic struggles were field-specific, and each relatively autonomous social world allowed (or disallowed) a "freer and more humane experience" in its own way.[6] Accordingly, each had to be studied on its own terms, with an eye not only to the (heteronomous) forces impinging on it from the outside, among which, as we shall see, money and power were preeminent, but also to its own (autonomous) structures and dynamics.

Bourdieu conceived of fields as "configuration[s] of objective relations between positions" (Bourdieu and Wacquant 1992: 97); any given field could be conceptualized as a structure of relations not between the concrete entities themselves but between the nodes which those entities happen to occupy. Positions in a field, including its dominant and dominated poles, needed to be analyzed in terms of the distinctive profiles of capital associated with them. For Bourdieu, capitals functioned both as weapons and as stakes in struggles to gain ascendancy within a field. Any field (from a synchronic perspective) was a structure or temporary state of power relations within what was also (from a diachronic perspective) an ongoing struggle for domination waged by the deployment or accumulation of relevant capitals, a struggle for successful monopolization "of the legitimate violence (specific authority) which is characteristic of the field in question" (Bourdieu 1993a [1980]: 73).

Bourdieu's perspective brought to the fore the structural tension between occupants of dominant and dominated positions in a given social space. It required that any field be conceptualized as a terrain of contestation among occupants of positions differentially endowed with the resources necessary for gaining and safeguarding an ascendant position. Indeed, much of the contestation among actors could be said to concern the legitimate valuation to be accorded the precise species of capital in which they happened, actually or potentially, to be well endowed. In making such arguments, Bourdieu placed structure, domination, and struggle at the very center of sociological analysis. From his action-theoretic starting point Dewey had been unable to move far in this direction, as had others in the pragmatist tradition, such as Hook and Mills, who also lacked the theoretical apparatus for pursuing such an agenda systematically.

Among the fields Bourdieu examined closely, perhaps the ones most directly relevant to the study of democracy were the field of power, the state (or what he called the bureaucratic field), and the political field. The field of power was the Marxian idea of a ruling class reworked in such a fashion that its substantialist features had been rendered thoroughly relational and transactional. Bourdieu conceived of it as a space in which the dominants of society, that is, the preeminent holders of its major assets or varieties of capital, were arrayed and pitted against each other in a ceaseless struggle for ascendancy. Crucial here was the contestation between dominants in the field of cultural production and dominants in the field of the capitalist economy: "The field of power . . . is a space of the relations of force between the different kinds of capital . . . whose struggles intensify whenever the relative value of [these capitals] is questioned (for example, the exchange rate between cultural capital and economic capital)" (Bourdieu 1998d [1994]: 34).

Bourdieu added that, despite this ongoing contestation, the dominants of their respective fields also shared in a certain complicity in, or commitment to, the field of power, resulting in what he termed, in a memorable phrase, an "organic solidarity in the division of the labor of domination" (Bourdieu 1996b [1989]: 386). In other words, underlying the mutual opposition of these powerful actors was a common investment in the perpetuation of a social order of which they were the beneficiaries. Key state officials, leading lawyers and jurists, top bankers, financiers, and corporate executives, prestigious literary, artistic, and scientific figures—all were structurally likely to favor strategies for conserving the social order, even as they sought also to undermine each other's legitimacy. In their contestations, the contours and dynamics of society as a whole were decisively determined.[7]

Bourdieu's conceptualization retained traces of its origins in Marxist thought: it was economistic (i.e., relative to the other forms of capital, economic capital was deemed the first among equals[8]); it focused on social as opposed to cultural relations (i.e., it emphasized the priority of the space of [social] positions vis-à-vis the space of [cultural] position takings[9]); and it said little about the alternative modes of civil association through which societal or institutional power might be contested (i.e., it failed to theorize the possibility of an oppositional public sphere, something about which we shall have more to say below[10]). Nonetheless, the idea of a field of power allowed Bourdieu to direct analytic attention to the workings of domination at the most elevated levels. It shed light on the structures and dynamics of power in the most privileged and rarefied of elite circles. Thereby, it marked a decisive step beyond Dewey's comparatively underdeveloped critiques of the ruling stratum in modern society. Any analysis of democracy and its prospects would have to take the field of power carefully and systematically into account.

Bourdieu asserted that the field of power arose historically in conjunction with the modern state, which he conceptualized as itself a space or field—specifically, as a field of bureaucratic powers. In contrast to prevailing conceptions of the state as "a well-defined, clearly bounded, and unitary reality" (Bourdieu and Wacquant 1992: 111), he conceived of it as "an ensemble of administrative or bureaucratic fields (they often take the empirical form of commissions, bureaus, and boards) within which agents and categories of agents, governmental and nongovernmental, struggle over this peculiar form of authority consisting of the power to *rule* via legislation, regulations, [and] administrative measures (subsidies, authorizations, restrictions, etc.)" (Bourdieu and Wacquant 1992: 111). For Bourdieu, the field of power was closely linked to the state insofar as the former constituted a "space of play in which [the] holders of various forms of capital struggle *in particular* for power over the [latter], that is, over the statist capital that grants power over the different species of capital and over their reproduction" (Bourdieu and Wacquant 1992: 114–15).

In a number of his political writings, especially toward the latter part of his career, Bourdieu elaborated a theory of the modern state that divided the major functions and ministries of that field into a right and a left hand: that is, an orientation toward security, taxation, law enforcement, and war making, on the one hand, and education, housing, health, and social welfare, on the other. With the retrenchment of the welfare state, he observed, "the left hand of the state has the sense that the right hand no longer knows, or, worse, no longer really wants to know what the left hand does. In any case, it does not want to pay for it" (Bourdieu 1998d: 2). In other words, the left hand of the state was increasingly undermined by budgetary cutbacks and sheer indifference, a failure or growing refusal on the part of the state in times of neoliberalism to serve as "the guardian of the public interest" (Bourdieu 1998d: 2). In Bourdieu's view, this failure had important implications for the poor and the downtrodden, as demonstrated in his coauthored ethnographic volume, *The Weight of the World* (Bourdieu and Accardo 1999); moreover, it was highly consequential for popular struggles on behalf of a more just, egalitarian, and progressive society. Not without reason, he became consumed with the fight against neoliberalism throughout the final decade of his life.

However, for Bourdieu the state was also the target of struggles not only over material resources but also over symbolic power. Its capacity to impose structures of thought, feeling, and action, categories "we spontaneously apply to all things of the social world—including the state itself" (Bourdieu 1998d [1994]: 35)—was, in fact, perhaps its most important feature. The state was able to impose these categories on minds and bodies alike through institutions as diverse as schooling, the census, and family policy. By such means, it produced a kind of "logical conformism" (Bourdieu borrowed the phrase from Durkheim) and rendered the social order legitimate, unquestionable, and natural. "The state does not necessarily have to give orders or to exercise physical coercion in order to produce an ordered social world, as long as it is capable of producing embodied cognitive structures that accord with objective structures and thus of ensuring . . . doxic submission to the established order" (Bourdieu 1998d [1994]: 56). No democracy would be possible so long as this symbolic power went unchecked. Much of Bourdieu's life's work was devoted to analyzing how the state operates outside the scope of democratic oversight—"beneath [the level of] consciousness and choice" (Bourdieu 1998d [1994]: 56–57)—to induce compliance. "When it comes to the state," he asserted, "one never doubts enough" (Bourdieu 1998d [1994]: 36).

The last of the fields analyzed by Bourdieu that bore important implications for democracy was the political field. Conceptually distinct from both the field of power and the state, it entailed all those phenomena typically associated with electoral politics: leaders, spokespersons, propagandists, and political parties; the consumers of these political products (i.e., the public, voters); and the campaigns in which political professionals compete for the people's vote. Among the most significant features of this field, Bourdieu contended, was the unequal distribution of political capital and of the authority to speak on behalf of others, that is, the monopolization of political power. Dominants of the political field—those who controlled "the instruments of production of an explicitly formulated representation of the social world" (Bourdieu 1991e: 171)—engaged with one another in a competitive, self-interested game as much as they struggled to represent and advance their constituents' interests. To a considerable degree, they inhabited a world far removed and insulated from the concerns of the dominated, an "*esoteric culture*," in Bourdieu's (1991e: 184) words, "comprised of problems that are completely alien or inaccessible to ordinary people, of concepts and discourses that are without referents in the experience of ordinary citizens and, especially, of distinctions, nuances, subtleties, and niceties that pass unnoticed by the uninitiated."

What counterbalanced this orientation inward on the part of political leaders was their need to appeal continually to a broader electorate, that is, to mobilize political support: "In order to triumph in their internal struggles, professionals have to appeal to forces which are not all, and not totally, internal" (Bourdieu 1991e: 189). Bourdieu stressed that, in making their appeals, leaders helped to constitute the very groups whose support they aspired to harness, those very groups from which they ultimately derived their power. Classes (and other such groups) were always constructed entities, products of efforts at political mobilization and group making, just as political power was always in turn the channeled or embodied energy of those groups once called into existence. "The group can exist," Bourdieu wrote, "only by delegating power to a spokesperson who will bring it into existence by speaking for it, that is, on its behalf and in its place. [It] is created by the person who speaks in its name, thus appearing as the source of the power that he exerts over those who are its real source" (Bourdieu 1991e: 249). By exploring these mutually reinforcing dynamics, Bourdieu focused attention on a question of fundamental importance: does political representation make for dispossession or for democracy? On this score, he himself seemed not entirely sanguine.

A final element in Bourdieu's portrayal of the political field was the concept of "rites of institution." This pertained to all those rituals, ceremonials, and formal practices that serve to demarcate boundaries and to signal who is in and who is out: "the important thing," he noted, "is the line" (Bourdieu 1991e: 118). One of the "essential effects" of such a rite of institution, Bourdieu observed, was "separating those who have undergone it, not from those who have not yet undergone it, but from those who will not undergo it in any sense, and thereby instituting a lasting difference between those to whom the rite pertains and those to whom it does not pertain" (Bourdieu 1991e: 117). It constituted one of the most significant means whereby arbitrary distinctions between groups are socially instituted and consecrated. This "social magic" (Bourdieu 1991e: 119) raised once again the issue of how arbitrary boundaries can be denaturalized, how barriers to entry can be delegitimized, and how excluded or profanized groups can contest their domination. Here, too, there seemed little possibility of a genuine way out. Would lines merely be replaced by other lines?

III

Bourdieu's sociology of fields was simultaneously a theory of the habitus. In this respect as well, Bourdieu can be said to have pursued questions closely parallel to those explored much earlier by the classical American pragmatists. Dewey was deeply concerned from the start with the educational process, in particular with how dispositions and habits are shaped through early childhood socialization. Indeed, he deemed education one of the primary means of constructing a more democratic society, underscoring in *Democracy and Education* (1985 [1916]: 93), his major contribution to educational philosophy, the importance to democracy of "deliberate and systematic" instruction. Dewey did not inquire, however, into how democratic dispositions and habits could be unified across different life circumstances (like the "affinity of style" among different practices alluded to by Bourdieu in *The State Nobility* 1996b [1989]: 272–73). Nor did he show how dispositions and habits could give rise to new patterns of action in response to unforeseen or novel situations.[11] By contrast, for Bourdieu the habitus was not only a system of dispositions, phenomenally perhaps distinct from one another but objectively unified, but also a generative principle—indeed, of actions that could be strikingly improvisatory and flexible.

Bourdieu (2000b [1997]: 164) argued that the habitus underwent continual development over the course of a lifetime, beginning with the "primary habitus" shaped by early family experience and evolving into one or more "specific habitus" (plural) corresponding to the various differentiated fields of modern social life. Since actors typically moved back and forth amidst a wide range of relatively autonomous spaces, it was even possible for them to develop a fractured or cleft habitus. Bourdieu first developed the idea of a fractured habitus in respect to rural Algerians faced with the dislocations of colonial rule and capitalist modernization. But in later writings he found a divided, tormented habitus in many other categories of people in modern society as well. Famously, he declared that even he himself, a provincial who had risen to the very apex of French academic life, suffered from a "cleft habitus" (Bourdieu 2008b: 100). Few if any antecedents for such an idea had existed in Dewey, although he did speak briefly in *Human Nature and Conduct* (1988b [1922]: 90) of "different institutions foster[ing] antagonistic impulses and form[ing] contrary dispositions." (One can also argue that neither thinker fully appreciated the possibility that, in a polysemic, complex, and contradictory world, cleft habitus might become, in fact, less the exception than the rule.)

Through his concept of the habitus, Bourdieu was able to illuminate the workings of what he termed symbolic violence. By this, he meant the perpetuation of domination by means of the active complicity of the dominated. Domination was not merely a matter of external coercion; it also operated internally (indeed, unconsciously) through "bodily emotions—shame, humiliation, timidity, guilt" (Bourdieu 2001b: 38); idealization of the oppressor; self-denigration; and acceptance of the principles of evaluation favored by the dominant. In Dewey, the idea of habitual conduct had never served double duty quite so explicitly as a theory of social reproduction, although his critique of traditionalism in education (he termed it custom [1988b (1922)]) did open up possibilities for just such a development. In Bourdieu, the concept of symbolic violence served as perhaps the lynchpin of his entire sociology.

Bourdieu stressed that the dominated were not to blame for their own victimization. His theory of symbolic violence was nothing if not a repudiation of such a stance. "If it is fitting to recall," he wrote, "that the dominated always contribute to their own domination, it is at once necessary to recall that the dispositions that incline them toward this complicity are themselves the effect, embodied, of domination" (Bourdieu 1996b [1989]: 4). However, the contribution of the less privileged to their own subjugation did need to be confronted squarely and not brushed aside, awkward as it might be to acknowledge. Symbolic violence was among the most important impediments to the realization of a democratic society. If social thinkers were to ignore it, they would be turning a blind eye to one of the principal means whereby humans' lack of freedom and suffering are perpetuated.

Among the best known of Bourdieu's critical analyses of the habitus and its role in the reproduction of domination was his inquiry into what it means to have—or not have—a political opinion. First in pieces such as "Public Opinion Does Not Exist" (1993a [1980]) and then in a celebrated chapter of *Distinction* (1984a: chap. 8), he explored how differences in specific political competence—

actors' "greater or lesser capacity to recognize a political question as political and to treat it as such by responding to it politically, i.e., on the basis of specifically political principles"—could be traced back to differences in actors' social standing and primary habitus. Their capacity to proffer a political opinion, as opposed to remaining silent or abstaining, was "inseparable from a more or less strong feeling of being *competent*, in the full sense of the word, that is, socially recognized as entitled to deal with political affairs, to express an opinion about them or even modify their course." In Bourdieu's view, authorized speech found its counterpart in "both impotence and objective and subjective exclusion ('That is none of my business'; 'That doesn't interest me')"; the result was at best a "selective democracy" (Bourdieu 1984a: 300).

Underlying Bourdieu's analyses of symbolic violence was the theme of the double historicity of the habitus. In his view, the habitus was nothing if not drenched in history—it was history embodied and incorporated—while the social structures whence it came were themselves "issued," as he put it, "out of the historical work of succeeding generations" (Bourdieu and Wacquant 1992: 139). Both habitus and field, in other words, were nothing but different and interrelated modes of existence of history. By means of such insights, Bourdieu further developed and radicalized the Deweyan notion that experience is fundamentally about eventfulness and process rather than fixity, stability, or permanence. Indeed, Bourdieu was always intent, from the very start of his career, on elaborating a radically temporalized theory of social life. Time was his great obsession, from his earliest work (inspired by Edmund Husserl) on the temporal orientations of protension and projectivity right up to his latest writings, such as the chapter "Social Being, Time, and the Sense of Existence" toward the end of *Pascalian Meditations*. We shall be discussing in greater detail below his use of the Husserlian distinction between protension and projectivity.

Bourdieu deployed his understanding of the historicity of experience, both societal and individual, "to step back," as he put it, "and gain distance from dispositions" (Bourdieu and Wacquant 1992: 136)—thereby also from symbolic violence. A line he liked to repeat in his writings was, "The Stoics used to say that what depends upon us is not the first move but only the second one." In other words, reflexivity could allow us to gain a limited but very real control over the inclinations of our habitus, transforming us from the agents of action into something more like the true subjects of action. This could happen, Bourdieu suggested, at the levels both of political practice and of sociological scholarship.

In politics, what was called for were efforts to "neutralize the mechanisms of the neutralization of history," to put "history in motion again," to denaturalize long-reified ways of thinking, feeling, and acting. Dispositions to-ward self-subordination before authority—the self-denying verdict that "this is not for the likes of us"—could not be allowed to stand. "To point out," wrote Bourdieu, "that what appears, in history, as being eternal is merely the prod-uct of a labour of eternalization performed by interconnected institutions such as the family, the church, the state, [and] the education system . . . is to reinsert into history, and therefore to restore to historical action, [processes] that the naturalistic and essentialist vision removes from them" (Bourdieu 2001b: viii). The hard cake of traditionalism and of mental structures favoring the dominant was indeed, as Dewey had also noted, the enemy of creative action.

The difficulty was that encrusted habits went all the way down. In a manner reminiscent of Dewey (1988b [1922]: chap. 2), who argued that wish and effort alone cannot fundamentally transform long-standing habits, Bourdieu stressed that deeply embedded and corporealized ways of being in the world had to be transformed slowly and laboriously; a sudden conversion of the will was un-feasible and would never do. What was urgently needed was not an effort at consciousness raising but a thoroughgoing reconstruction of the habitus. In *Democracy in America* (1966 [1835/40]: 287), Alexis de Tocqueville had sug-gested that liberty requires the cultivation of certain mores and "habits of the heart"; so, too, Bourdieu contended that overcoming symbolic violence and achieving a degree of freedom from domination entail a basic reshaping and reconstitution of dispositions. What would such a politics of the habitus look like? Although Bourdieu was not entirely clear, he indicated that the best way to proceed entailed targeting the full ensemble of social institutions (e.g., family, church, state, and education) responsible for producing habitus in the first place. If these institutions and the socialization processes taking place in them could be altered, then the cycle of reproduction of self-defeating, self-destructive habits could effectively be broken.

At the level of scholarship, Bourdieu spoke as well of the importance of gain-ing a critical distance from our dispositions. In *Pascalian Meditations* (2000b [1997]: chap. 1), he distinguished among three successively more searching and penetrating modes of critical reflexivity. Ideally, reflexivity would seek to make visible the effects on one's thinking of occupying a certain position in the social space; of adhering to the *doxa* that define specific and delimited fields within that space; and of being shaped by life experiences marked by distance from practical necessities (*skholé*), "of which the academic world represents the in-stitutionalized form" (Bourdieu 2000b [1997]: 13). The last of these was espe-cially significant, for social thinkers were often drawn by the conditions of their intellectual production and by the intellectual dispositions produced by those conditions to elaborate thoroughly ahistorical and atemporal ways of thinking. Given his abiding concerns with historicity and temporality, Bourdieu found this separation of sociological from historical inquiry deplorable, calling it a "*disastrous division*" (Bourdieu and Wacquant 1992: 90). Social thinkers would do well to turn a critical and reflexive gaze, he felt, back upon their own endeavors and objectify and historicize themselves as the professionals of historical objectification.

If social thinkers could become in this way reflexively more aware of the effects on their own work of scholastic privilege, of living and thinking at a remove from the urgencies of material existence, it would mark a crucial step toward the opening up of inquiry and an enlargement, at least to some degree, of their freedom from determination. In particular, it would allow sociological analysts of democracy to begin gaining some control over (and freedom with respect to) the unacknowledged forces otherwise working through them and behind their backs. Bourdieu stressed that such reflexive labor might be undertaken most effectively not by the solitary or heroic intellectual but by a community of inquirers bound together by a logic of peer competition and "regulated struggle" (Bourdieu 2004b: 62). In a fashion much more realistic than that of Dewey—he liked, after all, to invoke Machiavelli and the idea of a *Realpolitik* of reason—he looked to the rules of contestation within the scientific field to help further the work of critical socioanalysis. Much as Freud (1965 [1933]: 71) had once declared, "Where id was, there ego shall be," Bourdieu hoped that this mechanism of collective socioanalysis would help to emancipate social thinkers from the structures that constituted their own intellectual and scholarly unconscious.

IV

What might these terms *socioanalysis* and *unconscious* signify? Bourdieu used them in interesting, revealing ways. What strikes us as significant is that they lead directly into the more utopian and liberatory moment in Bourdieu's thought. They expose the hidden template to which he always returned in articulating this aspect of his vision. For in all his later writings, Bourdieu seemed to have Freud very much in mind, referring throughout to such notions as social defense mechanisms, the social unconscious, libido and cathexis, and the collective work of anamnesis; this was, in fact, a feature of his thought not stressed nearly enough by commentators.[12] To understand it, one must bear in mind that Freud, certainly more than Dewey or the other classical pragmatists, enjoyed a significant presence in France throughout the years of Bourdieu's early formation. Indeed, Bourdieu's mentor, Gaston Bachelard, spoke of the scientific enterprise in ways that evinced a profound debt to

Freudian thinking, referring to Freud often in his important work *The Forma-tion of the Scientific Mind* (2002 [1938]).

Deeply influenced by Bachelard, Bourdieu came to believe that socioanaly-sis could do more to help people comprehend and master the forces that dominate them than even the prolonged, arduous labors of psychoanalysis. At the very least it could complement psychoanalysis in a sort of joint labor of emancipation. Critical social science could gain some measure of conscious control over its otherwise unconscious dynamics of knowledge production. In this way it could generate not merely a spontaneous or folk sociology but a genuinely critical and liberatory self-knowledge. "Breach[ing] the *sacred boundary* . . . between *scholarship* and *commitment*," Bourdieu (2003b: 24) wrote, such a social science could contribute to the project of humanity's conquest of freedom.

For all that he learned from Freudian psychoanalysis, however, Bourdieu would have benefited at least as much, if not more, from Deweyan pragma-tism. Building as he did on psychoanalysis rather than on pragmatism, he missed out on valuable opportunities to speak to issues of democracy at the levels both of action theory and of theories of the public sphere. Bourdieu only incompletely developed something like a category of practical judgment or intelligence in action. Such a category was surely missing in Freud, al-though some might argue it was at least implied by the psychoanalytic ideal of ego rationality. Certainly it was present in Bourdieu, albeit latently; his discus-sions of "fuzzy logic," for example, in *The Logic of Practice* (1990a [1980]), are full of references to something on that order. However, to our mind, he never extended that notion from the domain of relatively unreflective action to that of more thoughtful, deliberate action guided by (or undertaken in the spirit of) modern science.

The only category Bourdieu presented as an alternative to those instances in which there is an immediate, spontaneous "fit between habitus and field" was strategic calculation, as in rational choice theory, which is not quite the same thing as Deweyan intelligence. "Times of crises," he said, "in which the routine adjustment of subjective and objective structures is brutally disrupted" —one will recognize here that Bourdieu was referring precisely to the type of situation the pragmatists had in mind when speaking of the initiation of in-quiry—"constitute a class of circumstances when indeed '*rational choice*' may take over" (Bourdieu and Wacquant 1992: 131). Bourdieu very likely found Deweyan ideas of intelligent judgment and practical wisdom highly congenial and appealing, but he fell short, in any case, in developing such ideas himself, resting content with the dualism of practical and rational action, perhaps the greatest of the dualisms unattended to and unresolved in his life's work.

If Freud failed to provide Bourdieu with a way out of this Procrustean bed, it was Husserl who, as mentioned earlier, was largely responsible for his constructing it in the first place. From the beginning of Bourdieu's career, during his graduate studies and while conducting his earliest ethnographies in Algeria, he was deeply shaped in his thinking by Husserl's dualist phenomenology of time consciousness. He later recalled, in fact, that "during the whole time that I was writing *Sociologie de l'Algerie* and conducting my first ethnological fieldwork, I continued to write every evening on the structure of temporal experience according to Husserl" (2004b: 419). In Husserl's philosophy, a sharp distinction was drawn between "pre-perceptive anticipation," in which subjects engage, in Bourdieu's (1998d: 80, 81) words, in "a sort of practical induction based on previous experience," and the project, understood as a "*plan*, as a design for the future in which the subject thinks of herself as positing a future and mobilizing all disposable means by reference to that future posited as such, as an end before explicitly being attained."

This distinction gave rise, in Bourdieu's (1979a) Algerian studies, to a host of parallel theoretical dualisms, such as those between practical reason and calculation, the implicit and the explicit, concrete and abstract, prudence and ambition, foresight and forecasting. These dualisms made themselves felt throughout his later sociology as well. Indeed, Bourdieu never gave up thinking in terms of these dualisms—we can hear echoes of them still in his very latest writings—and not even Freudian theory, resting as it did upon the same dualist, indeed Kantian, philosophic bases as Husserlian phenomenology, could help him to see beyond them. (Although it is a complicated issue, Freud had in some respects a very narrow understanding of ego rationality, which was his alternative to unconsciously driven or dispositional action; this understanding all too easily reduced to the same kind of dualism that Bourdieu took away from Husserlian philosophy.)

A pragmatist alternative would have served Bourdieu far better than Freudian theory in his analyses of the emancipatory and democratic possibilities in social action. While such an alternative was never clearly worked out by Dewey or the other classical pragmatists, it is possible at least to imagine the lineaments of such a framework. In brief, a pragmatism-inspired theory of agency would reconceptualize human agency as a temporally embedded process of social engagement, one that simultaneously entails agentic orientations toward the past, the future, and the present.[13] It would emphasize that one or the other of these three temporal orientations typically predominates in any given empirical instance of action. For instance, a predominant orientation toward the past involves stress on the iterational moment of agency, "the selective reactivation of past patterns of thought and action, as routinely incorporated in practical activity" (Emirbayer and Mische 1998: 971). It is this iterational moment that corresponds most closely to what Bourdieu had in mind by the practical strategies of action generated by the dispositions of the habitus.

However, there is also analytic space in such a theory for two other moments of human agency. Projectivity, of which we have already seen one conceptualization in Husserl, entails an orientation predominantly toward the future, "the imaginative generation by actors of possible future trajectories of action, in which received structures of thought and action may be creatively reconfigured in relation to actors' hopes, fears, and desires for the future" (Emirbayer and Mische 1998: 971). This moment captures the pragmatists' characteristic stress upon actors' capacity to envision alternative possible futures and to pursue them in search of "a fuller and richer issue of events" (Dewey 1988e [1929]: 171). Practical evaluation, for its part, involves "the capacity of actors to make practical and normative judgments among alternative possible trajectories of action, in response to the emerging demands, dilemmas, and ambiguities of presently evolving situations" (Emirbayer and Mische 1998: 971). It is highly compatible with the pragmatists' idea of open-ended experimentation and creativity on the model of play or art, and it points as well in the direction of their ideal of intelligence in action.

Bourdieu's intellectual commitments caused him to lay great stress upon the first of these three temporal moments, while attending to the other two either implicitly and unsystematically or, in the case of projectivity in particular, by recourse to a simple, misleading opposition between dispositional and strategic action. Having an integral and comprehensive theory of agency, one encompassing projectivity and practical evaluation as well as iteration, would have allowed him greater analytic leeway when analyzing instances of transformative action, an important subject matter for a historically oriented sociology of democracy. His sociological inquiries would also have enjoyed greater analytic scope had projectivity not been occluded in favor of protension and had the moment of practical evaluation, too, not been left outside his framework, based as it was on an iterational, dispositional understanding of action.

The fact that Bourdieu did not make these theoretical moves sheds light on the controversies surrounding his work, which has always been accused of evincing a reproductive or cyclical bias, that is, of underscoring how domination perpetuates itself over time rather than of also explaining how domination can be lessened or opposed. After all, Bourdieu himself frequently pointed out how little freedom there actually is in social life. Similarly, his work has been accused of implying that only the heroic few can lead truly creative lives—on the model of the "virtuoso ethic" spoken of by Weber (1964 [1946]: chap. 11)—while all the rest are trapped in the snares of their own social positions and dispositions. Only Gustave Flaubert and Edouard Manet could inaugurate new fields of artistic endeavor, while only Bourdieu was able to play such a role in the history of sociology, a discipline that, throughout his youth, was less a field of contestation than a static "apparatus" dominated by the "Capitoline triad" of Talcott Parsons, Robert Merton, and Paul Lazarsfeld (see, for example, Bourdieu 2008b). (In both cases, the tension was between a moment of creativity, on the one hand, and a moment of academic sterility, on the other, of which the paradigm was the academic style in French painting on the eve of the impressionist revolution [see Bourdieu 1993c: chap. 9].) According to these critiques, free, creative action was always the exception in Bourdieu, never the rule.

Accusations of this sort are in many respects a gross distortion. Bourdieu's life's work, after all, was profoundly concerned with understanding and exploiting the specifically social possibilities of creativity and innovation, as we have seen. Never in *Distinction* (1984a), *The Rules of Art* (1996a), or elsewhere did he imply any sort of heroic exceptionalism. Nonetheless, these charges do have a degree of truth to them at the level of action theory, for Bourdieu left the creativity of action distinctly underanalyzed. The twin factors of ignorance of the full scope of Bourdieu's social thought and selective and distorted appropriation of that thought cannot, alone or together, explain why the charge has stuck so tenaciously over time. In ways that the perspective of Freudian psychoanalysis never could, pragmatism in the Deweyan experimentalist mode would have helped to rescue Bourdieu from this limitation. Beyond that, however, Bourdieu's work in yet another dimension—namely, that of the study of collective democratic endeavors—would also have been given a sounder basis by Deweyan pragmatism and democratic theory. The normative goals of the psychoanalytic enterprise were to lessen human misery and unhappiness by freeing the rational ego from the dictates of its repressed unconscious, but the aims of Dewey's agenda were much more expansive: to promote a democratic way of life, understood, in his well-known formulation, as "a mode of associated living, of conjoint communicated experience" (1985 [1916]: 93). Dewey's idea was that democracy would liberate human potentialities and foster an ongoing process of transformation or growth. This normative ideal was arguably more resonant with Bourdieu's vision for a better society than were the ideals of Freud, who indeed had a conception of sublimation but never elaborated it systematically.

In particular, Dewey's alternative would more directly and seamlessly have connected Bourdieu's vision to the grand tradition of Western democratic thought. It is often noted that Bourdieu himself did not have a clearly worked out theory of democracy. He certainly did not believe in the idea of civil society, a concept with a long, distinguished pedigree in democratic theory. "It is not easy," he wrote, "to determine concretely where the state ends and 'civil society' begins. . . . In fact, abandoning the dichotomy, . . . we have rather to speak the language of differential access to specifically bureaucratic resources —law, regulations, administrative powers, etc.—and to power over these resources, which the canonical distinction, as noble as it is empty, leads us to forget" (Bourdieu 2005b [2000]: 163–65). Nothing could have been farther in spirit from Dewey's own conceptualization of democracy.

What might a better alternative have looked like? Most important, it would have posited, as a complement to the field of power, a field of publicity in which actors strive to extend their sway over and across the major differentiated fields of modern social life.[14] In *The Public and Its Problems* (1988d [1927]: 245–46) Dewey defined publics as "all those who are affected by the indirect consequences of transactions to such an extent that it is deemed necessary to have those consequences systematically cared for." Wherever new modes of association emerged, he argued, and wherever these generated new indirect consequences, new publics would correspondingly arise. Similar ideas about publicity and a public sphere animated the work of such pragmatists as Jane Addams, George Herbert Mead, Alain Locke, and W. E. B. Du Bois. Common to them all was the notion that, ideally at least, publics can aspire to a widening of the sway of creativity and self-determination.

Bourdieu could have added his own inflection to this line of reasoning, showing that actors engage in public life in diverse ways depending on what position they occupy in social space. Actors' capacities for public engagement are a kind of capital not equally available to all, as we saw in the discussion of public opinion. Additionally, Bourdieu could have pointed out that publics which themselves occupy different locations in the field of publicity contend with one another just as vigorously as they contend with the fields they seek to influence. Which is the most legitimate public? Which is the most oppositional? Which represents the general interest most authentically? Finally, Bourdieu could have explored how the field of publicity engages with the field of power. While specific individuals from the field of power may take part in the field of publicity, the two can be seen as exhibiting inverse logics, the latter's basic commitment to the conservation of legitimate authority being at odds with the former's abiding concern with its subversion. He could further have stressed in this regard that publicity's subversive energies only sometimes point in a democratic direction; there are many antidemocratic publics and movements, after all. Indeed, he might have acknowledged that it is impossible to state unequivocally that the field of power is to the field of publicity what self-interest is to solidarity or what particularism is to universalism.

While Bourdieu did not move unambiguously in the direction of a Deweyan theory of publicity, he did believe in struggles to universalize the sway of the universal, to institute, as he put it, "a universe where all agents and their actors would be subject—notably through critique—to a kind of permanent test of universalizability which is practically instituted in the very logic of the field" (1998d [1994]: 144). The dynamic he identified, one he might well have termed (recalling Norbert Elias's [1994 (1939)] "monopoly mechanism") the universality mechanism, was one in which actors in various fields all invoke disinterestedness and universalistic ideals as part of their strategies for advancement. These actors, whether civil servants, scientific researchers, jurists, or political leaders, all strive to advance their particular interests in the fields of which they are a part, but in so doing also serve to advance the universal interest (as in the dynamic highlighted by La Rochefoucauld's maxim, "Hypocrisy is the tribute that vice pays to virtue").

Bourdieu believed deeply in the progressive potential of this dynamic, not least because it asked so little of people in the way of democratic virtue, moving forward instead through the force of peer competition. "One is tempted to say," he wrote (2000 [1997]: 126), "contrary to the moralists who insist on pure intentions, that it is good that it should be so. No one can any longer believe that history is guided by reason; and if reason, and also the universal, moves forward at all, it is perhaps because there are profits in rationality and universality so that actions which advance reason and the universal advance at the same time the interests of those who perform them." Interestingly, Bourdieu showed that even those in the field of power can fall under the sway of this logic; even they can become constrained by the intrinsic force of universalism. Such insights further helped to complicate our understanding of the relation between power and publicity, making it possible for us to imagine scenarios in which universalism actually falls more to the side of power than of publicity, with high-level state bureaucrats speaking more to the public interest than even certain actors in the public sphere.

Bourdieu also sought to foster the development of what he termed a "collective intellectual" (a phrase meant to call to mind Jean-Paul Sartre's "total intellectual" and Michel Foucault's "specific intellectual"; see, for example, Bourdieu 1996a [1992]). This collectivity would gather together in a single working body a range of thinkers possessed of specific expertise in the given issue of wide concern, an expertise made possible by the autonomous inner development of their respective fields of learning. The collective intellectual would debunk folk assumptions as well as the so-called expert opinions propounded by media intellectuals and think tanks; it would also propose constructive, creative solutions to the problems addressed. In so doing it would contribute to broader public enlightenment. Bourdieu's vision, while falling short of the idea of a field of publicity as sketched out above, did at least presuppose a public sphere or a space of publicity in which something like public opinion could be found. Where, after all, would the collective intellectual otherwise intervene? (Recall that he specifically invoked "the public interest" in the quotation reproduced earlier about the state.) Bourdieu nonetheless provided no official "space" for this space of publicity in his broader, more systematic theory. Focusing on powers, he spoke hardly at all of publics.

V

Bourdieu's analyses would surely have been furthered by a more extensive engagement with pragmatist thought. He envisioned social science as assisting publics in the resolution of their problems—to recall the title of Dewey's (1988d [1927]) famous work of political theory—but he did not make entirely clear what alternatives to domination, symbolic violence, and power might look like or how they might be realized. Neither in his theory of action nor in his theory of public life did he clear out sufficient analytic space for the sociological study of creativity, self-determination, and democracy. It is because this aspect of his thinking was less than fully developed, in fact, that we have invoked in this essay the imagery of letting the Bourdieusian wine breathe in a Deweyan air.

Nonetheless, there is much to learn from Bourdieu, especially from a Bourdieu who has been read with Dewey in mind. We can begin by noting that all of Bourdieu's inquiries began with experience—for instance, late in his career — with the effects he saw neoliberalism as having all across the contemporary world. Dewey's social and historical inquiries, too, arose as a result of perplexities: in his case, those occasioned by the coming of an urban industrial society. Together these thinkers remind us that all scholarly inquiry, however many steps removed from the immediate conditions of its production, emerges from some sort of pragmatic engagement with the perplexities raised by those conditions and is itself a response to those perplexities. In *Experience and Nature* (1988c [1925]: 18), Dewey asked the following questions about such intellectual problem solving: "Does [the inquiry] end in conclusions which, when they are referred back to ordinary life-experiences and their predicaments, render them more significant, more luminous to us, and make our dealings with them more fruitful? Or does it terminate in rendering the things of ordinary experience more opaque than they were before?" These questions were about, among other things, the qualities of intelligence with which we can approach the problems that confront us, and how our inquiries can contribute to that intelligence.

Pondering Bourdieu now with such Deweyan concerns in mind, we can ask further how the historical sociology of democracy can be brought more effectively to bear upon problems and challenges in the present day, perhaps through individual scholars' self-organization into something like a "collective intellectual"; how such endeavors, whatever form they take, might contribute to more intelligent forms of action oriented toward social reconstruction, action marked not only by greater control and freedom but also by sound judgment and practical wisdom. Only by taking such challenges seriously will we be able to fulfill the vision Bourdieu laid out in his life's work, a vision so resonant with Dewey's own: the ideal of a genuinely scientific and critical scholarship with commitment.

Notes

1. It is true that Dewey was deeply engaged in psychology, even serving for a time as president of the American Psychological Association. He was convinced that "substantial bettering of social relations waits upon the growth of a scientific social psychology" (Dewey 1988b [1922]: 221). However, his contributions to social psychology were conceptual, not empirical, and his various works of social reflection and critique were primarily essayistic in nature.

2. For a parallel argument in respect to ethnomethodology, see Emirbayer and Maynard (2010). In both that paper and the present chapter, pathways leading from classical pragmatism to mid- to late twentieth-century sociology are explored. Yet another such path, besides ethnomethodology and Bourdieusian sociology, is that of symbolic interactionism; this approach is the one that most directly acknowledges its own continuities with pragmatist thinking. (Bourdieu did so to a lesser extent, and ethnomethodology hardly at all.)

3. Wacquant (2005: 10–11) similarly distinguishes between Bourdieu's personal politics, "politics as encountered in his personal writings," and "the politics *of* Bourdieu's works."

4. For a comparison of the ideas of Bourdieu and Mead, see Aboulafia (1999).

5. Dewey's arguments in this regard pertain primarily to Plato; it is questionable to what extent he got Aristotle right.

6. The phrase in quotation marks comes from the Dewey quotation with which the chapter began.

7. Since the field concept was meant to apply at all scales, from the most expansive to the most circumscribed, each of the more delimited social microcosms, too—down to singular institutionalized organizations—could also be said to feature something like its own field of power; for a fuller discussion, see Emirbayer and Johnson (2008).

8. In fairness to Bourdieu, we note that he always insisted on the historical specificity of any claims he made on behalf of the primacy of a given type of asset. For instance, when speaking of Soviet-style societies, he suggested that the most important principle of differentiation was political, not economic, capital (Bourdieu 1998d [1994]: 14–18). However, when speaking of most other societies, at least in the present day, Bourdieu easily resorted to formulations of an economistic nature; for a powerful critique along these lines, see Alexander (1995).

9. We do not engage directly with this issue here; for an attempt to rethink Bourdieusian sociology along more culturalist lines, see Emirbayer and Desmond (forthcoming).

10. Bourdieu also did less than might have been hoped for in theorizing social movements; for further discussion, see Emirbayer and Desmond (forthcoming).

11. An aristocratic habitus, for example, could conduce to a conservative or Burkean type of politics in one historical circumstance but to a radical or reactionary politics in another.

12. For a prominent exception, see Steinmetz (2006).

13. Much of the discussion that follows is drawn from Emirbayer and Mische (1998).

14. Much of the discussion that follows is drawn from Emirbayer and Sheller (1999).

SPACES BETWEEN FIELDS

The Theoretical Problem

I mean to critically engage here with Pierre Bourdieu's concept of field by posing the following questions: Are there spaces between fields? And if there are, what is their significance?

One of the crucial contributions of the concept of field is that it requires us to stop thinking in terms of entities, proper names, concrete individuals, and things and begin grasping all of these as bundles of relations. The prophet, the priest, or the magician, for example, in Bourdieu's (1987a [1971]) masterful conversion of Max Weber's *Sociology of Religion* are neither concrete individuals nor ideal types but certain intersections of the relations of dependence on and independence from the consumers of salvation, definite regions within the religious field. In my own work (Eyal 2003) I have followed Bourdieu in arguing that left and right in postcommunist politics or, indeed, in any politics should be grasped not as fixed ideological platforms but as constantly changing ideological packages assembled with respect to the crisscrossing pressures operating in the political field. This is what Bourdieu means by denoting his approach as relational. Yet while Bourdieu is quite rigorous in applying this relational approach to political programs, works of art, styles of life, and scientific theories, all of which are deconstructed into the bundles of relations that constitute them, he does not do the same thing with the distinction between fields themselves. Bourdieu constantly talks about the economic field, the artistic field, the political field, the bureaucratic field, the academic field, the legal field, the literary field, and so on. It is as if the relational approach stopped short before these entities—which are nothing but a fancy way of saying the economy, the political sphere, the state, academia, science, art, that is, proper names—and left them in their place as distinct spheres whose contents are clearly bounded and well distinguished from one another.

That this is a problem becomes clear when we consider, for example, the practices of gift giving, charity, and domestic money analyzed by Viviana Zelizer (1994), indeed even by Bourdieu himself (2000b; see also Callon 1998). All of these practices, wherein money is involved, have a double meaning, or a "twofold truth" as Bourdieu puts it: they can be seen as economic (i.e., interested, egoistic, calculable) or they can be seen as moral or social (i.e., altruistic, disinterested, nonquantifiable). It all depends, as Callon says, on the framing, particularly the temporal frame within which they are viewed. It follows, therefore, that there is no easy, clear-cut, self-evident criteria by which the various fields could be distinguished in terms of the content of the activity that takes place within them. Nothing is economic or scientific or artistic by itself. These are also shorthand for bundles of relations.

What would happen if we submit these entities as well to the relational method? if instead of treating them as given spheres, we would try to deconstruct them into bundles of relations? To do so means we would have to begin to think in terms of spaces between fields. The existence of these fields as separate spheres would have to be analyzed as a function of the struggles taking place in the spaces between them and of the mechanisms set up in the spaces between them.

The Empirical Problem

This problem has emerged for me in the context of my work on the history of expertise in Arab affairs in Israel, specifically, in my analysis of the relations between academic Middle Eastern studies and military intelligence. In an earlier article (Eyal 2002) I conceptualized these relations as taking place within a field of Orientalist expertise, but as I reworked these materials into a book-length manuscript I found myself in need of additional concepts and drawing on Bruno Latour in describing a "network of intelligence expertise" (Eyal 2006).

The problem I was seeking to understand is as follows: there is a branch of Israeli Middle Eastern studies, in fact, the dominant mainstream of this discipline ever since the late 1960s, typically practiced in academic research institutes, which is closely tied to military intelligence. Many of the scholars have served in military intelligence in the past and continue to provide services for it in the present, either as part of their reserve duty or as contract work. Moreover, critics have claimed that in terms of the selection of problems, the style of writing, and the methodology and mode of analysis there isn't really much difference between the two (Sivan 1979a, 1979b; Baer 1979; Porath 1984; Toleidano 1989).

What happens, therefore, to the distinction between the academic field and the bureaucratic field (or however else one might choose to denote the location of military intelligence)? There are ways of dealing with this issue, but they are unconvincing. One could deny, as many of these scholars do, that the contract work they do for military intelligence has anything to do with their real academic work. In short, they claim to be squarely within the academic field. Or one could imply, as many of their critics do, that these academics have betrayed their calling and crossed over into officialdom. I find these answers to be facile. All they seek to do is to save the distinction between academia and officialdom, to protect their appearance as distinct spheres whose contents are clearly bounded and well distinguished from one another. In short, they are forms of boundary work between science and its environment, and as such they may interest me as part of the object of study but not as reliable ways to conceptualize it. I became interested in other ways of approaching this form of expertise, without reducing it to this or that side of the opposition between the academy and the military. What would happen if we leave it where it is, in the space between them? what would happen if, like the gift, we permit it to hold onto its "double meaning" or "twofold truth"? As we will see below, Bourdieu's concepts did not hinder me from doing so, but they were not particularly helpful either, and I needed to twist them in a particular way to get at what I wanted. For this reason, I am now interested in exploring the idea of spaces between fields.

Objections

Bourdieu's theory can erect various lines of defense, as described in what follows, against my line of questioning.

RELATIONS BETWEEN FIELDS

The first line of defense might be to search in Bourdieu's theory for a set of relations that could do the job of accounting for the existence of fields as separate spheres. One plausible candidate is the relations between fields themselves. Terms like *economic field* and *political field*, the argument would go, denote not an essence (politics) or an entity (the economy) but a structure of relations itself determined by the total set of relations between fields as well as by the struggles in the field of power over the value of various forms of capital. This argument is illustrated by Bourdieu's visual device of depicting fields as nesting one within another, and all of them together within the field of power. I am not convinced by this answer. In Bourdieu's theory the relations between fields typically determine the degree of autonomy of a particular field, for example, how far they are, within the field of power, from the pole of dominant economic capital. Autonomy is a concept that refers to the orientations of actors and says very little about how to characterize the modality of their activities: are they economic or moral, scientific or artistic? It is a general, abstract characteristic that can pertain to many different spheres, without regard to the specific character of activities taking place therein. So the first conclusion I would like to derive is that the necessity for a concept of spaces between fields has to do with specifying the modality of activities rather than the orientations of actors.

EXCURSUS ON THE SCIENTIFIC FIELD

There is a brilliant economy to Bourdieu's (1975: 23) famous formulation that the specificity of the scientific field consists in that "the producers tend to have no possible clients other than their own competitors (and the greater the autonomy of the field, the more this is so)." But the tightness of the formulation comes at a heavy price. What Bourdieu is saying, after all, is that the more autonomous a field is, the more scientific, without needing to say anything about the type of activity taking place therein. Bourdieu intends this formulation to enable the distinguishing of real sciences, typically abstract, highly detached disciplines like theoretical physics or mathematics, from disciplines that are at a lower degree of scientificity or altogether false because the producers are heteronymously oriented to recognition by political, economic, and other actors. Whatever one may think of the wisdom of this endeavor, could this criterion really serve to identify the specificity of the scientific enterprise as distinct, say, from art or the intellectual field? Here Bourdieu is entering very dangerous terrain. He could argue that while artists and intellectuals may pretend they need no clients other than artists and intellectuals, they in fact are dependent on the recognition granted by larger groups of clients such as the reading public or art critics (see Bourdieu 1969). But the same could be said of psychologists and economists. Are they, therefore, lesser scientists, false scientists, artists, or intellectuals? I say this is dangerous terrain for Bourdieu because what becomes evident here is that the "specificity of science" is nothing but an idealization of the science or, even worse, an "ideal type." The irony is that Bourdieu developed the concept of field precisely in order to overcome the limitations of Weberian ideal type methodology (Bourdieu 1987a [1971]), but when it comes to differentiating the fields themselves from one another, he seems to recapitulate Weber's essentialism.

RELATIONS WITHIN THE FIELD

If the relations between fields cannot do the job, what about the relations within fields? Specifically, the struggles that take place in any field over the boundaries of the field itself, the criteria of membership in it, the costs of entry to it, in short, the struggles over boundary work. While the relations between fields set up the general parameters within which such struggles take place, it is up to boundary work to produce the distinction between fields, for example, the distinction between the academy and the state. I am not persuaded by this answer either. I can register my misgivings through the following rhetorical question: Where is boundary work itself located, inside the field or outside it? When scientists write op-ed pieces in order to expose charlatans, is this scientific or journalistic activity? Obviously, any answer to this question would be boundary work itself. Another question: Does the boundary separate or connect? To return to the example of gift giving and charity: What makes something a gift and not an investment or payment? The fact that I report it as such on my tax form, that is, it is excluded from the economic by being included in it (on the tax form) and vice versa, it is included in the economic by being excluded from it, as when my accountant calculates that I am better off contributing to charity now to avoid paying taxes later. So my second conclusion is that the necessity for a concept of spaces between fields has to do with the idea of boundary work. One cannot analyze boundary work, I would argue, without being armed with a set of concepts that make sense of what goes on inside the volume of the boundary. I propose that we cease to think of the boundary in Euclidean terms, as a fine line with no width to it, and begin to grasp it as a real social entity with its own volume, so to speak. As such, the boundary does not simply separate what's inside and outside the field, for example, what is economic and what is not, but is also a zone of essential connections and transactions between them. On the one hand, the volume of the boundary is where struggles take place to apportion actors and practices this way and that; on the other hand, it is also where networks provide for a seamless connection between fields. This also means that we could think of actors within the volume of the boundary as at once excluded from the field and yet included in it by virtue of this very exclusion, which apportions them a particular network role.

MISPLACED CONCRETENESS

At this point Bourdieu and his followers may retreat to their strongest and most fortified line of defense. All of this is a big misunderstanding, they would say. We are, in fact, in no disagreement. What you call a space between fields is nothing but another field. The point is that field is not a thing but a concept, a heuristic hypothesis, in a sense a fiction. There is no need to reify it and talk about spheres as if they actually existed. It is simply the point that in analyzing the actions of this or that politician or the words of this or that intellectual or the work of this or that scientist, one has to consider them as taking place in the context of a total set of relations; one has to take account of all the actors, proximate or distant, whose actions impinge on the politician/intellectual/ scientist and shape their likely conduct. Hence, there is also no need to define boundaries for the field, as the lines of force reach to infinity; they are only weaker at a longer distance. And fields therefore could easily overlap with one another. So, if you are interested in marginal actors who exist on the frontiers of fields where the lines of force become weaker, you can simply shift the focus and analyze the sphere of their activity as a different field, say, the field of generalized cultural production, the field of scientific popularization, the field of charity organizations, and so forth. This is a good answer, as far as it goes, but far from foolproof. First, it is a bit disingenuous because while we are given freedom to analyze fields wherever we see fit, it is still the case that Bourdieu almost always limits himself to the canonical distinctions between economy, politics, culture, and so on, and any additional fields analyzed are characterized negatively as less autonomous, less important. Second, we may agree that field is just a concept and hence there is no need to reify it, but the crucial question then becomes, What kind of a concept is it? What is it designed to do? If it is just a concept, we may decide not to use it if we do not think it can shed light on the problem at hand, if we do not think it will yield fruitful hypotheses. This is related to a problem I commonly face in trying to teach Bourdieu's theory and methodology and in guiding dissertation research. Invariably my students worry whether their case study, the activity they are analyzing, really qualifies as a field. Telling them it is a heuristic concept helps somewhat, but it would be more helpful to clarify what is the problem the concept is geared to address and what the alternatives are, what other concepts may be used heuristically to address other problems.

Bourdieu and Latour Compared

What kind of concept is field? and what is it designed to do? The main point is that it is not equipped to deal with the issues raised here, which are better addressed by the Latourian concept of network. The wager is whether it is possible to integrate the two approaches in some meaningful way, and this is exactly what I propose to do through the idea of spaces between fields.

Bourdieu (1985a) has already answered the question of what kind of concept field is and what it is designed to do: it is meant to overcome, he said, the false polarity between internalist and externalist explanations of artistic, intellectual, scientific, or political practices. I think this is true, but only with respect to a limited rendering of this problem: the concept of field is meant to overcome the false polarity between interpreting actors' actions as motivated by material self-interest (externalist explanation) as against construing their actions to be disinterested and guided only by a search for the truth, beauty, authenticity, and so forth (internalist explanation). What does it mean to overcome this polarity? Nothing grandiose or mysterious. For a long time now, everybody has known this is a false polarity. Certainly Karl Mannheim did. Overcoming it, however, means to invent a device that permits you to interpret the motivations for action without at any point occupying the Machiavellian position of the master strategist, the prince, who has full knowledge of his interests. It is not permissible to explain action as being disinterested—disinterest, explains Bourdieu (1975: 32), is nothing but orientation to "a system of specific . . . interests which implies relative indifference to the ordinary objects of interest—money, honors, etc."—but neither is it permissible to explain it as a rational calculation of interests. Bourdieu's solution, therefore, is to speak of actors as investing in the particular *illusio* of the field into which they enter, and thus even as they pursue their interests they are never masters of their own strategies. That this is what the concept of field is designed to do can be seen, for example, in the quote from Gaston Bachelard that Bourdieu (1975: 19) chose as the epigraph for his article about the scientific field: "The training of the scientific mind is not only a reform of ordinary knowledge, but also a conversion of interests." The concept of field concerns interests and motivations, and, correspondingly, it says very little about the problem at hand, namely, the modality of activities. Additionally, this is why it resorts to the image of a thin, strict boundary, since investment in the illusion of the field means that each actor orients his or her action to a limited set of recognized and recognizing actors.

Put differently, even if we shifted the lens and analyzed the space between fields as another field, we would gain very little. We would be guided toward conceiving of this field as a lesser one because the circle of recognizing others would be too heterogeneous and unstable—lesser, namely, less autonomous, therefore, less of a field. Similarly, we would be led to conceive of the actors in it as relatively weak and incapable of controlling their clientele instead of attending to their actual powers of invention and recombination.

Latour's concepts of network and hybridity, by comparison, deal precisely with the issues of modality and boundary neglected by Bourdieu. Yet they too have their blind side. This chapter is my modest attempt to negotiate peace between Bourdieu and Latour, between field theory and actor-network theory: I give fields to Bourdieu and the spaces between them to Latour.

Like Bourdieu, Latour (1988: 218) says his concepts are meant to overcome the false polarity between internalist and externalist explanations. That's good because it means these two enemies share an enemy (in fact, two other enemies) and the noble goal of defeating it. But on closer inspection it is clear that by this polarity Latour means something different than Bourdieu: not the opposition between self-interest and disinterest, but the opposition between objective fact (internalist) and social construction (externalist). What does it mean to overcome this polarity? To invent a device that permits one to explain scientific practices without at any point occupying the post hoc position of having full knowledge or the truth: it is not permissible, he says, to explain scientific practices as discoveries, that is, that they are somehow verified by our post hoc knowledge of what the truth about reality or nature is; but it is not permissible either to explain them as social constructions, thereby assigning society somehow greater reality and agency while trivializing scientists' actual, practical grappling with recalcitrant materiality. The concern of this approach, therefore, is with materiality, with specifying the modality and content of practices, precisely because it is no longer permissible to conceive of either nature or society as "really real." Latour's (1987: 86–90, 121–32) solution, therefore, is to speak of scientists neither as discovering nor as constructing but as recruiting, mobilizing, and striking alliances with the objects of their study. This means perforce that the boundaries between nature and society, reality and discourse, science and politics are thick and fuzzy and that they are crisscrossed by the networks scientists weave in order to recruit allies, or, as Latour puts it, the boundary is "internal to the network."

At the same time, what Latour (1987: 118–19) calls the "secondary mechanism" or "purification" is responsible for producing the appearance—what Timothy Mitchell (1991) calls the effect—of a strict and impassable boundary between two entities: the work of all the allies, from the microbes to the manufacturers of instruments to the public authorities that implement hygienist policies, is attributed to the ingenuity of Louis Pasteur, who discovered the microbes; the actions orchestrated by a strange network composed of Halliburton, of a vice president with one foot in each game, of private intelligence and interrogation contractors, of local turncoats with their own Pentagon-funded organizations, of a professional army and a national guard with their own private contractors are attributed to and appear as "state action."

This can explain why, aside from the vagaries of the French intellectual field, these two thinkers and their camps were so dismissive of each other. Indeed, I would argue that each is strongest precisely where the other is weakest, and each privileges precisely what the other discounts. Their omissions are, in a sense, symmetrical, and for this very reason, while their theories lead in different directions, they could also be complementary.

What Latour probably finds most problematic in Bourdieu's theoretical edifice is the strong insistence on the "epistemological break" between science and commonsense knowledge (as well as false science). This insistence is encapsulated in Bourdieu's claim that concepts such as space and field represent the objective moment of scientific inquiry with which it is possible to construct a representation of the total context of action. This claim is the complete inverse of Latour's sociology of science and of his careful avoidance of privileging any point of view as being the truth or as being objective. As Latour (1987: 78–79) says, what is deemed objective and what is deemed subjective are relative to "trials of strength" in specific settings. These are not qualities affixed once and for all to actors or theories because actors strive to fortify themselves so as to become objective and to deconstruct others so they become subjective. And his view of the epistemological break is no less scathing: "'Science'—in quotation marks—does not exist. It is the name that has been pasted onto certain sections of certain networks, associations that are so sparse and fragile that they would have escaped attention altogether if everything has not been attributed to them" (Latour 1988: 216). It is impossible, therefore, not to conclude that, from Latour's point of view, Bourdieu's treatment of his scientific practice is hopelessly internalist.

If they ever cared to pay attention to Latour, Bourdieu's camp probably should be the most riled up about his treatment of interests, encapsulated in the concept of translation. *Translation* is a general term meant to cover the process whereby the interests of both humans and nonhumans are interpreted, modified, and adjusted to one another so as to create alliances. It thus contains the important insight that oftentimes it is not interests that explain alliances, but the other way around; the fact of alliance is what explains how the interests of the various parties are construed and adjusted. Latour is insistent that the principle of symmetry requires that we treat alliances with humans and nonhumans as essentially the same and use the same language to describe them. From Bourdieu's point of view, however, such symmetry is bought at the price of an even more problematic asymmetry, that between the person whom Latour calls the "fact builder," almost always a scientist or an engineer, and those he or she aims to snare in his or her net as allies. The crucial section in *Science in Action* (Latour 1987: 108–21), I would note, where Latour expounds the idea of translation, is written completely from the point of view of the fact builder, and the language used to describe his actions is Machiavellian (Latour indeed pays homage to Machiavelli and seems proud to do so): the fact builder's problem is, to put it simply, how to recruit allies by convincing them to align their interests with his. Once they are recruited, their actions are still unpredictable, and the problem is how to control their actions and channel them toward the desired goal. Thus, the fact builder is the rational strategic actor par excellence. This is the complete inverse of Bourdieu's sociology of interest formation and of his careful avoidance of privileging any actor as the master strategist. If translation is the case, from Bourdieu's point of view the issue would be precisely how to take account—in some sort of parallel, not serial, processing—of all the translations that all the members of a network simultaneously operate on one another. First, no account is given of the processes by which the fact builder's own interests were formed or translated. These interests are taken to flow directly from the need to build and secure the said fact. No meaning or interpretation intervenes between this (imputed) need and action; nothing like habitus, socialization, or training serves to connect the interpretation of interests with social position. The second point is that no account is given of the processes of translation that the other parties to the alliance operate on the strategic actor. This is what I mean by asymmetry. Rationality is on the side of the Machiavellian actor, who translates, that is, aligns, adjusts, interprets, shapes, distorts, misrepresents, the interests of all the allies, who themselves are either led, misled, or resist. One could then shift the focus and describe the situation from the point of view of one of the allies, just as Bourdieu could shift the focus and describe a new field in between two old ones, but this is precisely the point: the Machiavellian language of translation is not geared to take into account all at once, symmetrically, all the members of a network as partially rational, partially determined actors.[1] I would argue that this is precisely what the language of field and habitus is adept at doing. It is impossible, therefore, not to conclude that, from Bourdieu's point of view, Latour's treatment of the question of interests is hopelessly externalist.

It is clear now what feats of juggling, of keeping one ball in the air at all times, it would take in order to negotiate peace between these two theories: in order to account for the formation and mutual adjustment of actors' interests, one would need to keep the concept of field. In order to account for the formation and mutual differentiation of practices, however, one would also need to keep Latour's concept of a network connecting humans and nonhumans and straddling the boundaries between what are known as science, society, politics, and nature. If these two concepts are to sit comfortably together, several provisions must be made: the theory of fields must shed the all-knowing narrator's voice that Bourdieu adopts, speaking from the point of view of scientific objectivity; actor-network theory, correspondingly, would need to part with the Machiavellian narrator's voice that Latour adopts, speaking from the point of view of the prince. Field theory will also have to make room for some of the insights contained in the concept of translation (particularly the point that distance, that objective measure par excellence in Bourdieu's theory, could be modified by interpretation); but at the same time, actor-network theory would have to grant more of a reality to the phenomenon of a bounded sphere, which it tends to treat as appearance or effect, and accept that to explain it one needs sturdier mechanisms than the flimsy secondary mechanism of attribution and purification. I do not know how to do all that, unless by means of a truce, a partition of jurisdictions: fields to Bourdieu and the spaces between them to Latour.

Back to the Problem of Orientalist Expertise

I first attempted to deal with the problem of the relations between Middle Eastern studies and military intelligence from within Bourdieu's research program, but with some telling modifications. I opted for the third line of defense discussed earlier and analyzed the exchanges between these two as taking place within a "field of orientalist expertise." To construct this field I had to ignore the boundary between the state and academia. In a sense, this was an intermediate field between the two.

Figure 1 presents a simplified sketch of this field, modeled after Bourdieu's conversion of Weber's *Sociology of Religion* and serving as a prototype for any field of expertise. The principal opposition in this field, along the horizontal axis, has to do with the degree of independence/dependence of the experts from the consumers of their services. As Weber and Bourdieu argue, experts seek to control the demand for their services, and their major coup in this respect is when they are able to completely dictate to the consumers what their needs are. The secondary opposition, along the vertical axis, has to do with the degree of openness/closure of expert knowledge and expert recruitment, that is, with the control over the supply of expertise. Weber and Bourdieu argue that experts seek to create artificial scarcity of their expertise, both by limiting access to the knowledge they produce, that is, making it esoteric, as well as by limiting access into their ranks through exams, ordeals, credentialing systems, and so forth.

I had, however, to modify Bourdieu's framework for my needs. Unlike Weber, Bourdieu did not seem to appreciate the extent to which the accumulation of resources and the attainment of domination within fields of expertise was a precarious balancing act. The thrust of his model was toward defining power as a situation in which experts fully control both the supply of and the demand for their expertise. How else to interpret Bourdieu's definition of the specificity of the scientific field? As you may remember, he defined it as the situation in which "the producers tend to have no possible clients other than their own competitors (and the greater the autonomy of the field, the more this is so)." Put differently, so great is the independence of the experts from their clients, that they have no clients! This definition was designed to maximize this element of control over demand, or, in other words, autonomy, and Bourdieu is also explicit that it is the result of a high degree of control over supply and a formidable accumulation of scientific capital, that is, power, autonomy, and full control over supply and demand are all equated in his scheme. But this is ridiculous! If they had no clients whatsoever, if nobody was interested in what they did, what kind of power would they have? and how would they have been able to control supply so well? (Unless it is because nobody wants to enter such a disconnected field.) On this point, see Latour's (1987: 145–75) devastating proof that if science is to have an inside, as he puts it, it is only by virtue of having an outside, and the more and harder inside it has, it is, first and foremost, owing to the extensive work performed outside.

My choice, therefore, was to conceptualize strength or domination or capital in a field of expertise as predicated on the capacity to balance the contradictory imperatives of independence versus dependence and closure versus openness (which, adopting Nikolas Rose's [1992] usage, I called generosity). I thought that, in fact, this way of thinking about the problem was much truer to Weber's analysis. The main point is that the opposition between independence from or dependence on the laity is truly a dilemma or a double constraint: too much dependence on the consumers exposes the group of producers to competition, critical appraisal, and devaluation; but too much independence may lead to isolation and loss of clientele (the ivory tower phenomenon). The same holds for the opposition between generosity and closure. Weber (1993), after all, notes that the closing of the scriptures and the monopolization of their interpretation at the hands of a small, select group leads to a peculiar form of tension within the priestly vocation, between those entrusted with maintaining the purity of the original revelation and those who engage in the everyday pastoral work among the laity. The pastoral workers, first of all, are more dependent on the needs of the laity. Not every household dispute, every confession of sin, every delicate business question can be answered by relating it to the doctrine of grace. The scriptures, the revelation, must be made to work and shown to be relevant to the life questions of the laity. In Rose's (1992) language, it must become possible to graft it onto other forms of knowledge, discourses, and technologies of the self. If they were to stick closely to the scriptures and remain distant from the needs of the laity, the pastors would become irrelevant and their place would be taken by magicians, soothsayers, oracles, diviners, witchdoctors, and the like. Moreover, they cannot afford to remain esoteric. They must make the laity understand at least portions of the revelation, appreciate its relevance to their life problems, and apply it to themselves. To put it more generally, there is an inverse relationship between how esoteric and monopolistic expert knowledge is and the capacity of the expert group to present itself as useful and relevant to the laity.

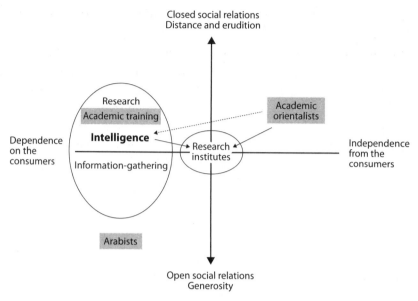

Figure 7.1. The field of Orientalist expertise.

Hence the position of the research institutes—where Middle Eastern studies and military intelligence intersect and fuse—at the center of figure 1. In my research (Eyal 2002, 2006) I have followed the actions of two generations of doctoral students and young lecturers at the Institute of Oriental Studies at the Hebrew University. I have shown that their professors exercised such strict control over the supply of their expertise as to greatly limit the mobility of these two groups. Moreover, they cultivated strict independence from the needs and demands of their possible clients, the political and military leadership, and thereby earned themselves and their students relative isolation and irrelevance. Nonetheless, as their students rebelled against this definition of orientalist expertise and moved to take up positions, first, in paramilitary intelligence and the Jewish Agency and then, later, after 1948, at military intelligence and the Foreign Office, they discovered that what they gained in relevance, influence, and proximity to their clients they lost in independence and the capacity to control the attribution and dissemination of their discourse. Put simply, while the leadership now listened to them, it did not have to acknowledge them, unless their predictions and assessments failed, in which case the blame could be apportioned to them. They were subordinate officers, taking orders and submitting reports. Whatever insights were contained in such reports the leadership could pass as its own.

I argued that the invention of midway research institutes provided a way out of this quandary, a means of balancing a measure of independence with proximity to clients' needs and of generosity with the capacity to control the attribution and dissemination of expert discourse. Top political and military decision makers are routinely invited to these institutes to participate in conferences and seminars, and some serve on their board of directors. Military intelligence officers and foreign office experts routinely spend a year as guest researchers at these institutes, and some move to full-time positions there after they finish their service. The result is that the professors who control the research institutes, who at the same time also lead academic departments of Middle Eastern studies, enjoy proximity to the men of power and prestige as independent commentators. The research institutes have become the site where multiple resources, financial, academic, administrative, and social connections, are accumulated and converted into political influence, academic power, and even high-level political appointments. In short, their leaders have managed to become the most dominant group within the field of orientalist expertise by balancing monopoly with generosity and independence with dependence.

I was not completely satisfied, however, with this way of conceptualizing my results. The main benefit of using the concept of field, reworked in this way, is that I no longer needed to attribute selfish motives per se to my actors, nor did I need to present them as grand strategists who have designed the research institute from scratch to solve their problems. I was able to show how their actions were guided by a philological habitus acquired in academic settings, then carried over to military intelligence wherein it generated homologous practices and institutions, thus permitting the formation of halfway institutions between the military and the academy. At no point did I need to add the device of rational calculation or disinterestedness to explain the motivations of my actors, who were guided by the acquired desire to recreate the social hierarchy of the philological modus operandi (composed of apprentice, pedant, and speculative interpreter) and to occupy its apex, that is, the position of the speculative interpreter, converted within military intelligence into the position of a researcher who assesses the intentions of the other side.

The main disadvantage, however, of deploying the concept of field in this way, even when modified by the idea of generosity, is that it requires us to maintain a somewhat artificial distinction between experts and clients. It is as if expertise was a thing, an entity (a set of skills), which could therefore be possessed by the experts and provided to the clients. But there were several aspects of my subject matter that defied such easy division. The most important had to do with the public and political functioning of the assessments written by the research branch of military intelligence as well as the commentaries written by Middle East experts at the research institutes. Such assessments and commentaries, it became clear to me, could not be analyzed as simply the opinion of the experts about what is likely to take place in the Middle East. They must be analyzed as political speech acts that are central to the Israeli political system (Peri 1983: 167). Intelligence assessments, for example, while they are officially submitted to the chief of staff and the government alone, have another, more important form of existence: their main points are almost immediately leaked to the press, either by politicians or by high-ranking intelligence officers who have developed their own set of give-and-take ties to military correspondents. The position of the research branch on this issue was summarized by one of its former commanders: "The principal points of the intelligence assessment should be passed to the media, so it would present them to the public. The public must know the truth; it is an important moral we drew from the Yom Kipur fiasco" (Amos Gilad, quoted in Schiff 2001). Such leaks permit intelligence officers to gain some power vis-à-vis the politicians. Even when political and military decision makers are interested in the supply of specific assessments and recommendations to support their policy choices, and when these may be different from the assessments of the research branch, they are forced to avoid, as much as possible, overt conflict with the research branch. Supply and demand must coincide. The result is a process of negotiation in which official policy and intelligence assessment are slowly adjusted to one another, facilitated by the social proximity between the commanders of military intelligence and the political hierarchy.[2] In essence, such leaks turn the intelligence officers into de facto political players. Much the same could be said of the Mideast specialists working at the research institutes. Sometimes they participate directly in the formulation of intelligence assessments. At other times they act as commentators in the media, reacting to the assessment, validating it, repeating it, unfurling its various implications, and hence contributing to its overall market value.

It follows, therefore, that intelligence assessments are not merely predictions about what may happen but policy tools, messages directed at politicians, the Israeli public, the enemy, or the international community and calculated to elicit certain performances. The intelligence assessment is at one and the same time the lens through which the enemy's actions are viewed as indicating certain intentions; a message to the other side that their schemes have been exposed (as well as a message to the Israeli public or the international community that this is the state of affairs, that is, propaganda or, in nicer language, public relations); and the interpretation guiding Israeli policy in reaction to these intentions. Raymond Cohen (1989) demonstrated how this mechanism worked in 1986, when tensions between Israel and Syria escalated to the brink of war: the research branch assessed that Syrian maneuvers indicated aggressive intentions. This assessment was leaked to the press, so as to warn the Syrians that the game was up. The Syrians, however, understood these leaks as a different kind of message, a threat that might indicate an Israeli intention to attack. As a result, they mobilized their forces. Israel responded in kind, and the resulting dynamic of escalation validated the original assessment. While Cohen sought to warn against the dangers of escalation inherent in such assessments, I think this is not necessarily the most important point. It is just as likely that the opposite scenario could have taken place, that is, that the Syrians would have canceled their maneuvers in order to avoid escalation. This was exactly the performance that the assessment sought to elicit. In this case, the assessment and the reaction to it would have been presented as a success because in this way the adversary's intentions were foiled, that is, it would have been validated all the same. With respect to this mechanism, it is difficult to make a strong distinction between experts (intelligence officers) and clients (politicians). In fact, if we consider how this mechanism functions in the long range to produce a stable state of affairs, it doesn't even make much sense to draw too strong of a distinction between the subject of knowledge (the expert) and the object of knowledge (the enemy) since the enemy's performances are part of what produces the stability and validity of the expert's assessments.

These considerations emerged for me once I was no longer preoccupied with explaining the interests and motivations of the actors who established the research institutes—for which I needed the device of an intermediary field—and when my attention turned to questions of modality, of characterizing the specific nature of the form of expertise practiced at the research institutes. This form of expertise now appeared to me to be a property neither of an individual nor even of an organized group (a profession), neither a given body of knowledge nor an acquired skills set, but a network connecting individuals in different positions and with different skills, as well as connecting them with arguments, devices, resources, demonstrated effects, and models. To say that expertise is a network means that we treat the distinctions between expert and client, or between subject and object, as provisional and internal to the network. There are no strong, impassable boundaries between those who are empowered to speak as experts; those who are empowered to listen to them and make decisions; those who produce knowledge but cannot speak, humans as well as nonhuman devices; and those about whom they speak—the network of expertise also involves a set of alliances or manipulations meant to secure from those about whom the experts speak, in this case, enemy leaders, a set of performances predicted by the experts.

For the network of expertise to function, all of these must be connected with one another, and certain mechanisms must control the flows of speech,

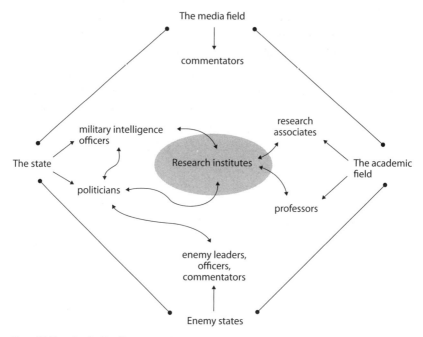

The media field

↓

commentators

military intelligence officers

The state

politicians

research associates

Research institutes

The academic field

professors

enemy leaders, officers, commentators

↑

Enemy states

Figure 7.2. The network of intelligence expertise.

work, information, and performances between them. Additionally, for the network to function it must also continually produce the appearance of a strong boundary between at least these four sets of actors: experts, clients, foot soldiers/technicians, and the enemy. But this is a secondary mechanism, superimposed on the more basic facts of connection, alliance, recruitment, and division of labor.

It follows, therefore, that this network could be described as straddling, at the very least, the boundaries of the state, the academic field, and the media field, crossing them rather promiscuously, indeed, even reaching across state borders to enemy states. Moreover, the position of the research institute, which plays an important role within this network, is best represented, as in figure 2 (loosely adapted from Medvetz 2007), as located in the *space between these fields*, in the volume of the boundary between them.

What Are These Spaces Good For?

Now that the idea of a space between fields has been indicated, I believe it is possible to give shape to this concept by asking about its utility. What analytical and conceptual tasks can it perform? How can it be put to use in the analysis of historical change? What advantages do we gain by thus supplementing the concept of field? I can think of at least two possible avenues.

Returning full circle to where I started, I would argue that the notion of a space between fields, of a thick boundary zone, is crucial in order to provide a fully relational account of the differentiation between fields. The key to such an account is the notion of boundary work. But the way this notion has been deployed up till now leaves much to be desired. Here is how Thomas Gieryn (1999: 4–5) defines it with respect to the field of science: "The discursive attribution of selected qualities to scientists, scientific methods and scientific claims for the purpose of drawing a rhetorical boundary between science and some less authoritative residual non-science." There are two problems with this definition. The first is the fact that boundary work is limited to rhetoric. The social mechanisms that limit the number of authoritative speakers, that assign their statements with differential values, that close off certain topics and devices from nonexpert inspection, that characterize something as calculable or not calculable, and so on, these mechanisms are far more robust than mere rhetoric. Rhetoric alone would never have been able to produce the relational reality of science or the economy or politics, and so forth. The second problem has already been noted: Where does boundary work itself fall? What is the status of the practices, symbolic materials, and persons who serve as boundary signs? While they mark the boundary between two sides, they themselves belong to neither side. They are hybrid. Put differently, the very act of drawing boundaries by the same token transgresses them. All of this serves merely to point out that, cartographically, it does not make sense to depict boundary work as taking place within neither side, neither inside the field nor outside it in another field; neither upstream nor downstream, as Gieryn would have it; it takes place in the space between fields, within the volume of a thick boundary. Fields secrete these thick boundary zones as an inevitable aspect of their functioning, as fuzzy zones of separation and connection.

Take, for example, the practices and mechanisms that constitute the economy. Michel Callon (1998) made the famous claim that "the economy is embedded in economics" or, more precisely, that economics and accounting format the economy. What does that mean? Something along the lines of the example I gave earlier, of the tax form. Callon points out the crucial role played in economic life by the identification of externalities, that is, certain objects or activities are identified as factors or consequences of the economic process but are nonetheless qualified as incalculable, outside the economy. This exclusion from the economic is, however, also a form of inclusion because the identification of an externality is the first move in disentangling it from its entanglements in social contexts, a first move toward bringing it within calculation, that is, reentangling it within a network of market devices. Callon suggests a far more robust and interesting concept of boundary work. Boundary work is real work. It is not just the rhetorical castigation of something as nonscientific, noneconomic, that is, drawing a fine line, but akin to the work of a border patrol: mapping the terrain, establishing connections to those who lie beyond it, transacting with them. Moreover, Callon notes that this work of identification, disentanglement, and reentanglement is typically performed by economics. Hence the subtitle of his introduction: "The Embeddedness of Economic Markets in Economics." Boundary work typically is not the work of the elite of the profession, university-based, highly abstract mathematical modelers, but of practical, hands-on, rank-and-file economists in government and corporations, who continuously identify externalities and devise means of measuring, calculating, and disentangling them. One gets the sense, therefore, that the constitution of the economy, of things economic, takes place in a boundary space between the economic field, the bureaucratic field, and the academic field and is carried out by actors who have a foot in each of these but by the same token are also somewhat marginal to each. What they do at once connects the economic field with the academic and bureaucratic ones—since to identify, measure, calculate, and disentangle externalities, that is, to qualify things as economic, to produce the specific modality of activities in the field, is a collaborative effort that requires the participation of scientists, politicians, administrators, and so on—and yet reproduces their separation since the very product of this collaborative, cross-boundary effort is the qualification of things and activities as economic or noneconomic.

Returning to the problem of the gift, we have seen how, on the page of the tax form, the gift straddles a space between the economic and the noneconomic. To report something as a gift on our tax form is boundary work in the simple sense of excluding it from things economic, but also in the more complex sense suggested above since in order to be excluded the gift is included as a candidate economic fact and is measured, probed, disentangled by the simple act of estimating and writing down its value. This sort of boundary work may serve as the basis for the Internal Revenue Service, for example, to intervene and determine that the gift is not a gift at all and is taxable. We all know that corporations use gifts to reduce their tax bill, hide money away, and so on. In short, included in the tax form, the gift becomes a boundary object (Star and Griesemer 1989), at once connecting and separating the economic and the noneconomic.

I want to return here to the case of Middle Eastern studies. Like the gift, the work carried out in research institutes functions simultaneously to connect and to separate Middle Eastern studies and military intelligence, the academy and the state. While at certain times the experts did not shy away from admitting that "papers [written] in university research institutes . . . were mostly prepared in the framework of projects connected to the defense establishment or of a similar nature" (Shamir 1979), on other occasions, when admission of such proximity became threatening, they averred that "we, as researchers, our role is to analyze, and not to educate or direct; to assess, without making recommendations that have a directive operative political application. As researchers our role is not to tell the government what to do" (Itamar Rabinovich, quoted in Eyal 1974). In both cases, they attempted to carve out for themselves, within the network, the position of those who deal with basic research or didactic intelligence, as they variously called it. The papers produced within the research institute, and more specifically the notion of assessment, were thus boundary objects between the military and the academy, at once connecting them (because they used data produced by military intelligence and aimed at the same goal of assessing intentions) and separating them (because they were basic and didactic, not operative). The research institute thus lay in the liminal space between the bureaucratic and academic and media fields, connected them, and yet also produced the relational reality of separate spheres.

A SPACE OF OPPORTUNITIES

A different way of thinking about the space between fields is as interstitial in Michael Mann's (1986: 15–6) sense, that is, as a space that is underdetermined, where things can be done and combinations and conversions can be established that are not possible to do within fields. In short, it is a space that has been opened up by some abrupt change and that can generate even more changes. There is, in fact, one place in which Bourdieu (1996a: 51–53) seems to make use of just such an idea. This is in his discussion of the salons hosted by mid-nineteenth-century French ladies of high society as "genuine articulations between the political and artistic fields." In these "bastard institutions" it was possible for writers and politicians to rub shoulders. The politicians, typically second tier, could acquire powers in the salons not available to them in the political sphere; the writers could intercede and act as a pressure group to secure material or symbolic rewards. Out of these exchanges and "shady deals" the structures and oppositions of a nascent literary field began to emerge. This example suggests several possible dynamics.

Field making: Bourdieu's story is about how such a space, or articulation, between fields became the site for the making of a new field, the literary field. Arguably, Tom Medvetz (2007) has similarly shown how the space in between academia, politics, business, and the media became the hothouse in which the contemporary American field of think tanks was hatched. But focusing on successful cases is dangerous because we may think that the space between fields is interesting not for its own sake but only if it serves to bring into being a new field. A less successful case has been studied by Lisa Stampnitzki (2008): terrorism expertise. In the early 1970s, especially after the attack on the Israeli athletes in Munich, various people became experts on terrorism. Some were academic political scientists or psychologists, others were defense analysts at RAND, others were former military intelligence officers, and others were journalists. One can describe, therefore, a space of terrorism studies that lies adjacent to or in between the academic, journalistic, and state fields. This space is characterized by (a) permeability: entry into it from all the other fields is relatively easy; (b) underregulation: rules about what one can legitimately do are relaxed there, as academics can study an object, terrorism, that is essentially defined by state activity, and state officials can engage in research that does not have clear policy implications; (c) high stakes: the prizes to be had in this space are relatively large, including government money, inside connections, and media fame, and cannot be had normally in the adjacent fields, precisely because this is (d) a space of articulation between the fields, where exchanges and alliances are contracted that cannot be done within the fields; (e) marginal actors: the actors that move into it are typically marginal in their own fields, hence they are more interested in venturing out; (f) stalemate: these marginal actors engage in field building (for example, the academics produce dubious chronologies of terrorism events and amass no-less-dubious bibliographies of terrorism-related knowledge; they even write dubious retrospective histories of the field's emergence), but the struggle over the type of expertise dominant in this space (which each brought with it)— military, social scientific, journalistic—was never decided. Unlike the field of think tanks, no clear division of labor and hierarchy of worth emerged.

Raid: Stalemate is not the only reason the idea of a space between fields, which is a space of opportunity, can be insightful. Such a space may be significant and long-lasting because it affords those in adjacent fields an opportunity to raid it, rapidly amassing profits, and rapidly retreat into their original fields, where these profits may be reconverted into currency that will improve one's formerly marginal position within it. A sort of gold rush image. For example, human behavioral genetics, studied by Aaron Panofsky (2006) is a subdiscipline that could be described as lying on the margins of the scientific field. It is considered by many practitioners of animal behavioral genetics to be quasi-scientific because the sort of controlled experiments performed with generations upon generations of lab animals are obviously impossible to perform with humans. On the other hand, this is a research site that generates a great deal of media attention and attracts a great deal of funding from foundations and the government. As a result, this space that lies between the natural and human sciences as well as between academia, the media, and the foundations field is the site of constant incursions by actors who are relatively marginal within their own fields or whose disciplines occupy a marginal or liminal position: failed animal behavioral geneticists, psychologists, professors of education, publicists, and science writers. Each perceives this in-between space as a site where combinations disallowed in their own field, the sort of "grafting" Rose describes (which in this case may connect, for example, identical twin studies from psychology with DNA mapping and socioeconomic stratification data), are permitted. Each actor perceives this in-between space as a site of opportunity, one in which resources could be accumulated and then possibly converted into an improved position within their home field. For this reason Latour's Machiavellian language may indeed aptly apply to describe the actions of these actors, but only because of how their habitus was shaped by their specific trajectory within given fields. Marginality is the mother of invention and improvisation, of seeing value in heterodox combinations and in exploiting fuzzy frontiers. Moving into the relatively unstructured space between fields, these marginal and heterodox actors may indeed approximate the Machiavellian model.

Fuzzification: It is also possible that the in-between status of the space between fields is valued for its own sake, not as a base for creating a new field or for a return to one's home field. Its fuzzy nature is therefore actively cultivated and reproduced. There are great advantages in staying liminal. This is true, for example, with respect to what Justin Lee (2004) calls "hybrid wellness practices," that is, alternative medicine, spiritual guidance, techniques of body/self improvement. The sociology of professions always assumed that professionalization (i.e., qualifying for entry into an existing field of expertise), either successful or failed, is the only option open to new forms of expertise or groups of experts. But a no less plausible option, especially for those who were not marginal actors in scientific or professional fields but entered the in-between space from another direction, is to remain within it and exploit the fact that it is an underregulated space. Instead of submitting to the close governmental and collegial regulation that comes with the status of professions, they may choose to suspend claims for scientificity or professionalism and remain in the space that straddles the medical field, the field of personal services, and so forth. The idea of a space between fields allows one to make sense, cartographically, of such choices. Such spaces of what I call fuzzification and hybridity are typically formed in response to massive cultural and social changes that deconstruct the existing system of distinctions and

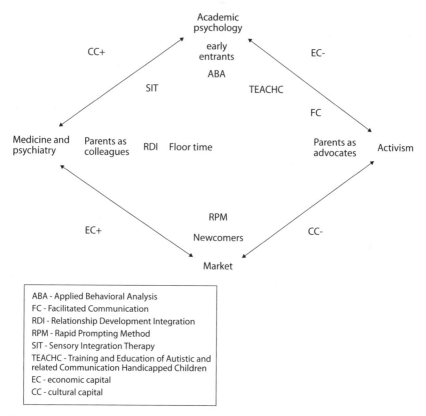

Figure 7.3. The space between fields of autism therapies.

classifications. A case in point is autism therapies (Eyal et al. 2010). The massive deinstitutionalization of mental retardation, which took place in the early 1970s, opened up a space of opportunity, as it destroyed the existing system of classification for childhood developmental disorders and shook the self-confidence of the reigning medical and psychiatric professions. Because of the massive and sudden nature of the change, barriers to entry in terms of credentials, funds, and licensing were rather low. At the same time, because deinstitutionalization meant that parents and schools were left to their own devices, in charge of kids who previously were institutionalized, there were vast opportunities for profits to be made in this space: monetary profits but also, more significantly, symbolic profits in terms of upgrading the prestige of practitioners and therapists who had been fairly marginal previously. Securing these profits, however, depended on striking a coalition with parents, which meant that techniques had to be kept simple and knowledge open. Low barriers to entry, high profits to be made, the necessity for keeping knowledge generous and open, all these meant that this was a space between fields, a space of opportunity into which entered all sorts of entrepreneurs from adjacent fields, including the academic field, medical field, the market, special education, and advocacy. Each new entrant was peddling a therapy that was low-tech, eclectic, not too attentive to psychiatric nosologies, and oriented toward an alliance with parents, in this way guaranteeing that the space would remain an in-between one, would not be colonized by adjacent, powerful professions, and, as represented in figure 3, would remain open to new entrants from the marketplace, advocacy organizations, and so forth.

To conclude, I have offered the idea of spaces between fields as strategic research sites or work spaces in which it is possible to combine field analysis and actor network theory in a fruitful way. Only time will tell if the idea sticks. Given, however, the current lack of productive interchange between field analysis, actor network theory, and the sociology of the professions, my hope is that this idea will at the very least foster dialogue between these divergent, competing approaches by bringing them together in this work space delineated by the notion of spaces between fields.

Notes

1. I would argue that the Machiavellian language of mobilizing allies and controlling their behavior is the price one has to pay if one wants to include in the account the nonhumans as actants and to provide a completely symmetrical account. Translation, when it comes to the nonhumans, does not have to include any account of meaning and understanding. So this dimension gets reduced and truncated in the Latourian treatment of humans as well. Latour would probably reply that the very idea of meaning as something that precedes and determines the act of translation is metaphysical. I agree. As Lakoff and Johnson (2003 [1980]: 59) have shown, it involves a container or conduit metaphor, according to which words contain and convey meaning. This metaphor is very useful for our everyday dealings but must be rejected as a serious account of language and meaning. Meaning is not inherent in words but is created in and through use. One could even say that meaning is what appears whenever one translates from one metaphor to the other. It exists in the space between words. But all of these considerations do not change the point that when it comes to humans, unlike nonhumans, an important dimension of translation is discursive and involves understanding. It involves linguistic persuasion aiming to get the other party to meaningfully understand their interests as aligned with the fact builder. The very term *discourse* conveys the point that while words do not contain meaning in and of themselves and could be interpreted and pushed in different ways, linguistic usage is anything but random. It is structured by systematic practices, rituals, and habits, which are themselves the product of concerted pedagogic action. From very early childhood and all the way through the rituals required in order to enunciate rarefied forms of discourse, pedagogic action works to stabilize and reproduce the meaning of linguistic formulations, first and

foremost through embodiment and habituation, i.e., it produces the very "metaphors we live by," those that model a less physical form of experience upon a more physical one (Bourdieu and Passeron 1977; Foucault 1986). It would be completely asymmetrical, therefore, to assume that the fact builder is somehow less determined by discourse, less subject to the embodiment of these practices, habits, and rituals, and freer in the use of linguistic formulations than the presumed allies. Obviously in some cases this may be true to some extent, but these are simply cases at the furthest pole of a continuum (in fact, the idea of a space between fields can make sense of these extreme cases, since it is a space of relative freedom, wherein marginality also means that actors are less determined). But such extreme cases are not the rule. This is why one needs concepts like field and habitus. With nonhuman allies, however, these considerations do not come into play at all.

2. There were notorious cases in which an open controversy erupted between the research branch and certain decision makers, but the status of these events as scandals shows that they are the exception that proves the rule. The most famous such scandal was the disagreement between the commander of military intelligence and Defense Minister Ariel Sharon over the scenario Sharon painted in order to justify extending the invasion of Lebanon in 1982 beyond previous, more limited plans (Yaari and Schiff 1984: 24, 99–122).

BOURDIEU'S TWO SOCIOLOGIES OF KNOWLEDGE

Not the least of Pierre Bourdieu's distinctions among the members of the sociological pantheon is his determination to make knowledge a primary focus of sociological inquiry. Whereas other leading figures of his generation, as of sociological generations past, barely touch the topic, save to render it small alongside big subjects like the economy, the state, and religion, Bourdieu stands almost alone in foregrounding the social dynamics of knowledge no less than the workings of the economy, the polity, and the domain of culture more broadly.[1] Future historians of the discipline will likely record that Bourdieu did more than any sociologist before him to move the study of knowledge from backstage to center stage.

Bourdieu's oeuvre treats many forms of human knowledge and does so as part of several diverse lines of work. From his early analyses of the scientific field to his final lecture course at the Collège de France, scientific knowledge of the kind associated predominately with the natural sciences constituted one of Bourdieu's major concerns. In his writings on Martin Heidegger, on various contemporary French philosophers, and on the French academy generally, philosophical knowledge, scholastic knowledge, scholarly knowledge, and academic knowledge likewise occupied his attention. These projects dovetailed with his extensive studies of cultural production in literature and art as well as with his late work on media, including that on the production, distribution, and consumption of journalistic knowledge. And social-scientific knowledge, sociological knowledge especially, formed a leitmotif of Bourdieu's work, a subject to which he continually returned as part of his lifelong campaign to transform sociology into a discipline imbued with greater reflexivity about its own practices of knowledge production. Indeed, Bourdieu believed strongly that "the sociology of sociology, . . . far from being a specialty among others, . . . is the necessary prerequisite of any rigorous sociological practice" (Bourdieu and Wacquant 1992 [1988]: 68).

Since a comprehensive study of this corpus of work is beyond the scope of a single chapter, I will approach Bourdieu's oeuvre in the spirit of this last statement of his. In other words, I will consider his writings on knowledge principally through the prism of what they contribute to the study of the production of *social-scientific knowledge*, sociological knowledge in particular. What is more, following Bourdieu's example, I will anchor my analysis in a concern with the problem of the "genesis of thought" (2000b: 43), that is, with the social practices and processes that shape the intellectual *content* of the work of social scientists. To seek the social basis of the content of texts is to pursue what Bourdieu called a "genetic sociology of the works themselves" (1993c [1986]: 190, 1988a: xxiv).

In view of sociologists' long-standing inattention to the production of social-scientific knowledge, Bourdieu's work holds the potential to open a new era. Capitalizing on this opportunity requires, nevertheless, a measured evaluation of his approach. On the whole, critical appraisals of Bourdieu's writings on culture have polarized between the extremes of filial loyalty (where the main critique is that Bourdieu left a few loose ends in his vast project) and blanket hostility (which condemns Bourdieu by hasty mischaracterization). The few more balanced analyses, notably those of Swartz (1997), Benson (1999), and Couldry (2002), have centered on aspects of Bourdieu's work other than his sociology of knowledge.

As a modest step toward rectifying this situation and enhancing the utility of his work for addressing the kinds of questions it poses about the "genesis" of social-scientific knowledge, this chapter proposes that Bourdieu's writings contain not one but two sociological approaches to knowledge production, one of them explicit and well marked out, the other less conspicuous and less systematically presented. For want of better terms, I call the first his programmatically stated model and the second his model-in-use. In the first section I describe the first of these models, and in the second I identify and attempt to integrate the principal components of the second model. In the third section I briefly assess which of the two models might better serve to ground a historical sociology of sociology, offering a few examples to illustrate their differences. The conclusion summarizes my argument.

The Programmatically Stated Model of Knowledge Production

Whether dealing with social-scientific knowledge or any other knowledge form, Bourdieu is careful to instruct his readers explicitly on how he believes a sociologist should set about to understand and explain knowledge production. He provides this instruction by presenting his own approach against the backdrop of what he sees as the two major preexisting approaches. These he labels "internal analysis" and "external analysis," in accord with the terms "internalism" and "externalism," which sociologists of knowledge have commonly used to designate the two scholarly approaches.

Bourdieu equates traditional internal analysis with exclusively "internal readings" of cultural works, that is, with hermeneutics of the kinds found in the work of literary scholars associated with New Criticism and of figures such as the Russian formalists and Michel Foucault (see esp. 1993c [1986]).[2] According to Bourdieu, this is a family of approaches that aims to achieve textual "interpretation" by "relating [cultural] works only to themselves" (1996a [1992]: 181, 1993c [1986]: 177–78)—"thus refus[ing] to relate works in any way to their social conditions of production" (1993c [1986]: 33). Owing to this refusal, cultural works emerge as "self-sufficient realities," comprehensible only insofar as the analyst enters "the enchanted circle of pure reading of [any particular] texts" in light of other prior or contemporaneous texts (Bourdieu and Wacquant 1992 [1988]: 151; Bourdieu 1996a [1992]: 306). When scholars use this perspective to examine scientific knowledge, the result is "the idea of 'pure' science, . . . developing according to its internal logic," with the corollary that the study of science is "the province of the epistemologist, which recreates the logic by which science creates its specific problems" (2004d [2001]: 45, 1975: 22).

By contrast, advocates of external analysis, according to Bourdieu's somewhat briefer account, seek the "explanation" of cultural works, scientific and otherwise, by turning away from texts to "external determinants," understood as the direct operation of macrosocial factors (1996a [1992]: 193, 1993c [1986]: 181). Bourdieu associates these practices with various branches of Marxism, including those that consider "the relationship between the social world and works of culture in terms of *reflection*," sometimes "directly link[ing] these works to the social characteristics (the social origins) of their authors" (1993c [1986]: 180). For Bourdieu the hallmark of the tradition of external analysis is that it "reduces [works] directly to the most general social and economic conditions" of an epoch, casting cultural production "for example, [as] the effect of economic crises, technical transformations or political revolutions" (Bourdieu and Wacquant 1992 [1988]: 151; Bourdieu 1993c [1986]: 181).

So characterized, conventional internalist and externalist approaches provide dichotomous counterpoints to Bourdieu's own approach to knowledge production, which he presents as "offering a route out of this forced choice . . . between an internal reading of the text which consists in considering the text in itself and for itself, and an external reading which crudely relates the text to the society in general. *Between the two there is a social universe that is always forgotten, that of the producers of the works. . . . To name this microcosm [is] to speak of the field*" (2005a [1995]: 32–33, emphasis added). According to Bourdieu, what proponents of internalism and externalism have "in common," for all their differences, is "a lack of recognition of the *field of production* as a space of objective relations" (1996a [1992]: 181).

One sees in these passages the reasoning by which Bourdieu's concept of field, which figures so significantly in his writings on the economy, the state, and religion, enters and becomes the centerpiece of his sociology of knowledge. Just as Bourdieu regards these other arenas of the social world each as a relatively autonomous universe of objective relations among hierarchically ordered positions—and hence as a site of struggle between agents in dominant and subordinate positions to conserve or transform those relations—so he extends this field conception into the realm of knowledge, treating philosophers, sociologists, and other specialized groupings of "professionals of symbolic production" as constituting a field each in its own right (1990d: 297). For Bourdieu, only "by taking into account *the field of specific production* [can] you avoid the complementary mistakes" of traditional internalist and externalist approaches (Bourdieu and Wacquant 1992 [1988]: 151, emphasis added).

This intervention leads Bourdieu to advocate an explicitly *dualist model* for the understanding and explanation of knowledge, scientific and otherwise: a model inclusive both of "the field of specific production" and of "general social and economic conditions."[3] For example, regarding scientific knowledge, he writes, "Science must be examined in its *two-fold relation*, on the one hand to the social cosmos in which it is embedded—the *external reading*—and on the other to the social microcosm constituted by the scientific universe, a relatively autonomous world endowed with its own rules of functioning which must be described and analyzed in themselves—the *internal reading*" (1990d: 298).[4] Similarly, he urges a "*double reading*" (Bourdieu and Wacquant 1992 [1988]: 152) of Heidegger's philosophy: "A simultaneously political and philosophical *dual reading* of writings which are defined . . . by their reference to two social spaces," that of the relatively autonomous "philosophical field" and that of "the political history of Germany" (1991a [1975]: 3, 41). In a somewhat related context Bourdieu speaks of knowledge producers as "*bi-dimensional beings*," "belong[ing] to an intellectually autonomous field" but not separate from "political activity outside it" (1989b: 99). And, with special reference to the social sciences, he lays down the following principle: "A comparative survey of the development of the social sciences suggests that a model designed to explain the historical and cross-national variations of these disciplines should take into account *two fundamental factors*"—on the one hand, the configuration of "dominant political and economic forces" and, on the other hand, the nature and degree of autonomy that the social-scientific field has acquired from these forces (1994b [1991]: 3).

The same message emerges on occasions when Bourdieu formulates general instructions for the sociological analysis of "fields of cultural production," whether "literary, artistic, philosophical, scientific, etc." (1996a [1992]: 214). In these contexts, he stipulates that "the science of cultural works" requires the following necessary "operations": "first, one must analyse the position of the literary (etc.) field within the [larger] field of power . . . ; second, one must analyse the internal structure of the literary (etc.) field" (1996a [1992]: 214; see also Bourdieu and Wacquant 1992 [1988]: 104–5). Bourdieu's collaborator and interpreter Loïc Wacquant describes the Bourdieusian approach precisely the same way: "An analysis of cultural works in terms of field entails [the following] closely interlinked operations. The first is locating the artistic (literary, poetic, musical, etc.) microcosm within the 'field of power.' . . . The second moment . . . consists in drawing a typology of the internal structure of the artistic [etc.] field" (1998: 300).[5]

One take on Bourdieu's program here would see Bourdieu as melding together the external and internal modes of analysis that, as he complains, were "traditionally perceived as irreconcilable" (1996a [1992]: 205). But this interpretation would miss the mark, for, with respect to the "dual reading" Bourdieu enjoins, "external" and "internal" acquire significantly new connotations, very different from the meanings that, in passages like those above, he gives these words when applying them to previous traditions of scholarship. To fail to notice these alterations of meaning is to overlook some of the points Bourdieu most wishes to emphasize.

Consider, first, "external." When Bourdieu uses "external" in reference to Marxist-style accounts, the term designates economic and other macrolevel factors operating on knowledge production directly. Yet one of his central arguments is that this thesis about direct influence rests on the "short-circuit fallacy": "seeking to establish a direct line between very distant terms, [the claim omits] the crucial mediation provided by the relatively autonomous space of the field of cultural production" in question (Bourdieu and Wacquant 1992 [1988]: 69). According to Bourdieu, "One cannot understand what happens, [even in] a very weakly autonomous field, simply on the basis of knowledge of the surrounding world; [instead, one must] understand the effects that the people engaged in the microcosm exert on one another" (2005a [1995]: 33). This break with the old externalism is essential because "the field *refracts*," receiving and filtering the force of external factors differentially at disparate locations within the field. Bourdieu puts this point as follows: "The efficacy of external factors, economic crises, technical transformations, political revolutions, or quite simply social demand . . . can *only* be exercised by the intermediary of the transformations of the structure of the field" (1988b: 544, 1996a [1992]: 204, emphasis added). These statements reveal that, although the "external" moment of a Bourdieusian reading includes some of the same kinds of "general social factors" found in traditional externalist accounts, the manner of incorporation has shifted from direct to field-mediated.

But Bourdieu reworks "internal" in a still more significant way, changing not only the manner of incorporation but also the very substance of the internal factors included. Whereas traditional internalist approaches, on Bourdieu's telling, exclude the "social" in favor of an asociological examination of texts in and of themselves, Bourdieu focuses on the objective relational structure and agonistic dynamics of a field, that is, on "the specific—and truly social—logic of the world of professional symbolic production and of symbolic producers" (1990d: 298). To be sure, texts (and other cultural works) are what professional symbolic producers produce; but in order to understand this process the internal moment in Bourdieu's analysis examines field forces and struggles, yielding a novel kind of "internal reading" that, as he states, centers not on texts per se but on the "functioning [of] the social microcosm" (1990d: 298).

Nor, according to Bourdieu's double reading, are the external and the internal moments coequal explanatory partners. To the contrary: the more autonomy a field of cultural production possesses, the more field forces and struggles take precedence, in his view, in a genetic account of the content of the works produced. In this specific sense, Karin Knorr-Cetina is quite right to describe Bourdieu's approach to the production of scientific knowledge as "internalism" (1981: 72, 1982: 106, 109),[6] even as Wacquant can equally correctly observe that Bourdieu stands "against all variants of internalist analysis propounded by neo-Kantian aesthetics, the Russian formalists, and structuralists from Roman Jakobson to Michel Foucault" (1998: 301). The internalisms Bourdieu opposes are all text-centered, as distinguished from what I have elsewhere called the "new sociological internalism" (Camic 2001). As exemplified in the United States particularly in the work of Randall Collins (1998), the new sociological internalism is an approach that (a) focuses on knowledge producers located within specialized intellectual fields; (b) posits that macrosocial factors affect knowledge production indirectly via their field effects; (c) rejects text-based internalist explanations; and, in consequence, (d) *views knowledge production mainly in terms of the social dynamics operating inside particular intellectual fields.* The paragraphs above have shown that points *a*, *b*, and *c* are fundamental, too, to Bourdieu's program for the analysis of knowledge production, and the paragraphs below will now document the same for point *d*. Taken together, they evidence Bourdieu's independent articulation and embrace of the tenets of the "new sociological internalism."

A note of clarification is in order. Throughout his writings on knowledge Bourdieu is careful to accord centrality to internal forces and struggles *only insofar* as the object of analysis is a *relatively autonomous* field of knowledge production. In his oeuvre as a whole, however, "relative autonomy" is a notoriously slippery concept, among other reasons because of Bourdieu's tendency to evade certain vexing questions, particularly questions as to whether relatively autonomous fields empirically produce the effects he theorizes by the tautological claim that a social space qualifies empirically as a relatively autonomous field only when it does produce the effects he theorizes (Bourdieu and Wacquant 1992 [1988]: 100).[7] Conveniently, however, when Bourdieu's topic is knowledge production, specifically knowledge production in Western societies during the past 125 years or so, he furnishes a less elusive way of identifying a relatively autonomous field. With respect to this particular historical context, he holds that "autonomization . . . takes place . . . in particular through the creation of some quite extraordinary realities . . .—namely, *disciplines*" (2004d [2001]: 49). Accordingly, he takes academic disciplines in the sciences, the social sciences, and the humanities as the preeminent illustration of knowledge production fields, instancing physics, mathematics, biology, economics, political science, sociology, history, philosophy, and literature, among others. In his view, "a discipline is a relatively stable and delimited field [which is] easy to recognize: it has an academically and socially recognized name (. . . such as sociology as opposed to 'mediology,' for example); it is inscribed in institutions, laboratories, university departments, journals, national and international fora (conferences), procedures for the certification of competences" and so forth (2004d [2001]: 64–65).

With regard to knowledge production in social spaces of *this* type, Bourdieu's dualist model assigns priority to internal field dynamics. The interrelated terms with which he characterizes these relatively autonomous arenas attest to this plank of the new sociological internalism in his program for the sociology of knowledge. On his account, each such field is

- "a world apart" (2004d [2001]: 32ff);
- a "closed vessel" (2005a [1995]: 35), "a closed, separate microcosm" (2000b [1997]: 19), "a separate social universe" (1993c [1986]: 162), a site "closing in . . . upon itself" (1996a [1992]: 204, 1993c [1986]: 162), a space of "(more or less total) closure" (2004d [2001]: 69);
- "the site of a logic and a necessity that are specific and irreducible to

those that regulate other fields" (Bourdieu and Wacquant 1992 [1988]: 97), a space that "fulfils its own logic" (1993c [1986]: 39) and "develop[s] its own necessity, its own logic, its own nomos" (2004d [2001]: 47);

- a microcosm possessing "its own laws of functioning independent of those of politics and the economy" (1993c [1986]: 162);
- a space constituted of "immanent forces" (1990e [1982]: 193), of "objective mechanisms immanent in the logic of the field" (1996a [1992]: 113);
- "a sort of well-regulated ballet in which individuals and groups dance their own steps" (1996a [1992]: 113);
- "a game apart" (2005a [1995]: 35), "a particular social game" (1993c [1986]: 162), a "game . . . of immanent necessity" (1996a [1992]: 247), a site operating by "the logic of the game itself" (2000b [1997]: 11);
- a battle "carried along by the internal logic[8] of [a] competitive fight" among combatants (1996a [1992]: 128);
- "a market [where] producers have only their own competitors as consumers" (1996b [1989]: 106; see also 1975, 23, 2004d [2001]: 54–56).

These recurring internalist metaphors—closed vessel, ballet, game, battle, market—are part and parcel of two broader arguments that constitute the sociological core of Bourdieu's model of knowledge production, as he exposits it in his writings on disciplines and similarly autonomous cultural fields. The first of these arguments concerns knowledge fields at any particular point in time and asserts a direct relationship between the objective social-relational location of knowledge producers within a field and the substance of the intellectual stances they adopt. According to Bourdieu, "fields of cultural production propose to those involved in them a *space of possibles* that tends to orient their research, . . . defining the universe of problems, references, intellectual benchmarks, . . . concepts," and so on (1993c [1986]: 176). Among these possibilities, moreover, producers do not select randomly. Rather, their substantive "position-takings" correspond to the field position that the different producers objectively occupy by virtue of the kinds and amounts of field-relevant capital they possess,[9] as Bourdieu explains: "Objective relations between [field] positions . . . are the *true principle* of the position-takings of different producers, of the competition which pits them against each other, of the alliances they form, of the works they produce or defend" (1996a [1992]: 204; see also 2004d [2001]: 58–59). By identifying the knowledge producer's field position as the "true principle" of his or her intellectual position taking, Bourdieu again makes plain the new internalist aspect of his thinking.

His second core argument reinforces the point. Turning from knowledge fields as they stand at any particular moment to how these fields change over time, Bourdieu holds that "the impetus for change in cultural works—language, art, literature, science, etc.—resides in the struggles that take place in the corresponding fields of production" (1993c [1986]: 183), above all "the struggle between established figures and the young challengers," that is, between those producers whose stake is to preserve the relations (and the distribution of capital) that define the field in its existing form and new entrants (still low in field-specific capital) who seek to transform the field to their advantage.[10] Contrasting this new internalist explanation with the old internalism, Bourdieu writes, "The motor of change . . . is not inscribed in the works themselves but in the opposition—which is constitutive of all fields of cultural production . . .—between orthodoxy and heresy" (1996a [1992]: 205). What is more, in relatively autonomous fields, he claims, this motor of positional opposition runs continually, now toward the consolidation, now toward the demise, of a succession of orthodoxies that furnishes the field with a "kind of cumulativity," such that "what happens in the field is more and more dependent on the specific history of the field, and more and more independent of external history" (1996a [1992]: 242–43, 1993c [1986]: 188).

Despite this emphasis on internal field dynamics, however, Bourdieu keeps to his policy of treating knowledge in its "two-fold relation" to the specific field of knowledge production *and* to the external social cosmos. In his view, even in regard to relatively autonomous cultural fields such as academic disciplines, this external relation retains importance for at least three reasons. First, under certain circumstances, members of these fields may themselves opt for extra-field engagement. Bourdieu describes, for example, "the free, critical thinker, the intellectual who uses his or her specific capital, won by virtue of autonomy and guaranteed by the very autonomy of the field, to intervene in the field of politics, following the model of Zola or Sartre" (1990e [1982]: 145; see also Bourdieu 1989b, 1996a [1992]: 129, 231–33). Second, although external factors affect autonomous fields only indirectly, they affect these fields nonetheless—most importantly, according to Bourdieu, by ensuring a supply of human knowledge producers and of the economic capital which supports specialized positions for them and which may also give one side or another an edge in struggles between the orthodox and the heterodox (1993c [1986]: 55, 184–85, 1996a [1992]: 127). In Bourdieu's analysis, external factors especially impinge around the "heteronomous" pole that arises in every field of cultural production and attracts those producers who are ill-prepared to acquire field-specific capital and are thus oriented outward (1993c [1986]: 186–87; Bourdieu and Wacquant 1992 [1988]: 184). By his account, this pole has exerted considerable force throughout the history of the social sciences, sociology in particular: "One always finds, at the very heart of the field, 'naifs' . . . who, for want of the theoretical and technical means to master the current problematic, import into the field certain social problems in a crude state" (1996a [1992]: 243). Third, the (relative) autonomy of a field of cultural production is never complete. In Bourdieu's reckoning, autonomy from external forces not only is a matter of "degree," but also is "a historical conquest, endlessly having to be undertaken anew" (2004d [2001]: 47). The latter circumstance, he maintains, has especially been the fate of the social sciences, which have repeatedly struggled "with external forces which hold back their 'take-off'" (2004d [2001]: 47).

Here, as in previous passages, one must understand Bourdieu's terminology precisely as he uses it within his program for the sociology of knowledge. When referring to "external" social factors in these and similar statements, Bourdieu neither retreats from his attack on the old externalism nor compromises what he seeks to achieve with his field concept. In his view, even a weakly autonomous field mediates and refracts external forces according to the dynamics of the "microcosm as such" (2005a [1995]: 33), while heteronomous cultural producers, too, accede "to the specific norms of the[ir] field" (1996a [1992]: 69; see also 1993c [1986]: 40). At the other extreme, the most autonomous producers, "in very autonomous fields, such as science or poetry, . . . tend to have no link with the social world [other] than the social conditions that ensure their autonomy with respect to that world" (2004d [2001]: 15). Bourdieu sometimes speaks of this latter state as one of "freedom from external determinations" (1996a [1992]: 301), anticipating, in his more optimistic moments, that sociology itself might eventually "escape" from and "limit the effects of historical and social determinisms" (2004d [2001]: 89–92). Whatever the likelihood of this prospect, one sees again how Bourdieu's dualist model of knowledge production refashions the externalism and internalism of the past in the light of his field theory.

The Knowledge Production Model-in-Use

The dualist model of knowledge production is a fixture in Bourdieu's oeuvre. On every occasion—or at least every occasion of which I am aware—where he explicitly formulates his approach to knowledge production, he proceeds in almost identical fashion: setting up the dichotomy between traditional internalist and externalist accounts; presenting his concept of a specialized field of cultural production as the crucial element missing from traditional accounts; recasting "internal" and "external" alike from the perspective of his field-conceptual apparatus; and then prescribing a dualist analysis of knowledge production, an analysis congruent with the principles of the new sociological internalism. The first part of this chapter cites a variety of Bourdieu's general statements about knowledge production to document his embrace of this model and identifies the model as well in his writings on empirical topics ranging from science and social science to philosophy and art.

Careful inspection of these same empirical writings, however, yields an unanticipated surplus: for when Bourdieu uses his model as a lens through which to view concrete subjects, he sometimes observes, in a less systematic way, other important aspects of the knowledge-production process. This kind of observational surplus is an outcome one expects when models meet the complexities of empirical cases, especially in the hands of observers like Bourdieu who are wary of conceptual straightjackets. In this sense, the presence of an observational surplus in his empirical writings is more a credit to than a criticism of Bourdieu and provides no warrant for charging him with any fundamental theoretical contradictions or inconsistencies. That said, I want to call attention to three fairly discrete currents in Bourdieu's empirical work on knowledge production that tend to overflow the banks of his dualist model. While a skilled exegete might render each of these currents compatible with the dualist model, my purpose here is instead to merge these currents together with one another in order to draw from Bourdieu an alternative model of knowledge production (especially in the social sciences), a model that may have wider historical range.

The first of these currents is Bourdieu's explicit inclusion, in his analysis of knowledge production, of a variety of social spaces in addition to those that underpin the dualist model. As I pointed out in the first part of this chapter, Bourdieu's model assigns particular meanings to "external" and "internal," associating "external" with the field-mediated effects of the macrosocial factors present in traditional sociology-of-knowledge accounts—"general social and economic conditions," "economic crisis, technical transformation, and political revolution," or the "field of power," in Bourdieu's terms—and "internal" with some specific field of knowledge production, typically an academic discipline.

Yet here and there in his empirical writings on knowledge production other elements briefly enter the equation. For example, having insisted on a double reading of Heidegger that attends to the philosophical and the political fields, Bourdieu attributes significance to "the position of the philosophical field in the structure of the university field and the intellectual field, etc.," and he adverts also to "literary movements outside the [philosophical] field" (1991a [1975]: 95, 46). Likewise, his dualist treatment of late nineteenth-century French novels makes passing reference to the need to consider "all the fields of cultural production together" and to take account of how "scientistic thought . . . dominated the whole intellectual field in the 1880s and . . . conquers the university field through the founders of the new sciences and the new university" (1996a [1992]: 132, 126). As well, his analysis of journalism notes the inter-play of several knowledge "fields—scientific, legal, philosophical, etc." (2005a [1995]: 44). Most important, perhaps, Bourdieu's final lecture course thrice interjects "that the various disciplines occupy positions in the *(hierarchized) space of disciplines* and that what happens in them partly depends on these positions" (2004d [2001]: 66; see also 32, 94).

To be sure, an interpreter wishing to square these heterogeneous elements with Bourdieu's dualist model could do so by simply arguing that the model contains these additional spaces—all fields of cultural production taken to-gether, the whole intellectual field, the hierarchy of academic disciplines, the university field, and so on—by tacit understanding: that is, that Bourdieu expects his readers to know that, whether regarded as external or internal forces, such fields belong in the picture. It is hardly typical of Bourdieu, however, to count on his audience to fill in missing terms for him; ordinarily, his practice is to lay out the conceptual apparatus of his work as fully as possible, lest readers overlook something important. That the additional spaces just listed go unmentioned when Bourdieu exposits his dualist model is therefore telling, and particularly so given that he himself elides these spaces when describing the sine qua non of a field, relative autonomy. On this issue, Bourdieu states repeatedly that, insofar as a discipline or other field of cultural production attains independence "with regard to external economic, political, and religious powers," that field then possesses the relative autonomy that makes it "a separate social universe having its own laws of functioning" (2005a [1995]: 105; 1993c [1986]: 162; see also 1996a [1992]: 61, 2004d [2001]: vii).[11] In statements like these, arenas such as the larger university field, the hierarch-ized space of disciplines, and so forth altogether vanish, begging questions about *their* status with regard to disciplinary autonomy.[12]

This is paradoxical, for in some ways Bourdieu is the sociologist par excel-lence of these other arenas, as he demonstrates particularly in *Homo Academ-icus*. Furthermore, as soon as one turns from his statements about knowledge production to other portions of his work, one immediately encounters the principle that "the concept of field can be used at different levels of aggrega-tion," that any "given field [is] itself nested in a network of hierarchical relations with other fields," and that fields may be "partially overlapping" (Bourdieu and Wacquant 1992 [1988]: 104n., 149, 113).[13] Consistent with this principle, Bour-dieu locates the field of any given academic discipline within "the field of the arts and social sciences," the "scientific field," the "university field as a whole," and the "intellectual field" (1988a [1984]: 114, 74).[14] In light of this, the puzzle is not that these additional spaces sometimes surface in his empirical writings on knowledge production, but that they surface there only briefly and occasionally.[15] My hunch as to why this is so is that Bourdieu's dualist language of internal/external and his language elsewhere of multileveled/nested/overlapping spaces do not graft naturally onto one another, and that the dualist perspective pushes the multilevel conceptualizing to the margins in both his programmatic and empirical writings on knowledge production because what frames his thinking in these cases is the internalism/externalism dichotomy.[16]

The alternative, in any event, would seem to be to liberate Bourdieu's sociology of knowledge from the dualist model and to reconstruct it in terms of a multiplex model that systematically includes not only specific knowledge production fields such as disciplines and macrolevel economic-political-religious powers, but also the full ensemble of additional fields that Bourdieu's empirical work on knowledge production mentions in passing.[17] And this, I believe, is a salutary move which his oeuvre clearly invites. Even so, it is a step that is less straightforward, less purely additive, than may seem to be the case. Recall, when Bourdieu takes knowledge production as his topic, his explanatory concern is with the substantive content of knowledge, with providing a "genetic sociology of the works themselves." When tackling other topics, however, his explanatory focus explicitly shifts. Thus, in *Homo Academicus* and elsewhere when he examines larger fields like that of the arts and sciences faculties or the university as a whole, Bourdieu naturally attends to other struggles, that is, to the specific game that defines each successive field, with its own stakes, positions, capital requirements, and so on—rather than, say, to the battles among specialists in a particular discipline and the content of the works that result.

How struggles in higher-level fields spill over onto the disciplinary battles is a question Bourdieu generally bypasses, however, aside from sometimes noting the effect of higher-level struggles on the supply to lower-level fields of knowledge producers and various material resources (1988a [1984]: 32–33). This effect exactly parallels the way in which external economic and other factors affect the internal dynamics of knowledge fields according to Bourdieu's dualist model, and it has equally little direct relationship to the shaping of content of knowledge. The lacuna is evident in his analysis of Heidegger, where, having briefly inserted the university field and the wider intellectual field into his dual philosophical-political reading, Bourdieu appraises these fields in terms of their impact on academic "career opportunities" and the "influx of students" into philosophy (1991a [1975]: 12–13), *not* in terms of their bearing on the actual substance of Heidegger's thought, as such content issues remain, for Bourdieu, matters connected with the inner dynamics of the philosophical field.[18] This example illustrates why elaborating Bourdieu's model of knowledge production involves more than simply adding in some of the other (multileveled, nested, and overlapping) spaces he examines else-where in his oeuvre, valuable as that first step is. One must also consider the status of these fields with respect to the genesis of the works that specialized knowledge producers produce.

For this purpose, a second current in Bourdieu's work bears notice: his occasional observations on the transfer of elements of content from one knowledge field into another. His most direct treatment of this issue appears in his discussion of the "exchanges between painters and writers" that went on in nineteenth-century France, as writers undertook "the first systematic for-mulations of the theory of art for art's sake," "sent" this theory and "the image of the artist as solitary hero" to painters, and then "took into [their own] discursive order the discoveries the painters were making in their practices, particularly with respect to the art of living" (1996a [1992]: 131–34). Elsewhere Bourdieu makes scattered mention of similar occurrences. Considering Gus-tave Flaubert, for example, he notices a one-directional version of the same transfer process: "The era is also that of Geoffroy Saint-Hilaire, [the Chevalier de] Lamarck, [Charles] Darwin, [Georges] Cuvier, of theories of the origins of species and evolution; Flaubert . . . borrows from the natural and historical sciences not only their erudite knowledge but also their characteristic mode of thought and the philosophy drawn from them—determinism, relativism, his-toricism" (1996a [1992]: 99). Bourdieu sprinkles his writings on the modern academy with many similar comments, pointing out

- that Roland Barthes made "liberal and often approximate borrowing from the combined lexicons of linguistics, psychoanalysis, and anthro-pology" (1988a [1984]: 117);
- that the "more advanced sciences [have served as sociology's] major suppliers not only of methods and techniques . . . but also of examples," as well as "norms and models" (1975: 37);
- that "borrowings between [the contemporary natural] sciences [in-volve] standardized procedures, tried and tested models, recognized protocols that researchers borrow and combine to devise new theories or new experimental devices" (2004d [2001]: 66).

While the language of these passages speaks simply of borrowers and bor-rowees, Bourdieu sometimes remarks further that who (that is, which field) actually borrows what from whom is the result of the positioning of the respective fields in higher-level spaces like the university field or the intellec-tual field. Regarding the French university field of the 1970s, for instance, he suggests, "What one might call the scientific syndrome, typical of most semi-ological work and of all the . . . combinations of the different lexicons of the social sciences, linguistics and psychoanalysis, psychoanalysis and economics, etc. . . . can be understood as an attempt by disciplines defined as doubly negative (neither arts nor science) to reverse the situation by inverting the signs, and to aggregate . . . literary (or philosophical) avant-gardism with . . . scientific avant-gardism" (1988a [1984]: 121). As well, Bourdieu notes obverse cases in which, because of their differing positions on a wider social space, what one knowledge production field draws from other fields are negative rather than positive templates for its work, as when the scientistic domination of the whole French intellectual field in the late nineteenth century led writers (post-Flaubert) to reject "reductionism, positivism, and materialism" in favor of the "classical humanities, Latin and Greek" (1996a [1992]: 126). Then, too, for similar reasons, positive and negative transfers may interweave, as Bourdieu illustrates when he describes recent substantive changes in French philosophy—once the "crown" in the French "hierarchy of disciplines" but later demoted following Claude Lévi-Strauss's Durkheimian rehabilitation of the social sciences (2000b [1997]: 35, 1988a: xx)—as these substantive changes relate to the content of social-scientific fields:

> The Durkheimian philosophy of man became rehabilitated . . . in opposition to the "philosophy of the subject" . . . that Sartre, [Raymond] Aron, and [Paul] Nizan, had set up in the thirties in opposition to . . . the Durkheimians, among others. But . . . the acknowledgement of the social sciences implies no unconditional surrender. Although each philosopher in his own way betrays his deference to or dependence on the social sciences—if only, like Derrida, by choosing them as the target of his criticism or by borrowing their themes, . . . the philosophers [keep] their statutory distance, [working to transfigure] the "historicist" philosophy which they borrow from social science along with many of its themes, its problems and its mode of thought. (1988a: xxiii; see also 2008b [2004]: 13)

Bourdieu does not dwell on the conceptual implications of these empirical examples,[19] almost all of which appear in asides to a larger argument about some different issue rather than as the focal issue itself. Even so, their implications are significant. Seeking a "genetic" account of cultural works, Bourdieu's dualist model conceptualizes a field of knowledge production—insofar as it commands relative autonomy from external economic, political, and religious forces—as a separate microcosm closed upon itself; constituted of objective relations that are the "true principle" that explains the content stances (position takings) of producers at any one time; and transformed over time in its substance by a "motor of change" that "resides in" positional struggles "immanent" in the field. Yet the various knowledge fields in the above examples, although they are social spaces that possess relative autonomy from economic, political, and religious forces,[20] are anything but closed in upon themselves in terms of their content. Rather, they are open, porous, even at times "dependent" on other fields for their erudite knowledge, critical targets, lexicons, methods, models, themes, problems, modes of thought, and theories. And this openness obtains, according to Bourdieu's description of these cases, not at the given field's heteronomous pole (that is, not among producers unable to acquire field-specific capital) but either at its autonomous pole, among those rich in the necessary capital, such as Flaubert, Barthes, and the top scientific researchers, or throughout a field more or less in its entirety, as with sociology and philosophy. Still further, as in the examples, this openness to other fields and the accompanying exchanges, intellectual borrowings, critical targetings, and so forth may fuel substantive transformations within the receiving field, providing another impetus change, as Bourdieu comments: "Innovation in the sciences is often engendered in the intersections . . . between disciplines [because such intersections] offer the possibility of extracting ideas and information from a large . . . number and range of sources" (2004d [2001]: 65).[21]

None of this is meant to exaggerate Bourdieu's examples of field openness. To point up the importance of field transfers is not to suggest that knowledge fields are *so highly* porous that they typically dissolve into one another, each disappearing in turn as an identifiable site of objective relations among agents constituted of field-specific capital and engaged in a game with its own stakes. Nonetheless, whether the content of works in a knowledge field or, better, whether particular aspects of the content of particular works in the field is attributable more to transfers from other knowledge fields without, more to the dynamic of the game within, or more to the way the two processes combine must be a matter for empirical determination on a case by case basis. To lay down the "true principle" of position takings and the "impetus for change," as if they were somehow preset and thus knowable in advance of empirical research into particular cases, is to close off the very avenues of investigation that Bourdieu's sociology of knowledge otherwise opens up. And this lesson applies not only to the question of whether a knowledge field's content is shaped more by internal struggles or by transfers across fields, but also to questions about the nature and extent of interfield transfers and to questions about which specific spaces outside the focal field are involved in the transfers: all of these are issues for the sociological researcher to unravel, historical case by historical case.

Nor is this cardinal point lost on Bourdieu. Rather, he implies it himself when observing how thoroughly knowledge production varies by historical context. This insight forms the third current that overflows Bourdieu's dualist model, though it is a current thinner and more subterranean than the two just discussed, largely confined to a single passage in *The Rules of Art*.[22] This pregnant passage appears as Bourdieu is far along in a line of argument that brings him around to the phenomenon that old-fashioned scholarship about the "spirit of an age" often noticed, namely, the presence within a particular country during a particular period, for instance, of similar ideas in multiple social spaces. Rejecting efforts to explain this phenomenon by invoking nebulous notions of the "'cultural unity' of an epoch and a society, which the history of art and of literature accepts as a tacit assumption," Bourdieu presents his field concept in a new light:

> If one realizes that each field—music, painting, poetry, or . . . linguistics, biology, etc.—has an autonomous history, . . . one sees that the interpretation by reference to the history unique to the field (or to the discipline) is the preliminary for an interpretation with respect to the contemporary context. . . . The fundamental question then becomes to know whether the social effects of chronological contemporaneity, or even spatial unity—like the fact of sharing the same specific meeting places (literary cafes, magazines, cultural associations, salons, etc.) or of being exposed to the same cultural messages, common works of reference, obligatory issues, key events etc.—are strong enough to determine, over and above the autonomy of different fields, a common problematic. . . . This brings up in a direct way the question of national traditions . . . which lend themselves to the promotion to a greater or lesser degree of the pre-eminence of a central cultural site, . . . and to encouraging more or less adequately the specialization within it (of genres, disciplines, etc.) or which, on the contrary, lend themselves to the interaction between members of different fields, or to consecrating a particular configuration of the hierarchical structure of the arts . . . or of the scientific disciplines. (1996a [1992]: 199–200)

From the perspective of the sociology of knowledge, several aspects of this dense passage stand out. Joining together the currents in his work already identified in this section, one sees that Bourdieu's knowledge production model-in-use takes two major steps beyond his programmatic model: first, it situates a given knowledge field in relation not only to external economic, political, and religious forces but also to a multiplicity of other social spaces; and, second, it attends to the transfer of elements of content across fields. The quotation from *The Rules of Art* extends this model-in-use further because what the passage addresses—that is, the appearance of the same messages, problematics, and so on across all cultural sites—roughly parallels the situation Bourdieu has described in the previous quotations about the presence of similar lexicons, problems, and modes of thought in more than one knowledge field.

In view of this parallel, one might read the passage from *The Rules of Art* as incorporating a third plank into Bourdieu's model-in-use. This is an emphasis on *historical variation* in how a given knowledge field is linked to multiple other social spaces and in which elements of content transfer across those linkages. For, in the passage, Bourdieu proposes that the wider configuration of fields to which any particular knowledge field is related varies systematically in time and space. In other words, just as a field's autonomy from economic and political forces is a variable condition, so a given knowledge field may "to a greater or lesser degree" be embedded, depending on the sociological ordering of the relevant (national) setting, in spaces ranging from "a central cultural site,"[23] to "a particular hierarchy of disciplines," to a pattern of interaction with other knowledge fields, to heterogeneous entities like professional associations and literary fora, "*etc.*" What is more, Bourdieu suggests that the bundle of contents that any knowledge field "is exposed to" by virtue of the wider configuration of fields in which it is embedded also varies temporally and geographically. In the quotation he speaks of the transfer of such diverse elements as "messages," "works of reference," "obligatory issues," "problematics," "*etc.*," again depending on the sociological ordering of the historical context in question.[24]

Furthermore, and perhaps most important in this regard, Bourdieu states that the *effect* of these variable linkages and transfers itself *varies in strength* in different times and places. In the passage his referent is cultural fields that have won enough independence from economic, political, and religious forces to have "an autonomous history." Even so, he now maintains, with regard to these fields, that in some contexts the "effects" of interfield linkages and exchanges "are strong enough to determine, *over and above the autonomy of different fields*, a common problematic," just as instances exist, "on the contrary," where these same effects are sufficiently minimal that disciplines and other knowledge fields determine their own "specialized" problematics (issues, reference works, etc.). What this variation in impact suggests, then, is that fields of the latter kind comprise a subset of the universe of autonomous fields of cultural production: special cases that arise under historical conditions where the impact of interfield connections and borrowings is sufficiently weak[25] as to dwindle before the force of internal field dynamics and, by so doing, to warrant the use of Bourdieu's dualist model of knowledge production as a kind of reduced form of the multiplex model required in the other temporal and geographical circumstances he alludes to here. Neither in *The Rules of Art* nor elsewhere does Bourdieu pursue his observations all the way to this conclusion, but he nonetheless brings the reader to the brink of this fundamental point.

Which Model for a Sociology of Sociology?

What I have called Bourdieu's programmatically stated model and his model-in-use have different implications for the sociological analysis of knowledge and knowledge production. The fact that Bourdieu sometimes explicitly invokes one model and sometimes implicitly invokes the other itself suggests that, depending on the theoretical or empirical issues under consideration, one model may be preferable to the other. Recognizing this point on principle, however, what I would nonetheless like tentatively to propose is that Bourdieu's model-in-use illuminates a wider range of historical cases.

That this is so is the tacit lesson of Bourdieu's empirical writings on knowledge production, which quietly introduce components of the model-in-use when treating concrete examples as diverse as nineteenth-century French novels, early twentieth-century German philosophy, mid-twentieth-century French philosophy, and late twentieth-century journalism and natural science. In addition, the lesson receives reinforcement from elsewhere, perhaps most explicitly from research in the sociology of science, where scholars have long since abandoned an earlier focus on scientific communities as relatively autonomous entities (which draw resources from economic, political, and religious groups) in favor of a concern with what Knorr-Cetina has called "variable transscientific fields"—relational networks that "go beyond the boundaries of a scientific community or scientific field, however broadly defined" (1981: 82; see also Knorr-Cetina 1982; 1999). This move is evident as well in studies of knowledge production in the natural sciences as associated with perspectives ranging from the actor network theory of Michel Callon and Bruno Latour to the social worlds approach of Adele Clarke and Joan Fujimura (Hess 1997 provides a good, short introduction to these lines of work; see also Hackett et al., 2008).

To be sure, none of these sites of natural knowledge production holds the same intense interest for Bourdieu as knowledge production in sociology itself.[26] Here, too, however, his model-in-use seems generally to prove more valuable than the programmatic dualist model. Again, Bourdieu suggests this point himself, observing in his various writings on late twentieth-century sociology how French sociology's different positionings "in the space of the disciplines" has affected the contents of the field, especially its conceptual and methodological "borrowing" from the natural sciences and the humanities (2004d [2001]: 108, 1988a [1984]: 30). Bourdieu does not indicate to what degree he would extend this sort of analysis to other times and places, but the sociology of sociology stands to gain considerably, I believe, from bringing his model-in-use to bear in the examination of other moments in the history of the field.

A couple of brief illustrations will serve to elaborate this claim. If sociological researchers approach the history of sociology through Bourdieu's dualist model, their analytic focus would naturally center on macrolevel economic, political, and perhaps religious forces and on internal field forces and struggles, and few scholars knowledgeable about the discipline's history would deny the importance of these "two fundamental factors." In some ways, historians of sociology have been attending to these same factors for generations,[27] albeit without the assist of Bourdieu's formalized field concept, which allows for a more rigorous and thorough treatment of the hierarchical structure and agonistic dynamics which characterized the discipline at every period that scholars have thus far studied. Yet only when one segues from this dualist approach to a more multiplex model can one come to terms with certain major episodes in the field's intellectual development, as the following two examples show. I select these cases from among many others I might cite because they go to the substantive core of sociology during the period they represent.[28] Both examples pertain to American sociology in the decades between the two world wars, during which time the field met all the criteria that Bourdieu lays down for a "discipline": the field had an academically and socially recognized name, it was inscribed in (approximately one hundred) college and university departments, it had its own journals, conferences, professional associations, certification requirements, and so on—and, as such, clearly passed the Bourdieusian test of "relative autonomy" from external economic, political, and religious forces.[29]

Example 1. Between 1918 and 1930 approximately, American sociology underwent a thoroughgoing transformation in its concept of the human individual. At the start of this period, sociologists thought in terms of "character," a holistic notion that referred (by various expressions) to an individual's overall mode or pattern of acting and reacting to his or her circumstances; by the period's end the prevalent concept was "personality," an atomizing notion that treated the individual (via different words) simply as the additive sum of his or her attitudes, beliefs, and values. However, although this conceptual shift swamped the discipline, it maps onto none of the struggles over which differently positioned sociologists were then fighting among themselves inside the field. Rather, in the short space of a half decade (c. 1925–30), sociologists both high and low in field position, both orthodox and heterodox, rich and poor alike in field-specific capital, turned away from character conceptions of the individual to personality conceptions—and (to the best of my knowledge) nowhere did they debate this move, discuss it in print, or even acknowledge that it was occurring. Nor have later historical scholars succeeded in identifying any macrolevel developments—for example, some "economic crisis, technical transformation, or political revolution," to follow Bourdieu's familiar listing—that might plausibly account, perhaps via various field-mediated processes, for the change.

Yet enlarge this double internal/external reading, and the sweeping change in content grows more sociologically comprehensible. During this era, sociology stood beneath but adjacent to the field of psychology in the hierarchized space of academic disciplines, and sociologists extensively borrowed templates, both positive and negative, from psychology, including, sometime before the period began, the notion of character, which had long been a distinguished presence in psychology and spread throughout sociology as well. Even so, psychologists of the 1920s were increasingly turning for their own intellectual tools to contemporary biology, a field that was then positioned nearby but above psychology in the disciplinary hierarchy and was in a phase of deep commitment to scientific objectivity, understood as disengagement from questions of morals and ethics. However, concurrently, academics in lowly teachers' colleges, aspiring to connect with the ethically charged Character Education Movement that then gripped the country's primary and secondary schools, heavily appropriated the concept of character from psychology in order to fertilize dozens of studies on how to train up good character traits and virtues in children. Compromised by this flagrant moralizing of "character" just when they were professing the ethical disengagement of the biologists, academic psychologists of the mid-1920s recoiled and very publicly abandoned the concept, widely declaring their preference for "personality" as the more scientifically objective idea. Not that sociologists of the time closely followed the work of either biologists or educational researchers, but the conceptual transformation throughout the field of psychology that resulted from its own linkages to the two fields reverberated almost immediately in sociology. For scarcely had psychologists substituted "personality" for "character" than sociologists of all positions and persuasions followed suit, importing into the discipline a conception of the human individual which has remained central to the field ever since[30]—and whose genesis comes to light only through this kind of more multiplex account. (See Camic 2001 for a fuller account.)

Example 2. If one compares sociological writings in 1927 and 1937 (again, approximate dates), one notices a pair of striking differences. In 1927 sociologists defined the subject matter of their discipline as "culture" in the extended sense in which anthropologists used the term, that is, as humankind's complete stock of material objects, customs, beliefs, attitudes, and institutions, economic, political, legal, religious, and familial; at the same time, sociologists voiced considerable reluctance to enter the arena of public debate except when members of the public called upon them for their technical expertise. By 1937 sociologists took their domain as "culture" in the more delimited sense of mores, attitudes, beliefs, and moral values (and the family and religious institutions from which these elements arise); simultaneously, they insisted that, in their capacity as sociologists, they had multiple contributions to make to the public sphere, whether or not the public called out for their services.

Here, unlike the situation in example 1, is a change in content that seems tailor-made for Bourdieu's dualist model. In the short interval between 1929 and 1937 American society experienced one of the most dramatic episodes of economic and political upheaval in its history—the Great Depression and the New Deal—and Bourdieu's bidimensional perspective suggests various hypotheses that would seem to account for intellectual transformations in the field of sociology under these macroconditions. Bourdieu's writings draw attention, for example, to the heteronomous pole of sociology and to the tendency of knowledge producers near this pole to look outward and to seize upon contemporary problems to elevate their field position. Viewed from this side, sociologists' proclamation, during the Depression, of their public role and their accompanying recasting of the substance of their discipline were perhaps the field-mediated effects of moves by the heteronomous players in the field to capitalize on the new social problems that the Depression presented. In the alternative, one might construct an explanation in terms of Bourdieu's analysis of the autonomous pole of a cultural field and of intellectuals like Sartre and Emile Zola who use their autonomy to intervene critically into the political realm. Were the intellectual changes in sociology during the 1930s perhaps field-refracted consequences of critical interventions into the national crisis by more autonomous sociologists?

In the historical instance at hand, however, explanations of these types fall short. Although internally divided among themselves on many issues, sociologists of the 1930s were virtually unanimous in regard to the changes at issue; their narrowing of their focus to culture in the sense of beliefs and moral values as well as their activist redefinition of their public role were shifts that occurred on a discipline-wide basis and appear in the work of heretical newcomers and established orthodox figures, the poorly positioned and the well positioned, the heteronomous and the autonomous. Further, while these changes were certainly connected to the national economic and political drama of the period and show the refracted intellectual effect of external conditions on the field of sociology, the timing of this effect was delayed for reasons that a dualist account would defocalize. Indeed, not until the mid-1930s, nearly five years after the Depression began and was already past its most severe phase, did sociologists even start to take cognizance of it in their meetings and publications and to pursue it as a topic of research. The reaction of some of the other social sciences was much swifter and more vigorous.

This last comment points, however, in the direction of a more multiplex account. During the early years of the Depression, experts from other intellectual fields—economics, political science, law, and social work—increasingly entered the political arena to debate the causes of and remedies for the contemporary crisis, to offer policy advice to state officials, to join the ranks of government departments confronting Depression Era problems, and so on. With few exceptions sociologists stood aside from these developments, still preferring a stance of political disengagement unless the public called upon them, as few in the public sphere were then doing. From late 1933 onward, however, sociologists more and more grasped the consequence; with New Deal programs and agencies bourgeoning, experts from these other fields now formed a vast presence on the national stage, occupying state positions at all levels. And, very suddenly, sociologists riveted to a social space outside the hierarchy of academic disciplines. In the academic hierarchy of the time, law still scarcely existed, political science stood at most as sociology's wan coequal, while economics, although well positioned, receded before the looming and more proximate discipline of psychology; yet on the wider intellectual field— newly ascendant on the field of power during the 1930s—these same disciplines were preeminent and furnished different templates for the sociologist's public role. Accordingly, in the mid-1930s, sociologists rose up, not with analyses of the Depression but in explicit outcry against a situation in which lawyers, legal scholars, economists, and political scientists dominated public discussion of the Depression despite the fact that sociology was, sociologists said, also an engaged discipline with an active public role to play. As to what this role was, that is something sociologists were still hammering out: their demand for inclusion came in advance of the specifics, goaded not by any immediate intellectual interest in the Depression and the New Deal but by the way these events affected other intellectual fields and thereby galvanized sociologists to rethink their own place in the public arena. From this rethinking followed the fundamental conceptual change that overtook the field almost immediately afterward, as sociologists from all corners of the discipline soon concurred that their subject matter was "culture" purged of the phenomena that these other fields treated—"culture" shorn of the economic, political, and legal institutions that had previously been elements in the sociological concept of culture. That is to say, sociology now concerned what the economists, the political scientists, and the legal professionals were neglecting: mores, beliefs, moral values. These factors were essential, or so sociologists decided as the Great Depression neared its end, to properly understanding the plight of the nation as a "moral crisis" whose solution required the public guidance of the sociologist rather than of experts from other locations on the broader intellectual field of the time. (See Camic 2007 for a fuller account.)

By no means are the two illustrations I have just given atypical. To the contrary, the history of sociology and, I would add, the history of the social sciences generally furnish numerous similar cases in which constructing an adequate "genetic" account of the works of knowledge which the agents involved in these cases produced entails moving beyond Bourdieu's programmatic dualist model of knowledge production in the direction the multiplex analytic approach suggested by his model-in-use—though, again, which model is the more useful is always an empirical question, open to different answers in regard to different historical instances.

Conclusion

My purpose has been to draw attention to Bourdieu's extensive writings on the sociology of knowledge and to argue that they contain two approaches to the analysis of knowledge production in the social sciences. One of these, which I have referred to as the programmatically stated model, represents the application to the study of knowledge of Bourdieu's celebrated concept of field and proposes a "double" or "dual reading" of cultural works. This reading situates spaces of knowledge production in relation to the "external" cosmos of economic, political, and religious forces; and it then proceeds to examine a space of this kind—to the extent that it maintains "relative autonomy" from these external forces—as "a closed, separate microcosm" that is "carried along by the internal logic" of the struggles that constitute the space as an academic discipline. Turning from Bourdieu's programmatic statements to his empirical writings on knowledge production, I next identified three currents not formulated in his dualist model: (i) attention to the multiplicity of social spaces—intermediate between the external macrocosm of economic, political, and religious forces and the internal microcosm of a particular discipline—in which knowledge fields are also situated; (ii) emphasis on the transfer of elements of content across these spaces; and (iii) recognition of historical variation in these spatial relations and content transfers. While Bourdieu does not himself integrate these currents, their combination constitutes what I have called his knowledge production model-in-use. Comparing the two models, I have argued that Bourdieu's model-in-use generally provides greater empirical traction than his programmatic model. To the extent that this is true, readers of Bourdieu's work who stop with his programmatically stated model ignore some of the most valuable aspects of his contribution to analysis of knowledge production.

At the end of a favorable assessment of Thomas Kuhn's ideas about science Bourdieu once commented, "I realize that . . . I have attributed to Kuhn the essential part of my own representation of the logic of the [scientific] field and its dynamic" (2004d [2001]: 13). A similar comment, I should point out, may very well apply to the proceeding reconstruction and defense of Bourdieu's model-in-use. This model, rather than Bourdieu's dualist model, closely resembles the approach I myself have advocated as an alternative to the new sociological internalism. Indeed, not only have I faulted the new sociological internalism for overlooking the multiple fields lying between any particular disciplinary field and macrolevel social forces; but I have further criticized the new sociological internalism for neglecting the linkages among such fields, the transfers of content that ensue from these linkages, and the variations that occur historically in these connections and transfers (Camic 2001).[31] This critique has no doubt alerted me to factors of this kind as I have read Bourdieu's work.

This personal interpretive bias notwithstanding, Bourdieu's writings on knowledge production do include a multiplicity of social spaces intermediate between a specific knowledge field and macrolevel forces, while also recognizing the various transfers of content that occur across fields and acknowledging patterns of temporal and spatial variation along these dimensions—even to the point of suggesting that a knowledge field driven by its own internal struggles and unaffected by transfers resulting from its linkages to other fields is but a special case of knowledge production fields more generally. On the other hand, Bourdieu's observations on all these matters lodge in the crevices of his empirical writings on particular knowledge fields, even as the dominant refrain of his oeuvre, when it addresses knowledge production in general terms, remains the dualist model, which sidelines the very factors his model-in-use brings to the fore. To the extent that Bourdieu himself seriously regarded his dualist model as but the reduced form of a more multiplex model of knowledge production, his unexplained decision to present his program for the sociology of knowledge in terms that urge a "double reading" of cultural works, emphasize the "twofold" nature of knowledge, and the "bidimensionality" of knowledge producers, characterize relatively autonomous knowledge fields as "separate microcosms closed in upon themselves," and stipulate the internal dynamics of these fields as the "true principle" of knowledge production—all of this is, to say the least, a decision both perplexing and misleading.

This warning entered for Bourdieu's readers, however, there can be no question of Bourdieu's accomplishment in resuscitating the sociology of knowledge, in anchoring it on strong conceptual foundations, and in equipping it to address questions about knowledge production in a genuinely historical manner. In offering not one but two knowledge production models, Bourdieu's writings invite careful attention to the ways in which knowledge production processes differ across time and place. By so doing, his two sociologies of knowledge open a wide terrain for investigation at the same time as they prepare researchers for some of the diverse conditions they may meet as they traverse this expanse. Should sociologists at long last embark on this path of inquiry and discover that they need to formulate additional models to understand the historical cases they encounter along the way, they will practice their craft in the spirit of Bourdieu's work.

Notes

This essay has benefited from the reactions of audiences at Yale, Northwestern, and the University of Oslo. I am grateful for the comments that I received on these occasions as well as for the valuable advice of Philip Gorski, Etienne Ollion, and David Swartz.

1. I say "almost alone" partially to exempt, among major sociological theorists of the twentieth century, Karl Mannheim, Robert Merton, and Randall Collins. Work in the sociology of science furnishes many additional exceptions, but to date this work has had (regrettably) little impact on sociological thinking at large.

2. The *locus classicus* of internal readings is sociology in the genre of the introductory textbook in sociological theory, where each succeeding theoretical approach is presented as a response to one or more prior theories.

3. To avoid misunderstanding, I emphasize that I use "dualist" in this chapter in a specific and restricted sense to refer to what (as this paragraph will indicate) Bourdieu himself calls a "dual" or "bi-dimensional" approach that encompasses both "internal" and "external" factors. I am aware that, according to its different meanings, "dualist" designates a tendency to align with one side of an either-or dichotomy (objectivist vs. subjectivist, structure vs. agency, external vs. internal)— and that Bourdieu, who spurned oppositions and antimonies of this kind, strongly opposed dualism in this second sense (see Brubaker 1985; Swartz 1997; Wacquant 1992).

4. Appearing in a festschrift for Robert Merton, this passage begins "Merton has established. . . ." I omit these words above because, as the context makes clear, Bourdieu is not simply describing Merton's position; rather, he is praising Merton for anticipating his own emphasis on this "two-fold relation." Save for the phrase "dual reading," which Bourdieu himself italicizes, all other emphases in this paragraph are mine.

5. Wacquant includes a third moment also. This "involves constructing the social trajectories of the individuals who come to vie within the field so as to uncover the socially constructed system of dispositions (habitus) guiding their conduct and representations in and out of the artistic sphere" (1998: 300). Here again he follows Bourdieu (Bourdieu and Wacquant 1992 [1988]: 105; Bourdieu 1996a [1992]: 214). Even so, since this element is less central than the former two in Bourdieu's writings

on cultural fields and has no bearing on the critical argument of this chapter, I bracket it here in the interest of economy.

6. I cite Knorr-Cetina because she focuses specifically on Bourdieu's analysis of knowledge production. Viewing Bourdieu's work through wider lenses, Swartz also draws attention to "the priority given [by Bourdieu] to the *internal analysis* of fields" (1997: 128). See also Pels (1995: 83).

7. Pels identifies a related problem, viz., that the condition Bourdieu describes as a field's relative autonomy "not only constitutes an empirical-historical variable but also erects a normative yardstick," yielding "not ostensive but performative definitions by means of which the sociologist forces the social facts that he defines into obedience and submission" (1995, 90).

8. Recall that Bourdieu criticizes the old internalism for proposing "the idea of 'pure' science, . . . developing according to its internal logic" (2004d [2001]: 45). Yet, once relocated to the context of his own internalism, the notion of an "internal logic" is one to which he no longer objects.

9. Here, too, however, Bourdieu emphasizes the role of habitus (see n. 5 above). He writes, "However great the effect of position, . . . it never operates mechanically, and the relationship between positions and position-takings is mediated by the dispositions of the agents" (1993c [1986]: 62).

10. Elaborating this point, Bourdieu writes the following: "Those who . . . more or less completely monopolize the specific capital, the basis of the specific power or authority characteristic of a few, are inclined to conservation strategies—those which, in the fields of production of cultural goods, tend to defend *orthodoxy*—whereas those least endowed with capital (who are often also the newcomers, and therefore generally the youngest) are inclined towards subversion strategies, the strategies of *heresy*. Heresy, heterodoxy . . . is what brings the dominant agents out of their silence and forces them to produce the defensive discourse of orthodoxy" (1993a [1980]: 73).

11. I would accent Bourdieu's inclusion here of religious powers, since he often includes these alongside economic and political powers, although not, as it so happens, in the particular passages I have cited up to this point. The on-again, off-again presence of religion in his conception of external is immaterial for the purposes of this chapter.

12. The question, for example, of whether a discipline's autonomy regarding external economic, political, and religious powers is positively or *inversely* related to its autonomy with respect to the university field.

13. I draw some of the quoted expressions that the text attributes to Bourdieu from Wacquant's questions to Bourdieu rather than from Bourdieu's answers since these answers presume Bourdieu's assent to the terms of the questions.

14. Just as Bourdieu uses his field concept to move to higher levels of aggregation, so he sometimes moves to lower levels, e.g., the disciplinary subfield (2004d [2001]: 36). For present purposes, his moves in the latter direction can be disregarded.

15. As this sentence states, my referent here is Bourdieu's writings on knowledge production. In his writings on other topics, most notably on the field of housing

construction, the circumstance that fields are multileveled, nested, and overlapping is central to Bourdieu's entire analysis (see Bourdieu 2005b [2000]).

16. I offer the suggestion in this sentence purely as speculation. Not only is the suggestion not central to the following argument, but the argument is independent of whether or not my hunch is correct.

17. While my concern is the sociology of knowledge and Benson (1999) deals with media studies, I believe that the multiplex alternative I propose here closely parallels his call to replace Bourdieu's "two-fold analysis" or "binary model" of media with a "three-dimensional" or "hexagonal" model.

18. A similar lacuna appears elsewhere in the Bourdieusian corpus and continues even at the forefront of Bourdieu-inspired research, e.g., in Sapiro's (2004a) meticulous analysis of the French literary field, which takes thorough account of the literary field itself, of the larger field of power, and also of other professional groups, including scholars in medicine, the humanities, and the social sciences—only then to sideline these additional groups when addressing the issue of content at stake in this analysis, i.e., the political position takings of members of the literary field. Cf. Ferguson (1998), Prevost (2002), and Topalov (1998), studies that also move Bourdieu's dualist model of knowledge production in directions of a more multiplex approach.

19. Neither, so far as I am aware, does Bourdieu attempt to theorize the exchanges and borrowings that he observes in these instances by applying to them the conceptual terminology he elsewhere uses in discussing how capital (symbolic and other) is transferred and exchanged across fields (see esp. Bourdieu 1996b [1989]).

20. Or at least Bourdieu treats them as relatively autonomous in this particular context.

21. I have quoted this passage in the way that is most generous to Bourdieu and gives him maximal credit for insight into interfield transfers. But the full passage (2004d [2001]: 65) furnishes grounds for more uncertainty: "There *may be* intersections between disciplines, *some empty*, some full, which offer the possibility of extracting ideas and information from a large *or not so large* number and range of sources. (Innovation in the sciences is often engendered in the intersections.)" With the words I have italicized, Bourdieu compromises a good bit of the main point, which he dilutes further by putting it inside parentheses. These moves are curious, but perhaps Bourdieu's way of granting recognition to interfield transfers, yet not so much recognition as to interfere with the internalist component of his knowledge production model. Be this as it may, the qualifiers do hint at a need to attend to the problem of variation. This hint comports with the current in Bourdieu's thought to which I turn in the paragraphs that follow. Cf. Bourdieu 1975.

22. Bourdieu offers brief intimations elsewhere.

23. An allusion, presumably, to the unique role of Paris in French intellectual life.

24. In an accompanying comment in *The Rules of Art*, Bourdieu observes that "direct exchanges" among fields of cultural production may "depend, in their form and very existence, on the positions occupied in their respective fields by the agents or institutions concerned, and hence on the structure of those fields, and also on the relative positions of the fields in the hierarchy established among them at the moment under consideration" (1996a [1992]: 199).

25. Or, to put this another way: sufficiently close in value to zero.

26. As Bourdieu writes, "In raising the problem of knowledge in the way that I have, I have constantly been thinking of the social sciences," sociology in particular (2004d [2001]: 85).

27. Coser (1971) is the classic work of this type and the paradigm for many subsequent studies up to the present. Studies of the history of sociology more congruent with what I am calling a multiplex model have also occasionally appeared: Bulmer (1984), Cravens (1978), Hinkle (1994), Lepenies (1985), Platt (1996), and Ross (1991).

28. I select these examples also because of my close familiarity with them; I have examined both at length elsewhere, drawing extensively on primary source materials. The studies I mention in the last sentence of the previous note also furnish many relevant illustrations.

29. This is not to say that sociology's autonomy from these forces matched the degree of autonomy that certain other disciplines had attained, nor to suggest that sociologists of the period took the autonomy they had gained for granted and ceased efforts to maintain and extend it.

30. Within sociology, Bourdieu's concept of habitus is arguably the most significant subsequent step in the opposite direction—i.e., to reinstate a more holistic conception.

31. My position here is congruent with the argument Gil Eyal develops in his chapter in this volume.

PART III **Historical Extensions**

T. H. MARSHALL MEETS PIERRE BOURDIEU
Citizens and Paupers in the Development
of the U.S. Welfare State

More than half a century after T. H. Marshall delivered his celebrated lecture "Citizenship and Social Class," it remains a touchstone for the sociology of the welfare state. This chapter builds on Marshall's contributions, including his threefold typology of civil rights, which are necessary for individual freedom and encompass the rights to own property, "conclude valid contracts," and "follow the occupation of one's choice"; political rights to participate in the exercise of political power; and social rights to at least "a modicum of economic welfare and security" (Marshall 1964 [1949]: 71–72, 75). At the same time, the chapter draws on Pierre Bourdieu's cultural sociology to complicate the evolutionary view typically ascribed to Marshall, in which a steady enrichment of the status of citizenship (i.e., the addition of new rights) accompanied a steady increase in the number of those on whom the status was bestowed.[1]

In the Anglo-American tradition, full citizenship was initially restricted to property owners on the grounds that property prevented their personal dependence and subordination. Propertyless wage earners were deemed unfit for full citizenship because, in the words of the English jurist William Blackstone, they had "no will of their own" and would therefore cast their votes "under some undue influence" (Keyssar 2000: 10). When propertyless white workingmen demanded and obtained voting rights in the United States in the first half of the nineteenth century, they expanded the boundaries of citizenship to encompass wage laborers as well as property owners. Although economic independence remained a prerequisite for full citizenship, propertyless white workingmen successfully challenged their classification as dependents by 1850, relocating themselves on the more privileged side of the boundary (Keyssar 2000: chap. 2). Paupers, who "lived not on wages but on poor relief," were left on the other side (Fraser and Gordon 1994: 315–16). Indeed, "states adopted 'pauper' exclusions as they moved to eliminate formal property qualifications for the vote. . . . Far from being anachronisms, pauper exclusions were integral to a new, nineteenth century way of defining full membership in a republican polity" (Steinfeld 1989: 335, 337; cf. Montgomery 1993: 21–22; Smith 1997: 126, 214–15; Keyssar 2000: 61–65). Whereas wage earners and recipients of poor relief had once occupied the same political status, the enfranchisement of wage earners and the exclusion of those who received poor relief divided "the undifferentiated propertyless of the colonial era . . . into two distinct categories" (Steinfeld 1989: 337). This division would endure well into the twentieth century. At the time of the Great Depression, "the constitutions of fourteen states [still] denied the franchise to paupers" (Piven and Cloward 1977: 42). Social welfare provision thus operated as a boundary institution in a double sense: it regulated not only the flow of workers into and out of the labor market (Piven and Cloward 1993 [1971]), but also their incorporation into the political community.

An important but neglected contribution of "Citizenship and Social Class" was to draw attention to this boundary work. As numerous commentators have observed, Marshall associated social rights with the twentieth-century welfare state. However, he did not claim that social rights were a creation of the welfare state. In fact, Marshall (1964 [1949]: 80) noted, social rights were established well before the modern welfare state, but they were "detached from the status of citizenship." In other words, paupers forfeited their civil and political rights in exchange for relief. Traditional poor relief "treated the claims of the poor, not as an integral part of the rights of the citizen, but as an alternative to them—as claims which could be met only if the claimants ceased to be citizens in any true sense of the word" (80). Furthermore, Marshall pointed out, "this divorce of social rights from the status of citizenship" was a gendered phenomenon that extended beyond relief to the regulation of labor markets (81). Legislators and judges, he observed, initially refused to apply protective labor laws "to the adult male—the citizen par excellence. And they did so out of respect for his status as a citizen, on the grounds that enforced protective measures curtailed the civil right to conclude a free contract of employment. Protection was confined to women and children, and champions of women's rights were quick to detect the implied insult. Women were protected because they were not citizens. If they wished to enjoy full and responsible citizenship, they must forgo protection" (81). In the nineteenth century full citizenship was equated with manly independence and liberty of contract, while relief and protective labor laws were understood to be incompatible with it. In Marshall's view, the modern welfare state broke with this legacy, not by establishing social rights but by incorporating social rights into the status of citizenship.[2]

Insofar as Marshall recognized the separation of paupers from the community of citizens, his perspective converges with more recent conceptions of citizenship as an instrument of social closure through which people monopolize valuable material and symbolic goods while excluding others (Brubaker 1992). This process is generally understood in terms of the exclusion of noncitizens from the rights and benefits conferred upon citizens. However, if citizenship is understood as a gradated category rather than a status that one either wholly possesses or completely lacks, then citizenship may also be seen as a means of internal social closure, an "instrument of social stratification" in Marshall's words (1964 [1949]: 110), which operates within the boundaries of the polity. From this perspective, people who are nominally citizens (i.e., members of the polity) but whose citizenship rights are circumscribed or curtailed also experience a form of civil exclusion: They are excluded from some, though generally not all, of the benefits associated with full citizenship.[3]

This chapter takes as its point of departure Marshall's suggestion that civil and political rights could be and sometimes were treated as an alternative to social rights rather than a foundation for them. However, it challenges Marshall's claim that the twentieth-century welfare state broke definitively with this practice. Instead, it suggests that the transition from poor relief to the welfare state was, at least in the United States, quite a bit messier. In the United States, major policy innovations that expanded the state's involvement in social provision often generated conflicts over whether to model the new policy on or sharply distinguish it from traditional poor relief. As in Britain, new policies were shaped by the "reaction against the poor law" and the search for "an alternative to poor relief" for those deemed deserving (Heclo 1974: 317). However, reformers in the United States were constrained again and again by conservatives (in the literal sense of the word), who drew different lessons from the past and sought to preserve or reproduce many of the features of traditional poor relief. At stake in these struggles were the citizenship status and rights of the policies' clients, who struggled not only to acquire new social rights, but also to avoid losing their civil and political rights in the process. These struggles continued to emerge well into the twentieth century, shaping the meaning and boundaries of American citizenship.

To illuminate and explain these struggles over the citizenship status and rights of welfare state claimants, I draw upon and extend the insights of Bourdieu (1984a, 1985b, 1989a, 1991e, 1994b).[4] More specifically, I bring Marshall into dialogue with Bourdieu in order to clarify why such struggles have emerged in the course of the development of the U.S. welfare state and why their outcomes have varied. Why, in other words, were some welfare state claimants classed as dependent paupers whose civil or political rights were curtailed while others successfully obtained recognition as independent, rights-bearing citizens? In brief, I argue that such struggles emerged soon after policy innovations created new groups of claimants, particularly when the new policy treated claimants in contradictory ways and when dominant elites were divided over whether to improve the claimants' status and rights. Historically, the outcomes of these struggles in the United States have been crucially shaped by the institutional structure of the policy and the manner and extent to which the policy became entangled in racial politics. Through most of American history African Americans enjoyed neither full civil and political rights (like white men) nor social protection (like white women). When new policies potentially challenged these racialized patterns of social closure— especially when they challenged both forms of closure simultaneously— claimants' efforts to preserve or expand their civil and political rights while acquiring new social rights met with greater resistance and less success.[5]

These claims are supported throughout the chapter with empirical evidence from a historical case study of the Works Progress Administration (WPA), an important but understudied component of the New Deal welfare state that provided temporary public employment for millions of able-bodied unemployed Americans from 1935 to 1942. The WPA was selected for this purpose because it was an important policy innovation that postdated traditional poor relief, it created an extensive new group of claimants whose status and rights were contested, and it coincided with and was part of a key moment of social crisis and reform during which political and judicial changes dramatically transformed American citizenship. Indeed, the WPA was central to the New Deal in terms of size, spending, and importance. By 1939 it "absorbed both the greatest amount of public spending and public attention" (Amenta 1998: 81), it was "Roosevelt's top priority in social policy" (Amenta 1998: 83), it "had become the most comprehensive, ambitious, and controversial government program" (Porter 1980: 61), and it was "regarded as the cornerstone of domestic relief" (Porter 1980: 70). To investigate the struggles that occurred over the citizenship status and rights of WPA workers, this chapter relies on a qualitative analysis of both archival records and secondary sources.

The Emergence of Classification Struggles in the Development of the U.S. Welfare State

Conflicts over the citizenship status and rights of welfare state claimants are a particular instance of what Bourdieu calls classification struggles. To be more precise, they are struggles to class claimants as citizens or paupers. At stake in classification struggles is "the power to make people see and believe, to get them to know and recognize, to impose the legitimate definition of the divisions of the social world and, thereby, to make and unmake groups" (Bourdieu 1991e: 221). The last point is perhaps the most important: Classification struggles are not merely struggles between existing groups over how to interpret the social world, but struggles that help form groups in the first place. Because classificatory schemes are "the basis of the representations of the groups and therefore of their mobilization and demobilization," struggles over classificatory schemes help to "bring into existence the thing named" and "*contribute to producing* what they apparently [only] describe or designate" (Bourdieu 1984a: 479, 1991e: 220, 223). In these struggles, stratifying factors like gender, race, and ethnicity may be constitutive of the groups formed, or they may constitute competing sources of social division (Swartz 1997: 153–58). Regardless of how and where people draw group boundaries, they include some in the group and exclude others, thereby defining the group's identity. While in Bourdieu's writings the concept of classification struggles is mainly used to explain the formation and mobilization of social classes, I show how it also helps to explain the formation and development of citizenship. (Indeed, one might say this chapter is concerned more with citizenship struggles than class struggles, though classification is an essential dimension of both.) In particular, I argue that historical struggles over the boundary between citizens and paupers have shaped both the meaning of American citizenship and access to the corresponding material and symbolic profits.

Classification struggles, Bourdieu suggests, cannot be understood apart from the social arenas or fields in which people struggle to accumulate and monopolize different kinds of resources, whether economic, cultural, social, or symbolic, which he describes as forms of capital. These fields are in turn structured by the amount and type of capital people possess. The dominant groups within the field struggle over the relative value of different types of capital, while dominated groups control little capital of any kind. This insight has been usefully extended to the sociology of the welfare state by Michel Peillon (1998, 2001), who postulates the existence of a "welfare field" wherein state officials, service providers, employers, clients, unions, and social movements struggle to convert the resources they possess, whether economic, political, cultural, or symbolic, into the kinds of capital they seek to accumulate, including greater legitimacy, better services and benefits, lower taxes, influence over policy administration, and so forth. From this perspective, citizenship itself may be seen as a form of political capital that, insofar as the citizenship status and corresponding rights of welfare state claimants are contested, constitutes both a stake of classification struggles and a resource that, insofar as citizenship rights enable one to acquire property (Marshall 1964 [1949]: 88), employment in the occupation of one's choice (75), a share in the exercise of political power (72), social protection (87), economic welfare and security (72), and so forth, people use to appropriate other valued goods.

The concepts of field and capital also encourage us to think about social welfare policy in relational terms, which in turn helps to explain when and why policies generate classification struggles. These struggles tend to emerge soon after the introduction of new policies, suggesting that policy innovations open a window of opportunity to establish the status and rights of the policy's clients relative to other clients in the field. Since the standing of clients is relational, existing policies serve as important benchmarks in these classification struggles, providing models to be avoided or standards of treatment to which clients can aspire. Furthermore, policies and their elite patrons frequently stand in a competitive relationship, which may contribute to classification struggles as well. The bureaucratic officials who administer a policy, for example, may have institutional, organizational, and professional interests in raising it to a dominant position, in terms of prestige and resources, within the welfare field. As in other fields, this is generally achieved through social distinction: administrators seek to distinguish their policy sharply from other policies, emphasizing its merits and, conversely, the flaws of competing policies. Such efforts need not be merely symbolic but may also involve efforts to incorporate and monopolize valued policy features. These policy features may therefore be seen as another form of capital over which social agents struggle in the welfare field. The classification of clients is shaped by these competitive struggles among policymakers and administrators. Finally, classification struggles are likely to emerge when clients occupy an intermediate position within the welfare field. Although "the objects of the social world" always include a degree of indeterminacy, vagueness, and "semantic elasticity" that make classification struggles possible, "it is in the intermediate positions of social space . . . that the indeterminacy and objective uncertainty of relations between practices and positions is at a maximum, and also, consequently, the intensity of symbolic strategies" (Bourdieu 1989a: 20). Within the welfare field, it is the clients of hybrid policies, positioned in some respects as rights-bearing citizens but in other respects as dependent paupers in need of discipline and supervision, who occupy these intermediate positions. Their indeterminate status is not merely a product of muddled minds or linguistic confusion, but also reflects how social provision is organized, which in turn reflects how classificatory schemes are institutionalized. When inconsistent or contradictory classificatory schemes are objectified in policies, the policies are likely to encourage classification struggles.[6]

This thesis is consistent with historical-institutionalist views of the welfare state. As previous studies have shown, institutions structure political struggles and their outcomes in a variety of ways. Institutions influence the formation of groups and their political capacities, ideas, and demands; they shape how individuals and groups define their interests and goals; and they provide models, schemas, or scripts for behavior (Skocpol 1985; Steinmo et al. 1992; Clemens and Cook 1999). From this perspective, "policies themselves must be seen as politically consequential structures" that restructure politics (Pierson 1994: 46). In other words, policies are not merely an outcome or consequence of past political struggles, but also influence subsequent struggles through their material and symbolic effects on political elites, interest groups, and mass publics (Pierson 1993; Mettler and Soss 2004). Historical institutionalists have described these effects as policy feedbacks (Skocpol and Amenta 1986: 149–51; Quadagno 1987: 118–19; Weir, Orloff, and Skocpol 1988: 25–27; Skocpol 1992: 57–60; Pierson 1994: 39–50). While stressing the causal importance of symbolic classification, I do not counterpose cultural with institutional influences. Rather, I proceed from the assumption that culture and institutions are inseparable, since classificatory schemes are objectified in institutions, and institutions have a cultural aspect or dimension (Meyer and Rowan 1991; Dobbin 1994).

These theoretical points are well illustrated by the struggles over the classification of WPA workers in the 1930s and early 1940s. Though modeled on earlier experiments with public works (Salmond 1967; Schwartz 1984; Sautter 1991), the WPA created a new group of welfare state claimants whose standing relative to those assisted by other policies was initially unclear. Would WPA employment reproduce disciplinary forms of work relief like those found in the poorhouse—an institution that had by no means disappeared in the 1930s (Wagner 2005)—or would it be sharply distinguished from them? Would the WPA provide relief as an alternative to citizenship rights or as an integral part of them? In the struggles that ensued, punitive forms of poor relief served as a model for WPA workers and sympathetic New Dealers to avoid, while New Deal labor policies set new standards against which they could measure injustices.[7]

The "Janus-like nature" of the WPA also contributed to uncertainty about WPA workers' status and rights. From its inception, "neither Congress nor administrative officials" ever clarified "how far the WPA should be regarded as a relief program as opposed to a work program" (Howard 1943: 246; see also 247, 251, 421–22; Lescohier 1939; Bremer 1975). The policy included features of both relief and public employment, which provided plausible bases for competing classificatory claims and encouraged political struggles to push it more consistently in one direction or the other (Goldberg 2005). Both the innovative nature of the WPA program and the intermediate position of WPA workers encouraged struggles over workers' status and rights.

Perhaps the most forceful advocate for WPA workers in these classification struggles was the Workers Alliance of America, a social movement organization that sought to mobilize and represent WPA workers from 1935 to 1941.[8] The Workers Alliance vigorously opposed the pauperization of WPA workers, which in practice meant striving to eliminate those policy features that the program shared with direct relief. At the same time, the Workers Alliance resisted threats to strip relief workers and relief recipients more generally of their civil and political rights. Such threats were very real in the 1930s. As millions of workers became relief recipients and new federal relief programs proliferated, controversy arose over how and to whom pauper exclusion laws applied. Some public officials tried to enforce the laws, and their efforts were accompanied by new proposals to curb or eliminate relief recipients' citizenship rights (Keyssar 2000: 237–44). Although most Americans opposed disfranchisement of relief recipients in the 1930s, a substantial minority supported the idea. According to a poll conducted in 1938 by the American Institute of Public Opinion, nearly one in five Americans, or 19 percent of those polled, supported disfranchisement of the unemployed on WPA and relief, and a similar survey conducted in 1939 by *Fortune* revealed that 18 percent of Americans favored disfranchisement of relief recipients (*Work*, October 22, 1938: 1; Keyssar 2000: 243). "National support [for disfranchisement] was sufficiently widespread that a countermovement was launched to promote a Twenty-second Amendment to the United States Constitution to guarantee the citizenship rights of the unemployed" (Keyssar 2000: 240). In this context, one of the principal aims of the Workers Alliance was to resist any "curtailment of citizenship rights to those receiving unemployment or public assistance" (*Work*, November 5, 1938: 2).

The Workers Alliance sought to expand the rights of WPA workers in addition to protecting their existing rights. Just as labor unions tried to create "a sort of secondary industrial citizenship" for workers in private industry through collective bargaining (Marshall 1964 [1949]: 93–94, 111), the Workers Alliance struggled to create something similar for WPA workers. By 1939 three-quarters of the members of the Workers Alliance were WPA workers, for whom the organization served as a kind of labor union. However, since the status of WPA workers as employees was contested, so too were their rights in the workplace. As the president of the Workers Alliance, David Lasser, ruefully noted, "The papers scoffed at our attempt to 'raise the wages of those on relief.' Reliefers, it was said, were being given charity. They should be thankful for whatever was bestowed!" (*Work*, July 16, 1938: 5). It was therefore imperative, as he demanded in 1936 in a letter to President Franklin D. Roosevelt, that WPA workers "be taken out of the twilight zone in which they are not on relief and yet have an essentially relief status. We WPA workers want to work and be treated as workers" (*New York Times*, August 25, 1936: 11). But what did it mean to be treated as workers? The material and symbolic profits that correspond to the name *worker* are not inherent in the category itself. To develop such an understanding, the Workers Alliance pointed to federal employees, Public Works Administration employees, and workers in private industry as salient reference groups with whom WPA workers could and should demand parity (Goldberg 2005). Moreover, parity with workers in private industry became a moving target as those workers won new gains. Successful labor struggles in private industry—especially the electrifying victories of the Congress of Industrial Organizations in 1936 and 1937—stimulated the mobilization of WPA workers as well (Seymour 1937: 45).[9]

As recently enacted New Deal labor policies encouraged and legitimized organizing efforts in private industry (Piven and Cloward 1977: 111–15; Skocpol 1980), the Workers Alliance invoked the same policies to encourage and legitimize protest among WPA workers. After Congress passed the National Labor Relations Act in 1935, making collective bargaining rights enforceable for workers in private industry, the Workers Alliance claimed the same rights for WPA workers. Similarly, though the applicability of the Fair Labor Standards Act (FLSA) of 1938 to WPA workers was contested, the Workers Alliance used it as a benchmark for defining the rights of WPA workers and invoked its minimum-wage provisions to make claims on their behalf (Goldberg 2005: 358–60). Invoking a discourse of industrial democracy that was resurgent and widespread during the New Deal, the Workers Alliance insisted that citizenship rights, including the right to organize, had to be extended to WPA workers to prevent the program from becoming "a system of forced labor in which the workers have no rights," a "situation abhorrent to democracy" (Roosevelt, Papers as President, Official File, File #2366). "Perhaps in Germany labor battalions fit the social and political scheme of things," Lasser wrote in 1939, "but we have no use for them here. And to tell free Americans that they must work at any wages fixed for them, or starve; to tell them that they will go to jail if they strike; to tell them that they are just 'reliefers' and have no rights, is an impossible situation" (*Work*, July 15, 1939: 6).

Like the Workers Alliance and sometimes in collaboration with it, WPA administrators also promoted recognition of WPA workers as rights-bearing citizen-workers. Their efforts were in part a response to the increasingly conservative and hostile policy environment in which the WPA operated. Early on, conservative opponents of the WPA sought to decentralize administration of the program or to replace it altogether with less costly direct relief (Howard 1943: chaps. 30, 31). Republican legislators in Congress began to push these competing policies as early as 1936 with the support of organizations like the U.S. Chamber of Commerce and the National Economy League (Howard 1943: 740, n. 2, 746–47, 760–61). In response, top-level WPA officials, including F. C. Harrington, Harry Hopkins, Howard Hunter, and Aubrey Williams, defended the continuation and national administration of the WPA in testimony to Congress, radio addresses to the public, and WPA press releases (Howard 1943: 735, 740, 743–44, 747–48, 761–62, 766, 768). President Roosevelt himself made a public "plea for the continuance of federal operation of the WPA program" in April 1939 (Howard 1943: 759). The conflict over whether to continue the WPA program and how to administer it had important implications for the status and rights of WPA workers. As Mettler (1998: 12–13) has shown, "Social citizenship determined by the states, judging by its ability to incorporate citizens on a broad and equal basis, has generally tended to be inferior to social citizenship with national standards for eligibility and administration." WPA officials were aware of these implications, and they used this very argument to discredit and ward off competing policy proposals from the right.

WPA officials emphasized the program's work aspects over its relief aspects and insisted that the WPA protected workers' citizenship rights better than competing policy proposals, which they equated with traditional poor relief. In 1938, for example, deputy administrator Williams of the WPA testified to Congress that the WPA's opponents sought to reduce "this whole thing [unemployment relief] to a level where you force people to accept the status of pauperism, denying them votes in many places, forfeiting their citizenship" (New York Times, June 28, 1938: 1; Howard 1943: 766). Similarly, in a press release dated May 15, 1939, WPA administrator Hunter declared, "People who propose to abandon the WPA for a system of grants-in-aid to States . . . do not like a program of work which enables these temporarily unemployed people to maintain their self-respect, bargaining power and rights of citizenship." Hunter went on to suggest that earlier attempts to administer relief through federal grants to states had failed in part because "there was no recognition given to the fact that these newly unemployed people . . . were a new kind of poor people. They were not the same old paupers who had normally been handled under the archaic poor-laws in most of our states. They were able-bodied unemployed citizens— the same kind of people as you and I" (Work, October 12, 1939: 4; Harry L. Hopkins, Container 35; Howard 1943: 761–62, 768).

The Workers Alliance, WPA officials, and their conservative opponents all understood that political and industrial citizenship were not only stakes in these classification struggles, but also forms of political capital that relief workers could use, in Lasser's words, for improving their "economic position" and "winning work and relief" (*Work*, September 10, 1938: 5). According to the Workers Alliance, disfranchisement was intended to curb "the growing economic and political power of the organized unemployed" (*Work*, April 23, 1938: 12; *Work*, October 22, 1938: 1). This power, whether real or exaggerated, was a major concern of the movement's opponents. When the Workers Alliance sent two thousand delegates on a job march to Washington in July 1937, Congressman Clifton Woodrum of Virginia warned that "the WAA would soon be a powerful political organization unless the federal government shifted relief back to the states and the municipalities. If this did not happen, said Woodrum, no congressman would be able to win reelection without acceding to WAA demands" (Folsom 1991: 421). A year later, an alarmed editorial in the *New York Times* (August 12, 1938: 16) warned that the Workers Alliance was becoming "an enormous pressure group compared with which the American Legion and the farm lobbies may pale into insignificance." These fears were deeply rooted in American history. Americans who favored decentralization of relief and disfranchisement of relief recipients "saw the nightmare that Blackstone had characterized and [the American jurist James] Kent had predicted: an army of 'dependents' marching to the polls; a mass of propertyless men ready to seize the property of others (through taxes); men 'with no will of their own' who easily could be manipulated by a clever politician or demagogue." They echoed eighteenth- and nineteenth-century fears when they denounced Roosevelt as "a masterful and manipulative politician" who used "federal tax dollars to build a national political machine" kept in power by "a permanent, government-supported army of indigents" (Keyssar 2000: 240–41).

The Outcomes of Classification Struggles in the Development of the U.S. Welfare State

Theoretical insights drawn from Marshall and Bourdieu help to explain why struggles emerge over the civic classification of welfare state claimants. But what about their outcomes? Why are some welfare state claimants classed as dependent paupers whose civil or political rights are curtailed while others successfully obtain recognition as independent, rights-bearing citizens? As previously noted, I focus on the institutional structure of the policy and the manner and extent to which it becomes entangled in racial politics as key determinants of these outcomes. However, this is not meant to imply that institutions or racial groupings are simply given features of the social world. Rather, in keeping with Bourdieu's constructionist structuralism, I suggest that the institutions and racial divisions that structure classification struggles are themselves constructed through past struggles. In this case—the struggles in the 1930s over the citizenship status and rights of WPA workers—the resources that were available to participants, their positions in social space, and the manner in which they grouped themselves and defined their interests, including their propensity to group themselves along racial lines, were shaped by previous struggles during Reconstruction and the Populist insurgency of the 1890s (Goldberg 2007). These earlier conflicts were more than struggles over classification, but classification struggles were an essential dimension of them. While it is beyond the scope of this chapter to fully demonstrate the historical legacies of past struggles, they should nevertheless be borne in mind as an important element of the explanation elaborated below.

As these remarks suggest, classification struggles and social policies are related in two ways. On the one hand, a successful classification struggle internalizes new classificatory schemes in the minds of social agents and objectifies them in policies, among other things. Recognition of welfare state claimants as rights-bearing citizens thus entails more than a change in discourse or categories of thought; it requires institutional changes as well. On the other hand, the institutional structures of existing policies shape subsequent classification struggles. The form of public provision—in other words, how the provision of benefits is organized—communicates something about the status of the recipients and thus serves an important symbolic function. The more isomorphic a new policy is with traditional poor relief (i.e., the more policy features they share), the more likely it is that clients of the new policy will be classed as paupers. Welfare state claimants are also more likely to be classed as paupers when the new policy is linked to or dependent upon traditional poor relief for distributing benefits, determining eligibility, and so forth. Conversely, policies confer dignity and independence to the extent that they are separated and differentiated from traditional poor relief. A variety of policy features have been used to accomplish this end. In the 1930s, for example, policymakers financed Old Age Insurance through payroll taxes in order to avoid any resemblance to relief. For similar reasons, policymakers rejected dependents' allowances for unemployment insurance and restricted eligibility to persons who were ordinarily and regularly employed (Mettler 1998: 126, 150). Though the particular means may vary, the separation and differentiation of a new social welfare policy from traditional poor relief is crucial to the favorable classification of the policy's clients.

Like policy structure, racial politics both reflects past struggles and influences subsequent struggles. Simply put, the clients of a policy are more likely to be classed as paupers when the policy's opponents mobilize a significant racial backlash against it. To be sure, this kind of backlash is not altogether independent of policy structure: Policies that become vehicles for the advancement of black citizenship rights, challenge racialized patterns of social closure, or expand the political or other forms of capital available to black workers are more likely to generate a racial backlash. In addition, because federal authorities have generally been more committed than local authorities to racial fairness, decentralized administration has also made policies more vulnerable to racial backlash. However, racial backlashes are not a product of policy structure alone; they also depend on political agency, including the symbolic work that is required to mobilize individuals along racial lines. Political entrepreneurs do not create racial divisions or racist sentiment *de novo*, but symbolic work is required to make racial divisions salient (and more so than competing sources of social division), activate racial antagonism, and turn potential racial groupings, what Bourdieu might call racial-groupings-on-paper, into real, mobilized racial groups. The success of those efforts is in turn shaped by the historical legacies of past classification struggles over the meaning and boundaries of American citizenship.

These theoretical points are again well illustrated by the struggle over the classification of wPA workers during the New Deal. The failure of this struggle is evident in three ways. First, it is apparent from public opinion. To be sure, large majorities of Americans favored continuation of the wPA (Schiltz 1970: 114–7) and opposed disfranchising wPA workers. In that respect, the existing political rights of wPA workers remained secure; the unemployed did not have to sacrifice them in exchange for new social rights. However, at a time when the citizenship rights of American workers were expanding, the public opposed the extension of these new rights to wPA workers. A poll in 1939 showed broad public support for the dismissal of striking wPA workers, and one in 1940 found that large majorities of the public believed that wPA workers should not be allowed to form unions and should not have the right to strike (*New York Times*, January 10, 1940: 13; *Work*, January 18, 1940: 3). In other words, public opinion supported continuation of the works program, but one shorn of the valued policy features that would have conferred industrial citizenship on wPA workers. Relative to workers in private industry, or at least those on the more privileged side of the gender and racial divide in the coverage of new U.S. labor standards, relief workers remained second-class citizens. Second, failure is also evident from the demise of the Workers Alliance itself in 1941. The collapse of the movement was in part a consequence of the classification struggles in which it was engaged and its failure to impose a favorable vision and division of the social world (Goldberg 2003). Third, the pauperization of relief workers is evidenced by the changing institutional structure of the wPA, which is addressed in more detail below. In sum, neither in people's minds nor in things, neither in agents' categories of thought nor in social institutions, were WPA workers ever classed as full citizens.

The most obvious explanation for this failure is the decline in mass unemployment as the United States became embroiled in the Second World War, which presumably rendered the WPA obsolete and made the civic classification of WPA workers a moot question. However, this explanation is inadequate upon closer examination. First, retrenchment of the WPA and repression of the Workers Alliance began in the late 1930s, when unemployment was still high—in fact, unemployment rose sharply during the recession of 1937–38— and before America's entry into the war. The war did not so much eliminate the rationale for the works program as reinforce political trends that had emerged beforehand. Second, there was no tight connection between the unemployment rate and political efforts to retrench or dismantle the WPA. Falling unemployment provided conservatives with an expedient justification for retrenchment, but so too did rising unemployment from 1937 to 1938, which conservatives blamed on the allegedly antibusiness policies of the Roosevelt administration (Rauch 1944: 295). Third, it was not certain that wartime recovery had eliminated the nation's need for a works program. Many elites and the general public, as shown by wartime public opinion polls, expected mass unemployment to return after the war ended, and New Dealers accordingly planned to make the works program a permanent feature of the postwar welfare state (Howard 1943: 361–68; Harvey 1989: 18–19, 106–7; Amenta 1998: 194–95, 199, 237–40, 2001: 264). Fourth, the WPA could have been reoriented to solve problems other than mass unemployment. Some congressmen envisioned an increase in WPA projects to assist the national defense, and some leaders of the unemployed movement sought cooperation with national defense agencies to promote the training of the unemployed (*Work*, November 23, 1939: 1; Howard 1943: 132–33; Rauch 1944: 314–15, 326; Roosevelt, President's Personal File, File #6794). Indeed, by 1942 the WPA was already "becoming more of a work agency to carry on defense and war projects than a work relief agency. Projects were then selected more on the basis of their value for the major task of the nation than on the basis of their suitability for furnishing employment to unemployed on relief rolls" (Meriam 1946: 403). These considerations suggest that economic recovery alone does not account for the retrenchment and eventual termination of the WPA or the failure of WPA workers to obtain recognition as full citizens. While changing economic conditions undoubtedly affected the fate of the WPA and its workers, the impact of those conditions was politically mediated.

Consistent with the theoretical framework sketched above, I argue that the WPA's institutional structure constrained efforts to obtain recognition of WPA workers as full citizens. First, the WPA incorporated several policy features that made it similar in form to traditional poor relief. For example, the WPA paid a monthly "security wage" deliberately fixed below those paid in private industry so as to encourage the unemployed to take jobs in private industry when they became available (Howard 1943: 255; Rose 1994: 98). This wage differential, rooted in the traditional poor relief principle of less eligibility, served to distinguish WPA workers from those in private industry.[10] The security wage also resembled the so-called supplemental wages historically paid to female dependents more than it did the family or living wage that served as "a benchmark of freedom, independence, and citizenship" for male workers (Glickman 1997: 3; see also Kessler-Harris 1990). Second, the WPA was structurally linked to traditional poor relief insofar as the program employed almost exclusively workers who were certified as needy and referred by local relief agencies (Howard 1943: 247, 354; Brown 1999, 73–74). Indeed, policymakers restricted WPA employment to relief recipients on the grounds "that if workers are to be brought to the realization that WPA employment is a form of relief rather than 'just another job,' it is necessary to require them to accept relief as an antecedent to a job" (Howard 1943: 409). The link to public relief was widely regarded as socially polluting. As the administrator of the New York City WPA Hugh Johnson put it, WPA employment failed to prevent "the humiliation of home relief," since "to go on work relief, the rules require that a man first go on home relief. To get there, he must submit to the equivalent of a pauper's oath" (quoted in Howard 1943: 412–13). These institutional features made it harder for WPA workers to obtain recognition as independent, rights-bearing citizen-workers.

While the WPA's institutional structure shaped classification struggles, classification struggles also shaped it. When the Workers Alliance formed in the mid-1930s, it mobilized relief recipients as workers (i.e., as part of the labor movement) and as members of the Popular Front against fascism, broadly inclusive identities that brought Communists and non-Communists together in the same organization.[11] However, in the late 1930s an incipient congressional coalition of Republicans and southern Democrats sought to delegitimize and disorganize the Workers Alliance by strengthening a cross-cutting division between Americanism and Communism. This boundary work, which was greatly facilitated by the nonaggression pact of 1939 between Nazi Germany and the Soviet Union, provided a new basis for excluding relief workers from full citizenship: disloyalty rather than dependency. More to the point, these congressional conservatives objectified their vision and division of the social world through a series of institutional reforms that (1) excluded Communists from participation in the federal works program, a provision used broadly against members of the Workers Alliance, not all of whom were Communists; (2) restricted the eligibility of foreigners, who were often viewed as social carriers of communism, for unemployment relief; and (3) limited WPA employment to eighteen months. By the time Congress terminated the WPA in 1942 conservative reforms had significantly transformed it, reinforcing the illiberal and disciplinary policy features it shared with traditional poor relief (Goldberg 2003). In this way, the changing institutional structure of the WPA reflected struggles over the classification of WPA workers as much as it influenced them.

These conservative reforms of the WPA were at odds with what New Dealers and WPA administrators envisioned. As we have seen, WPA officials sought to distinguish their program sharply from traditional poor relief in order to ward off competing policy proposals. However, their efforts to do so placed them in the contradictory position of denigrating the very relief programs to which the WPA remained tied. To be persuasive, their campaign required the institutional separation of the WPA from conventional poor relief, but the program's administrators lacked the authority to do so. Any such change required approval from Congress. Still, these institutional constraints only partly explain why WPA workers were classed as paupers. In fact, this explanation only pushes the question back a step. If WPA officials lacked the authority to upgrade the WPA and separate it from local and conventional forms of relief, why didn't Congress grant them the necessary authority or do the task itself? The answer to this question points to the deeper, underlying influence of racial politics: In brief, attempts to class WPA workers as rights-bearing citizen-workers rather than as reliefers with curtailed rights threatened powerful southern interests in Congress.

In the 1930s the southern economy was labor intensive, largely agrarian, and heavily dependent on a black workforce. As a result, southern politicians opposed social spending programs that "might reduce the supply of low-wage labor" or "provide sufficient benefits for African Americans to disrupt the Southern agrarian economy" (Manza 2000: 309; cf. Quadagno 1988b, 1994; Alston and Ferrie 1999; Brown 1999). At stake was not just the cost of labor, but the paternalistic method of labor control upon which the southern economy depended: "The political economy of the South . . . was based on the utter economic dependence of mostly black agricultural labor. Any welfare policy that gave Southern farm workers sources of income independent of the planter elite and the political institutions that it dominated had the potential to undermine the rigid racial and class structures of the South" (Lieberman 1998: 27; cf. Alston and Ferrie 1999: chap. 1). For similar reasons, southern planters and their political representatives in Congress opposed "nationalization of . . .

potentially intrusive labor market regulations" (Manza 2000: 309–10; cf. Katznelson et al. 1993; Alston and Ferrie 1999; Brown 1999).

These material interests did not necessarily lead southern congressmen to oppose social spending programs or federal labor standards during the New Deal, but they did demand that such policies accommodate their interests by sacrificing either federal control or inclusiveness (Lieberman 1998: 30, 37–38). Southern support was, in turn, crucial for the enactment of new policies because institutional arrangements in the 1930s and 1940s, most notably the disfranchisement of southern blacks and poor whites, the absence of significant party competition in the South, and the influence of southern Democrats over key congressional committees, created a powerful "Southern veto" in Congress (Katznelson et al. 1993). Southerners were willing to support policies such as Aid to Dependent Children and Old Age Assistance that sacrificed federal control, allowing states to set low benefit levels and restrict eligibility when expedient. Indeed, "Southern politicians aggressively embraced programs that combined federal resources with local control" (Manza 2000: 309–10; cf. Katznelson et al. 1993; Lieberman 1998: 37; Brown 1999). Alternatively, southerners were willing to support federally controlled social and labor policies that excluded African American workers and limited coverage as far as possible to white, urban industrial workers. For this reason Old Age Insurance and the FLSA covered neither agricultural nor domestic workers, occupational categories that accounted for two-thirds of black employment (Alston and Ferrie 1999: chap. 3; Amenta 1998, 226–27; Goldfield 1997: 211; Hamilton and Hamilton 1997: 29–30; Lieberman 1998; Mettler 1998: 186; Quadagno 1988a, 1988b; Valocchi 1994: 354; Palmer 1995).

In the WPA's existing form, four lines of defense mitigated its disruptive potential, ensuring that it would not pose a serious threat to the southern agrarian economy or arouse serious opposition from southern congressmen. First, regional differences in WPA wage rates minimized the danger that the WPA would reduce the dependence of black workers on southern planters or diminish the supply of low-wage labor. WPA wages varied widely among states and were set especially low in the South (Howard 1943: 182–83, 201, 206–7, 395, 770). Second, WPA officials set up elaborate administrative safeguards against the danger of labor shortages (Howard 1943: 487–88, 490). In the South this meant releasing black workers at harvest time, which "forced them to take low-paying, seasonal jobs in the fields" (Wolters 1970: 207–8; see also Rose 1994: 100–104; Valocchi 1994: 353; Hamilton and Hamilton 1997: 25; Brown 1999: 85–87). Third, some states established special restrictions on WPA employment of sharecroppers, tenants, and farm laborers, further minimizing any threat the WPA posed to the southern agrarian economy (Howard 1943:

506–9). Fourth, selective exclusion of African Americans from the WPA rolls also minimized the WPA's threat to the southern agrarian economy. Congress prohibited racial discrimination in WPA employment, and WPA administrators at the federal level were generally committed to racial fairness, but local authorities were able to circumvent the federal prohibition against racial discrimination in a variety of ways (Amenta 1998: 157–59; Brown 1999: 83; U.S. Department of Labor 1940: 638; Durant 1939; Foley 1997: 175, 178–80; Goldfield 1997: 208–9; Hamilton and Hamilton 1997: 24–26; Howard 1943: 285–87, 291–96, 386, 390, 452–53, 768–69; Rose 1994: 100–104; Valocchi 1994: 353; Wolters 1970: x–xi, 204). Although African Americans were sometimes overrepresented on WPA rolls elsewhere, local authorities made it difficult for them to get WPA jobs in the rural South, where the program would pose the greatest threat to the southern agrarian economy (Amenta 1998: 158; Brown 1999: 77–79, 84; Howard 1943: 288–89; U.S. Department of Labor 1940: 636; U.S. Federal Works Agency 1946: 45; Wolters 1970: 205–6).

While the WPA in its existing form did not pose a serious threat to southern interests, the struggle over the classification of WPA workers did. This struggle was not merely discursive. When the Workers Alliance demanded recognition of WPA workers as independent, rights-bearing citizen-workers, it sought to objectify this classificatory scheme by incorporating valued policy features into the WPA. Hence, the struggle over the classification of WPA workers had institutional implications and involved material as well as symbolic stakes. The struggle threatened southern interests in at least three ways: by potentially strengthening federal control, extending federal labor standards, and mobilizing black workers.

First, the struggle over the status and rights of WPA workers threatened the capacity of local authorities to selectively exclude black farm laborers from WPA employment. Insofar as local and state relief agencies certified the unemployed for WPA employment, the WPA allowed local authorities to exercise considerable control over who got onto its rolls. However, classification of WPA workers as independent, rights-bearing citizen-earners would have entailed the separation of the WPA from relief, which was in fact a key demand of the Workers Alliance. "We believe," Lasser testified to the Senate Appropriations Subcommittee in 1939, "that the W.P.A. program suffers from its characterization as a relief program, and because the W.P.A. workers are called 'relief workers.' We believe it should not be necessary for decent self-respecting Americans to reach the relief level before they can secure useful work and earn wages on a works program." Without the relief test, Lasser emphasized, the WPA "would not stigmatize the workers as 'relief clients'" (U.S. House of Representatives 1939–40: 34). While the Workers Alliance conceded that need should continue to be an important consideration in certifying the unemployed for WPA jobs, it insisted that need be determined "without forcing the unemployed to go through the relief rolls" (*Work*, May 7, 1938: 1). Separation of the WPA from relief would in turn have eliminated or minimized the role of local relief agencies in certifying the unemployed for WPA employment, thereby weakening the influence of local authorities and increasing federal control over certification.

Second, successful classification of WPA workers as independent, rights-bearing citizen-workers would have entailed the extension of federal labor standards to WPA workers. Although the National Labor Relations Act did not cover WPA workers, and application of the FLSA to WPA workers was unclear and contested, the extension of this legislation to WPA workers was another key demand of the Workers Alliance. In contrast, southern Democrats opposed the extension of federal labor standards, especially the minimum-wage provisions of the FLSA. To be sure, the FLSA provided "extremely low minimum wage rates: twenty-five cents an hour in 1938 increasing to a maximum of forty cents an hour by 1945" (Mettler 1998: 195). However, since WPA wages in the South were as low as fifteen cents an hour, extension of the newly established national minimum wage would have made possible "a substantial increase in the [wages of the] lowest paid WPA workers" (*Work*, September 24, 1938: 6). Some of these low-paid WPA workers were African American, and still more blacks would benefit if Congress reduced the role of local authorities in certifying the jobless for WPA employment. Applying the FLSA's wage protections to WPA workers would have made an end run around the law's occupational exclusions and potentially extended its coverage to many black workers who would otherwise be left out. The efforts of the Workers Alliance to extend federal labor standards to WPA workers, in the context of vocal support from some WPA officials for higher wages in the South and a marked rise in WPA wages in southern states after 1935, undoubtedly alarmed southern congressmen (Howard 1943: 159, 162, n. 3, 166).

Third, it was not only the demands of the Workers Alliance and the backing of WPA officials in Washington that alarmed southern Democrats, but also the efforts of the Workers Alliance to mobilize southern black workers in support of those demands. Such efforts were most evident in the alliance's southern organizing drive of 1936 and its campaign in 1938 to "raise the wages of 2,600,000 WPA laborers in low-wage categories," also primarily concentrated in the South (*Workers Alliance*, "Second March Issue" [1936]: 1; *Work*, July 16, 1938: 1; *Work*, August 26, 1939: 3). Black WPA workers, who were usually among the lowest paid, stood to benefit the most from the wage increases demanded and sometimes won by the Workers Alliance.[12] In addition, the Workers Alliance struggled to expand the civil and political rights of southern blacks in a variety of ways: opposing WPA discrimination against blacks, registering blacks to vote, and fighting for the abolition of the poll tax, which the alliance denounced as a tool for disfranchising the poor and unemployed (Bunche 1973: 422–24; Kelley 1990: 202; Porter 1980: 133; Sullivan 1996: 144–45; *Work*, May 7, 1938: 7; *Work*, July 16, 1938: 7; *Work*, September 24, 1938: 1; *Work*, October 22, 1938: 6; *Work*, December 3, 1938: 3; *Work*, April 8, 1939: 7; *Work*, June 17, 1939: 3; *Work*, July 29, 1939: 9; *Work*, September 14, 1939: 6; *Work*, September 28, 1939: 7; *Work*, October 12, 1939: 2; *Work*, October 26, 1939: 1, 4; *Work*, April 25, 1940: 1). The Workers Alliance also formed growing ties to black civil rights organizations in the late 1930s, including the National Negro Congress and the Southern Conference for Human Welfare (Krueger 1967: 22–23; *Work*, May 21, 1938: 5; *Work*, September 24, 1938: 1; *Work*, October 8, 1938: 9; *Work*, November 5, 1938: 5; *Work*, December 3, 1938: 5; *Work*, April 25, 1940: 1).

The classificatory demands the Workers Alliance made on behalf of WPA workers, the rights and policy changes that those demands entailed, and the alliance's endeavors to mobilize blacks in support of those demands generated a strong racial backlash against the movement, a backlash that sometimes expressed itself in the form of anti-Communism. This was not coincidental. Communists were active in the Workers Alliance, and they were also largely responsible for its efforts on behalf of southern blacks. In the 1930s the American Communist Party was an "aggressive advocate" of racial equality, elevating "black communists to the party's central committee" and expelling "white members who refused to socialize with blacks—gestures no other white organization was willing to match" (Babson 1999: 64; cf. Howe and Coser 1957: 204–16ff.; Goldfield 1997: chap. 6; Stepan-Norris and Zeitlin 2003: chaps. 8–9).

Southern racial conservatives were aware of the connection between Communism and black political mobilization, which helps to explain why prominent southern Democrats like Clifton Woodrum, the leader of the House Subcommittee on the Works Progress Administration, and Martin Dies, chairman of the House Special Committee on Un-American Activities, played leading roles in the anti-Communist crusade against the Workers Alliance and the WPA in the late 1930s. As Dies saw it, "Subversive elements [were] attempting to convince the Negro that he should be placed on social equality with the white people; that now is the time for him to assert his rights" (quoted in Gellermann 1944: 245–46). These southern Democrats worked with Republicans to delegitimize the Workers Alliance as a front for the Communist Party, discredit the WPA as a source of funding for Communist subversion, cut WPA expenditures, and eventually dismantle the program (Patterson 1967; Porter 1980; Sexton 1991; Goldberg 2003). Analysis of congressional roll call votes confirms this supposition. Although southern Democrats were generally favorable to the

WPA on budgetary votes during the program's early years, their support for spending declined over time, and by 1939 most of them were voting against WPA spending (either against increases or for reductions). In addition, most southern Democrats joined Republicans to maintain a prohibition on deficiency appropriations in 1938, oppose payment of prevailing wages in 1939, and support time limits on WPA work between 1939 and 1941. Of the thirty staunchest opponents of the WPA in the U.S. Senate, nearly half were from the South (Amenta and Halfmann 2000; Amenta 2001: 267–75). Opposition to the Workers Alliance and the WPA was not confined to southern Democrats or motivated exclusively by racism. However, "organized business and the Republicans could not have been effective as they were without the aid and leadership of southern Democrats" (Amenta 1998: 142, 219–25). Southern Democrats were therefore crucial to the failure of WPA workers to obtain recognition as rights-bearing citizen-workers.

The racial backlash against the Workers Alliance and the WPA was evident not only in the reaction of southern congressmen at the national level, but also in violent, often racially charged resistance to the movement at the local level. Members and organizers of the Workers Alliance were harassed, prohibited from meeting, forced out of town, tear-gassed, jailed, beaten, and shot (*New York Times*, December 22, 1935: 9; *Workers Alliance*, "Second January Issue" [1936]: 2; *Work*, May 7, 1938: 2; *Work*, June 4, 1938: 3, 9, 10; *Work*, June 18, 1938: 4; *Work*, July 15, 1939: 3; Bunche 1973: 501). Perhaps the most notorious attack came in Tampa, Florida, where a Workers Alliance organizer was tarred, feathered, and beaten to death by Ku Klux Klansmen (*Workers Alliance*, "First January Issue" [1936]: 1). In these instances, especially when the alliance's activities on behalf of relief workers challenged the exclusion of African Americans from the material and symbolic profits of full citizenship, its organizing efforts were aggressively and even brutally suppressed.

Despite the vigorous opposition of the leaders of the Workers Alliance to racial discrimination, a racial backlash emerged even within the ranks of the movement itself. For example, a Workers Alliance local in Atlanta had to be rid of "disturbing Ku Klux Klan elements," whom movement leaders expelled by December 1938 (*Work*, July 30, 1938: 2; *Work*, September 24, 1938: 11; *Work*, December 17, 1938: 4). Likewise, "racial equality and Communism were seen as two sides of the same coin" in Alabama, leading many whites to leave the organization "on the pretext that its racial practices alone proved it was a Communist front" (Kelley 1990: 156). To be sure, instances of racial backlash within the movement were more the exception than the rule. Most Workers Alliance members refused to make political claims on the basis of race and generally forswore the wages of whiteness. Nevertheless, these internal struggles weakened the alliance and undermined its efforts to secure work relief as an integral part of, not an alternative to, its members' citizenship rights.

The racial animus against and within the Workers Alliance may have merged with a broader racial backlash against the WPA in the late 1930s. Despite continued exclusion in the rural South, the proportion of blacks on WPA rolls grew nationwide because African Americans faced greater difficulty finding private employment and left the rolls less rapidly than whites (U.S. Federal Works Agency 1946: 45). Brown (1999: 77–79, 89) argues that this trend, combined with "widespread racist stereotypes" of black workers as "lazy, irresponsible, [and] indolent," "undoubtedly contributed to the erosion of public support after 1938 for expanding WPA and relief expenditures, despite continuing high levels of unemployment." In sum, once the Workers Alliance and the WPA became vehicles for challenging racialized patterns of social closure, both the movement and the program became targets of racial hostility at the elite and mass levels. This reaction made it difficult for WPA workers to establish new claims to social welfare provision without a concomitant curtailment of their civil, political, or industrial rights.

Conclusion
CLASSIFICATION STRUGGLES IN THE DEVELOPMENT OF THE U.S. WELFARE STATE

Combining insights from Marshall, Bourdieu, and historical institutionalism, I have offered here a general explanation of the emergence and outcomes of recurring struggles over the citizenship status and rights of welfare state claimants in the United States while applying this theory to the particular case of the WPA. Major innovations in social welfare policy, I have argued, typically generate struggles over whether to model the new policy on or distinguish it from traditional poor relief. At stake in these struggles are the citizenship status and rights of the policies' clients, who must struggle not only to preserve new social rights, but also to avoid losing their civil and political rights in the process. These conflicts, I have suggested, may be usefully conceptualized as classification struggles through which state officials, service providers, employers, clients, unions, and social movements seek to appropriate valuable symbolic and material resources in the field of social welfare provision. In the case of the WPA, the program created a new group of claimants within the welfare field whose status and rights relative to those of other claimants were initially uncertain. Furthermore, the policy's hybrid nature as both a relief program and a work program placed WPA workers in an intermediate position within the field, which provided a plausible basis for competing classificatory claims. In addition, the threat posed to the WPA by competing policy proposals encouraged WPA officials to emphasize the preservation of their clients' citizenship rights. By means of this strategy, they sought to distinguish their program in a manner that would legitimize it and discredit its competitors. Finally, the citizenship status and rights of relief workers were contested because citizenship itself was a valuable resource that facilitated, at least potentially, access to other kinds of resources. All of these conditions contributed to conflict over the status and rights of WPA workers in the 1930s and early 1940s.

The outcomes of these classification struggles, I argued, are crucially shaped by policy structure and racial politics. This theoretical claim is also evinced by the case of the WPA. The Workers Alliance sought not only to obtain recognition of WPA workers as independent, rights-bearing citizen-workers, but also to institutionalize that status. Achievement of this goal required structural reforms of the WPA to separate and distinguish it more clearly from existing relief arrangements—in short, strengthening the program's work aspects and minimizing its relief aspects. WPA officials had a shared interest in such reforms and generally supported them, but the alliance's activities and demands challenged racialized forms of social closure, especially in the South, and therefore triggered the "Southern veto" in Congress. Southern Democrats joined with Republicans to thwart the agenda of the Workers Alliance, repress the movement, and eventually dismantle the WPA. This reaction from congressional conservatives was compounded by a broader racial backlash at the local level, within the Workers Alliance itself, and perhaps in public attitudes toward WPA expenditures.

IMPLICATIONS FOR THE SOCIOLOGY OF THE WELFARE STATE

Although the findings presented in this chapter are limited to a single social spending program over seven years, they have broader implications for how we understand welfare state development in the United States. The WPA was by no means unique; other U.S. policies and programs have generated analogous struggles over the citizenship status and rights of their clients. Proponents of an expanded Civil War pension system, for example, successfully "defined [it] in opposition to charity or public programs for paupers at state and local levels" (Skocpol 1992: 149). Similarly but with less success, maternalist reformers sought to characterize mothers' pensions as compensation for mothers' service to the nation rather than poor relief or public charity. "We cannot afford to let a mother, one who has divided her body by creating other lives for the good of the state, one who has contributed to citizenship, be classed as a pauper, a dependent," declared the president of the Tennessee Congress of Mothers in 1911 (quoted in Skocpol 1992: 450). Likewise, Robert Doughton, the chairman of the House Ways and Means Committee in 1935, insisted then that recipients of old age insurance were "in a different class from the ordinary relief case" (quoted in Tynes 1996: 52), though the application of pauper exclusion laws to recipients of old age assistance remained contested into the 1950s (see, e.g., *Hines v. Winters*, 1957 OK 334, 320 P.2d 1114). More recent struggles have been fought over the classification of workfare workers and recipients of the Earned Income Tax Credit (Goldberg 2007). These examples suggest that struggles over the citizenship status and rights of welfare state claimants are a chronic feature of U.S. welfare state development in need of sociological explanation. The arguments put forward in this article in regard to WPA workers may help to explain these other struggles as well.

The findings presented here also have implications for how we understand the relations among work, welfare, and American political culture. According to a long-standing and influential view, Americans are generally hostile to social spending programs because of their historical commitment to classical liberal values of antistatism, laissez-faire and individualism. In line with this view, it is frequently assumed that policies that link benefits to work will receive more support in the United States because they are more consistent with liberal American values of self-reliance. The research presented here challenges or at least qualifies this view of how liberal values inhibit or facilitate the development of the American welfare state. The case of the WPA shows that the conditioning of new social rights upon work does not always legitimize them, nor does it ensure that claimants' other rights—civil, political, or industrial—will be respected. Just as antistatist antagonism to the welfare state grew stronger when the welfare state was linked to racial conflict and black political mobilization (Quadagno 1994), so too the work ethic generated less support for work-based social spending policies when those policies became linked to the pursuit of civil, political, and social rights for African Americans. The color of work mediated the effects of liberal values during the New Deal, much as the color of welfare mediated their effects thirty years later during the War on Poverty.

Theoretical Contributions

This chapter has built on the insights of Marshall and Bourdieu while developing and extending them in new directions. As Marshall is typically read, the modern welfare state represents the last stage in a steady development of citizenship over the past three centuries, from civil to political to social rights. This narrative of a cumulative expansion of citizenship rights provides the theoretical framework for most studies of the welfare state, which have mainly tried to explain why the development of (social) citizenship has advanced in some countries while lagging behind in others. In contrast, my reading of Marshall suggests a more complicated view of citizenship in which civil and political rights could be and often were treated as an alternative to social rights rather than a foundation for them. When welfare state development is viewed in this way, it raises a different set of questions: Why in some cases have newly established social rights been integrated into the status of citizenship while in other cases they were detached from it? To answer these questions, I drew upon Bourdieu's concept of classification struggles. However, rather than using the concept of classification struggles as Bourdieu did, that is, to explain the formation and mobilization of social classes, I have used it to investigate the boundary work through which social agents define the meaning of citizenship, regulate access to its material and symbolic profits, and link it to other social categories such as class, race, gender, and nation. This boundary work constitutes a promising new field of inquiry for the sociology of the welfare state.

Notes

This chapter originally appeared in slightly different form in 2008 in *Political Power and Social Theory* 19: 83–116. I thank the publisher of the journal for permission to reprint my article in this collection and the Center for European Studies at the University of Wisconsin, Madison, for a generous grant that made it possible for me to do so. Earlier drafts of this chapter were presented at the Conference on Bourdieuian Theory and Historical Analysis at Yale University in 2005; the meeting of the Law and Society Association in 2006; the Center for the United States and the Cold War, Tamiment Library and Robert F. Wagner Labor Archives, New York University, in 2007; and the meeting of the Social Science History Association in 2007. I am grateful to all those who offered suggestions and advice for improving the earlier drafts.

1. Following Marshall (1964 [1949]: 84), I use *citizenship* in this article to refer to a status with corresponding rights and duties that is bestowed upon the members of a political community. In principle, citizenship is a uniform status that confers equal rights and duties. However, as noted below, it may in practice be a gradated status that members possess to a greater or lesser extent.

2. Although Marshall's remarks about poor relief and protective labor laws refer to Britain, they are true of the United States as well. On the loss of civil rights through internment in almshouses and workhouses, see Rothman (1971: chap. 8). On the disfranchisement of paupers, which was not completely abolished until the 1960s, see Steinfeld (1989) and Keyssar (2000: 61–65, 271–72). On protective labor laws for women, see Skocpol (1992: 373–423); Mettler (1998: 34–37); and Glenn (2002: 84–85). Like courts in Britain, American courts struck down protective labor laws for men on the grounds that such laws violated their civil rights, in particular, their constitutionally guaranteed liberty of contract. This interpretation of the Fourteenth Amendment of the U.S. Constitution was enshrined by the Supreme Court in *Lochner v. New York* (1905) and not seriously challenged until the 1930s.

3. On social closure, see Weber (1978); Parkin (1979); and Murphy (1988).

4. Following Marshall, I use *claimant* as a generic term to indicate a person who claims state benefits, regardless of what form the benefits take (cash or in-kind),

how eligibility is determined, or how the benefits are financed. In this case study, the claimants were WPA workers. More generally, welfare state claimants included recipients of old-age or mothers' pensions, unemployment benefits, and so forth. I use *claimant* interchangeably with *client*, though the former has a more active connotation.

5. As these remarks indicate, some groups in the United States, most notably women and African Americans, lacked full civil and political rights during their struggles for new social rights. Rather than preserve their civil and political rights while acquiring new social rights, they had to struggle for civil, political, and social rights simultaneously.

6. Although Bourdieu (1985b, 1989a) emphasized the state's role in classification struggles as the "supreme tribunal" and the "holder of the monopoly of legitimate symbolic violence," this role must not be exaggerated. First, "the holders of bureaucratic authority never establish an absolute monopoly. . . . In fact, *there are always, in any society, conflicts between symbolic powers that aim at imposing the vision of legitimate divisions,* that is, at constructing groups" (Bourdieu 1989a: 22). These conflicts create opportunities for dominated groups to contest their classification. Second, in contrast to the "pessimistic functionalism" of social control theories, Bourdieu regarded the state itself as an arena of struggle, not a unified apparatus (Bourdieu and Wacquant 1992: 102, 111–15; Bourdieu 1994b). As a result of internal struggles, the state may unintentionally create indeterminacy through inconsistent and contradictory classifying practices, further expanding opportunities for dominated groups to contest their classification.

7. On eligibility for WPA employment, see Howard (1943: 269–527). Generally speaking, need and employability were the primary considerations. The WPA was prohibited from discriminating on the basis of sex or race, but women found it harder to get work for various reasons (278–85). Employment by the WPA was initially open to aliens but restricted after 1938 to "United States citizens, Indians, and others (such as Filipinos) owing allegiance to the United States" (303).

8. The Workers Alliance had its roots in earlier efforts to organize the unemployed by the Socialist Party, A. J. Muste's Conference on Progressive Labor Action, and the American Communist Party (Rosenzweig 1975, 1979, 1983; Piven and Cloward 1977, 68–76). The alliance's attempts to link work and citizenship reflected its organizational and ideological origins, the movement's growing ties to the new federal works program, and the rising proportion of Workers Alliance members who were WPA employees.

9. Although federal policy prohibited WPA workers from striking against the federal government, they engaged in strikes anyway (Ziskind 1940; Howard 1943: 222–27). "What is most noteworthy about this general consensus [that WPA workers had no right to strike]," observed one contemporary, "is that many who share it do so not because the struck jobs were 'government' jobs but because they were relief, not real, jobs" (Howard 1943: 222).

10. The principle of less eligibility stipulates that relief must always be less desirable than even the worst employment. The Emergency Relief Appropriation Act of 1938

required the wpa to pay its workers the prevailing wage or the federal minimum wage, whichever was greater. However, instead of raising the wpa security wage, Congress reduced "the hours of labor until the amounts of the original security wage translated into hourly terms equaled the prevailing wage" (Macmahon et al. 1941: 156). In 1939 Congress abandoned the prevailing wage policy and set hours uniformly at 130 per month (Rose 1994: 98).

11. Since wpa workers had diverse occupational backgrounds, they possessed varying amounts of economic and cultural capital and were thus dispersed in social space. This dispersion may have constrained efforts to mobilize wpa workers as part of the labor movement. wpa workers with white-collar or professional backgrounds, for example, may have been less likely to embrace such an identity and therefore less likely to join the Workers Alliance. Nevertheless, the Workers Alliance was able to mobilize hundreds of thousands of wpa workers, and it is apparent from newspaper evidence that the movement's membership included workers with professional backgrounds (see, e.g., *The Professional Worker*). This finding is consistent with Kocka (1980), who argues that white-collar employees in the United States have had relatively little difficulty identifying with the labor movement.

12. A sit-down strike of wpa workers led by the Workers Alliance in Birmingham, Alabama, is noteworthy because it was opposed by none other than Public Safety Commissioner Eugene "Bull" Connor. Connor gained notoriety in 1963 when he used fire hoses and police dogs against civil rights protesters in Birmingham. The strike led by the Workers Alliance twenty-five years earlier succeeded in raising the minimum wpa wage in Birmingham from $36 to $40.80 per month (*Work*, September 24, 1938: 3).

NATION-IZATION STRUGGLES
A Bourdieusian Theory of Nationalism

My goal in this chapter is to develop a Bourdieusian theory of nationalism, or at least to begin sharpening some of the tools that such a theory would require. The motivation for the paper is twofold. It is driven, on the one hand, by my dissatisfaction with many existing theories and the answers they give to the three cardinal questions about nationalism—what was it?, when did it emerge?, and why does it arise?—and, on the other hand, by a conviction that Pierre Bourdieu's approach can help us to overcome these old debates by providing a more satisfactory definition of nationalism and a more robust framework for analyzing it.

This is not to suggest that Bourdieu's writings contain a ready-made theory of nationalism; they do not. But they do contain at least one promising starting point for such a theory: the concept of "classification struggle," a concept Bourdieu uses to analyze the formation and dissolution of social groups (Bourdieu 1984a, 1991a). Since the concept was originally developed for analyzing processes of class formation within nation-states, it will need to be refined and reconstructed in various ways before it can be applied to processes of nation formation, what I will call nation-ization struggles.

The plan of the chapter is as follows. In the first section I will briefly review some key developments and debates in the study of nationalism, focusing on how English-language social science has addressed the what, when, and why questions. In the next section I will argue that considerable progress has been made on these questions, but that continued progress is being blocked or at least slowed by a failure to fully expunge the assumptions and aspirations of modern nationalist ideology from our definitions and typologies of national-ism. In the final sections I develop a general conceptual framework for the study of nation-ization struggles and suggest how it might be put into action.

Obstacles to Analysis: The Modernist Hypothesis and the Nationalist Unconscious of Nationalism Scholarship

The literature on nationalism is vast and complex, and it is neither possible nor necessary to subject it to a comprehensive analysis in this context; that has been done ably enough elsewhere (Delanty and Kumar 2006). Instead, I will focus on some recurring debates over the three cardinal questions about nationalism. I will argue that further progress in answering these questions is presently blocked by a misguided insistence in some quarters that nationalism is inherently modern and, moreover, that this insistence is rooted in a failure of many theorists of nationalism to break fully with the assumptions of nationalist ideology (Breuilly 1982; Gellner 1983; Hroch 1985; Hobsbawm 1992). In short, I will argue that the *modernist thesis is a symptom of a nationalist unconscious* and that the abandoning of this thesis will allow us to deepen our understanding of the whats and whys of nationalism.

By way of background, I begin with a thumbnail sketch of the English-language social science literature on nationalism. Vast as it is, this literature can be divided into four theoretically distinct, if temporally overlapping, waves. The first wave, which goes back at least to the early twentieth century, defined nationalism as an idea, ideology, principle, or creed on a par with liberalism, socialism, or fascism and located its origins in the late eighteenth century or early nineteenth but did not give any clear explanation of its emergence. It provided an intellectual genealogy of the national idea that pivoted around the work of French *philosophes* (e.g., J. J. Rousseau and the Abbé Sieyès) and German romantics (e.g., Johann Gottlieb Fichte and Johann Gottfried von Herder) and treated its subject in the manner of intellectual history (Meinecke 1908; Kohn 1946; Minogue 1967; Berlin and Hardy 1980; Kedourie 1993; Viroli 1997). The second wave, which began shortly after the Second World War, conceived of nationalism as a form of political community or identity, a competitor and successor to local identity, rooted in face-to-face relations, as well as to universal identity, derived from religion (Deutsch 1953; Weber 1976; Gellner 1983; Anderson 1991). It embedded the story of nationalism within a grand narrative about the arrival of modernity. Concretely, it focused on how various aspects of the modernization process (i.e., industrialization, democratization, secularization, and kindred processes) facilitated or necessitated the emergence of nationalism by expanding the scope of social integration and heightening its intensity. The third wave begins during the late 1960s and early 1970s. Scholars in this wave were inspired by neo-Marxian and neo-Weberian theory and were less interested in nationalism per se than in capitalist development and state formation. Consequently, they tended to see nationalism as an ideology in the sense of a ruling class ideology or strategy of legitimation—as instrumental, in other words. They emphasized the ways in which the expansion of markets and state bureaucracies promoted social integration on a national scale and the ways in which elites manipulated national symbols and loyalties to shore up their power (Tilly 1975; Breuilly 1982; Hroch 1985; Mann 1986; Balibar and Wallerstein 1991; Brass 1991). The fourth and most recent wave of scholarship began in the early 1990s (see, e.g., Hobsbawm and Ranger 1983; Brubaker 1992, 1996, 2004, 2006; Colley 1992; Laitin 1992, 1995, 2000; Calhoun 1993b, 1997; Porter 2000; Bell 2001; Snyder 2003) Like the first-wavers and unlike the second- and third-wavers, these scholars pay considerable attention to the symbolic dimension of nationalism. They look closely at national rituals and discourses. At the same time, they see the nation as a site of contestation and national identity as an ongoing construction. In this regard, they are more like third-wavers than first-wavers.

Surveying this literature, we see unmistakable signs of progress, particularly in answers to the what and why questions. Consider how answers to the what question have evolved. First-wavers usually defined nationalism in purely symbolic and even naively idealistic terms. Their analyses were based mainly on close readings of well-known social and political philosophers and typically gave scant attention to broader issues of sociopolitical power and institutions or, for that matter, to concrete processes of ideological production and reception. In sum, first-wavers gave short shrift to the material dimension of nationalism. Second-wavers responded by committing the reverse error. They turned their attention to material processes, to the ways in which modernization increased the resonance of national ideas and facilitated their diffusion. But they paid little if any attention to the ideas themselves. Indeed, their analyses rarely contain any extensive discussion of national rituals or discourses. Against this background, we might see the third wave as a first attempt at synthesis—as an attempt to relate the material and symbolic dimensions—but as a partial and inadequate synthesis which reduces the symbolic to the status of epiphenomenon or strategy by treating national identity as a side effect of underlying sociopolitical transformations and making nationalist ideology into a political tool of cynical rulers. In the fourth wave, finally, we see movement toward a fuller, more adequate synthesis, one which gives the material and the symbolic their proper due and highlights the interplay between them, though rarely with the systematicity and nuance permitted by a Bourdieusian approach.

Answers to the why question have followed a similar trajectory. They begin, in the first wave, with a more or less Hegelian analysis of ideas whose times have come and the world-historical thinkers who bring them into being. In the second wave the pendulum swings to the other extreme, with a focus on the material infrastructure through which ideas are transmitted, for example, the press, schools, railroads, etc. The third wave represents a first attempt at synthesis, in which nationalism is traced to the more or less conscious machinations of social elites. Finally, in the fourth wave we see a more balanced approach in which symbolic structures and cultural resources are given their proper due.

In sum, the naïve treatments of first-wavers, which located the origins of nationalism inside the heads of certain philosophers, gave way in the second wave to a non-Marxian materialism in which national identity simply bubbled up into individual minds from some deeper substrate of causation. Third-wavers refined this approach somewhat by alloying it with historical analyses of market growth, class conflict, and state formation, among other things, but only with the fourth wave is the causal force of the symbolic dimension fully recognized, via greater attention to ritual performances, discursive logics, and intellectual strata. If subjectivism and objectivism are the Scylla and Charybdis of social science, as Bourdieu argued, and if the road to progress in social science is via a media that steers between them while giving each its proper tribute, then the overall trajectory in the literature looks very much like progress.

But if there are signs of progress, there are also signs of stasis. They are most evident in answers to the when question. On this subject, there has been a surprising, indeed, suspicious, amount of agreement across all four waves. While some historians and, more recently, even some social scientists have begun to question the modernist thesis (Smith 1988, 2004; Beaune and Cheyette 1991; Colley 1992; Wormald 1994; Foote 1996; Hastings 1997; Pincus 1998; Gorski 2000, 2006; Marx 2003), the orthodox view has long been that nationalism is a modern phenomenon, not just in the incidental sense that it happens to have arisen in the period we conventionally call modern (i.e., a period beginning sometime between 1750 and 1800); but also in the deeper, developmental sense that it could not possibly have arisen prior to that time because certain necessary preconditions were not yet in place. Each wave identified a different set of preconditions. For the first-wavers it was simply the invention of a certain conception of the nation, typically on the French (civic) or German (ethnic) model. For second-wavers, the key precondition was a certain level of social and cultural modernization. In Ernst Gellner's account, for example, industrialization was the key; it gave rise to a society that was more mobile, more individualistic, more homogenized, and more educated, thereby creating the need for a new type of social integration, a need which nationalism was perfectly suited to fulfill (Gellner 1983). For the third-wavers it was the emergence of markets and states that were fully national in scope, as, for instance, in Michael Mann's account (1986). To the degree that they identify preconditions at all, fourth-wavers typically point to the impact of particular historical events on the crystallization of nationalism; the French Revolution is a favorite example (Giesen 1991; Bell 2001). This is not to say there is complete agreement about the birth date of nationalism. Some mainstream scholars place it as early as 1750; others as late as the 1870s (Weber 1976). And there have always been a few heterodox scholars who have located its origins several centuries further back during the early modern era (Ranum 1975). Still, the level of agreement about the when question has been, and still is, much greater than the level of agreement about the other cardinal questions.

The modernist position—the view that nationalism is inherently modern—is so much a part of the received wisdom in the social sciences that it may seem heretical to even question it. And yet there are some very simple and very obvious reasons for doubting it. After all, the term *nation* is hardly modern. Neither are kindred terms like *fatherland*, *people*, and *state*. Nor for that matter are discourses that interrelate or even equate some or all of these terms (Heissenbüttel 1920; Schönemann 1972–97). They can all be traced back through the ethnographic works of classical antiquity (Parsons 1929; Smith 2004; Patten 2006; Roshwald 2006), which catalogued and classified various nations and peoples, and beyond that to the Exodus saga of the Jewish Bible, which recounts the story of a chosen people's journey to a promised land where they establish a national state (O'Brien 1988; Grosby 1991, 2002; Hutchison and Lehmann 1994; Smith 2003). Nor did they disappear from scholarly and political discourse following the collapse of the empire. Discussions of nations and peoples recur again and again in the religious and political discourse of western Europe during the Middle Ages and even in the Dark Ages (Reynolds 1984; Beaune and Cheyette 1991; Wormald 1994; Foote 1996).

The modernists are not unaware of these objections, and they have developed various arguments to counter them. While none of these arguments can really survive closer scrutiny, it is important to look at them in some detail because they reveal the subtle ways in which many scholars of nationalism long were and still are ensnared in the web of nationalist ideology. We can distinguish four main counterarguments. The first is sociological and focuses on the scope of nationalist consciousness. Prior to the modern era, it is argued, national consciousness was confined to elite groupings, such as aristocrats and intellectuals. Only in the modern era, so the argument goes, did nationalism become a mass phenomenon. There is a great deal of evidence against this claim, and it is rarely heard today. This is because historians long ago found numerous premodern examples of nationalist discourse and what looks like nationalist consciousness (Kohn 1946).

A second and less sweeping defense makes organization and mobilization the litmus test for genuine nationalism. While national consciousness may have antedated the modern era, it is argued, nationalist movements and parties arise only in the modern era. This claim is also problematic, both empirically and theoretically. Nationalistic rhetoric played a considerable role in many early modern rebellions, revolutions, partisan struggles, and wars, including the Dutch Revolt against Spain, the Glorious Revolution in England, and the Anglo-Dutch Wars (Schama 1987; Pincus 1996, 1998, 2006; Gorski 2000). If one defines the terms *movement* and *party* in sufficiently modern terms, or if one insists they must refer to themselves as nationalist, a coinage first used after the French Revolution, then one will inevitably fail to find nationalist movements and parties until the nineteenth century. But we should not be taken in by tautological trickery of this sort, in which nationalism is found to be inherently modern because it is implicitly defined as such.

The third counterargument is semiotic. It focuses on the relationship between nationalist discourse and other discourses. Here, the argument is that genuine nationalism is, discursively, pure nationalism, a secular or democratic ideology (or both) unsullied by religious and authoritarian thinking (Hobsbawm 1992). This test does indeed screen out many possible instances of premodern nationalism, though certainly not all: one thinks, for example, of the civic patriotism of the Italian Renaissance, which was fully secular and republican (Trexler 1980, 1985; Villari 1997; Patten 2006). The problem is that it also screens out most accepted examples of modern nationalism as well. By this standard, for instance, modern Polish nationalism would not count as nationalism because it is so tightly intertwined with Roman Catholicism (Eile 2000; Zubrzycki 2006); much modern American nationalism, otherwise known as patriotism, would have to be disqualified on similar grounds (Tuveson 1968; Cherry 1998). Indeed, many modern nationalisms would have to be disqualified on these grounds (Akenson 1991; Hutchison and Lehmann 1994). And what about Nazism? It, too, would have to be excluded, not only because it was antidemocratic but also to the degree it embraced pre-Christian folk religions and a folk Christianity (Pois 1986; Bergen 2003; Babík 2006).

The fourth and final defense of modernism focuses on identity. The hallmark of genuine nationalism, according to this argument, is that it trumps all other identities—religion and region, clan and class, and so on. This argument comes in a strong and a weak version. In the strong version, national identity becomes *the* dominant identity of the modern era. In the weak version, individuals for whom national identity is the dominant identity first appear in the modern world; it makes the appearance of the radical nationalist the litmus test for modern nationalism. The strong argument is empirically implausible on its face and need not detain us for long. While national identity is certainly an important form of identity in the modern world, it does not preclude or displace other forms of identity and is not and probably never has been, except for brief moments, the predominant identity for any but a small minority. The weak argument appears more formidable, at least at first blush. But it too must be rejected. Radical nationalists may well be more numerous in modern times, but they can be found in the premodern era as well. And if we expand our purview to include historical nations—smaller nations that have been absorbed into larger ones and erased from memory, like the various nations of the British Isles, for example, Angles, Picts, Celts, or the nation of the Langue d'Oc—then this list could surely be expanded. One could also argue that the civic patriots of the Italian Renaissance were radical nationalists. While they were more apt to use the term *patria* than *nation*, they used it to connote many of the same things, such as birth, culture, community, and so on.

At the outset of this discussion I said that the various defenses of the modernist position reveal the degree to which scholars of nationalism qua phenomenon are still ensnared by the assumptions of nationalism qua ideology. What I meant by this, it should now be clear, is that modernist scholars of nationalism have long used and continue to use the aspirations of modern nationalists as criteria for what constitutes genuine nationalism. Thus the criteria of sociological scope are derived from the modern nationalist's hope for a nation that transcends social class and other social divisions; the criteria of party or movement from the belief that an organized avant-garde is needed in order to bring the nation back into being; the semiotic defense from the Jacobin vision of nationalism as the new religion of a secular age; and the identity defense from the hope that devotion to the nation becomes the supreme and universal loyalty. The root of the problem, in Bourdieusian terms, is a failure to make the necessary epistemological break from the subjective self-understanding of the social actors one is studying, a failure to draw a clear, sharp line between their categories of political practice and our categories of scientific analysis (Bourdieu, Chamboredon, and Passeron 1991).

It is this failure to break fully with nationalist ideology, I believe, that has enabled the modernist error to persist for so long. Because the aspirations of modern nationalists have never been fully realized—and (fortunately) probably never can be—they provide a litmus test that all instances of nationalism are doomed to fail from the start. This is why it has proven so easy for orthodox modernists to disqualify various episodes of premodern nationalism and why it proves equally easy for antimodernist critics to turn the tables on the modernists, by using their own criteria to disqualify key episodes of modern nationalism. However, because these aspirations are so utopian, it makes for a litmus test that few if any would-be nationalisms can pass, including the paradigms of modern nationalism. Nonetheless, because the aspirations of modern nationalists so deeply inform folk understandings of what a real nation is, and because these folk understandings have insinuated themselves into scientific discourse, the modernists' criteria appear intuitively plausible and even commonsensical to us, at least until we make them explicit and subject them to critique.

Once we begin this process of reflecting on and breaking with the folk theory of nationalism, we begin to see how its underlying assumptions have stunted investigations of nationalism. For example, while it is important to ascertain the sociological scope of nationalist mobilization, it is equally important to analyze the class bases of such mobilization. Rather than asking whether the scope of mobilization is sufficient to warrant the title of genuine nationalism, we should ask how we can measure the level and distribution of mobilization. Similarly, while we should attend to the degree and the form of nationalist mobilization, we should be equally attentive to the degree and form of nationalist symbolization. Rather than asking whether a truly nationalist movement or party exists and thereby assuming that nationalist mobilization necessarily takes this organizational form we should be open to the possibility that such mobilizations will occur through other types of sociopolitical organization (e.g., court cabals, fraternal brotherhoods, literary associations, etc.) (Conze, Engelhardt et al. 1992). Just as important, we should look at how nationalistic symbols and rituals are inserted into associative and intellectual life more generally, not only in print culture but in the built environment and material culture generally (Mukerji 1997; Koshar 2000). It is also important to recognize that the definition of the nation is itself an object of struggle, and that this struggle can be entwined with or refracted through sociopolitical struggles of many kinds, including those between clans, between dynasties, between crowns and estates, between aristocrats and gentrymen, between Catholics and Protestants, and so forth. Third, rather than searching in vain for some pure nationalism shorn of religion, monarchy and any other remnants of tradition, we would do better to catalogue the various discourses of which the national is composed and with which it has been mixed, the different alloys that have resulted, and the properties specific to each. We might ask how dynastic nationalist discourse differs from democratic nationalist discourse, how Protestant nationalism differs from Islamic nationalism, and so on. Fourth and finally, rather than embarking on a historical pilgrimage in search of the radical nationalist, that political antisaint, the one for whom the nation supersedes all, we would do better to look at how national identity becomes linked or opposed to other identities and with what effects. What happens, for example, when national identity is linked, as it often has been, with masculine identity, and how does the result differ when masculinity is defined in terms of blood nobility, in terms of blood on the battlefield, or in terms of civic virtue or economic success?

This is a wide-ranging and complex menu of questions. To hold them together, we need a systematic, coherent analytical framework. Bourdieu's sociology provides the methodological procedures and conceptual raw materials out of which such a framework can be constructed.

Analytical Preliminaries: Object, Method, Concepts
CONSTRUCTING THE OBJECT

The first step in sociological analysis, Bourdieu teaches, is "the construction of the object," meaning the object of analysis. Social scientists often begin their analyses with preconstructed objects, objects that have been constructed outside of the scientific field by social activists, policymakers, and lay intellectuals. But because these objects are inevitably freighted with and limited by the perspective of their producers, he warns, they can lead to distorted, one-sided analyses. The literature on nationalism is a textbook example of such dangers. This does not mean we need to replace nationalism with another term; it simply means that we need to use the term cautiously—which means reflectively.

We must construct nationalism properly, and the first step in this process is to deconstruct it, that is, to reflect on how it has been put together by previous analysts. Surveying the literature, one uncovers at least two recurring strategies. One, employed by many analysts, is to adduce a paradigmatic or originary case or text, such as revolutionary France or Emmanuel-Joseph Sieyès's "What Is the Third Estate?" or romantic-era Germany and Fichte's "Address to the German Nation." A second procedure, which builds upon the first, is to search for a common denominator across a number of cases and texts—France and Germany, say, or Sieyès and Herder—which then serves as the basis for a unitary definition.

At first glance these procedures may appear unobjectionable, but they turn out on closer inspection to rest on two highly problematic assumptions. The first is that nationalism, like an organism, is born in a particular time and place and that subsequent nationalisms are of the same species. The second is that the term *nation* has some core meaning or essence which can be discovered by means of induction since it is common to all its usages. It is not clear that we should accept either of these assumptions. Given the long history of nationalism and the many forms it has taken, why should we think of it as a single organism or even as a single species? If we are searching for an analogy, wouldn't it be more accurate to imagine it as a virus that is usually dormant but breaks out under certain conditions and evolves and mutates over time? If so, we should worry less about its putative origins and more about its epidemiology and evolution, that is, about the various strains of nationalism, the underlying mutations that generated them, the conditions under which they become virulent. Similarly, given the many uses to which the term *nation* has been put and the various contexts in which it has been deployed, why should we assume there is a common denominator among these uses? And even if such a common denominator did exist, which I frankly doubt, why should we assume that the common is the essential? Perhaps we should be less concerned with commonalities than with traits and distinguishing marks, with the things that set nationalisms apart from one another.

If the above procedures are not valid, then how should we go about constructing nationalism as an object of scientific analysis? I would propose that we focus on the form rather than the content, on the signifier rather than the signified. Specifically, I propose that we define nationalism as "any political practice or discourse that invokes the nation or an equivalent category."[1] The reasoning behind this approach is simple: because *nation* has had so many meanings, the only way to achieve a reasonably stable scientific definition is to base it on the national category itself. This is not to deny there are certain principles, tropes, symbols, and strategies that are regularly associated with nationalist discourse and practice; rather, it is to insist that these elements of nationalism are to be found in so many diverse permutations and combinations that a substantive definition of nationalism must always fail.

The advantage of the approach is clear: it does not exclude, as other definitions do, premodern nationalism, religious nationalism, and nondemocratic nationalism. The challenge it presents is also clear: it enormously expands the boundaries of the phenomenon. The history of nationalism no longer starts in the eighteenth century: it reaches back beyond the Common Era. Neither can we assume it is confined to the West.

APPROACHING NATIONALISM: BEYOND OBJECTIVIST AND SUBJECTIVIST ACCOUNTS

Having addressed the problem of object construction, at least in a preliminary fashion, we can turn to the problem of analysis proper. Here we face a somewhat different challenge: overcoming the opposition between objectivist and subjectivist approaches and the often sterile debates to which it gives rise.[2] The literature on nationalism has not been immune to such debates. Sometimes they have pitted open defenders of objectivism against open defenders of subjectivism, as in interchanges between social scientists, who argue that certain structural developments (e.g., state formation, print capitalism, market integration) form the objective basis for national identity and nationalist mobilization, and cultural historians, who protest that generalizing structural accounts of this sort fail to capture the subjective experience of a particular national identity, for example, what it means or feels like, say, to be English in the eighteenth century. For the most part, though, these two groups of scholars do not speak directly to one another. More common, in my experience, are debates among social scientists and social historians in which both parties vie for the title of objectivity by defining it in a way congenial to their perspective and implying that their opponents are subjectivistic. Rational choice theorists often claim their perspective is objective in the sense that it focuses on objective interests like individual utility and external objects, while they accuse their more sociological opponents of focusing on ineffable, subjective factors like internalized norms and lived experience. A neo-Durkheimian, conversely, might claim to be objective in the sense of focusing on objective, that is, suprapersonal, structures like norms and institutions, while denigrating her opponents as subjectivist in the sense of methodologically individualist. Historians are then left to defend subjectivist approaches that seek to recapture the meaning or experience, not of nationalism in general, but of particular nationalisms.

All four of these stances have some merit. The probability that a set of individuals will come to think of themselves as a group is at least partly a function of the number of interactions and interconnections between them. But this is hardly a sufficient condition for the emergence of a national identity and tells us nothing about the specific content of that identity. Similarly, the success or failure of a particular national project will have an impact on the distribution of power and profits that will benefit some individuals more than others. However, a national identity cannot be invented out of thin air but must draw on symbols and stories that resonate with members of the nation-to-be. So the question is not whether to adopt an objectivist or subjectivist approach but how to theorize the duality.

Social theorists have tried to address this problem in a variety of ways, none of which is entirely satisfactory. The oldest approach is essentialism, which involves mapping the objective and the subjective onto particular spheres of social practice and privileging one of them in the analyses. Most Marxists reserve the term *objective* for the sphere of material production and deride the sphere of cultural production as being subjective. The problem with essentialism is that it must draw a sharp boundary between the objective and subjective realms of society, for example, by denying the material aspects of culture or the objective limits on subjectivity. A second approach might be called partialism. This involves combining one aspect of subjectivism with one aspect of objectivism in an incomplete synthesis. Rational choice theory is an excellent example of partialism. It weds an objectivist theory of motivation to a subjectivist ontology of the social. On the one hand, it emphasizes utility and strategy while downplaying nonmaterial goals and nonstrategic action. On the other hand, it makes biological individuals the sole unit of analysis, denying the existence of any subindividual (e.g., psychodynamic) or supraindividual (e.g., social) reality. Another approach, more popular outside of economics and especially in contemporary sociology, is additive. This involves melding together an objectivist tradition with a subjectivist one—or, more accurately, the objectivist moment of an objectivizing tradition with the subjectivist moment of a subjectivizing one. Additive approaches are typically premised on the assumption that there is both an objective and a subjective dimension to social life, so that one needs two theories to analyze it. Thus historical sociologists often combine Marx and Weber. None of these approaches is entirely satisfying.

We have good reasons to prefer a nonessentializing, encompassing, systematic approach, and Bourdieu's sociology provides a model for such. It deploys two, related strategies. The first, which I have already touched upon, is to develop concepts that emphasize the objectivity of the subjective, and vice versa. The most important example of this strategy is the concept of the habitus, understood as the subjective dispositions that result from objective position. Conversely, we might consider how biological individuals can function as cultural signs: heroes, martyrs, and so forth. The second strategy is to treat objectivism and subjectivism not as regions or dimensions of social reality but as moments of social practice and scientific analysis. Procedurally, this means employing objectifying and subjectifying approaches serially and symmetrically rather than simultaneously or asymmetrically or both.[3] The question is how one could apply these two strategies to the study of nationalism.

CONCEPTUAL PRELIMINARIES: BOURDIEU'S THEORY OF CLASS

As I signaled early on, I think the answer to this question is to be found in Bourdieu's theory of classification struggles, struggles over the making and unmaking of classes. How does Bourdieu understand class? For Marx, class was defined objectively, in terms of one's relationship to the means of production. From Bourdieu's perspective, Marx's approach is too one-sided; it is objectivistic (Bourdieu 1991e). Accordingly, one of the main goals of Bourdieu's early work, and the central task of *Distinction*, his magnum opus, was to develop a subjectivizing approach to class that would emphasize the importance of the symbolic dimension of class formation, what Marx somewhat derisively referred to as ideology or consciousness. To this end he developed a number of concepts that allow us to grasp both moments of class, while emphasizing their interrelationship. These concepts are a fruitful starting point for thinking about nations and nationalism.

The first concept is "dis/position." The backslash marks an affinity and, more precisely, a relationship of circular causality: in Bourdieu's view, social position influences individual disposition, and vice versa, ad infinitum, if not in a wholly determinate or ineluctable fashion. By social position Bourdieu means position in a social space defined by the type and volume of capital. For example, position in the space of classes is largely determined by one's absolute and relative endowments with cultural and economic capital, roughly speaking, education and money. By individual disposition Bourdieu means individual tastes and distastes in the arena of consumption, construed broadly to include not only the consumption of market goods but of artworks, marriage partners, leisure activities, and so on—in a word, lifestyle. The key point here, for our purposes, is that the two spaces are homologous and interlinked: the space of lifestyles is divided up in much the same way as the space of classes—so that the one can be easily mapped onto the other—and the structure and dynamics of the two spaces are interlinked.

The second concept we need to borrow from Bourdieusian class analysis is "principles of di/vision" (Bourdieu 1990a). Here the backslash serves two functions: first, it marks the connection between the mental maps, or visions, that exist in people's minds and the us/them boundaries (di-visions) that are re/produced in and through interaction; second, it emphasizes that these principles are ultimately premised on binary oppositions (high/low, coarse/fine, male/female, and so forth) (visions), which create opposed perceptions of social reality (di-vision) (Bourdieu 1990a). Several points bear emphasis here. The first is that maps of social reality exist not only on paper and in theory (i.e., in the academic field) but also in minds and bodies and in nonscientific practice (i.e., outside the academic field) (Bourdieu 1990a, 2000b). The second is that although these maps are subjective, in the sense of being particular to and embodied in specific, biological individuals, their effects are objective, in the sense that they influence people's interactions and choices (e.g., whom they socialize with and what they buy) and thereby create patterns or structures. In this way the principles of individual vision help create boundaries of social division. The third is that because these principles of di/vision are always binaries whose meaning exists in and through their opposition to a second category, their application necessarily divides a complex and even continuous space into simplified and discontinuous spaces (Bourdieu 1996a). The fourth and last point is that the principles, once put into practice, tend to create a more binary reality: they impel men to be men and not women, artists to be artists and not bourgeois, blue-collar workers to be blue-collar workers and not bosses, and so on.

As noted earlier, Bourdieu's concept of class is elastic enough to take in most other types of social groups (more precisely, other principles of social division), including those normally designated by other names, for example, race, ethnicity, gender, confession, region—and nation (Bourdieu 1991e, 2001b; Wacquant 2003). However, Bourdieu's concept of class in this broader sense was initially developed for the study of class in the narrower sense of socioeconomic class and will require some adjustments before it can be applied to the study of nations.

Conceptual Foundations: From Classification Struggles to Nation-ization Struggles

Bourdieu's theory of classification struggle has three major inspirations: Marx's theory of class struggle, Durkheim's and Mauss's theory of primitive classifications, and Weber's theory of social stratification (Durkheim and Mauss 1963; Marx, Engels 1978; Weber 1978). Like Marx, Bourdieu sees classes rather than individuals as the key unit of social analysis, and class struggle as the driving force in historical development. Unlike Marx, however, he does not see material production as the only source of class divisions, nor does he see these divisions as objectively given; he gives equal weight to cultural production, at least in principle, and he sees the relative weight of these two sets of divisions as itself a source and an object of contention (Bourdieu 1996a). Like Durkheim and Mauss, Bourdieu believes that social divisions are founded on classificatory schemas and that these schemas permeate social interaction and are reinforced through ritual life (Bourdieu 1990a, 1991e). Unlike Durkheim and Mauss, however, he does not believe that each society has a single system of classification that is shared by all members of the society. Which schemata become the dominant ones determines which groups become the dominant ones, and vice versa. Like Weber, then, Bourdieu sees the actual system of class divisions within a given society as a contingent product of a social struggle which is both material and symbolic in nature.

How do we go about analyzing such struggles? Bourdieu does not afford us an explicit, codified method (he was opposed to "method" in this sense). But we can glean a sort of three-step procedure from his work (Bourdieu 1991a, 1996a). He begins by analyzing "social space," the objective space of classes, defined by the distribution of various material and nonmaterial resources or capitals (e.g., economic and cultural). Then he analyzes "the space of possibles," the symbolic space of classes, defined by various principles of di/vision and schemas of classification and the social structures that would result from the imposition of these principles. Finally, he narrates the unfolding game of position takings, the actual process of struggle in which sociocultural entrepreneurs seek to establish the saliency of particular schemas and thereby establish the dominance of certain groups. The first two steps focus on statics, the third on dynamics.

I would propose a similar three-step procedure for the analysis of nationization struggles. I begin by analyzing the (objective) space of nations; I then turn to the (symbolic) space of nation-izations; having done that, I will be in a position to narrate the dynamic process of nation-ization struggles. To define these terms more carefully, beginning with the space of nations: Much as Bourdieu conceives the space of classes as a two-dimensional space structured by the type of capital, economic or cultural, and the quantity of capital, more or less, I suggest we conceive the space of nations, at least initially, as having two major dimensions: territorial proximity and social interaction. By territorial proximity I mean the physical and temporal distance between individuals and populations. While physical distance is invariant, a natural fact, social distance is a historical variable, influenced by the available means of transport and communication. The underlying conjecture here is quite simple: sets of individuals that are close together in space or time or both are more likely to form nations than ones that are far apart. Yet territorial proximity can be a source of contention as well as of solidarity. The space of nations must therefore include a second dimension as well: social interaction. Of special importance here are the degree of economic cooperation and competition and the degree of cultural similarity and dissimilarity. The idea here is also very simple: economic cooperation and cultural similarity increase the likelihood of nation-ization; economic competition and cultural dissimilarity decrease it.

Now, an objectifying analysis of the space of nations gives us some sense of which nations will be more subjectively plausible at any given moment, which are most likely or unlikely to resonate and with whom, and therefore of which nations are the most objectively probable or improbable. But nations are also symbolic constructs—"imagined communities" in Benedict Anderson's oft-repeated phrase (1991). So to understand which are made or unmade and how, we also need to look at what I call the space of nation-izations. We may think of this space as having two dimensions as well: one discursive or linguistic, the other ritual and practical. This is the space in which real and possible nations are or can be imagined and enacted. It provides the store of symbolic resources through which nations are made and unmade. The discursive dimension consists of categories and narratives. By categories I mean the names of possible and real nations, which vary in their degree of possibility and reality across both space and time. By narratives I mean generic tropes about nations in general, for example, about the role of virtue and vice in the rise and fall of nations, as well as historic myths that are linked to a particular category, for example, the story of Romulus and Remus. On the ritual dimension one might distinguish between totemic rituals centered around a sacred object or personage such as a flag or a founder and historic rituals like Guy Fawkes Day or Fourth of July parades that reenact or commemorate crucial moments in a nation's mythohistory (Warner 1959).

The space of nations and the space of nation-izations form two moments in a static analysis; they lay the groundwork for a dynamic analysis of nation-ization struggles proper. In a nation-ization struggle, social and cultural actors propose and oppose various conflicting visions of the nation and of the sense of being a group more generally. They struggle both over how the nation should be defined and about its relative salience as a principle of group identity and action. This struggle is simultaneously symbolic and practical, and inextricably so. Every move is therefore a signal in both a symbolic and a practical sense. It is a symbolic signal in the sense that it must be encoded by the sender and decoded by the receiver; and it is a practical signal in the sense that it appeals to potential allies and alerts potential enemies (Hall 1980). The meaning of any given signal is a function of the receiver's location in social space and, more specifically, of the relative position of the senders and receivers. What appears as a signal of patriotism and solidarity to one actor will inevitably appear as a signal of treachery and divisiveness to another. Such signals vary not only in their meaning but also in their strength. Strength is a function of the sender's and receiver's relative positions in social and physical space. The signaling process is governed by a logic that is symbolic as well as strategic. The signal a political actor chooses is constrained not only by calculations of its effects but by the logic of its encoding. Indeed, to be strategically effective, a signal must be symbolically effective. This means that the dynamics of nation-ization struggle are unpredictable but not unreasonable. They are unpredictable because they involve a complex, open-ended series of interactions among numerous individuals, a game with no "dominant strategy" or "unique equilibrium." But they are not unreasonable because they deploy symbolic constructs which have a logic that can always be retrospectively reconstructed to some degree (Bourdieu 1990a).

Accounting for Change: Metaphors, Mechanisms, and Methods

To turn from structure to history, how can we use this framework to describe and account for change?

The most common metaphors in the study of nationalism have been origins, growth, and spread. I think we should stop using these metaphors or at least use them more carefully because they so quickly seduce us into sloppy thinking. The moment we begin to think of nationalism as a single organism that is born, matures, and reproduces, we fall into error. We then assume, whether implicitly or explicitly, that the origins of nationalism can be definitively localized in a unique time and place, that nationalism perdures through space and time, and that it has some essence that stands above space and time. These are all very problematic assumptions.

If it is metaphors we want, we might do better to think in terms of genes, mutations, contagiousness, and epidemics. I prefer the virological and epidemiological frame because it captures certain features of nationalism that I regard as very important. For example, genes suggests the existence of hidden codes within any given nationalism, while mutation emphasizes the instability of the code and the possibility that small and contingent changes in it may sometimes lead to large, enduring changes in morphology. Contagiousness suggests that nationalism is spread through social networks and that some individuals or groups may be more susceptible to it than others. Epidemics, finally, underlines the possibility of mass infection, but also of long periods of dormancy. And the spread of a virus to a new population can spark mutations in the virus.

I'll put this in less metaphorical and more sociological terms. For genes, read symbols and rituals. They act like a code, both in the linguistic sense of phonemes that convey information and in the cybernetic sense of a computer code that steers calculation and action. For mutations, read unintentional errors and intentional alterations in the transmission and enactment of national symbols and rituals. Whether such mutations are reproduced will hinge on a process of social selection, that is, on their functionality, on whether they elicit a response. Contagiousness might be translated as the affinity between a social class and a national classification, between a particular social location and a particular understanding of the nation. Affinity must be understood in probabilistic terms, that is, as the likelihood that an individual from a particular class will be attracted to a particular classification. An epidemic, finally, refers to a full-blown nation-ization struggle, a period in which nationalist practice and discourse infect many segments of a population and in which the salience and meaning of the nation become objects of massive, intensive struggle.

This conceptual schema suggests two main types of change: first, mutations of the genetic code, that is, transformations of symbols and rituals; second, the outbreak of an epidemic or, to put it less dramatically, a change in the scope or intensity of nationalist discourse and practice.

To shift from the description of change to the explanation of change, how might we explain mutations? Sometimes mutations are caused by developments which originate outside of the political field as such. Consider how the development of evolutionary biology led to a mutation of nationalist discourse in the late nineteenth century. National community, hitherto conceived in cultural and religious terms, could now be conceived in bioracial terms as well (Hull 1982; Weinberger 1988; Petzold 1989; Walton 1994; MacMaster 2000; Forsgård 2002). A second example: consider the role which the rediscovery of classical literature, especially ethnographic and historical writings, played in the development of civic patriotism in Italy and later of nationalist thinking throughout Europe (Martines 1979; Viroli 1997; Nauert 2006).

Developments in scholarly discourse do not automatically or inevitably result in mutations in political discourse. They must be transmitted from one discursive space to the other, a process often sparked by developments in social space, such as the emergence of new classes and their entry into politics. The development of civic patriotism went hand in hand with the foundation of universities in Italy, the resultant growth of a new class of legal and classical scholars, the entry of the new men into civic life, and so on. New kinds of nationalism are often the work of new groups of intellectuals. A similar pattern can be observed in late nineteenth-century Germany, where politically ambitious members of the dominated fraction of the intellectual strata, including schoolteachers, village pastors, lower-level civil servants, and so on, play a crucial role in the racialization of nationalist discourse (Puhle 1967; Harris 1976; Frankel 2003). And not only in Germany (Newman 1987).

Technological innovations sometimes play a catalytic role in the development of new types of ritual practice and thereby in the strengthening of national identifications (Mosse 1975). The development of public address systems and the related construction of amphitheaters are exemplary.

If some mutations are caused by developments outside the political field, others are triggered by struggles within the political field. One mechanism is what I term "recombinance": the juxtaposition or intertwining of two semantically distinct and hitherto separate symbolic or ritual frameworks. I call this recombinance because it involves grafting one code onto another. One form of recombinance I have encountered again and again in my work on nationalism in early modern Europe involves the intertwining of biblical and classical symbols and stories of nationhood (Gorski 2000). One salient example is the combination of biblical ideas of national chosenness with classical ideas of republican virtue in the claim that political liberty is a gift bestowed by God upon certain peoples (Tuveson 1968). This old idea has contemporary currency. Another mechanism is reencoding, or putting new symbolic substance into an old ritual form. The French Revolution contains a wealth of examples. Many of the new revolutionary rituals were closely modeled on the old Christian rituals they were supposed to replace (Ozouf 1988; Desan 1990; Bell 2001). The widespread use of the phrase "altars to the nation" is one clear instance of this.

So much for mutations. What about epidemics? How and why do they occur? Following is an inventory of causal mechanisms that can increase the intensity and scope of nation-ization struggles.

1. Changes in control over territory and populations, as in cases of conquest or colonization or both. The expansion of a polity's territorial boundaries often leads to a redefinition of the symbolic boundaries that define membership, boundaries that may be drawn in national terms, though also, for example, in racial, imperial, confessional, or dynastic terms. Here one thinks not only of the process of extra-European colonization from the sixteenth century on, which brought "white" sailors, soldiers, settlers, and administrators into contact with "native" populations, but also of the process of internal colonization within Europe that followed the collapse of Roman control, which led to the erasure of many historic nations and their symbolic integration into the so-called historic nations of contemporary Europe (Geary 1988, 2002).

2. Changes in the means of communications and transport. Two well-known and well-studied examples from European history are the reinvention of the printing press (actually invented in China) and the introduction of national railway systems (Weber 1976). The importance of the printing press in the emergence of a public sphere and the impact which ideals and practices of publicity eventually had on discourse about the nation, for example, in the English Civil Wars and the French Revolution, are well known (Habermas 1989; Zaret 2000). So, too, is the impact rail travel had on the development of popular tourism, on geographical mobility more generally, and thereby on the salience of national as opposed to local identity (Confino 1997).

3. Changes in the scale or structure of cultural or commercial networks. The role of German universities in the development of literary societies and fraternal orders is well known, as is the role of these organizations in the development and definition of a pan-German national identity. So, too, is the impact of the *Zollverein*, or customs union, which eliminated most barriers to trade between the various German principalities. Both of these developments increased the salience and probability of a German nation and were therefore opposed by those who conceived the nation differently. They did not simply increase German nation-ness; they sparked nation-ization struggles.

4. Large-scale movements of population owing to immigration and emigration. This trigger has been especially important in the history of the United States. The immigration of non-Christian Chinese to the West Coast and of south European Catholics and east European Jews to the Northeast had an enormous impact on the dominant conception of the United States as an Anglo-Protestant or at least north European nation and on the resulting conflicts over immigration, citizenship, integration, and so on (Higham 1955; Takaki 1989).

5. Transformations of capital, its distribution, composition, and value. Bourdieu posited at least three major types of capital, symbolic, economic, and cultural, as well as various subtypes, such as political, financial, and educational. The historical emergence of new types and subtypes and changes in its overall distribution or in their relative values (the "exchange rate") disrupt the status quo and spark struggles, including nation-izations struggles. The emergence and growth of nonclerical cultural elites often goes hand in hand with more secular understandings of nationhood or with an embrace of cosmopolitanism, both of which can spark conflict with defenders of religious understandings of the nation and with advocates of nationalism more generally. Similarly, the emergence of a class of salaried administrators, who advocate a less personalized, militaristic understanding of the state, can spark conflict with patrimonial and warrior elites about the nature of political rule.

6. The construction and propagation of new national categories or narratives or the disappearance of old ones. The names of Europe's historical nations can generally be traced to nation-ization struggles, in which they served as weapons and rallying cries. Many of the generic narratives that recur in that continent's nation-ization struggles entered into it at specific points in time and even through specific works. The rediscovery of Virgil's *Aeneid*, for example, led to feverish searches for and outlandish claims about the Trojan origins of many putative peoples beginning in the late Middle Ages (Appelt 1994; Linder 1978; Metz 1987; Abélard 1995). Tacitus's *Germania* was a boneyard for political antiquarians in northern Europe (Schama 1987; Kloft 1990; Kidd 1999; Vick 2003; Branford Smith 2004). The folklorists and amateur anthropologists of the late nineteenth century opened another vein that was mined for mythohistorical origins myths and national morality tales (Gellner 1983).

7. The invention of new ritual forms and techniques, often facilitated by developments in social or material technology that increase the potential scope or intensity of ritual life. Here, one thinks of examples from nineteenth-century Europe, including the invention of stadiums and

public address systems as well as industrial and engineering advances that facilitated the construction of massive national monuments of various sorts, all of which enabled the creation of new forms of national ritual and new types of national focal points (Koshar 2000).

How original any of these predictions are is debatable. Some are quite banal, and most have probably been advanced by others. What the theory of nation-ization struggles may have to offer is systematicity and scope: all of these mechanisms or predictions follow pretty clearly from the theory; and they can be applied across a wide range of cases, Western and non-Western, modern and premodern.

Now, it is one thing to inventory some descriptive typologies and explanatory mechanisms and quite another to apply them to particular cases. So I would like to conclude with some ideas about methodological strategies for analyzing particular nation-ization struggles.

One strategy is to map material positions to symbolic dispositions and, more specifically, to map the spaces of class and nation onto the spaces of classifications and nation-izations. Initially, one might begin by looking for affinities between interest and ideology in a kind of vulgar Marxist fashion. Ultimately, however, the goal must be to move from a semantic and reductionist approach that traces ideas directly to interests to a semiotic and relational approach that examines the dynamic interplay between social and symbolic oppositions and boundaries.

This sets the stage for a second strategy, which is to identify key oppositions and alliances at both the social and symbolic levels. Here, too, one might begin with a crude structural analysis that looks for a simple correspondence between the material and the symbolic. One might look for a simple correspondence between particular groups and particular discourses and treat the symbolic relationship between these discourses in public debate as an indicator of the social relationship between the corresponding groups. Juxtaposition of discourses would indicate an alliance; opposition would indicate antagonism. But, ideally, one would want to go beyond a simple structural analysis of this sort. For example, one would want to look at the symbolic strategies through which different categories or stories are equated or woven together, but also at the symbolic strains which these strategies generate within each discourse and among their respective carriers. Conversely, one would want to look for shifts in these symbolic juxtapositions and oppositions as indicators of changing social and political alliances.

This would set the stage for a third strategy, which is to narrate the actual sequence of symbolic and material moves in a particular struggle and reconstruct the strategies that underlay them. I have in mind here something akin to the Sunday morning chess column, which lists each player's moves, one by one, and then analyzes their respective strategies. Only in this way can the roles of cultural creativity and political entrepreneurship be fully appreciated and brought into focus.

This, finally, sets the stage for a fourth strategy, which is to focus on the social trajectories and political maneuvers of particular nationalist actors and thinkers. The point of such an exercise is not to exaggerate the power and creativity of particular actors, much less to celebrate individual agency and subjectivity in general. On the contrary, the first step in such an analysis, as I conceive it, is a crude sociologism that deprives the actors of all individuality and agency by reducing their political dispositions to their social positions and their political strategies to their social interests. Only then, I think, can we discover the true role of individual agency and the actual mechanisms of cultural creativity, by identifying how an individual's behaviors and utterances deviated from our expectations. Agency and creativity, it seems to me, are rooted in acts of reflexivity, which allow one to transcend social position, and in the ambiguities of symbolic forms, which create a certain elasticity in symbolic space.

Having done all of this—and I realize it is a lot to do—one should be in a position to assess the overall impact of a particular nation-ization struggle. In making such an assessment, I don't think the terms *success* and *failure* are helpful, since they really make sense only from a specific political standpoint. In social struggles, one person's failure is another's success. Rather, I would be inclined to pose questions of the following sort: what kinds of emotional traces did the struggle leave in certain regions of the social and national space, and how does this influence the probabilities of future alliances and oppositions? What kinds of symbolic traces did the struggle leave on various discourses and rituals, and how does this influence the probabilities of future juxtapositions or syntheses? Were new national symbols or discourse invented in the course of the struggle? Did the political valence of old ones change? Are there certain symbols, events, or rituals whose political valence was so contested and unresolved that they are likely to remain flash points around which future struggles may be ignited?

Conclusion

I strongly doubt that any of the foregoing predictions are altogether original. One could almost certainly find all of them in previous works. The advantage of the Bourdieusian framework I have developed here is not the originality of its predictions so much as the systematicity of its predictions, the fact, that is, that these predictions follow in a fairly straightforward and logical way from the framework itself.

The systematicity of this approach to nation-ization struggles sets it apart not only from more historicist approaches that focus on specific cases, but also from the sort of theoretical eclecticism practiced by most sociologists and many political scientists. I do not mean to suggest that systematicity is the only criterion or even the primary criterion by which an approach should be judged. Other things being equal, however, it does offer a number of distinct advantages. For example, it facilitates the task of theory building by providing a flexible repertoire of concepts that can be gradually expanded and refined in the course of empirical research on distinct cases. Further, it allows one to identify developments that are likely to spark nation-ization struggles and to anticipate or perhaps even avoid them, at least to some degree.

Bourdieu's is not the only systematic theory in the social sciences; other theories, such as Marxism and rational choice, are also highly systematic, in that they are universal in aspiration and application. But I believe the Bourdieusian approach has some distinct advantages over both of them. The two greatest shortcomings of Marxism, when seen from a Bourdieusian perspective, are its objectivism and its determinism. By objectivism I mean Marxism's one-sided focus on economic capital, social position, and principles of division and its attendant blindness to cultural capital, social disposition, and principles of vision; and by determinism I mean the wishful insistence that history has a single script which is distributed in advance to the elect rather than competing scripts that generate multiple casting calls. Rational choice has, in some sense, the reverse shortcomings: it is too subjectivist and voluntarist. It is subjectivist in the sense that it reduces dispositions to preferences, making something systematic and comprehensible—the link between disposition and position—into something random and mysterious.

Notes

1. Even this definition may be too narrow. How are we to deal with discourses that invoke kindred terms such as *fatherland* and *patriotism*, terms that have been closely connected to the national category and sometimes even interchangeable with it? And what are we to do with precolonial discourses in non-Western countries which did not invoke the term *nation* in the strict sense but may have employed analogous terms? These are not questions that can be settled a priori by definitional fiat.

2. This is not to suggest that these debates are inevitably sterile. They can, in time, generate more satisfactory conceptualizations and explanations. But such progress is often accompanied by insoluble metatheoretical debates about the primacy of

material or ideal factors, or ontological ones about the reality of society or the individual which rest on superficial and misleading dichotomies.

3. The order in which one proceeds will depend upon the circumstances with which one is confronted. For example, if subjectivist interpretations are predominant, as they tend to be in work on literature and the arts, one might choose to begin with an objectivizing analysis. Conversely, if objectivist strategies are predominant, as they tend to be in work on social class and economic life, then one might begin with a subjectivizing analysis. One's strategy might also be dictated by the available evidence. If one is studying the genesis of the literary field in nineteenth-century France, and one had more information about novels than about novelists, then it might be more fruitful to begin with a subjectivist analysis of literary dispositions before moving to an objectivist analysis of positions in the literary field.

11 GISÈLE SAPIRO
translated by Susan Emanuel

STRUCTURAL HISTORY AND CRISIS ANALYSIS
The Literary Field in France during the Second World War

A narrow reading of the work of Pierre Bourdieu has led to its reduction to a theory of reproduction. Yet Bourdieu, from his first research into the passage of traditional societies to capitalism and to modernity right up to his work on such political crises as May 1968, was always interested in situations of transition and crisis. And his theory includes factors for explaining change (Boyer 2003). In *Homo Academicus* (1984b) he develops, with respect to May 1968, an analytic model of political crises that tries to overcome the alternative between structural history and the history of events. Structural history relates general factors contributing to the transformation of social space (demography, economy, education, etc.) to the evolution of the different fields that compose it. The relative autonomy of fields, which translates exterior constraints according to their own logic and own temporality, means that structural history deals with several independent causal series. The historic event is precisely the product of the interaction of these independent causal series, of the synchronization of different fields' temporality and the harmonization of their agenda ("phase harmonization" in the English translation of *Homo Academicus*) during the crisis. Thus in this event "are expressed both at one and the same time the potentialities objectively inherent in the structure of each of them, and the relatively irreducible developments which are born of their conjunction" (Bourdieu 1984b: 227, 1988: 174).

The research I undertook on the French literary field under the German occupation during the Second World War (Sapiro 1999) concerned a crisis situation very different from May 1968: the military defeat, the foreign occupation, the scuppering of the government of the Republic, and the advent of an authoritarian regime combined to engender a profound economic and political crisis that would last throughout the four years of occupation. The political crisis turned into a deep crisis in national identity and in the legitimacy of the government. Was the defeat fatal and irreversible, as Marshal Philippe H. Pétain interpreted it? Should France sign the armistice and lay down arms? Should it accept the German occupation? On June 18, 1940, Gen. Charles de Gaulle, in a radio address, contested this interpretation: the war was not over, the armistice was a political and military error, the fight must be continued. These two opposing interpretations would divide the nation for four years, opening up a space of competition, a quite unequal one, among political forces that each tried to rally the majority to its cause. The political field was divided between the Occupied Zone, where the occupation forces ruled, the Southern Zone, where the Vichy regime was installed, the representatives of Free France who had emigrated to London, and the organizations of the Resistance, who set themselves up in clandestinity, notably around the Communist Party, which had been banned since 1939.

One of the characteristics of this crisis was not only the synchronization of all fields—economic, legal, medical, university, journalistic, literary, and so forth—but also their subordination to the political field. Synchronization always involves, to varying degrees, a loss of autonomy in fields. Within occupied France the degree of politicization and heteronomy was extreme, featuring economic collaboration with Nazi Germany, politicization of the judicial space, the interdiction of Jews from exercising the liberal professions and being civil servants, corporatist attempts to reorganize the liberal professions (the creation of a state corporate body to control doctors, for example), the firing of Jewish teachers, strict ideological control of the press via an elaborate propaganda apparatus, control of publishing, and so on. Nevertheless, the degree of subordination to the political field varied among the different fields. For example, one might suppose that, owing to both its distance from current affairs and the greater degree of autonomy of the academic world, the content of university courses was less affected than that of newspaper articles. Within the intellectual field, the literary world was situated between these two extremes.

Moreover, the "phase harmonization" of the different fields around the political agenda occurred according to the specific logics of each. Depending on the degree of relative autonomy, political stakes were more or less transformed or mediated by the stakes specific to the field. Structural history intervenes at this point. The schemes of interpretation used to analyze the crisis, the principles of division, and the factors of choice must be apprehended in the light of the stakes specific to each field and its history.

In turn, crisis situations have a revelatory effect: by constraining individuals to make choices and to take positions, by radicalizing the divisions, they reveal the structure of the field. But crises also have their own logics (Bourdieu

1984b, 1988; Dobry 1992). The politicization of the stakes and the loss of autonomy lead to a modification in power relations that gives rise to conjunctural alliances. They also cause new agents to appear—sometimes formerly marginal ones who take on importance because of the politicization of the stakes—and even new institutions to arise. Consequently, they can lead to a restructuring of the field. Moreover, while in ordinary times individuals might adjust their conduct to each of the fields in which they circulate, the phase harmonization of fields in periods of crisis constrains them to unify their conduct. This phenomenon can either accentuate inner divisions or induce unexpected changes in the configuration of alliances.

In the first section I will show how the structural history of the literary field explains its divisions during the occupation. In the second, I will deal with the specific effects of the crisis in the literary field. I will conclude, in the third section, with the reconstruction of the literary field after the liberation.

The Structural History of the French Literary Field

After the defeat in 1940 the literary field was restructured around a public debate called at the time "the quarrel of the bad masters [*mauvais maîtres*]." Coming from Switzerland, it benefited from the synchronization of fields that facilitated the rapid generalization of the issues at stake despite the strong territorial division. This quarrel was characteristic of the politicization of literary issues: it bore upon the intellectual responsibility for the defeat. Writers allied to the Vichy government accused interwar literature of sharing responsibility for the defeat. How could literature be responsible for a military defeat? By advocating the gratuitousness of art, subjectivism, pessimism, and defeatism, it supposedly had a noxious effect on youth. Writers like André Gide had proved irresponsible, they had been "bad masters." This scheme of analysis resonated with the more general interpretation of the defeat as the expiation of the sins of the Republic (Muel-Dreyfus 1996). Among these sins must be included the freedom of expression. The role of intellectuals was now to put their pens at the service of the program of "national revolution" elaborated by the Vichy government. This interpretation of the facts was opposed by two types of responses. The first, strictly literary, consisted of denying the social effects of literature, which merely describes reality and in any case reaches only a tiny elite. The second was more political and offered other explanatory schemes for the defeat, such as the Treaty of Versailles, the bankruptcy of elites, and the mistakes of the high command (Bloch 1990). But most of the contesters agreed on the harmful role played by certain intellectuals like the Monarchist leader Charles Maurras, judged to be complicit in the defeat and the sabotaging of the Republic, and they considered that writers should mobilize and participate in the struggle for the reconquest of national independence.

Even in this quick sketch, we can see the dual process of the politicization of the literary issues at stake and the translation of the political ones into literary terms. The struggle over the imposition of the definition of the causes of the crisis is inseparably a struggle for the imposition of the legitimate definition of literature and of the role of writers in occupied France. The harmonization of the literary field with the political field leads to homologous divisions, but in modes that remain specific to each of them. A long-term perspective is required to explain these principles of division of the literary field and to understand the categories applied by writers to interpret the defeat. The structural history of the literary field implies three levels of analysis: (1) the evolution of the position of the intellectual field within the field of power as a function of general social transformations like modernization and the development of education and of political regimes; (2) the evolution of the position of the literary field within the intellectual field and its relations with other fields (academic, journalistic, artistic, etc.) as a result of the progress in the division of expert labor; and (3) the structural history of the literary field, meaning the transformations of power relations constitutive of the structure of the field at different moments in its history. These levels articulate different causal series and different temporalities.

The first series concerns the rise of intellectual power in France since the middle of the eighteenth century, in tight correlation with geographical centralization, progress in secularization, which led to the separation of church and state in 1905, and the development of written culture (Darnton 1971a, 1971b, 1983; Chartier 2000). At the heart of the process of autonomization of the intellectual field, the claim for freedom of the press and the abolition of censorship, very provisionally acquired under the Revolution, was achieved under the Restoration in 1819 but would not be truly satisfactory until the Third Republic, with the liberal law of 1881. In this interval French society underwent major upheavals that affected the intellectual field. First and foremost, the industrialization of the press and of publishing enlarged the supply for intellectual producers while introducing the logic of economic profits (Charle 2004a). It gave birth to what Charles Sainte-Beuve called "industrial literature," symbolized by serialized novels (Thiesse 1984), and it would contribute, as a reaction, to the emergence under the Second Empire of an autonomous literary field that dissociates the literary value from the market value of works (Bourdieu 1992). In the second place, the development of education, which led to the shift from the direct mode of reproduction to a mode of reproduction with an educational component (Bourdieu 1996b [1989]), had a dual effect on the whole of society: on the one hand, it marked the rise of cultural capital as a foundation of power, but, on the other, it led to a devaluation of academic diplomas and a crisis in reproduction that culminated in the Third Republic, inasmuch as it relied on new elites—notably those coming from religious minorities such as Protestants and Jews against the traditional elites linked to local power, the France of the "notabilities" (Charle 2006b [1987]). These two factors led to a widened recruitment to the intellectual field and an affirmation of its symbolic power. This affirmation assumed a politicized form during the Dreyfus affair, at a moment when the professional development of the career of politician (Weber 1959), fostered by the advent of liberal democratic government, effected a differentiation between the political field and the intellectual field. But this event, which crystallized the symbolic unification of the intellectual field, also revealed lines of fracture within it, which leads us to its internal transformations (Charle 1990a).

From Voltaire to Émile Zola, men of letters have been the best representatives of this symbolic power. The leaders of the Revolution made Voltaire and Jean-Jacques Rousseau their predecessors, while the spokesmen of the counterrevolution accused them of being responsible for the social troubles that provoked the fall of the French monarchy. From both perspectives, men of letters were endowed with great symbolic power. At the beginning of the nineteenth century a differentiation occurred within the intellectual field: science began to professionalize, philosophy was incorporated under Napoléon in the new university system, which gave the status of civil servants to professors, neutralizing them politically (Ribard 2000). The writers had to redefine their social role. With the liberalization and the secularization of French society, the sacred was transferred from religion to literature (Bénichou 1996). Having inherited the critical function of the eighteenth-century *philosophes*, the writer would appear as the prophet of the new age, a figure most fully embodied by Victor Hugo.

Nevertheless, differentiation among intellectual activities with the growing division of intellectual and expert labor (Abbott 1988) dispossessed men of letters of certain of their domains of competence: in addition to the career of politician, already mentioned, we must include the professional development of the occupation of journalist and the emergence of the figure of the specialized scientist (Sapiro 2003a). These three groups of experts became professionalized by opposing to the literary and humanist culture a model of rationality and objectivity grounded on theoretical knowledge or on investigation, a model borrowed from the scientific paradigm: the science of governing; the investigatory objectivity of a journalism of news and information as opposed to the literary and political journalism of views that had prevailed in France;

specialization and the introduction of a scientific paradigm in the moral sciences over against social philosophy or rhetoric in the universities of the Republic.

Supported by political power, the rise in the scientific paradigm that accompanied the process of industrialization gave rise to a reaction among the literati in various countries, who contested it with culture in England, *Bildung* in Germany, and general culture in France (Williams 1983; Lepenies 1988; Ringer 1992; Sapiro 2004b). In Germany and in England, as in France, writers had participated in the building of a national culture that was, moreover, defined against French cultural imperialism of the eighteenth century (Thiesse 1998). But they had not accumulated symbolic power comparable to that of their French equivalents (Charle 1996; Casanova 2004 [1999]), whose sentiment of dispossession was thus all the stronger. It contributed, negatively, to precipitate the process of autonomization of the literary field that was at the same time being played out against political, religious, and economic powers (on the relations between the literary field and the religious field in France at that time, see Serry 2000). These factors of division were articulated around a cleavage between traditional elites and republican elites and explain the lines of fracture of the intellectual field during the Dreyfus affair: roughly speaking, men of letters and the other representatives of the old notabilities (professors of law and medicine) were largely in the anti-Dreyfus camp, while most of the scientists and the artistic and literary avant-gardes opted in favor of the appeal of Capt. Alfred Dreyfus's conviction (Charle 1990a). The "sublime engagement" (Suleiman 1993) of Zola in favor of Captain Dreyfus masks these principles of division, but it is also revelatory of the cleavages that structure the literary field itself and that constitute the third level of structural history.

In the eighteenth century the world of letters was principally structured around the opposition between the dominants and dominated, that is to say, on one side, the literary aristocracy, hired by the government, accumulating payments, official functions, and academic chairs, and the literary bohemia, stigmatized by Voltaire as "the riff-raff of literature" (Darnton 1983: 95). The process of autonomization of the literary field, precipitated by the advent of the market, operated around a new antinomy that now opposed autonomy and heteronomy: against the pole of large-scale production ruled by the market law of profit (sales), a pole of small-scale production was formed that decreed that aesthetic judgment could not be reduced to extraliterary values, whether economic, political, or moral (Bourdieu 1992). These two principles of polarization of the literary field, dominant/dominated, according to the overall volume of the capital of renown, and autonomy/heteronomy, according to the kind (symbolic or temporal) of renown, are not aligned but would

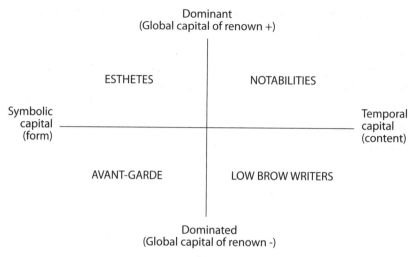

Dominant
(Global capital of renown +)

ESTHETES   NOTABILITIES

Symbolic   Temporal
capital ———————————————— capital
(form)   (content)

AVANT-GARDE   LOW BROW WRITERS

Dominated
(Global capital of renown -)

Figure 11.1. Structure of the literary field.

be articulated with each other to structure the field (Bourdieu 1991b; Sapiro 2003a).

At the temporally dominant pole, on the side of heteronomy, the writers we can ideal-typically call the notables, since they owe their consecration to high society (salons), the Académie Française, literary prizes, and sales, conceive of literature as an instrument of reproduction of elites and of the maintenance of social order; they subordinate aesthetic judgment to good taste and morality (figure 1). At the symbolically dominant pole, on the side of autonomy, the aesthetes, whose symbolic capital is founded upon recognition from their peers, promote the principle of art for art's sake, which asserts the autonomy of aesthetic judgment in relation to economic, political, and moral aspirations, as well as promoting the function of literature as artistic experimentation. At the dominated pole, one must distinguish between the subversive strategies of the avant-gardes, dominated temporally but oriented to the acquisition of symbolic capital by the resolution and overcoming of specifically literary problems (autonomy), and those writers who are dominated both temporally and symbolically, who bend to the expectations of the market and the press or to political demand (heteronomy): low brow writers, serial writers, journalistic writers, party writers.

These different poles struggle to impose their own conceptions of literature. For example, the notables reproach aesthetes like André Gide for their amoralism, the aestheticism that leads them to privilege form over content, and their conception of the gratuitousness of art. The notables confront them with the notion of a writer's responsibility, which ought to limit creative freedom in the name of morality. This position was theorized by the Catholic writer Paul Bourget in 1889, shortly after the adoption of the liberal law of 1881 vis-à-vis the press; it was reasserted by Catholic and nationalist writers after the First World War, a moment when the crisis favored, as it did in 1940, the imposition of nationalist morality within the literary field: they pit it against Gide and the *Nouvelle Revue Française* group who were at the time trying to reconquer the autonomy of the literary field. The notables also took it out on the Dadaist and surrealist avant-gardes, who from their point of view were the mischief makers fomenting the troubles that threatened the social order. And in fact, just as the symbolists had radicalized their subversive attitude by extending it into an anarchist political engagement, so the surrealists adopted an anticolonialist position during the war in Morocco in 1925 and made a rapprochement with the Communist Party.

Far from being masked, as in groups where esprit de corps prevails, these divisions were translated into struggles and permanent confrontations, especially in the crisis period. While professional development contributed at this time to the unification and homogenization of professional bodies by the closing down of social recruitment, the literary field experienced an inverse process and an increasing dispersion of its social recruitment. First, written culture, which constitutes the sole condition of access to its precincts, ceased to be a rare resource with widespread schooling. Second, while the emergence of a market and the enlargement of literacy increased the offer, the conditions of exercising the occupation, which remained very heterogeneous (ranging from *rentiers* to those who live from their writing and to those who have a second job), allowed writers to maintain investments in this space even without their gaining any positive sanctions. Third, the multiplication of the institutions of consecration in the nineteenth century and the absence of a monopolistic institution precluded any agreement on the legitimate definition of this activity and any uniting of the writing profession (Sapiro 2004c, 2007b; Sapiro and Gobille 2006). Linked to competition (Bourdieu 1971c), the paradigm of originality that, starting with romanticism, imposed itself justified the principle of evolution by revolutions, which differentiates the literary and artistic fields from other professional worlds. And so, weak professional development, the principle of permanent revolution, and the necessity of conferring universal bearing on what might appear to be simple parochial quarrels, all explain why the struggles therein often take a very politicized form. Therefore the politicization of the literary field predates the occupation: it goes back to the Dreyfus affair and was strengthened in the 1930s thanks to the international crisis, structuring the literary field around the opposition between antifascism and support for fascist regimes (Sapiro 2001). Radicalized by the circumstances of the occupation, these divisions would, in this world more than any part (except the political field), take the form of violent confrontations and boisterous splits.

The Literary Field in Crisis

The politicization of the literary field started in the 1930s, but it did not involve a loss of autonomy equivalent to what would take place under the occupation. This loss of autonomy relates principally to the material conditions of literary production, which was strictly controlled: a list of forbidden books, a self-censorship agreement adopted by the publishers' trade union, supervision of the press, repression. To this should be added the temporal gratifications granted to writers favorable to the occupier or to the Vichy regime: prizes, distinctions, promotions, translation into German, invitations to Germany, and so on. While in the 1930s the dissociation between literature and politics was still possible, under the occupation the very act of publishing became a political issue. Moreover, all the political forces on the scene had a stake in literature: at this time of crisis in national identity, politicians saw in the appropriation of the cultural patrimony a means for the charismatic legitimization of their enterprise, to use Max Weber's concept. The prestigious Goncourt prize awarded in 1941 to Henri Pourrat, eulogist of the return to the land, was thus a symbolic legitimation of the ideology of the National Revolution promoted by the traditionalists of the Vichy government. In his discourse of 1943 General de Gaulle cited the names of opposition writers: Gide, François Mauriac, Georges Bernanos. Lucien Rebatet answered him in the newspaper *Je Suis Partout* (issue of March 10, 1944), mentioning the most prestigious writers of the collaboration: Pierre Drieu La Rochelle, Henry de Montherlant, Louis-Ferdinand Céline. This game of citation illustrates the symbolic war being played out in parallel with the physical combat.

The literary field's synchronization with the political field, associated with the loss of autonomy, produced effects that are specific to crisis situations. In the first place, it opened the field to marginal agents, activists, and men of the party apparatus, all weakly endowed with specific capital but strong in a certain political capital. These people were given a chance, via politicization, to come to the fore: they are to be found at the most politicized poles of the literary field, in particular among the collaborationists (Lucien Combelle and Henri Poulain, for instance), but also in the intellectual Resistance, in particular, certain Communists. Roughly speaking, the degree of political engagement varies in inverse proportion to symbolic capital, with some notable exceptions such as Louis Aragon and Paul Eluard, who were both members of the Communist Party.

In the second place, quite typical of crisis situations, "the lifting of taboos" that are ordinarily imposed upon public debates "offers an opportunity to reveal social pretensions, or even impulses, often scantily veiled by an appearance of political generalization," as Bourdieu writes (1984b: 299, 1988:175). Under the occupation it opens the door not only to an overtly heteronomous discourse that reduces literary judgment to a judgment that is political, social, moral, and racial, but also to pamphleteering that is often muckraking in style, in which the trumps are insults, ad hominem attacks, and vulgarity. These impulses are expressed in the attempt to overturn the power relations constitutive of literary fields by recourse to extraliterary forces. An extreme example of this heteronomous logic is the attempt by Robert Brasillach and Lucien Rebatet to have the publication of Mauriac's *La Pharisienne* banned, though it was authorized by the Germans, and then the measures they took to boycott the book as well as the press campaign they mounted against the author. What seems at first sight to be an excess of zeal with respect to the occupier in fact relates to the settling of literary scores.

Recourse to such procedures, which are illicit from the standpoint of the rules of autonomy, in order to overturn internal power relations helps to explain the third effect that is typical of the "phase harmonization" of the literary and political fields, to wit, the restructuring of the former around principles homologous to those that organize the latter. The crisis touched individuals and institutions in ways which varied according to their social position: the most fragile—Jews, foreigners, Communists—were the most threatened and were reduced to silence or clandestinity, if not death, like Irène Némirovksy, who died in 1942 in Auschwitz. Literary institutions were more or less obliged to make guarantees to the temporal powers according to their age, legal status, prestige, and the symbolic stakes they represented: thus, while a very old institution like the Académie Française, an official body [*corps constitué*] of the French state, needed only to allow its principle of inertia to act in order to keep "being," the Académie Goncourt, an association of public utility created in 1904 that owed its symbolic power to the media repercussions of the annual prize it granted, had to adjust to the dominant ideology in order to continue to exist (as noted, in 1941 it awarded its prize to Pourrat, whose literature embodied the Vichy ideology of a return to the land).

Far from proving its solidarity in the face of the foreign occupation, the literary field was divided among political camps, with internal struggles taking a very radicalized form for the reasons mentioned above, weak professionalization, and extreme heterogeneity of social recruitment. These struggles extended throughout almost all the literary institutions: they were more muffled in the Académie Française, where an esprit de corps reigned, and they went so far as to take the form of rowdy splits in the Académie Goncourt.

How were the political and literary factors related? A statistical inquiry based on a population of 185 writers who were active in the 1940s identified relevant social and literary factors in order to explain the writers' political choices in this context of crisis. Part of this biographical data (58 out of 128 variables) was submitted to multiple correspondence analysis (MCA), a tool for geometric data analysis based on a contingency table. This tool has proved to be very powerful for exploring the social space (Benzécri 1992 [1980]; Rouannet and Leroux 1993), and it is especially well adapted to Bourdieu's relational and structural conception of the social space and of fields.[1]

The first axis of the MCA contrasted, roughly speaking, writers who supported the ruling forces, that is, the Vichy regime and the Germans, with resisting writers (figure 2; Sapiro 2002).[2] This opposition is superimposed upon principles of polarization that are specifically literary: age (old versus young), literary genre (novel versus poetry), and institutional membership (belonging to academies versus collaborating on small poetry magazines). While the majority of writers situated at the temporally dominant pole from the standpoint of age, institutional consecration, and literary genre rallied on the whole to the Vichy regime and to a lesser extent to collaboration (where we find the most writers both temporally and symbolically dominated), the writers who were temporally dominated—young poets publishing in small reviews—were the most numerous in the literary Resistance, thanks to their alliance with the dominated pole of the political field, the clandestine Communist Party. The process of autonomization of the literary field had placed the symbolic capital founded on peer recognition above the temporal forms of success (whether sales figures, success in high society, or institutional renown). Yet, a symptom of the crisis situation and of the loss of its autonomy, the harmonization of the literary field with the political field fostered the overthrow of this fundamental principle of the autonomy of the literary field, to the benefit of the heteronomous pole. Suddenly writers who had been symbolically dominant found themselves in a position of weakness and prey to diverse attempts at annexation, notably on the part of the Germans, who were trying to normalize the situation of occupation. In reaction to the conditions of heteronomy, they opted (not without hesitation, as in the case of Gide) to refuse to contribute to the authorized press, although they continued to publish books, and were sympathetic to the opposition to the regime, although such sympathy did not necessarily extend as far as underground engagement.

As we see, despite the loss of autonomy and the "phase harmonization" with the political field, the very logics according to which the literary field was

Figure 11.2. Structure of the French literary field in the 1940s.

restructured relates to the structural history of the literary field. As was the case with university faculties in May 1968 (Bourdieu, 1984), the political choices of writers are explained in large part by the positions they occupied in the literary field and its struggles prior to the defeat. The homology between political positions taken and positions occupied in the literary field is reinforced by the principle of unification of conduct specific to the harmonization process of fields going into phase with each other in times of crisis. "In obliging everyone to organize his political position with reference to the position held in a specific field and in that one alone, the crisis tends to substitute a *division* into clearly distinguished *camps* (according to the logic of a civil war) for progressive distribution between two poles, and for all the multiple, partly contradictory memberships which the separation of spaces and times allows to reconcile" (Bourdieu 1984b: 235, 1988: 181). Thereby, crisis also has the effect of revelator. The subordination of the economic field to the political field highlights the propensity of writers situated at the pole of large-scale production to sacrifice the rule of the autonomy of art to heteronomous logics—economic, political, media—and to ally with fractions who hold temporal power in order to defend or restore the social order. In contrast, it is when its autonomy is threatened that the pole of small-scale production reveals its subversive potential.

This opposition becomes more specific at several levels (especially within institutions) and is incarnated in the struggles in which different conceptions of literature and of the social role of the writer confront each other. These struggles, in which can be read the complex imbrication of ethical, aesthetic, and political dispositions, as well as the dynamics of collective assigning of positions (annexation, stigmatization, labeling, calls to order), refers back to the field's structural history, as illustrated by the quarrel of the bad masters evoked above.

As the children of the defeat by Germany in 1870, raised in fear of a revolution of which the Commune had given a foretaste, sons of ancient local notables who had been marginalized by the Republic, the literary notables were predisposed to interpret the defeat as the result of a modernity at once political (democracy, universal suffrage), economic (capitalism), scientific (industrialization, specialization, belief in the omnipotence of science), and artistic (gratuitousness of art, formalism, subjectivism, pessimism) and of modernity's consequences: de-Christianization, the disappearance of inter-mediary bodies, egoistic individualism, materialism, and so on, and hence they were predisposed to rally to the program of conservative revolution put into effect by the traditionalist pole of the Vichy regime (Paxton 2001). The crisis revealed the fact that their conservatism trumped national interest, of which they had made themselves the defenders since the Dreyfus affair, when nationalism moved to the right, and in the name of which they continued nevertheless to speak. But this discourse became less and less credible coming from the mouths of those who supported a regime that had just delivered two-thirds of France to Nazi occupation.

Slightly younger on average than the notables (they are around fifty years old), the collaborationist writers belong most often to the generation who participated in the First World War. They were not, like their elders, raised in the spirit of revenge with respect to Germany, and they maintain a more ambivalent relation to modernity. Situated in an intermediate position be-tween those who occupy the dominant positions and the rising generation, they found in the crisis an opportunity for an unexpected promotion; this was also the case for the youngest, like Brasillach and Rebatet, who profited from the fact that the Parisian scene was deserted.

By an apparent paradox, the literary Resistance grouped together, at least at the beginning, young poets and writers—they were between thirty and forty years old—who were turned more toward literary and political international-ism (pacifism, communism, Trotskyism, and so on) and in any case little inclined to nationalist sentiments. While opposition to Nazism and fascism had already united a number of them in the 1930s, their defense of universal principles such as liberty and humanism against barbarism made use of a reappropriation of the national patrimony, which they disputed with the opposite camp in the name of the "defense of the French spirit." By this means they rallied writers situated at the symbolically dominant pole.

While the crisis has a revealing effect, it also has, as we have seen, its own effects and a specific dynamic. Thus, from the standpoint of the recomposition of power relations, one of the effects of the crisis and the loss of autonomy it engendered is the tightening of the struggle that structures the field around the opposition between autonomy and heteronomy. While in ordinary times competition plays out largely between the avant-gardes and the aesthetes, the crisis favored an intergenerational alliance at the autonomous pole of the literary field. Heteronomous conditions of production, transgression of norms of literary debate by collaborationist intellectuals and their recourse to extra-literary forces in order to regulate the internal power relations contributed to knitting together writers of the opposition in a fight to reconquer literary autonomy, which merged with the ideological fight against the Nazi occupier and against the Vichy regime. The symbolic reunification of a literary field that had split apart into the two zones and exile operated primarily by means of a device for evading censure through coded language, which was called literary contraband: for example, speaking of the present by using the events of the national past as allegory. This device, which was decrypted by the initiated in the adversary camp, became too risky in 1942, however, when measures of control over printing hardened. At this time an underground literary activity commenced (Simonin 1994).

This underground activity would develop thanks to another type of im-probable alliance made possible by the crisis, namely, that between writers situated at the autonomous pole of the literary field but deprived of their habitual outlets and the clandestine Communist Party, which offered them the material means to become engaged with properly literary means. This alliance relates to another phenomenon that is typical of times of crisis: the central role played by political apparatuses in mobilizing an opposition (Bourdieu 1984b: 247–48, 1988: 191–92). Based on the literary affinities between Communists and non-Communists, this alliance was mediated by individuals who belonged to both groups: Jacques Decour, Aragon, and then Eluard, who joined the French Communist Party in 1942. Thanks to their prestige, they attracted young pretenders. Thus, clandestine recruitment in the southern zone relied on the literary networks Aragon had set up after the defeat around small literary magazines, where he had developed the device of poetic contraband.

From this alliance was born a new organization, the Comité National des Écrivains (CNE; National committee of writers). The appearance of this group is a specific effect of the crisis: it is the fruit of, on the one hand, the incapacity of traditional institutions like the Académie Française and the Académie Goncourt to defend the autonomy of the literary field in the face of enterprises of co-optation and the hijacking of symbolic capital; and, on the other, of the margin of maneuver open for individual initiatives within political organizations—here the Communist Party—in times of crisis. Its simultaneously literary and political character makes the CNE a typical organization of crisis periods. It also shows that in a conjuncture of crisis and loss of autonomy, the struggle to reconquer autonomy brings about new forms of dependence with respect to extraliterary forces—in this case, the clandestine Communist Party —and hence a new threat of heteronomy that the liberation would ultimately confirm.

Modes of Survival and Recomposition of the Literary Field at the Liberation

Emerging from a crisis situation implies neither an immediate return to normalcy nor the automatic reconquest of autonomy. Although the duration of the occupation was relatively short (four years), the crisis it engendered in the literary field persisted at least until 1953 and had long-lasting effects. This internal crisis reverberated according to its own logic, in a mediated manner, among the more general social effects of the political crisis, which intersected with long-term structural logics.

This is visible above all in the purge process. The purge, which touched all of French society, took place within the framework of the criminal law, with laws on treason, notably article 75 of the Penal Code, which punished with death the crime of "intelligence with the enemy," as well as within the framework of administrative and professional law (Novick 1968; Lottman 1986).

Symmetrically with the occupation, individuals and institutions were differently touched by the purge, too. The oldest institutions defended themselves best against outside pressure. The Académie Française, for example, from which four members were automatically expelled because they were convicted of "national indignity," did not replace two of them, Marshal Pétain and Charles Maurras, during their lifetimes, and it eulogized them after their deaths. It also resisted political pressure, from de Gaulle specifically, who wanted to get writers of the Resistance admitted. Inversely, the Académie Goncourt managed to survive by once again adjusting itself to the new dominant ideology: in 1945, while it did not manage to purge its most compromised members, like Sacha Guitry, it did award its prize for the first time to a woman in the same year women obtained the right to vote; the recipient, Elsa Triolet, was also a member of the Resistance close to the Communist Party and of Russian and Jewish origin, as well as the wife of Aragon, a Communist and the leading light in the CNE.

As for individuals, those who possessed the greatest amount of economic and symbolic capital were once again the best protected when faced with the purge. If intellectuals were more severely punished than economic collaborators, this was because they occupied a dominated position in the field of power

(Bourdieu 1979b), while at the same time being endowed with high symbolic power, which made them the most targeted objects of the exemplary punishments advocated by de Gaulle. But writers were affected differently as a function of their symbolic capital, the most severe punishments being reserved for those who enjoyed the least specific recognition. This relates also to each one's type of investment. While the writers most endowed with symbolic capital, like Montherlant, had limited their political engagement to the minimum necessary to take advantage of the conditions of promotion and had especially avoided implicating their literary works too directly, those who were promoted thanks to the circumstances, like Brasillach and Rebatet, were wholeheartedly engaged, which brought each of them a death sentence at the liberation, and Brasillach was indeed executed (Kaplan 2000; Sapiro 2006a). The maneuverability afforded by these strategies in ordinary times is reduced in times of crisis because of the harmonization of fields, which constrains individuals to unify their conduct and give it such coherence that readjustment in case of changing events becomes impossible: thus, after the German defeat at Stalingrad, the fascist writer Drieu La Rochelle thought for a time of joining the Communist Party, but this reconversion was impossible, and he committed suicide in March 1945, shortly after the execution of Brasillach.

While the purge is the direct expression of the overthrow of the political power relations in the literary field, writers did not remain outside this process. In fact, the resistant writers grouped in the CNE did not wait for legal measures to be set up to take charge of purging their own profession. Acting like a professional corporate body, although it did not possess such attributes, the CNE established a blacklist of writers compromised in the collaboration. Resistant writers refused to have any publishing contact with people on the list. This refusal amounted to a form of boycott at a time when publishers and newspapers were rushing to publish the authors of the Resistance so as to reestablish their respectability. The members of the CNE had even envisaged bringing a list of those most guilty to the Ministry of Justice, but they were prevented from doing so by Jean Paulhan, the former director of *La Nouvelle Revue Française*, in the name of the autonomy of the literary field and of solidarity among writers. The CNE nevertheless would become one of those bodies, along with the Société des Gens de Lettres (Literary society) and other professional organizations, entrusted with the power to bring complaints to the Comité d'Épuration des gens de lettres, auteurs et compositeurs (Committee for purging people of letters, authors, and composers), which was set up on the initiative of the Ministry of National Education in May 1945 to proceed with the purging of professionals (Lottman 1986: 6th part, IV–V; Sapiro 2003b). The Comité d'Épuration, which played a policing role in the profession equivalent to that of professional corporate bodies, had the power to pronounce sanctions ranging up to a two-year ban on publishing. Its activities led to violent controversies.

The assumption of a policing role in the profession is an indicator of the professionalization of the occupation of writer, and yet these controversies are revealing of the obstacles it encountered: the establishment of a code of ethics introduces criteria of morality that are incompatible with literary autonomy understood as pure aesthetic judgment.

In fact, the literary field was going to split around this question. While the lines of division follow to a large extent those of the political field, they cannot be reduced to them, and their principles are certainly not rooted in politics. In the debate over the purge the split between the indulgent and the intransigent generally coincided with the opposition between collaborators and Vichyists on one side and resisters on the other, and it was further differentiated within the resistant camp between right and left, Gaullists and Communists. But in the literary field, these divisions operated according to the logic and specific stakes derived from its history. As a result, the condemnation to death and execution of Brasillach at the beginning of 1945 raised a debate about the responsibility of the writer: while some people argued for limited responsibility, others considered it unlimited. The major split underlying these positions was generational. As Karl Mannheim explains (1990), crisis situations accelerate the crystallization of new generations, based on the implicit or explicit reference to this common event that they experience at a crucial moment in their personal development and which will structure their perception of reality. For writers of this new generation, best represented by Jean-Paul Sartre and Albert Camus, the experience of the occupation and of their engagement had been determining. It was as much the basis of their worldview as of their authority to speak in its name. They assimilated this experience into their intellectual vision of the world while valorizing it as a "moral capital" in order to impose themselves on the intellectual scene over and against their elders through one and the same notion: the notion of the responsibility of the writer.

It is this conception that Sartre theorized on the occasion of the first UNESCO conference (Sartre 1998) and that constituted the ground for his theory of committed literature. This debate assumes its full import if one relates it to the old belief in the responsibility of men of letters in the French Revolution and to the controversies over the responsibility of the writer raised by the laws on freedom of the press (Sapiro 2007b, Sapiro 2011). According to conservative writers, responsibility should impose limits on the freedom to create, research, and criticize, whereas Sartre saw responsibility as the end result of freedom; he conceived of the freedom of research and criticism as a duty of the intellectual (Sapiro 2006b). The crisis had made possible this overturning of the power relations between conservative writers and progressive writers. The redefinition of the concept of responsibility operated in favor of the reappropriation of nationalist morality by the Resistance. The propensity to valorize this moral capital at the liberation was all the greater when one was more deprived of specific capital—like the Communists or the newcomers who entered the field thanks to the crisis, such as Vercors and Pierre Seghers. However, the Communists who exercised hegemony in the intellectual field at the liberation gave a heteronomous meaning to the concept of responsibility in order to attempt to subordinate art to the political imperatives fixed by the party. Sartre, by contrast, held to an autonomous definition of the notion of the writer's responsibility, within the tradition of the critical intellectual, by constructing a genealogy that went from Voltaire to Zola to the writers of the Resistance. This largely explains his success at the liberation (Boschetti 1985).

As we see, although it was raised in a specific manner by the crisis situation, the question of professional ethics as debated in the literary world is not a simple reflection of the political stakes but derives from its own history. The same is true of other indicators of the professionalization of the writing occupation to which the liberation attested. These should be reinserted into the long-term process of professional development that had affected all occupations since the end of the nineteenth century (in particular since the law of 1884 authorizing trade unions and the law of 1901 on associations) and which culminated in the corporatist project of the Vichy regime: as witnessed by the numerous attempts to create professional corporate bodies, among which some succeeded (physicians, architects) and others failed (journalists, writers) (Sapiro 2004c). A pure product of the crisis, the project for a corporatist body of writers had nevertheless been reoriented to give new life to a prewar proposal to create—or rather recreate, since such a fund had existed between 1930 and 1935—a National Fund for Literature intended to aid literary creation. Set up in 1946, the new fund would not truly begin to function until a decade later, in parallel with the development of a new cultural policy (Surel 1997). In 1949 writers obtained an extension of the legislation on social security to include nonsalaried writers. They then claimed also that this fiscal status be assimilated to the salaried workforce rather than to the liberal professions. They would not be rewarded until twenty-five years later, upon emerging from another crisis, that of May 1968, which marked a supplementary stage in the professional development of the occupation of writer (Gobille 2003; Sapiro and Gobille 2006).

Conclusion

The crisis the literary field underwent during the occupation shows that even in a situation of extreme heteronomy, a margin of autonomy subsists, especially when it is a matter of a space that had previously achieved a high degree of autonomy. This signifies both that the reactions to the crisis and the logic of the restructuring of the field take place according to their own logics and temporalities, which derive from structural history, and that the forces of autonomy are able to resist the crisis, at least in the short and medium term. The crisis favored power taking by activists and a recourse to exterior forces to overthrow the power relations constitutive of the literary field. But while they managed to do so in appearance, the forces of autonomy and the logics of inertia were sufficiently powerful to prevent a complete upheaval, if not to reassert the principle of autonomy under oppression. The prolongation of the state of heteronomy—as in the East European countries under communism— may bring about the normalization of this situation (Karabel 1996). But even in such conditions, a form of (very) limited autonomy survives.

If structural history can illuminate the logics of functioning and the division of the field in times of crisis, crises in turn have the effect of revealing the structure of the field by the sole fact of radicalizing the oppositions and unifying people's behaviors. They also have effects of accelerating long-term processes like professional development and crystallization of new generations. In that, they are the vectors of change. They are such also by reason of their specific effects, which have more or less durable consequences: politicization, radicalization, restructuring of the field around the struggle between autonomy and heteronomy, which takes a politicized form, in improbable alliances that may generate new relations of dependence and new forms of heteronomy, investments with irreversible consequences.

This analysis of the functioning of fields in times of crisis can be extended to other professions. Similar patterns can be observed in the artistic field (Dorléac 1993), in the medical profession (Simonin 1997), and in the law profession (Israël 2005) in France during the occupation. As already stated, all fields experienced—in variable proportions—a loss of autonomy through the exclusion of members for nonprofessional reasons (for example, because of their identity or their political allegiance), through increased state control, and through the politicization of the inner issues at stake. Whereas these authoritarian measures were supported by the most heteronomous and conservative agents in these fields, those who defended autonomy adopted resisting practices, and some of them, namely, among those endowed with the highest symbolic capital, joined the intellectual Resistance organized by the

Communist Party in every domain. A systematic comparison of these fields would be required in order to understand the particularities of each of them according to its history, the specificity of its practice, and its relations with the political field.

The comparison could be extended to other authoritarian regimes, like the Nazi and the fascist ones (it has already proved fruitful for the Communist regimes; see Dragomir 2007). Bourdieu's analysis of the academic field in May 1968, Charle's analysis of the intellectuals' choices during the Dreyfus affair, and more recent studies on writers in May 1968 (Gobille 2003, 2005) as well as on the social movement of 1995 in France (Duval et al. 1998) suggest that this structural model based on field theory (namely, the oppositions between dominant/dominated and between autonomy/heteronomy) is relevant to understanding how political crises affect the intellectual professions beyond authoritarian contexts. Structural homology between fields, which makes the comparison possible, is also what fosters the synchronization process, one of the variables being time (duration of the crisis). Yet the patterns described here are specific to political crisis and result from the role of the political field. Research on the way economic crisis affects fields would probably reveal different mechanisms, but that still waits to be undertaken.

Notes

1. Multiple correspondence analysis (MCA) is a method of multivariable analysis: it relates all the categorical variables to each other, representing clusters of individuals who share the higher number of properties and, conversely, clusters of variables shared by the higher number of individuals.

2. There were 236 active modalities and 12 illustrative. Seventeen of the 185 writers were classified as illustrative, because they were too marginal as writers or because of lack of information. Two of the 58 variables were illustrative because of lack of information as well. The first three factors of MCA contributed, respectively, to 5.6 percent, 3.9 percent, and 3.2 percent of the overall inertia. The low percentage is due to the important number of variables and modalities.

THE TRANSMISSION OF MASCULINITIES
The Case of Early Modern France

In his book *Masculine Domination* (1998b), Pierre Bourdieu posed a challenge to those who wish to understand the history of masculinity and femininity. How, he asks, can we treat these apparently perennial phenomena as historical constructions without giving them at the same time "the allure of a natural essence"? To escape the trap of essentialism, he wrote, "we must not deny the permanences and invariants which, incontestably, make up a part of the historical reality; we must *reconstruct the historical work of dehistoricization* or, if one prefers, do the history of the continuous (re)creation of objective and subjective structures of masculine domination . . . , as *the history of the agents and institutions that permanently interact to assure these permanences*" (Bourdieu 1998b: 90; see also Collier and Yanagisako 1987: 14–50).

By "dehistoricization" Bourdieu means here the process by which gender difference is constantly produced and reproduced, feminizing and masculinizing women and men in ways that preserve difference as a transhistorical invariant. However, Bourdieu had nothing but disdain for the nominalistic "magic" of postmodern performativity and for linguistic theories that call action into being. The capacity of language to "make what it states . . . , does not lie, as some people think, in the language itself, but in the group that authorizes and recognizes it and, with it, authorizes and recognizes itself," the so-called officialization effect (Bourdieu 1990a: 109–10; Butler 1999: 113–28). In his view gender is performed according to scripts that are deeply embedded in "bodies and structures" that we feel to be and that are perceived by others to be natural. This socialization of the biological operates in a kind of circular causality with the naturalization of the social to implant particular qualities in bodies and to give gender difference a material and lived corporeality.

In the body of his work, Bourdieu showed how a sociocultural habitus reproduces cultural capital, emotional configurations, bodily dispositions, and esthetic tastes within discrete classes, and how elite institutions perpetuate a coherent culture in much the same manner (Bourdieu 1964, 1979b, 1989c). Bourdieu's initial demonstrations of the process of gender transmission were addressed in his early work in premodern or peasant societies among the Kabyle people of the Mahgreb and the modern peasantry of the Béarn, though, as has been pointed out, he did not initially make connections between them despite his early familiarity with Mediterranean area culture studies (Reed-Danahay 2005: 84–90). Though he was profoundly concerned with the multifarious ways in which males and females individually and collectively reproduced aspects of a gendered habitus in *Outline of a Theory of Practice* (1977) and *The Logic of Practice* (1990a [1980]), he did not use the word *gender* but rather "sexual identity" or "sexual division of labor" (1977: 89–94), terms that were interchangeable in his work of this period with masculinity and femininity. French intellectuals, including feminists, have been slow to accept Anglo-American gender analysis. Bourdieu may have merely been reflecting French usages, but it seems more likely that he did not automatically make the connections between power and gender among the Kabyle, the Béarn peasantry, and contemporary French men and women because of a misrecognition of his own society.

The conceptual tools for making these connections, however, existed in latent form in his early work. I refer to the clear presence of a deeply gendered honor culture in his work on Kabyle society and the matrimonial strategies employed by peasant families in the Béarn. Indeed, as he writes in the introduction to the revised essay on matrimonial strategies in *The Logic of Practice*, "The division of sexual labour, transfigured in a particular form of the sexual division of labour, is the basis of the *di-vision* of the world, the most solidly established of all collective—that is, objective illusions. . . . These principles, arising from social reality, contribute to the very reality of the social order by realizing themselves in bodies, in the form of dispositions" (46).

One task for the historian might be to identify and analyze the conditions under which this gendered embodiment occurs in historical societies, and the circumstances in which the forms and expressions of the honor culture are transformed over time. There are a few interesting ways in which this might be done. One is to follow Bourdieu's own guidelines for assessing matrimonial strategies and social reproduction. Another might be to follow an intergenerational process in which sociability and social skills and their related bodily dispositions are transmitted.

In this chapter I explore the first of these tasks in early modern Europe with special reference to France and then make a few suggestions about the role of masculine sociability in performing the transmission of technical and social skills. I am proposing here an analysis of the transmission of masculinities as an aspect of the intergenerational transmission of an honor culture. This is a highly complex matter that can be satisfactorily addressed only in interdisciplinary perspective, but I hope at least to clarify some of the epistemological issues that are raised by this very interesting process, about whose nature we all have a proximate intuitive sense. But even as we highlight the transformative nature of this process, the trick, as Bourdieu reminds us, is at the same time not to lose sight of the experience of inevitability associated with a social world and with bodies that are gendered (sexed, strictly speaking, to avoid historical anachronism) according to an order of masculine domination and feminine subordination.

Embodiment

Bourdieu's general aim as a sociologist/ethnologist/historian of culture has been to explore how culture reproduces itself in a rule-governed way while remaining open to innovation and new orientations. He breaks altogether with the structuralist anthropology of the generation of Claude Lévi-Strauss and follows the path of post-Wittgensteinian epistemology that emphasizes tacit knowledge and understanding as embedded social practice. He rejects the notion that culture is expressed exclusively in prepackaged, self-perpetuating, ahistorical linguistic forms, preferring to speak more loosely of the strategies that individuals enact and of the "generative principle" that creates and maintains culture and social institutions.

As Charles Taylor has explained, Bourdieu's method opposes the intellectualist standpoint altogether. The intellectualist outlook hypostatizes cultural and linguistic rules as representations and encourages us to "slide easily into seeing the rule-as-represented as somehow causally operative" (Taylor 1993: 55). The reification of rules is a distortion of the actual way in which culture evolves and is transmitted "on the ground." According to Bourdieu, we are guided in our social lives by a "practical sense" that he describes in *The Logic of Practice* as a "durably installed generative principle of regulated improvisations" (Bourdieu 1990a [1980]: 57). As Taylor describes this sense, "The practical ability exists only in its exercise, which unfolds in time and space. As you get around a familiar environment, the different locations in their interrelation don't all impinge at once. Your sense of them is different, depending on where you are and where you are going" (Taylor 1993: 55–56). The rule guides us, but "the practice not only fulfills the rule, but also gives it concrete shapes in particular situations. Practice is, as it were, a continual 'interpretation' and reinterpretation of what the rule really means" (Taylor 1993: 57).

Bourdieu and his critics alike are fascinated by the metaphor of sport or play in making clear the relation between rule and practice; it happens that this metaphor is also useful in understanding the process of embodiment. Bourdieu calls this "the feel for the game," in the case of culture, "a particular, historically determined game" that we acquire gradually through childhood:

> The good player, who is so to speak the game incarnate, does at every moment what the game requires. That presupposes a permanent capacity for invention, indispensable if one is to be able to adapt to indefinitely varied and never completely identical situations. This is not ensured by mechanical obedience to the explicit, codified rule (when it exists).... The habitus as the feel for the game is the social game embodied and turned into a second nature. Nothing is simultaneously freer and more constrained than the action of the good player. He quite naturally materializes at just the place the ball is about to fall, as if the ball were in command of him—but by that very fact he is in command of the ball. (Bourdieu 1990a [1980]: 63; also Calhoun 1993a: 78)

The use of the metaphor of sport (or dancing) to understand the process of the embodiment of rules or codes in social practice allows Bourdieu to explain the essentially unconscious nature (not the Freudian sense of repressed memory) of bodily understanding. Cultures, particularly certain institutions within them, subject bodies to disciplines that ensure individual obedience and corporate loyalty. Unlike Michel Foucault, Bourdieu is less interested in the authoritarian effects of such disciplines and their relation to embodied forms of power than he is in how individuals are able to reflexively interpret the rules these disciplines teach and follow a strategy that satisfies both individual interest and the rules of the game of culture (Bourdieu 1990a [1980]: 166–67).

Foucault's notion of bodily discipline was rooted in his understanding of the military pedagogy of the classical age and in the state's need of "docile bodies" for its projects (Foucault 1977: 135–70). Foucault argued that the process of conjoining of this passive disposition with the self-regulation of the autonomous modern individual was the great ruse of modern power, which regulated the body according to a logic of embodied discourses (Ehrenberg 1983). Foucault does not ignore the actual ways in which habit and repetition become second nature to bodies, but he is silent on the way in which discourses penetrate and influence bodies. Moreover, as critics have pointed out, Foucault's notion of embodiment does not permit an understanding of how discourses of power are embodied differentially according to gender. In addition, his "unidirectional account of power" leaves little room for individual experience and "results in an impoverished and over-stable account of the formation of gender identity" (McNay 1992: 47). By contrast, Bourdieu's approach to embodiment encompasses a certain degree of voluntarism and indeterminacy in the way individuals respond to social contingencies but still makes use of the notion of embodiment—rather than sociological *role*—as the way in which individuals appropriate culture (Karis 1993: 156–77; Le Hir 2000: 123–44).

It is largely accepted that Bourdieu initially learned about embodiment from Maurice Merleau-Ponty and perhaps Marcel Mauss, though Bourdieu converted their accounts of individual experience into a sociological and collective process (Lane 2000: 100–103; Reed-Danahay 2005: 102). The other great modern theorist whose perspective includes some notion of embodiment as cultural appropriation is Norbert Elias. Bourdieu learned much from Elias about how codes of etiquette and manners are incarnated in individuals to serve as guides to proper behavior, particularly at the inner promptings of shame and embarrassment. However, Elias was essentially an evolutionary thinker whose account of the West describes a scenario in which violence has been increasingly repressed in the wake of the continuing rise of standards of sensitivity and civility. Bourdieu's perspective resists the simple development of premodern societies into modern ones along some teleological course; he has used ethnographic analysis to see how much of traditional structures of habit and belief remains in modern societies. But Bourdieu also preserved a role for violence in the form of the symbolic violence experienced by individuals ensnared in complicit but subordinate relations of race, class, status, or gender according to the rules of the game.

In *Masculine Domination* Bourdieu finally developed in full for modern societies a version of the deeply gendered ethnology he undertook for the Kabyle people and the smallholders of the Béarn. What had been an analytical concept that explained the embodied transmission of class and social strata became a means of understanding the reproduction of gender in its broadest sense (Reed-Danahay 2005: 113). He made an effort to address the problem of the reproduction of masculine domination in the successive forms it has assumed in changing circumstances, building on what he had learned from less complex societies about the systematic alignments of gender difference according to domestic space, work, profession, matrimonial and inheritance strategies, family life, and sexuality. He identified the rites of passage that mark the stages of the bodily incorporation of culture for men, traced the aspects of the codes of honor and shame that gave form to the lives of (mostly) upper-class men, and described in general the ways in which the body and its gestures serve as emblems of culture for both sexes.

Though Bourdieu leaves us satisfied about the general, intuitive truth of his interpretive perspective—that gender is a naturalized way of seeing, feeling, and performing—he does not provide many instantiations of the process of transmission itself: how masculine domination adapts to new circumstances yet performs essentially the same functions, as his formulation puts it. Many of his illustrations continued to be drawn from ethnographic materials, which are synchronic and analytical in nature, not diachronic and transformational. He seemed content being the master of bravura analysis of the ethnological snapshot, the cataloguer of vestiges and embryonic forms.

I don't intend to supply either decisive examples or a grand scheme of historical change to demonstrate how masculinities are transmitted. My aim is more modest. I'd like to identify a few of the sociocultural circumstances in early modern and modern times that reveal a process of masculine embodiment at work. I shall not concentrate on those, like military training or rituals of violence, where the tacit aim is the development of the most aggressive forms of virility, but on marital strategies, inheritance practices, and masculine sociability, in which ostensibly what was being transmitted was social, economic, or cultural capital, not the naturalized materials of gender domination.

Inheritance and Social Reproduction

Between the end of the Middle Ages and the dawn of industrialization, the notion that noblemen were a separate and superior race descended from warrior elites was acknowledged in both custom and law. They embodied, so to speak, the principle of valor and were expected to comport themselves accordingly. They wore side arms, rode steeds, dressed in military garb, and expressed themselves through a linguistic and gestural repertory that was as distinctive in its own way as was the habitus of the clergy. By the sixteenth century, when the crusades and the era of constant warfare had come to an end, there emerged a discourse of noble apologetics that portrayed noblemen as possessing an "unequal aptitude for virtue," in effect personal qualities of valor and skill that were transmitted en bloc from ancestors who had exercised these qualities long enough for them to have become natural. This was, as Arlette Jouanna has written, a genuine theory of "acquired characters" *avant la lettre*, "fully buttressed by reference to the biological ideas of the era" (Jouanna 1977: 39–41). This body of beliefs served to guarantee the preeminence of individual lineages, but it also gave "to the orders of which they were a part, a personality at once biological, moral, and social; thus it made [nobles] socionatural types, kinds of mythical beings" (Jouanna 1977: 49).

As I have argued elsewhere, the quality of honor, which in early medieval times resided in a nobleman's *biens*, or properties, became by the sixteenth century a feature of his noble person and indistinguishable from his military vocation, which "accentuated," in Georges Duby's words, "the masculine nature of this social class" (Duby 1976: 39; Nye 1993: 18–21). But how was this sentiment of honor, which women did not possess except in the narrow sense of sexual chastity, transmitted? It passed through the blood but also by means of an apprenticeship at arms, in combat, and through associations with noble peers. In the words of a sixteenth-century jurist, so long as he "lived nobly" and could bring evidence from those who had seen "his father and grandfather living nobly, exercising their arms, going to war, . . . and doing other noble acts" a man could avoid derogation and keep his reputation and his patrimony intact (Grell and d'Arnau Ramière de Fortanier 1999: 230).

Over the course of the seventeenth century and the eighteenth, however, in the phrase of Ellery Schalk, noble identity shifted from "valor to pedigree," from being noble to proving noble lineage through legal proofs vetted by royal administrators (Schalk 1986), a point Bourdieu himself comments on in *In Other Words*, likening the Kabyle sense of honor with seventeenth-century usages, while Béarnaise honor was more aligned with modern forms (Bourdieu 1990a [1980]: 68). Blood now became the sign of nobility, its repository and guarantee, in place of the acts of daring or pugnacity that had previously defined the noble way of life. At the same time, nobles were obliged to spend time each year at court, where they found it necessary to learn an entirely new set of skills that went under the rubric *honnêteté*, including the elaborate manners and gestures required for courtiership. The honorable man now needed to invest energy in self-control and to master the subtle weapons of sociability that would preserve his status at court (Elias 1983: vol. 2). Most noble families still expected their sons to travel and serve at arms but also hoped they would learn the qualities of courtesy and civility that would endear them to the powerful (Stanton 1980; Dewald 1993: 45–63).

The usages of honnêteté continued but transformed the gender distinctions of the honor culture in ways that were appropriate to a mixed society. Indeed, one of the aims of honnêteté was to distinguish between men and women in speech, bearing, and dress. As one observer, Antoine Furetière, explained, "Women's honnêteté is their chastity, modesty, decency, discretion. Men's honnêteté concerns their behaviour—a manner of acting justly, sincerely, courteously, obligingly, civilly" (Cohen 1996: 18). The distinction preserved here is between active and passive, discriminating and discriminated, and this included the gestures and comportment appropriate to each one. Lord Chesterfield, who was familiar with French ways, advised his son in the early part of the eighteenth century that one must cultivate "the look, the tone of voice, the manner of speaking, the gestures, all must conspire to form that *je ne sais quoi* that everybody feels, although nobody can exactly describe" (Cohen 1996: 45).

Court society also provided the stage on which rich commoners and *noblesse de la robe* could learn the techniques of self-mastery necessary for success. Bourdieu was aware of the particular sensitivity robe nobles displayed in these settings: "Their special lucidity as regards aristocratic values and the symbolic foundations of authority, especially that of title, may well have owed something to the marginal position that inclined them towards the temporal powers of church or state, but this in no way invalidates the truth it reveals" (Bourdieu 2000b: 3). Indeed, studies on the emerging robe nobility in this period have found that this new class of royal officials followed an evolution similar to that of sword nobles, from reputations based on acts to faith in lineage. Although the acts that had earned this emerging elite its reputation were those of learning, efficiency, and work, not the valor or physical strength of nobles, they could be naturalized in precisely the same way as noble traits.

The historian Sarah Hanley has noted the emergence of a "family–state compact" in sixteenth-century France that laid down laws and procedures for extending state control over marriage and reproduction and assuring the reliable inheritance of property. The authority of the family patriarch was strengthened by these developments. His control over his children and his wife were affirmed by successive royal ordinances punishing fractious heirs, extending the age of majority, forbidding clandestine marriage, and imprisoning rebellious wives. Lineage property in the patriarchal line was favored over all other kinds. As Hanley writes, "Marriages were constructed financially from blood lines; inheritance followed suit" (Hanley 1989: 12). What emerged by the end of the century was a closed system of inheritance that established the security of property and the power of patriarchal authority, but that also placed unprecedented weight on the ability of the patriarch to translate the rules of inheritance into strategies for practical transgenerational success, in short, a perfect application of Bourdieusian practice.

Barbara Diefendorf has found that the humanist literature of the early sixteenth century advised bourgeois fathers to choose careers for their sons for which they had capacity and a natural disposition. The arduous course of legal studies required to become a Paris city counselor was not suited for a young man of little energy or taste for learning. Likewise, Jonathan Dewald has found that in the early years of the formation of the robe magistracy in sixteenth-century Rouen, the emphasis was on learning, experience, and the mastering of youthful impulses in favor of practical activity (Dewald 1980: 32, 68). Nor were these bourgeois elites contemptuous of their noble superiors; they claimed to respect and admire the profession of arms as simply another form of state service.

A study of wills over the sixteenth century and into the seventeenth finds in both Paris and Rouen, however, a narrowing of the class basis for recruitment to the magistracy, a growing marital endogamy, and, most important, a desire that the son follow the father's profession whether he was suited for it or not. Offices came increasingly to be inherited, as did the belief, as Diefendorf writes, "that the tendency toward virtue and superior moral character was inherited. . . . Jurists, social theorists, educators and even doctors believed that superior bloodlines coupled with carefully planned educations and marriages brought certain family lines, or *races*, to a higher moral plane than that of common society" (Diefendorf 1983: 168). In the parlance of the era, an *homme honorable* sought an office with a parallel rank of honorability. As noted above, inheritance strategies for both Parisian and Rouen magistrates were evolving toward greater stress on lineage than on disposable property. That is, more restrictions were put on what a married couple could do with the property that came to them through their families than had been true early in the sixteenth century, when a young man's talents and training were seen as the best guarantors of his success. The greatest of all dangers was *mésalliance*, which watered down or infected bloodlines, divided fortunes, and soiled the reputations of families hoping to rise in the world (Dewald 1980: 95–99; Diefendorf 1983: 168, 253–54, 277). Women in these milieux of early modern bourgeois society brought wealth and useful kinship relations to a match but were expected otherwise to be silent and chaste and to cultivate the domestic arts.

Mésalliance also helps clarify another assumption about inheritance held in early modern culture. As Gayle Brunelle has pointed out, among the seventeenth-century Norman nobility the belief that it was the father's blood that nourished the next generation of noble male heritors meant that charges of derogation brought against noblemen on account of mésalliance with bourgeois wives were less likely to succeed than those brought against noblewomen who had married down (Brunelle 1995: 83, 99). This principle effectively acknowledged that blood not only followed blood transgenerationally but did so preponderantly though sexual lineages. Like father, like son, for better or worse.

Further down the class hierarchy, the occupants of more humble professions experienced a similar tension between the need to demonstrate personal capacity and the debts and responsibilities they owed to families. In her study of notaries in early modern Nantes, Julie Hardwick has stressed the practices of patriarchal authority in the families of these petty legal officials. Everyone understood that the status claims and the family authority of these men depended on their managerial competence and diligence. Derogation and downward mobility were as possible for them as for a nobleman who showed cowardice in battle or on the field of honor. In good times notaries in Nantes could aspire to levels of professional function that would earn them the title *noble homme, maître, honorable homme, honnête homme,* or simply *sire,* all standing in hierarchical relation to one another and resting on some combination of marital alliance, inheritance, talent, and taste for work (Hardwick 1999: 9–11).

Hardwick traces the rough equivalence of honor, status, and masculine domestic authority in the marriage settlements and wills of notarial families. She found that lineage relations were prepared to intervene in situations where the managerial competence of the patriarch was in doubt, but that they rarely left his affairs and wealth in his wife's (or widow's) hands. Fathers had control over the lives and career choices of their sons until they were thirty and often postponed their own retirements as long as possible in order to prolong their domestic and legal authority. As Hardwick shows, "blood and property" were profoundly commingled in the imaginations of these petty officials, just as they were in more elevated social milieux where the combination of "reputation, rank, and resources" determined status and warranted authority over social inferiors, women, and minors. Not incidentally, being a *"good manager"* of his household was also an important criterion in creating mutual respect among the middling men who bore arms in the town militia. Militiamen were known to refuse to follow a militia leader who had fallen down in his household duties as patriarch (Hardwick 1999: 57–58, 205–7).

One can find pretensions to honorability in still lower social and occupational levels of early modern cities, linked in similar ways to inheritance practices, competence, and authority. James R. Farr has chronicled the slowly growing fortunes of master artisans in Dijon in the sixteenth century and seventeenth. As they accumulated goods and property, however modest in amount, master craftsmen, like peasant landlords in the Béarn, increasingly followed inheritance strategies that favored retaining property in lineage settlements rather than dispersing it in equal portions to all offspring. Fathers sought ever-greater control over the careers of their sons, and as patrimonies grew and the "stakes of a good marriage mounted ever higher, masters became ever more sensitive to the honor of their own marriages as well as the reputation of their daughters, beginning with the legitimacy of their birth" (Farr 1988: 187).

Like their social betters, master artisans "aspired to the ideal of the honorable man." They dressed and acted in a way they believed reflected their status and competence, were sensitive to a fault about insults or gestures aimed at stripping away or questioning their honor, and were extremely solicitous of their reputations as competent craftsmen and businessmen. They also reacted violently to affronts about their sexual behavior or tastes, especially any that concerned the waywardness of their wives, for that suggested they lacked authority at home (Farr 1988: 178–79). In short, like the notaries of Nantes, the town counselors of Paris, and the magistrates of Rouen, the master artisans of Dijon regarded reputation, competence, and honor as features of their personal identity. They and their contemporaries linked these features indissolubly with the property and assets that both reflected and warranted those qualities. Aided by the rigid sumptuary laws of the era and supported by a legal system protective of *état*, they took pains to appear to be what they were, no more and certainly no less.

By the second half of the eighteenth century an interesting debate had unfolded about whether nobles who engaged in trade, the so-called *noblesse commerçante*, automatically forfeited their noble status. The debate shows the extent to which contemporary opinion embraced the concepts of embodied inheritance we have seen operating throughout the early modern period at all levels of society. In this debate, Montesquieu's principle that nobles who were animated by the "prejudices" of honor and glory contributed to the good of society was subjected to a critique from bourgeois theorists. Lawyers and pamphleteers sought to establish an equivalence between commerce, with "its own services, its own dangers, its own combats," and the physical risks experienced by the military class (Smith 2000: 251). Some contributors to the debate were skeptical that the self-interested qualities of merchants could be transformed into the sacrificial and socially useful valor of the nobleman, but others optimistically endorsed educational schemes that would spread the noble qualities of honor and courage more widely through society or, on the other hand, praised as exemplary the courage, nobility, and patriotism of the commercial classes (Smith 2000: 369–72).

What most of these arguments had in common was a conviction that honor and the virile qualities it provoked and affirmed could, with some exceptions, be both acquired and lost. Even the most conservative old-regime defenders of the idea that only the nobleman was capable of virtue made allowances for a principle of acculturation very like that at the heart of Bourdieu's concept of gender embodiment. Thus the aphorist La Bruyère, writing in 1688, "Those . . . , whose birth distinguishes them from the common people, and who are exposed to the eyes of men, to their censures and praises, are capable of transcending their temperaments even if they are not naturally courageous; and this disposition of heart and mind, which passes from their ancestors to their descendents, is that courage so often found among persons of noble birth, and is perhaps nobility itself" (Shovlin 2000: 45).

By the end of the eighteenth century, notwithstanding a passionate rearguard debate about nobility, courage, and derogation, wealthy bourgeois could still aspire to marital alliances with increasingly endogamous aristocratic families, but on the whole urban elites continued to follow the reproductive and inheritance strategies that had elevated them in society (de Saint Martin 1993; Daumard 1988; Higgs 1987). A specifically bourgeois notion of family honor emerged from the repetition of these strategies. A noble patriarch needed only to produce an heir; the legal mechanism of primogeniture then switched on to ensure an orderly succession. The non-noble patriarch, however, needed an investment strategy that would permit the accumulation of wealth surely and not ignobly; an inheritance strategy that would maintain most of the wealth as a bloc; marital strategies that would enhance its growth and smooth transmission; and fertility strategies that would neither fragment the patrimony nor arrest its progress (Nye 1993: 37–39). These strategies required various degrees of self-denial, from the discipline of thrift and control of sexual impulses to the more serious sacrifices of celibacy and the renunciation of heritability by some of the heirs to foil fragmentation of the estate. Families attained a kind of honorability through these transgenerational practices; the claim to honor became, over time, inseparable from the honorable behavior that eventually procured it.

Bourdieu has written some memorable lines on the family as a "transpersonal person" in *In Other Words*. The "real fiction" of the family "as an objective social category (a structuring structure) is the basis of the family as a subjective social category (a structured structure), a mental category which is the matrix of countless representations and actions (such as marriages) which help to reproduce the objective social category" (Bourdieu 1990e: 67). This "structuring process" aims "to constitute the family by establishing it as a united, integrated entity which is therefore stable, constant, indifferent to the fluctuations of individual feelings." This process is both emotional and corporeal in nature. As Bourdieu puts it, "The structures of kinship and family as *bodies* can be perpetuated only through a continuous creation of family feeling, a cognitive principle of vision and division that is at the same time an affective principle of *cohesion*, that is, the adhesion that is vital to the existence of a family group and its interests" (Bourdieu 1998d: 68).

Bourdieu also reminds us that the authority of the patriarch, who was responsible for assuring that the family heritage, "which is always threatened by dilapidation and dispersion," must remain intact (Bourdieu 1998a: 70). Indeed, the personal qualities of the family patriarch that attained and maintained honor for him and his dependents derived from his comportment at work, his sexual life, and from his management of the "assets" of his fertility. These qualities were indistinguishable from his identity as a man of honor, which assumed a palpable and biological form that appeared, to all the participants in the expanding honor culture of the late eighteenth century, to be *embodied* in the man himself. If valor and prowess at arms were the inherited qualities of old-regime nobles, middle-class patriarchs expected their sons to possess the capacity for work and self-control that would preserve the patrimony, and their daughters to preserve their chastity and submit willingly to his notion of a suitable marital alliance (Daumard 1987: 242–43; Todd 1988; Darrow 1989: 128).

Foucault has written persuasively about how the bourgeoisie developed a "technology of sex" that promoted longevity, maximized vitality, and ensured fertile sexual relations that became a "political ordering of life" (Foucault 1980: 124–25). The European middle classes placed their faith, in short, in a form of sexual hygiene and comportment that, contrary to the supposed myth of Victorian repressiveness, celebrated the force of the sexual drive, sought to keep it pure from taint and disease, and invested all its hopes for the future in the numerous, healthy, and competent progeny good sexual hygiene could produce (Hull 1996). As Foucault wrote, the bourgeoisie's blood was its sex; that is, the personal and class identity of a middle-class man was subsumed into a moral and bodily discipline that stipulated the quantity and occasions for sex, confined it to the marital bed, and disdained nonprocreative, wasteful forms of sexual expenditure.

Proper sexual hygiene and the moral outlook associated with it have remained important to the transmission of masculinity and femininity up to our own time. But in one way or another the habitus appropriate to normative gender in the European middle classes was bound up with material property and assets in ways that made them utterly indistinguishable and that may therefore explain why it is that our ancestors continued to conflate biology with culture in ways that we moderns no longer take for granted. Historians must therefore continue to focus on the categories and assumptions that historical actors used when they thought they were acting to ensure the transmission of gender (and class and race) (Stolcke 1993: 17–37). For instance, in nineteenth-century German middle-class society, class and gender traits were bred into the body as a kind of aesthetics of bearing, conversation, dress, and manners, where they served as emblems of worthiness in future marital partners and heirs and thereby as warrants for the smooth transmission of property. As David Warren Sabean has argued, "The way a body was trained to move had everything to do with how capital was concentrated and property transferred. Families and clans provided the soil for the nursing of tender plants—in their protective environment, people were trained in style, tone, desire, and boundary marker recognition" (Sabean 1998: 486).

Likewise, in the mid nineteenth-century English middle class, educating a boy for success in commerce meant teaching him not the arts of business, but the character traits and habits of "self-instruction, self-command, and self-acting energy," that is, the manly qualities possessed by their fathers, whose own ascent to prosperity had been through apprenticeship and practical activity. The manhood of a middle-class man in Victorian Britain, was, in John Tosh's phrase, "mortgaged to the future" through his sons. Having sons was believed to be a marker of manliness, but in an era when education, examinations, and professional training were more important avenues to success than inheriting the family business, a boy's aptitudes for independent work, self-discipline, and personal autonomy were key traits. A father's own masculine apotheosis was realized through the character traits that ensured the financial independence of his sons. The celebrated English public school prospered throughout the last half of the nineteenth century to teach lads a "crash course in manliness" by demonstrating to them how to compete harmoniously with their peers (Tosh 1999: 110–18).

Sociability

Contemporary gender theorists weigh peer groups and sociability as heavily as they weigh the family as crucial influences on gender formation. Bourdieu discusses some of these matters in *Masculine Domination* and analogizes the maintenance of bourgeois dynasties to select clubs. Indeed, we are often startled when we learn about the extent of gender segregation our ancestors believed was necessary for the successful transmission of gendered traits. I have focused until now on the intrafamilial and the reciprocal transmission of personal qualities and property, but I would like to conclude with some observations on the ways in which sociability, beginning in the late eighteenth century, may have contributed to the transmission of masculinities. The turning of the century coincides with the rise of a new form of sociability based on all-male gatherings, in contrast to the mixed-sex salon culture that had dominated upper-class social life until then. Freemasonry was the first of these new forms to emerge; initially it united men of remarkably diverse social origins for the spreading of enlightenment, to be sure, but also for the pure democracy of sociability (Agulhon 1968; Jacob 1991). Eventually, in cities throughout Europe middle-class men gathered together in a variety of clubs and *cercles* for dining, gambling, recreation or to engage in serious activities of *emulation*.

It is not always appreciated that these gatherings did not specifically exclude women or, for the most part, require particular qualifications for membership; the entire process was based on word of mouth and recruitment of the right sort of man. Carol Harrison, who has studied the growth of *sociétés d'emulation* in small-town southeastern France, has found that the men who were asked to join were men of *capacité*, that is, they were hardworking bourgeois who had local stature, some talent for leadership, and subscribed to the vaguely progressive and scientific ideology of most such organizations (Harrison 1999: 51). Above all, these were men who wished to establish a presence in the public sphere and who were active participants in their self-construction as citizens. They openly contrasted their gatherings with the local fine arts academies, which they opined were only for girls, and with the mixed-sex sociability of the salons (Harrison 1999: 59–67).

Club society was, in other words, self-consciously masculine in outlook. The generations mixed together familiarly: young men were eagerly recruited and socialized, and fathers sought entry for their sons when they entered their majority. The ethos of such gatherings appears to have been both competitive and harmonious, with only the occasional incident leading to violence or requiring intervention by the leadership. This is not only because the groups were protective of their collective reputations, but also because they observed a kind of *bienséance* that was adapted from the masculine honor code that most of them already observed or aspired to in their personal lives. The practical ethics that guided masculine exchanges was concerned principally with elementary politeness, proper verbal formulas, subjects to avoid, such as politics, religion, and family matters, and the cultivation of frankness and courteousness in manners (Nye 1997: 60–79).

Everyone knew there were limits to what could be said or expressed in tone and gesture; the *point d'honneur* remained the last guarantor of a proximate civility everywhere in Europe until the 1850s, excluding Great Britain only after that date. Even though duels were infrequent in such settings, professional organizations widely adopted procedures for resolving differences between members that resembled the honor courts that sorted out disputes between brother officers in military life. On pain of expulsion, men were required to give satisfaction to someone they had offended, to make amends, and to have third parties mediate differences. The presence of such procedures suggests that club discourse encouraged tact, as Georg Simmel once observed, and a kind of impersonality that was unlikely to either offend or be offended (Simmel 1950: 45).

Obviously, the way masculinity was transmitted in club sociability was different from the processes of literal incarnation that occurred in family life, but masculine sociability taught disciplines for the body and decorum in speech that were reproduced not only in voluntary organizations, but also in all-male gatherings everywhere in the modern era: the military, schools, the professions, sports, and within masculine occupations and workplaces. The modern professions provide us with numerous examples of the ways in which male sociability inculcated distinctively masculine traits in doctors, lawyers, scientists, and engineers.

Though European states provided some regulatory and exclusionary protection for the all-male professions, it was the universities, professional schools, and professional organizations that ensured that neither women nor the "wrong kind of man" would gain entry to all-male professional domains (Witz 1992). When women did begin to penetrate these gender monopolies, they were effectively excluded from the social life of the profession by the masculine rituals and discourse of the male honor culture that required plain-spokenness, vigorous comportment, a willingness to back words with deeds, and other standards of an exclusively male culture. In the medical profession, the education and hospital training of physicians were profoundly masculine in nature well into the twentieth century, requiring of women a bodily *hexis* and a practical sense that were alien to them and, to say the least, discouraging. Historians and anthropologists have found Bourdieu's work very useful in explaining how medicine became and remained until recently an embodied masculine profession, surgery being the last bastion of male supremacy and a test case for the way in which a masculinized technique was transmitted down the generations (More 1999; Lawrence 1998: 156–202; Cassell 1998).

Though I have not the space to explore it here, there is some excellent recent historical work on the transmission of gender in the workplace. This was not a particular interest of Bourdieu's, but the acquisition of tacit skills, the operation of familiarizing and socializing mechanisms, and the gendering of work experience and of the employment of technologies make the workplace a site, like many others, for the analysis of gendered habitus. In the so-called deskilling of the workplace that occurred in twentieth-century industrialization, the blending of old and new workforces required a "remasculinization" or re-amalgamation of the rough and the respectable styles associated, respectively, with unskilled and skilled workers (Meyer 2001). The broadening of industrial unions to include male white collar workers required similar realignments (Taillon 2001). Extractive industries in particular employed initiation rites, myths, and specialized discourse to train new men in dangerous work (Quam-Wickam 2001). Machines and the mastering of tools have always been important aspects of building masculine solidarity between men in work settings. Tools operate as embodied prostheses by men who learn techniques for using them less through verbal cues than through observation and tacit experience (Mellstrom 2004).

I have tried to be suggestive here about the historical subjects we might study to appreciate fully Bourdieu's insights into the historical transmission of gender. I have only looked at a few of the cases in which this process operated historically and continues to operate today. Military training, sport, and other all-male contexts are even better suited to demonstrate how masculinity may be embedded in individuals. But the incarnation of favorable gender traits works no less well in the ways families raise their sons and hope to find in them the qualities that make a good heir and future progenitor. I have tried to locate a few of the situations that help illustrate Bourdieu's point about the ways in which social reproduction produces individuals with gender characteristics so utterly natural to them that they seem literally to have been inherited through the blood.

It is possible as well to see confirmation of Bourdieu's argument that these practices also operated to select embodied feminine qualities, preserving a relation of dominance in men's favor through the perpetuation of a hierarchy of perceived natural traits, including embodied emotions. As he writes in *Masculine Domination*, "The acts of knowledge and gratitude practiced on the magical frontier that separates the dominant and the dominated and that the magic of symbolic power affirms, in which the dominated themselves collaborate, . . . in their domination by accepting tacitly the limits imposed, often takes the form of corporeal emotions—shame, humiliation, timidity, anxiety, culpability—or of passions or sentiments—love, admiration, respect—; emotions all the more painful for the fact that they betray themselves visibly in blushing, verbal confusion, awkwardness, trembling, anger or helpless rage" (Bourdieu 1998b: 44).

Until recent times property has been transmitted transgenerationally together with the personal qualities in male heirs that would allow it to prosper. Since at least the beginning of the twentieth century, as Bourdieu tells us, property settlements have been less important in the establishment of the prosperity of heirs than social, cultural, and, especially, educational capital. At the same time, and not coincidentally, masculinity has seemed to us to be a product more of the biological body, a matter of genes and hormones, than of social or familial cultivation. This development stimulates the illusion that masculinity is, finally, a natural thing, not, as I have tried to demonstrate, culture made into nature. But it would be a mistake to regard masculinity as a natural thing. The biology of the gendered body is no less a social construction than the cultural traits whose origins we can ultimately identify in family and cultural life (Fausto-Sterling 2000; Bourdieu 1998b: 90).

THE MAKING OF A FIELD WITH WEAK AUTONOMY
The Case of the Sports Field in France, 1895–1955

As Nelson Goodman (1978) would say, the prospect of making a world from sports is a commonplace idea in sport itself, and that insight is elaborated by an American journalist in a book titled *Sportsworld* (Lipsyte 1975). Although this is an indigenous representation, it is not sufficient for the historical sociologist to produce a formalization in terms of field; she or he should precisely describe the relevant dimensions of the space of sports and the stages of its genesis, in a specific country, shaped through a singular social history.

Without going back to the set of methodological rules laid down by Pierre Bourdieu for the construction of a field analysis, I can say that my research on the genesis of the French "sports field" followed his proposal to proceed "in three necessary and internally connected moments (Bourdieu and Wacquant 1992: 104–5). First, one must analyze the position of the field vis-à-vis the field of power. . . . Second, one must map out the objective structure of the relations between positions occupied by the agents or institutions who compete for the legitimate form of specific authority of which the field is the site. And, third, one must analyze the *habitus* of the agents, the different systems of dispositions they have acquired by internalizing a determinate type of social and economic conditions, and which find in a definite trajectory within the field under consideration a more or less favourable opportunity to become actualized" (Bourdieu and Wacquant 1992: 104–5). In the case of the French sports field:

> First, the process through which the space of sports is produced is precisely a moment in struggles for the definition of what the scholastic/academic education of the children of the bourgeoisie should be, in both French *lycées* and universities during the 1880s and 1890s. On this point, the French case was similar to, but later than, the case in England (Mangan 1981).

Second, the structuring of the field led to a first configuration around 1900–30 and to a second one around 1930–60; they express the specific stakes defined in this sports world, and the balance of social powers described by a social and cultural history.

Third, the process through which sporting practices extricated themselves from social conventions and norms of ordinary conduct (norms of politeness, decency, honor), and through which they became specific practices, led to the definition of an ideal of bodily excellence specific to the field and to the increasingly intense inculcation of specific dispositions that prepare one for athletic competition. The definition of a sporting habitus became more precise and differentiated according to the kind of sport being practiced (boxing, track, soccer, and so forth). Apparatuses were developed to inculcate sporting dispositions and to certify their acquisition (curriculum, diplomas, sporting titles).

I. Genesis of the Sports Field

Sport became a significant practice in France at the end of the nineteenth century, although some sporting activities practiced in England, including horse racing, sailing regatta, and, sporadically, boxing, had been introduced as early as 1830 (Vigarello 1995). Sports imported from England after 1870, for example, athletic sports, were a catalyst in the making of the field, but other kinds of physical activities also played a role, notably cycle racing, which appeared in several industrial European countries just before 1870 and which was not an English import when it began in France (Poyer 2003: 98). The making of the field did not result from introducing isolated sporting techniques but presupposed that several sporting techniques were in competition and also that a kind of common principle between these practices existed. A condition for the crystallization of the field was that some formerly nonsporting but already institutionalized physical activities would be reshaped according to the principles of sportsmanship and transformed into sports.

HETEROGENEITY AND THE INITIAL STRUCTURE OF THE SPACE OF POSSIBLE PHYSICAL ACTIVITIES

The bodily activities subjected to a transformation process into sports were diverse. They belonged to diverse practical domains the logic of which could be completely different: for example, some practices in which you fight against and some in which you play with others; exercises which destroy the opponent's body and those which take care of your own body. By partially following a classification proposed by Roger Caillois that distinguishes idealized gestures derived from warfare, those derived from ball games, and those

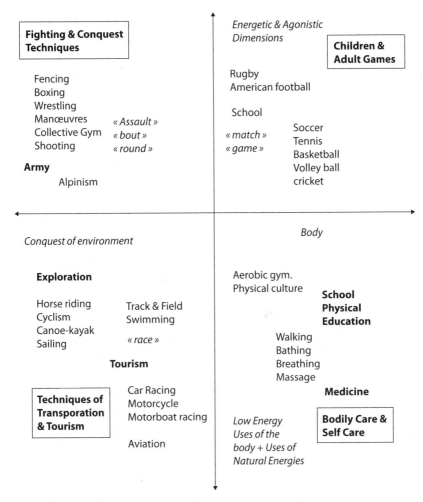

Figure 13.1. Physical activities in France at end of nineteenth century.

derived from everyday life and techniques (Caillois 1967), I shall distinguish four classes of activities according to their sociohistorical origins, from the older to the newer (figure 1).

Some bodily practices derived from the space of personal care techniques that individuals use to keep themselves in good health in their everyday life (see bottom right in figure 1). Medicine had formalized these practices, including physical exercise, diet, and living rhythms, since the eighteenth century, and it had reinforced them in many countries in Europe but controlled them only partially. Here, bodily exercise has a specific shape: walking, breathing, softening, climbing, bathing, swimming, and so on. Many imply contact with natural elements. They take place during sessions of exercise or a course of treatment.

The physical exercises that prepare one for fighting and struggle (see top left in figure 1) were, starting in the eighteenth century, broadly monopolized and organized by the armies in Europe following the Prussian example. They had a central place during the nineteenth century among the patriotic physical practices of countries like France, Germany, Switzerland, and Sweden: military walking with codified steps, running, jumping, shooting, fencing, boxing, military horse riding, attack–defense exercises, and so forth. Some of these activities take the form of fights or bouts.

Adults' and children's games were codified in some noble, bourgeois, and popular traditions or by school institutions (see top right in figure 1). Some, like basketball, expanded beyond the local festive world or the school world and became sporting games with national or international rules, while others, like pelota in the Basque country, remained local. The notions of play, match, and game are applied to these competitive activities.

Finally, some transportation techniques (see below left in figure 1) opened the opportunity for the playful and sporting uses of vehicles and machines that permitted movement. This took place mainly at the end of the nineteenth century and the beginning of the twentieth via motor vehicles. But horse races and horseback riding already existed. Here, sporting activities are organized in the form of races, speed and distance being relevant dimensions: skiing, cycling, car driving, sailing, rowing, civilian horse riding, and so forth all have the same competitive forms.

In that they came from distinct areas of social life and gathered different kinds of agents for different goals, these clusters of physical activities were originally practiced in separate places. The private sphere sheltered bodily care activities; the masculine space of the army contained the activities that prepared one for fighting (a space that was enclosed during the eighteenth century and the nineteenth); the local space, where community festivals and school took place, was the locus for adults' and children's games, which became athletic sporting games;[1] and, last, roads, lines of communication, and vacation resorts provided the arenas for games and sports derived from transportation techniques. All these activities found new sites and got closer to each other in modern sports facilities.

THE MAKING OF THE FIELD

When the sports field appeared in France, about 1885–1900, it was the result of a double process of transformation:

In parallel with the importation of some completely new activities (for example, athletic sports from England), already existing physical activities that belonged to diverse areas were dissociated from their habitual uses,[2] and they were transformed in shape and the way they were actualized so as to become sports. In the areas of military training, school and popular games, and transportation activities, this affected shooting, fencing, horse riding, walking, cycling, and the like. They gained autonomy from the logic to which they had been subject and took the form of sports (Vigarello 1988): military exercise was no longer practiced to prepare for war but to perform; school games were no longer played strictly for fun or education but for victory; transportation techniques were no longer used to move from one place to another but to stage a race.

As all these activities lost their original way of being performed, they tended to get closer to each other, to aggregate, to be incorporated into a common space, and to acquire some common features through a movement of coalescence (crystallization) through which the field was made.

"Much but by no means all of worldmaking consists of taking apart and putting together, often conjointly," says Goodman (1978: 7). So in the field that appeared about 1900, gymnastics, sports, and other forms of bodily exercises confronted each other and began to search for common principles and common forms of organization. We can speak, in that case, of a field of sports and physical activities rather than of a sports field.

Historical research shows that the original stake in France was to introduce bodily education into the academic training of children of the upper classes and, beyond that, to convert adults to a more active and competitive way of life. The making of the field took place at a very dynamic and conflict-ridden time in the social and political history of France. The working class had begun to organize itself into trade unions and political movements, which began to influence social relationships,[3] and the political system adopted modern features like an expanded masculine electorate, several mass political parties, and a free political press. The republican regime that reformed primary schools in the 1880s lost its reformist impetus after 1895–1900 and failed to reform secondary education (or did not try to do so). Sporting education was abandoned at this level of the school system, as were other points of the planned reform.

In this context, sports enthusiasts committed themselves to a kind of proselytism and began a true moral crusade (Gusfield 1963), proposing new ways to achieve physical salvation through bodily exercise (in Weber's term). The first actions of Pierre de Coubertin went in this direction, for example, the foundation of a Comité pour la Propagation des Exercices Physiques dans l'Education in 1887 (MacAloon 1981). Sporting education was proposed as part of a social reform program that encouraged the ruling classes to change their way of living and their manner of educating children and to adopt a new conception of education that transmitted a taste for action and physical effort.

When this attempt failed, sport developed outside the French school system. Sporting education remained foreign to the French public lycée: sporting activities were on the fringe, teachers gave preference to gymnastics practiced in a collective, patriotic manner rather than to the elite sports, and sporting activities were relegated to the "secondary pleasures of life" among the established bourgeoisie (Arnaud 1991).

However, the bourgeois milieux provided the core of the sporting population in many sports. Entrepreneurs invested money in sport business from 1900 onward, and the ruling positions in sport organizations were broadly held by members of the aristocracy and the bourgeoisie (Defrance 1987b). But on a cultural level and in relation to the school system, sport had low value. Sporting experience and competence, which began to constitute a capital in the sporting field, could not be converted into cultural capital, and so they remained defined as simply biological resources.

These facts attest that there were links between the sporting field and the field of power, but they also show the very dominated position of the sporting field in France (compared with the English case) during the first stage of its formation.

PROCESS OF COALESCENCE: A LOGICAL INTEGRATION INTO A WHOLE

The transformation of a set of practices of physical activity already established or newly imported into a sporting field took place as the scope of these activities began to broaden, and they all began to be called by the same word, *sport* (in French). In France the term was applied to the athletic sporting activities imported from England around 1880–85 (association football, rugby, track and field, rowing, and so on) as well as to other forms of physical activity that lacked the characteristic features of sport. The use of the word *sport* spread around 1900, and it had two meanings: it pointed to the generic category of bodily exercise broadly speaking (with uses like *le sport, les sociétés sportives*), and it was simultaneously applied to a specific category of physical activity, namely, athletic sports, implying that there were training programs, competitions, physical performances, and so on.

I don't mean that the sporting field existed only because a new linguistic use of the word *sport* appeared, but that this new use of the word, the semantic field of which was thereby widened and redefined, indicated the beginning of the logical integration of a set of formerly heterogeneous physical activities into a whole and the genesis of a classification that could conceive of their common features. From 1910 to about 1915, the Comité National des Sports (CNS) listed the following sporting and nonsporting organizations in five general categories: the *Saint Hubert* (hunting with hounds) under "equestrian and cynegetic sports"; the Union Vélocipédique de France (UVF; cycling) under "mechanical sports"; the Union des Sociétés Française de Sports Athlétiques (USFSA) under "athletic sports," which included athletics, football, "traditional games," which included Basque pelota after 1910; and the Union des Sociétés de Gymnastique de France (USGF) under "gymnastics."

This integration was also put into practice in the material organization of sport, with a duality of notions of sport, the definition of which was discussed in the field. On one side, there were encompassing organizations that used the term *sport*, like the CNS, an umbrella organization set up in 1908, although this committee included people who practiced exercises that did not have sporting characteristics and other people who rejected some of them, in particular systematic individual competition. This was the case of the gymnasts in the Union des Sociétés de Gymnastique de France, who preferred gymnastic festivals with collective tests rather than individual contests (Defrance 1987a). The term *sport* was used as a metacategory, a federative label for organizations that had very divergent positions about the purposes and orientations of physical education and about the social practice of physical activities. Simultaneously, the word *sportsman* (used in French) pointed to people who practiced pure sport, that is, a sport invented by the British and imitated by French promoters who had lived or traveled in England and who knew the methods of the British public schools.

PROCESS OF DISSOCIATION BETWEEN SPORT AND UTILITARIAN PHYSICAL ACTIVITY

As the field was generated and structured, tensions and debates grew over what should be the correct practices of physical activity. Contention over the definition of the right ways of practicing sport appeared, opposing useful sporting activity and pure performing sport, operating through several sets of relations.

One of these relations opposed hygienist-physicians and competitive sportsmen and bore upon the question of the right intensity of physical activity that would be beneficial to the health of youth. While the first national sporting organization, the USFSA, dated to 1887, the questioning of sporting practice by professors of medicine began almost immediately, in 1893, at the time of a convention of the French Association for the Advancement of Sciences,[4] an organization founded after the Franco-Prussian War in 1870 to raise the quality of French sciences to the level of the German ones (Digeon 1959). Some physicians took the initiative of defining and imposing a norm of moderation in the practice of physical activity: the Academy of Medicine placed its scientific power into the balance of forces (Arnaud 1980), and some medical writing tried to specify the conditions under which exercise produces useful effects from the standpoint of the biological sciences; there was also an experimental trial to create a medical specialty to supervise the hygienic and therapeutic practice of physical activity (Monet 2003). Physicians failed in this last initiative; however, they did succeed in defining the notion of physical exercise, which came to be distinguished from the notion of sport (Lagrange 1890) and kept health-oriented physical activities separate from the field of sport. But the growing strength of sport at the beginning of the 1920s led to new initiatives by physicians, who founded a medicine of physical education and sport to deal with the sporting field, while reviving the tensions between medical criteria of the utility of exercise for health, on the one hand, and sporting criteria of sportsmanship, on the other (Defrance and El Boujjoufi 2005).

Another tension brought schoolteachers into conflict with members of sporting clubs, and this conflict had more complex lines. French educators became attached to gymnastics at the end of the nineteenth century, the only kind of physical activity conceived as having a rational impact on children's bodies and instincts, and the only activity deemed to be methodical and delimited, observable and measurable. But as the reform of the school system reinforced gymnastics, competitive sport was excluded from the school curriculum and relegated to leisure activities for schoolboys (*associations sportives scolaires*). Educational gymnastics were opposed to sporting games. But two developments transformed this opposition. In gymnastics a competitive trend appeared, which tended to make some gymnasts specialize in a few difficult exercises listed in the program of the Olympic Games, a program formed by de Coubertin in 1896 without the agreement of gymnastics organizations (USGF and the International Federation). A sporting gymnastics ("useless," competitive, and individual) was in gestation. Conversely, in sporting milieux, a wide trend supported so-called useful sport, for which sporting practice was adapted; for educational sportsmen, the ideal was to refuse specialization in one sport, to dismiss competition, to minimize technical training, and so on, while emphasizing the effort and adaptation required by learning sports in general, the importance of personal relationships, respect for rules and players' dignity, and the goal of the complete physical and moral development of youth. In these conditions, gymnasts were no longer contrasted with sportsmen, as in 1890, for there were supporters of the gratuitousness of exercise among the former and supporters of the usefulness of exercise among the latter.

Finally, the most explicit tension was the one that opposed soldiers and sportsmen because it could be expressed in the common language of politics. It was formulated gradually but became an explicit opposition after the First World War.

In the first stage we observe some explicit divergences between gymnasts, who were close to the army and preferred a complete, useful, collective exercise that prepared youth for the defense of the country, and sportsmen, who chose so-called gratuitous activity practiced simply for the pleasure of competitive excitement. Political categories helped to structure the arguments, with notions like patriotism, equality, Republic, and so on (Defrance 1987a: chaps. 3–4). Depending on where they confronted each other, the opposition between gymnasts and sportsmen was more or less pronounced. This opposition was temporarily curtailed when sportsmen promoted an educative project and supported a varied practice aimed at developing the whole body, but it was revived in the 1910s, when sportsmen began to specialize in only one sport and focused on the unique pleasure of a single sporting game, association football (Wahl 1986). Expressing the wish to practice this kind of sport only, without any mention of military training or the collective values of patriotism, this trend became sharper after the First World War under the influence of pacifism, even if sportsmen didn't refer openly to such a political sensibility.[5] Ceremonies for sportsmen who had died in the war increased during the 1920s, and when a "circuit of the battlefields" was proposed to cycle racers,[6] a journalist suggested that public money would be better spent in building stadiums than in erecting war memorials.[7] Meanwhile, the sporting group in the National Assembly asked for the sports budget to be allocated to sporting federations, and not, via ministries, to military and school physical education.[8] For this group to dissociate itself from collective patriotic surges was not an insignificant development, but keeping that distance allowed sporting organizations to continue the trend toward specialization and, in spite of an attempt to reestablish a multisport umbrella group in the 1920s through the Union des Fédérations Françaises de Sports Athlétiques (UFFSA),[9] the specialized model definitively triumphed. At the same time, the control exercised by the army over school physical education and civilian sport was suppressed in 1927–28, when the public administration of physical education and sport was transferred from the Ministry of War to the Ministry of Education.

There remained one frontier of the field where the two logics of physical activity, the useful one and the competitive one, could almost be reconciled: the frontier that separated transportation and tourist activities from mechanical sports and exploration (see lower left in figure 1). Here there was an industrial pole that defined sport and the frontiers of the space of sports differently from other poles. A sociological analysis shows that positions in this pole were occupied by a professional and business bourgeoisie, whose liberal industrial values were more attuned to the gratuitous practice of sports. Here, the gap between sporting practice and useful activity decreased. Research has to be done on this topic, but many difficulties confront an empirical historical survey of this milieu, which requires locating of private archives.

Once I sketch this debate about the correct manner of practicing physical activity, that is, for its social utility or for itself, I can analyze the relations formed between the field of sports and physical activities and what is explicitly outside the field: meaning the physical exercise proposed by physicians, the physical education of teachers, the military training of the army, and transportation and exploration techniques promoted by the industries of transport and tourism.

II. Process of Achieving Autonomy and Fluctuation of Relative Autonomy

When a field is formed it maintains relations with the institutions from which it has become autonomous; relative autonomy does not mean isolation. The structures of relations in the field are a function of the relations on the frontiers, the relations that each sporting group forms with external forces, whether army, school, medicine, or industry. As Kurt Lewin said, "The boundary conditions of a field are essential characteristics of that field" (Lewin 1964: 57).

Two bundles of relationships with external forces produced divergence and long-standing debates and thus internal splits and new structural relationships in the sports field in France: (1) relationships of sportsmen with the economic market, given the attraction of competitions that promised prizes and the temptation of professionalism; and (2) relationships with politicized groups, religious or *anticlerical* groups, trade unions, and political parties. These two factors changed as sporting practices spread and gained autonomy. Without treating this subject in detail, I will briefly survey the dynamics of these relationships.

A SOCIAL HISTORY OF AMATEURISM

Controversies about professionalizing sporting activities pit economic groups willing to put up money for sport against their opponents, the amateurs, who denied having any financial motivation in their practice of sport. The denial had been built upon the aristocratic ethic of amateurism coming from England; it expressed the detachment of individuals with superior social status, exempted from earning their living and proud of their passion for sport. With the arrival of the first professional sportsmen of lower social extraction, such as cycle racers and some swimmers, disinterestedness could symbolize the taste for a sport played for itself, even if the values of self-control and self-education were not lacking.

With the spread of sport to the lower middle classes, the refusal of monetary benefit acquired a new meaning, all the more so since offers of payment became more numerous. The refusal of bonuses resulted no longer from financial affluence, but from an increasingly strained attachment to protecting youth from the corrupting power of money. The position taken by the physical educator Georges Hébert in 1925 conveyed this perception (Hébert 1925).[10] A moralizing amateurism was becoming stronger in the 1920s.

The conceptions became even more ambiguous in the 1930s, when the question of training necessary for managers and sporting educators (the term *coaches* was not yet in use) arose. The question was taken up by the state; public authorities began to support and subsidize amateur sports, and not only gymnastics. But at the same time, some in the senior civil service began to criticize voluntary sports organizations for their shortcomings, especially since expectations about sports were growing. The outcome was to discredit federal leaders, using schemas that participated in the symbolic reversal of the notion of amateur, already mentioned in sociological works (Freidson 1986). The amateur who in 1890 practiced an activity—whether politics, literature, or sports—because he liked it and had a passion for it had been considered a more reliable, more committed person than a professional who carried out the same activity for money. Later, values of professionalism were strengthened, and specific training gave professionals a better reputation, one of stability and competence. The image of the professional began to overshadow that of the amateur. The ascent of professions and the affirmation of technocratic ideologies in the 1930s constituted steps in the reinterpretation of these notions and stimulated a critique of amateur practices and voluntary organizations. This movement began in France in a context dominated by the antiparliamentary right, about 1929–34, when the attention of the sports press was focused on the Fascist Italian sports organization, which was taken as a model of organizational efficiency.[11] By comparison, French sports organization seemed rather weak.

As criticism of established organizations grew, some amateur federations reinforced their public positions in the early 1930s and decided to exclude athletes and clubs that had any contact with professionalism: for example, the Track and Field Federation expelled a very popular champion, the runner Jules Ladoumègue, in 1932; the image of voluntary organizations became a little more tarnished as the sports press attacked them tooth and nail (Lassus and Guillaume 2000). Other signs show that the denial of economic values and of the relationships with economic interests had changed between the first stage in the making of the field (1900–1927) and the second stage (1927–60). While the relationships between sport and the state became stronger, a tripolar structure of relations was now taking shape among sports, sponsoring corporations, and public bodies (a subject about which research should be developed).

UNEVEN AUTONOMY IN THE FIELD: NEUTRAL POLE AND COMMITTED POLE

The feeble autonomy of the field of sports and physical activities is well illustrated by the social history of gymnastics. The close relation between gymnastics and patriotic (moral) education that persisted into the twentieth century was the continuation of the orientations of the nineteenth century, which produced the *bataillons scolaires*, a kind of school military training combined with gymnastics in the primary school from 1882 up to 1890. This conception received new impetus just before the First World War and then declined. It was still represented by USGF, the gymnasts' organization, and by diverse unions for military training, the influence of which faded in the 1930s.

For defenders of such forms of physical activity, nothing was more absurd than wanting to practice exercise for itself (autonomy), that is, exercise without any social utility or meaning (rejecting moral, religious, or political purposes). Other groups besides patriots had the same viewpoint and chose activities related to superior principles borrowed from political, religious, or pedagogical thought (dependence). The period from 1895 to 1930, particularly the 1920s, was when one pole in the field clearly claimed its preference for dependence. A growing number of organizations managed sporting practices in the name of political convictions and religious beliefs and bound gymnastics or sport to morality as part of a policy for youth. Some organizations, like the Fédération des Patronages (1903) and the Union Chrétienne des Jeunes Gens (c. 1910–20), educated Catholic and Christian sportsmen and sportswomen; others, like the Fédération Sportive Socialiste (1908), were for young socialist sporting workers; still others, like the Fédération Sportive du Travail (1923) and the Fédération des Œuvres Laïques d'Education Physique (1927), served, respectively, future revolutionaries under the control of the Communist Party and young anticlericals. Each organization had its own championships, gymnastic festivals, and sporting competitions. As shown by Philippe Tichit in a monograph study of four industrial districts in the north of France, in the 1920s and 1930s sports associations in a single town would belong to federations with divergent philosophies and so never actually encountered each other (Tichit 1997). The organization of sport at the local level was divided in accordance with preexisting social divisions, this correspondence being a sign of the lack of autonomy vis-à-vis the field of social relationships. In separating the players, this kind of organization avoided direct conflicts between teams from the same town who diverged on ideological principles.

The profusion of organizations reached a peak about 1930, although sportsmen were not so numerous in France as in England and Germany. The division concerned the smallest associations as well as the biggest competitions. For example, working-class sports organizations created the Workers' Olympic Games (up to 1936); women, whose participation had been refused by the International Olympic Committee, had the Women's Olympic Games (up to 1934); there were Unionist International Games for the Protestants (1927) and Catholic International Contests (1932–39) (Dumons and Pollet 1992).

In that state of the field, when soccer players on a Catholic team took part in a competition they were always matched against regional clubs from the same parish, whether they were much superior or inferior in accomplishment. Therefore every year the match results could be the same. The priority was not to constitute homogeneous groups or leagues (divisions) or to offer a possibility of promotion to a higher league; rather, the aim was to revive a kind of community relationship among neighboring Christian assemblies. In other words, the structuring of sporting relationships reproduced lines of social divisions and, moreover, fostered and underlined social bonds that were not intrinsically sporting bonds. According to a monograph study of a rural community in the west of France, this situation persisted in some regions up until the early 1960s (Fradétal 1982).

Finally, the principle of a community of sporting interests, which intends to gather everyone who has a passion for the same sport and which is the *illusio* of the sports field, is less powerful than the principle of the community of social interests generated outside the sports field. These underlying heteronomous principles include the following:

Class relationships: select clubs remained apart from open clubs: the main thing for members of select clubs was to remain among others from high society.

Race relations: for example, segregation was the rule in the clubs of the colonies and was justified by racial categorizations (Deville-Danthu 1997: 51). (But attitudes were complex, and the sports press perceived segregation in other countries like the United States as more racist than the attitudes observed in France.)

Gender relations: men and women were separated; men were to stay among men, while women were to exercise among other women and beyond the gaze of men.

Religious and political convictions: believers and anticlericals were separated, as were the political right and left.

The fragmentation of sports organizations resulted in a weakening of sports during the 1910s and 1920s; they reached their weakest point about 1930, showing that the autonomy of sports practice from social and political involvements remained low.

But we have to take into account the divergence over the purposes of sports practice, which determined the formation of two opposite poles, one acting to foster and reinforce the bonds of sport with superior ends defined by established institutions, the other claiming to be neutral with respect to political ideologies. Consequently, the autonomization of the field was uneven and depended on which pole of the field is examined; it can no longer be globally measured.

THE QUESTION OF POLITICAL NEUTRALITY

The denial of economic interest and the rejection of political commitment show the will of some sportsmen to extricate themselves from bonds of dependence that they perceived to be an obstacle to the development of their practice. But fields are "open spaces, constrained to find necessary resources outside of themselves" (Bourdieu 1988: 49). The question of the neutrality of sport illustrates this point.

The theme of neutral sport emerged in the 1920s, in the face of workers' sports and of the sports policies of Fascist states. It was first promoted by sports that accepted professionalism and the help of economic interests, so that a dual structure appeared: on one side were sports backed by private corporations (cycling, association football), which proclaimed their ideological neutrality; on the other side were sports that claimed to be strictly amateur (demanded by the state, which granted subsidies), but that were involved in the education of youth and the alleged renovation of the race. Both sides claimed a form of independence but each was bound up in a kind of trusteeship.

Neutrality was loudly proclaimed by one of the most powerful sports leaders of the 1930s, Jules Rimet, president of the French Federation of Association Football (FFFA) and of the International Federation of Association Football (FIFA). Historical research can observe the conditions in which neutrality could be proclaimed and applied in action, at a time when authoritarian and technocratic policy models had much influence over French politics, first, up to 1934–35, particularly with a political figure like André Tardieu

(Monnet 1993), and then before the war, in 1938–39, when the government dispensed with the votes of the National Assembly. Any political attitude appeared to adopt a party line, and the denial of ties with party politics did not protect sport against involvement in subservience to dominant forces. Rimet admired the sports organization of Nazi Germany after 1936 and then devotedly supported the authoritarian regime of Vichy, thereby revealing the constraints and limits within which the neutral line could be expressed.[12]

However, there were some signs of a brief thrust in the autonomization of the field. An example is workers' sports after 1930. The two workers' sports organizations in France, Socialist and Communist, joined the International Workers' Sports Organizations in the 1920s, expressing their support for politicized policies. But after a period of repression of Communist militants and considering the low membership in politicized sport (in France), some members of the Fédération Sportive du Travail founded a Committee for the Independence of Workers' Sports in 1931. A debate about neutral sport was launched, and, in reaction to the politicized trajectory, a trend in favor of the separation of sports and politics took hold in workers' sports. We find this again after 1945 within the Fédération Sportive et Gymnique des Travailleurs (FSGT), in which one faction defended adhering to the Communist Party while the other defended autonomy. The organization was no longer part of the International Workers' Sports Organization but of a Social-Democrat International Committee, and it eventually joined Olympic sports, agreeing to the principles of neutrality that an institution occupying a central position in the sporting field was expected to adhere to.

The denial of external interests in relation to the field did not imply that the sports field broke every relation with economic and political forces: it meant that a relation developed between these forces and a field that now had a little more autonomy and took into account the autonomy of sporting affairs and their specific logics. (To illuminate this point, I am working on a history of the ways in which the state has intervened in French sports.)

III. Restructuring of the Field

The more the field is autonomous and acquires its own structures, the more the original divisions into types of physical activities (as shown in figure 1) fade away, and the more apparent new divisions and hierarchies become. These are the product of the specific history of the field and of the impacts refracted in that field by the social and cultural history of the practices which take place within it. From the 1930s on, new structural divisions appeared and were stabilized (figure 2).

The separate organization of each sport, whose principles and hierarchic

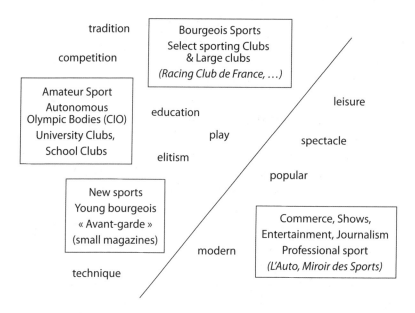

French Field of Physical Activities & Sports, 1930–1950

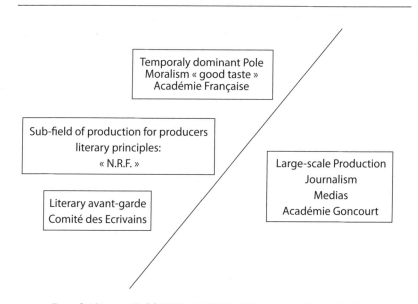

French Literary Field, 1930s & 1940–44 (borrowed from G. Sapiro)

Figure 13.2. French field of physical activities and sports, 1930–50, and French literary field, 1930s and 1940–44 (borrowed from G. Sapiro).

framework were consolidated near the end of the 1920s, cut each sport off from the others. In some of them, the distribution of players according to their positions in social space was concentrated among the upper classes (as in skiing, polo, tennis, and clay pigeon shooting), while some others were occupied by the popular classes (cycle racing, weightlifting, wrestling). The class character of sports, which was blurred in multisports organizations that blended very different sporting practices like boxing and rowing, became more clear-cut in specialized ones. Multisports groupings acquired a new meaning once they were opposed to specialized ones: their doctrinal character was more apparent when they could be compared with neutral federations whose gathering principle was only the choice of one sporting game. Divisions that had occurred before 1925–30 became sharper and began to play a structuring role and to replace earlier differentiating elements.

The distinctive social characteristics of sports in France in the decade 1925–35 have not been well documented, and work has to be done to specify the characteristic features of polo, tennis, track and field, association football, cycle racing, and boxing. But we can note that during this decade the social divisions produced specific impacts as they structured new cleavages in the space of sports.

A growing contrast in the distribution of players according to their position in social space separated sports that stayed amateur from those that (previously or newly) adopted professionalism. The professional ones like association football, cycle racing, and boxing dominated the French space of sporting spectacles and found a place in the growing sports press as it began using more illustrations in the 1920s and 1930s. These conditions in turn permitted their spread among the middle classes—and sometimes among the working classes. Conversely, exclusively amateur sports (at the beginning of the 1930s, track and field [Lassus and Guillaume 2000: chap. 2] and swimming [Terret 1998] succeeded in eradicating all forms of hidden remuneration) were perceived as being more rigorous and elitist practices, and their growth was slower than that of professional sports. More traditional, they were extended only through school practices and military training and so had a wider diffusion among men than among women.

Differences between bourgeois sports and popular sports sharpened, as each sport began to live its own life, to produce its own famous champions, and to be represented by its own leaders. Contrasts between players became stronger. A figure like Georges Carpentier, who was considered in the 1910s and 1920s a stylist and a gentleman boxer, could still give the impression that boxing could appeal to all social groups. But in the 1930s, boxers from working-class backgrounds became the rule. The contrast with the tennis champion was clear, for example, when four French tennis players won the Davis Cup in 1927: Jean Borotra, René Lacoste, Henri Cochet, and Jacques Brugnon. The same social contrast was true of sports leaders. After the breakup of the USFSA in 1920, some leaders managed several federations, for example, Frantz Reichel, who was president of the wrestling, boxing, weightlifting, and hockey federations and also filled positions in other sporting organizations. The representation of diverse sporting practices by the same president did not permit differentiating the image of each one. But Reichel died in 1932, and the sports newspaper *L'Auto* hailed him as one of the last defenders of an outmoded conception of sport (Desgrange 1932). The effort to maintain links among sports was no longer useful; the conception of specialization prevailed, and eventually the social and cultural specificity of each sport became more visible through its managing committee.

A new split began to separate all traditional sports, including bourgeois sports, from activities that have some sporting spirit but claim to be something other than a competitive sport, something more (and not gymnastics). Mountain and rock climbing, judo, and some other new activities thought of themselves as being on the fringe of the sports field, not sporting practices with competition and measurement, but cultivating values very similar to sport and offering very demanding physical activity. In contrast to these newer activities, the traditional character of established sports was reinforced, and some traditions were invented around them, as Eric Hobsbawm as shown in the case of England (Hobsbawm and Ranger 1983: chap. 7). For example, every year from 1929 on, the president of the French Republic attended the football cup final to present the trophy. So there was now a pole of sporting tradition with more social credit, as opposed to the pole of innovation, a kind of "sporting avant-garde." The distribution of those who practiced these new activities according to their positions in social space was almost the same as the distribution in traditional bourgeois sports: this is true of judo in the 1930s (Brousse 2005) and of the technical Alpinism of the Groupe de Haute Montagne, which detached itself from the French Alpine Club (Hoibian 2000). Oppositions between these two poles were encoded in ethical terms, while their social grounds were similar, differing only in the fractions of the bourgeoisie they could attract.

A new map of the space of sports could be drawn in which social differences in sporting practices are more relevant (see figure 2). This differentiation was going to last,[13] although some sports at each pole were revised: for example, at the avant-garde pole that constitutes itself under a logic of fashion. Although the differences were numerous, especially relevant was the opposition between sporting practices associated with the mass-circulation press and elitist sporting practices, more severe or more fashionable, which attracted mainly players from the bourgeoisie and the intellectual professions (on both sides of the oblique line in figure 2). On one hand, the sport was seen by many; on the other hand, it was performed by few. A critical discourse appeared (one that continues to the present) which denigrates the most popular practices, those most associated with the media, money, and professionalism, arguing that they mobilize passive sportsmen rather than true players. Conversely, the mass media developed a critique of amateur and elitist sports, arguing that they were suitable only for "the old legs of the established bourgeoisie" or to excite a few partisans of avant-garde activities.

Conclusion

As it won more autonomy, the field of sport acquired its own features, which in specific circumstances became pronounced. Analyzing the bursts of autonomization offers an opportunity to deepen the analysis of the mechanism through which the field appeared and found a form. From 1900 up to about 1930 the sports field was still forming, and internal struggles ended in the organization of federal monopolies and a hierarchy of powers from the local level up to the international one. At the end of the 1920s sporting powers claimed a margin of autonomy from established fields and with respect to the norms of everyday life. From 1930 up to 1960, in radically changing, often violent historical circumstances (the economic crisis, the Second World War), the sports field survived and defined more precisely its relationships with the state, local authorities, and the entertainment market; its autonomy fluctuated, with ups in 1936–37 and downs in 1940–44. As it stabilized into a hierarchical organization with its own emerging traditions, the sports field began to attract conservative political forces during the 1930s and was much cherished by the Vichy regime under German occupation.

As the field gained autonomy, the agents in the field expressed the stakes in increasingly specific language, which means that categories of thought, vocabulary, and preoccupations became more specific to sport. A proper sporting culture, with strong technical dimensions, was forming and took the place of heteronomous cultural schemes which had been in use in the field when it did not have much autonomy. I have showed how the heteronomous categories of eugenics were employed in the French field of sport and physical activities from 1910 to 1950, with a weakening in the 1930s (Defrance 2000). Afterward, these categories faded away and a technical culture emerged, with a first wave in the 1930s and a second after 1945 (Roger 2003).

The model prompts us to ask about the production and reproduction of a field, the integration and coherence of which are not natural things. Produced by a first phase of the integration of different kinds of physical activities, the field was outlined around 1900 but remained dominated by divisions reflected in the classifications of sporting activities, which were thought of as diverse but which could be gathered into a whole named sport. As the space of sports strengthened its frontiers, reinforced its specific character (for example, the intensity and specificity of bodily practices), and acquired more unified principles of organization, its expressed its autonomy. Political conditions during the 1930s in France led sports leaders to build relationships with the state, which, just before the Second World War, produced a system somewhat more like those of Germany and Italy rather than those of the English and North American models. International comparisons of national sports fields during critical phases of history, such as the period when social policies to combat economic crises were launched in different countries in the 1930s, will deepen this description for the period just outlined (Defrance et al. 1991; Harvey et al. 1993).

The centralized structure of the French sports field is a particular characteristic in comparison with other national sports fields. But the monopolistic power of the federations, almost all headquartered in Paris, remains to be analyzed more precisely.

Struggles to acquire a national federal monopoly over one sport occur in every country. In France the question was resolved for almost all the federations around 1929–35, and the state reinforced the unity of this system. The contrast with other countries is obvious, for example, the United States, where the competition in the sports entertainment market was so strong that it produced a dispersal of the organizing powers, as we see in the history of basketball leagues in the 1940s and 1950s (Vincent 1981). The stabilization of federal power permitted the imposition of institutional coherence in the French sports field (Simon 1990).

A centralized field is more manageable by the state, but it does provide sports leaders with more unified forces in negotiating with the state. However, a work in progress shows that centralization does not mean unity in this case: sports organizations do not show much solidarity with each other, and often the center tries to speak in the name of sport as a whole while dominating a profoundly divided space. Distance, tensions, and conflicts between the center and provincial clubs are common phenomena in this form of organization. Relations between a concentrated, centralized power and dispersed, grass-roots clubs that have limited membership are often strained and result in conflict. French relations are encoded in generic political symbols that set Paris in opposition to the regions, a phenomenon that a political sociology can grasp, as I showed in a study of conflicts in track and field during the 1970s and 1980s (Defrance 1989).

A contingent, that is, historical, fact is that the completion of the process of monopolization happened during the 1930s in France, in cultural and political conditions marked by crisis and the impact of authoritarian and antidemocratic political models. The effect was to produce a specific alliance between federal sports monopolies influenced by state control and antiparliamentary ideologies and parts of the civil service. As a result, private bodies became allied with public powers, even before the period of German occupation. We perceive here the "Republican roots of the Vichy regime," as the historian Gérard Noiriel says (Lenoir 2003; Noiriel 1999), and we disclose the origins of this original national organization, that of sport à la française, as Jean-Michel Faure and Charles Suaud put it (Faure 1999).

The sports field seems to be more clearly delimited than some other fields, for example, the literary field, and the positions of athletes in the specific hierarchy of positions in the field are better objectified than those of writers.[14] But positions in the sports field were not defined by competitive records alone, and the access to power positions resulted from many other conditions, which became specific to the sports field only when it gained autonomy. An analysis of the biographical trajectories of the leaders of sports organizations according to the autonomy of the field is ongoing.

Normalization of sporting events was one of the stakes of the federal monopolization of a national space (action which standardizes all the conditions in which performance takes place, so as to bring about strict equality among competitors). Once achieved at the national level, it was possible for the leaders to strive in the international space to impose the national standards onto other countries: on this point, French leaders were very competitive and occupied leading positions in many international federations in the 1920s. Sports leaders who were normalizing the conditions of sporting performance could actualize dispositions they had developed in economic affairs, where normalization was at issue (a private agency, the AFNOR, was created by industrialists to normalize products and services in 1926; then a public committee was organized within the Ministry of Trade and Industry in 1930, later than in England and the United States) (Igalens 1954).

I have outlined here a field analysis, from the genesis to the first outbursts of autonomy. The objective of structural history led to our asking whether observed transformations have some coherence, whether changes occur in some synchrony, and how the objects under study are related in a determinate

TABLE 1 States of the Field of Physical Activities and Sports, 1900–1975

	1900–1927/30	1927/30–1955	1955–1975
Useful activities/ "pure" sport	Useful ways of practice in every sport	Pure competitive sport challenging useful practices	Domination of competition
Sporting club life and relations	Sociability more important than training for competition	Sociability + training for competition with a few coaches	Preponderance of training and competitive culture
Federations	Multisports organizations (USFSA) or education-oriented organizations	Struggles between educational/ competitive orientations	Power of Technical National Managers (DTN), domination of specialized federations
Professionalism/ amateurism	Domination of amateurism, or reconciled with professionalism (cycling)	Ban on professionals, or schisms in organizations for professionalism (rugby in 1932)	Amateurism supported by the State plus "incomplete professionalism"
Formal training of teachers of physical education (P.E.)	No formal training for P.E. teachers or for coaches	Formal training in P.E. (1 year) 1927–: first federal training courses for coaches, 1929–	Extension of state certificate for coaches; Longer training for P.E. teachers (3, then 4 years)
Physical education curriculum	Gymnastics	Gymnastics and outdoor activities: French method 1925	Sporting P.E., 1961/67–
Access to management positions	Celebrities becoming sports managers	Managers stemming from sport's milieu	Managers stemming from sport's milieu plus State's Technical Managers
Central state organization	Administrative supervision: Ministry of Home Affairs and Ministry of War	Administrative supervision: Ministry of National Education or of Health; special body in 1940–44	Administrative supervision: separate ministry for youth and sport

social structure (Viala 1987). For that purpose, I analyzed a set of elements, of relations, and of organizational features, and I have discussed their transformations from the formational stage up to the middle of the twentieth century. Now a chronological outline can be proposed, with a table summarizing the transformations (table 1).

As we can see, doing social and cultural history as an observer armed with a theory, the sociological theory of Bourdieu in this case, still means working like a historian and requires much empirical work. But when we wonder what questions to ask, what files to open, what relations to scrutinize, and so on, the model of the social world that Bourdieu proposed helps us to articulate historical objects (Pinto 1998). The theoretical model—here, the idea of the space of sports; elsewhere, the notion of field of power—"provides us with . . . warnings and programmatic guidelines," as Bourdieu put it; it helps me to "choose my objects in a different way and . . . to maximize what I get out of monographs" (Bourdieu 1990e: 160). "The notion of field does not provide ready-made answers to all possible queries. . . . Rather, its major virtue . . . is that it promotes a mode of construction that has to be rethought anew every time. It forces us to raise questions: about the limits of the universe under investigation, how it is 'articulated', to what and to what degree, etc. It offers a coherent system of recurrent questions that saves us from theoretical vacuum of positivist empiricism and from the empirical void of theoretical discourse" (Bourdieu and Wacquant 1992: 110). That is to say, concepts and model work as a set of research questions and help give a coherence to historical inquiry. It does not provide answers, but it stimulates us to elaborate some hypotheses.

Notes

The translation was revised by Susan Emanuel.

1. Schools function in the local sphere, except for English private schools and French classic Collèges of the seventeenth century and the eighteenth. For France, see Chartier, Compère, and Julia (1976). For England, see Dunning (1977).

2. Dating the genesis of a sporting field is not dating the invention or the importation of a new activity that finds a place in it.

3. The main working-class trade union, the Confédération Générale du Travail, was founded in 1895, and the Socialist Party won growing representation in the Parliament.

4. Running is explicitly pointed out as a harmful practice by Bouchard (1893).

5. Pacifism is a fundamental value in the thought of Pierre de Coubertin. See Clastres (2004). For pacifism among war veterans, see Prost and Billois (1977).

6. Anonymous (1919).

7. Dudon (1920).

8. Neumeyer (1919).

9. This union tried to revive the old multisports union, the USFSA, which had been dissolved in 1920; it existed from 1920 to 1929 but didn't succeed in countering specialization.

10. For an analysis of its reception, see Defrance (1993).

11. Fascist Italy is mentioned in the French sports press in 1926 for its building of big stadiums and for the commitment of its political leaders to sporting affairs, for example, Anonymous (1928), which describes the Italian system without making any critical comment.

12. Jules Rimet's positions on this subject are covered in an article by Goddet (1940). It

is reported, just under the headline, that Rimet is ready to resign his post as president of CNS and that he supports the creation of a unique authoritarian body to control and manage all the federations. For an analysis, see Defrance (2007).

13. Some features of the French sports field remained as late as the end of the 1970s. See Defrance and Pociello (1993); Pociello (1981).

14. Comparisons between fields are possible. See, e.g., Bourdieu (1993a); Sapiro (1996).

BOURDIEUSIAN THEORY AND HISTORICAL ANALYSIS
Maps, Mechanisms, and Methods

The preceding chapters have given ample proof that it is both possible and fruitful to analyze sociohistorical change in Bourdieusian terms. The purpose of this conclusion is to elaborate, systematize, and reflect on the larger project of which these chapters are a part: the development of a Bourdieusian approach to historical analysis. I will divide these reflections into three parts. In the first and longest, entitled "Maps," I will show that Pierre Bourdieu's three master concepts, field, capital, and habitus, can be elaborated into a more general framework for describing sociohistorical change and tracing out causal interconnections. In the second and shorter part, entitled "Methods and Mechanisms," I will identify some of the basic methodological principles that underlie Bourdieu's explanatory practice, and I will do so via some reverse engineering on what is surely Bourdieu's most sophisticated piece of historical analysis and arguably his most methodologically sophisticated work *tout court*: *The Rules of Art* (Bourdieu 1996a). I will argue that Bourdieu's approach to sociological explanation is dialectical and dialogical and that his approach to historical transformation is conjunctural and mechanismic. In the third and final section I consider the relative advantages and disadvantages of Bourdieusian theory vis-à-vis rival theories and explanatory practices, particularly rational choice theory and cultural Marxism.

The emphasis in this conclusion on system and method will perhaps strike some readers as un-Bourdieusian. After all, wasn't Bourdieu a sworn enemy of "theoretical theory" and "methodologism," one who insisted that the best way to develop a theory was to confront it with new objects, and that we should choose our methods to fit our objects rather than the other way around? Indeed, he was and he did! But he was not a naïve historicist or empiricist who abjured theoretical and methodological reflection. On the contrary, two of his most influential books, *Outline of a Theory of Practice* and *The Logic of Prac-*

tice, are devoted entirely to reflections of this sort (Bourdieu 1977, 1990a [1980]). And in the years before he died, he was attempting to develop a general theory of fields.[1] His only concern was that the quest for generalization and routinization not lead us to reify particular concepts or fetishize particular methods. So what follows here should be construed not as an attempt to fix the meaning of his concepts or the tenets of his approach, but as an initial effort to develop some new conceptual tools and methodological axioms that might prove useful in and be sharpened through a new wave of sociohistorical research.

Maps

Bourdieu's *oeuvre* does not contain a general theory of social change of the sort contained in Karl Marx's "Communist Manifesto" or, even more succinctly, in his "Preface to the Critique..." (Marx and Engels 1978). Nor does it contain the sort of distilled narrative of world history embedded in Max Weber's "Religious Rejections of the World and Their Directions" (Weber 1964). What it does contain is a number of "sensitizing concepts" (Blumer 1954; Emirbayer and Mische 1998) that can be used to describe various forms and levels of sociohistorical change and to reconstruct the complex and variable causal connections between them. I am thinking, of course, of his master concepts of field, capital, and habitus. In what follows, I will inventory some of the ways in which Bourdieu himself used these concepts as mapping devices and propose various elaborations on these usages that could be useful for the historical researcher.

FIELDS

I begin, as Bourdieu himself generally did, with the concept of the field. In his efforts to elucidate this concept, Bourdieu often invoked the metaphors of the force field and the playing field (Bourdieu and Wacquant 1992). They are meant to be complementary. The metaphor of the force field evokes the objective character and structuring effects of the social field, the ways in which fields are external to actors and prior to actions. Just as a magnetic field causes iron filings to arrange themselves into particular patterns, Bourdieu suggests, so social fields cause individual actors to arrange themselves into structured relations (that is, hierarchical and doxical relations) (Bourdieu 1984b: 149). By contrast, the metaphor of the playing field suggests the role of subjective perceptions and strategic action in the dynamics of fields and, more generally, of the structuring effects of human action, of the ways in which actors and actions are phenomenologically prior to and constitutive of fields (Bourdieu and Wacquant 1992: 118). Like a playing field, a social field is a space for "serious play" governed by general rules and driven by both individual tactics and collective strategies. The two metaphors are thus complementary in the sense that they point not to two dimensions of fields, but to two *moments* in their analysis and existence: one objectivistic or static or both, the other subjectivistic or dynamic or both.

How can the field concept be used to map processes of change? Or, to put it in more constructivist terms, what sorts of change become visible on a map of fields? I begin, again, as Bourdieu usually does, by looking at objective changes, by which I mean changes in objective relations, either in the structure of positions within fields or in relations between fields. In what follows, I will discuss five forms of field change: genesis, autonomy, size, shape, and boundaries.

Genesis. The genesis of a new field—what is traditionally called functional or institutional differentiation—is the subject of *The Rules of Art*, which analyzes the emergence of the literary field in nineteenth-century France (Bourdieu 1996a). In what sense is the literary field new? Bourdieu does not mean to suggest that literary production did not begin until 1870; obviously, books and even novels of a generic sort were being written long before this. Rather, he contends that literary production prior to this time was subsumed within other fields and obeyed the logics of these other fields—a logic of patronage dictated by the court and the nobility, for instance, or a logic of the market, dictated by publishers and consumers. Only in the late nineteenth century, he contends, did some writers carve out a space and a logic of their own, the space of the avant-garde where literature was produced for literature's sake, thereby becoming literature, as opposed to mere fiction. The pioneers in this process, the ones who staked out and defined the new field, were heroic, bohemian writers like Charles Baudelaire and, even more, Gustave Flaubert. The genesis of this field was accompanied by the development of a new logic for the production and consumption of literature and by the formation of a new, dominant elite that articulated and also embodied this logic. Fields do not just appear; they also disappear, as in the case of "the court society" of the ancien régime so aptly described by Norbert Elias (Elias 2006). The monastic field met a similar fate in many parts of western Europe. How do we know that a new field has appeared or that an old one has disappeared? Objectively speaking, we look for the appearance or disappearance of a set of social positions and dispositions that is structured hierarchically and doxically. In standard sociologese, we look for a new elite and a new ideology—such as the avant-garde writers and the avant-garde principle (*l'art pour l'art*) that emerges in France in the late nineteenth century. In sum, a field exists if, and to the degree that, it has an autonomous elite and an autonomous logic.

Autonomy/Heteronomy. The autonomy of a field is not really an either/or proposition; it is a matter of degree. Objectively speaking, an autonomous field exists if and to the degree that we can identify a structured set of social positions. In assessing the autonomy of a field, we might focus on just how clearly specified, codified, and bounded this set of positions is. By this standard, for example, in contemporary America the university field is probably more autonomous, more fieldlike, than, say, the literary field since it is much clearer in the first case than in the second precisely what the price of entry into the field is (namely, a doctorate), who is and is not a serious player, which positions, that is, which universities, which disciplines, which specialties, are more and less prestigious and more and less orthodox, on the basis of, for example, student enrollments, faculty salaries, national rankings, and so forth. Within the literary field, by contrast, I suspect this would probably be a good deal harder to determine, not just for methodological or operational reasons, but because the literary field is objectively less fieldlike. Daniele Steele and Jonathan Lethem will probably not agree about the boundaries of literature or about the relative merits of other writers.

I would urge that we draw an additional distinction between autonomy and heteronomy, which are sometimes conflated. Autonomy may be defined as a function of the stucturedness of positions within a given field, while heteronomy is the degree to which this structuredness is influenced by other fields. The more systematic and explicit the structure and logic of a field are, the more autonomous it is; the more that structure and logic are distorted by actors and principles of neighboring fields, the more heteronomous it is. By this standard, one might hypothesize that the fields of legal education and business education (centered on law and business schools) are likely to be more heteronomous than, say, history or sociology departments, insofar as their internal structures, their hierarchies, and their *doxa* are probably more strongly influenced by the structures of other fields, specifically, the fields of private law practice and the corporate business world than is the case for history or sociology, which are not much influenced by or connected with the economic or the political fields.[2] The reverse is also true: as Bourdieu himself has amply shown in *The State Nobility*, academic titles and titleholders have become more and more important within the worlds of business and politics, and this has altered the internal structure of those fields. So heteronomy is a two-way street. That said, there may be more traffic in one direction than in the other. The relative volume of the traffic, however, is an empirical question rather than a theoretical one.

Size, Shape, and Boundaries. The foregoing forms of field change—appearance and disappearance, autonomy and heteronomy—have been analyzed by Bourdieu himself and by a number of the contributors to this book. But the field metaphor suggests other forms of change as well, such as changes in size, shape, and boundaries, which have not been explored so extensively here or elsewhere. To begin with size: this is relatively easy to conceptualize, though probably more difficult to measure. Personnel and resources are two potential indicators of size. In Bourdieusian terms, we might define a change in the size of a field as a change in the total population of individual positions contained within it. We could further distinguish between absolute and relative changes in the size of a field. Such changes in size are, in fact, a key indicator of transformations within the social space as a whole and a key dimension of variation between social spaces. For example, the fact that universities have generally grown in modern societies while churches have experienced more varied fates (growth in the United States, shrinkage in Europe) tells us much about the class structure of these societies and about how they differ from one another. The size and prestige of the Christian clergy in American society are certainly things that set it apart from that of many European societies. (Bourdieusians interested in studying relations within and between fields could learn a great deal from organizational sociologists and institutionalist theory.)

This line of questioning suggests another: changes in the boundaries of fields. This form of change is one Bourdieu occasionally mentioned but never explicitly theorized (Bourdieu 2004d [2001]: 43ff; Bourdieu and Wacquant 1992: 17). I suggest that we distinguish between two basic forms of boundary change: changes in location and changes in permeability. Changes in the location of a boundary can be of two types: zero-sum or non-zero-sum. By zero-sum boundary change I mean expansion of one field that occurs through encroachment on and contraction of a neighboring field or fields. The process commonly referred to as secularization can be conceived as a form of zero-sum boundary change in which religious officials, elites, and organizations cede positions and resources to nonreligious ones—to scientists and universities, to psychologists and clinics, to social workers and welfare programs, and so on (Chaves 1994; Martin 1978; Smith 2003). By non-zero-sum boundary change I mean expansion or contraction of one field that is not accompanied by contraction or expansion of another. Contraction occurs when a well-bounded, rule-governed arena of social life devolves into a more anarchic and anomic situation. An example of this would be the state of disorder—and possibility—that follows the collapse of state institutions, that is, revolution (Garcelon 2006). This would be an instance of negative-sum change. In positive-sum change relatively uncultivated (if not unoccupied) regions of social space are enclosed, that is, colonized and exploited to the profit of a particular class. The agricultural metaphor is not just a metaphor in this case; it is also the paradigmatic example of the primitive accumulation of capital through the enclosure of a common (Marx 1976). But it is hardly the only example. The growth of various helping and policing professions could be interpreted in very similar terms. Indeed, much of Foucault's lifework might be seen as an attempt to map this process through Western history—and to raise an anarchistic cry against it (Foucault 1995, 1978, 1980, 1988). Populist resistance to the enclosure of wild regions of social space can be an underlying motivation for certain forms of lower-class protest against the culturally dominant. Indeed, this may be the best way of understanding populism.

Changes in the location of boundaries can be distinguished from changes in the permeability of boundaries, which can be of two types: changes in degree and in directionality. By changes in degree I mean changes in the ease or fluidity with which actors and resources flow from one field to another. For example, how common and probable is it for a priestly intellectual to enter the scientific field—for a seminary-trained theologian to become president of a major research university—or for scientific intellectuals to enter the religious field—for a physicist or a sociologist to get an appointment in a divinity school? The former scenario is less likely than it used to be and is surely less probable than the latter at the present time (Marsden 1994). By changes in directionality, I mean changes in the net flows from one field or subfield to another. Consider, say, the relationship between political science and economics. This boundary has not only become more permeable; it also has a specific directionality, namely, from economics into political science, rather than the reverse.

Like playing fields, social fields can differ from one another not only in terms of their size or boundaries but also in terms of their shape. Bourdieu usually conceptualizes social fields two-dimensionally, in terms of a vertical and a horizontal dimension. The vertical dimension denotes hierarchy, meaning differences in power and prestige; the horizontal dimension is defined by orthodoxy, actors' relations to the *illusio* or *doxa* that holds the field together. Obviously, the degree of hierarchy and orthodoxy within a particular field can and does vary, and we can also conceive of these variations as variations in the shape of a field. In this sense, the more hierarchical a field is, the taller it is; and the less hierarchical a field is, the flatter it is. Similarly, a highly orthodox field would be thinner, while a more heterodox field would be thicker. One could argue that the university fields in the United States, the United Kingdom, and France, with their elite institutions (Harvard, Cambridge, ENA, and so on), are taller or more stratified than those in, say, the Germanic and Scandinavian countries, which lack equivalent institutions (but are now seeking to construct them).[3] Similarly, one could argue that the field of economics, which tolerates little heterodoxy, is thinner than the field of sociology, which has only

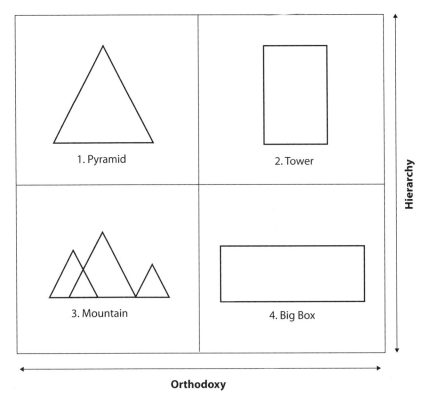

Orthodoxy

Figure 1. Field types.

a weak orthodoxy. Combining these two dimensions of variation yields four basic field shapes (figure 1): (1) Pyramids: a high degree of hierarchy and a high degree of orthodoxy, which increase with position in the hierarchy. Possible examples might include the Roman Catholic Church and the old Soviet state; (2) Towers: high degrees of hierarchy and low degrees of orthodoxy, so that disputes over orthodoxy do not vary with position in the hierarchy; they are intense at both the top and the bottom. Possible examples might include the U.S. academy and the art world of New York; (3) Mountains: low degrees of hierarchy and high degrees of orthodoxy, resulting in multiple and competing peaks or centers of orthodoxy, organized around a person or creed or both. Possible examples might include the religious fields in the United States and India, organized, respectively, around denominations and cultic centers. (4) Big boxes: low degrees of hierarchy and low degrees of orthodoxy but strong horizontal ties based on permeable organizations and overlapping networks. Possible examples might include radical subcultural milieux like punk and "social movement industries" (Hebdige 1991; McCarthy and Zald 1977).

The Subjective Moment. Up until now I have operationalized the various forms of field change primarily in objectivistic terms, in terms of changes in the structured relations between social positions. But it is possible, desirable, and often necessary to analyze fields in subjectivizing terms, that is, in terms of symbolic and cognitive structures. It is possible because fields are always also symbolic and cognitive constructs, which exist only in and through the interactions, investments, perceptions, and embodied habits of individual actors. It is desirable because the degree of homology between the objective and symbolic structures of a field is itself historically variable and sociologically consequential. And it is sometimes necessary because the bulk of the available evidence may well be symbolic rather than objective. This is often the case when the object of analysis is a historical one, about which we have more texts than tables.

Unfortunately, Bourdieu does not really give us too much guidance here. His conceptualization of (subjective) symbolic space is far less developed than his conceptualization of (objective) social space. Thus, in what follows I will try to provide some basic, orienting concepts for mapping change in social fields from a symbolic standpoint. Specifically, I will describe how the various types of relational change identified above (genesis, autonomy, size, boundaries, and shape) might be reconceptualized in symbolic terms. In doing so, I will draw heavily on Weber's sociology of religion and especially on his concept of "value spheres," which were two of the main inspirations of Bourdieu's sociology of culture and theory of fields (Bourdieu 1987a [1971]; Weber 1978 [1922]).

Genesis II. To revisit the problem of genesis: what sorts of changes within symbolic space would indicate the emergence of a new field? Drawing on Weber's theory of value spheres, we might hypothesize that the genesis of a new social field will be accompanied and indeed codetermined by the articulation of a new discourse of "ultimate value." By a discourse of ultimate value I mean a discourse which asserts that some family of social practices is not only inherently and relatively valuable, but also ultimately more valuable than all others, so that it can potentially provide an *ultima ratio* for individual and collective life. An ultimate value is, in short, something some people would rather die for than renounce. Weber himself identified seven such values in the modern West: family, religion, wealth, political community, scientific truth, art, and erotic love (Weber 1964). I would further suggest that such discourses tend to come in two basic forms: sociodicies and mythologies. By sociodicies I mean systematic and explicit theories about the general conditions of social order and the essential character of human flourishing, be it neoclassical economics, evangelical Christian theology or the Hindu caste system. By mythologies I mean the popular narratives of heroism and martyrdom that serve to inspire defense of the value, be it a valiant, anti-Communist dissident, a radical pro-lifer, or Krishna himself. Sociodicies and mythologies can be complementary, both symbolically and practically, and one can imagine many intermediate or mixed forms of ultimate-value discourses. One can easily imagine sociodicies and mythologies for each of the seven ultimate values identified by Weber, discourses that assert the ultimate value of religion, politics, truth, love, and so on, and of their particular historical variants.

Autonomy/Heteronomy II. How might we conceptualize and measure variations in the autonomy or heteronomy of a field from a symbolic vantage point? Here, too, Weber's theory of value spheres is a fruitful point of departure. For Weber the crystallization and development of a value sphere go together with a process of "theoretical and practical rationalization," in which the core value is made more explicit, its relationship to other values (and practices) is rendered more systematic, and the means to achieving it are refined and codified (Weber 1978 [1922]). For Weber the world religions are the paradigmatic example of such a rationalization process. Within each tradition, over the course of time, the nature of salvation (prosperity, heaven, nirvana, etc.), the means for achieving it (rational, ethical, contemplative, etc.), and the consequences which religious values have for worldly action are made more and more explicit and more and more consistent with one another. (In Weber's view this process of rationalization is accompanied and driven by the emergence of a class of religious specialists—magicians and mystagogues, priests and prophets [Weber 1978 (1922)].) Building on this formulation, we might hypothesize that the relative autonomy of a given field is indicated, in its symbolic moment, by the degree of rationalization of the corresponding discourse of ultimate value. Indicators of discursive rationalization might include the existence of (1) a named discourse or science (e.g., theology, economics) specific to the field; (2) a fully elaborated cosmology or social ontology based on this science (e.g., the Dantean world picture, the neoliberal worldview); and (3) a corresponding ethical theory (e.g., medieval casuistics, modern utilitarianism). A lack of rationalization would suggest a lack of autonomy. The lack of autonomy is distinct, analytically and sometimes also practically, from the existence of heteronomy, meaning the subordination of the symbolic logic of one field to that of another. Indicators of heteronomy might include (1) the subordination or cooptation of the core science to another science (e.g., theology becomes a branch of philosophy, political science becomes a subfield of economics); (2) the subordination of the core values to other values (as when religion is promoted as a source of physical well-being or social order, or when the political community is understood solely as a community of producers and consumers). The weakness of this neo-Weberian formulation is that it is overly intellectualistic; it emphasizes sociodicies but ignores mythologies. Put differently, it pays too much attention to the internal consistency of theological and cosmological systems and too little to processes of narrative and ritual rationalization. By narrative rationalization I mean the accumulation, editing, and canonization of a stock set of characters and tales that can be readily recounted and remembered. Plutarch's *Lives* is one example; Robert Heilbroner's classic history of economic thought another (Heilbroner 1953). By ritual rationalization I mean the equivalent process for collective rites. Here one thinks, for instance, of saints' days. There is no equivalent for economics (yet), though the recent takeover of the old quarters of the University of Chicago Divinity School by the newly established Milton Friedman Institute may mark a beginning.

Size II. What about the size of a field? From the symbolic vantage point, the size of a field could be conceptualized in terms of the scope of the circulation of the discourse of ultimate value, scope being understood here, as before, in terms of social rather than geographic space. The relative size of a field would then be measured in terms of the portion of the social space through which the discourse circulates, both via the spoken and printed word as well as through ritual and other embodied forms. The absolute and relative size of a field could be measured in terms of the absolute and relative number of people possessing some familiarity with (as opposed to complete mastery of) these concepts. In a contemporary context, the size of a field could be measured fairly easily and accurately, given the necessary resources and know-how, by means of content analysis and social surveys. Measuring them in a historical context involves less precise and more indirect methods. Here, one is typically compelled to make inferences about discursive scope based on circumstantial evidence, such as the sales of particular books, the accounts of historical observers, the diffusion of certain rituals, and so on, all common practices among professional historians.

Boundaries II. How might one assess changes in the boundaries of a field in symbolic terms? A zero-sum change in the location of a boundary should be manifested in a shift of discursive domination over a particular area of social practice from one field to another. For example, the gradual displacement of a Christian discourse about the cure of souls by a psychological discourse of mental health would indicate a shift of the boundary between the religious and scientific fields in favor of the latter (Reed 1997), as would the displacement of a discourse of patrimony and lineage in economic thinking by one dominated by considerations of profit and management (Adams 2005; Polanyi 2001). Non-zero sum boundary changes, on the other hand, would be manifested in increased or decreased rates of discursive production and diffusion. It should be noted that zero-sum and non-zero-sum changes are not necessarily exclusive of one another. One can easily imagine a situation in which the number of pastoral and psychological experts and publications are both increasing (non-zero-sum boundary change) even as the balance between them is shifting (zero-sum boundary change), such that private life would be more and more permeated by both pastoralist and therapeutic discourses, but with the latter being dominant. That is perhaps the situation which obtains in contemporary America, where the number of therapeutic and self-help tracts continues to increase without necessarily leading to a decrease in the volume of religious and spiritual books. Nor should we assume that such processes are irreversible. It seems quite possible and perhaps even probable that religious discourses of self-help have gained ground vis-à-vis therapeutic ones in recent years, at least in the United States.

How might changes in the degree and direction of permeability be assessed in symbolic terms? Consider the relationships between various scientific sub-fields, or disciplines, within the academic field in the contemporary United States. It is well established and well known by now that journal articles published by noneconomists cite the work of economists quite frequently, while articles published by economists rarely cite the work of noneconomists (Pieters and Baumgartner 2002). Moreover, it seems likely that this asymmetry in citation patterns has grown in recent years. Similarly, it is not uncommon at the moment for people with doctorates in economics to be hired by political science departments and even sociology departments, something that would have been almost unheard of, say, twenty years ago. The first example illustrates a change in directionality, the second a change in permeability. Both also suggest a basic strategy for tracking such boundary changes: patterns and rates of citation. Obviously, one cannot measure these patterns and rates as easily or precisely in a historical context as one can in contemporary academia. Nonetheless, the basic logic is the same.

Shape II. What about changes in the shape of a field? Variation along the vertical dimension, in the degree of hierarchy, could be conceptualized in terms of the relationship between official and lay discourse (i.e., between discourse in the dominant and the dominated regions of the field). For example, how big is the gap between the discourse of education school professors in Cambridge, Massachusetts, and elementary schoolteachers in Huntsville, Alabama? between Sri Lankan peasants and Buddhist monks in Colombo? Has it increased or decreased? What sets of signifiers or master narratives are used in the upper and lower regions of the field? and how great is the overlap between them? And what about those signifiers or narratives that are used in both regions? do they mean approximately the same thing? These are the sorts of questions one would need to ask; how one went about answering them would vary from context to context. Variation along the horizontal dimension, in the degree of orthodoxy, could be conceptualized in terms of the changing relationship between orthodoxy and heterodoxy within a field (i.e., between the established powers and their would-be challengers). Do the challengers seek incremental reforms within the dominant discourse? or do they advocate its complete overthrow? Do they advance critiques or alternative systems?

CAPITAL

Bourdieu's field concept is a novel and semantically rich one. It evokes various associations and can be elaborated in a number of different directions, including some Bourdieu himself did not pursue. The same is true of his second master concept: capital. The capital concept is hardly novel. It is central to modern economic thought, in its classical, Marxist, and neoclassical guises, whence its diverse and numerous associations. What Bourdieu does—and this is his singular innovation—is apply this economic concept to noneconomic domains, particularly the cultural field and its various subfields. This leads him to distinguish various forms or types of capital, of which cultural capital is probably the best known. Other key types include economic, symbolic, and social capital. In this section, I will explore some of the ways in which the capital concept can be used to map sociohistorical transformation. Before doing so, however, I want to briefly review a few crucial points about Bourdieu's theory of capital.

Capital, as Bourdieu understands it, is specific to a field. There are only particular kinds of capital; there is no such thing as capital in general, though symbolic capital can serve as a generalized medium of exchange, at least in modern, that is, state-dominated societies. Accordingly, Bourdieu is less interested in developing a general theory or definition of capital than in identifying particular types or forms of capital. And this he does: not just economic, cultural, social, and symbolic but also literary, academic, political, religious, and sexual, to name just a few. How are these types of capital related to one another? Bourdieu did not answer this question in an explicit or systematic way, probably because he thought the relationship was historically variable and that any attempt to fully systematize it would be a purely scholastic exercise. That said, it is clear he regarded symbolic, economic, and cultural capital as, respectively, the most fundamental (historically), the most powerful (socially), and the most important (politically). Symbolic capital is the most fundamental in the sense that it is the oldest. In undifferentiated, or primitive, societies that have little or no division of labor (e.g., only a sexual division of labor), symbolic capital is the only kind of capital, and it is held by men. It can be directly exchanged for economic capital; in effect, it is cultural and economic capital rolled into one. In differentiated, or historic, societies with a not exclusively sexual division of labor, cultural and economic capital become distinct from and to some degree opposed to one another. While Bourdieu regards symbolic capital as the most fundamental historically, economic capital is the most important socially. Why? Bourdieu speculates that the superior power of economic capital may derive from its inorganic and material nature, which makes it both more durable and more readily transferable than either embodied or cultural capital, which is inscribed in organic, mortal bodies, or symbolic capital, which is rooted in mutable, multivalent symbolic systems. Though it is neither as fundamental as symbolic capital nor as powerful as economic capital, cultural capital is, for Bourdieu, the politically most important form. Why? Because it represents a possible pole of opposition to economic capital. It is the source not only of legitimacy but potentially also of critique. In more differentiated societies (e.g., the agrarian empires of classical antiquity), the three major types of capital become relatively distinct from one another, as do the social fields in which they are produced and the elites who dominate them: the state (symbolic capital), religion (cultural capital), and the economy (economic capital). The other types of capital that Bourdieu identifies could be seen as arising out of subsequent processes of differentiation. Thus he suggests that the emergence of political capital is bound up with the differentiation of monarchical states into governments and party systems. Alternatively, one could conceive other types of capital as subtypes that emerge within subfields. Thus he suggests that literary capital might be seen as a subtype of cultural capital, much as financial capital might be seen as a subtype of economic capital. It is not clear whether these are two distinct processes or merely two different formulations.

The three major categories of field change—the genesis of fields, changes in relations between fields, and changes in relations within fields—can all be mapped through the capital concept. For example, the genesis of a field can also be conceptualized as a process of primitive accumulation, in which one actor or class amasses a stock of capital that is sufficient to establish a new and autonomous field. Bourdieu himself argues that European state formation can be theorized in this way. The state formation process begins when one noble house accumulates enough symbolic capital to establish itself as a *primus inter pares*. "The king, acting as 'head of the house,' makes use of the properties of the house (in particular, nobility as symbolic capital accumulated by a domestic group through a range of strategies, of which the most important is marriage) to construct a state, as administration and as territory, that gradually escapes from the logic of the 'house'" (Bourdieu 2004a: 30). Rivals' houses do not necessarily or inevitably consent to this process of primitive accumulation, but to the degree that they do, it is because they believe others are likely to do so: "The king occupies a distinct and distinctive position which, as such, ensures an initial accumulation of symbolic capital. As a feudal chieftain who has this particular property, that he is able to call himself king, with a reasonable chance of having his claim recognized. The effect, in accordance with the logic of the 'speculative bubble' so dear to the economists, is that he is found to believe he is king because the others believe (at least to some extent) that he is king, each having to reckon with the fact that the others reckon with the fact that he is the king" (Bourdieu 2004a: 33).[4] The longer this absence of dissent passes for the presence of consent, in other words, the more symbolic capital the king accumulates. This process, like all processes of primitive accumulation, involves not only physical coercion and violence, but also symbolic misrecognition and violence (Loveman 2007).

What about relations between fields? Bourdieu often speaks of the varying exchange rates between the forms of capital, between, say, economic and cultural capital. And he argues that changes in the exchange rate between two forms of capital indicate changes in the power relations between the fields in which they are produced. For example, if the rate at which educational credentials, a form of cultural capital, could be exchanged for monetary compensation, a form of economic capital, on the job market increases, this would indicate a change in the power relations between the cultural and economic fields, as would a decline in the monetary price paid for cultural capital of some form. The concept of exchange rate therefore gives us another way of thinking about the autonomy of a field. The stronger a field's currency is, in relation to other fields' currencies, the higher the exchange rate, or, in other words, the more autonomous the field is. Changes in the exchange rate signal changes in autonomy.

The capital concept also gives us another way of thinking about heteronomy. The crucial indicator here is the degree to which transactions within the field not only can be, but often must be conducted with forms of capital that are foreign to the field. Is social capital a sine qua non of mobility within the artistic field? Is economic capital a sine qua non of mobility within the political field? If so, the field is heteronomous. Seen in this way, a heteronomous field is a bit like a weak currency regime, in which strong foreign currencies are the preferred medium of exchange.

We can use the capital concept to think about boundaries as well. Non-zero-sum forms of boundary change could be assessed by tracing the circulation of field-specific capital across social space. Just as the monetization of trade in peasant communities or for basic commodities is often seen as indicating an expansion of the economic field in its modern, or capitalist, form, so, too, by the same logic, would the credentialization of labor markets in the lower regions of social space indicate an expansion of the cultural field in its modern, or scientific, form. Zero-sum boundary changes would be indicated by the disappearance of a field-specific capital from some area of social space. Are on-the-job-experience and union membership displaced by educational credentials in a particular segment of the economy? If so, this indicates a zero-sum change. There are many regions of social space where multiple forms of capital are in circulation. Here, one must be attentive to changes in the permeability and directionality of boundaries. They can be studied by monitoring changes in the negotiability of different forms of field-specific capital. When it becomes difficult or impossible to exchange one form of capital for another, a hardening of a boundary has occurred. In present-day America, for example, it is very, very difficult to exchange religious capital for scientific capital. Neither prophetic credentials such as a large radio or television audience nor priestly ones like an advanced degree in theology from a prestigious seminary provide much, if any, scientific credibility, though a degree is presumably somewhat more negotiable than prophetic credentials. (Though it does appear that they can be readily exchanged for political capital in the contemporary United States [Banerjee 2006].) Nor does a doctoral degree in physics or biology give a person much legitimacy among the faithful, with perhaps some exceptions, such as Episcopalians or Unitarians. Lest we hypostasize this state of affairs, I emphasize that this was not true as recently as a century ago, when the Baconian epistemology of Scottish commonsense realism created more space for dialogue between Christian theologians and natural scientists (Garroutte 2003).

What about changes within fields, what I have called changes in shape? Here, too, the capital concept offers some additional leverage. For example, we would expect that changes along the vertical axis, or degree of hierarchy, would be accompanied by changes in the distribution of field-specific capital or, what is the same thing, in rates of exploitation within the field. For example, if the practices governing stated authorship of scientific papers shifted from a situation in which the lab director or "PI" (Principal Investigator) was invariably given sole or first authorship to one in which multiple authorship or first authorship for junior researchers became more common, this would suggest a flattening of the field and an attendant decrease in the rate of (symbolic) exploitation. If, on the other hand, compensation practices within large corporations changed such that the ratio between the salaries of upper-level and lower-level managers increased, this would obviously indicate a peaking of the field, a shift in the direction of a pyramidal structure. Changes along the horizontal axis, or degree of orthodoxy, should be accompanied by changes in the composition of capital at each point in the field or, equivalently, in the portfolios held by actors in various parts of the field. The more diverse the portfolios, the more polarized the field; the less diverse, the more unified. For example, a highly polarized literary field would be one in which authors highly rich in economic capital were also very poor in literary capital and cultural capital more generally, and vice versa. One expects there to be an inverse relationship between these two forms of capital; but the slope of the line indicates the degree of heterodoxy. A highly unified academic field, to invoke a different example, would be one in which scientific prestige (cultural capital) was highly correlated with monetary compensation (economic capital).

I have shown how the capital concept can be used to track different types of field change. In doing so, I have translated from the language of fields into the language of capitals. This process of translation yields eight general propositions, namely,

1. The genesis of a new field is accompanied by the generation of new types of capital.

2. Changes in the relative autonomy of a field will be accompanied by changes in the rate of exchange commanded by the form of capital specific to that field.

3. Changes in the relative heteronomy of a field will be accompanied by the increasing use of foreign capital as the dominant medium of exchange or currency regime within the field.

4. Changes in the size of a field or non-zero-sum changes in the boundaries of a field (or both) will be reflected in the social scope of circulation of field-specific capital.

5. Non-zero-sum changes in a field's boundaries will be reflected in increased or decreased rates of production of field-specific capital.

6. Changes in the permeability and directionality of a boundary will be reflected in changes in the negotiability of field-specific capital.

7. Changes in the degree of hierarchy within a field will be marked by changes in the distribution of capital and, more specifically, in the degree of equality or inequality between the upper and lower regions of the field or, what is the same thing, by changes in the rate of exploitation within the field.

8. Changes in the degree of orthodoxy within the field will be marked by changes in the composition of capitals at every point in the field or, what is the same thing, by changes in the heterogeneity of portfolios held by actors across the field.

These general propositions could be understood in a variety of ways: as testable hypotheses, as laws governing the relationship between fields and capitals, or as mechanisms linking the states of fields and stocks of capitals. For my purposes, however, that is, for the purposes of a historical sociology, the translations themselves are more useful than the propositions because they provide an additional set of coordinates that can be used to map and track processes of sociohistorical change. New types of capital, rates of exchange, currency regimes, scope of circulation, negotiability, distributional equality or inequality, rates of exploitation, the heterogeneity of portfolios—all are themselves potentially fruitful objects of and powerful heuristics for sociologically informed historical investigation.

The Subjective Moment of Capitals. The foregoing analysis of capital change is of an objectivizing and materialist character. But Bourdieu's method requires that we complement an objectivizing and materialist analysis with a symbolic and subjectivizing one. How might we go about this? Bourdieu's analyses of cultural capital point to one general strategy. Drawing on Marx's celebrated analysis of "commodity fetishism" and on Durkheim's equally celebrated analysis of the social origins of religion, Bourdieu identifies two symbolic mechanisms that are crucial to the legitimation of cultural domination and the reproduction of cultural capital, namely, naturalization and misrecognition. He argues that the privileges and power conferred by cultural capital are legitimated if, and to the extent that, they are misrecognized as the results of natural talent or ambition, rather than as the fruits of cultural socialization and training. This basic argument could easily be extended to the legitimation and reproduction of other forms of capital as well.

But incisive as it is, this general strategy for analyzing the symbolic mechanisms of social reproduction is actually not that helpful when it comes to analyzing more specific processes of sociohistorical transformation. Here, it may be useful to return to Marx's original analysis of commodity fetishism. True to his materialist stance, Marx tends to see the commodity form as something that arises out of the material process of market exchange; in other words, he portrays it as ideological and epiphenomenal (Marx 1976: 168, 174). However, there are moments in this discussion where Marx slips, perhaps unwittingly, into a more symbolic mode of analysis, one that emphasizes the intellectual and theoretical work that goes into the naturalization of the commodity form (Marx 1976: 169, 177). Building on this thought and echoing Polanyi (2001), Espeland (1998), and Soto (2000), one might argue that the development and elaboration of the concepts of "price" and "value" and especially the notions of "market price" and "exchange value" are a key symbolic mechanism, perhaps *the* key mechanism, through which commodities are transformed into capital—into a form of generalized value abstracted from use value. To denaturalize this state of affairs and to realize the amount of symbolic work that is required to transform land and objects into property and property into capital, one need only turn one's attention from the capitalist core to the semicapitalist periphery, as Hernando de Soto has shown in *The Mysteries of Capital* (Soto 2000). Before a piece of land can become a piece of property, he shows, one needs not only the judicial category of private property but also surveys, plots, deeds, and a myriad of material practices and symbolic constructs. This approach to economic capital can easily be extended to the other types of capital as well and is a fruitful starting point for the symbolic and historical analysis of capital in general. The central point here is that the creation and legitimation of any form of capital involve considerable symbolic work and various symbolic processes, including abstraction, codification, commensuration, measurement, ranking, and so on (Espeland 1998). One of the central tasks of a Bourdieusian approach to historical analysis must therefore be to inventory these processes, track their transformations, and detail their workings for each of the various types and subtypes of capital.

How might one go about putting this agenda into practice? I begin with the problem of genesis. How could we analyze the emergence and development of a new form of capital in symbolic terms? One indicator might be the emergence and elaboration of a new form and metric of valuation. By this I mean a set of practical categories and symbolic operations through which people and things, in all their particularity and individuality, are ranked in a uniform, hierarchical fashion. In other words, a mechanism of commensuration, measurement, and ranking. In this perspective, the laws of supply and demand are not some kind of transhistorical law, but simply one metric of valuation among many others. The point, then, is not to stipulate how prices *should* be generated or to assess whether the prices are "right" or "efficient," but to investigate how prices *are* generated historically, to describe and inventory the relevant symbolic mechanisms, and, in short, to excavate the entire symbolic economy of the material economy. This would be a first step in identifying some of the historical forms economic capital has taken.

Such an approach would not need to be limited to economic capital. One could also study cultural capital from a symbolic perspective. This, too, would be a rich, illuminating field for comparative and historical study. Several strategies suggest themselves. One would be to look at a single subtype of cultural capital in several contexts. For example, one could compare the symbolic mechanisms through which bureaucratic capital was produced in, say, ancient China, the medieval papal Curia, and nineteenth-century Prussia.

What were the relevant properties of would-be bureaucrats? Through what means were they assessed? And how were these assessments translated into a hierarchical ordering? Another strategy would be to reconstruct the family tree of a general type of capital in a particular place across some period of time, by comparing the genesis and development of the various subtypes. For example, one might compare the mechanisms used to produce priestly, bureaucratic, academic, and artistic forms of cultural capital in, say, nineteenth- and twentieth-century France. In sum, one could proceed analytically or genealogically. One could also combine the analytical and genealogical strategies by looking at the breaks and continuities in the production of a particular subtype of capital in a specific place and period, say, the production of academic capital in the United States since the Second World War. This is the strategy employed so effectively by Bourdieu himself in *The State Nobility* (1996b [1989]). It would enable one to produce a fine-grained study rooted in primary source materials.

The other forms of change discussed in the preceding section could also be analyzed in symbolic terms. Consider changes in exchange rates. We would expect them to be accompanied and signaled by debates within the field of power over the value and valuations of various forms of capital. Should royal administrators be selected on the basis of blood and lineage? or of knowledge and skill? Should admission to Harvard be based solely on entrance examinations? or should "character" figure in as well (Karabel 2005)? What matters more in a prospective mate, a large dowry or a strong back? intelligence or breeding? When the conventional or institutional answer to such a question changes, we can infer movement in the rate of exchange. Thus we would expect that historical fluctuations in the value of the bureaucratic capital possessed by the Chinese literati should go hand in hand with changing assessments of the relative value of literary education for state administration —relative, say, to magical credentials, military experience, or commercial prowess. Ideally, one would want not only to explicate such movements, but also to identify the basic symbolic mechanisms through which they are accomplished. Is the logic of valuation being changed from, say, a cosmological to a utilitarian logic? or is it simply the metric of valuation that is being challenged, the means by which relative utility is assessed? Is the place of the literati within Chinese society being questioned? or just the utility of classical learning for state administration? or both?

In some cases it is not simply the rate of exchange that is in question, but also the very possibility of exchanging one form of capital for another, what I referred to above as negotiability. Where negotiability is at stake, we would expect to find debates about relative value and exchange rates and also about absolute value or commensurability of particular forms of capital or both. Is it legitimate to exchange economic capital for political favors? Are such exchanges to be understood as corruption or as gifts? Has there been a decline in the proportion of university presidents holding doctor of theology degrees relative to those holding doctor of philosophy degrees? If so and if the decline is due to changes in the negotiability of religious capital vis-à-vis academic capital, then we would expect this process to be accompanied by debate about the relevance of theology and religion to the mission of the university and the project of science, as it has been in historical fact (Marsden 1994; Reuben 1996).

Changes in the rate of exploitation can also be analyzed in symbolic terms. They should be signaled by claims about the relative contribution of the dominated and the dominant to the production of a particular form of capital. We might expect that changing rates of economic exploitation within contemporary industrial societies would be mirrored in changing discourses about entrepreneurship, engineering, and craftsmanship or their cultural and linguistic equivalents (Thelen 2004). If this hypothesis is correct, then we should find a strong correspondence between cults of entrepreneurship and high levels of inequality (e.g., in the U.S.) and, conversely, between cults of craftsmanship and low levels of inequality (e.g., in Germany). More generally, one would expect to find a strong correlation between increasing rates of exploitation and discourses about the individual nature of creativity and success—for example, about the artistic genius, the economic entrepreneur, the political leader, the military hero, and so on—and, conversely, between decreasing rates of exploitation and discourses about the collective nature of creativity and success—for example, about the great man behind the great woman, about the importance of economic teamwork or corporate spirit, about the genius of the nation or the people, about the greatest generation or the citizen-soldier, and so forth.

Even changes in the composition of capitals within a particular field should leave strong symbolic traces. In a thinner field, where portfolios are more homogeneous, for example, we would expect to find a relatively high degree of uniformity in and agreement about metrics of valuation; in a thicker field, by contrast, there would be less uniformity in practice and more contention in public. For example, one would probably find greater uniformity and agreement about, say, the relative merits of research papers in cell biology than of new works of avant-garde music. Similarly, one would expect that the injection of large amounts of a particular form of capital into an existing field—for example, through the entry of large numbers of trained engineers into middle management or the entry of large numbers of masters of business administration into televisions newsrooms—would bring about predictable shifts in valuation (Braverman 1975; Klinenberg 2002, 2007). Since such shifts apply not only to the products of the field but also to the people in it, one would also expect concomitant debates about what it means to be "called" in that field, who belongs in its pantheon, the basis of success and status within the field, and so on.

HABITUS

The habitus, as noted, is a set of embodied dispositions, schemas of perception, and recipes for action that are a function of an individual's location in and trajectory through social space. In his various attempts to explicate this concept, Bourdieu tends to invoke two metaphors. One is "deep grammar" à la Chomsky (1966). Like a grammar, a habitus is a set of rules that underlies a set of practices or, better, is implicit within them, a fuzzy logic that is deeply inscribed into human minds and that can be excavated by science. These rules allow individuals to interpret and respond to the social world in ways which are comprehensible both to themselves and to others, if not wholly predictable, much as grammatical rules allow individuals to understand and formulate linguistic statements which are subjectively and intersubjectively comprehensible but provide considerable leeway for individual creativity and improvisation. And just as variations in dialect or the absence of dialect locate speakers in geographical space, so variations in habitus locate individuals in social space.

The grammar metaphor has its limitations, however. It could lead one to assume that the habitus is in people's heads, that it is part of conscious awareness, and that it is wholly controlled from within by the individual will. Bourdieu would certainly not want the concept to be understood in this way. Perhaps that is why he often invokes another metaphor in his discussions of habitus: "feel for the game." Like the moves of a skilled athlete, the moves of social actors are largely preconscious, somatic responses triggered by a particular situation. They are produced by repetitive training, stored in muscle memory, and activated by the environment. The arms and legs of social actors, in Bourdieu's suggestive phrase, are "full of numb imperatives" (Bourdieu 2000b: 176).

Where do these imperatives come from? The most important influence on the individual habitus, Bourdieu repeatedly stresses, is early childhood socialization. In most societies, this means the family. Within modern, industrial societies, he adds, the most important source of secondary socialization is the educational system. By early adulthood, he implies, an individual's habitus is durably formed and fairly resistant to significant change. Adults are more apt to seek to change their surroundings to fit their habitus than the other way around.

If the individual habitus is resistant to change, as Bourdieu claims, then how can we use this concept to map and track sociohistorical transformation? Because the habitus is shaped by location in and trajectory through social space and, what is the same thing, by endowment with and accumulation of the various forms of capital, field theory strongly implies that changes in the shape of and boundaries within social space and (what is, once again, the same thing) in the volume and types of capital should be accompanied by predictable changes in habitus. Thus, the emergence of new fields and sub-fields and new types and subtypes of capital should be accompanied by the emergence of new types and subtypes of habitus. On the crudest, grandest historical scale, for example, one would expect that the differentiation of the economic and cultural fields and the emergence of the state and of their corresponding forms of capital should be accompanied by the formation of distinctive types of habitus within the field of power (e.g., the noble, the priest, the courtier). One could also look at the differentiation of these basic types into various subtypes, e.g., of the priestly classes into priestly priests (clerics *strictu sensu*) and worldly priests (clerks), of the worldly priests into worldly worldly priests (clerks in the economic sense) and priestly worldly priests (bureaucrats), and so on. How can one identify a new habitus? One could speak of a new type or subtype of habitus when and to the degree that clear symbolic boundaries emerge, boundaries which are marked both materially, in terms of lifestyle, but also symbolically, with a social category, and bound-aries whose underlying forms remain fairly constant, even if the material and symbolic marks of distinction change.[5]

The other types of change discussed above—changes in the shape of a field or the distribution of capital, for instance—should also be accompanied by changes in the distribution and composition of the habitus. For instance, the thickening or thinning of a field should be paralleled by increasing or decreas-ing levels of difference between orthodox and heterodox versions of the hab-itus. Growing tensions between, say, traditionalist and reformist monks should be reflected by growing differences in dress, speech, comportment, diet, and other outward manifestations of the habitus, as in fact occurred in the course of Buddhist and Catholic monastic reform movements in Asia and Europe (Friedrich-Silber 1995). The same would hold for the literary and academic fields. One thinks here of the clashes of 1968, of conservative professors in suits and ties and radical professors in jeans and peasant shirts. We would also expect a sharpening of the logical differences in the principles of di-vision that under-lie such outward differences, as manifested in, say, the rules of various monastic orders, the tone of academic debates, and so on. Peaking and flattening of the field should also have predictable consequences at the level of habitus, such as increasing or decreasing differences between the dominant and the dominated —in consumption patterns, child-rearing practices, aesthetic preferences, and so on. One would therefore anticipate that there would be greater lifestyle differences within the American professoriate, which is highly stratified, than within, say, the German or Swedish professoriates, which are far less stratified. Non-zero-sum boundary changes might be evidenced in increasing or decreasing levels of codification and formalization of certain aspects of social practice and thus of the individual habitus, while positive-sum boundary shifts should lead to heightened awareness and marking of certain lifestyle differences. In sum, changes in the structure of fields should generally occur in tandem with changes in the distribution of the habitus across social space.

There is another form of change in the habitus, namely, change in the composition of the habitus at a particular point in or region of social space. Such changes are driven by shifts not in the shape of a particular field but in the relationship between fields. When the balance of power between two fields shifts and the relative value of a particular kind of capital declines, the established mode of social reproduction is undermined, and the transmission of social status can be achieved only through altered strategies of investment. Though rational in a narrowly material sense, such strategies are costly in psychic terms, requiring as they do a symbolic disinvestment in the traditional way of life, and also in social terms, as they may occasion tumultuous intergenerational rifts. Such disinvestments and rifts are manifested in changes in the composition of the habitus. The daughter of a peasant family who became a salesclerk in a small city occupies a position in social space similar to her parents', at least in absolute terms, but she would have a rather different habitus, nonetheless. Here, one might speak of intergenerational drift in the habitus. Processes of collective rise and decline—upward or downward social trajectories, in Bourdieu's terms—may also inflect the political mediation of the class habitus. A class in decline, he argues, is typically more receptive to conservative politics, while a class on the rise is more apt to embrace progressive politics (though precisely what the content of these categories will be is highly variable and is determined by struggles within the political and cultural fields) (Bourdieu 1984a). This, it might be argued, is what explains the peculiar political career of the petty bourgeoisie, or small-scale merchants and artisans, a motor for change from the Reformation era up through the Age of Revolutions. During this time it was a class on the rise, by and large, but became an increasingly reactionary force with the advent of industrial capitalism, when large-scale commerce and production began to erode its economic position. Here, we might speak of transhistorical drift in the habitus.

The two forms of drift I have just described occur when the dynamics of one field disrupt those of another, threatening social reproduction. What happens when there are simultaneous and homologous disruptions in several fields? This, says Bourdieu, is precisely what happened in France—and not only there—in May 1968. A crisis in the cultural field, specifically the university field, coincided with a crisis in the economic field, which affected parts of the industrial working classes. This is not the place to recount Bourdieu's lengthy, subtle analysis of May 1968 (Bourdieu 1988). The outcome, in brief, was that certain segments of the intelligentsia and the labor movement came to see their situations as analogous, if only for a brief moment, and that led certain of their spokespersons to articulate a corresponding vision of the social world, in which university lecturers and factory hands were part of the same class or at least the same movement. Bourdieu seems to see the effects of this and similar episodes—he uses the term *synchronization*—as transitory. Is he correct? Perhaps not. There are plenty of good reasons to believe that crisis situations of this sort leave a lasting imprint on those who experience them and, through them, on subsequent generations as well. Wasn't the original habitus of many "68ers" undone or at least remade? and doesn't this continue to reverberate in the present? Couldn't the same be said of the generations of 1789, 1848, and 1915? (Goldstein 2005; Joas 2003; McAdam 1988). Could it not be that Bourdieu's a priori assertions about the stability of the individual habitus are too much informed by the stability of post–Second World War Europe?

There are still other types of long-term change in class habitus, including ones that involve changes in the symbolic structure of the habitus rather than in its practical composition. Perhaps the best example of such changes, and in any event the one that Bourdieu analyzes in greatest depth, is gender habitus (Bourdieu 2001b). Following certain well-established lines of feminist theorizing, Bourdieu suggests that while the outward markers of gender identity can and do undergo considerable change, the underlying principles of gender division can be and usually are extraordinarily durable, all the more so because they are symbolically anchored by "natural" or "biological" differences between the sexes. Building on this line of analysis, we might also theorize shifts in the symbolic content of the gendered habitus or, for that matter, of any class habitus. For the sake of discussion, I will conceptualize the symbolic moment of the gendered habitus as having the following three-dimensional structure: a horizontal axis of semiotic relations structured by relations of categorical opposition (à la Saussure) (1986), a vertical axis of semantic relations in which more explicit sets of oppositions are layered on and aligned with deeper ones; and a depth dimension of difference (à la Derrida) (1976), in which the given set of semiotic and semantic relations (gendered in this case) are stabilized and held in place by endless chains of reference that connect them with other lines of social di-vision (race, class, party, region, etc.). We might further stipulate, for this purpose, that the vertical, or semantic, dimension has three main layers or levels, a foundational one anchored by the opposition male/female, a meso level consisting of other deep oppositions (e.g., hard/soft, dry/wet, etc.), and a surface level consisting of the material and symbolic markers of gender. The foundational and surface levels are not very interesting, at least not to the historian or sociologist (though surely to the poet or fashion columnist) because the first almost never changes, while the second is constantly evolving. The real point of interest, to the historical sociologist or social historian is the meso level because it is there that we might discover forms of change that are both consequential and nonobvious. If, for example, the opposition inside/outside was reversed in the course of some great "transvaluation of values," this would have important consequences, not only in symbolic practices (e.g., in religious ritual), but also for material practices (e.g., in domestic architecture) (Bourdieu 1977). Indeed, because the gendered habitus is connected to other regions of the individual habitus and other social fields through extensive chains of shared and deferred significations, any changes in the gendered habitus are likely to have ripple effects—in the class habitus, for example, or in the artistic habitus. The model of the habitus I have just sketched suggests many other types of change that could be systematically explored, such as the emergence, displacement, or disappearance of oppositions at the meso level.

Explaining Sociohistorical Change: A Dialectical and Dialogical Approach

Having reflected at some length on how we might use Bourdieusian theory to map sociohistorical change, I want to consider how it could be used to explain change. Once we have identified some outcome of interest, once we have "constructed the object," how do we proceed? Bourdieu's own explanatory practice will be useful in answering this question. Typically, this practice involves some or all of the following three operations: a shift in perspective, a shift in language, or a shift in temporality.

By shift in perspective I mean one of the following two suboperations: a shift in the ontological level or a shift in the phenomenological moment. Shifting levels means explaining a whole in terms of its parts or vice versa or, more precisely and generally, a shift in relational scale, from habitus to field, say, or from field to capital. For example, the habitus of a group or individual —one set of relations—can often be at least partly explained in terms of their position in or trajectory through the field—a higher-order set of relations.

The dynamics of a field, conversely, can often be explained in terms of the types of capital at stake and their distribution through the fields; thus conflicts among culture producers often pit actors endowed with large amounts of economic capital, for example, economically successful artists or writers, against those with large amounts of cultural capital, say, highbrow or avant-garde producers. Here, a higher order set of relations is explained in terms of a lower order set. Bourdieu's explanatory practice thereby transcends the hoary opposition between holists and reductionists by giving wholes and parts their ontological dues.[6]

What does the second principle of explanation, a shift in the phenomenological moment, entail? Typically, it involves a shift from a practical or material perspective to a symbolic or cultural one. Thus patterns in symbolic or cultural practices, in speech, dress, leisure, and so on, can be traced to material or practical differences, such as economic capital or cultural capital. When one is studying culture, the shift to a materialist perspective enables one to establish epistemological distance. Conversely, patterns of identification and interaction within and between social groups can be traced to symbolic and cultural boundaries and practices. In cases where group boundaries are perceived as material, a symbolic perspective may be more useful in establishing the necessary distance. For Bourdieu, then, the adoption of a materialist or idealist perspective is not a methodological or ontological question but a practical or political one, determined by the object under investigation and the state of play in the scientific literature.

What does the shift in language involve? Bourdieu argues that the first step in scientific analysis is the "epistemological break," a break with the perspective of the social actors under investigation (Bourdieu, Chamboredon, Passeron 1991).[7] One means of achieving this break, the one Bourdieu most often recommends, is to abandon folk categories in favor of scientific ones. In this way, we establish a clear distinction between the "categories of practice," which social actors use to explain their practices to themselves and others, and the "categories of analysis," which social science uses to interrogate these practices. This break is important, first, because there is often a gap between what people say and what they do and, what is more, between what they think and what they do; second, because this gap is not always just a cognitive error but a process of misrecognition and repression, in which interests and motives are concealed from self and others; and, third, because these processes of misrecognition and repression are part and parcel of the social machinery that reproduces power and inequality and, as such, are themselves crucial objects of social scientific analysis. This principle applies equally to historical subjects.

This brings me to the third and final operation: a shift in temporal perspective. Bourdieu uses history in at least two distinct ways in his work: to critique and to explain. The necessity of historical critique derives from the role of naturalization in processes of misrecognition. One of the most common ways in which dominant actors conceal the arbitrary character of their power from themselves and others is by grounding it in nature. The paradigmatic example of this process, argues Bourdieu, is the grounding of masculine domination in sexual difference (Bourdieu 2001b). In this and other areas, historicization is a potent means of denaturalization, a way of uncovering the social that is concealed in the natural. Historicization is another means of establishing the epistemological distance toward folk explanations that makes scientific explanations possible. It can also be a form of explanation in and of itself. Bourdieu's most favored form of historical explanation is the conjunctural. I call this mode of explanation conjunctural insofar as it emphasizes interfield interactions that generate unintended consequences. Bourdieu's account of May '68 is an excellent example of a conjunctural explanation: increases in prosperity and fertility after the Second World War led to a rapid expansion of the educational system and the student population and an attendant expansion in the number of positions and faculties. These increases changed the pace of professorial reproduction and the composition of the professoriate and thereby sparked conflicts within the teaching corps; at the same time, changes within the field of material production were creating a homologous set of tensions among manual laborers. In sum, "morphological transformations" within the cultural and economic fields generated simultaneous crises in each, which led to an amplification and alignment of each crisis, with consequences that no one sought or foresaw. Bourdieu's conjunctural approach can therefore be seen as a means of transcending the old debate between determinism and contingency in history: while the laws or principles governing fields are, indeed, determinate ones, interactions between fields can lead to unexpected or contingent outcomes.

To sum up: Bourdieu's method might be fairly described as dialectical, dialogical, and conjunctural. It is dialectical in the sense that it proceeds by positing a particular ontological level or phenomenological moment of analysis or both and then negating it or them as a means of achieving a higher level of understanding. An analysis that begins from the whole proceeds to the parts; an analysis that begins with the symbolic proceeds to the material; and the outcome is, one hopes, a perspective that transcends these dualisms to some degree. Indeed, it is to be hoped that this dialectical procedure will eventually allow sociology to overcome the conceptual dualisms that guide the procedure: symbolic versus material, individual versus social, necessary versus contingent, and so on. The result will be not a unified field theory but another, deeper set of dualisms, since without dualisms there can be no dialectic and hence no increase in understanding. Bourdieu's method is also dialogical in the sense that it continually seeks to establish or reestablish a position from which we can question and interrogate the commonsensical folk view of the social world that is embedded in everyday practice. To the extent that this effort is successful, its categories will themselves enter into the folk view of the social world, necessitating a renewed epistemological break. For Bourdieu, then, the work of social science is never done. It is never done because there is always more to be learned through a negation of our present stance and because our hard-won scientific understandings are constantly being swallowed up into social practice. Finally, Bourdieu's method is conjunctural in the sense that it emphasizes how the lawful dynamics of one field can generate the reproductive equilibrium in another, and how simultaneous crises in multiple fields can amplify one another, all with outcomes that were not part of any actor's strategy.

Having examined Bourdieu's approach in a rather abstract way, I want to look at a concrete example, namely, how Bourdieu proceeds in *The Rules of Art*. The outcome which that work seeks to explain, to recall, is the emergence of avant-garde literature in France during the late nineteenth century. To achieve a break from his subject, Bourdieu does three things: first, he translates the folk term, *avant-garde literature*, into scientific terms; he speaks of the emergence of a literary field, of literary capital, and of the literary habitus, and so on; second, to counter the culturalistic, subjectivistic perspective that characterizes nativist understandings of the field, he starts with a materialistic and holistic perspective. In this materialist moment of the analysis, he looks at writing as a form of production, he looks at the aesthetic choices of writers as strategies of profit maximization, and he looks at how these individual choices are influenced by social position and trajectory. In the holistic moment of the analysis, he situates avant-garde writers in relation to conventional bourgeois writers, he shows how developments within the wider cultural and economic fields impacted the supply of writers and the demand for writing, and he shows how struggles within the cultural field were related to struggles within the economic field. This is the third operation: an emphasis on historical conjuncture and interfield relations. A "vulgar" sociology of this kind helps us to understand why, at this particular moment and in this particular place, a certain class of writers sought to change the rules of the game of literary production by challenging and, indeed, reversing the principles of supposed good literature and why some of them, such as Flaubert, were ultimately

successful. But it does not shed much light on the content of that new literature. To do that, we need to shift from a materialist, holistic perspective to a
more refined symbolic, subjective one. We would need to look at the various
styles and schools of literary production at this particular juncture in time
and, more deeply, at the symbolic oppositions that underlie these styles as well
as at the social composition of the various schools. And that is precisely what
Bourdieu does. This helps us to understand the particular set of aesthetic
choices that were open to would-be members of the avant-garde, the symbolic
distinctions through which they could achieve and manifest their social distinction. But it still does not tell us why some of those choices were chosen and
others not, why the choosers chose the way they did, and why some choices
proved successful while others did not. To do that, Bourdieu reintegrates the
results of the materialist moment of the analysis, by showing that those writers
who were best positioned to succeed, socially and economically, were inclined
to make certain aesthetic choices rather than others in ways that durably
affected the historical trajectory of the literary field itself.

A little reverse engineering on this explanatory model may identify some of
the methodological principles that underlie its construction. Three of them
should be familiar: the shift in moment, in language, in level, and in temporality. But there is much to be learned from seeing how Bourdieu actually
puts them into practice here. He begins with the materialist moment, presumably because this is the perspective that maximizes the epistemological distance between himself and his subjects. Literary producers and literary scholars are inclined to a hyperintellectualist, hypersubjectivist point of view and
are often devotees of the cult of creative genius. So our choice of stance follows
from our choice of object, not from any metaphysical or methodological
presuppositions. If we were analyzing, say, the emergence of the medical
profession in late nineteenth-century America, or of money and credit in late
twentieth-century America, we might actually want to begin with the symbolic moment (Abbott 1988; Zelizer 1994). Bourdieu is not a materialist, as has
often been claimed. If he frequently strikes up a materialistic stance, it is
because he often studies cultural objects. As for the shift in language, it has an
important effect: it results in a decomposition and multiplication of the naïve
object of analysis: instead of the avant-garde, a single object, we are now
confronted with at least three objects of explanation: a particular field, capital,
and habitus. Nor is Bourdieu content to anchor his explanations on one level
of analysis. His goal, in principle, is to trace lines of causal dependency across
the successive scales of social organization—to follow the formation of the
avant-garde habitus back to developments in the literary field, the cultural

field, and the space of power per se, and vice versa. There is also another specifically historical pattern of social causality at work: the expansion of higher education and the development of mass-market publishing, for example, have a major impact on literary production and are crucial factors in the emergence of the literary avant-garde. But they are the result of autonomous developments within the cultural and economic spheres.[8]

Taking apart *The Rules of Art*—probably Bourdieu's most methodologically sophisticated work—allows us to deepen our understanding of his basic methodological principles. We see, first, that we should choose the ontological and phenomenological starting points for our analysis in a way that maximizes the epistemological distance from the self-understanding of the dominant actors in the field under study. Thus, if we find that the study of the economy is dominated by, say, a hyperindividualist, utilitarian approach, then we should self-consciously begin our analyses of economic change from a holistic and symbolic perspective, one that looks, say, at fields rather than actors and at symbolic profits rather than material ones. Indeed, in keeping with the general principle of the epistemological break, we might even consider dropping the term *profits* altogether. While this term is useful in breaking with the doxa of cultural fields, where self-interest is supposedly excluded, it does not have this advantage where the economic field is concerned. In this domain we might derive more analytical leverage and greater critical distance from, say, a psychodynamic language of identity, cathexis, and gratification. Finally and, for our purposes, most important, *The Rules of Art* helps us to see how Bourdieu understands sociological explanation in general and sociohistorical explanation in particular. For Bourdieu there is no single, final, or even correct explanation of anything, only more complete, developed, adequate explanations—and for at least two reasons. Like Weber (and Heinrich Rickert), Bourdieu sees the social world as an infinite manifold of causal interdependencies; thus any outcome in which we are interested will be the result of a confluence of numerous causal chains (Bürger 1987; Weber 1949). Unlike the Weber of *The Protestant Ethic* (2001), however, and more like the later Weber (Weber 1924), Bourdieu is not content to reconstruct a single chain of causality but insists that we attempt to track multiple lines and levels of causation to whatever extent is practically possible, given time and data constraints. In this sense, sociological explanation as Bourdieu conceives it consists in the effort to reconstruct a web of causal interdependence. The concepts of field, capital, and habitus in their material and symbolic moments serve as heuristic, sensitizing devices that help us to discover and map these causal interrelationships. If sociological explanation focuses on causal connections, then specifically sociohistorical explanations focus on the causal conjunctions, on the intersection of "independent causal series," that occur in those spaces where fields overlap or collide.

As should be clear by now, Bourdieu's vision of sociohistorical explanation is quite different from those that currently dominate the social and historical sciences in the English-speaking world. So it may be useful to conclude this discussion of Bourdieu's methodology by comparing his explanatory practices to its rivals. To begin with the discipline of history, in truth, most historians do not reflect much on what it means to explain something. The cause and consequence of such lack of reflection is that their explanatory practices are often just sophisticated versions of folk practice. In mainstream historical discourse, as in most nonscientific discourses, to explain an event or action simply means to identify the sequence of events that preceded it or a complex of motives that animated it. From this perspective, something counts as explained to the extent that it has been successfully inserted into a narrative sequence or an interpretive framework. Explaining the French Revolution means recounting a series of crucial events, such as the French and Indian War, the calling of the Estates General, the abolition of feudalism, or reconstructing systems of values or ideas, such as *grandeur*, the Enlightenment, Jansenism, republicanism, that motivated actors.

Social scientists, by contrast, have engaged in considerable reflection about the meaning of explanation, or at least have engaged with philosophers of science who pretend to understand such things. Hence there is a substantial literature on this subject, if not a great deal of agreement, motivated by a strong desire to break with folk practices of explanation, including those prevalent in history. This break is typically achieved through two means. The first is to insist that explanations be general in form. From this perspective, it is not enough to narrate a series of events or reconstruct a system of motives, as historians do. Just what is enough, however, is a matter of considerable ongoing debate. The current state of play is roughly as follows. Inspired by Karl Popper, Carl Gustav Hempel, and Imre Lakatos, some social scientists insist that a genuine scientific explanation must invoke some kind of general law, ideally of a deterministic nature, which logically entails an observable outcome, thereby permitting "falsification" of the theory or at least of some version of the theory (Hempel 1965; Lakatos and Musgrave 1970; Popper 1959, 1962, 1972). This view of scientific explanation is generally referred to as the hypothetico-deductive model (Gorski 2004). It is most popular among economists and their acolytes in political science and sociology, and also among some practitioners of statistical modeling in the latter two disciplines. We might also call this the nomological approach, insofar as it insists that valid explanations invoke general laws that serve as the major premises in chains of deductive reasoning, enabling predictions about the observable world. Another model, inspired by realist philosophy of science, rejects the search for laws and makes the identification of underlying processes the evaluative standard (Gorski 2007). From this perspective a satisfactory explanation is one that identifies the causal mechanisms that produced a given outcome, *mechanisms* being understood here as patterns or sequences of events that recur across different contexts. This view is increasingly popular among sociologists and also among heterodox rational choice theorists, including a few within economics proper (Elster 1983a, 1989, 1999; Hedström and Swedberg 1998; Mahoney 2001, 2004; Tilly 1995, 2001). A third form of practice, prevalent among anthropologists and some cultural historians and sociologists, refuses the term *explanation* altogether, insisting instead on some form of interpretation, which is to say, an attempt to reconstruct and recover the deep structures of valuation and perception that motivate and underlie action (Dilthey, Makkreel, and Rodi 1989; Geertz 1973; Winch 1958). Insofar as it focuses on the way in which particular acts or utterances derive their meaning from larger systems of signification, interpretivism may also be seen as a holistic approach.

The second principal way in which social scientists attempt to break with folk theories is by invoking a dualistic social ontology of some sort. Sometimes the duality simply privileges one moment of social phenomena, usually some form of the symbolic ("identity," "culture," "discourse," "values," and so on) or the material ("interests," "practice," "utility," and so on). Sometimes it privileges one level or region of the social field, usually the whole, however conceived (for example, the "mode of production," the "value system," the "social system," the "world system," and so on) or some basic element or true foundation (for example, the "individual," "agency," the economy, the "lifeworld," and so on). Perhaps in hopes of grounding their criteria of scientific explanation even more firmly, most theoretical systems invoke both kinds of dualism. Marxism privileges the material and the whole, neoliberalism the material and the individual, neo-Durkheimianism the symbolic and the whole, ethnomethodology the symbolic and the individual. As diverse as these models are, they have one thing in common: they try to tame the phenomenal chaos of the social world by stipulating an unmoved mover, a moment in social space and a point in historical time at which causality begins and explanation stops. One might also call this approach ontological, insofar as it seeks to tame causal complexity by means of ontological reduction, or deistic because of its appeal to an unmoved mover.

Where does Bourdieu stand in these debates? A superficial and decontextualized reading of his work might suggest he is firmly aligned with the social scientists against the historians, with advocates of explanation against proponents of interpretation, with the holists against the individualists, and with the materialists against the culturalists. But this is a polemical and political stance rather than an epistemological and ontological one. It is true that Bourdieu loudly and frequently defended the pursuit of a social *science* that searches for regularities in and even laws of social life, against humanistic interpretation of the individual, the particular, and the unique, which he denounced as an "ideology of charisma" whose only use was to salve the narcissistic wounds of intellectuals. But it is also true that he saw social science as a means of assessing and enlarging the real possibilities of individual creativity and human freedom. In *The Rules of Art* Bourdieu argues that the only way of properly measuring the true genius of Flaubert is to fully appreciate the power of the constraints and conditionings to which his creative activity was subject and how difficult it was for him to create the social dis/position he embodied. It is also true that Bourdieu preached and practiced the principle of prioritizing the material and the holistic in sociohistorical analysis, even, or rather especially, in the analysis of culture. In all of his major empirical works—on class, on the state, on the academy, and on literature—he begins by reconstructing the field and analyzing the interests that attach to various positions within it. But it is also true that all of these works, including those on class and the state, pay systematic attention to the symbolic realm and that his later work on culture, as we have seen, analyzes even specific individuals. The priority he gives to science, to explanation, to the material, and to the social must be seen, first and foremost, as attempts to "twist the stick in the other direction," to overcome naïve understandings of the lifeworld, human action, individual freedom, and cultural dynamics, without denying their existence.

By exploding the claim that there is some single correct form of explanation in the social and historical sciences, or indeed that scientific explanation is the only proper end of these sciences, Bourdieu lays the groundwork for a fuller appreciation of the various forms that explanation (and interpretation) can take. Can we use the material to explain the symbolic? Certainly. Variations in social position go very far toward explaining variations in cultural dispositions. Taste in housing, food, sports, music, painting, and literature— these and many other elements of lifestyle and aesthetics can be and have been shown to correspond closely to an individual's stock of economic and cultural capital. The reverse is also true: a careful analysis of the space of lifestyles and aesthetics is a powerful tool for interpreting the operative lines of alliance and division within a given social space. Do the tastes and habits of the working class more closely resemble those of a business executive or of a university professor? The answer will tell you a great deal about party politics. But can we use the symbolic to explain the material as well? Certainly. As Bourdieu so powerfully shows in *Distinction*, the reproduction of social inequality and the unequal distribution of capital can be fully explained only in terms of symbolic processes of misrecognition and legitimation, such as the naturalization of socially produced differences or the expropriation of symbolic profits. Bourdieu's work also contains numerous strategies for explaining the properties and dynamics of certain parts in terms of the structure and development of some greater whole. For example, changes in the states of particular subfields (e.g., the degree of autonomy of the academic field), and in the relationship between fields (e.g., the permeability of the boundary between the scientific and religious fields) can be largely explained in terms of more general shifts within social space or within the field of power. Similarly, changes in reproduction and investment strategies in certain regions of social space (e.g., the amount that peasant families invest in education) can be largely explained in terms of the relative and absolute value of economic and cultural capital. Conversely, certain developments within a certain whole (e.g., in the structure of a field or of social space as such) can be largely explained in terms of developments within certain parts (e.g., in particular fields or subfields). The crisis of 1968—here I introduce a dynamic element—can be understood only in terms of the conjuncture and convergence of separate struggles across multiple fields. In such cases, Bourdieu speaks of the intersection of "independent causal series."

But if there is no single, correct form that explanations must take, then how do we evaluate them? Bourdieu never takes up this issue explicitly, perhaps because of his disdain for methodologism. Still, it is clear he would reject the logical criteria, espoused by the deductivists, that valid explanations must take the form of "covering laws," as well as any ontological criteria that make a particular entity into the unmoved mover of sociohistorical processes (class for Marxists, the individual for rational choice, and so on). In his research, he emphasized empirical engagement rather than logical form and championed a theoretical perspectivism rather than any one-sided ontology. Good work, he insisted, arises out of a deep engagement with the object of study and the determination to observe it from as many angles as possible. Progress in the social sciences is achieved through the careful construction of new objects of research—and the patient reconstruction of old ones—and through "epistemological vigilance" to our ontological blind spots, processes which require that we reflect on how our social position (i.e., as scholars) inflects our view of the social world (e.g., scholasticism). Good social science, he suggested, is less like architecture, where the final product is built according to a design stipulated in advance, than like painting or woodworking, where the final product is the result of multiple studies and successive adjustment and retouching (Bourdieu, Chamboredon, Passeron, 1991). Insofar as it emphasizes complexity and completeness over parsimony and precision, Bourdieu's vision of scientific progress is actually much closer to the vision of most historians than it is to the vision of many social scientists, and much closer to the mechanismic vision of social science than to deductivism or interpretivism.

Conclusion: Why and Whither Bourdieu?

The goal of this chapter, indeed of this book, has been to show that Bourdieusian theory provides powerful tools for analyzing sociohistorical transformation, that it is both possible and fruitful to study social change from a Bourdieusian perspective. Is it also preferable and desirable to do so? or should we choose some other general theory? or avoid general theory altogether? While I cannot fully address these questions here, I will attempt to outline my current thinking about them.

I begin with the universalizing theory du jour: rational choice. Rational choice theory stipulates that individuals seek to maximize utility, given certain subjective preferences and objective constraints. It is presently the dominant theory within the social sciences and, I would add, the dominant social science theory within public discourse. Initially developed to account for price formation within economic markets, it has gradually colonized the study of political life and is steadily encroaching on the study of social life as well. War and peace, movements and parties, crime and deviance, marriage and child rearing, traffic jams, and seating patterns: today there are few questions, political or social, great or small, for which a rational choice answer has not been proposed—and formalized. Nonetheless, I believe that the Bourdieusian David is actually more powerful than the rational choice Goliath, and in at least two crucial respects. First, it has an endogenous theory of preferences: it can predict the types of preferences (style, party, career, sexual mates, etc.) one is likely to find in certain regions of social space, and it can predict the way these preferences will be distributed across social space. After all, the theory of the habitus is, among other things, a theory of preferences. Rational choice theory, by contrast, does not have a predictive theory of preferences. It treats preferences as exogenous and subjective, as entities that are beyond the reach of the model and, indeed, beyond all explanation. A few rational choice theorists have attempted to develop an endogenous theory of preference, but they have not met with much success (Becker 1996). Second, while rational choice theory simply assumes that rationality is general and pervasive, that it is, so to speak, a built-in feature of human nature that everyone possesses in equal degree, Bourdieusian theory can actually account for variations in the degree and type of rationality across historical time and social space, something which new work in behavioral economics is also not equipped to do. At the most general level, it predicts that rationality will be greatest in periods of historical conjuncture and in the upper regions of social space, and it implies that rationality is somewhat field-specific—that knowing the rules of the game in the Chinese bureaucracy, the Catholic hierocracy, the corporate plutocracy, and the academic meritocracy are all somewhat different. For both of these reasons I believe Bourdieu is correct when he argues that rational choice theory is simply a subtheory within the theory of practice and that rational action is simply a particular form of practical action, and not necessarily the most common or important form.

Rational choice theory has made relatively few inroads into sociology and virtually none into history. Sociologists and historians who are interested in a universalistic theory of sociohistorical change have usually turned in a different direction: to Marxism. Like rational choice, Marxism is a formidable tradition of theorizing that has been developed over multiple generations and has been used in a number of disciplines to study a wide variety of topics, including economics, politics, culture, and so on. Marxism is a more fragmented and contentious tradition than rational choice, however, so it is always somewhat hazardous to speak of the Marxist theory of history. Still, most Marxists would probably agree on at least one premise: class struggle is the driving force of historical change. What advantages might Bourdieu have vis-à-vis Marx? Well, among other things, a more sophisticated theory of class struggle! There is no need to erect any vulgar Marxist straw men here. Since at least the early twentieth century Marxist theorists and activists have acknowledged that symbolic struggle is a crucial ingredient of class formation. And some, such as Antonio Gramsci, have even conceded the historical contingency of class formation. Still, because of its ontological commitment to materialism and its political commitment to the working class, Marxism has not been able to take these insights to their logical conclusion, the conclusion, that is, that class struggles are as much symbolic as material and that there is no prima facie reason to expect that economic class will always or inevitably trump other classifications, such as nation, race, gender, religion, and so on. The political history of the United States since the Great Depression provides ample proof of the mobilizing potential of such competing classifications and their capacity to undermine the salience of class in the Marxist sense. By contrast, Bourdieu's theory of classification struggles shows us a way to move beyond these limitations. It provides a set of conceptual tools and methodological procedures for analyzing the making and unmaking of groups that is arguably superior to even the most sophisticated versions of Marxist theory.

Grand theory is not much in fashion in sociology or history these days and has not been for some time. For most practicing researchers the real question is not which grand theory? but why grand theory? And there are surely plenty of reasons to be wary of grand theorizing. It can become disconnected from and uninformed by actual research, an endless exercise of textual exegesis. Or it can become a scholastic exercise, a never-ending quest for a coherent, closed set of concepts à la Parsons. It can spark insoluble and interminable metaphysical debates. In short, it can degenerate into mere ideology.

What alternatives are there? One can try to dispense with theory altogether by embracing some sort of radical descriptivism or subjectivism. The descriptivist stance has always had a substantial following within history, where it tends to attract methodological traditionalists and cultural conservatives. And the postmodern critique of master narratives and disciplinary objectivity has swelled the ranks of subjectivistic historians and sociologists content with the recovery of meaning. This is not to deny that descriptivists and subjectivists have produced a great deal of interesting, high-quality scholarship. Still, the shortcomings of these approaches are pretty obvious, at least to the sociologically minded. Even the most thoroughgoing descriptivism, which purports to narrate events or inventory facts, cannot avoid the use of certain natural categories (e.g., the event, the individual) and fundamental narrative devices (e.g., diffusion, sequence), which it thereby presents as natural and fundamental. Similarly, even the most careful subjectivism, one that is well aware of the perils of anachronism, is compelled to take actors' self-understandings more or less at face value, since it refuses to evaluate them against an objective background.

Common among historians, descriptivism and subjectivism are rarely, if ever, encountered among historical sociologists or other social scientists today.[9] Which is not to say that the current generation of historical sociologists is fond of grand theorizing; they are not.[10] At least not in public. In these quarters the standard practice is not so much a categorical rejection of grand theory as an opportunistic embrace of multiple grand theories: a little Marx, a little Weber, maybe a little Foucault or a little network theory, too. In historical sociology, grand theory is refused entrance at the front door, only to be quietly ushered in through the back. There is much to be said for the mix-and-match approach and for middle-range theorizing. This is what most of historical sociology—indeed, most of contemporary sociology—consists of. But there is also much to be said against it. A general theory does have certain advantages, both practical and theoretical. Practically, it provides a common language that facilitates dialogue between specialists; and it makes it easier to transmit research findings into public discourse. Theoretically, it yields more logically consistent representations of social reality, ones based on a single explicit ontology rather than on multiple implicit ones.

For those who regard such advantages as significant ones, there is really only one truly sociological theory that yields them, and that is Bourdieu's political economy of practice. This is not to say that Bourdieu's work is without spot or wrinkle. As we have seen, the framework remains somewhat underdeveloped in several areas. Three are of special moment: the symbolic, the subjective, and the transnational. Because so much of Bourdieu's work focused on the cultural field and because he wished to distance himself from the intellectualist and charismatic errors that characterize so many academic studies of culture, he inevitably gave added weight to the material and the objective. As a result, his methods of symbolic and subjective analysis remained somewhat anemic and underdeveloped. His analysis of symbolic spaces relied overmuch on an outmoded, Saussurean vision that emphasized binary oppositions, while his discussions of habitus rarely moved beyond the Chomskyan metaphor of generative structures. These are areas in which Bourdieu's theory would benefit from cross-pollination with kindred theories, such as Mikhail Bakhtin's sociolinguistics, Lacanian psychoanalysis, or recent work in cognitive psychology, all of which are broadly consonant with Bourdieu's sociology but much more fully elaborated both conceptually and methodologically (Bakhtin and Holquist 1981, 1986; Dimaggio 1997; Steinmetz 2005). Bourdieu has sometimes been criticized for being a "methodological nationalist" and rightly so (Beck and Sznaider 2006; Chernilo 2006). Like most social scientists and historians, he tacitly presumes the nation-state as the master unit of analysis. One need not subscribe to "nations are dead" versions of globalization theory to see that social science needs to pay more attention to trans- and supranational fields, and, indeed, some scholars have already begun doing so, by showing how global political and cultural structures can be conceived in field theoretic terms (Buchholz 2006; Go 2008). Here, Bourdieusian analysts would also do well to take account of the work of the Stanford school of organizational behavior, which has been analyzing global and transnational fields for almost a generation (Meyer and Scott 1983; Scott and Meyer 1994).

Bourdieusian theory might also benefit from a sustained dialogue with democratic theory of the sort essayed in chapter 6. If the two cardinal values of modern democracies are liberty and equality, there is no doubt that equality has weighed more heavily in Bourdieu's thinking. Indeed, it is no exaggeration to say that equality forms the normative horizon toward which most of his lifework was dedicated. This is not to say Bourdieu was unconcerned with democracy. But his writings on this subject rarely went beyond revealing its limits. What is needed, perhaps, is a positive theory of democracy that takes account of the subtle dynamics of exclusion and domination of which Bourdieu was the consummate analyst. But that is a subject for another book.

Notes

1. Loïc Wacquant, personal communication, April, 2006.
2. Another way of expressing this state of affairs is to say that law and business schools are closer to the heteronomous pole of the university field, while history and sociology are closer to the autonomous pole; economics and political science would then occupy an intermediate position. But this does not really give us much analytical purchase on variations in heteronomy, which is what we are interested in capturing here.
3. This is not to say there are no differences in prestige. The universities of Konstanz and Uppsala, for example, are more prestigious than those in, say, Giessen or Linköping. But the difference in prestige cannot be compared to that between, say, Yale, the University of Connecticut, and Gateway (a community college in New Haven).
4. For a brilliant extension of this analytic strategy, see Loveman (2005).
5. It would be wrong to assume some ineluctable and irreversible trend toward differentiation. One can just as easily imagine processes of de-differentiation and even of extinction. Is the distinction between the habitus of the entrepreneur and that of the manager as sharp as it was a century ago? Probably not, at least not in America. And what has become of the courtier, an important sociopolitical subtype not so long ago? The disappearance of a field or a change in its autonomy should also generate effects at the level of the habitus and vice versa.
6. At first glance, the Bourdieusian approach might appear to be similar to Coleman's "macro-micro-macro" model and related strategies (Coleman 1990). But a number of important differences exist. Rational choice models typically have only two ontological levels (e.g., individual and society). In Bourdieu's model, by contrast, the number of levels is equal to or greater than three. I say "equal to" because Bourdieu's three master concepts—field, capital, habitus—can also be conceived as three levels of a nested or scalar hierarchy, with fields determining the types of capital and the distribution of capital structuring the habitus—but also the reverse. But I say "greater than" because each level can be scaled up or down. For instance, the major fields of modern societies—economic, cultural, and political—are related to one another in an emergent field of power. But they can also be broken down into subfields. The cultural field in modern societies typically contains a scientific, artistic, and religious field, for example, to which correspond various subtypes of capital. Symbolic capital, meanwhile, can be thought of as a higher-order form of capital that emerges from the various pure types (e.g., economic and cultural).

Even the habitus can be scaled down or up. Thus we can speak of a class habitus that is characteristic and constitutive of a particular group. Similarly, we can break the individual habitus down in at least two ways: (1) into archaeological strata: the primary habitus acquired in the family, the secondary habitus acquired in school, and a tertiary habitus acquired in one's work life; and (2) into psychodynamic elements of an individual habitus: thus Bourdieu sometimes speaks of a "fractured habitus," in which a habitus specific to one field is logically incongruent and psychologically at odds with that specific to another field. In short, Bourdieu's model contains more than just the micro and the macro.

7. Sometimes, this break is already achieved by means of the shift in perspective. In America, for example, most laypeople and more than a few social scientists tend to view the world through the lens of a hyperindividualistic social ontology—so much so that many of them deny the very existence of society and of supraindividual entities *tout court*. In this context, invoking categories like class and field already constitutes a break with folk understandings. (In an earlier historical context invoking categories such as the individual or utility enabled a break. Whence the faint scent of radicalism that still lingers about neoclassical orthodoxy.)

8. Similarly, his analyses of the reproduction crisis within peasant families, both in Algeria and in France, give considerable weight to exogenous processes—demographic, epidemiological, logistical, educational, and so on. In fact, different as they are substantively, these two analyses are quite similar in formal terms: the rise of the avant-garde and the transformation of peasant households can both be seen as the result of crises of sociocultural reproduction triggered by shifting equilibria in other fields. While disruption and disequilibration are probably the forms that such cross-field interactions have most often taken historically, they are by no means the only one: sometimes crises across fields align, resulting in a synchronization of struggles and sometimes in a broad social crisis that unites actors occupying homologous positions across various fields.

9. The descriptivist stance is a minority one within sociology, though one does find partisans, especially in ethnomethodology and conversation analysis and, to a lesser extent, within the ethnographic tradition. Radical subjectivism, meanwhile, is mostly banished to cultural studies, but a more disciplined version of it can be found in the "strong program" of cultural sociology advocated by Jeffrey Alexander and others.

10. One does find it in an earlier generation of historical sociologists influenced by Parsons, and there is a small group within the current generation that embraces rational choice qua general theory.

APPENDIX 1

English Translations of Bourdieu's Works

The initial receptions of Bourdieu's works in Anglophone sociology are marked with an asterisk.

1962: *The Algerians*

1977: *Reproduction* (w. Passeron)*

1977: *Outline of a Theory of Practice**

1979: *Algeria 1960**

1979: *The Inheritors* (w. Passeron)*

1984: *Distinction**

1988: *Homo Academicus*

1990: *Logic of Practice*

1990: *In Other Words*

1990: *Photography*

1991: *Craft of Sociology*

1991: *Political Ontology of Martin Heidegger*

1991: *Language and Symbolic Power*

1992: *Invitation to Reflexive Sociology* (with Wacquant)

1993: *Field of Cultural Production*

1993: *Sociology in Question*

1995: *Free Exchange* (with Haacke)

1996: *Rules of Art*

1996: *State Nobility*

1998: *On Television*

1998: *Practical Reason*

1998: *Acts of Resistance*

2000: *Pascalian Meditations*

2001: *Masculine Domination*

2003: *Firing Back*

2004: *Science of Science and Reflexivity*

2005: *Social Structures of the Economy*

2007: *Celibates' Ball*

2008: *Sketch for a Self-Analysis*

2010: *Uprooting*

Original titles are in parentheses. Works marked by an asterisk have not yet been translated.

1958: *Algerians* (*Sociologie de l'Algérie*)

1964: *Travail et travailleurs en Algérie**

1964: *Uprooting* (*Le Déracinement*)

1964: *Etudiants et leurs etudes* (with Passeron)*

1964: *The Inheritors* (*Héritiers*) (with Passeron)

1965: *Photography* (*Art moyen*) (with Boltanski et al.)

1966: *Love of Art* (*Amour de l'art*)

1968: *The Craft of Sociology* (*Métier de sociologue*)

1970: *Reproduction* (*Reproduction*)

1972: *Outline of a Theory of Practice* (*Esquisse d'une théorie de la pratique*)

1977: *Algeria 1960* (*Algérie 60*)

1979: *Distinction* (*Distinction*)

1980: *Sociology in Question* (*Questions de sociologie*)

1980: *Logic of Practice* (*Sens pratique*)

1982: *Language and Symbolic Power* (*Ce que parler veut dire*)

1984: *Homo Academicus*

1987: *In Other Words* (*Choses dites*)

1988: *The Political Ontology of Martin Heidegger* (*Ontologie politique de Martin Heidegger*)

1989: *The State Nobility* (*Noblesse d'état*)

1992: *The Rules of Art* (*Règles de l'art*)

1994: *Free Exchange* (*Libre-échange*) (with Hans Haacke)

1996: *On Television* (*Sur la télévision*)

1997: *Pascalian Meditations* (*Méditations pascaliennes*)

1998: *Firing Back* (*Contre-feux*)

1998: *Masculine Domination* (*Domination masculine*)

2000: *Social Structures of the Economy* (*Structures sociales de l'économie*)

2001: *Science of Science and Reflexivity* (*Science de la science et réflexiviae*)

2002: *The Celibates' Ball* (*Bal des célibataires: crise de la société paysanne en Béarn*)

2004: *Sketch for a Self-Analysis* (*Esquisse pour une auto-analyse*)

WORKS CITED

Abbott, Andrew D. 1988. *The System of Professions: An Essay on the Division of Expert Labor*. Chicago: University of Chicago Press.

Abélard, J. 1995. "Les *Illustrations de Gaule* de Jean Lemaire de Belges: Quelle Gaule? Quelle France? Quelle Nation?" *Nouvelle Revue du Seizième Siècle* 13(1): 7–27.

Aboulafia, Mitchell. 1999. "A (neo) American in Paris: Bourdieu, Mead, and Pragmatism." *Bourdieu: A Critical Reader*, ed. Richard Shusterman, 153–74. Oxford: Blackwell.

Abraham, Karl, and Ernest Jones. 1927. *Selected Papers of Karl Abraham, M. D.* London: L. and Virginia Woolf [etc.].

Adams, Julia. 2005. *The Familial State: Ruling Families and Merchant Capitalism in Early Modern Europe*. Ithaca: Cornell University Press.

Agulhon, Maurice. 1968. *Pénitents et Francmaçons de l'ancienne province*. Paris: Fayard.

Akenson, Donald Harman. 1991. *God's Peoples: Covenant and Land in South Africa, Israel, and Ulster*. Montreal: McGill-Queen's University Press.

Alexander, Jeffrey C. 1995. "The Reality of Reduction: The Failed Synthesis of Pierre Bourdieu." *Fin de Siécle Social Theory: Relativism, Reduction, and the Problem of Reason*, 128–217. New York: Verso.

Alston, Lee J., and Joseph P. Ferrie. 1999. *Southern Paternalism and the American Welfare State: Economics, Politics, and Institutions in the South, 1865–1965*. New York: Cambridge University Press.

Althusser, Louis. 1971. *Lenin and Philosophy, and Other Essays*. London: New Left Books.

———. 1979. *For Marx*. London: Verso.

Amenta, Edwin. 1998. *Bold Relief: Institutional Politics and the Origins of Modern American Social Policy*. Princeton: Princeton University Press.

———. 2001. "Who Voted with Hopkins? Institutional Politics and the WPA." *Journal of Policy History* 13(2): 251–87.

Amenta, Edwin, and Drew Halfmann. 2000. "Wage Wars: Institutional Politics, WPA Wages, and the Struggle for U.S. Social Policy." *American Sociological Review* 65(4): 506–28.

Anderson, Benedict R. O. G. 1991. *Imagined Communities: Reflections on the Origin and Spread of Nationalism*. London: Verso.

Anonymous. 1919. "Le Circuit des Champs de Bataille." *L'Auto*, January 5, April 24– May 12, front pages.

———. 1928. "Mussolini et le Sport." *Le Miroir des Sports*, May 15, 300.

———. 1935. (Les Sports Athlétiques: Le Sport Mondial) "L'organisation du Sport en Italie." *L'Auto*, September 6, 5.

Anzieu, Didier. 1986. *Freud's Self-Analysis*. London: Hogarth Press and the Institute of Psycho-analysis.

Appelt, U. F. 1994. "'Another Troy to Burn': History, Origin, and the Politics of Descent in Tudor England." Ph.D. diss., University of Virginia.

Archer, Margaret. 1993. "Bourdieu's Theory of Cultural Reproduction: French or Universal?" *French Cultural Studies* 4(12): 225–40.

Arnaud, Pierre. 1980. "L'actualité de l'Histoire: Le Surmenage des écoliers." *Travaux et Recherches en E.P.S., INSEP* 6: 136–51.

Arnaud, Pierre, and Maurice Agulhon. 1991. *Le Militaire, l'écolier, le Gymnaste: Naissance de L'éducation Physique en France: 1869–1889*. Lyon: Presses Universitaires de Lyon.

Atsma, Hartmut, and André Burguière, eds. 1990. *Marc Bloch Aujourd'hui: Histoire Comparée and Sciences Sociales*. Paris: Editions de l'Ecole des Hautes Etudes en Sciences Sociales.

Babík, Milan. 2006. "Nazism as a Secular Religion." *History and Theory* 45(3): 375–96.

Babson, Steve. 1999. *The Unfinished Struggle: Turning Points in American Labor, 1877–Present*. New York: Rowman and Littlefield.

Bachelard, Gaston. 1949. *Le Rationalisme Appliqué*. Paris: Presses Universitaires de France.

———. 1980. *La Formation de L'esprit scientifique: Contribution à une Psychanalyse de la Connaissance Objective*. Paris: J. Vrin.

———. 1984. *The New Scientific Spirit*. New York: W. W. Norton.

———. 2002 [1938]. *The Formation of the Scientific Mind*. Translated by Mary McAllester Jones. Manchester: Clinamen.

Baer, Gabriel. 1979. "Orientalism in Israel in the Last 30 Years." *Hamizrach Hachadash* 28(3–4): 175–81. [Hebrew]

Bakhtin, Mikhail M., and Michael Holquist. 1981. *The Dialogic Imagination: Four Essays*. Austin: University of Texas Press.

———. 1986. *Speech Genres and Other Late Essays*. Austin: University of Texas Press.

Balibar, Etienne, and Immanuel Wallerstein. 1991. *Race, Nation, Class: Ambiguous Identities*. London: Verso.

Banerjee, Neela. 2006. "Students Flock to Seminaries, But Fewer See Pulpit in Future." *New York Times*. 17 March.

Bastide, Roger. 1958. *Le Candomblé de Bahia (Rite Nagô)*. Paris: Mouton.

———. 1970–71. "Mémoire collective et bricolage." *L'Année Sociologique*, ser. 3, 21: 65–110.

Beaune, Colette, and Fredric L. Cheyette. 1991. *The Birth of an Ideology: Myths and Symbols of Nation in Late-Medieval France*. Berkeley: University of California Press.

Beck, Ulrich, and Natan Sznaider. 2006. "Unpacking Cosmopolitanism for the Social Sciences: A Research Agenda." *British Journal of Sociology* 57(1): 1–23.

Becker, Gary S. 1996. *Accounting for Tastes*. Cambridge: Harvard University Press.

Bell, David A. 2001. *The Cult of the Nation in France: Inventing Nationalism, 1680–1800*. Cambridge: Harvard University Press.

Bender, Thomas. 2006. *A Nation among Nations: America's Place in World History*. New York: Hill and Wang.

Bénichou, Paul. 1996. *Le Sacre de L'écrivain 1750–1830: Essai sur l'Avènement d'un Pouvoir Spirituel Laïque dans la France Moderne*. Paris: Gallimard, 1973.

Benson, Rodney D. 1999. "Field Theory in Comparative Context: A New Paradigm for Media Studies." *Theory and Society* 28: 463–98.

Benson, Rodney D., and Erik Neveu. 2005. *Bourdieu and the Journalistic Field*. Malden, Mass.: Polity.

Benzécri, Jean-Paul. 1980. *Pratique de l'Analyse des Données*, 1. *Exposé Élémentaire*. Paris: Dunod. English trans., 1992, *Handbook of Correspondence Analysis*. New York: Dekker.

Bergen, Doris L. 2003. "Die 'deutschen Christen' 1933–1945: Ganz Normale Glaubige und eifrige Komplizen?" *Geschichte und Gesellschaft* 29(4): 542–74.

Berlin, Isaiah, and Henry Hardy, eds. 1980. *Against the Current: Essays in the History of Ideas*. New York: Viking.

Best, Heinrich. 1990. *Die Männer von Bildung un Besitz: Struktur und Handeln Parlamentarischer Führungsgruppen in Deutschland und Frankreich (1848/49)*. Düsseldorf: Droste Verlag.

Bhaskar, Roy. 1979. *The Possibility of Naturalism: A Philosophical Critique of the Contemporary Human Sciences*. Atlantic Highlands, N.J.: Humanities.

Biernacki, Richard. 1995. *The Fabrication of Labor: Germany and Britain, 1640–1914*. Berkeley: University of California Press.

Bloch, Marc. 1953 [1928]. "Toward a Comparative History of European Societies." *Enterprise and Secular Change: Readings in Economic History*, ed. Frederic C. Lane, and Jelle C. Riemersma, 494–521. Homewood, Ill.: R. D. Irwin.

———. 1990. *L'Étrange Défaite*. Paris: Gallimard.

Blumer, Herbert. 1954. "What Is Wrong with Social Theory?" *American Sociological Review* 19(1): 3–10.

Bordwell, David, and Kristin Thompson. 1979. *Film Art: An Introduction*. Reading, Mass.: Addison-Wesley.

Boschetti, Anna. 1985. *Sartre et les Temps Modernes*. Paris: Minuit.

Bouchard, M. 1893. "Actes, 1. partie." In *Association Française pour l'Avancement des Sciences*, vol. 1. Besançon: Au Secrétariat de l'Association.

Bourdieu, Pierre. 1959. "La Logique Interne de la Civilisation Algérienne Traditionnelle" and "Le Choc des Civilizations." *Le sous-développement en Algérie*, ed. S. S. d'Alger, 40–64. Algiers: Éditions du Secrétariat Social d'Alger.

———. 1961. *Sociologie de l'Algérie*. Paris: Presses Universitaires de France.

———. 1962. *The Algerians*. Boston: Beacon Press.

———. 1964. *Les Héritiers: Les Etudiants et la Culture*. Paris: Minuit.

———. 1969. "Intellectual Field and Creative Project." *Social Science Information* 8(2): 89–119.

———. 1971a. "Champ du Pouvoir, Champ Intellectuel et Habitus de Classe." *Scolies* 1: 7–26.

———. 1971b. "Intellectual Field and Creative Project." *Knowledge and Control: New Directions for the Sociology of Education*, ed. M. F. D. Young, 161–88. London: Collier-Macmillan.

———. 1971c. "Le Marché des Biens Symboliques." *L'Année sociologique* 22: 49–126.

———. 1975. "The Specificity of the Scientific Field and the Social Conditions of the Progress of Reason." *Social Science Information* 14(6): 19–47.

———. 1977. *Outline of a Theory of Practice*. Translated by Richard Nice. Cambridge: Cambridge University Press.

———. 1979a. *Algeria 1960: The Disenchantment of the World: The Sense of Honour: The Kabyle House or the World Reversed: Essays*. Translated by Richard Nice. Cambridge: Cambridge University Press.

———. 1979b. *La Distinction: Critique Sociale du Jugement*. Paris: Minuit.

———. 1984a. *Distinction: A Social Critique of the Judgment of Taste*. Translated by Richard Nice. Cambridge: Cambridge University Press.

———. 1984b. *Homo Academicus*. Paris: Minuit.

———. 1985a. "The Genesis of the Concepts of Habitus and Field." *Sociocriticism* 2(2): 11–24.

———. 1985b. "The Social Space and the Genesis of Groups." *Theory and Society* 14(6): 723–44.

———. 1986a. "The Biographical Illusion." *Working Papers and Proceedings for the Center for Psychosocial Studies*, 1–7.

———. 1986b. "The Forms of Capital." *Handbook of Theory and Research for the Sociology of Education*, ed. John G. Richardson, 241–58. New York: Greenwood.

———. 1987a [1971]. "Legitimation and Structured Interests in Weber's Sociology of Religion." *Max Weber: Rationality and Modernity*, ed. Scott Lash and Sam Whimster, 119–36. London: Allen and Unwin.

———. 1987b. "What Makes a Social Class? On the Theoretical and Practical Existence of Groups." *Berkeley Journal of Sociology* 32: 1–18.

———. 1988a. *Homo Academicus*. Translated by Peter Collier. Stanford: Stanford University Press.

———. 1988b. "Flaubert's Point of View." *Critical Inquiry* 14: 539–62.

———. 1989a. "Social Space and Symbolic Power." *Sociological Theory* 7(1): 14–25.

———. 1989b. "The Corporatism of the Universal: The Role of Intellectuals in the Modern World." *Telos* 81: 99–110.

———. 1989c. *La Noblesse d'Etat: Grandes écoles et Esprit de Corps*. Paris: Minuit.

———. 1990a [1980]. *The Logic of Practice*. Translated by Richard Nice. Stanford: Stanford University Press.

———. 1990b. "La Domination Masculine." *Actes de la Recherche en Sciences Sociales* 84(3): 2–31.

———. 1990c. "The Scholastic Point of View." *Cultural Anthropology* 5(4): 380–91.

———. 1990d. "Animadversiones in Mertonem." *Robert K. Merton: Consensus and Controversy*, ed. Jon Clark, Celia Modgil, and Sohan Modgil, 297–301. London: Falmer.

———. 1990e. *In Other Words: Essays Towards a Reflexive Sociology*. Translated by Matthew Adamson. Stanford: Stanford University Press.

———. 1990f. *Photography, a Middle-Brow Art*. Stanford: Stanford University Press.

———. 1991a [1975]. *The Political Ontology of Martin Heidegger*. Translated by Peter Collier. Oxford: Polity.

———. 1991b. "Le Champ Littéraire." *Actes de la Recherche en Sciences Sociales* 89: 4–46.

———. 1991c. "Genesis and Structure of the Religious Field." *Comparative Social Research* 13: 1–43.

———. 1991d. "The Peculiar History of Scientific Reason." *Sociological Forum* 6: 3–26.

———. 1991e. *Language and Symbolic Power*. Edited John B. Thompson. Translated by Gino Raymond and Matthew Adamson. Cambridge: Harvard University Press.

———. 1992. *Les Règles de l'Art: Genèse et Structure du Champ Littéraire*. Paris: Seuil.

———. 1993a [1980]. *Sociology in Question*. Translated by Richard Nice. London: Sage.

———. 1993b. "Concluding Remarks." *Bourdieu: Critical Perspectives*, ed. Craig Calhoun, Edward LiPuma, and Moishe Postone, 263–75. Chicago: University of Chicago Press.

———. 1993c. *The Field of Cultural Production*. Edited by Randal Johnson. New York: Columbia University Press.

———. 1994a. "Avant-Propos Dialogué." *L'Autobiographie d'un Paranoïaque: L'abbé Berry (1878–1947) et le Roman de Billy Introïbo*, ed. J. Maître, v–xxii. Paris: Anthropos.

———. 1994b. "Rethinking the State: Genesis and Structure of the Bureaucratic Field." *Sociological Theory* 12(1): 1–18.

———. 1996a [1992]. *The Rules of Art: Genesis and Structure of the Literary Field*. Translated by Susan Emanuel. Stanford: Stanford University Press.

———. 1996b. *The State Nobility: Elite Schools in the Field of Power*. Translated by Lauretta C. Clough. Stanford: Stanford University Press.

———. 1997. *Les Usages Sociaux de la Science: Pour une Sociologie Clinique du Champ Scientifique: Une Conférence-Débat*. Paris: Institut National de la Recherche Agronomique.

———. 1998a. *Acts of Resistance: Against the Tyranny of the Market*. Translated by Richard Nice. New York: New Press.

———. 1998b. *Masculine Domination*. Paris: Seuil.

———. 1998c. *On Television*. Translated by Priscilla Parkhurst Ferguson. New York: New Press.

———. 1998d. *Practical Reason: On the Theory of Action*. Stanford: Stanford University Press.

———. 1998e. "The Essence of Neoliberalism." *Le Monde Diplomatique*, 1–7.

———. 1998f [1994]. "A Paradoxical Foundation of Ethics." *Practical Reason: On the Theory of Action*, 141–45. Stanford: Stanford University Press.

———. 1999 [1995]. "On the Relationship between Sociology and History in Germany and France." *Social Time and Social Change: Perspectives on Sociology and History*, ed. Fredrik Engelstad and Ragnvald Kalleberg, 157–86. Oslo: Scandinavian University Press.

———. 2000a. *Les Structures Sociales de l'économie*. Paris: Seuil.

———. 2000b. *Pascalian Meditations*. Translated by Richard Nice. Stanford: Stanford University Press.

————. 2001a. *Contre-feux 2: Pour un Mouvement Social Européen.* Paris: Raisons d'Agir.

————. 2001b. *Masculine Domination.* Translated by Richard Nice. Stanford: Stanford University Press.

————. 2001c. *Science de la Science et Réflexivité: Cours du Collège de France, 2000–2001.* Paris: Raisons d'Agir.

————. 2002a. "Les Conditions Sociales et la Circulation Internationale des Idées." *Actes de la Recherche en Sciences Sociales* 145: 3–8.

————. 2002b. *Ein Soziologischer Selbstversuch.* Frankfurt am Main: Suhrkamp.

————. 2002c. *Interventions, 1961–2002: Science Sociale et Action Politique.* Marseille: Agone.

————. 2003a. "Participant Objectification." *Journal of the Royal Anthropological Institute* 9: 281–94.

————. 2003b. *Firing Back: Against the Tyranny of the Market 2.* Translated by Loïc J. D. Wacquant. London: Verso.

————. 2003c. *Images d'Algérie. Une affinité elective,* ed. Franz Schultheis and Christine Frisinghelli. Arles: Actes Sud.

————. 2004a. "From the King's House to the Reason of State: A Model of the Genesis of the Bureaucratic Field." *Constellations* 11(1): 16–36.

————. 2004b. "Algerian Landing." Translated by Richard Nice and Loïc Wacquant. *Ethnography* 5: 415–43.

————. 2004c. *Esquisse pour une Auto-Analyse.* Paris: Raisons d'Agir.

————. 2004d [2001c]. *Science of Science and Reflexivity.* Chicago: University of Chicago Press.

————. 2005a [1995]. "The Political Field, the Social Science Field, and the Journalistic Field." *Bourdieu and the Journalistic Field,* ed. Rodney Benson, 29–47. Malden, Mass.: Polity.

————. 2005b [2000]. *The Social Structures of the Economy.* Cambridge: Polity.

————. 2008 [2002]. *Political Interventions: Social Science and Political Action.* London and New York: Verso.

————. 2008a. *Esquisses Algériennes.* Paris: Seuil.

————. 2008b. *Sketch for a Self-Analysis.* Translated by Richard Nice. Chicago: University of Chicago Press.

————. 2008c. *The Bachelors' Ball: The Crisis of Peasant Society in Béarn.* Translated by Richard Nice. Chicago: University of Chicago Press.

Bourdieu, Pierre. 1999. *The Weight of the World: Social Suffering in Contemporary Society.* Translated by Priscilla Parkhurst Ferguson. Stanford: Stanford University Press.

Bourdieu, Pierre, and Luc Boltanski. 1981. "The Educational System and the Economy: Titles and Jobs." *French Sociology: Rupture and Renewal since 1968,* ed. Charles Lemert. New York: Columbia University Press.

Bourdieu, Pierre, Luc Boltanski, Robert Castel, J.-C. Chamboredon, and Dominique Schnapper. 1990 [1965]. *Photography: A Middlebrow Art.* Cambridge: Polity.

Bourdieu, Pierre, Jean-Claude Chamboredon, and Jean-Claude Passeron. 1991. *The Craft of Sociology: Epistemological Preliminaries,* ed. Beate Krais. Translated by Richard Nice. Berlin: Walter de Gruyter.

Bourdieu, Pierre, Christophe Charle, Hartmut Kaelble, and Jürgen Kocka. 1995. "Dialogue sur L'histoire Comparée." *Actes de la Recherche en Sciences Sociales* 106–7: 102–4.

Bourdieu, Pierre, and Alain Darbel. 1963. *Travail et Travailleurs en Algérie*. Paris: Mouton.

Bourdieu, Pierre, Alain Darbel, J.-P. Rivet, and C. Seibel. 1995 [1963]. *Travail et travailleurs en Algerie*. Paris and The Hague: Mouton.

Bourdieu, Pierre, Alain Darbel, and Dominique Schnapper. 1990 [1966]. *The Love of Art: European Art Museums and Their Public*. Translated by Caroline Beattie and Nick Merriman. Stanford: Stanford University Press.

Bourdieu, Pierre, and Jean-Claude Passeron. 1967. "Sociology and Philosophy in France since 1945: Death and Resurrection of a Philosophy without Subject." *Social Research* 34: 162–212.

——. 1977. *Reproduction in Education, Society and Culture*. Beverly Hills: Sage.

——. 1979. *The Inheritors: French Students and Their Relation to Culture*. Chicago: University of Chicago Press.

Bourdieu, Pierre, Jean-Claude Passeron, and Jean-Claude Chamboredon. 1968. *Le Métier de Sociologue*. Paris: Mouton.

Bourdieu, Pierre, Frank Poupeau, and Thierry Discepolo. 2002. *Interventions, 1961–2001: Science Sociale et Action Politique*, ed. Frank Poupeau and Thierry Discepolo. Marseilles and Montréal: Agone.

Bourdieu, Pierre, and Lutz Raphael. 1995. "Sur les Rapports entre l'Histoire et la Sociologie en France et en Allemagne." *Actes de la Recherche en Sciences Sociales* 106–7: 108–22.

Bourdieu, Pierre, and Abdelmalek Sayad. 1964. *Le Déracinement, la Crise de l'Agriculture en Algerie*. Paris: Editions de Minuit.

Bourdieu, Pierre, and Loïc Wacquant. 1992. *An Invitation to Reflexive Sociology*. Chicago: University of Chicago Press.

——. 2000. "The Organic Ethnologist of Algerian Migration." *Ethnography* 1: 173–82.

Boyer, Robert. 2003. "L'anthropologie économique de Pierre Bourdieu." *Actes de la Recherche en Sciences Sociales* 150: 65–78.

Brass, Paul R. 1991. *Ethnicity and Nationalism: Theory and Comparison*. Newbury Park, Calif.: Sage.

Braungardt, Jürgen. 1999. "Theology after Lacan? A Psychoanalytic Approach to Theological Discourse." *Other Voices* 1(3). http://www.othervoices.org/1.3/jbraungardt/theology.php.

Braverman, Harry. 1975. *Labor and Monopoly Capital; The Degradation of Work in the Twentieth Century*. New York: Monthly Review Press.

Bremer, William W. 1975. "Along the 'American Way': The New Deal's Work Relief Programs for the Unemployed." *Journal of American History* 62: 636–52.

Breuer, Josef, Sigmund Freud, and A. A. Brill. 1950. *Studies in Hysteria*. New York: Nervous and Mental Disease Monographs.

Breuilly, John. 1982. *Nationalism and the State*. London: Manchester University Press.

Brousse, Michel. 2005. *Les Racines du Judo Français*. Bordeaux: Presses Universitaires de Bordeaux.

Brown, Michael K. 1999. *Race, Money, and the American Welfare State*. Ithaca: Cornell University Press.

Brubaker, Rogers. 1985. "Rethinking Classical Sociology: The Sociological Vision of Pierre Bourdieu." *Theory and Society* 14(6): 745–75.

——. 1992. *Citizenship and Nationhood in France and Germany*. Cambridge: Harvard University Press.

——. 1993. "Social Theory as Habitus." *Bourdieu: Critical Perspectives*, ed. Craig Calhoun, Edward LiPuma, and Moishe Postone, 212–34. Chicago: University of Chicago Press.

——. 1996. *Nationalism Reframed: Nationhood and the National Question in the New Europe*. New York: Cambridge University Press.

——. 2004. *Ethnicity without Groups*. Cambridge: Harvard University Press.

——. 2006. *Nationalist Politics and Everyday Ethnicity in a Transylvanian Town*. Princeton: Princeton University Press.

Brunelle, Gayle K. 1995. "Dangerous Liaisons: Mésalliance and Early Modern French Noblewomen." *French Historical Studies* 19(1): 75–104.

Bryson, Norman. 1994. "Géricault and 'Masculinity.'" *Visual Culture: Images and Interpretation*, ed. Norman Bryson, Michael Ann Holly, and Keith Moxey, 228–58. Hanover: University Press of New England.

Buchholz, Larrisa. 2006. "Field Theory and the Globalization of Art: Rethinking 'Interdependency.'" Paper presented at the conference "Practicing Pierre Bourdieu: In the Field and across the Disciplines," University of Michigan. September 29.

Bulmer, Martin. 1984. *The Chicago School of Sociology*. Chicago: University of Chicago Press.

Bunche, Ralph J. 1973. *The Political Status of the Negro in the Age of FDR*, ed. Dewey W. Grantham. Chicago: University of Chicago Press.

Bürger, Thomas. 1987. *Max Weber's Theory of Concept Formation: History, Laws, and Ideal Types*. Durham: Duke University Press.

Butler, Judith. 1997. *The Psychic Life of Power: Theories in Subjection*. Stanford: Stanford University Press.

——. 1999. "Performativity's Social Magic." *Bourdieu: A Critical Reader*, ed. Richard Shusterman, 113–28. Oxford: Blackwell.

Caillois, Roger. 1967. *Jeux et Sports*. Paris: Gallimard.

Calhoun, Craig J. 1993a. "Habitus, Field, and Capital: The Question of Historical Specificity." *Bourdieu: Critical Perspectives*, ed. Craig Calhoun, Edward LiPuma, and Moishe Postone, 61–88. Chicago: University of Chicago Press.

——. 1993b. "Nationalism and Ethnicity." *Annual Review of Sociology* 19: 211–39.

——. 1995. *Critical Social Theory*. Oxford: Wiley-Blackwell.

——. 1997. *Nationalism*. Minneapolis: University of Minnesota Press.

——. 2002. "Existing Cosmopolitanism." *Debating Cosmopolitics*, ed. D. Archibugi, 86–116. London: Verso.

——. 2011. "Pierre Bourdieu." *The Blackwell Companion to the Major Social Theorists*, ed. George Ritzer, 696–730. Cambridge: Blackwell.

——. Forthcoming. "The Democratic Integration of Europe: Interests, Identity, and the Public Sphere." *Remapping Europe*, ed. Mabel Berezin and Martin Schain. Baltimore: Johns Hopkins University Press.

Callon, Michel. 1998. "Introduction: The Embeddedness of Economic Markets in Economics." *The Laws of the Markets*, ed. Michel Callon, 1–57. Oxford: Blackwell.

Camic, Charles. 2001. "The Eclipse of 'Character': A Case Study in the Sociology of Ideas." Paper presented at Princeton University.

——. 2007. "On Edge: Sociology during the Great Depression and the New Deal." *Sociology in America: A History*, ed. Craig Calhoun, 225–80. Chicago: University of Chicago Press.

Carles, Pierre (Director). 2001. *Sociology Is a Martial Art*. France: C-P Productions et VF Films présentent; Brooklyn: Icarus Films.

Casanova, Pascale. 1999. *La République Mondiale des Lettres*. Paris: Seuil. English trans. 2005, *The World Republic of Letters*. Cambridge: Harvard University Press.

——. 2004 [1999]. *The World Republic of Letters*. Translated by M. B. DeBevoise. Cambridge: Harvard University Press.

Cassell, Joan. 1998. *The Woman in the Surgeon's Body*. Cambridge: Harvard University Press.

Champagne, Patrick, René Lenoir, Dominique Merllié, and Louis Pinto. 1989. *Introduction à la Pratique Sociologique*. Paris: Dunod.

Charle, Christophe. 1979. *La Crise Littéraire à l'époque du Naturalisme*. Paris: Presses de l'Ecole Normale Supérieure.

——. 1985. *Les Professeurs de la Faculté des Lettres de Paris: Dictionnaire Biographique*, Vol. 1 *(1809–1908)*. Paris: Editions du CNRS-INRP.

——. 1986. *Les Professeurs de la Faculté des Lettres de Paris: Dictionnaire Biographique*, Vol. 2 *(1909–1939)*. Paris: Editions du CNRS-INRP.

——. 1987. *Les Élites de la République 1880–1900*. Paris: Fayard.

——. 1988. *Les Professeurs du Collège de France: Dictionnaire Biographique (1901–1939)*. Paris: Editions du CNRS-INRP.

——. 1989. *Les Professeurs de la Faculté des Sciences de Paris: Dictionnaire Biographique (1901–1939)*. Paris: Editions du CNRS-INRP.

——. 1990a. *Naissance des 'Intellectuels' 1880–1900*. Paris: Minuit.

——. 1990b. "A la Recherche des Bourgeoisies Européennes." *Le Mouvement Sociale* 153: 91–97.

——. 1994a. *La République des Universitaires (1870–1940)*. Paris: Seuil.

——. 1994b. *A Social History of France in the Nineteenth Century*. Translated by Miriam Kochan. Oxford: Berg.

——. 1996. *Les Intellectuels en Europe au XIXe Siècle: Essai d'Histoire Comparée*. Paris: Seuil.

——. 1997. "Légitimités en Péril: Eléments pour une Histoire Comparée des élites et de l'Etat en France et en Europe Occidentale (XIXe–XXe siècles)." *Actes de la Recherche en Sciences Sociales* 116–17: 39–52.

——. 1998. *Paris Fin de Siècle: Culture et Politique*. Paris: Seuil.

——. 2001. *La Crise des Sociétés Impériales*. Paris: Seuil.

——. 2002. "L'Europe des Intellectuels en 1848." *1848: Actes du Colloque International du Cent-Cinquantenaire de la Révolution de 1848*, ed. J.-L. Mayaud, 421–47. Paris: Créaphis.

———. 2004a. *Le Siècle de la Presse (1830–1939)*. Paris: Seuil.

———. 2004b. "Chapter Two: Patterns." *A History of the University in Europe*, ed. Walter Rüegg, 33–80. Cambridge: Cambridge University Press.

———. 2004c. "Intellectuals in Europe in the Second Half of the Nineteenth Century: Elements for a Comparison." *The European Way*, ed. Hartmut Kaelble, 186–204. Oxford: Berghahn.

———. 2005. "Intellectuels et Ecrivains en France et en Allemagne dans les Années 1950: Les Fondements du Rapprochement." *Mutations et Intégration: Les Accords de Paris de 1954 dans le Processus des Rapprochements Franco Allemands d'après-Guerre*, ed. Hélène Miard-Delacroix and Rainer Hudemann, 267–89. Munich: Oldenbourg.

———. 2006a. "The Crisis of 'Imperial Societies.'" *Reading Bourdieu in a Dual Context: Essays from India and France*, ed. Roland Lardinois and Meenakshi Thapan, 56–76. London: Routledge.

———. 2006b [1987]. *Les Élites de la République (1880–1900)*. Paris: Fayard.

———. 2007a. "French Intellectuals and the Impossible English Model (1870–1914)." *Anglo-French Attitudes*, ed. Christophe Charle, Julien Vincent, and Jay Winter, 235–55. Manchester: Manchester University Press.

———. 2007b. "Les intellectuels et le *Sonderweg* Britannique." *Archives Européennes de Sociologie* 3: 477–84.

———. 2008. *Théâtres en Capitales: Naissance de la Société du Spectacle à Paris, Berlin, Londres et Vienne (1860–1940)*. Paris: Albin Michel.

Charle, Christophe, ed. 2009. *Le Temps des Capitales Culturelles en Europe XVIIIe–XXe Siècles*. Seyssel: Champvallon.

Charle, Christophe, Edwin Keiner, and Jürgen Schriewer, eds. 1993. *Sozialer Raum Akademische Kulturen: Studien zur Europäischen Hochschullandschaft im 19. und 20. Jahrhundert/ A la Recherche de l'Espace Universitaire Européen: Etudes sur l'Enseignement Supérieur aux XIXe et XXe Siècles*. Frankfurt: Peter Lang.

Charle, Christophe, and Daniel Roche, eds. 2004. *Capitales Culturelles, Capitales Symboliques: Paris et les Expériences Européennes XVIIIe–XXe siècles*. Paris: Editions rue d'Ulm.

Charle, Christophe, Jürgen Schriewer, and Peter Wagner, eds. 2004. *Transnational Intellectual Networks: Forms of Academic Knowledge and the Search for Cultural Identities*. Frankfurt: Campus.

Charle, Christophe, and Jacques Verger. 2007 [1994]. *Histoire des Universités*. Paris: Presses Universitaires de France.

Charle, Christophe, Julien Vincent, and Jay Winter, eds. 2007. *Anglo-French Attitudes: Comparisons and Transfers between English and French Intellectuals since the Eighteenth Century*. Manchester: Manchester University Press.

Chartier, Roger. 1993. "Social 'Figuration and Habitus.'" *Cultural History: Between Practices and Representation*, ed. Roger Chartier and Lydia Cochrane, 71–94. Cambridge: Polity.

———. 2000. *Les Origines Culturelles de la Révolution Française*. Paris: Seuil.

Chartier, Roger, Marie-Madeleine Compère, and Dominique Julia. 1976. *L'éducation en France du XVI au XVIII Siècle*. Paris: SEDES-CDU.

Chaves, Mark. 1994. "Secularization as Declining Religious Authority." *Social Forces* 72(3): 749–74.

Chernilo, Daniel. 2006. "Social Theory's Methodological Nationalism: Myth and Reality." *European Journal of Social Theory* 9(1): 5–22.

Cherry, Conrad, ed. 1998. *God's New Israel: Religious Interpretations of American Destiny*. Chapel Hill: University of North Carolina Press.

Chevallier, Stéphane, and Christiane Chauviré. 2010. *Dictionnaire Bourdieu*. Paris: Ellipses.

Chomsky, Noam. 1966. *Topics in the Theory of Generative Grammar*. The Hague: Mouton.

Chong, Denis. 1991. *Collective Action and the Civil Rights Movement*. Chicago: University of Chicago Press.

Clastres, Patrick. 2004. "La Refondation des Jeux Olympiques au Congrès de Paris (1894). Initiative Privée, Transcendantalisme Sportif, Diplomatie des Etats." *Le Pouvoir des Anneaux: Les Jeux Olympiques à la Lumière de la Politique, 1896–2004*, ed. P. Milza, F. Jequier, and P. Tétard, 39–60. Paris: Vuibert.

Clemens, Elisabeth S., and James M. Cook. 1999. "Politics and Institutionalism: Explaining Durability and Change." *Annual Review of Sociology* 25: 441–66.

Cohen, Margaret. 1999. *The Sentimental Education of the Novel*. Princeton: Princeton University Press.

Cohen, Michele. 1996. *Fashioning Masculinity: National Identity and Language in the Eighteenth Century*. London: Routledge.

Cohen, Raymond. 1989. "Threat Assessment in Military Intelligence." *Intelligence and National Security* 4(4): 741–49.

Coleman, James. 1986. "Social Theory, Social Research, and a Theory of Action." *American Journal of Sociology* 91(6): 1309–35.

———. 1990. *Foundations of Social Theory*. Cambridge: Harvard University Press.

Colley, Linda. 1992. *Britons: Forging the Nation, 1707–1837*. New Haven: Yale University Press.

Collier, Jane, and Sylvia Yanagisako. 1987. "Toward a Unified Analysis of Gender and Kinship." *Gender and Kinship: Essays toward a Unified Analysis*, ed. Jane Collier and Sylvia Yanagisako, 14–50. Stanford: Stanford University Press.

Collini, Stefan. 2006. *Absent Minds: Intellectuals in Britain*. Oxford: Oxford University Press.

Collins, Randall. 1993. "Emotional Energy as the Common Denominator of Rational Action." *Rationality and Society* 5(2): 203–30.

———. 1998. *The Sociology of Philosophies: A Global Theory of Intellectual Change*. Cambridge: Harvard University Press.

Confino, Alon. 1997. *The Nation as a Local Metaphor: Württemberg, Imperial Germany, and National Memory, 1871–1918*. Chapel Hill: University of North Carolina Press.

Conway, Stephen. 1997. "The Reproduction of Exclusion and Disadvantage: Symbolic

Violence and Social Class Inequalities in 'Parental Choice' of Secondary Education."
Sociological Research Online 2(4).

Conze, Werner, et al. 1992. *Gesellschaft, Staat, Nation: Gesammelte Aufsätze*. Stuttgart:
Klett-Cotta.

Coquery-Vidrovitch, Catherin. 1969. "Recherches sur un Mode de Production Afri-
caine." *La Pensée* 144: 61–78.

Corcuff, Philippe, ed. 2004. *Pierre Bourdieu: Les Champs de la Critique*. Paris: Editions
de la Bibliothèque publique d'information.

Coser, Lewis A. 1971. *Masters of Sociological Thought*. New York: Harcourt.

Couldry, Nick. 2002. "Media Meta-Capital: Extending the Range of Bourdieu's Field
Theory." *After Bourdieu: Influence, Critique, Elaboration*, ed. David L. Swartz, and
Vera L. Zolberg, 165–92. Boston: Kluwer.

Cravens, Hamilton. 1978. *The Triumph of Evolution*. Philadelphia: University of Penn-
sylvania Press.

Crossick, Geoffrey, and Heinz-Gerhard Haupt. 1996. *The Petite Bourgeoisie in Europe*.
Oxford: Oxford University Press.

Crossley, Nick. 2003. "From Reproduction to Transformation: Social Movement Fields
and the Radical Habitus." *Theory Culture Society* 20(6): 43–68.

Darnton, Robert. 1971a. "The High Enlightenment and the Low-Life of Literature in
Prerevolutionary France." *Past and Present: A Journal of Historical Studies* 51: 81–115.

———. 1971b. "Reading, Writing, and Publishing in Eighteenth-Century France: A Case
Study in the Sociology of Literature." *Daedalus* 100(1): 214–56.

———. 1983. *Bohème Littéraire et Révolution: Le Monde des Livres au XVIIIe Siècle*. Paris:
Gallimard/Seuil.

Darrow, Margaret. 1989. *Revolution in the House: Family, Class, and Inheritance in
Southern France, 1775–1825*. Princeton: Princeton University Press.

Daumard, Adeline. 1987. *Les Bourgois et la Bourgeoisie en France Depuis 1815*. Paris: Aubier.

———. 1988. "Noblesse et Aristocratie en France au XIXe Siècle." *Noblesses Européenes au
XIXe siècle* 107: 89–104.

Davidoff, Leonore, and Catherine Hall. 2002. *Family Fortunes: The Men and Women of
the English Middle Class*. London: Routledge.

Davies, James Chowning. 1962. "Toward a Theory of Revolution." *American Sociological Review* 27: 5–18.

Defrance, Jacques. 1987a. *L'Excellence Corporelle: La Formation des Activités physiques et
sportives modernes. 1770–1914*. Rennes: Presses Universitaires de Rennes, STARS.

———. 1987b. "Patronat, Patronage et Patriotisme." *Les Athlètes de la République*, ed.
Pierre Arnaud, 223–33. Toulouse: Privat.

———. 1989. "Un Schisme Sportif: Clivages structurels, scissions et oppositions dans les
sports athlétiques, 1960–1980." *Actes de la Recherche en Sciences Sociales* 79: 76–91.

———. 1993. "'Le Sport Contre l'Education Physique' et sa Publication." *Education Physique et Sport* 242: 41–44.

———. 2000. "Les Gymnastiques et L'idéologie Eugéniste en France, Pendant la Première
Moitié du 20ème Siècle." *Stadion: Revue Internationale d'Histoire du Sport* 26: 155–77.

———. 2007. "Le Sport Français dans L'entre-deux-Guerres (La Croissance des Pratiques

Sportives et L'élargissement du Monde Fédéral, 1914–1939)." *Du Second Empire au Régime de Vichy, Histoire du Sport en France*, ed. Philippe Tétard, 100–101. Paris: Vuibert.

Defrance, Jacques, and El Boujjoufi Taieb. 2005. "La Construction Sociale d'une Compétence Médico-Sportive, entre Holisme et Spécialisation (Années 1910–1960)." *Regards Sociologiques* 29: 75–93.

Defrance, Jacques, Jean Harvey, and Rob Beamish. 1991. "Les Caractères Originaux de L'histoire Sportive Française: Comparaison du Rôle de l'Etat dans les Années 1930 en France, au Canada et en Grande-Bretagne." *Jeux et Sport dans l'histoire* 1: 189–203.

Defrance, Jacques, and Christian Pociello. 1993. "Structure and Evolution of the Field of Sport in France (1960–1990)." *International Review for the Sociology of Sport* 28: 1–21.

Delanty, Gerard, and Krishan Kumar. 2006. *The Sage Handbook of Nations and Nationalism*. Thousand Oaks, Calif.: Sage.

Derrida, Jacques. 1976. *Of Grammatology*. Baltimore: Johns Hopkins University Press.

Desan, Matt. 2010. *The Concept of Capital in Marx and Bourdieu*. Ann Arbor: University of Michigan Press.

Desan, Suzanne. 1990. *Reclaiming the Sacred: Lay Religion and Popular Politics in Revolutionary France*. Ithaca: Cornell University Press.

Desgrange, Henri. 1932. "La mort d'un preux." *L'Auto*.

Deutsch, Karl W. 1953. *Nationalism and Social Communication: An Inquiry into the Foundations of Nationality*. Cambridge: Technology Press of MIT and Wiley.

Deville-Danthu, Bernadette. 1997. *Le Sport en Noir et Blanc: Du Sport Colonial au Sport Africain dans les Anciens Territoires Français d'Afrique Occidentale (1920–1965)*. Paris: L'Harmattan.

Dewald, Jonathan. 1980. *The Formation of a Provincial Nobility: The Magistrates of the Parlement of Rouen, 1499–1610*. Princeton: Princeton University Press.

———. 1993. *Aristocratic Experience and the Origins of Modern Culture*. Berkeley: University of California Press.

Dewey, John. 1972 [1897]. "Ethical Principles Underlying Education." *John Dewey: The Early Works, 1895–1898*, Vol. 5, ed. Jo Ann Boydston, 54–83. Carbondale: Southern Illinois University Press.

———. 1985 [1916]. *Democracy and Education. John Dewey: The Middle Works, 1899–1924*, Vol. 9, ed. Jo Ann Boydston. Carbondale: Southern Illinois University Press.

———. 1988a [1920]. *Reconstruction in Philosophy. John Dewey: The Middle Works, 1899–1924*, Vol. 12, ed. Jo Ann Boydston. Carbondale: Southern Illinois University Press.

———. 1988b [1922]. *Human Nature and Conduct. John Dewey: The Middle Works, 1899–1924*, Vol. 14, ed. Jo Ann Boydston. Carbondale: Southern Illinois University Press.

———. 1988c [1925]. *Experience and Nature. John Dewey: The Later Works, 1925–1953*, Vol. 1, ed. Jo Ann Boydston. Carbondale: Southern Illinois University Press.

———. 1988d [1927]. *The Public and Its Problems. John Dewey: The Later Works, 1925–1953*, Vol. 2, ed. Jo Ann Boydston. Carbondale: Southern Illinois University Press.

———. 1988e [1929]. *The Quest for Certainty. John Dewey: The Later Works, 1925–1953*, Vol. 4, ed. Jo Ann Boydston. Carbondale: Southern Illinois University Press.

Dewey, John, and Arthur F. Bentley. 1991 [1949]. *Knowing and the Known. John Dewey: The Later Works, 1925–1953*, Vol. 16, ed. Jo Ann Boydston, 1–294. Carbondale: Southern Illinois University Press.

Dezalay, Yves, and Bryant G. Garth. 2002. *The Internationalization of Palace Wars: Lawyers, Economists, and the Contest to Transform Latin American States*. Chicago: University of Chicago Press.

Diefendorf, Barbara. 1983. *Paris City Councillors in the Sixteenth Century: The Politics of Patrimony*. Princeton: Princeton University Press.

Digeon, Claude. 1959. *La Crise Allemande de la Pensée Française, 1870–1914*. Paris: Presse Universitaires de France.

Dilthey, Wilhelm, Rudolf A. Makkreel, and Frithjof Rodi. 1989. *Introduction to the Human Sciences*. Princeton: Princeton University Press.

Dimaggio, Paul. 1997. "Culture and Cognition." *Annual Review of Sociology* 23(1): 263–87.

Dobbin, Frank R. 1994. "Cultural Models of Organization: The Social Construction of Rational Organizing Principles." *The Sociology of Culture: Emerging Theoretical Perspectives*, ed. Diana Crane. Cambridge, Mass.: Blackwell.

Dobry, Michel. 1992. *Sociologie des Crises Politiques*. Paris: Presse de la FNSP.

Dorléac, Laurence Bertrand. 1993. *L'Art de la Défaite*. Paris: Seuil.

Dragomir, Lucia. 2007. *L'Union des Ecrivains: Une Institution Littéraire Transnationale à l'Est: L'Exemple Roumain*. Paris: Belin.

Du Bois, W. E. B. 1962 [1935]. *Black Reconstruction in America*. New York: Free Press.

Duby, Georges. 1976. "Lineage, Nobility, and Chivalry in the Region of Macon during the Twelfth Century." *Family and Society: Selections from the Annales*, ed. Robert Forster and Ores Ranum, trans. Elborg Forster and Patricia M. Ranum, 16–40. Baltimore: Johns Hopkins University Press.

Dudon, Henry. 1920. "Du Bronze? Non, des Stades." *L'Echo des Sports*, January 28: 1.

Dumons, Bruno, and Gilles Pollet. 1992. "Eglises Chrétiennes et Sport International dans la Première Moitié du XX siècle." *Jeux et Sport dans l'Histoire* 1: 205–18.

Dunning, Eric. 1977. "Power and Authority in the Public Schools (1780–1850)." *Human Figurations: Essays for Norbert Elias*, ed. P. Gleichmann, J. Goudsblom, and H. Krote, 225–57. Amsterdam: Amsterdams Sociologisch Tijdschrift.

Durant, Ruth. 1939. "Home Rule in the WPA." *Survey Midmonthly* 75: 273–75.

Durkheim, Emile. 1951. *Suicide, a Study in Sociology*. New York: Free Press.

———. 1966. *The Rules of Sociological Method*. New York: Free Press.

Durkheim, Emile, Carol Cosman, and Mark Sydney Cladis. 2001. *The Elementary Forms of Religious Life*. Oxford: Oxford University Press.

Durkheim, Emile, and Marcel Mauss. 1963. *Primitive Classification*. London: Cohen and West.

Duval, Julien Christophe Gaubert, Frédéric Lebaron, Dominique Marchetti, and Fabienne Pavis. 1998. *Le "Décembre" des Intellectuels Français*. Paris: Liber-Raisons d'Agir.

Ehrenberg, Alain. 1983. *Le Corps Militaire: Politique et Pédagogie en Démocratie*. Paris: Aubier.

Eile, Stanislaw. 2000. *Literature and Nationalism in Partitioned Poland, 1795–1918*. London: Macmillan and St. Martin's.

Elias, Norbert. 1983. *The Civilizing Process*. Vol 2. *The Court Society*. Oxford: Blackwell.
———. 1994 [1939]. *The Civilizing Process*. Translated by Edmund Jephcott. Oxford: Blackwell.
———. 2006. *The Court Society*. Translated by Edmund Jephcott. Edited by Stephen Mennell. Dublin: University College Dublin Press.
Elliott, Anthony. 2005. "Psychoanalysis and the Theory of the Subject." *The Politics of Method in the Human Sciences*, ed. George Steinmetz, 427–50. Durham: Duke University Press.
Elster, Jon. 1983a. *Explaining Technical Change: A Case Study in the Philosophy of Science*. Cambridge: Cambridge University Press.
———. 1983b. *Sour Grapes*. Cambridge: Cambridge University Press.
———. 1986. "Introduction." *Rational Choice*, ed. Jon Elster, 1–33. Oxford: Basil Blackwell.
———. 1989. *Nuts and Bolts for the Social Sciences*. Cambridge: Cambridge University Press.
———. 1999. *Alchemies of the Mind: Rationality and the Emotions*. Cambridge: Cambridge University Press.
———. 2000. "Rational Choice History: A Case of Excessive Ambition." *American Political Science Review* 94(3): 685–95.
Emirbayer, Mustafa. 1997. "Manifesto for a Relational Sociology." *American Journal of Sociology* 103(2): 281–317.
Emirbayer, Mustafa, and Matthew Desmond. Forthcoming. *The Racial Order*. Chicago: University of Chicago Press.
Emirbayer, Mustafa, and Victoria Johnson. 2008. "Bourdieu and Organizational Analysis." *Theory and Society* 37: 1–44.
Emirbayer, Mustafa, and Doug Maynard. 2011. "Pragmatism and Ethnomethodology." *Qualitative Sociology* 34(10): 221–61.
Emirbayer, Mustafa, and Ann Mische. 1998. "What Is Agency?" *American Journal of Sociology* 103: 962–1023.
Emirbayer, Mustafa, and Mimi Sheller. 1999. "Publics in History." *Theory and Society* 27: 727–79.
Ermakoff, Ivan. 2008. *Ruling Oneself Out: A Theory of Collective Abdications*. Durham: Duke University Press.
———. 2010. "Theory of Practice, Rational Choice, and Historical Change." *Theory and Society*, 39:527–53.
Espagne, Michel. 1999 [1994]. "Sur les Limites du Comparatisme en Histoire Culturelle." *Les Transferts Culturels Franco-Allemands*, 35–49. Paris: Presses Universitaires de France.
Espeland, Wendy Nelson. 1998. *The Struggle for Water: Politics, Rationality, and Identity in the American Southwest*. Chicago: University of Chicago Press.
Eyal, Eli. 1974. "The Orientalists' Polemics after the Agranat Report." *Ma'ariv Weekend Magazine*, April 26, 1974, 12–13. [Hebrew]
Eyal, Gil. 2002. "Dangerous Liaisons: The Relations between Military Intelligence and Middle Eastern Studies in Israel." *Theory and Society* 31(5): 653–93.

———. 2003. *The Origins of Postcommunist Elites: From the Prague Spring to the Breakup of Czechoslovakia*. Minneapolis: University of Minnesota Press.

———. 2006. *The Disenchantment of the Orient: Expertise in Arab Affairs and the Israeli State*. Stanford: Stanford University Press.

Eyal, Gil, Brendan Hart, Emine Onculer, Neta Oren, and Natasha Rossi. 2010. *The Autism Matrix: The Social Origins of the Autism Epidemic*. London: Polity Press.

Fabiani, Jean-Louis. 1984a. "Review of Francine Muel-Dreyfus, *Le Métier D'éducateur: Les Instituteurs de 1900, les Educateurs Spécialisés de 1968*." *Revue Française de Pédagogie* 68: 89–93.

Farr, James R. 1988. *Hands of Honor: Artisans and Their World in Dijon, 1550–1650*. Ithaca: Cornell University Press.

Faure, Jean-Michel. 1999. *Le Football Professionnel à la Française*. Paris: Presses Universitaires de France.

Fausto-Sterling, Anne. 2000. *Sexing the Body: Gender Politics and the Construction of Sexuality*. New York: Basic.

Feierabend, Ivo, and Rosalind Feierabend. 1966. "Aggressive Behavior within Polities, 1948–1962: A Cross-National Study." *Journal of Conflict Resolution* 10: 249–71.

———. 1972. "Systematic Conditions of Political Aggression: An Application of Frustration-Aggression Theory." *Anger, Violence, and Politics*, ed. Ivo Feierabend and Rosalind Feierabend, 136–83. Englewood Cliffs: Prentice-Hall.

Ferguson, Priscilla Parkhurst. 1998. "A Culture Field in the Making: Gastronomy in 19th-Century France." *American Journal of Sociology* 104: 597–641.

Foley, Neil. 1997. *The White Scourge: Mexicans, Blacks, and Poor Whites in Texas Cotton Culture*. Berkeley: University of California Press.

Folsom, Franklin. 1991. *Impatient Armies of the Poor: The Story of Collective Action of the Unemployed, 1808–1942*. Niwot: University Press of Colorado.

Foner, Eric. 1988. *Reconstruction, 1863–1877: America's Unfinished Revolution*. New York: Harper and Row.

Foote, Sarah. 1996. "The Making of *Anglecynn*: English Identity before the Norman Conquest." *Transactions of the Royal Historical Society* 6(6): 25–49.

Forsgård, N. E. 2002. "En Nationall strategi?" *Historisk Tidskrift* 2: 209–19.

Foucault, Michel. 1977. *Discipline and Punish: The Birth of the Prison*. Translated by Alan Sheridan. New York: Pantheon.

———. 1978. *The History of Sexuality: An Introduction*. Vol. 1. Translated by Robert Hurley. New York: Pantheon; Random.

———. 1980. *The History of Sexuality*. Vol. 2. New York: Vintage.

———. 1986. "The Discourse on Language." *Critical Theory since 1965*, ed. Adams Hazard and Leroy Searle, 148–62. Tallahassee: Florida State University Press.

———. 1988. *The History of Sexuality*. Vol. 3. New York: Vintage.

———. 1995. *Discipline and Punish: The Birth of the Prison*. Translated by Alan Sheridan. New York: Vintage.

Fourny, Jean-François, and Meaghan Emery. 2000. "Bourdieu's Uneasy Psycho-analysis." *SubStance* 29: 103–12.

Fowler, Bridget. 1987. *Pierre Bourdieu and Cultural Theory*. London: Sage.

Fradétal, Bernard. 1982. "Le Football: Un Lieu Stratégique." *Cahiers de l'Observatoire du changement social* 7: 83–112.

Frankel, Richard. 2003. "From the Beer Halls to the Halls of Power: The Cult of Bismarck and the Legitimization of a German Right, 1898–1945." *German Studies Review* 26(3): 543–60.

Fraser, Nancy, and Linda Gordon. 1994. "A Genealogy of Dependency: Tracing a Keyword of the U.S. Welfare State." *Signs: Journal of Women in Culture and Society* 19: 309–36.

Freidson, Eliot. 1986. *Professional Powers: A Study of the Institutionalization of Formal Knowledge*. Chicago: University of Chicago Press.

Freud, Sigmund. 1897. "Letter 75. November 14, 1897." In James Strachey, ed., *The Standard Edition of the Complete Psychological Works of Sigmund Freud*, Vol. 1 (1886–1899): Pre-Psycho-Analytic Publications and Unpublished Drafts. London: Hogarth.

———. 1955. "Group Psychology and the Analysis of the Ego." *The Standard Edition*, Vol. 18: 67–143, ed. J. Strachey. London: Hogarth.

———. 1965 [1933]. *New Introductory Lectures on Psychoanalysis*. Translated by James Strachey. New York: W. W. Norton.

———. 1977. *Five Lectures on Psycho-Analysis*. New York: Norton.

Freud, Sigmund. 1962. *The Ego and the Id*. London: Hogarth Press and the Institute of Psycho-Analysis.

Freud, Sigmund. 1953. *The Standard Edition of the Complete Psychological Works of Sigmund Freud*. London: Hogarth.

Friedrich-Silber, Ilana. 1995. *Virtuosity, Charisma, and Social Order: A Comparative Sociological Study of Monasticism in Theravada Buddhism and Medieval Catholicism*. Cambridge: Cambridge University Press.

Furet, François. 1992 [1988]. *Revolutionary France 1770–1880*. Oxford: Blackwell.

Garcelon, Marc. 2006. "Trajectories of Institutional Disintegration in Late-Soviet Russia and Contemporary Iraq." *Sociological Theory* 24(3): 255–83.

Garcia, F. V. 1999. "Historicidad de la Razón y Teoría Social: Entre Foucault y Bourdieu." *Revista Mexicana de Sociología* 61(2): 189–212.

Garroutte, E. M. 2003. "The Positivist Attack on Baconian Science and Religious Knowledge in the 1870s." *The Secular Revolution*, ed. Christian Smith, 197–215. Berkeley: University of California Press.

Gartman, David. 2002. "Bourdieu's Theory of Cultural Change: Explication, Application, Critique." *Sociological Theory* 20(2): 255–77.

Gaulejac, Vincent de. 2004. "De l'inconscient Chez Freud à l'inconscient selon Bourdieu: Entre Psychanalyse et Socio-Analyse." *Pierre Bourdieu: Les Champs de la Critique*, ed. P. Corcuff, 75–86. Paris: Editions de la Bibliothèque publique d'information.

Geary, Patrick J. 1988. *Before France and Germany: The Creation and Transformation of the Merovingian World*. New York: Oxford University Press.

———. 2002. *The Myth of Nations: The Medieval Origins of Europe*. Princeton: Princeton University Press.

Geertz, Clifford. 1973. *Interpretation of Cultures: Selected Essays*. New York: Basic.

Gellermann, William. 1944. *Martin Dies*. New York: John Day.

Gellner, Ernest. 1983. *Nations and Nationalism*. Ithaca: Cornell University Press.

Gieryn, Thomas F. 1983. "Boundary Work and the Demarcation of Science from Non-Science: Strains and Interests in Professional Ideologies of Scientists." *American Sociological Review* 48 (December): 781–95.

———. 1999. *Cultural Boundaries of Science: Credibility on the Line*. Chicago: University of Chicago Press.

Giesen, Bernhard. 1991. *Nationale und kulturelle Identität: Studien zur Entwicklung des kollektiven Bewusstseins in der Neuzeit*. Frankfurt: Suhrkamp.

Gilcher-Holtey, Ingrid. 1995. *Die Phantasie an die Macht. Mai 68 in Frankreich*. Frankfurt: Suhrkamp.

Glenn, Evelyn Nakano. 2002. *Unequal Freedom: How Race and Gender Shaped American Citizenship and Labor*. Cambridge: Harvard University Press.

Glickman, Lawrence B. 1997. *A Living Wage: American Workers and the Making of Consumer Society*. Ithaca: Cornell University Press.

Go, Julian. 2008. "Global Fields and Imperial Forms: Field Theory and the U.S. and British Empires." *Sociological Theory* 26(3): 201–29.

Gobille, Boris. 2003. "Crise Politique et Incertitude: Regimes de Problématisation et Logiques de Mobilisation des Écrivains en Mai 68." Ph.D. diss. Paris: EHESS.

———. 2005. "Les Mobilisations de L'avant-Garde Littéraire Française en Mai 1968. Capital Politique, Capital Littéraire et Conjoncture de Crise." *Actes de la Recherche en Sciences Sociales* 158: 30–53.

Goddet, Jacques. 1940. "Rebâtir le Sport Français, mais dans la Cohésion. Même si le C.N.S. n'a Jamais Fait ouvre Utile, le Contact Est Indispensable entre les Pouvoirs Actuels et les Dirigeants d'Hier," *L'Auto* 27, July, 1–2.

Goldberg, Chad Alan. 2003. "Haunted by the Specter of Communism: Collective Identity and Resource Mobilization in the Demise of the Workers Alliance of America." *Theory and Society* 32: 725–73.

———. 2005. "Contesting the Status of Relief Workers during the New Deal: The Workers Alliance of America and the Works Progress Administration, 1935–1941." *Social Science History* 29(3): 337–71.

———. 2007. *Citizens and Paupers: Relief, Rights, and Race, from the Freedmen's Bureau to Workfare*. Chicago: University of Chicago Press.

Goldfield, Michael. 1997. *The Color of Politics: Race and the Mainsprings of American Politics*. New York: New Press.

Goldstein, Jan. 2005. *The Post-Revolutionary Self: Politics and Psyche in France, 1750–1850*. Cambridge: Harvard University Press.

Goldstone, Jack. 1994. "Is Revolution Individually Rational?" *Rationality and Society* 6: 139–66.

Goodman, Nelson. 1978. *Ways of Worldmaking*. Indianapolis: Hackett.

Goodwyn, Lawrence. 1976. *Democratic Promise: The Populist Moment in America*. New York: Oxford University Press.

Gorski, Philip S. 1995. "The Protestant Ethic and the Spirit of Bureaucracy." *American Sociological Review* 60(5): 783–86.

———. 2000. "The Mosaic Moment: An Early Modernist Critique of Modernist Theories of Nationalism." *American Journal of Sociology* 105(5): 1428–68.

———. 2004. "The Poverty of Deductivism: A Constructive Realist Model of Sociological Explanation." *Sociological Methodology* 34(1): 1–33.

———. 2006. "Premodern Nationalism: An Oxymoron? The Evidence from England." *Sage Handbook of Nationalism*, ed. Gerard Delanty and Krishan Kumar, 143–55. New York: Russell Sage.

———. 2007. *The ECPRES Model: A Critical Realist Approach to Causal Mechanisms.* New Haven: Yale University Press.

Green, Donald, and Ian Shapiro. 1994. *Pathologies of Rational Choice Theory.* New Haven: Yale University Press.

Green, Nancy L. 1990. "L'Histoire Comparative et le Champ des études Migratoires." *Annales ESC* 6: 1335–50.

Grell, Chantal, and d'Arnaud Ramière de Fortanier, eds. 1999. *Le Second Ordre: l'idéal Nobiliaire.* Paris: Presses Universitaires Sorbonne Nouvelle.

Grenfell, Michael J. 2005. *Pierre Bourdieu: Agent Provocateur.* London: Continuum.

Grosby, Steven. 1991. "Religion and Nationality in Antiquity: The Worship of Yahweh and Ancient Israel." *Archives Européennes de Sociologie* 32(2): 229–65.

———. 2002. *Biblical Ideas of Nationality: Ancient and Modern.* Winona Lake, Ind.: Eisenbrauns.

Gurr, Ted Robert. 1968. "A Causal Model of Civil Strife: A Comparative Analysis Using New Indices." *American Political Science Review* 27: 1104–24.

———. 1970. *Why Men Rebel.* Princeton: Princeton University Press.

Gusfield, Joseph R. 1963. *Symbolic Crusade: Status Politics and the American Temperance Movement.* Urbana: University of Illinois Press.

Habermas, Jürgen. 1989. *The Structural Transformation of the Public Sphere: An Inquiry into a Category of Bourgeois Society.* Cambridge: MIT Press.

Hackett, Edward J., Olga Amsterdamska, Michael Lynch, and Judy Wajcman, eds. 2008. *The Handbook of Science and Technology Studies.* 3d ed. Cambridge: MIT Press.

Hage, Ghassan. 2000. *White Nation: Fantasies of White Supremacy in a Multicultural Society.* London: Routledge.

Hall, Stuart. 1980. "Cultural Studies: Two Paradigms." *Media, Culture and Society* 2: 57–72.

———. 1988. "The Toad in the Garden: Thatcherism among the Theorists." *Marxism and the Interpretation of Culture*, ed. Cary Nelson and Lawrence Grossberg, 35–74. Urbana: University of Illinois Press.

Hamilton, Dona Cooper, and Charles V. Hamilton. 1997. *The Dual Agenda: Race and Social Welfare Policies of Civil Rights Organizations.* New York: Columbia University Press.

Hammoudi, Abdellah. 2009. "Phenomenology and Ethnography: On Kabyle Habitus in the Work of Pierre Bourdieu." *Bourdieu in Algeria*, ed. P. A. Silverstein and J. E. Goodman, 199–254. Lincoln: University of Nebraska Press.

Hanley, Sarah. 1989. "Engendering the State: Family Formation and State Building in Early Modern France." *French Historical Studies* 16(1): 4–27.

Hardwick, Julie. 1999. *The Practice of Patriarchy: Gender and the Politics of Household Authority in Early Modern France.* University Park: Penn State University Press.

Harker, Richard K. 1984. "On Reproduction, Habitus and Education." *British Journal of Sociology of Education* 5(2): 117–27.

Harris, James F. 1976. "Franz Perrot: A Study in the Development of German Lower Middle Class Social and Political Thought in the 1870s." *Studies in Modern European History and Culture* 2: 73–106.

Harrison, Carol E. 1999. *The Bourgeois Citizen in Nineteenth-Century France: Gender, Sociability and the Uses of Emulation.* Oxford: Oxford University Press.

Harsanyi, John C. 1967. "Games with Incomplete Information Played by 'Bayesian' Players, I-III. Part I. The Basic Model." *Management Science* 14(3): 159–82.

——. 1969. "Rational-Choice Models of Political Behavior vs. Functionalist and Conformist Theories." *World Politics* 21(4): 513–38.

——. 1995. "Games with Incomplete Information." *American Economic Review* 85(3): 291–303.

Hartmann, Michael. 2000. "Class-Specific Habitus and the Social Reproduction of the Business Elite in Germany and France." *Sociological Review* 48(2): 262–82.

Harvey, Jean, Jacques Defrance, and Rob Beamish. 1993. "Physical Exercise Policy and the Welfare State: A Framework for Comparative Analysis." *International Review for the Sociology of Sport* 28: 53–64.

Harvey, Philip. 1989. *Securing the Right to Employment: Social Welfare Policy and the Unemployed in the United States.* Princeton: Princeton University Press.

Hastings, Adrian. 1997. *The Construction of Nationhood: Ethnicity, Religion, and Nationalism.* New York: Cambridge University Press.

Haupt, Heinz-Gerhard. 1995. "La Lente Émergence d'une Histoire Comparée." *Passés Recomposés*, ed. Jean Boutier and Julia Dominique, 196–207. Paris: Autrement.

Haupt, Heinz-Gerhard, and Jürgen Kocka. 1996. *Geschichte und Vergleich.* Frankfurt: Campus.

Heath, Stephen. 1986. "Joan Riviere and the Masquerade." *The Formations of Fantasy*, ed. V. Burgin, J. Donald, and C. Kaplan, 45–61. London: Methuen.

Hebdige, Dick 1991. *Subculture: The Meaning of Style.* London: Routledge.

Hébert, Georges. 1925. *Le Sport Contre L'éducation Physique.* Paris: Vuibert.

Heclo, Hugh. 1974. *Modern Social Politics in Britain and Sweden: From Relief to Income Maintenance.* New Haven: Yale University Press.

Hedström, Peter. 2005. *Dissecting the Social: On the Principles of Analytical Sociology.* Cambridge: Cambridge University Press.

Hedström, Peter, and Richard Swedberg. 1998. *Social Mechanisms: An Analytical Approach to Social Theory.* Cambridge: Cambridge University Press.

Hegel, Georg Wilhelm Friedrich. Trans. J. B. Baillie. 1967. *The Phenomenology of Mind.* New York: Harper and Row.

Hegel, Georg Wilhelm Friedrich. Trans. Leo Rauch. 1983. *Hegel and the Human Spirit:*

A Translation of the Jena Lectures on the Philosophy of Spirit (1805–6) with Commentary. Detroit: Wayne State University Press.

Heilbroner, Robert L. 1953. *The Worldly Philosophers: The Lives, Times, and Ideas of the Great Economic Thinkers*. New York: Simon and Schuster.

Heissenbüttel, K. 1920. *Die Bedeutung der Bezeichungen für "Volk" und "Nation" bei den Geschichtschreiben des 10. bis 13. Jahrhunderts*. Göttingen: Dieterichischen Univ.-Buchdruckerei (W. Fr. Kaestner), Universität Göttingen.

Hempel, Carl Gustav. 1965. *Aspects of Scientific Explanation and Other Essays in the Philosophy of Science*. New York: Free Press.

Herzfeld, Michael. 1997. *Cultural Intimacy*. London: Routledge.

Hess, David J. 1997. *Science Studies: An Advanced Introduction*. New York: New York University Press.

Higgs, David. 1987. *Nobles in Nineteenth-Century France: The Practice of Inegalitarianism*. Baltimore: Johns Hopkins University Press.

Higham, John. 1955. *Strangers in the Land; Patterns of American Nativism, 1860–1925*. New Brunswick: Rutgers University Press.

Hinkle, Roscoe C. 1994. *Developments in American Sociological Theory, 1915–1950*. Albany: State University of New York Press.

Hobsbawm, Eric J. 1992. *Nations and Nationalism since 1780: Programme, Myth, Reality*. Cambridge: Cambridge University Press.

Hobsbawm, Eric J., and Terence O. Ranger. 1983. *The Invention of Tradition*. Cambridge: Cambridge University Press.

Hoibian, Olivier. 2000. *Les Alpinistes en France, 1870–1950: Une Histoire Culturelle*. Paris: L'Harmattan.

Honneth, Axel. 1995. *The Struggle for Recognition: The Moral Grammar of Social Conflicts*. Cambridge: MIT Press.

Hopkins, Harry L. 1938–39. Container 35. File: Federal Emergency Relief Administration: Works Progress Administration: Releases, Speeches, etc., 1938–39. Franklin D. Roosevelt Presidential Library, Hyde Park, N.Y.

Horney, Karen. 1942. *Self-Analysis*. New York: W. W. Norton.

Howard, Donald S. 1943. *The WPA and Federal Relief Policy*. New York: Russell Sage Foundation.

Howe, Irving, and Lewis Coser. 1957. *The American Communist Party: A Critical History (1919–1957)*. Boston: Beacon Press.

Hroch, Miroslav. 1985. *Social Preconditions of National Revival in Europe: A Comparative Analysis of the Social Composition of Patriotic Groups among the Smaller European Nations*. New York: Cambridge University Press.

Hull, Isabel V. 1982. "The Bourgeoisie and Its Discontents: Reflections on 'Nationalism and Respectability.'" *Journal of Contemporary History* 17(2): 247–68.

——. 1996. *Sexuality, State, and Civil Society in Germany, 1700–1815*. Ithaca: Cornell University Press.

Hutchison, William R., and H. Lehmann. 1994. *Many Are Chosen: Divine Election and Western Nationalism*. Minneapolis: Fortress Press.

Igalens, Jacques. 1954. *La Normalisation*. Paris: Presses Universitaires de France.

Inderbitzin, L. B. and S. T. Levy. 2001. "Fantasy and Psychoanalytic Discourse." *International Journal of Psychoanalysis* 82: 795–803.

Israël, Liora. 2005. *Robes Noires et Années Sombres: Avocats et Magistrats en Résistance Pendant la Seconde Guerre Mondiale*. Paris: Fayard.

Jacob, Margaret C. 1991. *Living the Enlightenment: Freemasonry and Politics in Eighteenth-Century Europe*. New York: Oxford University Press.

Joas, Hans. 1996. *The Creativity of Action*. Translated by Jeremy Gaines and Paul Keast. Chicago: University of Chicago Press.

———. 2003. *War and Modernity*. Cambridge: Polity.

Johnson, Barbara. 1981. "Translator's Introduction." *Dissemination*, ed. J. Derrida, vii–xxxv. Chicago: University of Chicago Press.

Jouanna, Arlette. 1977. *Ordre social: Mythes et hierarchies dans la France du XVIe siècle*. Paris: Hachette.

Julien, Philippe. 1994. *Jacques Lacan's Return to Freud: The Real, the Symbolic, and the Imaginary*. New York: New York University Press.

Kaelble, Hartmut. 1989. *Social History of Western Europe, 1880–1980*. Translated by Daniel Bird. Dublin: Gill and Macmillan.

———. 1991. *Nachbarn am Rhein: Entfremdung und Annäherung der Französischen und Deutschen Gesellschaft seit 1880*. Munich: Beck.

———. 1995. "La Recherche Européenne en Histoire Sociale." *Actes de la Recherche en Sciences Sociales* 106–7: 67–79.

———. 1999. *Der historische Vergleich: Eine Einführung zum 19. und 20. Jahrhundert*. Frankfurt: Campus.

Kant, Immanuel. 1987. *Critique of Judgment*. Translated by Werner S. Pluhar. Indianapolis: Hackett.

Kaplan Yaeger, Alice. 2000. *The Collaborator: The Trial and Execution of Robert Brasillach*. Chicago: University of Chicago Press.

Karabel, Jérôme. 1996. "Towards a Theory of Intellectuals and Politics." *Theory and Society* 25: 205–23.

———. 2005. *The Chosen: The Hidden History of Admission and Exclusion at Harvard, Yale, and Princeton*. Boston: Houghton Mifflin.

Karady, Victor. 1999. *Gewalterfahrung und Utopie: Juden in der Europäischen Moderne*. Frankfurt: Fischertaschenbuchverlag.

Karis, Beate. 1993. "Gender and Symbolic Violence: Female Oppression in the Light of Pierre Bourdieu's Theory of Social Practice." *Bourdieu: Critical Perspectives*, ed. Craig Calhoun, Edward LiPuma, and Moishe Postone, 156–77. Chicago: Chicago University Press.

Katznelson Ira, Kim Geiger, and Daniel Kryder. 1993. "Limiting Liberalism: The Southern Veto in Congress." *Political Science Quarterly* 108(2): 283–306.

Katznelson Ira, and Barry R. Weingast. 2005. "Intersection between Historical and Rational Choice Institutionalism." *Preferences and Situations: Points of Intersection between Historical and Rational Choice Institutionalism*, ed. Ira Katznelson and Barry R. Weingast, 1–24. New York: Russell Sage.

Kedourie, Elie. 1993. *Nationalism*. Oxford: Blackwell.

Kelley, Robin D. G. 1990. *Hammer and Hoe: Alabama Communists during the Great Depression*. Chapel Hill: University of North Carolina Press.

Kessler-Harris, Alice. 1990. *A Woman's Wage: Historical Meanings and Social Consequences*. Lexington: University Press of Kentucky.

Keyssar, Alexander. 2000. *The Right to Vote: The Contested History of Democracy in the United States*. New York: Basic.

Kidd, Colin. 1999. *British Identities before Nationalism: Ethnicity and Nationhood in the Atlantic World, 1600–1800*. Cambridge: Cambridge University Press.

Kingston, Paul W. 2001. "The Unfulfilled Promise of Cultural Capital Theory." *Sociology of Education* 74: 88–99.

Kiser, Edgar, and Joachim Schneider. 1995. "Rational Choice versus Cultural Explanations of the Efficiency of the Prussian Tax System." *American Sociological Review* 60(5): 787–91.

Klinenberg, Eric. 2002. *Heat Wave: A Social Autopsy of Disaster in Chicago*. Chicago: University of Chicago Press.

———. 2007. *Fighting for Air: The Battle to Control America's Media*. New York: Metropolitan.

Kloft, Hans. 1990. "Die *Germania* des Tacitus und das Problem eines Deutschen Nationalbewusstseins." *Archiv für Kulturgeschichte* 72(1): 93–114.

Knorr-Cetina, Karin D. 1981. *The Manufacture of Knowledge*. Oxford: Pergamon.

———. 1982. "Scientific Communities or Transepistemic Arenas of Research." *Social Studies of Science* 12: 101–30.

———. 1999. *Epistemic Culture: How the Sciences Make Knowledge*. Cambridge: Harvard University Press.

Kocka, Jürgen. 1980. *White Collar Workers in America, 1890–1940: A Social-Political History in International Perspective*. Translated by Maura Kealey. Beverly Hills: Sage.

Kocka, Jürgen, and Ute Frevert. 1988. *Bürgertum im 19. Jarhundert*. 3 vols. Munich: DTV.

Kocka, Jürgen, and Allan Mitchell, eds. 1993. *Bourgeois Society in Nineteenth-Century Europe*. Oxford: Berg.

Kohn, Hans. 1946. *The Idea of Nationalism: A Study in Its Origins and Background*. New York: Macmillan.

Koshar, Rudy. 2000. *From Monuments to Traces: Artifacts of German Memory, 1870–1990*. Berkeley: University of California Press.

Krueger, Thomas A. 1967. *And Promises to Keep: The Southern Conference for Human Welfare, 1938–1948*. Nashville: Vanderbilt University Press.

Lacan, Jacques. 1988. *Freud's Papers on Technique, 1953–1954*. New York: W. W. Norton.

———. 1991. *The Ego in Freud's Theory and in the Technique of Psychoanalysis, 1954–1955*. New York: W. W. Norton.

Lacan, Jacques, and Bruce Fink. 2002. *Ecrits: A Selection*. New York: W. W. Norton.

Lagache, Daniel. 1961. "La Psychanalyse et la Structure de la Personnalité." *La Psychanalyse* 6: 5–58.

Lagrange, Fernand. 1890. *L'hygiène et L'exercice Physique chez les Enfants et les Jeunes Gens*. Paris: Alcan.

Laitin, David D. 1992. *Language Repertoires and State Construction in Africa*. Cambridge: Cambridge University Press.

———. 1995. *Identity in Formation: The Russian-Speaking Nationality in Estonia and Bashkortostan*. Glasgow: Centre for the Study of Public Policy, University of Strathclyde.

———. 1998. *Identities in Formation: The Russian-Speaking Populations in the Near Abroad*. Ithaca: Cornell University Press.

———. 2000. *Culture and National Identity: "The East" and European Integration*. San Domenico di Fiesole, Italy: European University Institute, Robert Schuman Centre.

Lakatos, Imre, and Alan Musgrave. 1970. *Criticism and the Growth of Knowledge*. Cambridge: Cambridge University Press.

Lakoff, George, and Mark Johnson. 2003 [1980]. *Metaphors We Live By*. Chicago: University of Chicago Press.

Lamont, Michèle, and Virag Molnar. 2002. "The Study of Boundaries in the Social Sciences." *Annual Review of Sociology* 28: 167–95.

Lane, Jeremy F. 2000. *Pierre Bourdieu: A Critical Introduction*. London: Pluto.

Laplanche, Jean, and J. B. Pontalis. 1974. *The Language of Psycho-Analysis*. New York: Norton.

Lareau, Annette, and Elliot B. Weininger. 2003. "Cultural Capital in Educational Research: A Critical Assessment." *Theory and Society* 32(5/6): 567–606.

———. 2004. "Cultural Capital in Educational Research: A Critical Assessment." *After Bourdieu: Influence, Critique, Elaboration*, ed. David L. Swartz and Vera L. Zolberg, 105–44. Dordrecht: Kluwer Academic.

Lassus, Marianne, and Pierre Guillaume. 2000. *L'affaire Ladoumègue: Le débat Amateurisme/Professionalisme dans les Années Trente*. Paris: L'Harmattan.

Latour, Bruno. 1987. *Science in Action*. Cambridge: Harvard University Press.

———. 1988. *The Pasteurization of France*. Cambridge: Harvard University Press.

Lawrence, Christopher. 1998. "Medical Minds, Surgical Bodies: Corporeality and the Doctors." *Science Incarnate: Historical Embodiments of Natural Knowledge*, ed. Christopher Lawrence and Stephen Shapin, 156–202. Chicago: University of Chicago Press.

Lee, Justin. 2004. "Investigating the Hybridity of 'Wellness' Practices." Paper presented at the Graduate Student Conference on Categories, Columbia University in the City of New York, October 22.

LeHir, Marie-Pierre. 2000. "Cultural Studies Bourdieu's Way: Women, Leadership, and Feminist Theory." *Pierre Bourdieu: Fieldwork in Culture*, ed. Nicholas Brown and Imre Szeman, 123–44. New York: Rowman and Littlefield.

Lenoir, Rémy. 2003. *Généalogie de la Morale Familiale*. Paris: Seuil.

Lepenies, Wolf. 1985. *Between Literature and Science: The Rise of Sociology*. Cambridge: Cambridge University Press.

———. 1988. *Between Literature and Science: The Rise of Sociology*. Cambridge: Cambridge University Press.

Lescohier, Don D. 1939. "The Hybrid WPA." *Survey Midmonthly* 75: 167–69.

Levi, Margaret. 1988. *Of Rule and Revenue*. Berkeley: University of California Press.

Lewin, Kurt. 1964. *Field Theory in Social Science: Selected Theoretical Papers*. New York: Harper and Row.

Lieberman, Robert C. 1998. *Shifting the Color Line: Race and the American Welfare State*. Cambridge: Harvard University Press.

Lindenberg, Siegwart. 1989. "Social Production Functions, Deficits, and Social Revolutions, Prerevolutionary France and Russia." *Rationality and Society* 1(1): 51–77.

Linder, Amnon. 1978. "Ex Mala Parentela bon Sequi seu Oriri non Potest: The Troyan Ancestry of the Kings of France and the "Opus Davidicum" of Johannes Angelus de Legonissa." *Bibliothèque d'Humanisme et Renaissance* 40(3): 497–513.

Lipsyte, Robert. 1975. *Sportsworld: An American Dreamland*. New York: Quadrangle.

Lizardo, Omar. 2004. "The Cognitive Origins of Bourdieu's *Habitus*." *Journal for the Theory of Social Behavior* 34: 375–401.

Lottman, Herbert R. 1986. *The Purge*. New York: Morrow.

Loveman, Mara. 2005. "The Modern State and the Primitive Accumulation of Symbolic Power." *American Journal of Sociology* 110(6): 1651–83.

——. 2007. "Blinded Like a State: The Revolt against Civil Registration in Nineteenth-Century Brazil." *Comparative Studies in Society and History* 49(01): 5–39.

Lunbeck, Elizabeth, and Bennett Simon. 2003. *Family Romance, Family Secrets: Case Notes from an American Psychoanalysis, 1912*. New Haven: Yale University Press.

Lutz, Raphael, and Pierre Bourdieu. 1995. "Sur les Rapports entre l'Histoire et la Sociologie en France et en Allemagne." *Actes de la Recherche en Sciences Sociales* 106–7 (March): 108–22.

MacAloon, John J. 1981. *This Great Symbol: Pierre de Coubertin and the Origins of the Modern Olympic Games*. Chicago: University of Chicago Press.

MacHardy, Karin J. 1999. "Cultural Capital, Family Strategies and Noble Identity in Early Modern Habsburg Austria 1579–1620." *Past and Present* (163): 36–75.

Macmahon, Arthur W., John D. Millett, and Gladys Ogden. 1941. *The Administration of Federal Work Relief*. Chicago: Public Administration Service.

MacMaster, Neil. 2000. " 'Black Jew–White Negro': Anti-Semitism and the Construction of Cross-Racial Stereotypes." *Nationalism and Ethnic Politics* 6(4): 65–82.

Mahoney, James. 2001. "Beyond Correlational Analysis: Recent Innovations in Theory and Method." *Sociological Forum* 16(3): 575–93.

——. 2004. "Revisiting General Theory in Historical Sociology." *Social Forces* 83(2): 459–89.

Malatesta, Maria. 1999. *Le Aristocrazie Terriere nell' Europa Contemporanea*. Rome: Laterza.

Mamdani, Mahmood. 1996. *Citizen and Subject: Contemporary Africa and the Legacy of Late Colonialism*. Princeton: Princeton University Press.

Mangan, J. A. 1981. *Athleticism in the Victorian and Edwardian Public School: The Emergence and Consolidation of an Educational Ideology*. Cambridge: Cambridge University Press.

Mann, Michael. 1986. *The Sources of Social Power*. Cambridge: Cambridge University Press.

Mannheim, Karl. 1990. *Le Problème des Générations*. Paris: Nathan.

Manza, Jeff. 2000. "Political Sociological Models of the U.S. New Deal." *Annual Review of Sociology* 26: 297–322.

Marsden, George M. 1994. *The Soul of the American University: From Protestant Establishment to Established Nonbelief.* Oxford: Oxford University Press.

Marshall, T. H. 1964 [1949]. "Citizenship and Social Class." *Class, Citizenship and Social Development*, 65–122. Garden City: Doubleday.

Martin, David. 1978. *A General Theory of Secularization.* New York: Harper and Row.

Martin-Criado, Enrique. 2008. *Les deux Algéries de Pierre Bourdieu.* Broissieux: Éditions du Croquant.

Martines, Lauro. 1979. *Power and Imagination: City-States in Renaissance Italy.* New York: Knopf.

Marx, Anthony W. 2003. *Faith in Nation: Exclusionary Origins of Nationalism.* Oxford: Oxford University Press.

Marx, Karl. 1976. *Capital: A Critique of Political Economy.* Translated by David Fernbach. Harmondsworth: Penguin.

Marx, Karl, and Friedrich Engels. 1978. *The Marx–Engels Reader.* Edited by Robert C. Tucker. New York: Norton.

Mayer, Arno. 1981. *The Persistence of the Old Regime: Europe to the Great War.* New York: Pantheon.

——. 2000. *The Furies: Violence and Terror in the French and Russian Revolutions.* Princeton: Princeton University Press.

McAdam, Doug. 1988. *Freedom Summer.* New York: Oxford University Press.

McCarthy, John D., and Mayer N. Zald. 1977. "Resource Mobilization and Social Movements—Partial Theory." *American Journal of Sociology* 82(6): 1212–41.

McNay, Lois. 1992. *Foucault and Feminism: Power, Gender and the Self.* Oxford: Polity.

Medvetz, Thomas M. 2007. "Merchants of Expertise: Think Tanks and Intellectuals in the U.S. Field of Power." Ph.D. diss., University of California, Berkeley.

Meinecke, F. 1908. *Weltbürgertum und Nationalstaat: Studien zur Genesis des Deutschen Nationalstaates.* Munich: R. Oldenbourg.

Mellstrom, Ulf. 2004. "Machines and Masculine Subjectivity." *Men and Masculinities* 6(4): 368–82.

Mendras, Henri. 1988. *La Seconde Révolution Française 1965–1984.* Paris: Gallimard.

Meriam, Lewis. 1946. *Relief and Social Security.* Washington: Brookings Institution.

Mettler, Suzanne. 1998. *Dividing Citizens: Gender and Federalism in New Deal Public Policy.* Ithaca: Cornell University Press.

Mettler, Suzanne, and Joe Soss. 2004. "The Consequences of Public Policy for Democratic Citizenship: Bridging Policy Studies and Mass Politics." *Perspectives on Politics* 2(1): 55–73.

Metz, Karl Heinz. 1987. "'A Tale of Troy': Geschichtserfahrung und die Anfange der Nationwerdung in Irland, 1641–1652." *Geschichte in Wissenschaft und Unterricht* 38(8): 466–77.

Meyer, John W., and Brian Rowan. 1991. "Institutionalized Organizations: Formal Structure as Myth and Ceremony." *The New Institutionalism in Organizational Analysis*, ed. Walter W. Powell and Paul J. DiMaggio. Chicago: University of Chicago Press.

Meyer, John W., and W. Richard Scott. 1983. *Organizational Environments: Ritual and Rationality*. Beverly Hills: Sage.

Meyer, Stephen. 2001. "Work, Play, and Power: Masculine Culture on the Automotive Shop Floor." *Boys and Their Toys? Masculinity Technology and Class in America*, ed. Roger Horowitz, 13–32. New York: Routledge.

Minogue, Kenneth R. 1967. *Nationalism*. London: Batsford.

Mitchell, Timothy. 1991. "The Limits of the State: Beyond Statist Approaches and Their Critics." *American Political Science Review* 85(1): 77–96.

Moi, Toril. 1999. *What Is a Woman and Other Essays*. New York: Oxford University Press.

Monet, Jacques. 2003. "Emergence de la Kinésithérapie en France, à la fin du XIX et au début du XX siècle, Une spécialité Médicale Impossible: Genèse, acteurs et intérêts de 1880 à 1914." Paris: Sociology, Université Paris I—Sorbonne.

Monnet, François. 1993. *Refaire la République: André Tardieu, une Dérive Réactionnaire (1876–1945)*. Paris: Fayard.

Montgomery, David. 1993. *Citizen Worker: The Experience of Workers in the United States with Democracy and the Free Market during the Nineteenth Century*. New York: Cambridge University Press.

More, Ellen S. 1999. *Restoring the Balance: Women Physicians and the Profession of Medicine*. Cambridge: Harvard University Press.

Mosse, George L. 1975. *The Nationalization of the Masses: Political Symbolism and Mass Movements in Germany from the Napoleonic Wars through the Third Reich*. New York: H. Fertig.

Muel-Dreyfus, Françine. 1983. *Le Métier d'éducateur: Les Instituteurs de 1900, les Educateurs Spécialisés de 1968*. Paris: Les éditions de minuit.

———. 1996. *Vichy et L'éternel Feminine: Contribution à Une Sociologie Politique de L'ordre des Corps*. Paris: Seuil. English translation: 2002. *Vichy and the Eternal Feminine*. Durham: Duke University Press.

Mukerji, Chandra. 1997. *Territorial Ambitions and the Gardens of Versailles*. Cambridge: Cambridge University Press.

Murphy, Raymond. 1988. *Social Closure: The Theory of Monopolization and Exclusion*. Oxford: Clarendon Press.

Nauert, Charles G. 2006. *Humanism and the Culture of Renaissance Europe*. Cambridge: Cambridge University Press.

Neumeyer, Gaston. 1919. "Les Étrennes de l'Education Physique." *L'Ere Nouvelle*, 29 December, 7.

Newman, Gerald. 1987. *The Rise of English Nationalism: A Cultural History, 1720–1830*. New York: St. Martin's Press.

Noiriel, Gérard. 1999. *Les Origines Républicaines de Vichy*. Paris: Hachette Littératures.

North, Douglass C. 1981. *Structure and Change in Economic History*. New York: Norton.

———. 1990. *Institutions, Institutional Change and Economic Performance*. Cambridge: Cambridge University Press.

Novick, Peter. 1985 [1968]. *The Resistance versus Vichy: The Purge of Collaborators in*

Liberated France. London: Chatto and Windus. French translation: *L'Épuration française 1944–1949*. Paris: Balland.

Nye, Robert A. 1993. *Masculinity and Male Codes of Honor in Modern France*. New York: Oxford University Press.

——. 1997. "Medicine and Science as Masculine Fields of Honor." *Osiris* 12: 60–79.

O'Brien, Conor Cruise. 1988. *God Land: Reflections on Religion and Nationalism*. Cambridge: Harvard University Press.

Olson, Mancur. 1965. *The Logic of Collective Action*. Cambridge: Harvard University Press.

O'Neill, Barry. 2001. *Honor, Symbols, and War*. Ann Arbor: University of Michigan Press.

Ozouf, Mona. 1988. *Festivals and the French Revolution*. Cambridge: Harvard University Press.

Palmer, Phyllis. 1995. "Outside the Law: Agricultural and Domestic Workers under the Fair Labor Standards Act." *Journal of Policy History* 7(4): 416–40.

Panofsky, Aaron. 2006. "Fielding Controversy: The Structure and Genesis of Behavior Genetics, 1960–2004." Ph.D. diss., New York University.

Parkin, Frank. 1979. *Marxism and Class Theory: A Bourgeois Critique*. London: Tavistock.

Parsons, A. E. 1929. "The Trojan Legend in England." *Modern Language Review* 24(3): 17–38.

Passeron, Jean-Claude. 1992. *Le Raisonnement Sociologique*. Paris: Nathan.

Patten, Alan. 2006. "The Humanist Roots of Linguistic Nationalism." *History of Political Thought* 27(2): 223–62.

Patterson, James T. 1967. *Congressional Conservatism and the New Deal: The Growth of the Conservative Coalition in Congress, 1933–1939*. Lexington: University of Kentucky Press.

Paxton, Robert O. 2001 [1972]. *Vichy France: Old Guard and New Order 1940–1944*. New York: Columbia University Press.

Peillon, Michel. 1998. "Bourdieu's Field and the Sociology of Welfare." *Journal of Social Policy* 27(2): 213–29.

——. 2001. *Welfare in Ireland: Actors, Resources, and Strategies*. Westport, Conn.: Praeger.

Pels, Dick. 1995. "Knowledge Politics and Anti-Politics: Toward a Critical Appraisal of Bourdieu's Concept of Intellectual Autonomy." *Theory and Society* 24: 79–104.

Peri, Yoram. 1983. *Between Battles and Ballots: Israeli Military in Politics*. Cambridge: Cambridge University Press.

Pettit, Philip. 1997. *Republicanism: A Theory of Freedom and Government*. Oxford: Oxford University Press.

Petzold, Joachim. 1989. "Rassismus, Sozialdarwinismus, Geopolitik—Theoretische Grundpfeiler der Ideologischen Kriegsvorbereitung durch den Deutschen Imperialismus." *Revue Internationale d'Histoire Militaire* (71): 44–56.

Pierson, Paul. 1993. "When Effect Becomes Cause: Policy Feedback and Political Change." *World Politics* 45: 595–628.

——. 1994. *Dismantling the Welfare State? Reagan, Thatcher, and the Politics of Retrenchment.* New York: Cambridge University Press.

Pieters, Rick, and Hans Baumgartner. 2002. "Who Talks to Whom? Intra- and Interdisciplinary Communication of Economics Journals." *Journal of Economic Literature* 40(2): 483–509.

Pincus, Steven C. A. 1996. *Protestantism and Patriotism: Ideologies and the Making of English Foreign Policy, 1650–1668.* Cambridge: Cambridge University Press.

——. 1998. "'To Protect English Liberties': The English Nationalist Revolution of 1688–9." *Protestantism and National Identity*, ed. Tony Claydon and Ian McBride, 75–103. Cambridge: Cambridge University Press.

——. 2006. *England's Glorious Revolution, 1688–1689: A Brief History with Documents.* New York: Palgrave Macmillan.

Pinto, Louis. 1995. *Les Neveux de Zarathoustra: La Réception de Nietzsche en France.* Paris: Seuil.

——. 1998. *Pierre Bourdieu et la Théorie du Monde Social.* Paris: A. Michel.

Piven, Frances Fox, and Richard A. Cloward. 1977. *Poor People's Movements: Why They Succeed, How They Fail.* New York: Vintage.

——. 1993 [1971]. *Regulating the Poor: The Functions of Public Welfare.* Rev. ed. New York: Vintage.

Platt, Jennifer. 1996. *A History of Sociological Research Methods in America, 1920–1960.* Cambridge: Cambridge University Press.

Plotke, David. 1992. "The Political Mobilization of Business." *The Politics of Interests*, ed. M. Petracca. Boulder: Westview.

Pociello, Christian. 1981. *Sports et Société: Approche Socio-Culturelle des Pratiques.* Paris: Vigot.

Pois, Robert A. 1986. *National Socialism and the Religion of Nature.* New York: St. Martin's.

Polanyi, Karl. 2001. *The Great Transformation: The Political and Economic Origins of Our Time.* Boston: Beacon Press.

Popper, Karl R. 1959. *The Logic of Scientific Discovery.* New York: Basic.

——. 1962. *Conjectures and Refutations: The Growth of Scientific Knowledge.* New York: Basic.

——. 1972. *Objective Knowledge: An Evolutionary Approach.* Oxford: Clarendon Press.

Porath, Yehoshua. 1984. "On the Writing of Arab History by Israeli Scholars." *Jerusalem Quarterly* 32: 28–35.

Porter, Brian. 2000. *When Nationalism Began to Hate: Imagining Modern Politics in Nineteenth-Century Poland.* New York: Oxford University Press.

Porter, David L. 1980. *Congress and the Waning of the New Deal.* Port Washington, N.Y.: Kennikat.

Postone, Moishe, Edward LiPuma, and Craig Calhoun. 1993. "Introduction: Bourdieu and Social Theory." *Critical Social Theory: Culture, History, and the Challenge of Difference*, ed. Craig Calhoun, Edward LiPuma, and Moishe Postone, 1–13. Oxford: Blackwell.

Poyer, Alex. 2003. *Les Premiers Temps des véloce-club: Apparition et Diffusion du Cyclisme associatif Français entre 1867 et 1914.* Paris: L'Harmattan.

Prevost, Jean-Guy. 2002. "Genèse Particulière d'une Science des Nombres: l'Autono-
misation de la Statistique en Italie entre 1900 et 1914." *Actes de la Recherche en Sciences Sociales* 141–42: 98–109.

Professional Worker, The. 1936–37. Berkeley: Union of Professional Workers (Workers
Alliance affiliate). Tamiment Library and Robert F. Wagner Labor Archives, Elmer
Holmes Bobst Library, New York University.

Prost, Antoine, and Philippe Billois. 1977. *Les Anciens Combattants et la Société Française, 1914–1939.* Paris: Fondation Nationale des Sciences Politiques.

Puhle, Hans-Jürgen. 1967. *Agrarische Interessenpolitik und preussischer Konservatismus
im wilhelminischen Reich (1893–1914) Ein Beitrag zur Analyse des Nationalismus in
Deutschland am Beispiel des Bundes der Landwirte und der Deutsch-Konservativen
Partei.* Hannover: Verlag für Literatur u. Zeitgeschehen.

Quadagno, Jill. 1987. "Theories of the Welfare State." *Annual Review of Sociology* 13:
109–28.

———. 1988a. "From Old Age Assistance to Supplemental Security Income: The Political
Economy of Relief in the South, 1935–1972." *The Politics of Social Policy in the United
States,* ed. Margaret Weir, Ann Shola Orloff, and Theda Skocpol, 244–45. Princeton:
Princeton University Press.

———. 1988b. *The Transformation of Old Age Security: Class and Politics in the American
Welfare State.* Chicago: University of Chicago Press.

———. 1994. *The Color of Welfare: How Racism Undermined the War on Poverty.* New
York: Oxford University Press.

Quam-Wickham, Nancy. 2001. "Rereading Man's Conquest of Nature: Skill, Myths,
and the Historical Construction of Masculinity in Western Extractive Industries."
Boys and Their Toys?, ed. Roger Horwitz, 91–110. New York: Routledge.

Rand, Nicolas. 2004. "The Hidden Soul: The Growth of the Unconscious in Philosophy, Psychology, Medicine, and Literature, 1750–1900." *American Imago* 61: 257–80.

Ranum, Orest A. 1975. *National Consciousness, History, and Political Culture in Early-
Modern Europe.* Baltimore: Johns Hopkins University Press.

Rauch, Basil. 1944. *The History of the New Deal, 1933–1938.* New York: Creative Age Press.

Reed, Edward. 1997. *From Soul to Mind: The Emergence of Psychology, from Erasmus
Darwin to William James.* New Haven: Yale University Press.

Reed-Danahay, Deborah. 2005. *Locating Bourdieu.* Bloomington: Indiana University
Press.

Requate, Jörg. 1995. *Journalismus als Beruf: Die Entstehung und Entwicklung des Jour-
nalistenberufs im 19. Jahrhundert: Deutschland im internationalen Vergleich.* Göttingen: Vandenhoeck et Ruprecht.

Reuben, Julie A. 1996. *The Making of the Modern University: Intellectual Transformation and the Marginalization of Morality.* Chicago: University of Chicago Press.

Reynolds, Susan. 1984. *Kingdoms and Communities in Western Europe, 900–1300.*
Oxford: Oxford University Press.

Ribard, Dinah. 2000. "Philosophe ou Ecrivain? Problème de Délimitation entre Histoire Littéraire et Histoire de la Philosophie en France, 1650–1850." *Annales HSS* 2:
355–88.

Richter, Rudolf. 2002. "Pierre Bourdieu and the Penetration of the Social World." *Innovation: European Journal of Social Sciences* 15(2): 167–69.

Ringer, Fritz K. 1992. *Fields of Knowledge: French Academic Culture in Comparative Perspective 1890–1920*. Cambridge: Cambridge University Press.

Riviere, Joan. 1986. "Womanliness as a Masquerade." *The Formations of Fantasy*, ed. V. Burgin, J. Donald, and C. Kaplan, 35–44. London: Methuen.

Robbins, Derek. 2004. *The Work of Pierre Bourdieu: Recognizing Society*. London: Continuum.

Roger, Anne. 2003. "L'Entraînement en Athlétisme en France (1919–1973): Une Histoire de Théoriciens?" Doctoral thesis, Université de Lyon 1.

Roosevelt, Franklin D. 1935–42. Papers as President, Official File. File 2366 (Workers Alliance of America, 1935–42). Franklin D. Roosevelt Presidential Library, Hyde Park, N.Y.

Roosevelt, Franklin D. N.d. President's Personal File. File 6794 (American Security Union). Franklin D. Roosevelt Presidential Library, Hyde Park, N.Y.

Rose, Nancy Ellen. 1994. *Put to Work: Relief Programs in the Great Depression*. New York: Monthly Review Press.

Rose, Nikolas. 1992. "Engineering the Human Soul: Analyzing Psychological Expertise." *Science in Context* 5(2): 351–69.

Rosenzweig, Roy. 1975. "Radicals and the Jobless: The Musteites and the Unemployed Leagues, 1932–1936." *Labor History* 16(1): 52–77.

———. 1979. "'Socialism in Our Time': The Socialist Party and the Unemployed, 1929–1936." *Labor History* 20(4): 485–509.

———. 1983. "Organizing the Unemployed: The Early Years of the Great Depression, 1929–1933." *Workers' Struggles, Past and Present: A "Radical America" Reader*, ed. James Green. Philadelphia: Temple University Press.

Roshwald, Aviel. 2006. *The Endurance of Nationalism: Ancient Roots and Modern Dilemmas*. Cambridge: Cambridge University Press.

Ross, Dorothy. 1991. *The Origins of American Social Science*. Cambridge: Cambridge University Press.

Rothman, David J. 1971. *The Discovery of the Asylum: Social Order and Disorder in the New Republic*. Boston: Little, Brown.

Rouannet, Henri, and Brigitte Leroux. 1993. *L'Analyse des Données Multidimensionnelles*. Paris: Dunod.

Saada, Emmanuelle. 2000. "Abdelmalek Sayad and the Double Absence: Toward a Total Sociology of Immigration." *French Politics, Culture, and Society* 18(1): 28–47.

Sabean, David Warren. 1998. *Kinship in Neckarhausen, 1700–1870*. Cambridge: Cambridge University Press.

Saint Martin, Monique de. 1993. *L'Espace de la noblesse*. Paris: Métailié.

Sallaz, Jeffrey J., and Jane Zavisca. 2007. "Bourdieu in American Sociology, 1980–2004." *Annual Review of Sociology* 33: 21–41.

Salmond, John A. 1967. *The Civilian Conservation Corps, 1933–1942: A New Deal Case Study*. Durham: Duke University Press.

Sapiro, Gisèle. 1996. "La Raison Littéraire: Le champ Littéraire Français sous l'Occupation (1940–1944)." *Actes de la Recherche en Sciences Sociales* 111: 3–36.

———. 1999. *La Guerre des Écrivains, 1940–1953.* Paris: Fayard. English trans.: Forthcoming, *French Writers' War.* Duke: Duke University Press.

———. 2001. "De l'usage des Catégories de Droite et de Gauche Dans le Champ Cittéraire." *Sociétés et Représentations* 11: 19–53. English trans.: "The Importation of the Categories of Right and Left in the Literary Field," *The Autonomy of Literature at the Fins de Siècles (1900 and 2000): A Critical Assessment,* ed. Liesbeth Korthals-Altes. Louvain: Peeters, 2007.

———. 2002. "The Structure of the French Literary Field during the German Occupation (1940–1944): A Multiple Correspondence Analysis." *Poetics* 31(5–6): 387–402.

———. 2003a. "Forms of Politicization in the French Literary Field." *Theory and Society* 32: 633–52. Reprinted in David Swartz and Vera Zolberg. 2004. *After Bourdieu: Influence, Critique, Elaboration.* Dordrecht: Spring.

———. 2003b. "L'épuration du Monde des Lettres." *Une Poignée de Misérables: L'épuration de la Société Français après la Seconde Guerre Mondiale,* ed. Marc Olivier Baruch, 243–85. Paris: Fayard.

———. 2004a. "Forms of Politicization in the French Literary Field." *After Bourdieu: Influence, Critique, Elaboration,* ed. David L. Swartz and Vera L. Zolberg, 145–64. Boston: Kluwer.

———. 2004b. "Défense et Illustration de 'L'honnête Homme': Les Hommes de Lettres Contre la Sociologie." *Actes de la Recherche en Sciences Sociales* 153: 11–27.

———. 2004c. "Entre Individualisme et Corporatisme: Les Écrivains dans la Première Moitié du XXe siècle." *Corporations et Corporatisme en France, XVIIIe–XXXe Siècles,* ed. Steven Kaplan and Philippe Minard, 279–314. Paris: Belin.

———. 2006a. "Portrait of the Writer as a Traitor: The French Purge Trials (1944–1953)." *EREA* 4/2. http://www.e-rea.org.

———. 2006b. "Responsibility and Freedom: Foundations of Sartre's Concept of Intellectual Engagement." *Journal of Romance Studies* 6(1–2): 31–48.

———. 2007a. " 'Je N'ai Jamais Appris à Ecrire': Les Conditions de Formation de la Vocation d'écrivain." *Actes de la Recherche en Sciences Sociales* 168: 13–33.

———. 2007b. "The Writer's Responsibility in France: From Flaubert to Sartre." *French Politics, Culture and Society* 25(1): 1–29.

———. 2011. *La Responsabilité de l'écrivain: Littérature et Morale en France (19ᵉ–20ᵉ siècles).* Paris: Seuil.

Sapiro, Gisèle, and Boris Gobille. 2006. "Propriétaires ou Travailleurs Intellectuels? Les Ecrivains Français en Quête de Statut." *Le Mouvement Social* 214: 119–45.

Sartre, Jean-Paul. 1998. *La Responsabilité de l'écrivain.* Paris: Verdier.

Saussure, Ferdinand de. 1986. *Course in General Linguistics,* ed. Charles Bally and Albert Sechehaye, with the collaboration of Albert Riedlinger. Translated and annotated by Roy Harris. LaSalle, Ill.: Open Court.

Sautter, Udo. 1991. *Three Cheers for the Unemployed: Government and Unemployment before the New Deal.* New York: Cambridge University Press.

Sayad, Abdelmalek. 1999. *La Double Absence: Des Illusions de L'émigré aux Souffrances de L'immigré*. Paris: Seuil.

Sayer, Andrew. 1999. "Bourdieu, Smith and Disinterested Judgment." *Sociological Review* 47(3): 403–31.

Schalk, Ellery. 1986. *From Valor to Pedigree: Ideas of Nobility in France in the Sixteenth and Seventeenth Centuries*. Princeton: Princeton University Press.

Schama, Simon. 1987. *The Embarrassment of Riches: An Interpretation of Dutch Culture in the Golden Age*. New York: Knopf.

Schelling, Thomas. 1980. *The Strategy of Conflict*. Cambridge: Harvard University Press.

Schiff, Zeev. 2001. "A New Challenge for Mr. Intelligence." *Haaretz*, July 20, 17.

Schiltz, Michael E. 1970. *Public Attitudes toward Social Security, 1935–1965*. Washington: U.S. Government Printing Office.

Schönemann, B. 1972–97. "Volk, Nation." *Geschichtliche Grundbegriffe: Historisches Lexikon Zur Politisch Sozialen Sprache in Deutschland*, ed. O. Brunner, W. Conze, and R. Kosseleck, 7: 141–431. Stuttgart: E. Klett.

Schultheis, Franz. 2002. "Nachwort." *Ein soziologischer Selbstversuch*, ed. Pierre Bourdieu, 133–51. Frankfurt: Suhrkamp.

Schumpeter, Joseph A. 1942. *Capitalism, Socialism, and Democracy*. New York: Harper and Brothers.

Schwartz, Bonnie Fox. 1984. *The Civil Works Administration, 1933–1934: The Business of Emergency Employment in the New Deal*. Princeton: Princeton University Press.

Scott, W. Richard, and John W. Meyer. 1994. *Institutional Environments and Organizations: Structural Complexity and Individualism*. Thousand Oaks, Calif.: Sage.

Sedler, Mark J. 1983. "Freud's Concept of Working Through." *Psychoanalytic Quarterly* 52: 73–98.

Serry, Hervé. 2000. *Naissance de L'intellectuel Catholique*. Paris: La Découverte.

Sewell, William H., Jr. 1987. "Theory of Action, Dialectic, and History: Comment on Coleman." *American Journal of Sociology* 93(1): 166–72.

Sexton, Patricia Cayo. 1991. *The War on Labor and the Left: Understanding America's Unique Conservatism*. Boulder: Westview.

Seymour, Helen. 1937. "The Organized Unemployed." Ph.D. diss., University of Chicago.

Shamir, Shimon. 1979. "Letter to the Editor: The Decline of Nasserism." *Haaretz*, Literary Supplement, June 22.

Shovlin, John. 2000. "Toward a Reinterpretation of Revolutionary Antinobilism: The Political Economy of Honor in the Old Regime." *Journal of Modern History* 72: 35–66.

Siegrist, Hannes. 1995. *Advokat, Bürger und Staat: Sozialgeschichte der Rechtsanwälte. in Deutschland, Italien und der Schweiz (18–20 Jahrhundert)*. 2 vols. Frankfurt: M. V. Klostermann.

Silverman, Kaja. 1988. *The Acoustic Mirror: The Female Voice in Psychoanalysis and Cinema*. Bloomington: Indiana University Press.

——. 1996. *The Threshold of the Visible World*. New York: Routledge.

Silverstein, Paul. 2004. "Of Rooting and Uprooting: Kabyle Habitus, Domesticity, and Structural Nostalgia." *Ethnography* 5(4): 553–78.

Silverstein, Paul A., and Jane E. Goodman. 2009. "Bourdieu in Algeria." *Bourdieu in Algeria*, ed. J. E. Goodman and P. A. Silverstein, 1–62. Lincoln: University of Nebraska Press.

Simiand, François. 1987 [1903]. "Méthode Historique et Science Sociale." *Méthode Historique et Sciences Sociales*, ed. Maria Cédronio, 146. Lausanne: Editions des Archives Contemporaines.

Simmel, Georg. 1950. *The Sociology of Georg Simmel*. Translated and edited by Kurt H. Wolff. Glencoe, Ill.: Free Press.

Simon, Gérald. 1990. *Puissance Sportive et Ordre Juridique Etatique: Contribution à L'étude des Relations entre la Puissance Publique et les Institutions Privées*. Paris: LGDJ.

Simon, Herbert A. 1978. "Rationality as Process and as Product of Thought." *American Economic Review* 68(2): 1–16.

——. 1985. "Human Nature in Politics: The Dialogue of Psychology with Political Science." *American Political Science Review* 79(2): 293–304.

Simonin, Anne. 1994. *Les Éditions de Minuit 1942–1955. Le devoir d'insoumission*. Paris: IMEC.

——. 1997. "Le Comité Médical de la Résistance: Un Succès Différé." *Le Mouvement Social* 180: 159–78.

Sivan, Emmanuel. 1979a. "The Annual Survey of the Shiloh Institute." *Hamizrach Hachadash* 28(3–4): 300. [Hebrew]

——. 1979b. "The Decline of Nasserism or the Decline of Orientalism?" *Haaretz* (7/17): 23. [Hebrew]

Skocpol, Theda. 1979. *States and Social Revolutions: A Comparative Analysis of France, Russia and China*. Cambridge: Cambridge University Press.

——. 1980. "Political Response to Capitalist Crisis: Neo-Marxist Theories of the State and the Case of the New Deal." *Politics and Society* 10: 155–201.

——. 1985. "Bringing the State Back In." *Bringing the State Back In*, ed. Peter B. Evans, Dietrich Rueschmeyer, and Theda Skocpol. New York: Cambridge University Press.

——. 1992. *Protecting Soldiers and Mothers: The Political Origins of Social Policy in the United States*. Cambridge: Harvard University Press.

Skocpol, Theda, and Edwin Amenta. 1986. "States and Social Policies." *Annual Review of Sociology* 12: 131–57.

Smith, Anthony D. 1988. "The Myth of the 'Modern Nation' and the Myths of Nations." *Ethnic and Racial Studies* 11(1): 1–26.

——. 2003. *Chosen Peoples: Sacred Sources of National Identity*. Oxford: Oxford University Press.

——. 2004. *The Antiquity of Nations*. Cambridge: Polity.

Smith, Branford W. 2004. "Germanic Pagan Antiquity in Lutheran Historical Thought." *Journal of the Historical Society* 4(3): 351–74.

Smith, Christian. 2003. *The Secular Revolution: Power, Interests, and Conflict in the Secularization of American Public Life*. Berkeley: University of California Press.

Smith, Jay M. 2000. "Social Categories, the Language of Patriotism and the Origins of the French Revolution: The Debate over the *Noblesse Commerçante.*" *Journal of Modern History* 72: 339–74.

Smith, Rogers M. 1997. *Civic Ideals: Conflicting Visions of Citizenship in U.S. History.* New Haven: Yale University Press.

Snyder, Timothy. 2003. *The Reconstruction of Nations: Poland, Ukraine, Lithuania, Belarus, 1569–1999.* New Haven: Yale University Press.

Soto, Hernando de. 2000. *The Mystery of Capital: Why Captialism Triumphs in the West and Fails Everywhere Else.* New York: Basic.

Stampnitzky, Lisa. 2008. "The Rise of the Terrorism Expert." Ph.D. diss., University of California, Berkeley.

Stanton, Domna. 1993. *The Aristocrat as Art: A Study of the Honnête Homme and the Dandy in Seventeeth- and Nineteenth-Century French Literature.* Berkeley: University of California Press.

Star, Susan Leigh, and James R. Griesemer. 1989. "Institutional Ecology, 'Translations' and Boundary Objects: Amateurs and Professionals in Berkeley's Museum of Vertebrate Zoology, 1907–39." *Social Studies of Science* 19(3): 387–420.

Stavrakakis, Yannis. 2002. "Creativity and Its Limits: Encounters with Social Constructionism and the Political in Castoriadis and Lacan." *Constellations* 9: 522–36.

Stedman Jones, Gareth. 2004. *An End to Poverty?: A Historical Debate.* London: Profile.

Steinfeld, Robert J. 1989. "Property and Suffrage in the Early American Republic." *Stanford Law Review* 41: 335–76.

Steinmetz, George. 1999. "Introduction: Culture and the State." *State/Culture: State-Formation after the Cultural Turn*, ed. George Steinmetz, 1–49. Ithaca: Cornell University Press.

——. 2004. "The Uncontrollable Afterlives of Ethnography: Lessons from German 'Salvage Colonialism' for a New Age of Empire." *Ethnography* 5: 251–88.

——. 2005. *The Politics of Method in the Human Sciences: Positivism and Its Epistemological Others.* Durham: Duke University Press.

——. 2006. "Bourdieu's Disavowal of Lacan: Psychoanalytic Theory and the Concepts of 'Habitus' and 'Symbolic Capital.'" *Constellations* 13: 445–64.

——. 2007a. "American Sociology before and after World War II: The (Temporary) Settling of a Disciplinary Field." *Sociology in America. The* ASA *Centennial History*, ed. Craig Calhoun, 314–66. Chicago: University of Chicago Press.

——. 2007b. *The Devil's Handwriting: Precoloniality and the German Colonial State in Qingdao, Samoa, and Southwest Africa.* Chicago: University of Chicago Press.

——. 2008. "The Colonial State as a Social Field." *American Sociological Review* 73(4): 589–612.

——. 2009a. "How Bourdieu's Theory of Symbolic Capital Might be More Fruitfully Utilized to Study Global Inequality." Paper presented at "The Cultural Wealth of Nations" conference at the University of Michigan, Ann Arbor, March 27–28.

——. 2009b. "Neo-Bourdieusian Theory and the Question of Scientific Autonomy: German Sociologists and Empire, 1890s–1940s." *Political Power and Social Theory* 20: 71–131.

——. 2011. "Bourdieu, Historicity, and Historical Sociology." *Cultural Sociology* 11(1): 45–66.

Steinmo, Sven, Kathleen Thelen, and Frank Longstreth, eds. 1992. *Structuring Politics: Historical Institutionalism in Comparative Analysis*. New York: Cambridge University Press.

Stepan-Norris, Judith, and Maurice Zeitlin. 2003. *Left Out: Reds and America's Industrial Unions*. New York: Cambridge University Press.

Stigler, George, and Gary Becker. 1977. "De Gustibus Non Est Disputandum." *American Economic Review* 67(2): 76–90.

Stolcke, Verena. 1993. "Is Sex to Gender as Race Is to Ethnicity?" *Gendered Anthropology*, ed. Teresa de Valle, 17–37. London: Routledge.

Suleiman, Susan Rubin. 1993. "L'engagement Sublime: Zola comme Archétype d'un Mythe Culturel." *Les Cahiers naturalistes* 67: 11–24.

Sullivan, Alice. 2001. "Cultural Capital and Educational Attainment." *Sociology* 35(4): 893–912.

Sullivan, Patricia. 1996. *Days of Hope: Race and Democracy in the New Deal Era*. Chapel Hill: University of North Carolina Press.

Surel, Yves. 1997. *L'État et le Livre: Les Politiques Publiques du Livre en France, 1957–1993*. Paris: L'Harmattan.

Suter, Andreas. 1997. *Der Schweizerische Bauernkrieg von 1653: Politische Sozialgeschichte—Sozialgeschichte eines politischen Ereignisses*. Tübingen: Bibliotheca Academica.

Swartz, David L. 1997. *Culture and Power: The Sociology of Pierre Bourdieu*. Chicago: University of Chicago Press.

——. 2003. "From Critical Sociology to Public Intellectual: Pierre Bourdieu and Politics." *Theory and Society* 32(5–6): 791–823.

——. 2005. "Le Capital Culturel dans la Sociologie de L'éducation Américaine." *Rencontres avec Pierre Bourdieu*, ed. Gérard Mauger, 453–65. Bellecombe-en-Bauges, France: Éditions du Croquant.

——. 2013 (forthcoming). Chapter 2, *Symbolic Power, Politics, and Intellectuals: The Political Sociology of Pierre Bourdieu*. Chicago: University of Chicago Press.

Taillon, Paul Michel. 2001. "To Make Men Out of Crude Material: Work Culture, Manhood, and Unionism in the Railroad Running Trades." *Boys and Their Toys?* ed. Roger Horowitz, 33–54. New York: Routledge.

Takaki, Ronald T. 1989. *Strangers from a Different Shore: History of Asian Americans*. Boston: Little, Brown.

Taylor, Charles. 1993. "To Follow a Rule . . ." *Bourdieu: Critical Perspectives*, ed. Craig Calhoun, Edward LiPuma, and Moishe Postone, 45–60. Oxford: Polity.

Taylor, Michael. 1988. "Rationality and Revolutionary Collective Action." *Rationality and Revolution*, ed. Michael Taylor, 63–97. Cambridge: Cambridge University Press.

Terret, Thierry. 1998. *L'institution et le Nageur: Histoire de la Fédération Française de Natation (1919–1939)*. Lyon: Presses Universitaires de Lyon.

Thelen, Kathleen A. 2004. *How Institutions Evolve: The Political Economy of Skills in Germany, Britain, the United States, and Japan*. Cambridge: Cambridge University Press.

Thiesse, Anne-Marie. 1984. *Le Roman du Quotidien: Lecteurs et Lectures Populaire à la Belle Époque*. Paris: Le chemin vert.

———. 1999. *La Création des Identités Nationales. Europe XVII siècle–XXe siècle*. Paris: Seuil.

Tichit, Philippe. 1997. "Industrialisation et Développement du Sport dans Quatre Communes Industrielles Ouvrières du Nord (au XX*f*g siècle)." *Sciences du Sport*, Université Paris 11 Orsay, Paris.

Tilly, Charles. 1975. "Revolutions and Collective Violence." *Handbook of Political Science*, Vol. 3, ed. Fred Greenstein and Nelson Polsby, 483–541. Reading, Mass.: Addison-Wesley.

———. 1984. *Big Structures, Large Processes, Huge Comparisons*. New York: Russell Sage Foundation.

———. 1995. "To Explain Political Processes." *American Journal of Sociology* 100(6): 1594–1610.

———. 2001. "Mechanisms in Political Processes." *Annual Review of Political Science* 4(1): 21.

Tilly, Charles, ed. 1975. *The Formation of National States in Western Europe*. Princeton: Princeton University Press.

Tocqueville, Alexis de. 1966 [1835/40]. *Democracy in America*. Translated by George Lawrence. Edited by J. P. Mayer. New York: Harper and Row.

Todd, Emmanuel. 1988. *The Explanation of Ideology: Family Structures and Social Systems*. New York: Basil Blackwell.

Toleidano, Ehud. 1989. "The Silence of the Orientalists." *Politika* (November): 16–19. [Hebrew]

Tombs, Isabelle, and Robert Tombs. 2006. *That Sweet Enemy: The French and British from the Sun King to the Present*. London: Heinemann.

Tombs, Robert. 1994. "Was There a French Sonderweg?" *European Review of History* 2: 169–78.

Topalov, Christian. 1998. "Les Usages Stratégiques de l'histoire des Disciplines." *Pour une Histoire des Sciences Sociales*, ed. Johan Heilbron, Rémi Lenoir, and Gisèle Sapiro, 127–57. Paris: Fayard.

Tosh, John. 1999. *A Man's Place: Masculinity and the Middle-Class Home in Victorian England*. New Haven: Yale University Press.

Toulmin, Stephen. 1990. *Cosmopolis: The Hidden Agenda of Modernity*. New York: Free Press.

Trexler, Richard C. 1980. *Public Life in Renaissance Florence*. New York: Academic.

———. 1985. *Persons in Groups: Behavior and Identity Formation in Medieval and Renaissance Europe*. Binghamton: Medieval and Renaissance Texts and Studies.

Tsebelis, George. 1990. *Nested Games: Rational Choice in Comparative Politics*. Berkeley: University of California Press.

Tullock, Gordon. 1971. "The Paradox of Revolution." *Public Choice* 1: 89–99.

Tuveson, Ernest. L. 1968. *Redeemer Nation: The Idea of America's Millennial Role*. Chicago: University of Chicago Press.

Tversky, Amos, and Daniel Kahneman. 1986. "Rational Choice and the Framing of Decisions." *Journal of Business* 59(4): S251–S278.

Tynes, Sheryl R. 1996. *Turning Points in Social Security: From "Cruel Hoax" to "Sacred Entitlement."* Stanford: Stanford University Press.

United States. Department of Labor, Bureau of Labor Statistics. 1940. "Negroes under WPA, 1939." *Monthly Labor Review* 50 (March): 636–38.

United States. Federal Works Agency. 1946. *Final Report on the WPA Program, 1935–43.* Washington: U.S. Government Printing Office.

United States. House of Representatives. 1939–40. Hearings before the Subcommittee of the Committee on Appropriations, 76th Congress, 1st sess., Acting under House Resolution 130. Record Group 233, National Archives, Washington.

Valocchi, Steve. 1994. "The Racial Basis of Capitalism and the State, and the Impact of the New Deal on African Americans." *Social Problems* 41(3): 347–62.

Viala, Alain. 1987. "Synchronie Classique: Le Dispositif des Quatre Référents." *Oeuvres et Critiques* 12: 9–18.

Vick, Brian. 2003. "The Origins of the German Volk: Cultural Purity and National Identity in Nineteenth-Century Germany." *German Studies Review* 26(2): 241–56.

Vigarello, Georges. 1988. *Une Histoire Culturelle du Sport: Techniques d'hier—et d'aujourd'hui.* Paris: R. Laffont.

———. 1995. "Le Temps du Sport." *L'Avènement des Loisirs: 1850–1960,* ed. A. Corbain, 193–221. Paris: Aubier.

Villari, Rosario. 1997. "Patriottismo e Riforma Politica." *Dimensioni e Problemi della Ricerca Storica* 2: 7–16.

Vincent, Julien. 2004. "The Sociologist and the Republic: Pierre Bourdieu and the Virtues of Social History." *History Workshop Journal* 58: 128–48.

Vincent, Ted. 1981. *Mudville's Revenge: The Rise and Fall of American Sport.* New York: Seaview.

Viroli, Maurizio. 1997. *For Love of Country: An Essay on Patriotism and Nationalism.* Oxford: Oxford University Press.

Wacquant, Loïc. 1992. "Toward a Social Praxeology: The Structure and Logic of Bourdieu's Sociology." *An Invitation to Reflexive Sociology,* by Pierre Bourdieu and Loïc Wacquant. Chicago: University of Chicago Press.

———. 1998. "Artistic Field." *Encyclopedia of Aesthetics,* ed. Michael Kelly. Oxford: Oxford University Press.

———. 2002. "The Sociological Life of Pierre Bourdieu." *International Sociology* 17: 549–56.

———. 2003. *Body and Soul: Notebooks of an Apprentice Boxer.* Oxford: Oxford University Press.

———. 2004. "Following Pierre Bourdieu into the Field." *Ethnography* 5: 387–414.

———. 2005. "Pointers on Pierre Bourdieu and Democratic Politics." *Pierre Bourdieu and Democratic Politics,* ed. Loïc Wacquant, 10–28. Cambridge: Polity.

Wacquant, Loïc, and Pierre Bourdieu. 2005. *Pierre Bourdieu and Democratic Politics: The Mystery of Ministry.* Cambridge: Polity.

Wacquant, Loïc, and Craig Calhoun. 1989. "Intérêt, rationalité et culture." *Actes de la Recherche en Sciences Sociales* 76(1): 41–60.

Wagner, David. 2005. *The Poorhouse: America's Forgotten Institution.* Lanham, Md.: Rowman and Littlefield.

Wahl, Alfred. 1986. "Le Footballeur Français: de L'amateurisme au Salariat (1890–1926)." *Le Mouvement Social* 135(2): 7–31.

Walton, Robert C. 1994. "The Holocaust: Conversion to Racism through Scientific Materialism: 'The People Like Us Who Killed Jews.'" *History of European Ideas* 19(4): 787–94.

Warner, Lloyd W. 1959. *The Living and the Dead: A Study of the Symbolic Life of Americans.* New Haven: Yale University Press.

Weber, Eugen J. 1976. *Peasants into Frenchmen: The Modernization of Rural France, 1870–1914.* Stanford: Stanford University Press.

Weber, Max. 1924. *Wirtschaftsgeschichte.* Munich: Duncker and Humblot.

———. 1949. *The Methodology of the Social Sciences.* Translated and edited by Edward A. Shils and Henry A. Finch. New York: Free Press.

———. 1951 [1915]. "The Social Psychology of the World Religions." In H. H. Gerth and C. W. Mills, eds., *From Max Weber: Essays in Sociology.* London: Routledge.

———. 1959. *Le Savant et le Politique.* Paris: Plon.

———. 1964 [1946]. *From Max Weber: Essays in Sociology.* Translated, edited, and with an introduction by H. H. Gerth and C. Wright Mills. New York: Oxford University Press.

———. 1978 [1922]. *Economy and Society: An Outline of Interpretive Sociology.* Edited by Guenther Roth and Claus Wittich. Berkeley: University of California Press.

———. 1993 [1963]. *The Sociology of Religion.* Translated by Ephraim Fischoff. Boston: Beacon Press.

———. 2001. *The Protestant Ethic and the Spirit of Capitalism.* Translated by Talcott Parsons. Introduction by Anthony Giddens. London: Routledge.

———. 2002. *The Protestant Ethic and the "Spirit" of Capitalism and Other Writings.* Edited, translated, and with an introduction by Peter Baehr and Gordon C. Wells. New York: Penguin.

Weber, Samuel M. 1991. *Return to Freud: Jacques Lacan's Dislocation of Psychoanalysis.* Cambridge: Cambridge University Press.

Weinberger, Ota. 1988. "Geistesgeschichtliche und Philosophische Voraussetzungen für Hitlers Radiklen Antisemitismus." *Geschichte und Gegenwart* 7(4): 313–27.

Weir, Margaret, Ann Shola Orloff, and Theda Skocpol. 1988. "Understanding American Social Politics." *The Politics of Social Policy in the United States,* ed. Margaret Weir, Ann Shola Orloff, and Theda Skocpol, 3–35. Princeton: Princeton University Press.

Weisz, George. 1983. *The Emergence of Modern Universities in France (1863–1914).* Princeton: Princeton University Press.

Wilfert, Blaise. Forthcoming. *La Nation des Écrivains: Importations Littéraires et Nationalisme.* Paris: Belin.

Williams, Raymond. 1983 [1958]. *Culture and Society 1780–1950.* New York: Columbia University Press.

Winch, Peter. 1958. *The Idea of Social Science and Its Relation to Philosophy.* London: Routledge and Kegan Paul.

Witz, Anne. 1992. *Professions and Patriarchy.* London: Routledge.

Wolters, Raymond. 1970. *Negroes and the Great Depression: The Problem of Economic Recovery.* Westport, Conn.: Greenwood.

Woodward, C. Vann. 1957. "The Political Legacy of Reconstruction." *Journal of Negro Education* 26(3): 231–40.

Work. 1938–40. Newspaper of the Workers Alliance of America. Washington, D.C., April 9, 1938–November 1940. Microfilm R1568, Tamiment Library and Robert F. Wagner Labor Archives, Elmer Holmes Bobst Library, New York University.

Workers Alliance, The. 1935—36. Newspaper of the Workers Alliance of America. Milwaukee, August 15, 1935–September 1936. Microfilm R1569, Tamiment Library and Robert F. Wagner Labor Archives, Elmer Holmes Bobst Library, New York University.

Wormald, Patrick. 1994. *"Engla Land:* The Making of an Allegiance." *Journal of Historical Sociology* 7(1): 1–24.

Yaari, Ehud, and Zeev Schiff. 1984. *A War of Deceit.* Jerusalem: Schocken.

Zaret, David. 2000. *Origins of Democratic Culture: Printing, Petitions, and the Public Sphere in Early-Modern England.* Princeton: Princeton University Press.

Zelizer, Viviana A. Rotman. 1994. *The Social Meaning of Money.* New York: Basic.

Ziskind, David. 1940. "Strikes on Public Employment Projects." *One Thousand Strikes of Government Employees.* New York: Columbia University Press.

Žižek, Slavoj. 1989. *The Sublime Object of Ideology.* London: Verso.

——. 1997. *The Plague of Fantasies.* London: Verso.

Zubrzycki, Genevieve. 2006. *The Crosses of Auschwitz: Nationalism and Religion in Post-Communist Poland.* Chicago: University of Chicago Press.

CONTRIBUTORS

Craig Calhoun is the director of the London School of Economics and Political Science and past president of the Social Science Research Council. He has published widely in the areas of social theory, political philosophy, and political and historical sociology. He coedited the seminal volume entitled *Bourdieu: Critical Perspectives.*

Charles Camic is John Evans Professor of Sociology at Northwestern University. His recent publications include *Social Knowledge in the Making*, edited with Michele Lamont and Neil Gross (2011), and *Essential Writings of Thorstein Veblen*, edited with Geoffrey Hodgson (2011).

Christophe Charle is professor of contemporary history at the Sorbonne (Paris 1) and the director of the Institut d'histoire moderne et contemporaine. He worked closely with Bourdieu and has written extensively on the intellectual field in nineteenth-century France, on transnational intellectual networks, and on comparative social and cultural history of Europe. His works include *Les Intellectuels en Europe au XIXe siècle: Essai d'histoire comparée* (1996), *La crise des sociétés impériales: Essai d'histoire sociale comparée de l'Allemagne, de la France et de la Grande Bretagne* (2001), and *Théâtres en capitales, naissance de la société du spectacle à Paris, Berlin, Londres et Vienne (1860–1914)* (2008); he has edited, with Julien Vincent and Jay Winter, *Anglo-French Attitudes: Comparisons and Transfers between English and French Intellectuals since the Eighteenth Century* (2007).

Jacques Defrance is professor of social sciences in the Sports Sciences Department at the West Paris—Nanterre University. He wrote his doctoral dissertation under Pierre Bourdieu, with Luc Boltanski and Claude Grignon, on the sociogenesis of modern physical education in France from 1770 to 1914. His research interests include the relations between education, medicine, and science and the question of the relative autonomy of specialized fields vis-à-vis political and economic powers. He is the author of *L'Excellence Corporelle: La Formation des Activités physiques et sportives modernes. 1770–1914* (1987) and *Sociology of Sport* (1995; 6th ed., 2011).

Mustafa Emirbayer is professor of sociology at the University of Wisconsin, Madison. He is the author of numerous papers on Bourdieusian sociology, including, with Eva Williams, "Bourdieu and Social Work" (*Social Service Review*, 2005); with Victoria Johnson, "Bourdieu and Organizational Analysis" (*Theory and Society*, 2008); and "Tilly and Bourdieu" (*American Sociologist*, 2010). He is also coauthor with Matthew

Desmond of two works on race in America, both informed by Bourdieu: *Racial Domination, Racial Progress* (2009), and *The Racial Order* (forthcoming).

Ivan Ermakoff is professor of sociology at the University of Wisconsin, Madison. He is the author of *Ruling Oneself Out: A Theory of Collective Abdications* (2008) and several articles on normative shifts and political transitions, including "Prelates and Princes" (*American Sociological Review*, 1997), "Strukturelle Zwänge und zufällige Geschehnisse" (*Geschichte und Gesellschaft*, 2001), "Patrimonial Rise and Decline" (*Political Power and Social Theory*, 2008), and "Theory of Practice, Rational Choice and Historical Change" (*Theory and Society*, 2010).

Gil Eyal is professor of sociology at Columbia University. His most recent book is *The Autism Matrix* (2010).

Chad Alan Goldberg is professor of sociology at the University of Wisconsin, Madison. His research interests include American political development; the sociology of citizenship, the welfare state, and social movements; and social theory. He is the author of *Citizens and Paupers: Relief, Rights, and Race, from the Freedmen's Bureau to Workfare* (2007).

Philip S. Gorski is professor of sociology and religious studies at Yale University, where he directs the European and Russian Studies Program and codirects the Center for Comparative Research and the MacMillan Initiative on Religion, Politics, and Society. His research interests include social and political theory, the philosophy of the social sciences, and religion and politics in Western Europe and North America. He is currently completing a book on American civil religion.

Robert A. Nye is Thomas Hart and Mary Jones Horning Professor of the Humanities and Professor of History Emeritus, Oregon State University, Corvallis.

Gisèle Sapiro is professor of sociology at the École des hautes études en sciences sociales and research director at the CNRS. She is also head of the European Center for Sociology and Political Science in Paris. Her interests include the sociology of intellectuals, literature, translation, and the international circulation of ideas. She is the author of *La Guerre des écrivains, 1940–1953* (1999; forthcoming in English from Duke University Press) and of *La Responsabilité de l'écrivain* (2011). Among the books she has edited are *Pierre Bourdieu, sociologue* (2004) and *L'Espace intellectuel en Europe* (2009).

Erik Schneiderhan is assistant professor of sociology at the University of Toronto. His research is on deliberative democracy and pragmatist social theory. His most recent work is "Pragmatism and Empirical Sociology: The Case of Jane Addams and Hull-House, 1889–1895" (*Theory and Society*, 2011). Currently he is at work on a book on Jane Addams and the dilemmas of social provision in America.

George Steinmetz is Charles Tilly Collegiate Professor of Sociology and German at the University of Michigan. He is the author of *The Devil's Handwriting: Precoloniality and the German Colonial State of Qingdao, Samoa, and Southwest Africa* (2007), and editor of *Sociology and Empire: The Imperial Entanglements of an Empire* (Duke University Press, 2013).

David L. Swartz is assistant professor of sociology at Boston University. He is the author of *Culture and Power: The Sociology of Pierre Bourdieu* (University of Chicago Press, 1997), and *Symbolic Power, Politics, and Intellectuals: The Political Sociology of Pierre Bourdieu* (University of Chicago Press, forthcoming, 2013), and the coeditor with Vera L. Zolberg of *After Bourdieu: Influence, Critique, Elaboration* (Kluwer Academic Publishers, 2004). He is a senior editor and book review editor of *Theory and Society*.

citizenship (*cont.*)

    relief and, 215–16, 217; property owner-ship and, 215; social rights and, 216–17; wage earners and, 215, 216; Workers Alliance of America defense of, 222, 223, 224–25

civil rights: T. H. Marshall on, 215

class, 139

classification, 47–49

classification struggles, 48–49, 255–57; analysis of, 255–56; capital in, 219–20; in Civil War pension program, 237; client positions and, 220; conceptual foundations of, 254–55; group making/unmaking and, 219, 221; historical struggles and, 225–26; institutional structures and, 226; in mothers' pension program, 237; in nation formation (*see* nationalism; nation-ization struggles); in old age insurance program, 237–38; policy-related emergence of, 220, 226; position takings in, 220, 256; race and, 226–27; social space analysis in, 254, 255; space of possibles in, 255–56; state in, 220, 221, 226, 240n6; in U.S. welfare state development, 218–25 (*see also* Works Progress Administration [WPA])

closure/generosity, 169–72

club society, 299–300

cognitive capacity: in rational choice theory, 95

collective bargaining, 222, 223

collective intellectual, 154–55

collective unrest: explanations of, 98–99

Collini, Stefan, 81

Comité de'Épuration, 281–82

Comité National des Écrivains, 279–80, 281

Comité National des Sports, 309

commodity fetishism, 343

Communists: in French literary field crisis, 274, 278, 279, 283; in Workers Alliance of America, 229–30, 234

comparative history, 69–76; analytic frameworks in, 70–71; binary comparisons in, 75; constructing the object in, 69–70; cross-fertilizing transfers in, 76, 81–82;

experimentation analogy to, 73–74; historical perspective on, 67–69; macro vs. micro, 72–73, 75–76; purpose of, 73–75; resistance to, 68–69; scale of division in, 70; semantics in, 76; vs. specialization, 69; standard of sources for, 75–76; transnational concepts in, 71–72, 76–84; of university field, 76–84

consciousness: double, 94, 123; nationalist, 246–47; rational choice theory and, 91–93, 94, 106n10; theory of practice and, 92–93

correspondence analysis, 34n16

Craft of Sociology, The (Bourdieu, Chamboredon, and Passeron), 124, 125

creativity, 151–52

crisis, 93–94; consciousness and, 91–94; of French literary field (*see* French literary field [WWII] crisis); of May 1968, 10–11, 93, 98–100, 350, 353; multiple modes of response to, 100–103; rational choice and (*see* rational choice theory); reflexivity in, 93–94; self-defeating response to, 100–101

cross-tabular analysis: in field construction, 29

cultural capital, 21, 28, 57, 58, 117, 339; education and, 11; Marxism and, 111; misrecognition of, 343; social reproduction and, 6–8

culture, 51; idealization of, 47, 51–52; inequality and, 47–48; social-scientific knowledge about, 203–6

dehistoricization, 286

democracy, 131–57, 364–65; bureaucratic field and, 141–42; civil society and, 153; Dewey on, 131–32, 139, 152–53; field specificity of, 139; political field and, 143–44; political opinion and, 145–46; power field and, 140–42; publicity field and, 153–54; scholarship and, 147–48; symbolic power and, 142; symbolic violence and, 145; workers' rights and, 223

Democracy in America (de Tocqueville), 147

denegation, 110

Descartes, René, 134–35
descriptivism, 363–64, 366n9
desire, 117, 118
Dewey, John, 131–57; antifoundationalism
of, 134–35; on democracy, 131–32, 139,
152–53; on education, 144; on experience,
135, 155–56; on habits, 136, 145, 147; on
inquiry, 135–36, 155–56; on psychology,
156n1; on publics, 153
discourse, 181–82n1; boundary change
effects on, 336–37; dominant/dominated,
337–38; nationalist, 247, 249, 263n1; rationalization of, 335–36; social space of, 336;
of ultimate value, 334–35
disfranchisement: of relief recipients, 222,
225, 239n2
disinterestedness, 48–49, 53, 56, 164
disposition, 31–32. See also habitus
dis/position, 254
dispossession, 98–100
Distinction (Bourdieu), 2, 3–8, 12, 47–49,
253–55; political opinion topic of,
145–46
di/vision, 254–55
dominant/dominated, 116–19, 140; collu-
sion in, 40, 41, 42; discourses of, 337–38;
recognition/misrecognition and, 117–18
domination, 13, 21, 145–46; conservation of,
141; masculine, 112–114, 353 (see also
masculinities)
double consciousness, 94, 123
doxic attitude, 39, 65n8, 137, 147
Dreyfus affair, 270, 271
dualisms, 150
Durkheim, Emile, 22, 38, 48, 255

economic capital, 52, 56, 57, 58, 157n8, 339,
344, 346
economics: boundary work and, 175–76;
disinterestedness and, 48; vs. noneconomic realms, 58, 66n15; politics
and, 59
economism, 56–62, 58
economy: habitus and, 8–9, 39–40, 41, 122–
23; neoliberalism and, 56–62; post-
WWII, 43–44; revolution and, 10–11

education, 43–49; cultural capital and, 11;
Dewey on, 144; field of, 46 (see also intellectual field; university field); in France,
11, 12, 44–46, 61, 100–101; inequality and,
45–46, 47–48, 60; Kabyle, 40, 45, 65n5;
openness of, 60
ego-ideal, 115–16
Elementary Forms of Religious Life, The
(Durkheim), 38
Elias, Norbert, 41, 65n6, 154, 290
embodiment, 288–91
empiricism, 19–20, 23, 135–36
emulation, 299–300
epistemological break, 21–22, 165–66, 248–
49, 352, 356
epistemology: vs. ontology, 9–10, 358
Espagne, Michel, 70–71
ethnomethodology, 156n2
European Union, 62
exchange rates, 345–46
exchange value, 343–44
Experience and Nature (Dewey), 155–56
expertise, 171–74
explanation, 351–61; causation in, 355–57,
358; of collective unrest, 98–99; conjunctural, 353, 354; dialectical, 353–54;
dialogical, 354; evaluation of, 360–61;
general form of, 357–58, 359; hypothetico-
deductive model of, 357–58; vs. interpretivism, 358; multiple forms of, 359–61;
narrative, 357; ontological, 358; shift in
language and, 352, 355; shift in perspective
and, 351–52, 354–55, 356, 366n7; shift in
temporal perspective and, 353

fact builder, 166–67
Fair Labor Standards Act (1938), 223, 233
family, 297
Fanon, Frantz, 41
fantasy, 109–10, 113, 120, 121, 129n6
father: son's relation to, 110, 127, 293, 295,
298–99
Feudal Society (Bloch), 68
field(s), 21, 26–29, 49–56, 128n5, 156n7, 328–
38; autonomy of, 37, 139, 160–61, 189–90,
192, 194, 329–30, 335–36, 340; boundaries

field(s) (*cont.*)

of (*see* field boundaries); capital and (*see* capital); change within, 190–91, 209n10; conservatism of, 50; construction of, 22, 24, 27–29; content transfers/exchanges between, 196–98, 200, 210n21, 210n24; contraction of, 331–32; definition of, 26–27, 90, 140, 162–63; democratic struggles and, 139; expansion of, 331–32; fuzzification between, 179–81; generosity vs. closure and, 169–72; genesis of, 22, 37, 50–51, 177–78, 329, 334–35, 339–40; heteronomy of, 329–30, 335–36, 340, 365n1; hierarchy in, 332–33, 341; historical context of, 198–200; horizontal dimension of, 332–33, 341–42; knowledge production and, 185–86, 187–91, 197–98; multi-leveled/nested/overlapping, 160, 194–95, 209n14; vs. network, 163–68; orthodoxy in, 28–29, 30, 332–33, 341–42; permeability of, 332, 337; raiding of, 178–79; refracted external factors of, 187–88; relations between, 30–31, 160–61, 194–98, 200 (*see also* field boundaries); relations within, 161–63, 190–91, 209n10, 275–79, 282–83; shape of, 332–33, 337–38, 341–42; size of, 330–33, 336; spaces between, 158–60, 174–81; symbolic analysis of, 334–38; transformation of, 187–88, 190–91, 202–5; underdetermined spaces between, 177–81; vertical dimension of, 332–33, 341

field boundaries, 30; changes in, 331–32, 336–37, 340–41; field-specific capital circulation and, 340–41; internal field work on, 160, 161–62, 175–77; locational change in, 331–32, 336–37; permeability change in, 332, 337, 341; symbolic aspects of, 336–37

Fields of Knowledge (Ringer), 73

Flaubert, Gustave, 10, 52–56, 152

Formation of the Scientific Mind, The (Bachelard), 148–49

Foucault, Michel, 289, 298

foundations: illusion of, 136–37

framing, 159

freemasonry, 299

French literary field: autonomy/heteronomy polarization of, 271–72; dominant/dominated polarization of, 271–73; education and, 269–70, 273; nineteenth century, 52–56, 196, 269–74, 329, 354–57; vs. scientific field, 270–71; structural history of, 268–74. *See also* French literary field (WWII) crisis

French literary field (WWII) crisis, 267–85; biographical multiple correspondence analysis in, 276, 277; causes of, 268–269; collaborationist writers in, 277, 278; Comité National des Écrivains and, 279–80, 281; Communists and, 274, 278, 279, 283; dominant/dominated polarization and, 273–74; emergence from, 280–83; field restructuring and, 267–68, 274–75; heteronomy in, 275, 276–79; internal field struggles with, 275–79, 282–83; literary Resistance in, 277, 278; loss of autonomy with, 274, 276–79; notables in, 277, 278; phase harmonization of fields in, 267, 268, 275–77; political field and, 267–68, 274–80; purge process in, 280–82; quarrel of the bad masters and, 268–69; question of professional ethics and, 281–83; symbolic capital and, 276–78, 281; underground activity and, 278

French Revolution, 68–69, 74

Freud, Sigmund, 108–10, 124, 129nn8,9, 129n13, 148, 150

fuzzification, 179–81

fuzzy logic, 134–38, 149

gender: citizenship and, 216; dehistoricization of, 13, 286; dominant/dominated and, 13, 302; intellectual field and, 79; symbolic analysis of, 350–51; transmission of, 286–87 (*see also* masculinities); in workplace, 301

general science of practices, 23

generosity, 169–72

Gide, André, 268, 272–73

gift giving, 159, 162, 176

globalization, 60, 61, 62

Goffman, Erving, 32

Goncourt prize, 274
Great Depression, 204–5. *See also* Works Progress Administration (WPA)
guilt, 127
gymnastics, 310–11, 312, 314

habitus, 6–8, 347–51; agency and, 32, 42–43; in colonized cultures, 119, 120, 122–23; composition of, 348–50; construction of, 32; as defense mechanism, 121–22; definition of, 31–32, 34–35n20, 41–42, 90, 92, 137, 347; development of, 120–21, 144–45; disjunctural, 93, 120, 122–23; domination and, 145–46; double historicity of, 146–47; economic change and, 8–9, 39–40, 122–23; failed social reproduction and, 8–9, 40–41, 100; field changes and, 348–50; formation of, 348; game metaphor of, 347; gendered, 350–51; grammar metaphor of, 347; historical perspective on, 41, 119; integrated, 120; intergenerational drift of, 349–50; knowledge production and, 208–9n5, 209n9; masculine, 113 (*see also* masculinities); political competence and, 145–46; positions and, 31, 32; of researcher, 24, 147–48; self-reflexive critique of, 147–48; social reproduction and, 6–7, 8–9; split, 120, 123, 127, 144–45; subordination and, 42; successful social reproduction and, 9; symbolic structure of, 350–51; at times of crisis, 93; transformation of, 147–48; transhistorical drift in, 349–50
Haupt, Heinz-Gerhard, 68
Hegel, Georg Wilhelm Friedrich, 116, 117
Heidegger, Martin, 2, 9–10, 186, 193, 195
heterodoxy, 28–29, 30, 209n10, 332–33, 341–42
heteronomy, 329–30, 335–36, 340, 365n1; capital and, 340, 342; of French literary field, 271–72, 275, 276–79
historical rationalism, 64
historicization, 353
history: explanation in, 357; periodization and, 74; specialization and, 69. *See also* comparative history; sociohistorical change

Homo Academicus (Bourdieu), 2, 4–8, 10–11, 45, 62, 267; Lacan's absence from, 109
honor, 40, 287, 291–92, 296–97, 300
human behavioral genetics, 178–79
human individual: social-scientific knowledge about, 202–3
Human Nature and Conduct (Dewey), 145
Husserl, Edmund, 41, 150–51
hybridity, 179–81

ideology, 117–18
imaginary: concept of, 120–22
Inheritors, The (Bourdieu and Passeron), 3, 44, 62
In Other Words (Bourdieu), 297
intellectual activism, 24–26, 59–61, 62–64, 66n18, 133, 138; during Great Depression, 204–5
intellectual field, 76–84; autonomization of, 79; biographical analysis in, 80; critical reflexivity within, 147–48; European, 78–80, 82–84; field of power and, 78–79; French, 71, 76–79, 82–83, 269–71; gender and, 79; geography and, 80; German, 71, 76–78, 82; morphological analysis of, 79–80; political conjunctures and, 80, 83–84; religion and, 79; traditional elites in, 79
Intellectuals en Europe au XIXe Siéle, Les (Charle), 78–80
internalism: sociological, 188–90, 209n8
interpretivism, 358
Invitation to Reflexive Sociology, An (Bourdieu and Wacquant), 33n1, 132
Israeli Middle Eastern studies, 168–74; academic field vs. bureaucratic field and, 159–60; boundary work and, 176–77; field generosity vs. closure and, 169–71; network of intelligence expertise and, 173–74; research institutes of, 159, 170–71, 173, 177
Israeli military intelligence, 159–60, 168–74; assessments by, 171–74
Italy: civic patriotism in, 259

Kabyle, 64–65n1; double domination of, 38; doxic attitude of, 39, 65n8; economy of,

Ministry of Culture, 47
misrecognition, 118, 343
monasticism, field of, 329, 348
monopoly mechanism, 154
monothetic reason, 57
Mysteries of Capital, The (Soto), 344
mythologies, 334–35

narrative: as explanation, 357; nation-
ization struggles and, 261
narrative rationalization, 336
nation, 249, 250, 254n1; in comparative history, 70. *See also* nationalism; nation-
ization struggles
National Fund for Literature, 283
national identity, 247–48, 252
nationalism: additive objectivist and subjectivist accounts of, 253; Bourdieu's theory of class and, 253–55; common
denominator analysis of, 250–51; construction of, 250–51; deconstruction of,
250–51; definition of, 244, 251; dis/posi-
tion and, 254; di/vision and, 254–55;
essentialism approach to, 252; historical
events and, 246; as idea, 243, 244, 245;
identity and, 243, 247–48, 249–50, 252;
industrialism and, 245–46; as instrumental ideology, 243–44, 245; modernist
hypothesis of, 243, 245–49; movements
and parties and, 247, 249; nation-ization
struggles and, 256–63; objectivist
accounts of, 251–53; origins of, 244–48,
257–58; paradigmatic case analysis of,
250–51; partialism approach to, 252–53;
as political community, 243, 244, 245;
preconditions for, 245–46; premodern,
246, 247, 251; secular, 247, 249; subjectivist accounts of, 251–53; symbolic dimension of, 244, 245, 246, 249; virus analogy
and, 251. *See also* nation-ization
struggles
nationalist consciousness, 246–47
National Labor Relations Act (1935), 223,
233
nation-ization struggles, 255–63; actors and
thinkers in, 263; analytic assessment of,

262–63; capital transformations and, 261;
communication and transport innovation and, 260; conquest and/or colonization and, 260; contagiousness metaphor
for, 258; cultural and/or commercial networks and, 260; epidemic metaphor for,
258, 260–62; metaphors for, 258–62;
mutation metaphor for, 258–60; narrative and, 261; population movements
and, 261; ritual inventions and, 261–62;
space of nation-ization in, 256–57, 262;
space of nations in, 256, 257, 262; symbolic dimensions of, 262–63
neoliberalism, 37, 43, 56–62, 142
network: concept of, 163–68; of intelligence
expertise, 173–74
noblemen, 291–93
non-domination, 50

object: construction of, 22, 69–70, 250
Old Age Insurance, 226, 231, 237–38
ontology, 9–10, 358
orientalist expertise, field of, 159–60, 168–74
orthodoxy, 28–29, 30, 209n10, 332–33, 341–42
Outline of a Theory of Practice (Bourdieu),
2, 3–8, 287, 328–29

Pascalian Meditations (Bourdieu), 64, 111–
12, 116, 132
paupers: citizenship and, 215–16
peasant society, 37. *See also* Béarn; Kabyle
periodization, 74
Persistence of the Old Regimen, The (Mayer),
74–75
philosophy, field of, 186, 195; field transfers/
exchanges and, 197
photography, 65n9
policy: in classification struggle, 220, 221
Political Ontology of Martin Heidegger, The
(Bourdieu), 2, 4, 7, 8, 9–10, 186, 193, 195
political opinion, 145–46
politics, field of, 143–44, 177, 186–87; French
literary field and, 267–68, 274–80
poor relief, 226; citizenship and, 215–16, 217;
vs. WPA, 221–23, 224, 226, 229, 230, 232–
33. *See also* U.S. welfare state

position(s), 26, 28–30, 34n19; capital and, 140; in classification struggles, 220, 256; field of, 31, 32; in French literary field, 276–78; knowledge production and, 190

Pourrat, Henri, 274

power: classification and, 24; sociology of, 21. *See also* capital; power, field of

power, field of, 13, 21, 140–42; education and, 45–46; field of sport and, 308; intellectual field and, 78–79; publicity field and, 153–54

practical evaluation, 151

practical sense, 288

pragmatism (Deweyan), 132, 134–38, 149–51, 155–56

preferences: theory of, 361–62

pre-perceptive anticipation, 150

project (plan), 150

projectivity, 146, 150, 151

protension, 146

psychoanalysis, 108–14, 152; in *Masculine Domination,* 112–14; in *Pascalian Meditations,* 111–12; in *The Weight of the World,* 110. *See also* socioanalysis

psychology, field of, 203

Public and Its Problems, The (Dewey), 153

publicity, field of, 153–54

Quest for Certainty, The (Toulmin), 134

race: WPA and, 226–27, 231–32, 234–36

rational choice theory, 89–107, 149, 361–63; agency and, 97–98; autonomy and, 92–93; beliefs and, 95–96; cognitive capacity and, 95; consciousness and, 91–93, 94, 106n10; constraints and, 94, 95–96, 105n5; cost assessment and, 96; crisis conjunctures and, 91, 93–94, 96–98, 102–3, 149, 362; dispossession/maladjusted expectations and, 98–100; full knowledge and, 91–92, 95; incomplete information and, 95; maximization of benefits and, 90, 94–95, 97–98; ontological levels in, 365–66n6; personal commitments and, 106n16; preferences in, 95–96, 361; routine times and, 97–98, 102, 104; scope

conditions and, 96–97; universalist nature of, 101–2, 106n18; utilitarianist view of, 105n1

rationalization, 335–36

Realphilosophie (Hegel), 116

reason: monothetic, 57

received views: rejection of, 21–22, 33n8, 165–66, 248–49, 352, 356

recognition, 115–18

reflexivity, 23–24, 34n13; critical, 146, 147–48; in times of crisis, 93–94

relationality, 22–23, 34n10

religion, field of, 45–46, 169, 209n11, 341

reproduction: theme of, 2–6, 8–9, 11–13

Reproduction (Bourdieu), 2, 3, 4, 7, 8, 44

République des universitaries, La (Charle), 77–78

revolution: comparative history of, 74–75

revolutionary subject, 10

rights, 50

Ringer, Fritz K., 73

rites of institution, 143–44

ritual rationalization, 336

rule, 288

Rules of Art, The (Bourdieu), 2, 4–8, 10, 11, 52–56, 109–10, 199–200, 328, 354–57

salons (literary), 177–78

Sartre, Jean-Paul, 52, 59, 92, 282–83

scholastic bias, 43

scholasticism, 136–37

science, field of, 137–38, 161, 164–69, 175, 341

scientific syndrome, 196–97

security wage, 229, 240–41n10

Seignobos, Charles, 67

self-analysis, 124–27

self-exclusion, 40

short-circuit fallacy, 139, 187

Simiand, François, 67

Sketch for a Self-Analysis (Bourdieu), 123–27

sociability, 299–302

social capital, 21, 57, 58

social history, 22

social rights, 215, 216–17. *See also* U.S. welfare state

social-scientific knowledge, 183–84, 201–6;

about culture, 203–6; about human individual, 202–3; critique of, 33n8

social space, 123, 139, 141

social space analysis: in classification struggles, 254, 255

social welfare. *See* U.S. welfare state

sociétés d'emulation, 299–300

socioanalysis, 108–30, 148–55; Deweyan pragmatism and, 149, 150–51, 152–53; dualisms in, 150; father-son relationship and, 110; Freud and, 109–10, 148–49, 150; habitus and, 119–24; Lacan and, 108–10, 112, 115–19, 120–21, 127–28; Marxism and, 111; of masculine domination, 112–14 (*see also* masculinities); self-, 124–27; subject formation and, 111–12, 120–22; symbolic capital and, 115–19; terminological origin of, 114

sociodicies, 334–35

sociohistorical change, 1, 6–13, 351–61; causation in, 355–57; conjunctural explanation of, 354; dialectical explanation of, 353–54; dialogical explanation of, 354; in literature field (*see* French field of literature [WWII] crisis); in masculinity (*see* masculinities); nationalist (*see* nationalism; nation-ization); shift in language for explanation of, 352, 355; shift in moment for explanation of, 355; shift in perspective for explanation of, 351–52, 354–55, 356, 366n7; shift in temporal perspective for explanation of, 353; in sport field (*see* sport [France], field of); in U.S. welfare state (*see* Works Progress Administration [WPA]). *See also* explanation

Sociologie d'Algerie (Bourdieu), 38

Sociology of Religion (Weber), 158, 161, 168, 334–35

Southern agrarian economy: vs. WPA, 230–36

sport (France), field of, 303–26; amateurism and, 312–14, 319; autonomy of, 312–17; centralization of, 322–23; child and adult games and, 305, 306; class and, 319–21; coalescence of, 308–9; community of social interests and, 315–16; educator initiatives and, 310–11; field of power and, 308; fighting and conquest activities and, 305, 306; genesis of, 304–12, 323–24; gymnastics and, 310–11, 312, 314; metaphor of, 288–89; military training and, 311; moral aspects of, 307–8, 314–15; neutral sport and, 316–17; noncompetitive activities and, 320; normalization of events and, 323; personal care activities and, 305–6; physician initiatives and, 309–10; political and religious organizations and, 314–16, 317; possible physical activities in, 304–6; professionalism and, 313–14; restructuring of, 317–21; transformation of, 306–8; transportation tourism activities and, 305, 306, 311–12; vs. utilitarian physical activities, 309–12; word *sport* in, 308–9

stances, field of, 29–30

state, 141–42. *See also* power, field of; nation

State Nobility: Elite Schools in the Field of Power, The (Bourdieu), 4, 7, 8, 11, 13, 330

structuration, 50

subjectivism, 363–64, 366n9

supplemental wage, 229

symbolic analysis, 364; capital and, 343–47; exchange rates and, 345–46; exploitation rate and, 346; field autonomy/heteronomy and, 335–36; field boundaries and, 336–37; field genesis and, 334–35; field shape and, 337–38; field size and, 336; habitus and, 350–51

symbolic capital, 57, 115–19, 338–39; definition of, 116; recognition and, 58, 116–18

symbolic interactionism, 156n2

symbolic power, 21, 42, 142; struggles against, 25–26; of writers, 270, 276–78

symbolic violence, 21, 42, 145; classification and, 48; in education, 44, 46

terrorism: expertise on, 178

text: external analysis of, 185–86, 187–88, 191–92; internal analysis of, 185–86, 188–91. *See also* knowledge production

theory, 23; bias of, 24

theory of practice, 103, 137, 364–65; crisis

theory of practice (*cont.*)
conjuncture and, 89, 93–94, 102–3, 149, 362; levels in, 365–66n6; maximization of benefits and, 97–98; preferences in, 361; vs. rational choice theory (*see* rational choice theory); routine times and, 102. *See also* capital; habitus
theory of symbolic order, 117–18, 120, 121, 123
thinking: relational, 22–23, 34n10; substantialist, 22
time, 146; Husserl on, 150
Tocqueville, Alexis de, 147
Toulmin, Stephen, 134
transformation: theme of, 2–3, 9–13, 36–38
translated works, 3
translation: human/nonhuman, 166–67, 181–82n1

ultimate values, 334–35
unconscious, 112–13, 148
unification: of economic fields, 43
universalism, 50, 154
university field: European, 78–80; French, 76–78; German, 76–78; of May 1968, 10–11, 350. *See also* intellectual field
U.S. welfare state: citizenship rights and, 215–17, 238–39; claimant in, 239n4; classification struggles in, 215–18, 236–38 (*see also* Works Progress Administration [WPA]); development of, 218–25; liberal values and, 238

wage earners: citizenship and, 215, 216
Weber, Max, 158, 161, 168, 328, 334–35, 356
Weight of the World, The (Bourdieu), 110, 142

welfare, field of, 219–20
welfare state: French, 37, 43–49; neoliberalism and, 37, 43, 56–62, 142; U.S., 215–25, 236–39 (*see also* Works Progress Administration [WPA])
Workers Alliance of America (WAA), 222, 240n8; African American mobilization by, 233–34; citizenship defense by, 222, 223, 224–25; Communists in, 229–30, 234; demise of, 227; political power of, 225; professional mobilization by, 241n11; racial backlash against, 234–36
Works Progress Administration (WPA), 218; African American political mobilization and, 233–34; citizenship and, 222, 223–25, 227–28, 239n2; conservative opposition to, 224–25, 229–30, 234–36; employment restrictions in, 231–32, 240n7; failure of, 227–29; federal labor standards and, 233; federal vs. state control in, 232–33; vs. poor relief, 221–23, 224, 226, 229, 230, 232–33; racial backlash against, 226–27, 234–36; racial discrimination in, 231–32; regional wage differences in, 231; right to strike and, 223, 227, 240n9, 241n12; seasonal worker releases in, 231; security wage of, 229, 240–41n10; southern African American worker exclusion from, 231–32; Southern agrarian economy and, 230–36; word *worker* and, 223–24
World War II, French literary field during. *See* French literary field (WWII) crisis)

Zola, Emile, 271

Philip S. Gorski is professor of sociology and religious studies
and co-director of the Center for Comparative Research at Yale
University.

Library of Congress Cataloging-in-Publication Data
Bourdieu and historical analysis / Philip S. Gorski, ed.
p. cm. — (Politics, history, and culture)
Includes bibliographical references and index.
ISBN 978-0-8223-5255-6 (cloth : alk. paper)
ISBN 978-0-8223-5273-0 (pbk. : alk. paper)
1. Bourdieu, Pierre, 1930–2002—Political and social views.
2. Political sociology. I. Gorski, Philip S. II. Series: Politics,
history, and culture.
HM479.B68 B66 2012
306.2—dc23   2012011601